WHITAKER'S OLYMPIC ALMANACK

An Encyclopaedia of the Olympic Games

FITZROY DEARBORN PUBLISHERS

CHICAGO • LONDON

Published in the United Kingdom by
The Stationery Office Ltd
51 Nine Elms Lane, London SW8 5DR

Published in the United States of America by
Fitzroy Dearborn Publishers
919 North Michigan Avenue,
Chicago, Illinois 60611

A Cataloging-in-Publication record for this book is available
from the Library of Congress.

ISBN 1-57958-136-6

First published in the UK and USA 2000

Edited by Kim Yarwood and Arlene Zuccolo
Picture Research by Lauren Hill and Vanessa Taylor
Typeset by Spire Origination, Norwich, United Kingdom
Printed and bound by MPG Books, Cornwall, United Kingdom
Cover design by Compendium
Cover photography © Allsport UK Ltd, Corbis
Internal photography © Allsport UK Ltd

Acknowledgements

I am greatly indebted to the original research by Olympic historians Erich Kamper (AUT), Volker Kluge (GER), Wolf Lyberg (SWE), Bill Mallon (USA) and Ian Buchanan (GBR). After extensive research, particularly by Wolf Lyberg, new participation figures have been agreed by the International Society of Olympic Historians (ISOH). My main sources alphabetically, by author:

The Associated Press and Grolier, *Pursuit of Excellence, The Olympic Story* (1979)
Sandor Barcs (HUN), *The Modern Olympics Story* (1964)
Pat Besford (GBR), *Encyclopaedia of Swimming* (1976)
Ian Buchanan (GBR), *British Olympians* (1991)
John Durant (USA), *Highlights of the Olympics* (1961)
Erich Kamper (AUT), *Enzyclopadie der Olympischen Spiele* (1972), *Lexicon der Olympischen Winter Spiele* (1964), *and Lexicon der 14, 000 Olympioniken* (1983)
Erich Kamper (AUT) and Bill Mallon (USA), *The Golden Book of the Olympic Games* (1992)
Lord Killanin (IRE) and John Rodda (GBR), *The Olympic Games* (1976)
Volker Kluge (GER), *Die Olympischen Spiele von 1896 bis 1980* (1981); *Winter Olympia Kompakt* (1992) and *Olympische Sommerspiele I 1896–1936* (1998);*II 1948–1964* (1998)
Bill Mallon (USA) and Ian Buchanan (GBR), *Quest for Gold* (1984)
Bill Mallon (USA), *The Olympic Record Book* (1988)
Peter Matthews (GBR), *Track and Field Athletics, The Records* (1986)
Norris and Ross McWhirter (GBR), *The Guinness Book of Olympic Records* (1980)
David Wallechinsky (USA), *The Complete Book of the Olympics* (1984, 1988, 1992); *The Complete Book of the Summer Olympics* (1996) and *The Complete Book of the Winter Olympics* (1998)
Melvyn Watman (GBR), *The Encyclopaedia of Track and Field Athletics* (1981)

Other experts and organizations whose publications and personal help have been invaluable include:

Richard Ayling, Howard Bass, Anthony Bijkerk (NED), Harry Carpenter, Jim Coote, Peter Diamond (USA), Maurice Golesworthy, John Goodbody, Mark Heller, Richard Hymans, Peter Johnson, Ove Karlsson (SWE), Ferenc Mezo (HUN), Rebecca Middleton, Jan Patterson, Ron Pickering, Jack Rollin, Bob Sparks, Stuart Storey, Dave Terry, John Tidy, Lance Tingay, Martin Tyler, David Vine, Alan Weeks, Ture Widlund (SWE), Dorian Williams, Don Wood. The Association of Track and Field Statisticians (ATFS), British Olympic Association, The International Society of Olympic Historians (ISOH), International Amateur Athletic Federation (IAAF), International Olympic Committee (IOC), International Weightlifting Federation, National Ski Federation of Great Britain, National Union of Track Statisticians (NUTS), New York Times, Sports Illustrated, The Times, Track and Field News, L'Equipe, and many national and international bodies and individuals.

I particularly thank Keith Greenberg for assistance with typing and checking, Paul Sparks for his technical help, Carole Greenberg for her good humour and understanding and Arlene Zuccolo for her excellent proof reading. Where contradictions have been found in different sources I have invariably arrived at my own, hopefully correct, conclusion. The recent political upheavals of the former East European bloc have caused Olympic chroniclers some problems. I have taken my own attitude to such matters and made my own, perhaps unique, medal compilations. However, I have given all necessary data so that readers with different views can reconstruct tables to their own liking

Stan Greenberg
London 2000

Key to notes in text

G = gold or gold medallist	km/h = kilometres per hour
S = silver	mph = miles per hour
B = bronze	yd = yard
M = medallist	m = metres

Contents

Abbreviations

All member countries, present and past, have an official Olympic three-letter abbreviation, used in results. These can be found under the entry 'Participation, by Country'.

Albertville 1992
XVI Winter Games (8–23 February)

Attended by representatives of 64 countries, comprising 1801 competitors of which 489 were women.

In October 1986 the IOC awarded the Games to Albertville, in the Savoie region of France, ahead of six other sites in six other countries. The 1968 triple gold medallist, Jean-Claude Killy, was co-president of the organising committee. With a population of less than 20 000 Albertville was the smallest place ever to host an Olympic Games. The 13 different venues were very widespread, which gave rise to complaints that 'atmosphere and spirit' were lacking when compared to previous celebrations. Nevertheless, the Games were highly successful, with a record number of competitors and participating countries. These included newcomers from Swaziland, Senegal, Ireland and the Virgin Islands. The political upheavals in eastern Europe manifested themselves in various ways: there was a combined German team for the first time since 1964; Latvia, Estonia and Lithuania competed independently again after 56 years, having been incorporated into the Soviet Union in 1940; competing under the title of the Unified Team (EUN) were the National Olympic Committees (NOCs) of Russia, Belarus, Ukraine, Kazakhstan and Uzbekistan — they used the Olympic flag, and Beethoven's *Ode to Joy* for victory ceremonies. The break-up of Yugoslavia meant that Croatia and Slovenia also competed separately for the first time.

As usual the world's media attended in force, trying to cope with the logistical problems caused by the multi-venued sports facilities. CBS paid some $243 million for the American television rights. There was a remarkable opening ceremony with the Games declared open by François Mitterand , the President of France. The flame was lit by soccer star, Michel Platini, and a local child, François-Cyrille Grange, and figure skater Surya Bonaly took the oath.

A record 57 events included the newly accepted sports of short-track speed skating and freestyle skiing. Overall, there were nine extra events since the previous Games, plus demonstration sports of curling, speed skiing, and two forms of freestyle skiing not in the Games 'proper'. Another change was that in figure skating compulsory exercises had been eliminated.

Unusually, the Alpine skiers did not produce the stars in this Games as in the past. Italy's Alberto Tomba gained a lot of attention by becoming the first Alpinist to successfully defend a title, but no skier

really dominated. Indeed, only Petra Kronberger of Austria won more than one event, and the 30 available medals in the sport were spread among 25 skiers. Surprisingly, the Swiss won only a single bronze, while female skiers from Sweden and New Zealand won the first such medals from their areas.

Nordic skiing made a big impact, and, with good television coverage, some of the cross-country competitors became stars. The Norwegians, Vegard Ulvang and Bjørn Dæhlie, got due recognition for winning three golds and a silver each. They made good media copy too, especially Dæhlie, who deliberately skied backwards over the line for his last gold medal in the relay. But the most successful competitor at Albertville was their female equivalent, Lyubov Yegorova of the Unified Team, who won three golds and two silvers — a record total of medals in Winter Games. That was matched by her team-mate, Yelena Valbe, with four individual bronzes and a gold in the relay. The inclusion of women's biathlon events enabled Anfissa Reztsova (URS/EUN) to become the first Winter Olympian to win gold medals in two separate sports — she had previously gained a gold in the 1988 cross-country relay.

Austrian ski jumpers put up a surprising challenge to the Finns, especially in the team event, and it was mainly the superb jumping of the young Toni Nieminen that won the day. Another closely fought contest involving Austria came in the 4-man bob when their team beat Germany by a mere 0.02 of a sec after four rounds, the smallest margin of victory ever. In lugeing, the Neuner sisters, also from Austria, took first and second places, matching the feat of the French Goitschel sisters in the 1964 Alpine skiing. By winning the ice hockey the Unified Team, in effect, extended the Soviet Union's victory run to eight since first entering the Games in 1956.

Despite the new rules most of the favourites won the medals in figure skating, with Viktor Petrenko (EUN) taking his country's first individual skating gold since 1908. In speed skating both sprint titles were retained by the 1988 champions, Bonnie Blair (USA) and Uwe-Jens Mey (GER) respectively. However, the surprise here, and in the new short-track events, was the rise of Asia, whose skaters, from China, Japan and the Koreas, won 13 medals.

Toni Nieminen, the Finnish gold medallist in the 120m ski-jump individual and team events, was only 16 years and 259 days when he gained his first title, thereby becoming the youngest ever male Winter Olympics champion. A member of the Unified Team, Raisa Smetanina, was the oldest ever female gold medallist as a member of the 4 × 5km relay team, just 12 days short of her 40th birthday. She set another record by winning medals in five consecutive Games, between 1976 and 1992. She said her secret was that she is really only 10 years old — being her birthday on 29th February! The oldest male champion was Fritz Fischer (GER) in the biathlon, aged 35 years and 146 days, while the oldest medallist was Maurilio De Zolt (ITA) with a silver in the 50km cross-country, aged 41 years and 150 days. The youngest medallist was Nikki Ziegelmeyer (USA) with a silver in the women's short-track speed skating relay at 16 years and 149 days, while the youngest competitor was figure skater Krisztina Czakó (HUN), aged 13 years and 66 days, whose father/coach Gyorgy had skated in the 1952 Games.

These were the last Winter Games to be held in the same year as the Summer celebration. In future the Winter Games would be held on the even-numbered years between the editions of the Summer Games.

1992 MEDALS (WINTER)

	G	S	B
Germany	10	10	6
Unified Team	9	6	8
Norway	9	6	5
Austria	6	7	8
United States	5	4	2
Italy	4	6	4
France	3	5	1
Finland	3	1	3
Canada	2	3	2
Korea	2	1	1
Japan	1	2	4
The Netherlands	1	1	2
Sweden	1	–	3
Switzerland	1	–	2
China	–	3	–
Luxembourg	–	2	–
New Zealand	–	1	–
Czechoslovakia	–	–	3
North Korea (PRK)	–	–	1
Spain	–	–	1

Two silvers, and no bronze in Women's Giant Slalom

Alpine Skiing

Separate Alpine skiing events were first introduced into the Games in 1948, but this style had been contested in 1936 as an Alpine combination event consisting of an aggregate of points scored in a downhill and a slalom race. Anton Sailer (AUT) in 1956 and Jean-Claude Killy (FRA) in 1968 both won a record three gold medals. Vreni Schneider (SUI) was the first woman to win three golds (1988 and 1994), and set an all-time record of five medals (three gold, one silver, one bronze). The latter was equalled by Katja Seizinger (GER) and Deborah Compagnoni (ITA), both 1992–98. The total of five medals was also matched by Kjetil André Aamodt (NOR) 1992–94 (one gold, two silver, two bronze), and Alberto Tomba (ITA) 1988–94 (three gold, two silver), the latter also becoming the first Alpine skier to win medals in three consecutive Games (Tomba's coach, Gustav Thöni, won the 1972 giant slalom). However, Deborah Compagnoni (ITA) became the first Alpine skier to win gold medals in three Games (1992–98).There

were a record 131 competitors in the 1992 giant slalom, representing a record 47 countries. In 1998 Lasse Kjus of Norway won two silver medals on the same day, firstly in the postponed downhill race, and then, four hours later, in the combined event. Graham Bell (GBR) was the first Alpine skier to compete in five Olympic Games, 1984–98.

The oldest gold medallist was Jean-Luc Crétier (FRA) who won the 1998 downhill, aged 31 years and 291 days, while the youngest was Michaela Figini (SUI), aged 17 years and 314 days when winning the 1984 downhill. The youngest male winner was Anton Sailer (AUT), aged 20 years and 73 days in the 1956 slalom, and the oldest female champion was Ossi Reichert (GER) in the 1956 giant slalom, aged 30 years and 33 days. Heinrich Messner (AUT) was the oldest medallist with the downhill bronze in 1972, aged 32 years and 159 days, and the youngest medallist was Gertraud 'Traudl' Hecher (AUT), aged 16 years and 145 days with the bronze in the 1960 downhill race. The youngest male medallist was Alfred Matt (AUT) with the 1968 slalom bronze, aged 19 years and 281 days, and the oldest female medallist was Dorothea Hochleitner (AUT), aged 30 years and 201 days when she won the 1956 giant slalom bronze. When Edwina Chamier (CAN) competed in the 1936 Alpine combination she became the oldest ever female Winter Olympian at the age of 45 years and 318 days.

The highest average speed attained in an Olympic downhill race was 107.532km/h (66.817mph) by Jean-Luc Crétier in 1998. The highest by a woman was 102.403km/h (63.630mph) by Katja Seizinger in the downhill portion of the combined event in 1998.

The greatest margin of victory in downhill was 4.7sec by Madeleine Berthod (FRA) in 1956, while the best in the male race was 4.1sec by Henri Oreiller (FRA) in 1948. The smallest margin was 0.04sec in the 1994 men's race, while for women it was 0.05sec in the 1984 event. The greatest margin in slalom was 11.3sec by Cristl Cranz (GER) in the 1936 combination event, while the men's equivalent was 5.9sec by Franz Pfnür (GER). Since then Anton Sailer (AUT) won by 4.0sec in 1956 and Anne Heggtveit (CAN) the 1960 women's race by 3.3sec. The smallest margin was 0.02sec in the 1972 women's event, which was equalled in the 1994 men's race. The tie for silver in the 1992 women's slalom was the first such tie since the introduction of automatic timing.

In the giant slalom the biggest margin was 6.2sec by Sailer in 1956, while for women it was 2.64sec by Nancy Greene (CAN) in 1968. The smallest margin was 0.1sec (before electronic timing) by Yvonne Ruegg (SUI) in 1960, and 0.12sec by Kathy Kreiner (CAN) in 1976. The smallest for men was 0.20sec by Henri Hemmi (SUI) in 1976. The greatest margin in the super giant slalom was 1.30sec by Franck Piccard (FRA) in 1988, and for women it was 1.41sec by Deborah Compagnoni (ITA) in 1992. The smallest for men was 0.08sec by Markus Wasmeier (GER) in 1994, and for women it was 0.01sec by Picabo Street (USA) in 1998 — the latter being the smallest margin of victory in any Olympic Alpine skiing event.

AVERAGE SPEEDS IN THE OLYMPIC DOWNHILL RACES

Men			Women	
Year	km/h	Winner	km/h	Winner
1936	47.599	Ruud (NOR)	39.031	Schou-Nilsen (NOR)
1948	66.034	Oreiller (FRA)	43.695	Schlunegger (SUI)
1952	57.629	Colò (ITA)	50.420	Jochum-Beiser (AUT)
1956	72.356	Sailer (AUT)	55.484	Berthod (SUI)
1960	88.429	Vuarnet (FRA)	67.426	Biebl (GER)
1964	81.297	Zimmermann (AUT)	74.496	Haas (AUT)
1968	86.808	Killy (FRA)	77.080	Pall (AUT)
1972	85.291	Russi (SUI)	78.568	Nadig (SUI)
1976	102.828	Klammer (AUT)	85.286	Mittermaier (FRG)
1980	102.677	Stock (AUT)	99.598	Moser-Pröll (AUT)
1984	104.532	Johnson (USA)	96.428	Figini (SUI)
1988	94.702	Ortlieb (AUT)	88.600	Lee-Gartner (CAN)
1994	103.319	Moe (USA)	99.109	Seizinger (GER)
1998	107.532	Crétier (FRA)	101.977 [1]	Seizinger (GER)

[1] In downhill segment of combined event Seizinger achieved 102.403 km/h

ALPINE SKIING MEDALS (NOT INCLUDING FREESTYLE SKIING)

	Men			Women			
	G	S	B	G	S	B	Total
Austria	15	14	17	9	13	10	78
Switzerland	6	11	9	10	8	6	50
France	9	4	7	3	7	7	37
United States	3	4	1	7	9	3	27
Germany	3	2	1	7	5	6	24
Italy	7	5	2	4	2	4	24
Norway	5	6	5	–	–	1	17
Canada	–	–	2	4	1	3	10
FRG	–	1	–	3	4	1	9
Liechtenstein	–	1	3	2	1	2	9
Sweden	2	–	3	2	1	–	8
Slovenia	–	–	1	–	–	2	3
Luxembourg	–	2	–	–	–	–	2
Spain	1	–	–	–	–	1	2
Yugoslavia	–	1	–	–	1	–	2
Japan	–	1	–	–	–	–	1
New Zealand	–	–	–	–	1	–	1
Russia	–	–	–	–	1	–	1
Australia	–	–	–	–	–	1	1
Czechoslovakia	–	–	–	–	–	1	1
Soviet Union	–	–	–	–	–	1	1
	51	52 [1]	51 [2]	51	54 [3]	49	307

[1] Two silvers in 1998 super giant slalom
[2] Two bronzes in 1948 downhill
[3] Two silvers in 1964 and 1992 giant slalom

American Football

A demonstration sport at Los Angeles in 1932. Two teams representing the East and West of the United States played an exhibition which the West won 7–6.

Amsterdam 1928
IX Olympic Games (17 May–12 August)

Attended by representatives of 46 countries, comprising 3014 competitors, of which 290 were women.

After unsuccessfully applying for the Games of 1916, 1920 and 1924, the Dutch were finally rewarded and built a new 40 000 capacity stadium on reclaimed land in Amsterdam. The size of the running track, 400m, encircled by a cycling track, was then standardised for future Games. The design of the stadium won the architect, Jan Wils, an Olympic prize in the architecture competition. One innovation was the erection of a large results board; others included the release of pigeons at the opening ceremony to symbolize peace and the burning of an Olympic flame throughout the period of competitions. The formal opening was conducted by HRH Prince Hendrik, the consort of Queen Wilhelmina who was on a state visit to Norway, although the Queen herself did hand out medals at the end of the Games. The record number of countries included Rhodesia and Panama for the first time, and Germany made its return to the Olympics in great strength.

After much argument in world sporting circles, and despite the opposition of Baron de Coubertin, women were allowed to compete in track and field, albeit in only five events. World records were set in all five, although there were such harrowing scenes of distress at the end of the 800m that it was then omitted from the programme until 1964. In winning that 800m Lina Radke won the first ever Olympic track and field gold medal for Germany. Her team-mate, Anni Holdmann, became the first woman to win an Olympic track race by finishing first in heat 1 of the 100m on 30 July. Another first in the sport was a gold medal for Japan by Mikio Oda in the triple jump.

The Finns again dominated the athletics, although the fabulous Paavo Nurmi only won one gold and two silvers. Looking far older than his 31 years due to his increasing baldness, the dour Finn offered some light relief when he competed in the steeplechase: unused to the event, he had problems with most of the barriers, and in his heat ignominiously fell into the water jump. Another competitor, a Frenchman, Lucien Duquesne, stopped and courteously helped him to his feet. Obviously grateful, Nurmi uncharacteristically acknowledged and thanked him, and then proceeded to 'shepherd' the French runner for the rest of the race, even inviting him to break the tape first. This Duquesne, to his eternal credit, declined to do. Despite running his fifth distance race in seven days, Nurmi won the silver medal in the final. It was later

reported that the great Finn had damaged his famous stopwatch in the fall.

The unheralded Canadian youngster, Percy Williams, took both sprints, and with Lord Burghley becoming the first member of the British House of Lords to win an Olympic athletic title (400m hurdles), and Douglas Lowe (GBR) successfully defending his 800m title, the Americans had a lean time. A pointer for the future was the victory in the marathon of Boughèra El Ouafi, representing France, but an Algerian and the pathfinder for future great African distance runners. The US team was under the control of the President of the US Olympic Committee, Major-General Douglas MacArthur, later in command of the victorious Americans in the Pacific theatre of the Second World War.

In the swimming pool another threat to United States' dominance came from the Japanese. In Amsterdam they won their first ever swimming medals, giving an indication of things to come. American honour was saved by Johnny Weissmuller in the 100m and relay. Dorothy Poynton (USA) won a silver medal in springboard diving when only 24 days past her 13th birthday, one of the youngest medallists ever. She won gold medals at the next two Games. There was an unfortunate mix-up in the result of the men's high diving when Farid Simaika of Egypt was initially awarded the gold on the basis of his greater points score. The result was later reversed and the title given to Ulise 'Pete' Desjardins (USA) as more first place decisions had been made in his favour by the judges. Canadian-born Desjardins had been the first Olympic diver to be awarded a score of 10, in the 1924 springboard event.

Another Egyptian, Ibrahim Moustafa, won the light-heavyweight wrestling title to become the first non-European to take a Greco-Roman event. Not for the first time, nor last, boxing was beset with protests about the standard of officiating. In yachting, Crown Prince Olav, later King Olav V of Norway, gained the first Olympic victory by a member of a Royal house when he was a crew member of the 6m yacht *Norna*. (His son, Crown Prince Harald, also competed in Olympic yachting 1964–72, but not with his father's success.) In the soccer tournament Uruguay retained its title, beating another South American country, Argentina, in the final. In front of 50 000 people India won the first of their six consecutive hockey gold medals, retaining the title until 1960. Their goal-keeper, Richard Allen, did not concede a single goal in the tournament.

A team-mate of the Crown Prince in *Norna*, Johan Anker, a champion from 1912, was the oldest gold medallist in Amsterdam, aged 57 years and 44 days. The youngest gold medallist, and male medallist, also water-borne, was the Swiss pairs cox Hans Bourquin, aged 14 years and 222 days. The youngest female champion was Elizabeth Robinson (USA) who won the 100m sprint, aged 16 years and 343 days, while the oldest woman to win a gold medal was Virginie Hériot (FRA) in the 8m yachting, aged 38 years and 15 days. The youngest medallist was Luigina Giavotti (ITA), silver in gymnastics, aged 11 years and 302 days —

she remains the youngest ever female medallist in Olympic history.

1928 MEDALS (SUMMER)

	G	S	B
United States	22	18	16
Germany	10	7	14
Finland	8	8	9
Sweden	7	6	12
Italy	7	5	7
Switzerland	7	4	4
France	6	10	5
The Netherlands	6	9	4
Hungary	4	5	–
Canada	4	4	7
Great Britain	3	10	7
Argentina	3	3	1
Denmark	3	1	2
Czechoslovakia	2	5	2
Japan	2	2	1
Estonia	2	1	2
Egypt	2	1	1
Austria	2	–	1
Australia	1	2	1
Norway	1	2	1
Poland	1	1	3
Yugoslavia	1	1	3
South Africa	1	–	2
India	1	–	–
Ireland	1	–	–
New Zealand	1	–	–
Spain	1	–	–
Uruguay	1	–	–
Belgium	–	1	2
Chile	–	1	–
Haiti	–	1	–
Philippines	–	–	1
Portugal	–	–	1

Ancient Games

The Olympic Games originally evolved from legendary conflicts among the Greek Gods and the religious ceremonies held in their honour. Historical evidence dates the Games from about 900BC, but there is good reason to believe that a similar festival existed four centuries previously. Indeed the modern word 'athlete' is said to derive from Aethlius, King of Elis. The area in which Olympia lies is in the plain of Elis, on the banks of the River Alpheios. It was a successor, Iphitus, who was instrumental in reviving the then faltering concept in the late ninth century BC. He also arranged for the truce between the continually warring states of the region which recognised the neutrality and sanctity of Olympia, and which lasted for the period of the Games. The first firm record dates from 776BC, and the Games were numbered at four-yearly intervals from then. At that time there was only one event, the stade race, and the winner, the first recorded Olympic champion, was Coroibis of Elis. The stade was 192.27m (210.26yd) long, reputably 60 times the length of the god Heracles' (Hercules) foot. After 13 Olympiads, in 724BC, a race of two stade, the diaulus, was also contested, and in the following celebration the 24-stadia dolichus, about 4.5km (2.8 miles) in length, was instituted. In 708BC came the pentathlon, consisting of running, jumping (with the aid of hand-held weights), throwing the discus and javelin, and wrestling. Eventually, chariot racing, running in armour and boxing were included, and in 648BC the pankration, a brutal mix of boxing and wrestling. Numerous variants of these sports appeared over the years, as did activities of a less sporting nature, such as contests for trumpeters.

Initially, contestants wore simple shorts-like garments, but from about 720BC they competed in the nude, and until 692BC the Games only lasted for a single day. This was later increased to two days, and in 632BC to a total of five days, of which the middle three were for actual competitions. For the next six centuries the fame of Olympia spread throughout the known world, and many famous people visited the Games. Victors, in those early days, won only a crown of wild olive leaves, but were often richly rewarded by their home states, and sometimes became very wealthy. Crowd figures were not published but archaeologists have estimated that the Stadium at Olympia could hold over 20 000 spectators.

For reasons not fully understood today, women, and slaves, were strictly forbidden, under pain of death, to even attend the Games. An exception does appear to have been made for high-ranking priestesses of the most important gods. However, it was possible for a woman to gain an Olympic prize. This was because in the chariot race the chaplet of olive leaves was awarded to the owner of the horses and not the drivers. One of the first women to win an Olympic title in this way was Belistike of Macedonia in 268BC as owner of the champion two-horse chariot. It is recorded that some women did defy the rules and disguised themselves, but, on discovery, were thrown over a cliff to their deaths. There is a story, perhaps apocryphal, that Pherenice of Rhodes acted as a second to watch her son, Pisidores, win his event. In her excitement she gave herself away, but, when it was realised that not only her son, but also her father and brothers had all been Olympic champions, she was pardoned.

Possibly the most famous champion of early times was Leonidas of Rhodes who won the three 'track' events on four consecutive occasions 164–152BC, making a total of 12 victories that has not been surpassed since. The first recorded triple gold medallist at one Games was Phanas of Pellene in 512BC, while the Spartan runner 'Chionis' won the stade in three successive Games 664–656BC. Other excellent champions included Theagenes of Thassos who won eight titles at boxing, wrestling and pankration from 468–456BC, and Milon of Croton who won six wrestling titles 536–516BC. Eventually, the very success of the Games gave rise to its downfall. The importance of winning at

Olympia, and the reflected glory it bestowed on the winner's birthplace, led cities to hire professionals and bribe judges. With the dawn of the Christian Era the religious and physical backgrounds of the Games were attacked. An irreversible decline set in under Roman influence, so much so that in AD 67 a drunken Emperor Nero was crowned victor of the chariot race despite the fact that there were no other entrants (who could blame them) and he did not even finish the course. According to accepted belief, in AD 393 the Roman Emperor Theodosius I issued a decree in Milan that prohibited the Games. Recent archaeological evidence seems to suggest that the Games may have continued — in some form — for another 100–120 years, but then, the ravages of foreign invaders, earthquakes and flooding virtually obliterated the site of Olympia, and the world forgot the glory that once had been.

There was a resurgence of interest in Ancient Greece in the 17th and 18th centuries and references to the Olympic Games in the poems of Pindar and other Greek poets were noted. In Britain, the Cotswold Olympic Games were inaugurated in the early 17th century, and in 1850 the Much Wenlock Olympic Society was founded by Dr William Penny Brookes. At the end of the 18th century, in Germany, the famed founder of modern gymnastics, Johann Guts Muths, had suggested the revival of the Olympic ideal. Some 50 years later a fellow countryman, Ernst Curtius, who had done archaeological work at Olympia (started by the French in 1829) reiterated the idea in a lecture he gave in Berlin in 1852. In Greece itself, Major Evangelis Zappas organised a Pan-Hellenic sports festival in 1859 which attracted a great deal of public support, and which was revived at intervals over the next 30 years. However, the true founder of the modern Olympic Games is commonly acknowledged to be Pierre de Fredi, Baron de Coubertin, of France. In 1889 he met Brookes of the Much Wenlock Olympic Society, and formed his concept of a revived Games, which he first propounded publicly at a lecture in the Sorbonne, Paris, on 25 November 1892. In the following year, he met with representatives of the top American universities. In June 1894 he convened an international conference, also in the Sorbonne, the outcome of which was a resolution on 23 June, calling for competitions along the lines of the Ancient Games to be held every fourth year. The International Olympic Committtee (IOC) was inaugurated under the presidency of Demetrius Vikelas of Greece with de Coubertin as Secretary-General. The Frenchman had hoped to herald the new century with the first Games in Paris in 1900, but the delegates were impatient. There was strong sentiment in favour of London or Budapest but, at the instigation of Vikelas, Athens was finally selected and the date set as 1896.

Antwerp 1920
VII Olympic Games (20 April–12 September)

Attended by representatives of 29 countries, comprising 2668 competitors, of which 77 were women.

When the venue of the VI Games, due in 1916, came to be discussed in Stockholm, three cities were put forward as candidates: Budapest, Alexandria and Berlin. It is said that the latter was chosen in an attempt to avert the war that was then threatening Europe. With the outbreak of hostilities in 1914, hopes of holding the Games virtually disappeared, although the Germans still made preparations for them believing that the war would not last very long. In 1920, although Antwerp was sorely affected by the human tragedy and economic ruin of the conflict, the organising committee under Count Henri de Baillet-Latour, later IOC President, overcame all difficulties to hold the Games. The recent enemies, Germany, Austria, Hungary and Turkey, were not invited but still a record number of countries and competitors attended. These included New Zealand as a separate entity (previously it had been part of an Australasian team), Argentina and Brazil. The Games were opened by King Albert, and the concept of the Olympic oath was introduced . This was taken by Victor Boin, who had competed in two previous Games, winning medals at water polo, and in Antwerp he gained another at fencing. Another newcomer at these Games was the newly devised Olympic flag, which consisted of five interlaced rings coloured blue, yellow, black, green, and red, from left to right. The rings were meant to symbolize the friendship of the human race, with the colours, including the white background of the flag itself, representing all nations, as every national flag contains at least one of the colours used.

Unfortunately the 400m running track at the new 30 000-seat stadium was very poor (Charles Perry, the famous groundsman, had not been able to do much with it) and was badly affected by the persistent rain. The combination of the weather and the economic aftermath of the recent conflict meant that spectator attendance was low. The competitors were housed in school buildings, which caused something of a revolt among the US team — though they were much more incensed by the intolerable conditions experienced aboard the old freighter that had brought them to Belgium.

For the first time, Finland competed under its own flag, having gained independence in 1917, and they celebrated the occasion by halting the American track and field juggernaut by winning as many athletic gold medals as the United States team. The track star of 1912, Hannes Kolehmainen, made a surprise return to win the marathon. However, his mantle had been taken over by another outstanding Finnish runner, Paavo Nurmi, who, although he lost his very first Olympic final (over 5000m) to the gassed French war veteran, Joseph Guillemot, was at the start of a brilliant career in which he won a record 12 Olympic medals, nine of them gold, and set 29 world records of one type or another. Britain's Albert Hill who had fought throughout the war, here won the 800m/1500m double, a feat not repeated for 44 years. In addition, Hill also gained a silver medal in the 3000m team race. In second place in the 1500m was Philip Baker (GBR) who, later in life as Philip Noel-Baker MP was the recipient of the 1959 Nobel Peace

Prize — a unique achievement for an Olympian. Charley Paddock retained the 100m sprint title for the United States, delighting the spectators with his spectacular jump finish. (Later, he found work in the movie industry, was killed in World War II as a Marine Corps Captain, and posthumously had a ship named after him.) The most successful competitors at these Games were, Willis Lee (USA) who won five golds, one silver and one bronze, and his team-mate, Lloyd Spooner, who won four golds, one silver and two bronzes, both as shooting competitors. This sport also produced the first gold medal won by a South American country, when Guilherme Paraense (BRA) took the rapid-fire pistol title. Yet another shooter, the phenomenal Oscar Swahn (SWE), became the oldest ever Olympic medallist, with a silver, aged 72 years and 280 days. Also outstanding was fencer Nedo Nadi (ITA) who won two individual and three team golds. His younger brother, Aldo, added another three to the family total.

Returning to Olympic competition for the first time since 1906, when he won two golds and a silver, was archer Hubert van Innis (BEL) who won four golds and two silvers, and was the oldest champion at these Games, aged 54 years and 187 days. The youngest gold medallist was tiny (1.43m) diver Aileen Riggin (USA) at 14 years and 119 days. Indeed, she was the youngest Olympic champion ever at the time, but almost lost the honour to Sweden's Nils Skoglund who finished a very close second in high-diving when only three months younger. Riggin won a diving silver four years later and, more unusually, a bronze in the 100m backstroke. The youngest male gold medallist was Franciscus Hin (NED) in the yachting, aged 14 years and 163 days. The oldest female champion was Winifred McNair (GBR) in tennis, aged 43 years and 15 days.

Swimming was dominated by two Americans, who captured three gold medals each. Ethelda Bleibtrey, who had suffered from polio as a child, won all events open to her, in world-record times. The year before she had been arrested in America and charged, under local decency laws, for swimming 'nude' at a public beach, when all she had done was to remove her stockings! Norman Ross won the 400m, 1500m and was part of the winning relay team, also figured in an unusual incident when he was disqualified in the 100m final for impeding an Australian swimmer. The race had been won by the Hawaiian Duke Kahanamoku in world-record time. He also won the re-swim but in slower time. Another incident, of a more serious nature, occurred in the soccer final when the Czechoslovakian team were disqualified for leaving the field after 40 minutes of play in protest at decisions by the British referee. Belgium were leading 2–0 at that point.

Daniel Carroll completed an unparalleled double in the rugby final when he won a second gold medal as part of the US team. He had played in the victorious Australian team of 1908, but had since emigrated. The tennis events presented one of the greatest players in the game, Suzanne Lenglen (FRA), eventual six-times winner of the Wimbledon title. The winner of the single sculls and, teamed with his cousin, for the double sculls, was John Kelly. Earlier in the year, the American had been refused entry to the Henley Regatta in England on the grounds that 'as a bricklayer' he had an unfair advantage over 'gentlemen'. Ironically, after he had become a millionaire, his son John Jr won at Henley in 1947, and his daughter, Grace, the film actress, became Princess of Monaco. Coincidentally, these were the first Games at which Monaco participated.

Two winter sports were also held, ice hockey and figure skating, attracting 73 men and 12 women from 10 countries. Figure skating witnessed the first gold medals won by a married couple, in the pairs champions German-born Ludowika and Walter Jakobsson of Finland. Also this year, it may be that the first Olympic marriage was that of American diver Alice Lord and high jump champion Dick Landon, soon after they returned home. One final note on the subject of matrimonial bliss: it was revealed after the competitions that the ladies skating champion, Magda Mauroy-Julin (SWE), was three months pregnant.

1920 MEDALS (SUMMER)

	G	S	B
United States	41	27	27
Sweden	19	20	25
Finland	15	10	9
Great Britain	14	15	13
Belgium	13	11	11
Norway	13	9	9
Italy	13	5	5
France	9	19	13
The Netherlands	4	2	5
Denmark	3	9	1
South Africa	3	4	3
Canada	3	3	3
Switzerland	2	2	7
Estonia	1	2	–
Brazil	1	1	1
Australia	–	2	1
Japan	–	2	–
Spain	–	2	–
Greece	–	1	–
Luxembourg	–	1	–
Czechoslovakia	–	–	2
New Zealand	–	–	1

Archery

The sport made its first appearance in the 1900 Games at Paris with six events on the programme. Some Olympic historians consider that another, live pigeon shooting was an official event, but the majority think not, and this book follows that opinion. The contests were held in Continental style, with each archer shooting a single arrow at a time in competition order (as opposed to the British method of three arrows at each turn). The eligibility of the 1904 archery competitions is also disputed by some, particularly as only American archers took part. However, the majority of historians and this author accepts them as Olympic events. The competitors in the 1904 women's contests were among the first women to compete in the Olympics, with only the tennis players in 1900 having a prior claim. The competitions of 1908 were accorded a much higher status than before despite only three nations taking part. The men's York Round was won by William Dod (GBR), and his remarkable sister, Charlotte, took the silver behind Queenie Newall (GBR) in the women's event. Charlotte Dod, then over 36 years old, was one of the greatest sportswomen of her, or, indeed, of any other generation. She had won the Wimbledon tennis singles five times, the British Ladies golf crown in 1904, and had represented England at hockey. She also excelled at skating and tobogganing. She and William were also the first brother and sister, in any sport, to win medals at the same Olympic Games.

Archery was not included in the 1912 Games but, reflecting Belgium's great interest in the sport, there were ten events at Antwerp in 1920, all in the Belgian style of shooting. With only three countries present again, Hubert van Innis (BEL), now 54, brought his total medals to a record six gold and three silver. The most successful woman has been Kim Soo-nyung (KOR) with three gold medals and a silver in 1988–92. The sport was dropped from the Games until 1972 when events were standardised into contests of Double (Fédèration Internationale de Tir à l'Arc (FITA))

Rounds for men and women. A FITA Round consists of 144 arrows, comprised of 36 each, over distances of 90m, 70m, 50m and 30m for men, and 70m, 60m, 50m and 30m for women. There have been a number of rule changes over the years, but currently after the qualifying round of 144 arrows, the top 32 competitors compete in knock-out stages of 12-arrow contests over 70m.

The oldest gold medallist was the Revd Galen Spencer (USA) in the winning 1904 team two days past his 64th birthday. A fellow team member, Robert Williams Jr, a youngster at 63 years, was the only known Olympic gold medallist to have fought for the South in the American Civil War. The youngest champion was Yun Young-sooh (KOR), aged 17 years and 21 days in the winning 1988 women's team. The youngest male winner was Park Sung-soo (KOR) in the 1988 team, aged 18 years and 135 days, while the oldest female champion was Lida Howell (USA) in 1904, aged 45 years and 25 days. The oldest ever medallist was Samuel Harding Duvall (USA), aged 68 years and 194 days winning a silver in the 1904 team contest, while the youngest medallist was Denise Parker (USA) with a team bronze in 1988, aged 14 years and 294 days. The youngest male medallist was Henry Richardson (USA) with a team bronze in 1904, aged 15 years and 126 days. Hubert van Innis (BEL) won gold medals over a record span of 20 years (1900–20). The first paraplegic to compete in a standard Olympic event was Neroli Fairhall (NZL), who, from her wheelchair, finished 35th in the 1984 women's archery event.

ARCHERY MEDALS

	Men			Women			
	G	S	B	G	S	B	Total
United States	9	5	4	4	2	3	27
France	6	10	6	–	–	–	22
Belgium	10	6	3	–	–	–	19
Korea	1	3	1	7	2	2	16
Soviet Union	–	1	1	1	2	4	9
Great Britain	1	1	3	1	1	1	8
Finland	1	1	1	–	–	1	4
China	–	–	–	–	3	–	3
Italy	–	–	3	–	–	–	3
Sweden	–	2	–	–	–	–	2
Japan	–	1	1	–	–	–	2
Poland	–	–	–	–	1	1	2
The Netherlands	1	–	–	–	–	–	1
Spain	1	–	–	–	–	–	1
Germany	–	–	–	–	1	–	1
Indonesia	–	–	–	–	1	–	1
Ukraine	–	–	–	–	–	1	1
	30 [1]	30	23 [2]	13	13	13	122

[1] Only a gold medal awarded in two 1920 events
[2] No bronze medals in one 1900 and six 1920 events

Athens 1896

I Olympic Games — Athens, Greece (6–15 April 1896) (25 March–3 April by the Julian Calendar)

Attended by representatives of 14 countries, comprising 211 competitors (no women).

Although the Greek government was apparently not consulted and were beset with internal financial and political problems, the Greek public were very enthusiastic. However, it was not until Crown Prince Constantine set up a committee and began organising and collecting funds that the project became feasible and the prospect of Budapest securing the honour by default faded. The turning point came with the generosity of a Greek businessman, Georges Averoff (formerly Avykeris) who actually lived in Alexandria, Egypt. He offered to pay for the reconstruction of the Panathenean Stadium in Athens at a cost of 920,000 drachma (£36,500 at the 1896 exchange rate). The stadium had first been built in 330BC by the orator Luycurgus, a disciple of Plato. It was rebuilt 500 years later by Herodes Atticus, but had gradually disintegrated and was covered up until 1870 when King George of Greece had arranged for its excavation by the German, Herr Ziller. The new track measured 333.33m, had very sharp turns, and the competitors ran in a clockwise direction. There was supposed to be a total of 50 events, but the seven rowing competitions were cancelled due to inclement weather in Phaleron Bay.

The opening of the Games coincided with the 75th anniversary of the declaration of Greek independence from Turkish rule. Over 40 000 spectators in the stadium, plus thousands more on the surrounding hills, saw King George I formally open the proceedings. The majority of the competitors were from Greece itself. Many athletes, including holidaymakers, entered privately and the British contingent included two employees of the Embassy in Athens. Another member of the British team was an Irishman, John Boland, who was on holiday in Greece at the time and entered the tennis events. He won the singles and, partnering a German, also won gold in the pairs. A further nice touch of the period was provided by a French sprinter who insisted on wearing his gloves as he was running before royalty.

Not for the last time a gymnast, Hermann Weingärtner (GER), was the most successful competitor, with three first places, two seconds and a third; a Frenchman, Paul Masson, won three cycling events; but perhaps the most outstanding achievement was that of Carl Schuhmann of Germany who not only won three gymnastic events but also won the wrestling title. Another competitor to gain medals in two sports was gymnast Fritz Hofmann (GER) whose total of five placings included a silver medal in the 100m. In shooting, John and Sumner Paine (USA) became the first brothers to win Olympic gold medals, in military pistol and free pistol respectively. Their father had successfully defended yachting's America's Cup some years before, and John's great-granddaughter later sculled in the 1996 Games.

The first competition of the modern Olympic Games was heat 1 of the 100m. It was won, in 12.5sec, by the American Francis Lane of Princeton University, thus carving a niche in history for himself. The first gold medallist of modern times was James Brendan Connolly (USA) who won the hop, step and jump (now known as the triple jump). In fact, the American team, composed exclusively of college students, dominated events in the stadium, despite arriving only the day before the start of the competitions, having travelled by ship to France and then by train to Greece. Victors actually received a silver medal and a crown of olive leaves; runners-up were given bronze medals and a crown of laurel; no awards were made for third place.

Two new sporting events were introduced at these Games: the discus throw and the marathon. Both were based on Greek antiquity and the hosts were eager to win them. However, the former was taken by Robert Garrett (USA) who had inadvertently practised with an implement much larger and heavier than the one actually used at Athens. The marathon had been proposed by Frenchman Michel Breal, to commemorate the legendary run of a Greek courier, possibly Pheidippides, with the news of a Greek victory over the Persians in 490BC. He is supposed to have run from the site of the battle and, after crying out "Rejoice! We conquer", collapsed and died. To the great delight of the spectators the race was won by a Greek shepherd, Spiridon 'Spyros' Louis, who was escorted into the stadium by Crown Prince Constantine and Prince George.

The oldest gold medallist was Georgios Orphanidis (GRE) in the free rifle contest, aged 36 years and 102 days, while the youngest was swimmer Alfréd Hajós (HUN), aged 18 years and 70 days when he won the 100m and 1200m freestyle events. A member of the Greek bronze medal team in gymnastics has been reported to have been under 11 years of age, but some doubt exists about the veracity of this claim. In view of the modern saturation coverage of the Olympics by the media, it is noteworthy to record that the British press gave little space to reports from Athens, despite an earlier complaint in The Times about the lack of knowledge of the occasion and Britain's inadequate representation. Nevertheless the Games were a tremendous success and Greece looked forward to the next celebration, which they also expected to host.

1896 MEDALS

	G	S	B
United States	11	7	1
Greece	10	19	18
Germany	7	5	2
France	5	4	2
Great Britain	3	3	1
Hungary	2	1	3
Austria	2	–	3
Australia	2	–	–
Denmark	1	2	4
Switzerland	1	2	–

Athens 1906
The Interim or Intercalated Games (22 April–2 May)

Attended by representatives of 20 countries, comprising 826 competitors, of which 6 were women.

After two debacles, in Paris and St Louis, something was needed to revive the flagging Olympic movement. Baron de Coubertin, with some misgivings, agreed a series of four-yearly meetings, interspersed with the main Games, to be held in Athens. Although these had the blessing of the IOC, it was decided that the Interim Games would not be numbered in sequence. This has caused an ambivalence in Olympic historians when writing about the Games, leading to the ludicrous situation where some refuse to include these Games in their narratives, but do include the medals won in their totals. This author considers that as these Games were sanctioned by the IOC, numbered or not, they were genuine Olympic Games, and should be treated as such. In the event, only this meeting of the projected series was ever held. Again the Greeks showed their enthusiasm and large crowds, missing for the past ten years, were in evidence. The marble stadium in Athens was full to capacity, and enthusiasm often helped to smooth over organisational mishaps.

The 20 countries included the first 'official' American team, selected and sent by the US Olympic Committee, so ending the practice of colleges, clubs and private individuals entering. Also present was the first ever team from Finland, with the doyen of the famous Järvinen family, Werner, gaining his country's first Olympic gold medal. The programme of track and field events was altered by a reduction in the number of sprint and hurdles races, and the addition of a pentathlon and the javelin throw.

There were some excellent performances, especially by some of the 1904 champions such as the perennial Ray Ewry and the New York policeman, Martin Sheridan. Another American, with the apt name of Paul Pilgrim, had only been added to the team at the last moment after he had privately raised the money for his fare. He had won a gold medal in 1904 as a member of the New York Athletic Club relay team, but in Athens he surprisingly won both the 400m and 800m titles, a feat not equalled again until 1976.

The new pentathlon event, consisting of a 192m run, standing long jump, discus and javelin throws, and Greco-Roman wrestling, was won by Hjalmar Mellander of Sweden. In third place was his countryman Erik Lemming who also gained bronze medals in the shot and tug-of-war as well as winning the first of three Olympic javelin titles. There was a real surprise in the 1500m walk, (also the scene of a number of purely chauvinistic decisions by the various national judges). The American distance runner George Bonhag had disappointed in the 1500m and 5 mile runs, and had entered the walk, an entirely new event to him, in a last effort to win a medal. Owing mainly to the excessive number of disqualifications, all the favourites were ruled out and he won the gold. With all three previous Olympic marathons having been won by the host country, the Greeks were hopeful of continuing the tradition, but despite half of the entrants coming from Greece it was won by William Sherring of Canada by a massive margin of nearly seven minutes. In addition to his medal he was given a goat. The most successful competitor at the Games was shooter Louis Richardet (SUI) who won three gold and three silver medals.

The oldest gold medallist was Maurice Lecoq (FRA), aged 52 years and 31 days when he won the rapid fire pistol event. The youngest was the coxswain of the Italian fours crew, Giorgio Cesana, aged 14 years and 12 days. The youngest female champion was Marie Decugis (FRA), in tennis, aged 21 years and 261 days. She and her husband, Max became the first married couple to win Olympic gold medals. The oldest medallist was fencer Charles Newton-Robinson (GBR) at 52 years and 195 days.

Despite the soft cinder track in the stadium, poor facilities for the swimmers in the sea at Phaleron, complaints about food and judging decisions, these, since much maligned, Interim Games succeeded in putting the whole Olympic concept back on the path towards de Coubertin's ideal.

1906 MEDALS

	G	S	B
France	15	9	16
United States	12	6	6
Greece	8	11	13
Great Britain	8	11	5
Italy	7	6	3
Switzerland	5	6	4
Germany	4	6	5
Norway	4	2	–
Austria	3	3	2
Denmark	3	2	1
Sweden	2	5	7
Hungary	2	5	3
Belgium	2	2	3
Finland	2	1	1
Canada	1	1	–
The Netherlands	–	1	2
Australia	–	–	3
Czechoslovakia	–	–	2
South Africa	–	–	1

Athens 2004
XXVIII Olympic Games (August 13–29)

There was preliminary interest shown by 14 cities around the world but, in September 1997 the IOC decided on Athens, the site of the inaugural modern Games in 1896. The city has an ongoing pollution problem which the authorities have promised to alleviate by the time of the Games.

Athletics
(See also Tug-of-War)

The track and field events have been the centre-piece of every Olympic Games since 1896. From 1920 until the International Amateur Athletics Federation (IAAF) inaugurated their first world title meeting in 1983, the Olympic events were also official world championships. In the early Games quite large numbers of entries per country were allowed in an event, e.g. 12 in 1908, but in 1928 it was limited to four and in 1932 to three. After Barcelona in 1992 a suggestion was made to reduce the number to two, but has not been acted on to date. The first champion in modern Olympic history was James Connolly (USA) who won the triple jump (then called the hop, step and jump) on 6 April 1896. He also won medals in the high and long jumps, and went on to become a novelist and war correspondent. The first winner of an Olympic event was Francis Lane (USA) who had won the first heat of the 100m earlier the same day. Women's events were introduced in 1928, and the first female gold medallist was Halina Konopacka (POL) in the discus. As with the men, the first winner of an Olympic women's event was Anni Holdmann (GER) who took the first heat of the 100m the day before.

A record ten gold medals were won by Ray Ewry (USA) in the standing jumps between 1900 and 1908. It is a feat unsurpassed in any sport, and achieved despite the fact that Ewry had contracted polio as a child. The Finnish distance runner Paavo Nurmi won a total of 12 medals between 1920 and 1928, comprising nine golds and three silvers. He won them in an unmatched seven different events, and his five golds in 1924 is a record for a single Games. Carl Lewis (USA) equalled Nurmi's nine gold medals, 1984–96, as a sprinter/long jumper, adding a silver as well. Incidentally, Ewry had won three of his titles on a single day in 1900. However, the most individual titles at one Games is four by Alvin Kraenzlein (USA) in 1900. This total of four golds was equalled by Jesse Owens (USA) in 1936 and Carl Lewis (USA) in 1984, but they only gained three individual events — 100m, 200m and long jump — with the fourth gold medal in the relay. Fanny Blankers-Koen of The Netherlands matched them in 1948 with golds in the 100m, 200m, 80m hurdles and relay. Nurmi's team-mate, Ville Ritola, won a record of six medals in 1924, consisting of four golds and two silvers, incurring eight distance races in eight days. In 1912 the forerunner of all 'Flying Finns', Hannes Kohlemainen, had won six such races within nine days.

Four gold medals have been won by four women: Fanny Blankers-Koen (NED) in 1948, which is also a female record for one Games, as is the three individual titles included; Betty Cuthbert (AUS) in 1956 and 1964; Bärbel Wöckel (née Eckert) (GDR) in 1976 and 1980; and Evelyn Ashford (USA) between 1984 and 1992. Shirley Strickland (later de la Hunty) (AUS) won a record seven medals between 1948 and 1956, comprising three golds, one silver and three bronzes.

This total was equalled by Irena Szewinska (née Kirszenstein) (POL) with three golds, two silvers and two bronzes between 1964 and 1976, and Merlene Ottey (JAM) with two silvers and five bronzes in 1980, 1984, 1992 and 1996. This last compilation, of medals in four Games over a 16-year period, is a unique achievement for a female athlete. Szewinska, Ashford and Jackie Joyner-Kersee (USA) are the only women to win medals at three successive Games – in Szewinska's case uniquely in five different events. A 1975 study of photo evidence indicates that Strickland also came third in the 1948 200m, not fourth, but no move has been made to change the result officially.

A further remarkable track and field achievement was the four successive gold medals in the discus won by Al Oerter (USA) 1956–68. This was matched by Carl Lewis (USA) in the long jump 1984–96. Almost as worthy were the three golds and one silver won by Viktor Saneyev (URS) in the injury-prone triple jump events 1968–80. Mildred Didrikson (USA), who later achieved golf fame as 'Babe Zaharias', achieved a triple in 1932 when she won medals in a run (80m hurdles — gold), a jump (high jump — silver) and a throw (javelin — gold). Another unusual spread of medals was by Micheline Ostermeyer (FRA) in 1948 with golds in the shot and discus and a bronze in the high jump. Perhaps even more surprising was the fact that she was a concert pianist. The foremost male equivalent was Robert Garrett (USA) with golds in the shot and discus, and silvers in the high and long jumps, in 1896. Stanley Rowley won bronze medals in the 60m, 100m and 200m in 1900 representing Australasia (he was an Australian), and then was drafted into the British team for the 5000m team event, and won a gold medal although he did not finish the race.

The oldest gold medallist was Patrick 'Babe' McDonald (USA) winning the 56lb weight throw in 1920, aged 42 years and 23 days. The youngest gold medallist was Barbara Pearl Jones (USA) in the 1952 sprint relay, aged 15 years and 123 days, while the youngest individual event champion was Ulrike Meyfarth (FRG) who won the high jump in 1972 aged exactly one year older. The youngest male champion was Robert Mathias (USA) who won the 1948 decathlon, aged 17 years and 263 days, and in 1966, after a brief movie career, became a US Congressman. The oldest female champion was Lia Manoliu (ROM) in the 1968 discus, aged 36 years and 176 days. She (1952–72), and British javelin thrower, Tessa Sanderson (1976–96), hold the record of attending six Games. The male record, for athletes, of five Games, is held by 10 men. Manoliu's and Sanderson's 20-year spans of competition match the record of Dorothy Odam-Tyler (GBR) and Toyoko Yoshino-Nakamura (JPN), both 1936–56, and Francie Larrieu-Smith (USA), 1972–92. The greatest span of competition in Olympic athletics is 24 years by discus thrower Frantisek Janda-Suk of Bohemia and Czechoslovakia, 1900–24. The oldest medallist was Tebbs Lloyd Johnson (GBR) in the 50km walk of 1948, aged 48 years and 115 days, and the oldest female medallist was Dana Zátopková (TCH) in the 1960 javelin, aged

37 years and 348 days. Barbara Pearl Jones (USA) was also the youngest medallist, while the youngest male medallist was Mikhel Dorizas (GRE) in the 1906 stone throw, aged 16 years and 11 days. The oldest competitor ever in Olympic athletics was Percy Wyer (CAN), aged 52 years and 199 days when 30th in the 1936 marathon. The oldest female competitor was Joyce Smith (GBR), aged 46 years and 282 days when placing 11th in the 1984 marathon.

The first brothers to win medals were Richard and Lewis Sheldon (USA) in the 1900 throws and jumps respectively. The first to gain medals in the same event were Platt and Ben Adams (USA) who won gold and silver in the 1912 standing high jump. The most successful siblings were the Press sisters (URS), Tamara with three golds and a silver, and Irina with two golds, in 1960 and 1964. The only twins to win medals were Patrick and Pascal Barré (FRA) in the bronze medal sprint relay of 1980. Father and son gold medallists are represented by two families. Werner Järvinen (FIN) won the 1906 Greek style discus, his son, Matti, won the javelin in 1932, and another son, Akilles, gained silver medals in the 1928 and 1932 decathlons. In 1948, Imre Németh (HUN) won the hammer and 28 years later his son, Miklós, won the javelin with a world-record throw. The only father/daughter medal combination was that of Lennox Miller (JAM) with a 1968 100m silver and Inger Miller (USA) with a gold in the 1996 sprint relay.

The most successful mother/daughter combination was Elisabeta Bagriantseva (URS) with a silver in the 1952 discus, and Irina Nazarova with a gold in the 4 × 400m relay of 1980. Violet Webb (GBR) and her daughter, Janet Simpson, both won bronze medals in the 4 × 100m relay, in 1932 and 1964 respectively. One of the more poignant Olympic stories relates to Marie Dollinger who was one of the women involved in dropping the baton in the 1936 sprint relay when the German women 'couldn't lose'. One imagines the thoughts of her daughter, Brunhilde Hendrix, in the 1960 relay final — happily she won a silver medal. Incidentally, it has recently been suggested that the disaster to the usual machine-like precision changes of the 1936 German team was due to a last-minute change in their order to match similar changes to the American team's. Remarkably, Dollinger had first run in the Olympics in 1928, in the inaugural 800m, and in 1931 had equalled the 800m world record — not the usual curriculum vitae of a world class sprinter.

The first married couple to win gold medals were Emil and Dana Zátopek (TCH). Even more remarkable is the fact that Dana won her javelin title on the same afternoon as one of Emil's in 1952 — both of them were also born on the same day! The only other couple were Victor Bryzgin (URS), 4 × 100m in 1988, and his wife, Olga, gold medallist in the 400m and 4 × 400m. Frank Wykoff (USA) was the only sprinter to win gold medals in three Games, in relay teams between 1928 and 1936, until he was equalled by Evelyn Ashford (USA), also in relay teams, 1984–92, and Carl Lewis (USA) 1984–92.

The first Olympic athlete to be disqualified for contravening the drug regulations was Danuta Rosani (POL) in the 1976 discus. By far the biggest uproar occurred with the positive testing of Ben Johnson (CAN), after he had won the 1988 100m title in an apparently fabulous new world-record of 9.79sec. The repercussions on world attitudes to drug testing were immense. The scrutiny of 'sex testing' of women was introduced into the Games in 1968, many years too late in the opinion of many. They had in mind the case of Dora Ratjen (GER) who placed fourth in the 1936 high jump and was later found to be a man posing as a woman. There was also the case of Stella Walasiewicz (later Walsh), Polish-born but later an American citizen, who won gold and silver medals in the 100m of 1932 and 1936 respectively, and was reported, after her violent death in 1980, to have 'primary male characteristics'.

The shortest time that an athlete has held an Olympic record was 0.4sec by Olga Rukavishnikova (URS) in the 1980 pentathlon. That is the difference between her second place time of 2min 04.8sec in the final 800m event of the five-event contest, and the time of the third-placed Nadyezda Tkachenko (URS) whose overall points score exceeded her team-mate's by 146. Only three athletes have lost a title and then won it back. Nina Romashkova-Ponomaryeva (URS) won the discus in 1952, came third in 1956, then won again in 1960. Similarly Ulrike Meyfarth (FRG) won the high jump in 1972, did not make the final in 1976, but won again in 1984. The only man was Vladimir Golubnichiy (URS) in the 20km walk, winning in 1960, third in 1964 and first again in 1968. (Incidentally he also placed second in 1972). Meyfarth's 12 years between gold medals is matched by only Al Oerter, Carl Lewis and Irina Szewinska.

The largest number of competitors in a single event was the 124 runners in the 1996 men's marathon — 111 finished. The largest women's field was also in the 1996 marathon, with 86 starters of which 65 finished. The use of starting blocks was allowed in the Games for the first time in 1948. (See also Automatic Timing).

A number of Olympic athletics medallists have later made their mark in Hollywood films. In particular, they have come from the ranks of the decathletes — Jim Thorpe, Glenn Morris, Bob Mathias, Rafer Johnson, C. K. Yang, Floyd Simmons and Bruce Jenner. The 1924 pole vault champion, Lee Barnes, doubled for Buster Keaton for a vault sequence in his excellent film College. The 1928 silver medallist in the shot, Herman Brix, changed his name to Bruce Bennett and had many serious roles after an initial Tarzan appearance. Norman Pritchard (GBR), a 1900 medallist, made many silent films, while more recent additions to the Hollywood scene have been 1952 sprint relay gold winner Dean Smith (USA) and 1968 pole vault champion Bob Seagren (USA). The film industries of other countries have welcomed Tapio Rautavaara (FIN), the 1948 javelin champion, Giuseppe Tosi (ITA), the 1948 discus silver medallist, Giuseppe Gentile (ITA), 1968 triple jump bronze, and Adhemar Ferreira da Silva (BRA) the 1952 and 1956 triple jump champion.

The 1996 marathon champion, Josiah Thugwane (RSA), is thought to be the smallest male Olympic gold medallist in athletics ever at 1.58m tall and weighing 45kg. Merlene Ottey (JAM) is the only athlete to be a finalist in the same event, the 200m in her case, at five Games, 1980–96. For 2000, at Sydney, the pole vault and hammer events for women have been added, and the women's 10km walk has been replaced by the 20km event.

OLYMPIC RECORDS

Men

100m	9.84sec	Donovan Bailey (CAN)	1996
200m	19.32sec	Michael Johnson (USA)	1996
400m	43.49sec	Michael Johnson (USA)	1996
800m	1min 42.58sec	Vebjørn Rodal (NOR)	1996
1500m	3min 32.53sec	Sebastian Coe (GBR)	1984
5000m	13min 05.59sec	Said Aouita (MAR)	1984
10 000m	27min 07.34sec	Haile Gebrselassie (ETH)	1996
Marathon	2hr 9min 21sec	Carlos Lopez (POR)	1984
110m hurdles	12.95sec	Allen Johnson (USA)	1996
400m hurdles	46.78sec	Kevin Young (USA)	1992
3000m steeplechase	8min 05.51sec	Julius Kariuki (KEN)	1988
20km walk	1hr 19min 57sec	Jozef Pribilinec (TCH)	1988
50km walk	3hr 38min 29sec	Vyacheslav Ivanenko (URS)	1988
4 × 100m	37.40sec	United States	1992
4 × 400m	2min 55.74sec	United States	1992
High jump	2.39m	Charles Austin (USA)	1996
Pole vault	5.92m	Jean Galfione (FRA)	1996
Long jump	8.90m	Bob Beamon (USA)	1968
Triple jump	18.09m	Kenny Harrison (USA)	1996
	18.17m [1]	Mike Conley (USA)	1992
Shot	22.47m	Ulf Timmermann (GDR)	1988
Discus	69.40m	Lars Riedel (GER)	1996
Hammer	84.80m	Sergei Litvinov (URS)	1988
Javelin	89.66m	Jan Zelezny (TCH)	1992
Decathlon	8847pts	Daley Thompson (GBR)	1984

Women

100m	10.62sec [2]	Florence Griffith-Joyner (USA)	1988
	10.54 sec [1]	Florence Griffith-Joyner (USA)	1988
200m	21.34sec	Florence Griffith-Joyner (USA)	1988
400m	48.25sec	Marie-José Pérec (FRA)	1996
800m	1min 53.43sec	Nadyezda Olizarenko (URS)	1980
1500m	3min 53.96sec	Paula Ivan (ROM)	1988
5000m	14min 59.88sec	Wang Junxia (CHN)	1996
10 000m	31min 01.63 sec	Fernanda Ribeiro (POR)	1996
Marathon	2hr 24min 52sec	Joan Benoit (USA)	1984
100m hurdles	12.38sec	Yordanka Donkova (BUL)	1988
400m hurdles	52.82sec	Deon Hemmings (JAM)	1996
4 × 100m	41.60sec	GDR	1980
4 × 400m	3min 15.17sec	USSR	1988
10 000m walk	41min 49sec	Yelena Nikolayeva (RUS)	1996
High jump	2.05m	Stefka Kostadinova (BUL)	1996
Pole vault	new event		
Long jump	7.40m	Jackie Joyner-Kersee (USA)	1988
Triple jump	15.33m	Inessa Kravets (UKR)	1996
Shot	22.41m	Ilona Slupianek (GDR)	1980
Discus	72.30m	Martina Hellmann (GDR)	1988
Hammer	new event		
Javelin	4.68m	Petra Felke (GDR)	1998
Heptathlon	291pts	Jackie Joyner-Kersee (USA)	1988

[1] There has always been confusion as to whether wind-assisted performances should be considered as Games records. Both are given here
[2] In preliminary round

YOUNGEST AND OLDEST MEDALLISTS, BY EVENT

Men

Event	Medal	Youngest Yr/Dy	Name/Country/Date	Oldest Yr/Dy	Name/Country/Date
100m	G*	19–128	Reggie Walker (RSA) 1908	32–121	Linford Christie (GBR) 1992
	M*	18–234	Donald Lippincott (USA) 1912	32–121	Linford Christie (GBR) 1992
200m	G	20–47	Percy Williams (CAN) 1928	28–30	Pietro Mennea (ITA) 1980
	M	17–287	Dwayne Evans (USA) 1976	30–170	Barney Ewell (USA) 1948
400m	G	19–135	Steve Lewis (USA) 1988	30–323	Mike Larrabee (USA) 1964
	M	19–135	Steve Lewis (USA) 1988	30–323	Mike Larrabee (USA) 1964
800m	G	20–237	Ted Meredith (USA) 1912	31–147	Albert Hill (GBR) 1920
	M	20–35	Earl Jones (USA) 1984	32–58	Arthur Wint (JAM) 1952
1500m	G	21–62	Peter Rono (KEN) 1988	31–149	Albert Hill (GBR) 1920
	M	21–62	Peter Rono (KEN) 1988	31–149	Albert Hill (GBR) 1920
5000m	G	20–321	Joseph Guillemot (FRA) 1920	36–78 [1]	Miruts Yifter (ETH) 1980
	M	19–237	Fita Bayissa (ETH) 1992	36–78 [1]	Miruts Yifter (ETH) 1980
10 000m	G	21–42	Brahim Boutayeb (MAR) 1988	36–73 [1]	Miruts Yifter (ETH) 1980
	M	20–104	Richard Chelimo (KEN) 1992	36–73 [1]	Miruts Yifter (ETH) 1980
Marathon	G	20–301	Juan Carlos Zabala (ARG) 1932	37–176	Carlos Lopes (POR) 1984
	M	19–178	Ernst Fast (SWE) 1900	40–90	Mamo Wolde (ETH) 1972
3km steeplechase	G	20–33	Matthew Birir (KEN) 1992	32–211	Kipchoge Keino (KEN) 1972
	M	20–33	Matthew Birir (KEN) 1992	32–211	Kipchoge Keino (KEN) 1972
110m hurdles	G	20–304	Fred Kelly (USA) 1912	30–237	Mark McKoy (CAN) 1992
	M	20–304	Fred Kelly (USA) 1912	33–50	WillieDavenport(USA) 1976
400m hurdles	G	20–329	Edwin Moses (USA) 1976	29–207	Roy Cochran (USA) 1948
	M	18–325	Eddie Southern (USA) 1956	33–252	Kriss Akabusi (GBR) 1992
4 x 100m	G	18–118	Johnny Jones (USA) 1976	31–38	Carl Lewis (USA) 1992
	M	17–229	Ture Persson (SWE) 1912	33–292	Jocelyn Delecour(FRA) 1968
4 x 400m	G	19–100	Edgar Ablowich (USA) 1932	32–62	Arthur Wint (JAM) 1952
	M	17–+	Pál Simon (HUN) 1908	33–254	Kriss Akabusi (GBR) 1992
20km walk	G	22–25	Jefferson Perez (ECU) 1996	33–110	Peter Frenkel (GDR) 1972
	M	21–253	Noel Freeman (AUS) 1960	37–71	Peter Frenkel (GDR) 1976
50km walk	G	25–103	Norman Read (NZL) 1956	38–128	Thomas Green (GBR) 1932
	M	25–26	Antal Róka (HUN) 1952	48–115	Tebbs Lloyd Johnson (GBR) 1948
High jump	G	19–214	Jacek Wszola (POL) 1976	30–3	Con Leahy (GBR) 1906
	M	18–140	Valeri Brumel (URS) 1960	30–3	Con Leahy (GBR) 1906
Pole vault	G	17–360	Lee Barnes (USA) 1924	30–280	Bob Richards (USA) 1956
	M	17–360	Lee Barnes (USA) 1924	30–280	Bob Richards (USA) 1956
Long jump	G	19–17	Randy Williams (USA) 1972	35–28	Carl Lewis (USA) 1996
	M	19–17	Randy Williams (USA) 1972	35–28	Carl Lewis (USA) 1996
Triple jump	G	20–225	Gustaf Lindblom (SWE) 1912	31–195	Peter O'Connor (GBR) 1906
	M	20–38	Arnoldo Devonish (VEN) 1952	34–296	Viktor Saneyev (URS) 1980
Shot	G	19–167 [2]	Ralph Rose (USA) 1904	32–151	Wladyslaw Komar (POL) 1972
	M	19–167 [2]	Ralph Rose (USA) 1904	37–59	Denis Horgan (GBR) 1908
Discus	G	20–69	Al Oerter (USA) 1956	35–240	Ludvik Danek (TCH) 1972
	M	19–170	Ralph Rose (USA) 1904	37–46	John Powell (USA) 1984
Hammer	G	20–161	József Csermák (HUN) 1952	35–187	John Flanagan (USA) 1908
	M	19–165	Ralph Rose (USA) 1904	45–205	Matt McGrath (USA) 1924
Javelin	G	20–34	Erik Lundkvist (SWE) 1928	33–149	Tapio Rautavaara (FIN) 1948
	M	20–34 [3]	Erik Lundkvist (SWE) 1928	38–332	József Várszegi (HUN) 1948
Decathlon	G	17–263	Bob Mathias (USA) 1948	30–102 [4]	Helge Løvland (NOR) 1920
	M	17–263	Bob Mathias (USA) 1948	30–102 [4]	Helge Løvland (NOR) 1920

YOUNGEST AND OLDEST MEDALLISTS, BY EVENT *continued*

Women

Event	Medal	Youngest Yr/Dy	Name/Country/Year	Oldest Yr/Dy	Name/Country/Year
100m	G	16–343	Elizabeth Robinson (USA) 1928	30–98	Fanny Blankers-Koen (NED) 1948
	M	16–343	Elizabeth Robinson (USA) 1928	36–78	Merlene Ottey (JAM) 1996
200m	G	18–254	Betty Cuthbert (AUS) 1956	30–102	Fanny Blankers-Koen (NED) 1948
	M	17–116	Raelene Boyle (AUS) 1968	36–83	Merlene Ottey (JAM) 1996
400m	G	19–340	Monica Zehrt (GDR) 1972	30–66	Irena Szewinska (POL) 1976
	M	18–152	Christina Brehmer (GDR) 1976	30–66	Irena Szewinska (POL) 1976
800m	G	20–251	Madeline Manning (USA) 1968	28–194	Svetlana Masterkova (RUS) 1996
	M	20–100	Inge Gentzel (SWE) 1928	33–205	Fita Lovin (ROM) 1984
1500m	G	24–29	Hassiba Boulmerka (ALG) 1992	29–47	Ludmila Bragina (URS) 1972
	M	19–227	Qu Yunxia (CHN) 1992	34–13	Maricica Puica (ROM) 1984
3000m/5000m	G	23–201	Wang Junxia (CHN) 1996	34–12	Maricica Puica (ROM) 1984
	M	23–201	Wang Junxia (CHN) 1996	34–12	Maricica Puica (ROM) 1984
10 000m	G	20–139	Derartu Tulu (ETH) 1992	28–120	Olga Bondarenko (URS) 1988
	M	20–139	Derartu Tulu (ETH) 1992	32–28	Lynn Jennings (USA) 1992
Marathon	G	22–223	Fatuma Roba (ETH) 1996	30–86	Rosa Mota (POR) 1988
	M	22–223	Fatuma Roba (ETH) 1996	37–61	Lorraine Moller (NZL) 1992
80m/100m hurdles	G	17–19	Maureen Caird (AUS) 1968	32–101	Ludmila Engquist (SWE) 1996
	M	17–19	Maureen Caird (AUS) 1968	34–95	Karin Balzer (GDR) 1972
400m hurdles	G	22–115	Nawal El Moutawakel (MAR)1984	28–161	Debbie Flintoff-King (AUS) 1988
	M	22–115	Nawal El Moutawakel (MAR)1984	29–353	Sandra Farmer-Patrick (USA) 1992
4 x 100m	G	15–123	Barbara Pearl Jones (USA) 1952	35–115	Evelyn Ashford (USA) 1992
	M	15–123	Barbara Pearl Jones (USA) 1952	36–85	Merlene Ottey (JAM) 1996
4 x 400m	G	18–154 [5]	Christina Brehmer (GDR) 1976	30–235	Maria Pinigina (URS) 1988
	M	17–236	Mabel Fergerson (USA) 1972	30–235	Maria Pinigina (URS) 1988
10km walk	G	24–124	Chen Yueling (CHN) 1992	30–179	Yelena Nikolayeva (RUS) 1996
	M	22–134	Gao Hongmiao (CHN) 1996	30–179	Yelena Nikolayeva (RUS) 1996
High jump	G	16–123	Ulrike Meyfarth (FRG) 1972	31–131	Steka Kostadinova (BUL) 1996
	M	16–115	Dorothy Odam-Tyler (GBR) 1936	31–131	Stefka Kostadinova (BUL) 1996
Long jump	G	20–256	Tatyana Kolpakova (URS) 1980	29–67	Viorica Viscopoleanu (ROM) 1968
	M	17–332	Willye White (USA) 1956	34–12	Jackie Joyner-Kersee (USA) 1996
Triple jump	G	29–300	Inessa Kravets (UKR) 1996	29–300	Inessa Kravets (UKR) 1996
	M	25–72	Sarka Kaspárková (CZE) 1996	29–300	Inessa Kravets (UKR) 1996
Shot	G	21–186	Galina Zybina (URS) 1952	34–255	Ivanka Khristova (BUL) 1976
	M	21–186	Galina Zybina (URS) 1952	35–244	Svetlana Krachevskaya (URS)1980
Discus	G	20–121	Evelin Schlaak (GDR) 1976	36–176	Lia Manoliu (ROM) 1968
	M	20–100	Ruth Osborn (USA) 1932	36–176	Lia Manoliu (ROM) 1968
Javelin	G	17–86	Mihaela Penes (ROM) 1964	33–190	Herma Bauma (AUT) 1948
	M	17–86	Mihaela Penes (ROM) 1964	37–348	Dana Zátopková (TCH) 1960
Heptathlon	G	23–267	Glynis Nunn (AUS) 1984	30–152	Jackie Joyner-Kersee (USA) 1992
	M	22–154	Jackie Joyner-Kersee (USA) 1984	30–344	Sabine John (GDR) 1988

1 Questionable date of birth would result in revised age of 20 days less
2 Mikhel Dorizas (GRE) was third in the 1906 stone throw aged 16 years and 11 days
3 Mikhel Dorizas (GRE) was second in the 1908 javelin (freestyle) aged 18 years and 90 days
4 Thomas Kiely (GBR) won the 1904 all-round title aged 34 years and 134 days
5 Grit Breuer (GDR) only ran in heats of 1988 event, but received a gold medal aged 16 years and 228 days
* G — Gold medallist
* M — Medallist

ATHLETICS MEDALS (excluding Tug-of-War)

	Men			Women			
	G	S	B	G	S	B	Total
United States [1]	260	191	160	39	25	17	692
Soviet Union	37	37	42	34	29	35	214
Great Britain	42	61	43	5	20	14	185
Finland	47	33	30	1	2	–	113
GDR	14	14	14	24	23	21	110
Germany	7	23	26	9	12	14	91
Sweden	18	25	41	1	–	3	88
Australia	6	9	12	11	10	12	60
France	8	20	18	6	1	4	57
Canada	12	10	17	2	5	7	53
Italy	13	7	20	3	6	3	52
Poland	10	8	5	6	8	7	44
FRG	4	8	12	8	6	5	43
Hungary	7	13	16	3	1	2	42
Kenya	13	15	11	–	1	–	40
Jamaica [2]	4	11	5	1	5	5	31
Romania	–	–	1	9	10	6	26
Greece	3	7	14	1	1	–	26
Czechoslovakia [3]	8	7	3	3	2	2	25
Cuba	3	6	4	2	2	4	21
New Zealand	7	1	7	1	–	2	18
South Africa	5	5	4	1	2	1	18
Japan	4	5	6	–	2	1	18
Bulgaria	1	–	1	3	7	5	17
Ethiopia	6	1	6	2	–	1	16
Norway	4	2	7	–	1	1	15
The Netherlands	–	–	5	6	2	1	14
Brazil	3	2	6	–	–	–	11
Belgium	2	6	2	–	–	–	10
China	–	–	1	2	3	4	10
Morocco	3	2	3	1	–	–	9
Russia	–	2	–	3	3	1	9
Spain	2	3	3	–	–	–	8
Switzerland	–	6	2	–	–	–	8
Mexico	3	3	1	–	–	-	7
Nigeria	–	1	1	1	1	3	7
Portugal	1	1	1	2	–	1	6
Austria	–	–	–	1	1	4	6
Trinidad and Tobago	1	1	4	–	–	–	6
Ireland	4	1	–	–	–	–	5
Argentina	2	2	–	–	1	–	5
Ukraine	–	1	2	1	–	1	5
Tunisia	1	2	1	–	–	–	4
Namibia	–	4	–	–	–	–	4
Belarus	–	1	1	–	1	1	4
Czech Republic	1	–	1	–	–	1	3
Denmark	–	1	1	–	–	1	3
Algeria	1	–	–	1	–	–	2
Korea	1	1	–	–	–	–	2
Uganda	1	–	1	–	–	–	2
Bahamas	–	–	1	–	1	–	2
Chile	–	1	–	–	1	–	2
Tanzania	–	2	–	–	–	–	2
Yugoslavia	–	2	–	–	–	–	2
Estonia	–	1	1	–	–	–	2
Latvia	–	1	1	–	–	–	2

ATHLETICS MEDALS (excluding Tug-of-War) *continued*

| | Men | | | Women | | | |
	G	S	B	G	S	B	Total
Chinese Taipei	–	1	–	–	–	1	2
Panama	–	–	2	–	–	–	2
Philippines	–	–	2	–	–	–	2
Burundi	1	–	–	–	–	–	1
Ecuador	1	–	–	–	–	–	1
Lithuania	1	–	–	–	–	–	1
Luxembourg	1	–	–	–	–	–	1
Syria	–	–	–	1	–	–	1
Haiti	–	1	–	–	–	–	1
Iceland	–	1	–	–	–	–	1
Ivory Coast	–	1	–	–	–	–	1
Senegal	–	1	–	–	–	–	1
Slovenia	–	–	–	–	1	–	1
Sri Lanka	–	1	–	–	–	–	1
Zambia	–	1	–	–	–	–	1
Barbados [2]	–	–	1	–	–	–	1
Colombia	–	–	–	–	–	1	1
Djibouti	–	–	1	–	–	–	1
Mozambique	–	–	–	–	–	1	1
Qatar	–	–	1	–	–	–	1
Turkey	–	–	1	–	–	–	1
Venezuela	–	–	1	–	–	–	1
	573	573	573	194	196	193	2302

[1] Includes 2 extra golds when Jim Thorpe reinstated to 1912 decathlon/pentathlon titles
[2] Two bronzes counted for joint British West Indies 4 × 400m relay team in 1960
[3] Split into Czech Republic and Slovakia from 1996

Atlanta 1996
XXVI Olympic Games (19 July–4 August)

Attended by representatives of 197 countries, comprising 10 310 competitors, of which 3513 were women.

The 1996 Games celebrated the 100th anniversary of the rebirth of the Modern Olympics, and Athens was thought by many to be the obvious venue. The somewhat surprising decision, in September 1990, was in favour of Atlanta. It was immediately suggested that many in the IOC were swayed by the financial support that the city would receive from American television and other corporate sponsors. (American television rights were sold for a record $456 million.) In the event there was much criticism of the chauvinistic coverage by NBC, with the excessive emphasis on American performances reaching ludicrous levels. However, it was reported that the television company received some $700 million in advertising revenue for the Games period. It was expected that Atlanta would provide the model of top-flight organisation and excellent technology — but it didn't. There was much criticism of the extreme commercialisation and of the organisational failures, particularly in the areas of transportation. The cost of hotels and the high price of tickets was another

area of foreign concern. On the plus side was the undoubted goodwill and friendliness of the city's inhabitants, and the generally good, albeit hot and humid, weather. Also, it was one of the most centralized Games of recent years with most of the sports held within the periphery of the city, although yachting was held on the Georgia coast at Savannah. Although cut-backs to the number of sports and events in the Games have been mooted for years, there were a record 29 sports and 271 events. Newcomers included softball, beach volleyball, mountain bike racing, and soccer for women. However, it had been agreed that demonstration sports would no longer be held as part of this and future celebrations. Other changes included the holding of the modern pentathlon on only one day, and the replacement of the Flying Dutchman 2-man yachting class by a single-handed Laser class. Many new, excellent facilities were built, including an 85 000-seat stadium and a remarkable equestrian centre.

The Games were officially opened by President William Jefferson Clinton, and the overlong opening ceremony witnessed, for the first time, a full turnout of all 197 countries then affiliated to the Olympic movement. New countries — in addition to those coming from the break-up of the former Soviet Union and Czechoslovakia included Burundi, Guinea-Bissau, Nauru and Palestine. Other debuts included the first female competitor ever from Iran, in the shooting events. Entries exceeded 10 000 for the first time, and there were over 17 000 representatives of the world's media. The American team numbered 697, the largest ever national contingent since the enormous French team (884) at Paris in 1900.

An unusual scenario for the end of the traditional Olympic torch run had representatives of, white and black, male and female, and current and first Olympic hosts. Thus, in the last few changeovers: Al Oerter (4-time champion) passed to Evander Holyfield (bronze 1984); he was joined by Paraskevi Patoulidou (1992 women's 100m hurdles gold for Greece); and then the torch was handed to Janet Evans (4-time swimming gold medallist), who took it up the stairs in the stadium. There she passed it to the one-time boxing champion, Muhammed Ali, sadly a shadow of his former self, who finally lit the stadium flame, an exceptionally moving moment. The oath, on behalf of all the competitors, was taken by American basketball player Teresa Edwards.

In all, 79 countries won medals, another record, including the first ever medal (a gold) for Hong Kong, in board sailing, on what will probably be its last appearance, as a separate entity, on the Olympic stage. The most successful competitor was Amy Van Dyken (USA), who won four gold medals in swimming, while Alexei Nemov of Russia won six gymnastic medals (two gold, one silver, three bronze). Over 32 000 spectators packed the gymnastics hall to see injured US gymnast Kerri Strug complete her final vault to guarantee the hosts the team gold medal. Overall there were excellent attendances at all venues, with an unprecedented 8.6 million tickets sold for the 17 days competitions. In the athletics stadium, later converted for baseball, Michael Johnson set an astounding time of 19.32sec for 200m, while team-mate Carl Lewis won his fourth consecutive long jump title to take his career total to nine Olympic golds. The star of the swimming pool was the Irishwoman, Michelle Smith, who was not only her country's first ever swimming finalist, but won three gold medals and a bronze. She was the target of much innuendo about drug-taking, especially from some of the US swimming team and American press. In rowing, Britain's Steve Redgrave took his fourth gold medal in as many Games; France's Jeannie Longo-Ciprelli won the cycling women's road race, improving on her Barcelona silver, at the age of 37 years; and Hubert Raudaschl of Austria competed in a record breaking, for any sport, ninth Olympic Games. The first Australian Aborigine athlete to win a gold medal was Nova Peris-Kneebone in the victorious Australian women's hockey team. Primarily a sprinter she will almost certainly make the athletics team in 2000. Appallingly, halfway through the Games a bomb went off in Centennial Park, a popular place for fans and general public alike, which resulted in two deaths, with over 100 others injured. This happened despite an enormous outlay on security, which involved some 30 000 operatives — yet another record.

The youngest gold medallist was swimmer Amanda Beard (USA) at 14 years and 269 days as a member of the winning medley relay squad. She was the youngest medallist three days earlier when she took silver in the 100m breaststroke. The youngest male champion was Michal Martikan (SVK), aged 17 years and 70 days winning the canoeing C1 slalom event, while individual pursuit cyclist, Alexei Markov (RUS) won a bronze just eight days younger. The oldest gold medallist and medallist at Atlanta was Klaus Balkenhol (GER) taking gold in the dressage team event, aged 56 years and 235 days. The oldest female champion was Jeannie Longo-Ciprelli (FRA), aged 37 years and 264 days when she won the cycling road race. Softball player Jocelyn Lester (AUS) was the oldest female medallist at 38 years and 130 days. The oldest competitor at Atlanta was Faustino Puccini (ITA) in the dressage event, aged 63 years and 267 days.

1996 MEDALS (SUMMER)

	G	S	B
United States	44	32	25
Russia	26	21	16
Germany	20	18	27
China	16	22	12
France	15	7	15
Italy	13	10	12
Australia	9	9	23
Cuba	9	8	8
Ukraine	9	2	12
Korea	7	15	5
Poland	7	5	5
Hungary	7	4	10
Spain	5	6	6
Romania	4	7	9
The Netherlands	4	5	10
Greece	4	4	–
Czech Republic	4	3	4
Switzerland	4	3	–
Denmark	4	1	1
Turkey	4	1	1
Canada	3	11	8
Bulgaria	3	7	5
Japan	3	6	5
Kazakhstan	3	4	4
Brazil	3	3	9
New Zealand	3	2	1
South Africa	3	1	1
Ireland	3	–	1
Sweden	2	4	2
Norway	2	2	3
Belgium	2	2	2
Nigeria	2	1	3
North Korea	2	1	2
Algeria	2	–	1
Ethiopia	2	–	1
Great Britain	1	8	6
Belarus	1	6	8
Kenya	1	4	3
Jamaica	1	3	2
Finland	1	2	1
Indonesia	1	1	2
Yugoslavia	1	1	2
Iran	1	1	1

1996 MEDALS (SUMMER) continued

	G	S	B
Slovakia	1	1	1
Armenia	1	1	–
Croatia	1	1	–
Portugal	1	–	1
Thailand	1	–	1
Burundi	1	–	–
Costa Rica	1	–	–
Ecuador	1	–	–
Hong Kong	1	–	–
Syria	1	–	–
Argentina	–	2	1
Namibia	–	2	–
Slovenia	–	2	–
Austria	–	1	2
Malaysia	–	1	1
Moldova	–	1	1
Uzbekistan	–	1	1
Azerbaijan	–	1	–
Bahamas	–	1	–
Latvia	–	1	–
Philippines	–	1	–
Taiwan	–	1	–
Tonga	–	1	–
Zambia	–	1	–
Georgia	–	–	2
Morocco	–	–	2
Trinidad and Tobago	–	–	2
India	–	–	1
Israel	–	–	1
Lithuania	–	–	1
Mexico	–	–	1
Mongolia	–	–	1
Mozambique	–	–	1
Puerto Rico	–	–	1
Tunisia	–	–	1
Uganda	–	–	1

Australian Rules Football

A demonstration sport at Melbourne in 1956. Two amateur Australian teams played an exhibition that resulted in a 250–135 score.

Automatic Timing

The debut for electrical/photo-timing equipment was tried out for the athletic events at the Stockholm 1912 Games. The photograph produced by the system was used to determine second and third placings in the 1500m. However, the first use of 'modern' photo-timing was at Los Angeles in 1932, with the film made available to the Jury of Appeal, but times not officially given. In 1948, at London, photo-finish equipment used for horse-racing was employed at the athletic events, but only to help the judges decide on placings, not timings. At these Games, in at least one event the women's 200m final an incorrect result was allowed to stand (see Athletics). Although automatic timing devices were in use from 1952, they were not officially recognised and hand-timings were used. (However, these automatic timings have been published after research by statistician Bob Sparks.) Timings in athletics, to two decimal places in the short races, were first used officially in 1972 at Munich.

Badminton

Introduced for the first time in 1992, badminton had been a demonstration sport in 1972, when the men's singles was won by Rudy Hartono of Indonesia. Because officials felt it necessary to control the number of entries a mixed doubles competition was not included until 1996.

The youngest gold medallist was Ge Fei (CHN) in the 1996 women's doubles, aged 20 years and 175 days, while the youngest male champion/medallist was Kim Dong Moon (KOR) in the 1996 mixed doubles, aged 20 years and 314 days. The oldest champion was Poul-Erik Hoyer-Larsen (DEN) 1996 singles champion, aged 30 years and 316 days, and the oldest female winner was Young Ah Gil (KOR) in the 1996 women's doubles at 26 years and 111 days. The youngest medallist was Mia Audina (INA) taking the silver in the 1996 women's singles at 16 years and 345 days. The oldest male medallist was Rashid Sidek (MAS) with a singles bronze in 1996, aged 34 years and 56 days, while the youngest female medallist was Guan Weizhen (CHN) at 28 years and 62 days in the

BADMINTON MEDALS

	Men [1]			Women			
	G	S	B	G	S	B	Total
China	–	1	2	1	2	5	11
Korea	2	1	–	2	2	1	8
Indonesia	2	2	2	1	–	–	7
Denmark	1	–	1	–	–	–	2
Malaysia	–	–	2	–	–	–	2
	5	4	7	4	4	6	30

[1] Including mixed doubles

1992 women's doubles. Barcelona female gold medallist Susi Susanti, Indonesia's first ever Olympic champion, later married her countryman, the male singles winner Alan Budi Kusuma. Brothers Razif and Jalani Sidek won the bronze in the 1992 men's doubles, for Malaysia's first ever Olympic medal.

Bandy

A demonstration sport at the Oslo Winter Games in 1952, bandy is similar to ice hockey, but played with a ball instead of a puck. A tournament was held, and final placings were decided on goal average, with Sweden winning over Norway and Finland.

Barcelona 1992
XXV Olympic Games (25 July–9 August)

Attended by representatives of 169 countries, comprising 9364 competitors, of which 2707 were women.

After intense 'politicking', the 1992 Summer Games were awarded to Barcelona, Spain, in October 1986. Barcelona had been promised the Games in 1924 but Baron de Coubertin had changed his mind and opted for Paris. Barcelona was then suggested for the 1936 celebration, but by then the spectre of civil war decided the IOC in favour of Berlin. The stadium intended for those Games, built in 1929 on Montjuic, was completely refurbished and served as the main venue for 1992. Most of the other venues were within city limits, with only football (preliminary games), rowing, canoeing and road cycling sites at any great distance. Television revenue set what was then a record, with NBC paying $401 million for the American rights. As well as two new sports — baseball and badminton — being added to the official programme there were also a number of extra events. These included seven for women in judo, a women's 10km walk, a dinghy sailing competition for women, and four canoe-slalom contests, of which one is for women. There were 26 sports and the total number of medal events was 259 (with the distribution of 815 medals in all). An outbreak of African equine plague in Spain in 1989 originally cast considerable doubt as to whether the equestrian events would be held, but it was curtailed in time. There were three demonstration sports: pelota basque, tae kwon do, and roller hockey.

Prior to the Games, as always, there were the familiar cries from media doom-mongers that the Olympics were finished, and that there was no point in holding them again. It was stated that most sports had their own world championships and thus the importance of the Olympic Games was diluted. What these critics seem never to understand is that the world's sportsmen and women still consider an Olympic medal as the pinnacle of sporting achievement. In 1992, for the first time in many years not a single nation boycotted the occasion, and there were a record number of countries and competitors, which caused the IOC to discuss the need for 'quotas' to limit numbers in future Games. The Baltic states were independent again and Germany competed as one team. Yugoslavia was split into Bosnia-Herzogovina, Croatia and Slovenia who competed independently, with competitors from Serbia and Macedonia competing as Independent Olympic Participants (IOP). South Africa returned to the Olympic fold after 32 years. The 169 countries marching in the parade were joined by Afghanistan, despite not having any competitors. Media representatives, including the critics, outnumbered the competitors.

The Barcelona Games were a tremendous success overall — many thought it one of the best Games ever. The only sour note was caused by transport shortcomings for fans billeted way out of town. Happily, fears of terrorist activity proved to be unfounded, but security arrangements were reported to have cost $90 million. Tennis professionals and the US basketball 'Dream Team' with Earvin 'Magic' Johnson, Michael Jordan, Larry Bird and Charles Barkley, was one of the highlights of the Games. Because of their presence these sports were given greatly increased television coverage, even outside the United States. The disintegrating Soviet Union, known here as the Commonwealth of Independent States (CIS) or Unified Team (EUN), made its last appearance. King Juan Carlos, an Olympic yachtsman in 1972, declared the Games open during a colourful ceremony, and the oath was taken by Luis Doreste Blanco, who later won a gold medal in the Flying Dutchman class. He had won gold in the 1984 470 class, while his brother José-Luis had won the 1988 Finn event. Incidentally, the King's son, Felipe, placed sixth in the Barcelona Soling, and his daughter, Christina, had been in the 1988 Tornado class. Their uncle, Constantine of Greece, had been a yachting gold medallist in 1960. The flame on the stadium pedestal was spectacularly lit by paraplegic archer Antonio Rebollo symbolically shooting an arrow at the torch tower. Recent research indicates that Spain's first Olympic champion, Lucius Minicius, winner of the chariot race in AD 129, was born in Barcelona, and his ghost must have been smiling as Spain gained a record number of medals, nearly doubling its total from the 16 previous Games. In all, 64 countries won a medal — another record to that time — and of these, 37 won a gold.

Although the heat did affect a number of sports adversely, the overall standard was very high, with perhaps the outstanding individual performances of the Games being the 1500m freestyle of 14min 43.48sec by swimmer Kieren Perkins (AUS), and the 400m hurdles in 46.78sec by Kevin Young (USA). In the swimming pool there was a fine swansong by the Unified Team as Alexander Popov won two gold and two silver medals, and Yevgeni Sadovyi took three golds. The most successful competitor was their compatriot gymnast Vitali Scherbo who won six gold medals. Although he only placed 20th in the Star yacht class Hubert Raudaschl (AUT) equalled a record, of competing in eight Games, 1964–92 — he has since added another. Indonesian-born Chrisilot Hanson-Boylen (CAN), 12th in the dressage competition, set a new record for women, also in her eighth Games, and also equalled the 28 year span of competition.

The youngest gold medallist/medallist was the diver Fu Mingxia (CHN), aged 13 years and 345 days, while the youngest male winner was her diving team-mate, Sun Shuwei at 16 years and 185 days. The oldest gold medallist was Klaus Balkenhol (GER) in the dressage team, aged 52 years and 243 days, with the oldest female champion, Gillian Rolton (AUS), in the three-day event team at 36 years and 88 days. The oldest medallist was the 1972 gold medallist Swedish shooter Ragnar Skanåker, in his sixth Games at 58 years and 48 days, while the oldest female medallist was, Carol Lavell (USA) in the dressage, aged 49 years and 118 days. The youngest competitor was rowing cox Carlos Barrera of Spain, aged 11 years and 256 days. The youngest female competitor was Hungarian swimmer Judit Kiss at 12 years and 184 days.

1992 MEDALS (SUMMER)

	G	S	B
Unified Team	45	38	29
United States	37	34	37
Germany	33	21	28
China	16	22	16
Cuba	14	6	11
Spain	13	7	2
Korea	12	5	12
Hungary	11	12	7
France	8	5	16
Australia	7	9	11
Canada	7	4	7
Italy	6	5	8
Great Britain	5	3	12
Romania	4	6	8
Czechoslovakia	4	2	1
North Korea (PRK)	4	–	5
Japan	3	8	11
Bulgaria	3	7	6
Poland	3	6	10
The Netherlands	2	6	7
Kenya	2	4	2
Norway	2	4	1
Turkey	2	2	2
Indonesia	2	2	1
Brazil	2	1	–
Greece	2	–	–
Sweden	1	7	4
New Zealand	1	4	5
Finland	1	2	2
Denmark	1	1	4
Morocco	1	1	1
Ireland	1	1	–
Ethiopia	1	–	2
Algeria	1	–	1
Estonia	1	–	1
Lithuania	1	–	1
Switzerland	1	–	–

1992 MEDALS (SUMMER) continued

	G	S	B
Jamaica	–	3	1
Nigeria	–	3	1
Latvia	–	2	1
Austria	–	2	–
Namibia	–	2	–
South Africa	–	2	–
Belgium	–	1	2
Croatia	–	1	2
IOP	–	1	2
Iran	–	1	2
Israel	–	1	1
Chinese Taipei	–	1	–
Mexico	–	1	–
Peru	–	1	–
Slovenia	–	–	2
Mongolia	–	–	2
Argentina	–	–	1
Bahamas	–	–	1
Colombia	–	–	1
Ghana	–	–	1
Malaysia	–	–	1
Pakistan	–	–	1
Philippines	–	–	1
Puerto Rico	–	–	1
Qatar	–	–	1
Surinam	–	–	1
Thailand	–	–	1

Baseball

There were six occasions when American baseball was demonstrated, plus an exhibition of Finnish baseball in 1952. In 1912, the USA team, containing many track and field medallists, beat Sweden 13–3. In 1936 a 'World Amateurs' team beat an American 'Olympic' team in front of 100 000 spectators in the Berlin Olympic Stadium. In 1956, an American Services team beat an Australian team 11–5 before an estimated 114 000 people, then a record crowd for a baseball game anywhere. At Tokyo in 1964, a USA team beat two Japanese teams, and in 1984 Japan won an eight-nation tournament. In 1988 the USA also won an eight-nation tournament, beating Japan in the final. Finally, in 1992, baseball became an official medal sport.

The greatest margin of victory, and the highest score, was the 20–0 victory by Chinese Taipei over Spain in the 1992 competition. In 1996 Cuba beat Italy 20–6 to equal the highest score, and set an aggregate record of 27 when beating Australia 19–8. Orestes Kindelan (CUB) scored 11 home runs in the 1996 competition, and team-mate Omar Linares scored a record 12 home runs 1992–96. Luigi Carrozza (ITA) has had the best batting average with .571 at Atlanta, while the pitcher Tomohito Ito (JPN) achieved 20 strikeouts at Barcelona in 1992.

The oldest gold medallist/medallist was Lourdes Gurriel (CUB), aged 35 years and 133 days in 1992, while the youngest winner was Giorge Diaz (CUB) at 21 years and 324 days in 1992. Jong Yeu-jeng (TPE) played for the 1992 silver medal team, aged 18 years and 217 days.

BASEBALL MEDALS

	G	S	B	Total
Cuba	2	–	–	2
Japan	–	1	1	2
Chinese Taipei	–	1	–	1
United States	–	–	1	1
	2	2	2	6

Basketball

The game made its official Olympic debut in 1936, although it was demonstrated in 1904, and the analogous Dutch game, Korfball, was demonstrated in 1928. The 1936 tournament was played outdoors, and the final score was very low due to a downpour which made the ground slippery and the ball slimy. Interestingly, one of the referees in that tournament was Avery Brundage (USA), later to become President of the IOC, while the man who had devised the modern game, Dr James Naismith, was among those who presented the medals. The tournament was won by the United States, beginning a winning streak of seven titles and 63 victories. The run began with a walkover against Spain, whose team had returned home to fight in the Spanish Civil War, and ended when they were beaten by the Soviet Union 51–50 in the 1972 final. That final was much disputed, with the Americans claiming that too much overtime was played during which the Soviet Alexander Belov (who tragically died six years later) scored the winning basket. With one second to go, and the USA in the lead 50–49, the Soviet inbounds pass had been deflected and everyone thought the game was over. However, the Soviet team was given another inbounds pass chance, but did not score. Again the game seemed to be over. But Dr William Jones (GBR), Secretary-General of Fédération Internationale de Basketball Amateur (FIBA), stated that play was incorrectly restarted at one second and that there should have been three seconds remaining. The clock was reset to three seconds and the Soviet team scored. The USA team protested vigorously and refused to accept the silver medals. Unbeaten again until another defeat by the Soviet Union in the 1988 semi-final, and unbeaten in 1992 and 1996, the overall Olympic tally of USA teams is now 11 golds, one silver and one bronze.

After various changes and qualifying conditions since 1976 the IOC accepted 12 teams in both the men's and women's competitions at Atlanta. Eleven US players have won two gold medals each, but only David Robinson (1988–96) additionally won a bronze. Two men have won medals at four Games; Gennadi Volnov (URS) with a gold, two silvers and a bronze, 1960–72, and Sergei Belov (URS) with a gold and three bronzes 1968–80. In April 1989 it was decided to allow professional players to compete in the Olympic tournaments. Thus the American 'Dream Team' for 1992 included all-time NBA greats Earvin 'Magic' Johnson, Larry Bird, Michael Jordan, Patrick Ewing, Charles Barkley and David Robinson. This team averaged 117.25 points per game. In 1999 Barkley, by then a senator, became a US presidential candidate.

The oldest gold medallist was Larry Bird (USA) in 1992, aged 35 years and 245 days, while the youngest was Spencer Haywood (USA), aged 19 years and 186 days in 1968. The oldest medallist was Sergejus Jovaisa (LTU) in 1992, aged 37 years and 235 days, while the youngest medallist was Vladimir Tkachenko (URS) in 1976, aged 18 years and 311 days. The highest aggregate score in a game is 238 points when Brazil beat China 130–108 in 1988. In that same tournament Brazil also scored the highest ever by a team in Olympic contests when they beat Egypt 138–85. The biggest margin of victory is 100 points, when Korea beat Iraq 120–20, and when China beat Iraq 125–25, both in 1948. The highest score by an individual in a single game is 55 points by Oscar Schmidt (BRA) in a 1988 qualifying round encounter in which Spain beat Brazil 118–110. In Seoul, he scored 338 points and averaged a record 42.2 points a game. Schmidt, 1980–96, and Teofilo Cruz (PUR), 1960–76, have competed in a record five Olympic basketball tournaments. In 1996, Schmidt, for the third time, was the highest scorer in the tournament, aged 38 years and 171 days, and brought his total points in Olympic competition to a remarkable 1093.

In the women's game, Japan beat Canada 121–89 for an aggregate record of 210 points in 1976, while the highest total was 122 by the Soviet Union against Bulgaria (83) in 1980. The biggest margin was 66 points when the Soviet Union beat Italy 119–53 in 1980. Yevladia Stefanova (BUL) scored a record 39 points against Korea in 1988. The most successful female player has been Teresa Edwards (USA) with three gold medals and a bronze 1984–96. She is also the only woman to play in four Games, and only player, male or female, to win three gold medals. Edwards became the oldest female gold medallist, in 1996, aged 32 years and 16 days, and she was also the youngest in 1984, aged 20 years and 19 days. The oldest medallist was a member of the silver medal Brazilian team in 1996, Hortencia Marcan Oliva at 36 years and 315 days, while the youngest medallist was Zheng Haixia (CHN) in 1984 at 17 years and 151days. When the Soviet men's team beat the USA at Seoul, their coach was Alexander Gomelsky, and when the Unified women's team beat the American women in Barcelona their coach was his brother, Yevgeni. A member of the winning American men's team in 1996, Reggie Miller, is the brother of the star of the 1984 gold medal women's team, Cheryl Miller.

The tallest player in Olympic basketball, and the tallest medallist in any sport, was Tommy Burleson (USA), silver in 1972, at 2.23m (7ft 4in). Also reported in some quarters as the same height, but actually some 2cm less, was Arvidas Sabonis, who won gold in the 1988 Soviet team, and bronze in the 1992 Lithuanian team. The tallest female player, and the tallest Olympic female gold medallist ever, was Iuliana Semenova (URS) at 2.18m (7ft 1¾in) in 1976 and

BASKETBALL MEDALS

| | Men | | | Women | | | |
	G	S	B	G	S	B	Total
United States	11	1	1	3	1	1	18
Soviet Union	2	4	3	3	–	1	13
Yugoslavia	1	4	1	–	1	1	8
Brazil	–	–	3	–	1	–	4
Bulgaria	–	–	–	–	1	1	2
China	–	–	–	–	1	1	2
Lithuania	–	–	2	–	–	–	2
Uruguay	–	–	2	–	–	–	2
Canada	–	1	–	–	–	–	1
Croatia	–	1	–	–	–	–	1
France	–	1	–	–	–	–	1
Italy	–	1	–	–	–	–	1
Korea	–	–	–	–	1	–	1
Spain	–	1	–	–	–	–	1
Australia	–	–	–	–	–	1	1
Cuba	–	–	1	–	–	–	1
Mexico	–	–	1	–	–	–	1
	14	14	14	6	6	6	60

1980. She was also the heaviest female gold medallist ever at 129kg (284lb). Incidentally, during the first tournament in 1936 there was a move to ban all players taller than 1.90m (6ft 2¾in), but happily this was withdrawn. In the 1996 tournament there was an Olympic basketball record of 34 447 spectators to watch the US men's team beat China 133–70 in the Georgia Dome, and the women's semi-final between USA and Australia (93–71) drew a female match record of 33 952.

Beach Volleyball

The sport appears to have originated in Santa Monica, California in the early 1930s. In 1996, at Atlanta, beach volleyball became an Olympic sport. Special sand courts were built within the city's Olympic complex and the separate contests for men and women gained much spectator and media support.

The oldest gold medallist was Karch Kiraly (USA), aged 35 years and 268 days. He had won two gold medals in the standard sport indoors in 1984 and 1988, and thus becomes the most successful volleyball player, of either category, with three golds. The oldest medallist was Michael Dodd (USA) who won a silver medal, aged 39 years and 343 days. The oldest female gold medallist was Jacqueline Silva (BRA) at 31 years and 165 days. She had played indoor volleyball in the 1980 and 1984 Games. The youngest winner was her partner, Sandra Pires, aged 23 years and 41 days. The youngest medallist was Natalie Cook (AUS), aged 21 years and 190 days winning the bronze. The youngest male champion was Kent Steffes (USA) at 28 years and 35 days. The youngest male medallist was Mark Heese (CAN) with the bronze, aged 26 years and 348 days. Chris St John 'Sinjin' Smith (USA) whose pair finished equal fifth was 39 years and 80 days old.

Berlin 1936
XI Olympic Games (1–16 August)

Attended by representatives of 49 countries, comprising 4066 competitors, of which 328 were women.

These Games were awarded to Berlin just prior to the rise of Adolf Hitler and the National Socialist (Nazi) Party to power. Abhorrence of Germany's policies under this government led many countries, not least the United States, to propose a boycott, but the President of the US Olympic Committee, Avery Brundage, was strongly in favour of participation, and won the day. In Germany itself the notorious Heinrich Himmler was opposed to the Games being held, but Josef Goebbels convinced Hitler that they would present tremendous propaganda opportunities. Political overtones overshadowed the Games until the last moment when Spain withdrew owing to the outbreak of the civil war.

BEACH VOLLEYBALL MEDALS

| | Men | | | Women | | | |
	G	S	B	G	S	B	Total
Brazil	–	–	–	1	1	–	2
United States	1	1	–	–	–	–	2
Australia	–	–	–	–	–	1	1
Canada	–	–	1	–	–	–	1
	1	1	1	1	1	1	6

The original intention had been to enlarge the stadium that had been built for the aborted 1916 Games, but Hitler decreed that a new 100 000 capacity stadium be built. The architects were Werner and Walter March, whose father had designed the 1916 stadium. Other fine stadia and halls were erected, plus a magnificent 'village' of 150 buildings for the competitors. Yachting events were held at Kiel on the north-west coast. At the instigation of Carl Diem, the main organiser, a torch relay was inaugurated to bring the sacred Olympic flame from the Temple of Zeus at Olympia, where it was lit by 'priestesses' Koula Pratsika and Aleka Katseli, who handed it to Greek runner, Kyril Kondylis, the first of 3331 runners. The flame crossed seven countries (3187km, 1980 miles) in 10 days. The last runner into the stadium to light the cauldron was athlete Fritz Schilgen. The Games were formally opened by Chancellor Hitler, as a specially commissioned 16½ ton bell was rung and thousands of pigeons set free. As the massive, 348-strong German contingent entered, the giant airship *Hindenburg* flew over the stadium.

The German team, with full government backing, was probably the best prepared team ever in the Games. As a sop to foreign criticism it contained one athlete of Jewish origin, Helene Mayer, persuaded to return from America with the promise of full 'Aryan' classification. Ironically, she placed second in the foil to the Hungarian Jewess, Ilona Elek, with another Jewish fencer in third. Perhaps even more ironic, at the opening ceremony was the 1896 marathon victor, Spiridon Louis, attired in national dress, presented Hitler with an olive branch (signifying peace) from Olympia. In the march-past of teams, a number of them gave the Nazi salute, but the United States and Great Britain, to their credit and to the annoyance of the crowd, merely made the traditional 'eyes right'. The music for the ceremony was conducted by the famous composer, Richard Strauss. An indication of the future came with the first ever use of television at the Games. Very high sporting standards were reached at these Games, and at the forefront of the record breaking were the ten black members of the US track and field team. Anathema to the German propaganda machine, which dubbed them 'Black Auxiliaries', they won seven gold, three silver and three bronze medals — more than any national team, including their own white team-mates. Outstanding among them was Jesse Owens with four gold medals, in the 100m, 200m, long jump, and as a member of the 4 × 100m relay team. The runner-up in the 200m was Mack Robinson, whose brother, Jackie, was the first black Major League Baseball player. It should be noted that the attitude of the German government to Owens was not shared by the majority of the fans — and he was in tremendous demand by autograph hunters.

Much has been written about Hitler refusing to meet and congratulate Owens and the other black gold medallists. In fairness it should be realised that after he had made a point of personally greeting the German victors on the first day, he was rebuked for the practice by the President of the IOC, Henri de Baillet-Latour, who informed him that only IOC designated people performed such duties in an Olympic stadium. After that he refrained from further congratulatory meetings, although it is reported that he met all German medallists in private. Thus, if he did snub anybody, it would have been the only black winner on the first day, high jumper Cornelius Johnson.

Other track highlights included the superb sprinting of Helen Stephens (USA); the decathlon victory of team-mate Glenn Morris, later to be a screen *Tarzan*; and the 1500m world record by Jack Lovelock (NZL). This last event was considered by many to have been the highlight of the Games. The Finns took all three places in the 10 000m as well as the first two places in the 5000m and steeplechase, Volmari Iso-Hollo successfully defending his title in the latter. Outstanding in the pool were the Dutch women led by Hendrika Mastenbroek, who won three golds and a silver. The winner of the women's springboard diving, Marjorie Gestring (USA), became the youngest female gold medallist as well as the youngest individual event champion, aged 13 years and 268 days. The oldest gold medallist at Berlin was Friedrich Gerhard (GER) in the dressage team, aged 52 years and 20 days. The youngest male champion was fencer Edoardo Mangiarotti (ITA), aged 17 years and 124 days, while the oldest female champion was gymnast Friedl Iby (GER) at 31 years and 128 days. In taking the bronze medal in the 200m breaststroke, Inge Sörensen (DEN) became one of the youngest ever Olympic medallists, aged 12 years and 24 days.

Robert Charpentier (FRA) won three gold medals in cycling, in which Toni Merkens (GER) won the 1000m sprint despite being fined, but not disqualified, for obstruction in the first race. In wrestling, Kristjan Palusalu of Estonia matched the achievement of Ivar Johansson (SWE) in 1932 by winning titles in both freestyle and Greco-Roman styles. Interestingly, the list of gold medallists at Berlin includes the name *Nurmi*, but in this case it is the name of the horse ridden by Ludwig Stubbendorff (GER) to his easy victory in the tough three-day event. Of the 14 teams that started, only four finished with sufficient scorers. These included Great Britain, whose final placer, Captain Richard Fanshawe, gained his team bronze medal despite numerous penalty points incurred from having to chase his horse for 4km (2.5 miles) before remounting.

In the single-handed Olympia class yachting the bronze medal went to Peter Markham Scott, son of the tragic Antarctic explorer, and later himself a world-famous naturalist. Canoeing and basketball made their official debuts in 1936, with the inventor of the latter, Dr James Naismith, on hand to see the USA team begin its remarkable sequence of victories. At the end of the Games a magnificent film, *Olympische Spiele*, was produced by Leni Riefenstahl which, although criticized as propaganda, is still the best documentary record of an Olympic Games. In addition to their traditional awards, gold medallists were given oak tree seedlings. Forty years later research by the US

Olympic Committee indicated that at least 16 of the trees were still alive and well.

1936 MEDALS (SUMMER)

	G	S	B
Germany	33	26	30
United States	24	20	12
Hungary	10	1	5
Italy	8	9	5
Finland	7	6	6
France	7	6	6
Sweden	6	5	9
Japan	6	4	8
The Netherlands	6	4	7
Great Britain	4	7	3
Austria	4	6	3
Czechoslovakia	3	5	—
Argentina	2	2	3
Estonia	2	2	3
Egypt	2	1	2
Switzerland	1	9	5
Canada	1	3	5
Norway	1	3	2
Turkey	1	—	1
India	1	—	—
New Zealand	1	—	—
Poland	—	3	3
Denmark	—	2	3
Latvia	—	1	1
Romania	—	1	—
South Africa	—	1	—
Yugoslavia	—	1	—
Mexico	—	—	3
Belgium	—	—	2
Australia	—	—	1
Philippines	—	—	1
Portugal	—	—	1

Biathlon

The combination of skiing and shooting was introduced for men in 1960 and for women in 1992. Alexander Tikhonov (URS) set a Winter Games record by winning a gold medal in the relay on four successive occasions 1968–80. The most successful women have been Myriam Bédard (CAN) and Anfissa Reztsova (RUS/EUN), both of whom won two golds and a bronze in 1992–94. However, Ursula 'Uschi' Disl (GER) has won a total of six medals (one gold, three silver, two bronze), 1992–98. The oldest gold medallist/medallist was Fritz Fischer (GER) in the 1992 relay, aged 35 years and 147 days. The oldest female champion was Reztsova in the 1994 relay, aged 29 years and 71 days. The youngest winner and medallist was Corinne Niogret (FRA) in the 1992 relay at 19 years and 86 days, while the youngest male winner was Yuri Kachkarov (URS) in the 1984 relay, aged 20 years and 75 days. Frank-Peter Roetsch (GDR) was the youngest male medallist when he won a silver in the 20km event in 1984, aged only 19 years and 298 days. Alfred Eder (AUT) competed in a record six Games, 1976–94. In 2002 there will be an additional two events, one each for men and women.

Bicycle Polo

A demonstration sport at London in 1908. Consisted of a match between a German team and one from the Irish Bicycle Polo Association.

Bobsledding

An Olympic bob competition for 4-man sleds was first held in 1924. The rules allowed for 4- or 5-men teams in 1924 and 1928. The 2-man event was introduced in 1932. Both competitions have been held ever since

BIATHLON MEDALS

	Men			Women			Total
	G	S	B	G	S	B	
Soviet Union	10	6	5	1	1	2	25
Germany	4	4	1	2	4	3	18
Norway	5	4	2	—	—	1	12
GDR	3	4	4	—	—	—	11
Russia	2	1	2	2	1	—	8
Finland	—	4	2	—	—	—	6
FRG	1	2	2	—	—	—	5
Sweden	1	—	4	—	—	—	5
France	—	—	1	1	1	1	4
Canada	—	—	—	2	—	1	3
Italy	—	1	2	—	—	—	3
Belarus	—	—	1	—	1	—	2
Ukraine	—	—	—	—	1	1	2
Bulgaria	—	—	—	1	—	—	1
	26	26	26	9	9	9	105

except for 1960 when the Squaw Valley Organising Committee refused to build a run. In 1952 a situation arose which led to changes in the rules governing the overall weight of teams and bobs. The Germans combined their heaviest men from their two vehicles into one 4-man sled averaging 117kg (258lb) per man, and won easily. Resulting complaints led to rules that currently stipulate that the maximum weight of the bobs, with crews, must not exceed 390kg (860lb) (2-man) and 630kg (1389lb) (4-man), but that extra weights may be added within those limits. In 1994 Gustave Weder (SUI) was the first to retain a 2-man title, and Wolfgang Höppe (GER) became the only man to win medals in four Winter Games. The most gold medals won by an individual is three by Bernhard Germeshausen (GDR) and Meinhard Nehmer (GDR) both 1976–80. The most medals won is seven by Bogdan Musiol (GDR), comprising one gold, five silver and one bronze, 1980–92. The oldest gold medallist was Jay O'Brien (USA) in the 4-man in 1932, aged 48 years and 359 days, which also makes him the oldest gold medallist in Winter Games' history. The youngest champion was William Fiske (USA) who piloted the winning 5-man bob in 1928, aged 16 years and 260 days. The youngest medallist was Thomas Doe Jr (USA), aged 15 years and 127 days in the 1928 silver medal team. The oldest medallist was Max Houben (BEL), aged 49 years and 278 days in the 1948 4-man event. He had been a member of the sprint relay squad at Antwerp in 1920.

The 1932 American 4-man team had unusually eventful lives outside bobsledding. Fiske had the distinction of being the first American to join the RAF in the Second World War — he was killed in the Battle of Britain. O'Brien married silent-film star Mae Murray. British-born Clifford 'Tippy' Gray was reportedly a songwriter, and Eddie Eagan, a Rhodes scholar, lawyer and wartime colonel, was the only man to win gold medals in both Summer and Winter Games. The tallest gold medallist was Edy Hubacher (SUI) in the 1972 4-man bob at 2.01m (6ft 7in). He also competed in the 1968 Summer Games shot put event. Carl-Erik Eriksson (SWE) was the first Olympic competitor to compete in six Games, 1964–84. The first brothers to win bob gold medals were Alfred and Heinrich Schläppi (SUI) in the 4-man of 1924, while the inaugural 2-man event of 1932 was won by siblings Hubert and Curtis Stevens (USA).

The closest finishes in Olympic bobsledding have occurred in the 2-man events of 1968 and 1998. In 1968, at Grenoble, Italy I and FRG I had identical aggregate times after the four runs. The title went to Italy, driven by the 40-year-old Eugenio Monti, as they had the fastest single run. In 1998, at Nagano, the same thing happened with Italy I and Canada I tieing after four runs. However, this time they were both awarded joint first place. Incidentally, the Canadian pair had the fastest single run. The greatest margin of victory was in 1924 when the Swiss 4-man won by 3.29sec, and the smallest margin in 4-man was 0.02sec between Austria and Germany after four runs in 1992. The fastest speed attained (average for a run) was by

the 1994 Germany II 4-man team of 95.10km/h (59.09mph), although a momentary speed of 143km/h (88.8mph) was recorded by the Swiss team at Calgary in 1988. In 2002 there will be a bobsledding event for women.

BOBSLEDDING MEDALS

	G	S	B	Total
Switzerland	9	9	8	26
United States	5	4	5	14
GDR	5	5	3	13
Italy	4	4	3	11
Germany	4	2	5	11
FRG	1	3	2	6
Great Britain	1	1	2	4
Soviet Union	1	–	2	3
Austria	1	2	–	3
Canada	2	–	–	2
Belgium	–	1	1	2
France	–	–	1	1
Romania	–	–	1	1
	33 [1]	31	33 [2]	97

[1] Tie in 1998 2-man
[2] Tie in 1998 4-man

Boxing

Contests were included in the ancient Games in 688BC, when competitors wore leather straps on their hands. As the status of the Games deteriorated in Roman times, metal studs were added. Later still boxers wore metal knuckledusters. One of the earliest known champions was Onomastos of Smyrna. The last known champion before the Games were abolished was Varazdetes (or Varastades), the winner in AD 369, who later became King of Armenia. This type of boxing should not be confused with the pankration event, which was a brutal combination of boxing and wrestling in which virtually anything was permitted. It is recorded that Arrachion of Phigalia was awarded that title in 564BC, as his opponent 'gave up' — although Arrachion himself was by then lying dead in the arena. Boxing was included in the modern Games in 1904 when the USA won all the titles. A pattern was set by the first heavyweight champion, Samuel Berger, when he turned professional after his victory. Incidentally, he was a member of the San Francisco Olympic Club that had also produced 'Gentleman' Jim Corbett who had won the world title in 1892. Over the years the weight limits for the various classes have changed, and new classes have been added. Bronze medals for losing semi-finalists were not awarded until 1952.

Two men have won three golds László Papp (HUN), a southpaw, won the middleweight division in 1948 and the light-middleweight class in 1952 and 1956, while Teofilo Stevenson (CUB) won the heavyweight class between 1972 and 1980. In 1904 Oliver Kirk (USA) won two events at the same Games, also unique (but he only fought one bout in each class). The first boxer to defend a title successfully was Harry Mallin (GBR) with the midddleweight crown in 1920 and 1924. In those latter Games the standard of refereeing was highly suspect, not least because the European custom of seating the referees outside the ring was followed. Mallin was continually fouled by his French opponent in a preliminary bout, and ended the fight with teeth marks on his chest. Despite this the outclassed Frenchman was declared the winner of the bout. An immediate appeal, backed by a threat of withdrawal of all English-speaking countries, was upheld. A strange occurrence was the disqualification of Ingemar Johansson (SWE) in the 1952 heavyweight final, and the withholding of the silver medal due to 'inactivity in the ring'. In 1959, he won the world professional title, and 30 years after the Games, on his 50th birthday, he was finally presented with his medal.

The oldest gold medallist/medallist was Richard Gunn (GBR), the 1908 featherweight champion, aged 37 years and 254 days. The youngest was Jackie Fields (né Jacob Finkelstein) (USA) winning the 1924 featherweight crown, aged 16 years and 162 days. Both of these records can no longer be broken as current rules specify that boxers must be over 17 and under 37 prior to start of the particular Games. Floyd Patterson (USA) won the 1952 middleweight title, aged 17 years and 211 days, and four years later became the youngest world professional heavyweight champion. The first black African to win a gold medal was Robert Wangila (KEN) in 1988. A number of brothers have won medals, but the only known father and son medallists are Jose Villanueva (PHI), bronze bantamweight in 1932, and Anthony Villanueva (PHI), silver featherweight in 1964.

Many Olympic boxing champions, and even more minor medallists, have won world professional titles. Only two, Joe Frazier (USA—1964) and George Foreman (USA—1968), won the Olympic heavy-weight title and then became undisputed professional heavyweight champions. Note also that 1988 super-heavyweight gold medallist Lennox Lewis, then of Canada, won the undisputed professional world heavyweight title in 1999 representing Great Britain. Perhaps more unusually, the 1908 middleweight champion, John Douglas (GBR), later captained the England cricket team against Australia, in 1911. Just as unusual was the fact that his opponent in the 1908 final, Reg 'Snowy' Baker, also competed in spring-board diving and was a member of the Australian 4 × 200m swimming team which placed fourth. Incidentally, over the years there has been an unsubstantiated story that their final bout was refereed by Douglas's father. Recent research indicates that the official in charge was Eugene Corri.

The Val Barker Cup is presented by the Association Internationale de Boxe Amateur (AIBA) (Val Barker was a former President) to the competitor adjudged the best stylist at the Games.

In the 1988 tournament, because of a record 441 entries, two rings were used simultaneously. In 1992 elimination contests were held to limit entries to 32 per class. Despite pressure to drop boxing from the Olympic programme, the introduction of new gloves, safer protective helmets and three rounds of three minutes, seems to have reprieved the sport, at least for the foreseeable future. In Sydney 2000 contests of four rounds of two minutes each will be in force. In 1992, an electronic scoring system was introduced in which the judges had to simultaneously push a button to record a scoring point. Despite this innovation there was still considerable criticism of the scoring during the tournament, especially in the early bouts. The 1992 tournament was also noteworthy for the virtual eclipse of American boxers, with only one medal of each colour — their worse ever showing — and the domination of the Cubans, with seven golds and two silvers out of nine finals reached.

VAL BARKER CUP WINNERS

1936	Louis Lauria (USA)	bronze — flyweight
1948	George Hunter (SAF)	gold — light-heavyweight
1952	Norvel Lee (USA)	gold — light-heavyweight
1956	Dick McTaggart (GBR)	gold — lightweight
1960	Giovanni Benvenuti (ITA)	gold — welterweight
1964	Valeri Popentschenko (URS)	gold — middleweight
1968	Philip Waruinge (KEN)	bronze — featherweight
1972	Teofilo Stevenson (CUB)	gold — heavyweight
1976	Howard Davis (USA)	gold — lightweight
1980	Patrizio Oliva (ITA)	gold — light-welterweight
1984	Paul Gonzales (USA)	gold — light-flyweight
1988	Roy Jones (USA)	silver — light-middleweight
1992	Roberto Balado (CUB)	gold — super-heavyweight
1996	Vasili Jirov (KZK)	gold — light-heavyweight

BOXING MEDALS

	G	S	B	Total
United States	47	21	34	102
Soviet Union	14	20	19	53
Great Britain	12	10	21	43
Poland	8	9	26	43
Cuba	23	13	5	41
Italy	14	12	13	39
Germany	5	12	8	25
Argentina	7	7	10	24
Romania	1	8	13	22
Hungary	10	2	7	19
South Africa	6	4	9	19
Canada	3	7	7	17
Bulgaria	4	5	7	16
Korea	3	6	7	16
Finland	2	1	11	14
GDR	5	2	6	13
France	3	4	6	13
Denmark	1	5	6	12
Yugoslavia	3	2	6	11
Mexico	2	3	6	11
Sweden	–	5	6	11
Ireland	1	3	5	9
Kenya	1	1	5	7
Czechoslovakia	3	1	2	6
North Korea (PRK)	2	2	2	6
The Netherlands	1	1	4	6
FRG	1	–	5	6
Nigeria	–	3	3	6
Puerto Rico	–	1	5	6
Norway	1	2	2	5
Venezuela	1	2	2	5
Thailand	1	1	3	5
Algeria	1	–	4	5
Australia	–	2	3	5
Philippines	–	2	3	5
Belgium	1	1	2	4
Kazakhstan	1	1	2	4
Russia	1	–	3	4
Uganda	–	3	1	4
New Zealand	1	1	1	3
Japan	1	–	2	3
Chile	–	1	2	3
Ghana	–	1	2	3
Spain	–	1	2	3
Turkey	–	1	2	3
Colombia	–	–	3	3
Ukraine	1	–	1	2
Cameroon	–	1	1	2
Mongolia	–	–	2	2
Morocco	–	–	2	2
Tunisia	–	–	2	2
Estonia	–	1	–	1
Tonga	–	1	–	1
Bermuda	–	–	1	1
Brazil	–	–	1	1
Dominican Republic	–	–	1	1
Egypt	–	–	1	1
Guyana	–	–	1	1
Niger	–	–	1	1

BOXING MEDALS *continued*

	G	S	B	Total
Pakistan	–	–	1	1
Tunisia	–	–	1	1
Uruguay	–	–	1	1
Uzbekistan	–	–	1	1
Zambia	–	–	1	1
	192	192	322 [1]	706

[1] The official 1908 report only notes a single bronze medal awarded

Brothers

Many brothers have competed together in the Games, especially in fencing, rowing and yachting. The first gold medallists were John and Sumner Paine (USA) who won the military pistol and free pistol events respectively in 1896. However, the first to win gold medals together were Reggie and Laurie Doherty (GBR) in the men's tennis doubles in 1900. The three Gossler brothers, Oscar, Gustav and Carl, were in the winning German rowing four in 1900, the latter as cox and the French Thubé brothers, Amédée, Gaston and Jacques, won golds in the 1912 6m class yachting. At the next Games, in 1920, they were eclipsed by Henrik, Jan, Ole and Kristian Østervold of Norway, who crewed the winning 12m (1907 rating) yacht.

Probably the most successful brothers were two sets of sibling fencers. Nedo and Aldo Nadi (ITA) won a total of nine golds and one silver in 1912 and 1920, while their countrymen, Edoardo and Dario Mangiarotti, amassed seven golds, seven silvers and two bronzes between 1936 and 1960. Also worthy of note are: Dhyand Chand Bais and Roop Singh Bais of India in hockey, with the former gaining three gold medals 1928–36, and the latter two, 1932–36; the rowing Abbagnale brothers of Italy, Carmine and Giuseppe, won the coxed pairs in 1984–88, and a silver in 1992, and Agostino won gold in the 1992 quadruple sculls and 1996 double sculls.

Budo

A demonstration sport at Tokyo in 1964, when exhibitions of a combination of Japanese archery, wrestling and fencing were given.

Calgary 1988
XV Winter Games (13–28 February)

Attended by representatives of 57 countries, comprising 1425 competitors, of which 313 were women.

Having had three unsuccessful bids previously, Calgary was finally awarded these Games in 1981. Most of the venues were close together except for Mounts Allan and Kenmore, some 90km away, where the Alpine and Nordic skiing took place. The programme was stretched to 16 days to include three weekends, particularly favourable for television coverage — for which ABC paid $309 million for the American rights, over three times the sum for the Sarajevo (1984) coverage. There were a number of new events: Nordic combination for teams, team ski jumping, Alpine combination, super giant slaloms for men and women, and a 5000m speed skating event for women. In all there were 46 events, as well as the demonstration sports of curling, short track speed skating and freestyle skiing. Five teams made their Winter Games debuts: Fiji, Guam, Guatemala, Ireland and Jamaica. The official opening was performed by the Governor-General of Canada, Jeanne Sauvé, on behalf of Queen Elizabeth II. The torch was brought into the stadium by a couple, speed skater Cathy Priestner and skier Ken Read, and then handed to a 12-year-old girl skater, Robyn Perry, who lit the flame. Incidentally, that flame was easily the highest ever as it was set at the top of the Calgary Tower, which stands 191m (616ft) high. The oath was taken by Pierre Harvey, a Nordic skier who had also represented Canada at cycling in the 1984 Olympics. The facilities in the main were excellent, and the expected local transport problems were few and far between. Accommodation was at a premium with so many teams and competitors — some officials were based in an establishment which had previously been a 'house of ill-repute'. However, one unforeseen occurrence caused real problems, and that was a dramatic climatic change caused by a 'chinook' wind, which gave spring-like weather and strong winds, causing havoc in the timetable. These conditions, which primarily affected the bob sledding, luge and ski jumping events, resulted in some unexpected results. The exposed ski jumps were very dangerous at times, and caused the Nordic combination event, comprising of jumping and cross-country skiing, to be contested all on one day.

Nevertheless, there were many excellent performances, although the 'star' of these Games was an unknown British ski jumper. Despite, or more likely because of, being totally inept by world standards Michael 'Eddie the Eagle' Edwards stole the media attention from the great and famous, to the amusement of many and the chagrin of some. Britain's first Olympic entrant ever in this sport, he finished last in both jumps, albeit with a British record of 71m, over 20m behind the rest of the competitors.

The most successful competitors were Yvonne van Gennip (NED) who won three speed skating titles, and Matti Nykänen (FIN) who won all three gold medals open to him. The Finn totally dominated ski-jumping and leapt to 118.5m on the 90m hill, the greatest distance ever achieved in the Games. In Alpine skiing Vreni Schneider (SUI) and Alberto Tomba (ITA) both won their slalom and giant slalom events. Frank-Peter Roetsch (GDR) became the first man to win both individual biathlon races in a single Games, while the Soviet Union won the relay for the sixth consecutive time. The Soviet women hardly made an error in the Nordic skiing taking seven of the nine individual medals as well as the relay. Although

not in that relay, 35-year-old Raisa Smetanina (URS) gained a silver and a bronze to raise her total from four Games to a record nine medals for the sport.

After the shocks of Sarajevo the GDR lugers were back winning all three golds, two silvers and a bronze. Steffi Martin-Walter was the first luger to retain an individual title, and led her team-mates to a clean sweep. Incidentally, one of the British competitors in this sport was Nick Ovett, whose older brother Steve won the 1980 Olympic 800m. The bobsleigh course was likened to sandpaper as the winds had blown so much dirt on the track, and many of the top crews were upset. There was bitter rivalry between the Swiss and GDR 4-man crews with officials of both teams checking the legality of each others' sleds. The coach of the Swiss team was 1980 gold medallist Erich Schärer, while the GDR coach was Horst Hörnlein who had won gold in the 2-man luge in 1972. After the fourth and final run the Swiss were triumphant by 0.07 of a second, the smallest margin ever in the event. The drama was heightened even further when the rather unlikely crew from Jamaica crashed badly, but happily no one was seriously hurt. Bogdan Musiol (GDR) with two silver medals raised his total to a record-equalling six. Placed 25th (of 41) in the 2-man bob was Prince Albert of Monaco, partnered by a croupier from the principality's casino. Himself a member of the IOC, Prince Albert's grandfather and uncle, both named John Kelly, had won Olympic rowing medals.

Katarina Witt (GDR) was the first individual skater since 1952 to retain a figure skating title, amid some criticism about her skimpy costumes — not shared by the spectators. In third place, Debbie Thomas (USA) was the first Afro-American skater to win an Olympic skating medal. Speed skating was held indoors for the first time at the Olympics, in the superb $39 million Olympic Oval. It proved to be the fastest circuit in the world with world records in seven of the nine events, and as many as 29 skaters bettering the world mark in the men's 5000m. Karin Kania (née Enke) (GDR) added two silvers and a bronze for a record medal haul of eight since 1980. Monika Pflug-Holzner (FRG), the 1972 1000m champion competed in her fifth Games, then a record number of appearances for a female Winter Olympics competitor. The Soviet Union moved past Canada in ice hockey with its seventh title, while the host nation and the United States, who won in 1980, failed to gain a medal. A small consolation prize for Canada was that the most prolific goal-scorer, with seven, in the tournament was Serge Boisvert. There was only one competitor in Calgary who failed a dope test (a Polish ice hockey player).

The youngest gold medallist was Ekaterina Gordiyeva (URS) in the pairs skating, aged 16 years and 264 days, while the oldest was Ekkehard Fasser (SUI) in the 4-man bob, aged 35 years and 178 days. The youngest male champion was Ari Pekka Nikkola (FIN) in the 90m team ski-jumping at 18 years and 284 days, and the oldest female gold medallist was Christa Rothenburger (GDR) who won the 1000m speed skating, aged 28 years and 84 days. Competitors' ages ranged from a 14 year old North Korean girl skater to a 52 year old bobsledder, Harvey Hook, from the US Virgin Islands.

1988 MEDALS (WINTER)

	G	S	B
Soviet Union	11	9	9
GDR	9	10	6
Switzerland	5	5	5
Finland	4	1	2
Sweden	4	–	2
Austria	3	5	2
The Netherlands	3	2	2
FRG	2	4	2
United States	2	1	3
Italy	2	1	2
France	1	–	1
Norway	–	3	2
Canada	–	2	3
Yugoslavia	–	2	1
Czechoslovakia	–	1	2
Japan	–	–	1
Liechtenstein	–	–	1

Canoeing

Official canoeing competitions were first held in 1936, although kayak and Canadian events were demonstrated in 1924. In 1972 at Munich, four slalom events were held and, after a gap of 20 years, slalom racing was reintroduced at Barcelona. The most successful canoeist has been Gert Fredriksson (SWE) with six golds, one silver and a bronze between 1948 and 1960, all in kayaks. The most medals won by a woman is five golds and three silvers by Birgit Fischer-Schmidt, first representing GDR and then Germany, in 1980, 1988, 1992 and 1996. Two men, Vladimir Parfenovich (URS) in 1980, and Ian Ferguson (NZL) in 1984, have won three gold medals at one Games. The best by a woman at one Games is two golds and a silver, by Agneta Andersson (SWE) in 1984 and Birgit Fischer-Schmidt (GDR) in 1988.

The highest speed achieved in the Games over the standard 1000m course is 20.98km/h (13.03mph) when the German K4 clocked 2min 51.52sec in 1996. In 1992 the Hungarian K4 team achieved an average speed of 21.94km/h (13.63mph) over the first 250m, in a heat. The fastest by a female crew over the 500m

CANOEING MEDALS

	Men			Women			
	G	S	B	G	S	B	Total
Soviet Union	22	12	6	8	2	3	53
Hungary	8	19	15	2	4	5	53
Germany	13	9	11	5	6	1	45
Romania	8	9	9	1	1	3	31
GDR	8	5	8	6	2	1	30
Sweden	11	8	2	3	2	2	28
France	2	6	14	–	–	1	23
United States	5	2	4	–	2	2	15
Bulgaria	3	1	7	1	2	1	15
Canada	3	5	3	–	2	1	14
Austria	3	4	4	–	1	1	13
Czechoslovakia	7	4	1	–	–	–	12
Denmark	2	4	4	1	–	1	12
Australia	1	2	6	–	1	1	11
Poland	–	3	5	–	–	3	11
Finland	4	2	3	1	–	–	10
Italy	3	3	2	–	–	1	9
Norway	2	3	3	–	–	–	8
The Netherlands	–	1	3	–	2	2	8
New Zealand	5	1	1	–	–	–	7
FRG	1	1	1	1	2	1	7
Czech Republic	2	2	–	1	–	–	5
Yugoslavia	2	2	1	–	–	–	5
Spain	–	2	2	–	–	–	4
Latvia	–	2	–	–	–	–	2
Slovenia	–	2	–	–	–	–	2
Slovakia	1	–	–	–	–	–	1
Great Britain	–	1	–	–	–	–	1
Moldova	–	1	–	–	–	–	1
Switzerland	–	–	–	–	1	–	1
Russia	–	–	1	–	–	–	1
	116	116	116	30	30	30	438

course is 19.76km/h (12.27mph) when the German K4 clocked 1min 31.07sec in 1996. In that race the German K4 achieved an average speed of 20.20km/h (12.55mph) over the first 250m. The closest finish in an Olympic canoeing final occurred in the 1952 K2 1000m when the time-keepers were unable to separate the first and second placed pairs. The closest finish in women's canoeing was in the 1988 K1 500m when the winning margin was 0.12sec. This was equalled in the 1992 K2 final.

The oldest ever canoeing gold medallist/medallist was Gert Fredriksson (SWE), aged 40 years and 292 days in the 1960 K2 over 1000m. The youngest was Bent Peder Rasch (DEN) in the 1952 C2 at 1000m, aged 18 years and 58 days. However, Michal Martikan (SVK) won the C1 slalom event in 1996, aged 17 years and 70 days, making him easily the youngest champion in Olympic canoeing events. The youngest female champion was Birgit Fischer (GDR), aged 18 years and 158 days in 1980, while the oldest was Sylvi Saimo (FIN) in 1952, aged 37 years and 259 days. The youngest medallist was Francine Fox (USA), with a silver in the 1964 K2 at 15 years and 220 days. (Incidentally, her partner was 20 years older.) The youngest male medallist was Gábor Novák (HUN) in 1952, aged 17 years and 348 days, and the oldest woman to win a medal was Antonina Seredina (URS) in 1968 at 37 years and 307 days. Ivar Patzaichin (ROM) won gold medals over a 16-year period, 1968–84, in the Canadian events. This was matched by Birgit Fischer (GER) 1980–96. When Philippe Renaud (FRA) won a bronze in the 1988 C2 500m, he was the latest success of an Olympic family: his brother, Eric, won a canoe bronze in 1984; their father, Marcel gained a canoe silver in 1956; and a great-uncle won a cycling bronze in 1924.

Celebrations of the Games

(New research has resulted in revised figures for participation in some celebrations of the Games)

Summer

Year	Venue	Date	Nations	Women	Men	Total
I 1896	Athens, Greece	6–15 April [1]	14	–	211	211
II 1900	Paris, France	20 May–28 October	25	19	1206	1225
III 1904	St Louis, USA	1 July–23 November	13	6	681	687
1906 [2]	Athens, Greece	22 April–2 May	20	6	820	826
IV 1908	London, England	27 April–31 October	22	36	1999	2035
V 1912	Stockholm, Sweden	5 May–22 July	28	57	2490	2547
VI 1916	Berlin, Germany	Not held due to war	–	–	–	–
VII 1920	Antwerp, Belgium	20 April–12 September	29	77	2591	2668
VIII 1924	Paris, France	4 May–27 July	44	136	2956	3092
IX 1928	Amsterdam, The Netherlands	17 May–12 August	46	290	2724	3014
X 1932	Los Angeles, USA	30 July–14 August	37	127	1281	1408
XI 1936	Berlin, Germany	1–16 August	49	328	3738	4066
XII 1940	Tokyo, Japan, then Helsinki, Finland	Not held due to war	–	–	–	–
XIII 1944	London, England	Not held due to war	–	–	–	–
XIV 1948	London, England	29 July–14 August	59	385	3714	4099
XV 1952	Helsinki, Finland	19 July–3 August	69	518	4407	4925
XVI 1956	Melbourne, Australia [3]	22 November–8 December	67	371	2813	3184
XVII 1960	Rome, Italy	25 August–11 September	83	610	4736	5346
XVIII 1964	Tokyo, Japan	10–24 October	93	683	4457	5140
XIX 1968	Mexico City, Mexico	12–27 October	112	781	4749	5530
XX 1972	Munich, Germany	26 August–10 September	121	1058	6065	7123
XXI 1976	Montreal, Canada	17 July–1 August	92	1247	4781	6028
XXII 1980	Moscow, Soviet Union	19 July–3 August	80	1124	4093	5217
XXIII 1984	Los Angeles, USA	28 July–12 August	140	1567	5230	6797
XXIV 1988	Seoul, Korea	17 September–2 October	159	2186	6279	8465
XXV 1992	Barcelona, Spain	25 July–9 August	169	2707	6657	9364
XXVI 1996	Atlanta, USA	19 July–4 August	197	3513	6797	10310
XXVII 2000	Sydney, Australia	15 September–1 October	–	–	–	–
XXVIII 2004	Athens, Greece	13–29 August	–	–	–	–

1 Actually 25 March–3 April by the Julian Calendar then in use in Greece
2 This celebration (to mark the tenth anniversary of the modern Games) was officially intercalated, but not numbered
3 Equestrian events held in Stockholm Sweden, 10–17 June, with 158 competitors, from 29 countries, of which 13 were women

Winter

Year	Venue	Date	Nations	Women	Men	Total
I 1924	Chamonix, France	5 January–4 February	16	13	281	294
II 1928	St Moritz, Switzerland	11–19 February	25	27	468	495
III 1932	Lake Placid, USA	4–15 February	17	32	274	306
IV 1936	Garmisch-Partenkirchen, Germany	6–16 February	28	80	675	755
– 1940	Sapporo, Japan, then St Moritz, Switzerland, then Garmisch-Partenkirchen, Germany	Not held due to war				
– 1944	Cortina d'Ampezzo, Italy	Not held due to war				
V 1948	St Moritz, Switzerland	30 January–8 February	28	77	636	713
VI 1952	Oslo, Norway	14–25 February	30	109	623	732
VII 1956	Cortina d'Ampezzo, Italy	26 January–5 February	32	132	686	818
VIII 1960	Squaw Valley, USA	18–28 February	30	144	521	665
IX 1964	Innsbruck, Austria	29 January–9 February	36	200	891	1091
X 1968	Grenoble, France	6–18 February	37	211	947	1158
XI 1972	Sapporo, Japan	3–13 February	35	206	800	1006
XII 1976	Innsbruck, Austria	4–15 February	37	231	892	1123
XIII 1980	Lake Placid, USA	13–24 February	37	233	839	1072
XIV 1984	Sarajevo, Yugoslavia	8–19 February	49	274	1000	1274
XV 1988	Calgary, Canada	13–28 February	57	313	1112	1425
XVI 1992	Albertville, France	8–23 February	64	489	1312	1801
XVII 1994	Lillehammer, Norway	12–27 February	67	519	1217	1736
XVIII 1998	Nagano, Japan	7–22 February	72	787	1390	2177
XIX 2002	Salt Lake City, USA	9–24 February	–	–	–	–
XX 2006	Turin, Italy	–	–	–	–	–

Chamonix/Mont Blanc 1924
I Winter Games (25 January–4 February)

Attended by representatives of 16 countries, comprising 294 competitors, of which 13 were women.

After skating (1908, 1920) and ice hockey (1920) these events were held previously as part of the Summer Games and it was finally decided to hold a separate Winter festival. Although initially opposed by the Scandinavian countries, who felt that a Winter Olympics would detract from their own Nordic Games, an 'International Winter Sports Week' was held at Chamonix, France. In 1926 it was accorded the title of Winter Games retrospectively. The French Under-Secretary for Physical Education, Gaston Vidal, formally opened the proceedings, and the oath was taken by all the flag bearers, that of France being by a skier, Camille Mandrillon. Sixteen countries marched in the opening ceremony, joined by Estonia despite not having any competitors. The first ever official Olympic Winter gold medallist was Charles Jewtraw (USA) who won the 500m speed skating on 26 January, which also made it the earliest gold medal ever won in an Olympic year. It was the only speed skating medal won by a competitor from somewhere other than Finland or Norway. Clas Thunberg (FIN) won three golds, one silver and a bronze (tied) to dominate the sport. In skiing only the Nordic variety was held as Alpine skiing was still in its infancy. Norway's Thorleif Haug won three gold medals. He was also, originally awarded the

bronze in the special jumping event, but 50 years later a Norwegian sports historian, Jakob Vaage, discovered that the points had been added incorrectly, and that the fourth placed jumper, Anders Haugen, a Norwegian-born American, had beaten Haug. In place of her deceased father, Haug's daughter presented the bronze medal to the 86-year-old Haugen in 1974. Canada retained its title from 1920 in ice hockey, scoring 110 goals to 3 against in five matches. In figure skating, Gillis Grafström (SWE) gained the second of his three gold medals. He was later to gain even more fame as coach of Sonja Henie (NOR) who as an 11-year-old competitor in Chamonix placed eighth and last in the women's skating. Aside from her Olympic successes she was to earn an estimated $47 million from her film and ice show activities, making her the richest ever female Olympian. The inaugural 4-man bobsled contest was won by the Swiss, the first of a record five titles they have won in this discipline. Curling and a military patrol were held as demonstration events.

The oldest champion was speed skater Julius Skutnabb (FIN), aged 34 years and 229 days, and the youngest was Heinrich Schläppi, in Swizerland's 4-man bob, aged 18 years and 279 days. The oldest medallist was pairs skater Walter Jakobsson (FIN), aged 41 years and 357 days, although it is possible that the Belgian bobsledder, René Mortiaux, was over 42 years. It is of note that Jakobsson and his partner/wife, Ludowika (herself well over 39 years) are the oldest married couple ever to win Winter Olympic medals. Two days before the closing ceremony, a meeting established the Fédèration Internationale de Ski (FIS).

1924 MEDALS (WINTER)

	G	S	B
Norway	4	7	6
Finland	4	3	3
Austria	2	1	–
United States	1	2	1
Switzerland	1	–	1
Canada	1	–	–
Sweden	1	–	–
Great Britain	–	1	2
Belgium	–	–	1
France	–	–	1

Consecutive Medals

The only competitor to win six consecutive gold medals in the Olympic Games is Aladár Gerevich (HUN) who was a member of the winning sabre fencing team 1932–60. His team-mate, Pál Kovács, won five golds consecutively 1936–60. Hans-Günter Winkler (FRG) also won medals in six consecutive Games in show jumping, but they were not all gold. A countryman, Reiner Klimke, won gold medals at five Games between 1964 and 1988, but they were not consecutive. The only woman to win medals at five consecutive Games is fencer Ildikó Ságiné-Uljakiné-Rejtő (HUN), 1960–76. In the Winter Games, cross-country skier Raisa Smetanina (URS/EUN) is the only competitor to win medals in five Games 1976–92.

Cortina d'Ampezzo 1956
VII Winter Games (26 January–5 February)

Attended by representatives of 32 countries, comprising 818 competitors, of which 132 were women.

Most of the money spent on these Games came from the Italian Soccer Pools, but despite excellent facilities there were still problems with the weather. Once again snow needed to be 'imported' for some venues. The President of Italy, Giovanni Granchi, formally opened the Games. Guiliana Chenal-Minuzzo, who won the 1952 bronze medal in downhill skiing, became the first woman in Olympic history to pronounce the oath on behalf of all competitors. The last runner in the torch relay, speed skater Guido Caroli, fell as he completed a circuit of the arena but happily the flame did not go out. The entry of the Soviet Union provided the first Russian competitors in Olympic 'Winter' events since 1908. These were the first Winter Games to be televised, which undoubtedly resulted in smaller numbers of spectators than previously.

Most attention was gained by the Austrian plumber Anton Sailer who gained a grand slam of all three Alpine titles — downhill, slalom and giant slalom — winning in treacherous conditions by outstanding margins of 3.5sec, 4.0sec and 6.2sec respectively.

Second in the slalom was Asia's first Winter medallist, Chiharu Igaya (JPN), an American college student, who had to wait anxiously while the jury investigated an unsubstantiated claim, by Sweden and the United States, that he had missed a gate. Madeleine Berthod (SUI) won the women's downhill by a still record margin of 4.7sec.

The most medals won at Cortina was by Sixten Jernberg (SWE) with one gold, two silvers and a bronze in Nordic skiing. Hallgeir Brenden (NOR) successfully defended his 1952 Nordic skiing title, the distance now reduced from 18km to 15km. Using a new style the Finns dominated the ski jumping, and the Norwegians, who had won 15 of the 18 medals available in the sport since 1924, failed to place in the top six. Though Germany competed as a single team, the jumping bronze, won by Harry Glass, is claimed by the GDR as its first Olympic medal. The speed skating surface on Lake Misurina, at an altitude of 1755m (5756ft), was considered to be the fastest ever, and witnessed an assault on the record book. The winner of the 500m title, Yevgeni Grishin (URS) had been a member of the Soviet cycling team in Helsinki. In figure skating Hayes (gold) and David (bronze) Jenkins were the first brothers to win medals in the same skating event. Their team-mate, women's champion Tenley Albright (USA), had been a victim of polio as a child.

A member of the winning Swiss 4-man bob, Franz Kapus at 46 years and 298 days was the oldest gold medallist at Cortina. The youngest champion was Elisabeth Schwarz (AUT) in pairs skating, aged 19 years and 260 days. The youngest male winner was Anton Sailer (AUT) in the giant slalom, aged 20 years and 73 days, and the oldest female champion was Siiri Rantanen (FIN) in the cross-country relay aged 31 years and 49 days. The youngest medallist was skater Ingrid Wendl (AUT) with a bronze at 15 years and 260 days, and the youngest male medallist was speed skater Alv Gjestvang (NOR) at 18 years and 137 days. The Soviet competitors won a total of 15 medals to head the unofficial medal table — a position they were rarely to forfeit in future Winter Games.

1956 MEDALS (WINTER)

	G	S	B
Soviet Union	7	3	6
Austria	4	3	4
Finland	3	3	1
Switzerland	3	2	1
Sweden	2	4	4
United States	2	3	2
Norway	2	1	1
Italy	1	2	-
Germany	1	–	1
Canada	–	1	2
Japan	–	1	–
Hungary	–	–	1
Poland	–	–	1

Creed

The Olympic Creed has been displayed on the score-board at every opening ceremony since the 1932 Games at Los Angeles. The words are: 'The most important thing in the Olympic Games is not to win but to take part, just as the most important thing in life is not the triumph but the struggle. The essential thing is not to have conquered but to have fought well.' They are attributed usually to Baron de Coubertin, but were actually based on words used by Ethelbert Talbot, the Bishop of Central Pennsylvania, in a sermon at St Paul's Cathedral in London on 19 July 1908.

Cricket

Cricket was played once at the Games, in 1900. Great Britain, represented by the Devon Wanderers CC beat a French team, consisting of mainly expatriate Britons, in a 12-a-side match scoring 117 and 145 for five declared, against the French score of 78 and 26.

Croquet

It was only contested in 1900 when all the competitors were French. There were two singles competitions, and a doubles in which only a gold medal was awarded.

Curling

After many appearances as a demonstration sport curling finally became a medal sport at Nagano in 1998. Prior to this a three-country contest was held in 1924, won by Great Britain from Sweden and France. In 1932 there were four Canadian provincial and four American club teams. The Canadians took the first four places with the title won by Manitoba. In 1936 eight teams from Austria (three), Germany (three) and Czechoslovakia (two) competed in a specialised version of the game, German curling, with the Austrian number one team from the Tyrol winning. The Austrians demonstrated the game in 1964 at Innsbruck, and it was a demonstration sport again in 1988 and 1992.

The curling events in 1998 were held at the Kazakoshi Park, Karuizawa, which had been the site for the show jumping contests in the 1964 Summer Games, thus making it the first venue to host both Winter and Summer Games' events. In the men's competition the highest score, and margin of victory, was when the Canadian team beat the USA team 11–3. The greatest aggregate score was when Norway beat Canada 10–8. The youngest gold medallist was Dominic Andres (SUI), aged 25 years and 132 days, while the oldest was his team-mate Patrik Loertscher at 37 years and 333 days. The oldest medallist was Paul Savage (CAN) of the silver winning team at 50 years and 235 days, while the youngest was his team-mate Mike Harris, aged 20 years and 251 days.

In the women's competition the biggest margin of victory came when the USA beat Japan 10–2. The highest score, and greatest aggregate, was when Sweden beat Japan 12–6. The youngest gold medallist was Atina Ford (CAN), aged 26 years and 126 days, while the oldest was her team-mate Jan Belker at 37 years and 211 days. The youngest medallist was Margaretha Lindahl (SWE) taking a bronze, aged 23 years and 118 days, and the oldest was Jane Bidstrup of Denmark at 42 years and 178 days.

Cycling

The first Olympic cycling champion was Léon Flameng (FRA), winner of the 100km race in 1896, which was held on a 333.33m cement track and involved 300 circuits. Four men have won three gold medals: Paul Masson (FRA) in 1896; Francisco Verri (ITA) in 1906; Robert Charpentier (FRA) in 1936; and Daniel Morelon (FRA) in 1968 (two) and 1972. Of these only Morelon won a bronze as well. He also won a record seven world amateur titles. Initially, the seven 1904 cycling events were not considered official, as there were no foreign entries. However, recent thinking has 'reinstated' them. Thus it should be noted that Marcus Hurley (USA) won a record four titles, and a bronze medal, at that Games. His team-mate, Burton Downing, also set a record at St Louis with six medals, comprising two gold, three silver and a bronze. The only woman to win two gold medals is Erika Salumäe, who won the 1988 sprint representing the Soviet Union, and the 1992 title for Estonia. Both Jeannie Longo-Ciprelli (FRA) and Ingrid Haringa (NED) won a record three medals each 1992–96. The latter had competed as a speed skater at the 1988 Winter Games in Calgary. The first pair of brothers to win a medal were the Götze duo, Bruno and Max, of

CURLING MEDALS

	Men			Women			
	G	S	B	G	S	B	Total
Canada	–	1	–	1	–	–	2
Switzerland	1	–	–	–	–	–	1
Denmark	–	–	–	–	1	–	1
Norway	–	–	1	–	–	–	1
Sweden	–	–	–	–	–	1	1
	1	1	1	1	1	1	6

Germany with a tandem silver in 1906. The greatest family performance in Olympic cycling was achieved by the Pettersson brothers of Sweden: Gösta, Sture, Erik and Tomas. The first three, with Sven Hamrin, won a bronze in the 1964 team road race, and then, in 1968 with their younger brother, won the silver. Two extremes of sportsmanship have been highlighted in Games cycling. In 1936 Robert Charpentier beat his team-mate Guy Lapébie by 0.2sec at the end of the 100km, the latter inexplicably slowing down just before the line. A photograph showed that Charpentier had pulled his rival back by his shirt. More credit-worthy was another Frenchman, Léon Flameng, who, when far

ahead of his only opposition, a Greek, in 1896, stopped when the man's cycle broke down. After waiting for it to be replaced, Flameng still went on to win by six laps. After the 1984 Games it was admitted that many of the USA cycling team had indulged in 'blood-boosting' procedures — not illegal at the time. Those Games also witnessed numerous 'space-age' innovations, especially in the composition and construction of wheels. Of the many excellent facilities that have been built for Olympic cycling programmes, one of the most remarkable sites was the magnificent Hachioji velodrome in Tokyo 1964. Built at a cost of $840,000, it was used for only four days during the Games, and within a year

CYCLING RECORDS

Men

1000m Time-Trial	1min 02.712sec	Florian Rosseau (FRA)	1996
4000m Individual Pursuit	4min 19.153sec	Andrea Collinelli (ITA)	1996
4000m Team Pursuit	4min 05.930sec	France	1996

Women

3000m Individual Pursuit	3min 32.371sec	Antonella Bellutti (ITA)	1996

CYCLING MEDALS

	Men			Women			
	G	S	B	G	S	B	Total
France	29	16	22	3	3	–	73
Italy	30	15	6	2	–	–	53
Great Britain	9	21	16	–	–	–	46
United States [1]	10	11	13	1	2	3	40
The Netherlands	9	13	4	1	1	3	31
Germany	7	8	8	1	1	1	26
Australia	5	9	7	1	2	1	25
Soviet Union	10	4	8	1	–	1	24
Belgium	6	6	10	–	–	–	22
Denmark	6	7	8	–	–	–	21
GDR	6	5	4	–	1	–	16
FRG	4	4	4	–	1	1	14
Sweden	3	2	8	–	–	–	13
Canada	–	3	3	–	1	2	9
Switzerland	2	4	2	–	–	–	8
South Africa	1	4	3	–	–	–	8
Poland	–	5	3	–	–	–	8
Czechoslovakia	2	2	2	–	–	–	6
Greece	1	3	1	–	–	–	5
Spain	2	1	–	–	–	–	3
Austria	1	–	2	–	–	–	3
Russia	–	1	–	1	–	–	2
Norway	1	–	1	–	–	–	2
Japan	–	–	2	–	–	–	2
Estonia	–	–	–	1	–	–	1
Jamaica	–	–	1	–	–	–	1
Latvia	–	–	1	–	–	–	1
Mexico	–	–	1	–	–	–	1
New Zealand	–	–	1	–	–	–	1
	144	144	141 [2]	12	12	12	465

[1] Includes seven events in 1904 formerly excluded
[2] No bronzes in 1896 100km, 1972 road team trial and individual race

was demolished. Track cycling was held indoors for the first time in 1976.

The greatest speed ever achieved in Olympic cycling was in the altitude of Mexico City in 1968 when Daniel Morelon and Pierre Trentin (FRA) clocked 9.83sec for the last 200m in the tandem race, an average of 73.24km/h (45.50mph). The greatest speed by an individual rider was 71.08km/h (44.16mph) by Gary Niewand (AUS) in the elimination rounds at Atlanta 1996, when he clocked 10.129sec for the last 200m in the 1000m sprint. The fastest by a female rider was 64.21km/h (39.89mph) by Michelle Ferris (AUS), also in 1996, when she clocked 11.212sec. The longest ever held in the Games, at any sport, was the 1912 cycling road race over a distance of 320km (198.8 miles). The largest entry in any Olympic event came in the 1996 men's road race which had 183 competitors.

Few future top professionals competed at the Games successfully as amateurs, but now professionals are allowed to compete. Of the four men who have won the Tour de France a record five times , only Miguel Induráin (ESP) has won at the Games, in 1996. Eddy Merckx (BEL) and Jacques Anquetil (FRA), both finished 12th in the Olympic race, in 1964 and 1952 respectively. However, the latter won a bronze in the team race. The only other Olympic gold medallist to also win the Tour de France was Joop Zoetemelk (NED), a member of the winning quartet in the 1968 team time-trial. British rider Chris Boardman, riding a high-tech carbon-fibre bike with a revolutionary frame design, won the 1992 4km pursuit final by uniquely catching his opponent with a lap to go.

The youngest gold medallist was Dmitri Nelyubin (URS) in the 1988 team pursuit, aged 17 years and 229 days, while the oldest was Maurice Peeters (NED), aged 38 years and 99 days in the 1920 1000m sprint. Winning a bronze four years later in the tandem, Peeters at 42 years and 83 days, was the oldest ever medallist as well. The youngest medallist was Alexei Markov (RUS) in the silver medal team pursuit squad in 1996 at 17 years and 62 days. The oldest female champion was Jeannie Longo-Ciprelli (FRA) who won the 1996 road race, aged 37 years and 264 days. She was also the oldest medallist at 37 years and 278 days when second in the time trial at Atlanta. The winner of that race, Zulfiya Zabirova (RUS) became the youngest ever female gold medallist, aged 22 years and 228 days, while the youngest female medallist was Sandra Schumacher (FRG) in 1984 at 17 years and 217 days. In 1984, the first race for women, (a road race), was won by Connie Carpenter-Phinney (USA), whose husband, Davis, won a bronze in the 100km team event. She had competed in the 1972 Winter Games as a 14-year-old speed skater.

In 1996 mountain bike events for men and women were introduced. At Sydney in 2000 there will be the addition of three track events for men; the Madison, Keirin and the Olympic sprint (a team event) and a 500m time-trial for women.

De Coubertin

The accolade of founder of the modern Olympic Games is universally given to Pierre de Fredi, Baron de Coubertin of France. He was born in Paris on 1 January 1863, and early on studied the impact that sport had, and could have, on society at large, particularly appreciating the Greek ideal of developing the body and mind at the same time. He was also influenced by the ideas of the British educationalist, Thomas Arnold, and from a young age concentrated his energies on improving general education in France. He vigorously propounded the importance of exercise and fitness as a cornerstone of education.

In 1890, as part of a French government commission to study physical culture methods, he visited Dr William Penny Brookes and his Much Wenlock Olympic Society in Britain. Much impressed by this and other visits, he developed his concept of a revived Games. He put forward his ideas publicaly in a lecture at the Sorbonne, Paris, on 25 November 1892. They were received enthusiastically, and this encouraged him to meet with representatives of top American universities in the following year. In June 1894 he called an international conference, again at the Sorbonne, which was attended by 12 countries, and received messages of support from another 21. A resolution, dated 23 June, called for competitions along the lines of the ancient Olympic Games to be held every four years. An International Olympic Committee (IOC) was formed with de Coubertin as Secretary-General. Two years later he was appointed President, and retained that position until 1925, when he retired. He was then given then title of Honorary President until his death, at Geneva, Switzerland, on 2 September 1937. He was buried at Lausanne, but his heart was interred in a marble monument at Olympia in Greece. He wrote a number of books, and in 1912, under a pseudonym, won a gold medal in the Artistic Olympics for *Ode to Sport*.

Demonstration Sports

It was decided by the IOC that after 1992 there would no longer be any demonstration sports held at the Games. Since 1904 there had been a variety of such demonstrations held but not as official events eligible for medals. Some of them later became official sports and they have been mentioned elsewhere. Other than those there have been the following:

American Football (1932); Australian Rules Football (1956); Bandy (1952); Bicycle Polo (1908); Budo (1964); Dog Sled Racing (1932); Gliding (1936); Jeu de Paume (1928); Korfball (1920); Lacrosse (1928, 1932, 1948); Military Patrol (1924, 1928, 1936, 1948); Pelota Basque (1924, 1968, 1992); Roller Hockey (1992); Speed Skiing (1992); Water Skiing (1972); Winter Pentathlon (1948). *See also* separate alphabetical headings.

Discontinued Sports

In the early celebrations of the Games there were a number of sports included that were often of a purely local interest to the host country. The last of these was polo which had its final outing in 1936. Below are listed all such sports, and the years they were held.

Cricket (1900); Croquet (1900); Golf (1900, 1904); Jeu de Paume (1908); Lacrosse (1904, 1908); Motor Boating (1908, 1900, 1908, 1920, 1924, 1936); Roque (1904); Rackets (1908); Rugby Union (1900, 1908, 1920, 1924). *See also* separate alphabetical headings.

Diving

Part of the aquatics programme, men's diving was introduced into the Games in 1904, and for women in 1912. In 1996 new rules came into operation that provide for three rounds instead of two, but with fewer dives in each round. The most successful diver has been Greg Louganis (USA) with four golds (a double 'double') in 1984–88, and a silver in 1976. Austrian-born Klaus Dibiasi (ITA) won three gold and two silver medals between 1964 and 1976, winning the same event three times and gaining medals in four Games. Pat McCormick (USA) set a female record of four golds in 1952 and 1956. Her daughter, Kelly, won a silver in 1984 and a bronze in 1988. Dorothy Poynton-Hill (USA) 1928–36 and Paula Myers-Pope (USA) 1952–60 both won medals in three separate Games. Isabella White (GBR), 1912–28, Nicole Pellissard-Darrigrand (FRA), 1968–80, and Juno Stover-Irwin

(USA), 1948–60, competed in four Games. Only White, a bronze, and Stover-Irwin, a silver and a bronze, won medals.

The oldest gold medallist was Hjälmar Johansson (SWE), aged 34 years and 186 days in the plain diving at London 1908, and also the oldest ever medallist four years later in Stockholm with a silver, aged 38 years and 173 days. The oldest female champion was Micki King (USA) in 1972, aged 28 years and 33 days, while the oldest female medallist was Mary Ellen Clark (USA) with a bronze in 1996 at 34 years and 215 days. The youngest champion, and the youngest individual Olympic champion in any Summer Games sport, was Marjorie Gestring (USA) who won the 1936 springboard title, aged 13 years and 268 days. The youngest male diving champion was Sun Shuwei (CHN) in 1992, aged 16 years and 185 days. Dorothy Poynton-Hill (USA) was the youngest medallist in 1928, aged 13 years and 23 days, while the youngest male medallist was Nils Skoglund (SWE), aged 14 years and 10 days, also in 1928. Greg Louganis (USA) won both diving titles in 1984 by the biggest margins ever recorded at the Games.

Four divers, three women and a man, have also won medals at swimming. The most successful was Aileen Riggin (USA) with gold and silver diving medals in 1920 and 1924, and a bronze in the backstroke at Paris. Georg Hoffmann (GER) won silvers in 1904 at diving and the 100m backstroke; Katherine Rawls (USA) won a silver in the 1936 springboard and a bronze in the relay; Hjördis Töpel (SWE) won bronzes at diving and the relay in 1924.

The most successful husband and wife team were Clarence and Elizabeth (née Becker) Pinkston (USA), who between them won three golds, two silvers and two bronzes between 1920 and 1928. Elizabeth won

DIVING MEDALS

| | Men | | | Women | | | |
	G	S	B	G	S	B	Total
United States	27	20	20	19	20	21	127
Germany	3	6	5	3	2	2	21
Sweden	4	5	4	2	3	3	21
China	2	5	4	7	1	–	19
Soviet Union	2	1	4	2	5	3	17
Italy	3	4	2	–	–	–	9
Mexico	1	3	4	–	–	–	8
GDR	1	–	–	1	2	3	7
Great Britain	–	–	2	–	1	2	5
Canada	–	–	–	1	–	2	3
Czechoslovakia	–	–	–	1	1	–	2
Russia	1	–	–	–	1	–	2
Denmark	–	–	–	1	–	1	2
Egypt	–	1	1	–	–	–	2
Australia	1	–	–	–	–	–	1
France	–	–	–	–	1	–	1
Austria	–	–	1	–	–	–	1
	45	45	47 [1]	37	37	37	248

[1] Two bronzes awarded in a 1904 and a 1908 event

her second gold medal, in 1928, on the second birthday of her twin children. Two male divers, Giorgio Cagnotto (ITA), 1964–80, and Niki Stajkovic (AUT), 1972–80 and 1988–92, have competed at five Games. In 2000, at Sydney, two events of synchronized diving will be added.

Dog Sled Racing

A demonstration sport held at the Lake Placid Winter Games in 1932. A race of 12 sled teams, seven dogs to a sled, was held. There were actually two races of approximately 40km (25 miles) each, with the aggregate times added together. Emile St Goddard (CAN) won easily finishing first both times in a combined 4hr 23min 12.5sec, nearly eight minutes ahead of Lennard Seppala (USA).

Doubles Across Sports

There have been a number of multi-talented sports people who have won Olympic medals in different sports. The only one to win gold medals in both Summer and Winter Games was Eddie Eagan (USA) who won the 1920 light-heavyweight boxing title, and was a member of the 1932 winning 4-man bob sled. His closest rival has been Jacob Tullin Thams (NOR) who won the ski jump in 1924, and then took a silver in yachting in 1936. The most outstanding woman in this line of endeavour was Christa Rothenburger-Luding (GDR) who won a gold and a silver at speed skating at Calgary in 1988, and then came second in the sprint cycling at Seoul later the same year.

In the Summer Games the earliest double gold winner at two sports was Carl Schuhmann (GER), with three gymnastic events and the wrestling in 1896. At the same Games, Edwin Flack (AUS) won the 800m/1500m double on the track, and joined with British discus thrower George Robertson to win the tennis doubles bronze medal on the morning of the 800m final. He also started the marathon two days later, but dropped out some 4km short of the finish. Also at Athens, Viggo Jensen (DEN) won a gold and silver in weightlifting, a silver and a bronze at shooting, and was fourth in the rope climb. Fritz Hofmann (GER) won the silver medal in the 1896 100m, and is also included in the gold medal gymnastics team in some sources. Morris Kirksey (USA) won gold medals in the 4 × 100m relay and as a member of the American Rugby team in 1920. Daniel Norling (SWE) won gymnastic golds in 1908 and 1912, and then an equestrian gold in 1920. John Derbyshire (GBR) and Paul Radmilovic (GBR) won golds at swimming and the allied sport of water polo. Examples of women excelling in two Summer Olympic sports are rare, with the most outstanding being Roswitha Krause (GDR) who won a 1968 silver in the 4 × 100m freestyle, and then won silver and bronze in the 1976 and 1980 handball tournaments.

Anfissa Reztsova (URS/EUN) was the first Winter Games Olympian to win gold medals at two sports, in cross-country skiing in 1988 and the biathlon in 1992. One of the more unusual doubles was that of Fernand de Montigny (BEL), who won a gold, two silver and two bronze medals in fencing in five Games, 1906–24, and another bronze on the hockey field in 1920. Although Otto Herschmann's double, of a bronze in the 1896 100m freestyle and a silver in the 1912 sabre fencing team, is not particularly outstanding, he was at the time of his fencing medal he was the President of the Austrian Olympic Committee, and is the only competitor holding such a position to win an Olympic medal. However, even more unique is Frank Kungler (USA), who has the unmatched distinction of winning medals at three sports at the same Games. (*See* Trebles.)

Drugs

Distance runners at the end of the 19th century took small doses of strychnine as a stimulant, and it is known that the winner of the 1904 Olympic marathon was administered a dose during the race. However, under the regulations of the time this was not illegal.

The first Olympic drug abuse scandal occurred in the 1960 100km cycling race when two Danish competitors collapsed, and one, Knut Jensen, died from what was originally thought to be sunstroke. It transpired that they had both taken overdoses of a blood-circulation stimulant. Random testing was introduced at the 1964 Games at Tokyo for cycling, and then, in 1968 at the Grenoble Winter Games and Mexico City, testing for all sports was instituted. At Munich in 1972, the American swimmer Rick DeMont lost the gold medal in the 400m freestyle after testing positive for a prohibited substance, though it should be stated that as an asthmatic DeMont apparently did not realise that the drug was in his regular medication. Also at Munich came the first judo contestant to fail a drugs test, when Bakhaavaa Buidaa (MGL) was disqualified after taking the silver medal in his class. There was a spate of disqualifications in weightlifting at Montreal in 1976, and the first athlete at that Olympics to fail a test was the Polish female discus thrower, Danuta Rosani. An even higher-profile case occurred in the 1984 10 000m, when the second-placed finisher, Martti Vainio of Finland, was disqualified after a test. It was reported that as many as 17 'A' samples were found to be positive at Los Angeles, but as the athlete's code numbers mysteriously disappeared, no 'B' samples were tested.

Without doubt the biggest drugs 'scandal' at the Games was when the Canadian sprinter, Ben Johnson, was disqualified after winning the 100m, in a sensational 9.79sec, at Seoul in 1988. In 1992 International Weightlifting Federation (IWF) changed all weight categories (thus eliminating all existing world records) after the Olympic Games of that year, in a move to counter results made during a period of suspected drug abuse. In the 1990s there surfaced irrefutable evidence that the East German (GDR) state sponsored the supply of drugs to East German sportsmen and women, especially the latter.

Equestrianism

In the ancient Games the first known event using horses was a chariot race in 680BC. Horses with riders came into the Games in 648BC. The first equestrian gold medallist of the modern Olympics was Aimé Haegeman (BEL) on *Benton II* in the 1900 show jumping. In 1956 the equestrian events were held at Stockholm separately from the main Games at Melbourne, due to the strict Australian quarantine laws. The most gold medals won by a rider is six (one individual and five team events) by Reiner Klimke (FRG) 1964–88. Klimke's total of eight medals, comprising the six golds and two bronzes, also constitutes a record for equestrianism, as does his feat of winning golds in five separate Games over a 24-year period. The medals won by Gustav-Adolf Boltenstern Jr (SWE) over a similar 24-year period, 1932–56, were not all gold. A record competition span by a woman of 28 years was set by British-born Anne Jessica Ransehousen (née Newberry) (USA) in 1988.

The oldest gold medallist was Josef Neckarmann (FRG) in the 1968 dressage team, aged 56 years and 141 days. The oldest individual event winner was Ernst Linder (SWE) in the 1924 dressage, aged 56 years and 91 days. The youngest individual champion was Edmund Coffin (USA) in the 1976 three-day event, aged 21 years and 77 days. However, Mary Tauskey (USA) won a gold medal in the three-day team event in 1976, aged 20 years and 235 days. The d'Inzeo brothers of Italy, Raimondo and Piero, competed in a record eight Games, 1948–76. Raimondo won a gold, two silver and three bronze medals, while Piero gained two silvers and four bronzes. The female record in competition is six Games by Christilot Hansen-Boylen (CAN), over a record period of 28 years, 1964–92. A Bulgarian, Kroum Lekarski, competed in the three-day event for a record period of 36 years between 1924 and 1960, but actually only competed in four Games. Women first competed in 1952, and Lis Hartel (DEN) won the first female medal with a silver in the dressage, and then repeated the feat in 1956. The most successful woman has been Nicole Uphoff (GER) with four golds in 1988–92. Since 1984 equestrianism has been the only Olympic sport in which men and women compete against each other in individual events.

The only horse to be ridden to medals in three Games was *Absent* in the Soviet dressage team, with a gold and two bronzes under Sergei Filatov in 1960 and 1964, and a silver with Ivan Kalita in 1968. The most successful father and son have been Gustav-Adolf Boltenstern Sr and Jr (SWE), with the former winning a dressage individual bronze in 1912, and the latter two golds, a silver and a bronze, also in dressage, 1932–56. Liselott Linsenhöfen (FRG) won two dressage golds and a silver in 1968–72, and her daughter, Ann-Kathrin, won a gold in 1988. A unique equestrian participation record is that held by the family of William Roycroft (AUS), himself the oldest medallist in the sport at 61 years and 130 days in 1976. His son, Wayne, won a bronze in the same team, as he also had in 1968, while two other sons, Clarke (1972) and Barry (1976 and 1988) also competed well. In addition, Wayne's wife, Vicki, competed in 1984 and 1988, so that a Roycroft was in Australian teams between 1960 and 1988, and Wayne coached the winning Australian three-day event team in 1996.

In 1936 Germany completed the only six gold medal 'clean sweep' in Games' equestrian history. In the 1912 and 1920 individual dressage, Sweden took the three available medals both times, a unique occurrence.

Show Jumping

This was the first equestrian event to be included in the Games, along with high and long jumping contests, in 1900. From 1924 until 1968 teams comprised of three members, all counting for the final score. This led to many teams not finishing, as in 1932 when no team medals were awarded at all, and in 1948 when only four of the 14 competing teams finished. Since 1972 teams have consisted of four riders with the best three scoring. The most gold medals won are five by Hans-Günter Winkler (FRG) 1956–72. His total of seven medals, including a silver and bronze, is also a record for the discipline, as is his feat of winning medals in six Games. Only Pierre Jonquères d'Oriola (FRA) has won the individual title twice. The first woman to win a medal was Pat Smythe (GBR) in the 1956 team event, while the first individual medallist was Marion Coakes (GBR) in 1968.

The oldest gold medallist was Hans-Günter Winkler in 1972, aged 46 years and 49 days, while the oldest individual champion was Jonquères d'Oriola, aged 44 years and 266 days in 1964. Bill Steinkraus (USA) won medals over a 20-year period 1952–72, a record matched by Winkler 1956–76. The youngest gold medallist was Jim Day (CAN) in the 1968 team, aged 22 years and 117 days.

The lowest score obtained by a winner is no faults by Frantisek Ventura (TCH) on *Eliot* in 1928, Jonqueres d'Oriola (FRA) on *Ali Baba* in 1952, Alwin Schockemöhle (FRG) on *Warwick Rex* in 1976, and Ludger Beerbaum (GER) on *Classic Touch* in 1992. The most successful horse was Winkler's *Halla* with three golds in 1956 and 1960.

Dressage

The most successful rider was Reiner Klimke (as noted at the start of this section), but Henri St Cyr (SWE), 1952–56, and Nicole Uphoff (GER), 1988–92, won the individual title twice. Remarkably when Reiner Klimke (GER) won his last gold, it was in the 1988 team event which included Ann-Kathrin Linsenhoff, the daughter of his gold-winning team partner of 20 years before. In all, St Cyr won a record four golds, as did Nicole Uphoff. Undoubtedly St Cyr's total would have been more but his team was disqualified in 1948, having finished first, because one of its members, Gehnäll Persson, was not a fully commissioned officer — a requirement at that time. With the rules changed Persson was in the 1952 and 1956 winning teams. This Swedish team of St Cyr, Persson, and Gustav-Adolf Boltenstern Jr, uniquely finished in top place three times in a row, and can claim to be the most successful combination in Olympic history.

The first woman to win a medal was Lis Hartel. Amazingly, she was a polio victim who had to be helped on and off her horse.The first female gold medallist was Liselott Linsenhoff (FRG) in 1972. The silver medallist that year, Yelena Petushkova (URS), won gold in the team event, and was, for a time, married to Valeri Brumel, the 1964 Olympic high jump champion. The oldest gold medallist was Josef Neckarmann (FRG), who was also the oldest medallist in 1972, aged 60 years and 96 days. Incidentally, the oldest competitor in Olympic equestrian history was General Arthur von Pongracz (AUT) who began his Olympic career in 1924, aged 60 years and finished it in 1936, just missing a bronze medal, aged 72 — one of the oldest ever Olympians. The oldest woman ever to compete in the Olympic Games, at any sport, was Lorna Johnstone (GBR) who placed twelfth in the 1972 dressage five days after her 70th birthday. The youngest rider to win a gold medal was Nicole Uphoff (FRG) in the 1988 team event, aged 22 years and 244 days. The most successful horse has been *Rembrandt* ridden by Nicole Uphoff (FRG) to four golds in 1988 and 1992. They competed again in 1996 but failed to reach the final.

Three-Day Event

Competitions actually last four days as the dressage segment now occupies two days. Charles Pahud de Mortanges (NED) won the individual title twice, in 1928 and 1932, as did Mark Todd (NZL), in 1984 and 1988. However, the Dutchman also won a record total of four golds and a silver between 1924 and 1932. His Dutch team, including Gerard de Kruijff and Adolph van der Voort van Zijp, won two team titles with the same team members. The most appearances and the longest span of competition is seven Games and 28 years by Mickey Plumb (USA) 1964–92. His Games total would have been a record-equalling eight except for the US boycott of Moscow in 1984. The first female competitor was Helena Dupont (USA), 33rd in 1964, while the first female gold medallists were Mary Gordon-Watson and Bridget Parker (both GBR) in 1972. The first individual medals won by women were in 1984 by Karen Stives (USA) and Virginia Holgate (GBR).

The oldest gold medallist was Derek Allhusen (GBR), aged 54 years and 286 days in 1968, while the youngest was Mary Tauskey (USA) in 1976, aged 20 years and 235 days. The oldest medallist was William Roycroft (AUS) with a bronze in 1976, aged 61 years and 130 days. The youngest medallist was Charles Hough (USA), aged 18 years and 92 days in 1952. The most successful horse was *Marcroix* ridden by Charles Pahud de Mortanges (NED) to three golds and a silver in 1928 and 1932. Both *Silver Piece*, ridden by Adolph Van der Voort van Zijp (NED), 1924 and 1928, and *Charisma*, ridden by Mark Todd (NZL),

1984 and 1988, also won three golds. Two members of the 1996 winning USA team were husband and wife David and Karen O'Connor.

The 1936 cross-country course was so tough that only four teams out of 14 finished. One of the members of that fourth-placed team, Otomar Bures of Czechoslovakia, had over 18 000 penalty points against him at the finish, having taken over 2¾ hours to catch his horse after a fall. Britain's Captain Richard Fanshawe, with a similar problem with his horse, *Bowie Knife*, having gained over 8000 penalty points, but had the satisfaction of finishing with a team bronze. In 1920 the dressage was excluded with two cross-country runs, at 20km (12.4 miles) and 50km (31.06 miles), added to the jumping.

EQUESTRIANISM MEDALS

	G	S	B	Total
Germany	20	12	11	43
Sweden	17	8	14	39
United States	8	17	13	38
France	11	12	11	34
FRG	11	5	9	25
Italy	7	9	7	23
Great Britain	5	7	9	21
Switzerland	4	9	7	20
The Netherlands	6	7	2	15
Soviet Union	6	5	4	15
Belgium	4	2	5	11
Australia	5	1	2	8
New Zealand	3	2	3	8
Mexico	2	1	4	7
Poland	1	3	2	6
Denmark	–	4	1	5
Canada	1	1	2	4
Austria	1	1	1	3
Portugal	–	–	3	3
Spain	1	1	–	2
Chile	–	2	–	2
Romania	–	1	1	2
Czechoslovakia	1	–	–	1
Japan	1	–	–	1
Argentina	–	1	–	1
Bulgaria	–	1	–	1
Norway	–	1	–	1
Brazil	–	–	1	1
Hungary	–	–	1	1
	115 [1]	113	113 [2]	341

[1] Two golds in 1900 high jump
[2] No bronze in 1932 three-day team event

Ever Present, Countries

Only five countries have never failed to be represented at celebrations of the Summer Games since 1896 (including 1906): Australia, France, Greece, Great Britain and Switzerland. (Prior to 1924, Irish competitors were members of the Great Britain team, and did not then represent Ireland. In 1956 Switzerland only competed in the Stockholm segment of the Games.) Of those five, only France, Great Britain and Switzerland have been present at all Winter Games as well. Only Great Britain competed in the skating and ice hockey events of 1908 and 1920, the 'winter' events included in those Summer Games.

Ever Present, Events

There have been 16 individual events that have been contested at every modern Olympic Games. The athletics programme includes: 100m, 400m, 800m, 1500m, marathon, 110m hurdles, high jump, pole vault, long jump, triple jump (originally the hop, step and jump), shot and discus. In fencing, there has been the individual foil and sabre contests; in weightlifting, the unlimited class. In swimming, the 1500m freestyle may be included although the event was actually 1200m in 1896, 1000m in 1900, and 1 mile in 1904 and 1906.

Ever Present, Sports

Only five sports have been contested at every modern Games since 1896. They are athletics, cycling, fencing, gymnastics and swimming. Rowing should have been included, but rough seas caused the cancellation of these events in 1896.

Families

There have been some remarkable family achievements in the Olympic Games. (See also under Brothers and Sisters.) Outstanding among them have been the Gyarmati family of Hungary. The patriarch was Dezső who won three golds, one silver and a bronze in water polo 1948–64; his wife Éva Székely, won one gold and one silver as a breaststroke swimmer 1952–56; their daughter, Andrea, won one silver and one bronze in 1972 at backstroke and butterfly; Andrea married Mihály Hesz who had won one gold and a silver in canoeing 1964–68. Also noteworthy were the yachting Lunde family of Norway. Eugen won a gold in the 1924 6m class, his son, Peder, daughter-in-law, Vibeke, and Vibeke's brother, won a silver in the 1952 5.5m class; and grandson, Peder Jr, won a gold in the 1960 Flying Dutchman class. Similarly, the Gerevich family of Hungary made an impact on fencing: Aladár won a record seven golds, one silver and two bronzes 1932–60; his wife, Erna Bogen, won a bronze in 1932; her father, Albert Bogen (AUT), won a silver in 1912; and Aladár and Erna's son, Pál, won two bronze medals in 1972 and 1980. Many other father/son, mother/daughter, brother/sister, and husband/wife combinations have enriched the Games and they are noted under the specific sports.

Fencing

Fencing was one of the original sports held in 1896, when the first Olympic champion was Emile Gravelotte (FRA) in the foil. Until recently it was the only sport in which professionals had openly competed in the Games, as special events for fencing masters were held in 1896 and 1900. At the latter Games they even competed against amateur competitors, so that Albert Ayat (FRA) beat his pupil Ramón Fonst (CUB) in the épée. When Leon Pyrgos won the foil contest for fencing masters in 1896 he became the first Greek Olympic champion of modern times. A foil competition for women was introduced in 1924 and a team contest for them in 1960. In 1996 team and individual épée events for women were introduced. Electronic scoring equipment was used for épée in 1936, for foil in 1956, and for the sabre in 1992.

Aladár Gerevich (HUN) won a record seven gold medals in the sabre between 1932 and 1960. The record for most medals is 13 by Edoardo Mangiarotti (ITA) in foil and épée 1936–60, comprising of six golds, five silvers and two bronzes. His elder brother, Dario, won a gold and two silvers in 1948 and 1952. Nedo Nadi (ITA) won an unequalled five golds at one Games in 1920, and his younger brother, Aldo, added three more golds and a silver — a family record total at a Games. The most individual event gold medals is three, achieved by Ramón Fonst (CUB) in 1900 and 1904 (two), and by Nedo Nadi (ITA) in 1912 and 1920 (two). The only man, in any sport, to win Olympic gold medals at six consecutive Games was Aladár Gerevich; his medal-winning span of 28 years is also a record. Great Britain's Bill Hoskyns also competed at six Games, 1956–76, but only won two silver medals, while Norman Armitage (USA) attended six celebrations, 1928–56, and gained a bronze in 1948. The equal longest span of competition by any Olympic competitor is 40 years by Ivan Osiier (DEN) who fenced between 1908 and 1948, in a record seven Games. During this time he won a silver medal in 1912, and became the oldest Olympic fencer in 1948, aged 59 years and 240 days. His fencer wife, Ellen, won a gold medal in 1924.

Four fencers have won individual medals in all three disciplines at one Games. Both Nedo Nadi and his brother, Aldo, won golds in each of the team events in 1920. Roger Ducret (FRA) won foil and épée golds and a sabre silver in 1924. In the sparsely supported 1904 events American born Albertson Van Zo Post (CUB) won a foil silver and bronzes in the other two disciplines. The oldest gold medallist was Aladár Gerevich (HUN) in 1960, aged 50 years and 178 days, while the youngest was Ramón Fonst (CUB), aged 16 years and 289 days in 1900. The family of Aladár Gerevich has a unique position in Olympic fencing as he won seven golds, one silver and two bronzes; his wife, Erna Bogen, won a bronze in 1932; his father-in-law, Albert Bogen, won a silver in 1912; and Aladár's son, Pál, won bronze medals in 1972 and 1980.

Foil

Only Nedo Nadi (ITA) in 1912 and 1920, and Christian d'Oriola (FRA) in 1952 and 1956 have won two individual titles. In addition, d'Oriola won two team golds and two silvers for a record six medals. The oldest gold medallist was Henri Jobier (FRA) who was over 44-years-old in the winning 1924 team, while the youngest was Nedo Nadi (ITA) in 1912, aged 18 years and 29 days. In the 15 Games from 1920 to 1984 France only failed once to gain a team competition medal.

Épée

Ramón Fonst (CUB) was the only double winner of the individual title, but the most successful was Edoardo Mangiarotti (ITA) with five gold, one silver and two bronze medals 1936–60. The oldest gold medallist was Fiorenzo Marini (ITA), aged 46 years and 179 days in the 1960 team, and the youngest was Fonst. Charles Newton-Robinson, a member of the silver winning British team in 1906 was 52 years and 197 days, the oldest ever Olympic fencing medallist.

Sabre

Jean Georgiadis (GRE), Jenö Fuchs (HUN), Rudolf Kárpáti (HUN), Viktor Krovopouskov (URS) and Jean François Lamour (FRA) have all won two individual titles. Aladár Gerevich (HUN) won a record seven gold medals (only one individual) and was also the oldest gold medallist. The youngest was Mikhail Burtsev (URS), aged 20 years and 36 days in the 1976 team event. Hungarians have dominated the discipline to an unparalleled extent, winning 12 gold, six silver and eight bronze individual medals. They won the individual title every year between 1908 and 1964, except in 1920 when they were not invited. They have won the team title 11 times, placed second once, and third on three occasions, and won 46 consecutive contests between 1924 and 1964. Their 1960 team included Gerevich, Kárpáti and Pál Kovács, who between them amassed a total of 19 gold medals. The winning Hungarian teams of 1948 and 1952 comprised the same members. An interesting coincidence is that Kárpáti and IOC President, Juan Antonio Samaranch, were born on the same day.

Women's Foil

Only Ilona Elek (HUN) has won two individual titles, in 1936 and 1948, but Yelena Novikova-Belova (URS) won a record four golds between 1968 and 1976. The record for most medals is seven, by Ildikó Ujlakiné-Rejtó of Hungary in a record five Games, 1960–76. Surprisingly she was born deaf. Ellen Müller-Preis (AUT) competed over a record 24-year period 1932–56. This was matched by Kerstin Palm (SWE) from 1964–88, but she notched up a record seven Games — the most attended by any female Olympic competitor, in any sport. The period of 24 years is also

FENCING MEDALS

	Men			Women			
	G	S	B	G	S	B	Total
France	34	32	30	4	2	2	104
Italy	32	32	20	5	4	4	97
Hungary	27	14	20	5	6	6	78
Soviet Union	14	14	15	5	3	3	54
Poland	4	7	7	–	–	1	19
United States [1]	2	6	11	–	–	–	19
Germany	4	3	3	2	3	3	18
FRG	4	6	–	3	2	1	16
Belgium	5	3	5	–	–	–	13
Romania	1	–	2	1	3	4	11
Cuba [1]	5	3	2	–	–	–	10
Great Britain	–	6	–	1	3	–	10
Greece	3	3	2	–	–	–	8
The Netherlands	–	1	7	–	–	–	8
Russia	4	2	–	–	–	1	7
Sweden	2	3	2	–	–	–	7
Austria	–	1	3	1	–	2	7
Demark	–	1	1	1	1	2	6
Switzerland	–	2	3	–	–	–	5
Bohemia (Czech)	–	–	2	–	–	–	2
China	–	–	–	1	1	–	2
GDR	–	1	–	–	–	–	1
Mexico	–	–	–	–	1	–	1
Argentina	–	–	1	–	–	–	1
Portugal	–	–	1	–	–	–	1
	141	140	137	29	29	29	505

[1] Double counting for 1904 team gold medal

a record span of competition for any female Olympian.

Ilona Elek was the oldest gold medallist in 1948, aged 41 years and 77 days, and the oldest medallist four years later with a silver, aged 45 years and 71 days. The youngest champion/medallist was Helene Mayer (GER) in 1928, aged 17 years and 225 days. When Gillian Sheen (GBR) won her gold medal in 1956 there were hardly any members of the British press corps on hand as they considered that fencing was a 'minor' sport, and anyway she had not been expected to achieve anything of note.

Women's Épée
First held in 1996, with individual and team competitions. The youngest gold medallist was Laura Flessel (FRA), aged 24 years and 258 days in 1996. The oldest gold medallist/medallist was Sophie Moresee-Pichot (FRA) in the winning team in 1996, aged 34 years and 112 days, while the youngest medallist was Karina Aznavuryan (RUS) in the bronze team, aged 21 years and 308 days.

Figure Skating

Ice skating had been included in the original programme of events for the 1900 Games, but was withheld. Thus, the first Olympic title at a Games event was won by Ulrich Salchow (SWE) in 1908 at the Prince's Rink, London. Salchow gave his name to one of the most popular jumps. Also in the 1908 Games there was a special figures event that was won by a Russian, Nikolai Panin, who had been too ill to compete in the main event. The first women's title went to Madge Syers (GBR), who six years previously had entered the World Championships, ostensibly for men only, and had placed second to Salchow. The most gold medals won by a figure skater is three, achieved by Gillis Grafström (SWE) 1920–28, Sonja Henie (NOR) 1928–36, and Irina Rodnina (URS) in the pairs 1972–80. Of these, only Grafström also won a silver, in 1932, aged 38, and thus is the only skater to win medals in four Games. No skater has doubled with complete success in singles and pairs at the Games. The best have been Ernst Baier (GER) with the pairs gold and a singles silver in 1936, and Madge Syers (GBR) with a singles gold and a pairs bronze in 1908.

The oldest gold medallist was Walter Jakobsson (FIN) who won the 1920 pairs with his German-born wife, Ludowika, aged 38 years and 80 days. Ludowika became the oldest ever female winner, aged 35 years and 276 days. The youngest was Maxi Herber (GER), aged 15 years and 128 days in the 1936 pairs with Baier, whom she later married. The youngest individual event champion was Tara Lipinski (USA) in 1998, aged 15 years and 255 days. The youngest male champion was Richard Button (USA), aged 18 years and 202 days winning the 1948 singles. The youngest medallist was Scott Allen (USA) two days short of his 15th birthday taking the 1964 singles bronze, while the youngest female medallist was Manuela Gross (GDR)

just ten days past her 15th birthday in the 1972 bronze-winning pairs. The oldest medallist was Martin Stixrud (NOR) with the 1920 singles bronze, aged 44 years and 78 days, while the oldest female medallist was Ludowika Jacobsson (FIN) with a pairs silver in 1924, aged 39 years and 189 days. The youngest ever Winter Games competitor was Cecilia Colledge (GBR), who was 11 years and 73 days at the 1932 Games. She gained the silver medal in 1936, behind Sonja Henie. The youngest male competitor was Jan Hoffmann (GDR), aged 12 years and 110 days in 1968. Twelve years later he gained the silver medal.

Sonja Henie won three Olympic, six European and ten World titles before turning professional and making an estimated $47 million in ice shows and films. The film world attracted a number of other Olympic skaters. Down the field (16th) in 1936 was Gladys Jepson-Turner (GBR) who had a Hollywood career as *Belita*, and Vera Hruba (TCH), one place behind the British woman, married the head of *Republic Pictures* and starred in many films as Vera Hruba Ralston. Sonja Henie is usually credited with introducing jumps into the women's event, but in 1920 Theresa Weld (USA), the bronze medal winner, included a salchow in her programme, which brought a reprimand from the judges and a threat that she would be penalized if she continued with such unfeminine behaviour. In the 1992 Games, Surya Bonaly (FRA) attempted the first ever quadruple jump, in competition, by a woman.

The sport has always been plagued by accusations, often thought to be merited, that many of the judges indulge in so-called 'protocol judging', or judging on reputation rather than actual performance. A change of marking in the sport was brought about by Trixi Schuba (AUT) winning the 1972 title primarily on the basis of her excellent set figures (she had only placed seventh in free skating). At that time the marks were divided 50–50 between sections, but they were changed to give greater emphasis to free skating. Set figures were skated for the last time at Calgary in 1988, and are no longer be included in Olympic competition. On the subject of marks, Jayne Torvill and Christopher Dean (GBR) were awarded a maximum nine 6.0 for their artistic impression in the 1984 ice dancing event, as well as another three 6.0 for technical merit — unsurpassed marking at the Games. In 1994, stricter rules governing skimpy clothing were introduced, but have not always been enforced.

In 1972, although Irina Rodnina and Aleksei Ulanov (URS) won the pairs, it was the latter's dalliance with Ludmila Smirnova, silver medallist with Andrei Suraikin, which caught the media interest. The result was a break-up of the top Soviet pair. Rodnina then teamed with Alexander Zaitsev, while Ulanov and Smirnova got married. In the World Championships the Rodnina/Zaitsev partnership beat the other pair and, getting married themselves in 1975, they went on to win two Olympic titles, the second less than a year after the birth of their son. Artur Dmitriyev (RUS/EUN), with Natalya Mishkutienok, won the 1992 pairs title. At Nagano in 1998 he appeared with a new partner, Oksana Kazakova, and won the gold again, making it the 10th consecutive victory in this event for Russian pairs (i.e. URS, EUN, RUS). Also in 1998 Yevgeni Platov and Oksana Grischuk became the first couple to successfully defend the ice dance title.

FIGURE SKATING MEDALS

	G	S	B	Total
United States	12	13	14	39
Soviet Union	13	10	6	29
Austria	7	9	4	20
Canada	2	7	9	18
Great Britain	5	3	7	15
Russia	7	4	–	11
France	2	2	7	11
Sweden	5	3	2	10
GDR	3	3	4	10
Germany	4	4	1	9
Norway	3	2	1	6
Hungary	–	2	4	6
Czechoslovakia	1	1	3	5
The Netherlands	1	2	–	3
Finland	1	1	–	2
Belgium	1	–	1	2
Switzerland	–	1	1	2
FRG	–	–	2	2
China	–	–	2	2
Ukraine	1	–	–	1
Japan	–	1	–	1
	68	68	68	204

Firsts

The first person to win an event in the Modern Olympics was Francis Lane (USA), who won heat 1 of the 100m in 1896. The first gold medallist was James Brendan Connolly (USA) the winner of the 1896 hop, step and jump (now known as the triple jump). *See also* under Women.

Flag

The Olympic flag was devised by Baron de Coubertin, based on a design depicted on an ancient Greek symbol found at Delphi. It consists of five interlaced rings in two rows, coloured blue, yellow, black, green and red, from left to right. The rings are meant to symbolize the friendship of humankind, with the colours, including the white background of the flag itself, representing all nations. Every national flag contains at least one of the colours. It was originally presented to the IOC in 1914, and first flown at the Games in 1920 at Antwerp. In 1984, Korea presented a new flag to the IOC and it was first flown at

the Seoul Games in 1988. At the end of a Games the flag is placed in the safe keeping for the host city of the next celebration.

Flame

The Olympic flame was introduced to the modern Games at Amsterdam in 1928, and since then has always burned throughout the duration of a Games. It symbolizes the endeavour for perfection and struggle for victory. It is first lit by the rays of the sun in an enactment of an ancient ceremony at Olympia, the site of the original Games. (*See also* Torch Relay.) The tables below list those who have lit the Olympic flame in the stadium:

Summer
1936	Fritz Schilgen
1948	John Mark
1952	Paavo Nurmi (Hannes Kolehmainen on tower)
1956	Ron Clarke
1960	Giancarlo Peris
1964	Yoshinori Sakai
1968	Enriqueta Basilio
1972	Gunter Zahn
1976	Stephane Prefontaine and Sandra Henderson
1980	Sergei Belov
1984	Rafer Johnson
1988	Ching Sun-man, Kim Won-tuk and Sohn Mi-chung
1992	Antonio Rebollo
1996	Muhammad Ali

The first flame to burn at a Winter Games was at Oslo in 1952. It was lit at the home of Sondre Nordheim, the founder of modern skiing, at Morgedal in southern Norway, and brought by a relay of skiers to the Bislett stadium at Oslo. Thereafter the flame came from Olympia.

Winter
1952	Eigil Nansen
1956	Guido Caroli
1960	Ken Henry
1964	Joseph Rieder
1968	Alain Calmat
1972	Hideki Takada
1976	Christl Haas and Josef Feistmantl
1980	Dr Charles Morgan Kerr
1984	Sandra Dubravcic
1988	Robyn Perry
1992	Michel Platini and François-Cyrille Grange
1994	Crown Prince Haakon
1998	Midori Ito

Football

See under separate headings of *American, Australian Rules, and Soccer.*

Freestyle Skiing

Freestyle skiing, for men and women, was a demonstration sport in 1988 comprising of ballet, aerials and mogul events. Mogul events became an Olympic medal sport in 1992, with aerials added in 1994. Marking is complicated but can best be compared to diving as each manouevre has a degree of difficulty which affects the final marks.

The most successful competitors have been Edgar Grospiron (FRA), with a gold and a bronze 1992–94, and Stine Lise Hattestad (NOR) equalling him in the women's events. Hattestad was also the oldest female champion, aged 27 years and 292 days winning the 1994 moguls; the oldest male winner was Eric Bergoust (USA) who won the 1998 aerials at 28 years and 175 days. The youngest winner, of the 1994 moguls, was Jean-Luc Brassard (CAN), aged 21 years and 176 days, while the youngest female champion was Tae Satoya (JPN), aged 21 years and 244 days. The youngest medallist was Yelizaveta Kozhevnikova (RUS/EUN) in the 1992 moguls, aged 19 years and 48 days, and the youngest male to win a medal was Dimitri Daschinsky (BLR) with an aerials bronze in 1998 at 20 years and 101 days. Elizabeth McIntyre (USA) was the oldest medallist in the 1998 moguls, aged 33 years and 229 days. When Satoya won the 1998 moguls title she became the first ever winner of a Winter Olympics gold medal by a Japanese woman.

Garmisch-Partenkirchen 1936
IV Winter Games (6–16 February)

Attended by representatives of 28 countries, comprising 755 competitors, of which 80 were women.

It is not always remembered that when the Winter and Summer Games of 1936 were awarded to Germany five years previously, Adolf Hitler was virtually unknown. However, by the year of the Games they were seen by many as a test case of how the German Olympic Committee would react to the demands of the National Socialist government of Germany. There had been much heated discussion around the world as to the advisability of attending these, or the later Summer Games, due to the racial policies of that government. In spite of this a record entry included teams from Bulgaria, Turkey, Australia, Spain and Liechtenstein for the first time. The Games were declared open by Chancellor Adolf Hitler, and Wilhelm Bogner, a cross-country skier, took the oath on behalf of competitors. By the end of the competitions, over 500 000 paying spectators had watched the six different sports. These now included Alpine skiing, although the only event was a combination one, for both men and women.

Birger Ruud (NOR) successfully defended his ski jumping title, and then caused a major surprise by winning the downhill segment of the men's Alpine combination. By a 5.9sec margin of victory in the slalom

FREESTYLE SKIING MEDALS

	Men			Women			
	G	S	B	G	S	B	Total
United States	2	–	1	2	1	–	6
France	1	2	1	–	–	–	4
Norway	–	–	–	1	–	3	4
Canada	1	1	1	–	–	–	3
Switzerland	1	–	–	–	–	1	2
Finland	–	1	1	–	–	–	2
Russia	–	1	–	–	–	1	2
Japan	–	–	–	1	–	–	1
Uzbekistan	–	–	–	1	–	–	1
China	–	–	–	–	1	–	1
Germany	–	–	–	–	1	–	1
Soviet Union	–	–	–	–	1	–	1
Sweden	–	–	–	–	1	–	1
Belarus	–	–	1	–	–	–	1
	5	5	5	5	5	5	30

segment the title went to Franz Pfnür (GER) and Ruud fell back to fourth place. In the women's event there was a similar situation when the downhill race was won by 16-year-old Laila Schou Nilsen (NOR), who, a year later, broke five world speed skating records. She had entered the skiing in the absence of such events for women. In the slalom Christl Cranz (GER), who was eventually to win 12 world skiing championships, won by the quite astounding margin of 11.3sec and took the overall gold medal, Nilsen gaining the bronze.

The top medal winner was speed skater Ivar Ballangrud (NOR) with three golds and a silver. Contrary to the Lake Placid conditions of four years earlier the racers competed under European-style rules with pairs of skaters racing against the clock. Instead of four gold medals the Americans gained a solitary bronze. Sonja Henie (NOR) won her third consecutive figure skating title, to add to her ten world championship wins, and then went off to Hollywood, followed sometime later by the 16th-placed British girl, Gladys Jepson-Turner, who gained cinematic fame as *Belita*, and 17th placed Vera Hruba (TCH). The British caused a major upset by winning the ice hockey, albeit with a team containing some Anglo-Canadians. Also in this competition appeared Rudi Ball, one of only two athletes of Jewish origin selected by Germany in 1936. Ball, a bronze medallist from 1932, was especially requested to return from his exile in France. The hosts hoped to offset criticism of their attitude to Jewish competitors by this act.

A most unusual double nearly came the way of Ernst Baier (GER) who won the pairs skating, but came second in the men's singles. It was still the best such double placing ever. His pairs partner, Maxi Herber, was the youngest gold medallist, aged 15 years and 128 days, whilst sister and brother Ilse and Erik Pausin (AUT), the pairs silver medallists, were the youngest ever couple to gain a medal in the event, their ages totalling a mere 32 years and 307 days. The oldest gold medallist was Carl Erhardt (GBR) one day past his 39th birthday in the ice hockey final. The demonstration events were German curling and the military patrol.

1936 MEDALS (WINTER)

	G	S	B
Norway	7	5	3
Germany	3	3	–
Sweden	2	2	3
Finland	1	2	3
Austria	1	1	2
Switzerland	1	2	–
Great Britain	1	1	1
United States	1	–	3
Canada	–	1	–
France	–	–	1
Hungary	–	–	1

Gliding

A demonstration sport at Berlin in 1936. Fourteen countries took part in an exhibition, but the main participants were German gliders.

Golf

George Lyon, a former Canadian pole vault record holder, was 46 years and 59 days when he won the 1904 title. The most successful player was Chandler Egan (USA) who won a team gold and individual silver in 1904. Also in that gold medal team was his brother, Walter. Charles Sands (USA) who won the inaugural competition in 1900, was one of the few people to compete in three sports at the Games, as he had played in the tennis tournament in 1900, and took part in Jeu de Paume in 1908. The winner of the only women's competition, in 1900, was Margaret Abbott, aged 20 years and 110 days, who became the first American woman to win an Olympic gold medal. Her mother, Mary, placed seventh in a rare case of mother and daughter competing in the same event at a Games.

Grenoble 1968
X Winter Games (6–18 February)

Attended by representatives of 37 countries, comprising 1158 competitors, of which 211 were women.

There were complaints that venues at Grenoble were very widespread, with some 40km distant, but the new 12 000-seat indoor ice stadium delighted everyone. For the first time gender tests for female competitors were held. The political split between East and West Germany was finally acknowledged and separate teams accepted. Morocco made its debut, and the official opening was performed by the President of France, Charles de Gaulle. The last relay runner was Alain Calmat, the 1964 skating silver medallist, and the oath was taken by Léo Lacroix, a 1964 skiing silver medal winner. The IOC attempted to control the exploitation of the Games from commercial interests by banning the use of trade names on competitors' equipment. Following the threat of a withdrawal by some leading skiers, who relied very heavily on ski company sponsorship, it was finally agreed that they need only remove the equipment before appearing in photographs or on television.

The undoubted star of these Games was Jean-Claude Killy (FRA), who emulated Anton Sailer's 1956 record by winning all three Alpine skiing events. However, in the last of the three events, the slalom, Karl Schranz (AUT) claimed that in his second round run he had been distracted by a policeman cutting across the course in front of him. He was allowed another run, which he accomplished in a faster time to become the overall winner. Then it was decided that on his first attempt he had already missed a gate before the policeman incident, and his rerun was disqualified. He was to be even unluckier four years later. The best of the women Alpinists was Canada's Nancy Greene with a gold in the giant slalom and a silver in the slalom. The latter was won by Marielle Goitschel (FRA) to keep the title in the family — her sister had won in 1964.

The most successful Nordic skier was Finnish-born Toini Gustafsson (SWE) with two gold and a silver in the women's events. By winning the 30km race Franco Nones (ITA) became the first ever non-Scandinavian winner in cross-country skiing. Another shock to Scandinavian sensibilities occurred in the two jumps and the combination event, when they only won a single bronze from the nine medals available. Yet another upset was in the women's luge, where the GDR women, in first, second and fourth places, were disqualified for illegally heating their sled runners. The bob run at Alpe d'Huez, which was badly sited and considered to be very dangerous, was the scene of total triumph for Eugenio Monti, who was the good sport of Innsbruck four years previously. The Italian, nine times a world-champion bobsledder, won both Olympic gold medals. In the 2-man event the total times after four runs for Monti's bob and that of the German bob were equal. The tie was decided in the Italian's favour as he had the fastest single run. Aged 40 years and 24 days, Monti was the oldest gold medallist at Grenoble.

The youngest champion was skater Peggy Fleming (USA), aged 19 years and 198 days. The youngest male gold medallist was Wolfgang Schwarz, winning Austria's first skating title since 1936, aged 20 years and 155 days. Ludmila Belousova and Oleg Protopopov (URS) retained their pairs title, with Ludmila the oldest female champion at 32 years and 84 days. In 26th place in the men's figure skating was Jan Hoffmann (GDR), aged 12 years and 110 days — the youngest ever male competitor in Olympic Winter Games. Twelve years later he won the silver medal. The oldest female medallist was Nordic skier Alevtina Koltschina (URS) with a bronze in her fourth Games at 37 years and 97 days.

This was the only occasion that multiple victories were not gained. The women's 500m was reminiscent of the men's event of 1948 and 1964 as three women tied for the silver medal. Making this occasion unique was the fact that all three of them were from the same country, the United States. For the last time, Norway topped the medal table. In future, until 1998, the first two places would be taken by the Soviet Union and the GDR.

Gymnastics

In artistic gymnastics there are eight inter-linked events for men and six for women. A team competition comes first, comprising one compulsory and one optional exercise for each separate discipline. For men these are: floor exercises, pommel horse, rings, horse vault, parallel bars and horizontal bar. For women they are floor exercises, asymmetrical bars, horse vault and balance beam. Each competitor is marked out of 10.00 for both the compulsory and optional exercises at each discipline. The best total of five gymnasts per country decides the team competition. The best 36 individuals (but a maximum of three per country) then qualify for the individual all-round competition. They each complete a further optional exercise for each discipline, and are awarded new marks. Prior to 1992 these were added to the average of their previous best total from the team competition, but from then they are started from scratch. The best eight in each discipline go forward to the individual final for that event. With the exception of 1948, when scores were marked out of 20.00 points, since 1936 are of some comparative value. After 1996 there were no compulsory exercises. In 1984 an individual modern rhythmic event for women was introduced, and in 1996 there was a team event.

The first gymnastics gold medal was won by the German team on the parallel bars event in 1896, and the first individual champion was Carl Schuhmann of that team in the vault. Due to the large number of disciplines, each with their own medals awarded, gymnasts are among the greatest collectors of Olympic medals. The most successful was Larissa Latynina (URS) who won a record 18 medals between 1956 and 1964, comprising nine golds (the most by any female Olympian), five silvers and four bronzes unsurpassed in any sport. The most individual gold medals was won by Vera Cáslavská (TCH) in 1964 and 1968, an Olympic record in any sport by a woman. The most gold medals won by a man is eight by Sawao Kato (JPN) 1968–76, but the male record for individual golds is six achieved by Boris Shakhlin (URS) and

1968 MEDALS (WINTER)

	G	S	B
Norway	6	6	2
Soviet Union	5	5	3
France	4	3	2
Italy	4	—	—
Austria	3	4	4
The Netherlands	3	3	3
FRG	2	2	3
United States	1	5	1
Finland	1	2	2
GDR	1	2	2
Czechoslovakia	1	2	1
Canada	1	1	1
Switzerland	—	2	4
Romania	—	—	1

GYMNASTICS MULTI-MEDAL WINNERS

	G	S	B
Larissa Latynina (URS) 1956–64	9	5	4
Sawao Kato (JPN) 1968–76	8	3	1
Nikolai Andrianov (URS) 1972–80	7	5	3
Boris Shakhlin (URS) 1956–64	7	4	2
Vera Cáslavská (TCH) 1960–68	7	4	0
Viktor Chukarin (URS) 1952–56	7	3	1

Nikolai Andrianov (URS). The latter also holds the absolute Olympic record for most medals by a male competitor, in any sport, with a total of 15. In 1980 Alexander Ditiyatin (URS) became the only male gymnast to gain medals in all eight events at one Games, while in 1992 Vitali Scherbo (EUN) won six gold medals at the one Games.

In recent years the sport has caught the imagination of the public due to a tremendous increase in media, especially television coverage. In 1968 it was the attractive blonde Czech, Vera Cáslavská, who drew the attention by defeating the Soviet women only two months after the invasion of her country. At Munich, it was Olga Korbut (URS) who was the focus of all, even though she was outshone, technically, by her illustrious team-mate Ludmila Tourischeva. In 1976 the unsmiling Nadia Comaneci (ROM) deserved all the adulation as she scored the ultimate 10.00 on seven occasions, while the photogenic Nelli Kim (URS) attained that score twice. Alexander Ditiatin stole the

show from the women in 1980, and also gained the first Olympic 10.00 by a man in the horse vault. At Los Angeles the television cameras made a superstar of Mary Lou Retton (USA) in the absence of the East Europeans. The television pictures of the injured Kerri Strug (USA) successfully vaulting to clinch the American's team gold at Atlanta in 1996, was beamed around the world.

The oldest gold medallist was Masao Takemoto (JPN), aged 40 years and 344 days in the 1960 team event. Only 24 days younger was Heikki Savolainen (FIN) in the 1948 team event, who competed in a record five Games over a record span of 24 years between 1928 and 1952. The oldest male medallist was Lucien Démanet (FRA) at 45 years and 266 days in 1920. The youngest champion was Nadia Comaneci (ROM), aged 14 years and 252 days in 1976, while the oldest female champion was Agnes Keleti (HUN) in 1956, aged 35 years and 331 days. The oldest female medallist was Ethel Seymour

GYMNASTICS MEDALS

| | Men | | | Women | | | |
	G	S	B	G	S	B	Total
Soviet Union	45	42	19	38	30	30	204
Japan	27	28	30	–	–	1	86
United States [1]	22	17	19	4	6	9	77
Romania	–	2	2	16	13	18	51
Switzerland	15	19	13	–	–	–	47
Hungary	6	6	4	7	6	10	39
GDR	3	3	10	3	10	7	36
Czechoslovakia	3	7	9	9	6	1	35
Germany	12	7	11	1	1	–	32
Italy	13	7	9	–	1	–	30
China	8	9	5	2	3	1	28
Finland	8	5	12	–	–	–	25
France	4	7	9	–	–	–	20
Yugoslavia	5	2	4	–	–	–	11
Russia	2	1	3	1	2	1	10
Greece	4	2	3	–	–	–	9
Sweden	4	1	–	1	1	1	8
Bulgaria	2	1	2	–	2	1	8
Ukraine	1	–	1	3	1	1	7
Norway	2	2	1	–	–	–	5
Denmark	1	3	1	–	–	–	5
Belarus	–	–	4	–	–	–	4
Austria [1]	2	1	–	–	–	–	3
Korea	–	1	2	–	–	–	3
Great Britain	–	1	1	–	–	1	3
Spain	–	–	–	1	1	–	2
Belgium	–	1	1	–	–	–	2
Poland	–	1	–	–	–	1	2
FRG	–	–	1	–	–	1	2
Canada	–	–	–	1	–	–	1
The Netherlands	–	–	–	1	–	–	1
North Korea (PRK)	1	–	–	–	–	–	1
	190	176	176	88	83	84	797

[1] Double counting for 1904 men's team title

(GBR) in 1928, aged 46 years and 222 days. The youngest male to win a gold medal was Harald Eriksen (NOR) in 1906, aged 17 years and 292 days. The youngest medallist was Dimitrios Loundras (GRE) who gained a bronze in the parallel bars team event of 1896, aged 10 years and 218 days. However, it should be noted that some doubt exists about his exact age. The youngest ever female medallist was Luigina Giavotti (ITA) in 1928, aged 11 years and 303 days. In 1984 it was decided that minimum ages should be set for competitors: 16 years for males and females 15 years, for Sydney 2000 the minimum age for all is 16 years. Recent revelations suggest that in the past some countries in the Eastern bloc faked the ages of their young female performers, presenting them as older than in fact they were.

The closest margin of victory in the individual all-round contest for men was 0.025 of a point in 1984 when Koji Gushiken (JPN) beat Peter Vidmar (USA). In 1992 there was a tremendous duel for the women's all-around title between Tatyana Gutsu (EUN) and Shannon Miller (USA) which ended in the Ukrainian girl winning by the smallest ever margin of 0.012pts. There had been some controversy over the inclusion of Gutsu, who had failed to make the cut-off after the team competition, but was a replacement for an allegedly injured team-mate. On two occasions there has been a triple tie for a gold medal, both times in the pommel horse event, in 1948 and 1988. Since the Soviet Union entered Olympic competition in 1952 they have won the women's team title nine times (they were not present in 1984). In 1992, under the guise of the Unified Team they not only won for the 10th time, but as their swansong took the men's and women's individual and team titles plus the rhythmic

crown. With the Soviet Union broken up, it was Russia that took the 1996 men's title.

One of the most amazing competitors in Olympic history must be the American gymnast George Eyser, who won six medals, including three golds, in the 1904 Games. He was well over 30 years of age, but even more remarkably had a wooden leg. Despite this he competed in the all-round contest, the forerunner of the decathlon, in the track and field programme. In 1988 Vladimir Gogoladze (URS) performed a triple somersault in the team floor exercises — the first achieved in the Olympics. In the 1988 modern rhythmic competition, Marina Lobatch (URS) scored the maximum possible 60.00 points.

The largest crowd to watch an Olympic gymnastic event was the 32 600 at the Georgia Dome in 1996 for the final of the women's team contest. Prior to 1928 it has been suggested that there were no individual medal events, merely competitors as part of the all-round title. However, in this book, these are shown in the tables of results and added to the medal lists until more evidence comes to light to indicate otherwise. At Sydney, in 2000, two trampolining events have been added to the gymnastics programme.

Handball

The sport was introduced in 1936, appropriately since it was a German invention, and was played as an outdoor 11-a-side game. When reintroduced in 1972 it was as an indoor seven-a-side competition. The most successful players have been Zinaida Tourchina (URS) and her team-mate Larissa Karlova, who won gold medals in 1976 and 1980, and then a bronze in

HANDBALL MEDALS

	Men			Women			Total
	G	S	B	G	S	B	
Soviet Union	3	1	–	2	–	2	8
Yugoslavia	2	–	1	1	1	–	5
Korea	–	1	–	2	2	–	5
Romania	–	1	3	–	–	–	4
GDR	1	–	–	–	1	1	3
Norway	–	–	–	–	2	–	2
Sweden	–	2	–	–	–	–	2
Hungary	–	–	–	–	–	2	2
Croatia	1	–	–	–	–	–	1
Denmark	–	–	–	1	–	–	1
Germany	1	–	–	–	–	–	1
Austria	–	1	–	–	–	–	1
Czechoslovakia	–	1	–	–	–	–	1
FRG	–	1	–	–	–	–	1
China	–	–	–	–	–	1	1
France	–	–	1	–	–	–	1
Poland	–	–	1	–	–	–	1
Spain	–	–	1	–	–	–	1
Switzerland	–	–	1	–	–	–	1
	8	8	8	6	6	6	42

1988. Four male Romanian players have also won medals in three Games, but none of them was gold.

The oldest gold medallist was Yuri Klimov (URS), aged 36 years and 1 day in 1976, while the oldest female was Ludmila Poradnik (URS) in 1980, aged 34 years and 200 days. Tourchina's bronze in 1988 was achieved at the age of 42 years and 135 days and the oldest male medallist was Mats Olsson (SWE), winning silver in 1996, aged 36 years and 205 days. The youngest gold medallist/medallist was Larissa Karlova (URS), aged 17 years and 356 days in 1976, while the youngest male winner was Günther Ortmann (GER), aged 19 years and 257 days in 1936. Willy Hufschmid (SUI) won a bronze medal in 1936, aged 17 years 310 days.

The greatest margin of victory was 34 when Yugoslavia beat Kuwait 44–10 in 1980. The comparable margin among the women was 30 when Yugoslavia beat Congo 39–9, also in 1980. The greatest aggregate score was 70 when the Danish women beat Korea 37–33 in the 1996 final, after extra time. The comparable men's figure is 62 when the FRG team beat Korea 37–25 in 1984, and equalled when Croatia beat the United States 35–27 in 1996. The record score by an individual in one game was 17 by Jasna Kolar-Merdan for the Yugoslavian women when they beat USA 33–20 in 1984. The male record is 13, by István Varga (HUN) against the United States in 1972, and by Kenji Tamamura (JPN) against Hungary in 1988.

A member of the GDR winning team in 1980 was Hans-Georg Beyer, the brother of 1976 shot put champion, Udo (who also won a bronze in 1980). To complete an outstanding family trio, their sister Gisela narrowly missed a bronze medal in the women's discus in Moscow. Their countrywoman, Roswitha Krause, a member of the silver medal handball team of 1976, and of the bronze medal team in 1980, had been a silver medallist in the 4 × 100m freestyle swimming quartet in 1968.

Heaviest

The heaviest person to win an Olympic medal, and indeed the heaviest known to have competed in the Games, was probably Chris Taylor (USA) the 1972 super-heavyweight wrestling bronze medallist. He weighed between 182kg (401lb) and 190kg (419lb). Another contender for the 'title' is the American weightlifter Mark Henry who weighed in at 184.92kg (407.5lb) in the 1996 Games. The heaviest woman to win a gold medal at the Games was Iuliana Semenova, a member of the Soviet gold medal basketball teams in 1976 and 1980 — she weighed 129kg (284lb) (*See also* Tallest). Perhaps it should be noted that the famed sumo wrestler, Akebono, (actually born Chad Rowan in Hawaii), who played a prominent part in the opening ceremony of the 1998 Winter Games at Nagano, weighed in at 234kg (516lb). The heaviest gold medallist, and indeed competitor, at the Winter Games was Friedrich Kuhn (GER), a member of the winning 4-man bob at Oslo in 1952, who weighed in at 140kg (308lb). The team totalled 468kg (1032lb) — an average of 117kg (258lb) — leading to a change in the rules limiting the overall weight of the manned bob.

Helsinki 1952
XV Olympic Games (19 July–3 August)

Attended by representatives of 69 countries, comprising 4925 competitors, of which 518 were women.

One of the greatest Olympian countries, Finland, finally became hosts of the Games. President Juho Paasikivi formally opened the Games in the smallest city ever to be host — Helsinki had a population of only 367 000. There were two dramatic moments during the ceremony. Firstly, when a so-called 'Angel of Peace', an apparently mentally unstable German girl in a flowing white robe, ran around part of the track. More appropriate to the occasion was the moment when the last relay runner was due and the scoreboard indicated the first letter of his name. The stadium erupted to cheers as 55-year-old Paavo Nurmi, arguably the greatest distance runner the world has seen, ran a lap and lit the flame in the stadium. He then passed the torch to 62-year-old Hannes Kolehmainen, the original 'Flying Finn', who ascended the stadium tower, and lit another flame there.

After 40 years Russia returned to the Olympics, now in the guise of the Soviet Union. Fears of confrontation between them and the United States team proved unfounded, as the competitors seemed to treat each other quite cordially, if somewhat coolly. Attending the Games for the first time were teams from the Bahamas, Gold Coast (now Ghana), Guatemala, Dutch Antilles, Hong Kong, Indonesia, Israel, Nigeria, Thailand, Vietnam, and for the only time ever, the Saar. Because mainland China had been invited, the Nationalist Chinese (Taiwan) had withdrawn. Although they all marched together there were two Olympic villages; surprisingly the IOC had allowed the Soviet bloc to set up their own at Otaniemi, while everybody else was at Kapyla.

The athlete of these Games was the Czech runner Emil Zátopek who won an unprecedented triple in the 5000m, 10 000m and marathon. To crown his achievements, his wife, Dana, born on the same day, also won a gold medal, in the javelin, within an hour of his 5000m victory. The outstanding female track athlete was Australia's Marjorie Jackson who set world records winning the 100m and 200m but dropped the baton when certain to win a third gold in the sprint relay. Incidentally, she retrieved the baton and finished in fifth place. In the winning American team was Barbara Pearl Jones who became the youngest ever track and field gold medallist, aged 15 years and 123 days. However, the youngest gold medallist at Helsinki was French cox Bernard Malivoire at 14 years and 94 days in the pairs event. Once again small nations did well, with Jamaican runners invincible over 400m, and Josy Barthel causing the band some problems as they tried to find the anthem of his native Luxembourg when he scored an upset win in the 1500m.

The 1948 100m sprint champion, Harrison Dillard (USA), won the 110m hurdles and taking his fourth gold medal in the sprint relay. His team-mate, Horace Ashenfelter, gained America's first win in a distance run since 1908 when he set an inaugural official world record for the 3000m steeplechase. The Press had great fun with the fact that Ashenfelter, an FBI agent, was followed home by a Russian. The Soviet Union's first ever Olympic gold medal was won by Nina Romashkova in the women's discus. Highly questionable disqualifications by blatantly biased judges marred the 10 000m track walk, but did not stop the Swiss and Russian second and third place medallists literally running the last 30m to the line, outsprinting the judge who vainly tried to reach them to rule them out. Incidentally, the judge was Giorgio Oberweger (ITA), who had won a bronze medal in the 1936 discus before becoming a walking official. The event was dropped from future Games. The winner of the high jump, Walt Davis (USA), was, at 2.04m, (6ft 8¼in) probably the tallest competitor ever to win an individual event , in any sport, at the Games. In the swimming pool the Hungarians won four of the five events for women. Almost matching the Zátopeks were Éva Székely, who won the 200m breaststroke, and her husband Dezsö Gyarmati, a member of the victorious Hungarian water polo team four days later. Much media attention was gained in the 400m freestyle for men when the father of the winner, Jean Boiteux (FRA), jumped into the pool fully clothed to congratulate his son. In diving, Dr Sammy Lee, an American of Korean origin, became the first man to successfully defend a diving title, in this case the highboard. He later coached the next man to achieve the feat, Bob Webster, in 1960 and 1964.

The gymnastics competitions were dominated by the Soviet teams, led by Viktor Chukarin, four golds and two silvers, and his female counterpart Maria Gorokhovskaya, with two golds and five silvers. The latter's total of seven is the most medals ever won by a woman at one Games in any sport. The Finnish veteran, Dr Heikki Savolainen, (who had taken the oath at the opening ceremony), gained a team bronze, the fifth consecutive Games at which he had won a medal, was just two months short of his 45th birthday. Other veterans did well in 1952. Ilona Elek (HUN) added a silver to her two fencing golds at the age of 45 years and 71 days. In the dressage André Jousseaume (FRA) won an individual bronze medal two days after his 58th birthday, and 20 years after his gold medal at Los Angeles. In all, he placed in the top five positions in five Games. Another great sportsman, Károly Takács (HUN), won the rapid-fire pistol for the second time. Before the War he had won the European title as a right-handed shooter, but in 1938 he had lost his right hand when a grenade exploded while he was holding it. He painstakingly taught himself to shoot with his left hand and won two Olympic titles. On a less uplifting note, there was the disqualification of Ingemar Johannson (SWE) in the heavyweight boxing final for 'not trying'. His silver medal was withheld for 14 years. In 1959 he won the world professional title from the 1952 Olympic middleweight champion, Floyd Patterson (USA).

The oldest gold medallist at these Games was Everard Endt (USA) in the 6m yachting, aged 59 years and 112 days. Another yachtsman, Ernst Westerlund (FIN), was the oldest medallist, 19 days older than Endt. The youngest male and female champions were Bernard Malivoire and Barbara Pearl Jones. The oldest female winner was Sylvi Saimo (FIN) in the 500m kayak event, aged 37 years and 260 days. At the end of the Games a then-record 43 countries had won medals in Helsinki, and it was announced that Avery Brundage (USA) had taken over the Presidency of the IOC from the retiring Sigfrid Edström.

1952 MEDALS (SUMMER)

	G	S	B
United States	40	19	17
Soviet Union	22	30	19
Hungary	16	10	16
Sweden	12	13	10
Italy	8	9	4
Czechoslovakia	7	3	3
France	6	6	6
Finland	6	3	13
Australia	6	2	3
Norway	3	2	–
Switzerland	2	6	6
South Africa	2	4	4
Jamaica	2	3	–
Belgium	2	2	–
Denmark	2	1	3
Turkey	2	–	1
Japan	1	6	2
Great Britain	1	2	8
Argentina	1	2	2
Poland	1	2	1
Canada	1	2	–
Yugoslavia	1	2	–
Romania	1	1	2
Brazil	1	–	2
New Zealand	1	–	2
India	1	–	1
Luxembourg	1	–	–
Germany	–	7	17
The Netherlands	–	5	–
Iran	–	3	4
Chile	–	2	–
Austria	–	1	1
Lebanon	–	1	1
Ireland	–	1	–
Mexico	–	1	–
Spain	–	1	–
Korea	–	–	2
Trinidad and Tobago	–	–	2
Uruguay	–	–	2
Bulgaria	–	–	1
Egypt	–	–	1
Portugal	–	–	1
Venezuela	–	–	1

Hockey

The first Olympic hockey game was won by Scotland, who beat Germany 4–0 in 1908, with the first goal scored by Ian Laing only two minutes after the start. In those Games four of the six teams competing represented England, Ireland, Scotland and Wales. From 1928 until 1984, Olympic hockey tournaments were dominated by teams from the Indian sub-continent, with India winning eight times and Pakistan three. However, it should be noted that Great Britain, probably the world's strongest team at the time, did not participate in 1932 and 1936. The long-awaited meeting between them and India came in the 1948 final which India won 4–0. In 1988, for the first time in 60 years, no member from the sub-continent won a medal. Interestingly, after years of decline, in 1984 the Great Britain team was a last-minute replacement for the boycotting Soviet Union, and they won the bronze — their first medal for 32 years. Then, in 1988, the British team won the gold medal again, after 68 years. Women's competition was instituted in 1980.

Several members of Indian teams have won a record three gold medals: Dhyan Chand 1928–36, Richard Allen 1928–36, Randhir Singh 1948–56, Balbir Singh 1948–56, Leslie Claudius 1948–56, Ranganandhan Francis 1948–56, and Udham Singh 1952, 1956 and 1964. Of these, only Claudius and Udham Singh also won a silver, each in 1960. The oldest gold medallist/medallist was Dharam Singh (IND) in 1964, aged 45 years and 278 days. The youngest winner was Russell Garcia (GBR) in 1988, aged 18 years and 103 days, and the youngest medallist was Haneef Khan (PAK) at 17 years and 26 days in 1976. The youngest female champion was Maider Goni (ESP) in 1992,

aged 19 years and 24 days, although Arlene Boxhall was under 19 as a member of the 1980 Zimbabwe women's team but she did not actually play in the tournament. The oldest female gold medallist was the Zimbabwe coach/player Anthea Stewart, aged 35 years and 253 days. Iveta Sramkova (TCH), in the 1980 silver medal team, was only 16 years and 304 days of age.

The highest score ever achieved in Olympic hockey was when India beat the United States 24–1 in 1932. The highest score in a final was also in 1932 when India beat Japan 11–1. Roop Singh (IND), the brother of the team captain Dhyan Chand, scored a record 12 goals in the above mentioned match against the United States. In their six successive wins 1928–56, India scored 178 goals and conceded only seven. They did not concede a single goal during the 1928 tournament (five games). The longest game in Olympic hockey lasted 2hr 25min (into the sixth period of extra time) when The Netherlands beat Spain 1–0 in Mexico in 1968.

The biggest margin of victory in the women's contests came in 1980 when the Soviet Union beat Poland 6–0. This was matched by Australia in 1996 beating Argentina 7–1, their score being the highest ever in the women's competitions. The greatest aggregate was 10 in 1988 when Korea and Australia tied 5–5.

Andreas Keller's gold medal in Germany's 1992 team capped a wonderful family achievement: his father, Carsten, won gold in 1972, and his grandfather, Erwin, silver in 1936. Keller's girlfriend, Anke Wild, also won a silver in the 1992 women's tournament. The 1988 Olympic competitions were particularly noteworthy for family achievements. Sisters Lee and Michelle Capes gained gold medals in the Australian women's team, and the Dutch siblings, Marc and Carina Benninga, gained bronze medals in their country's respective third-placed teams.

HOCKEY MEDALS

	Men			Women			
	G	S	B	G	S	B	Total
India	8	1	2	–	–	–	11
Great Britain	3	2	4	–	–	1	10
The Netherlands	1	2	3	1	–	2	9
Pakistan	3	3	2	–	–	–	8
Australia	–	3	2	2	–	–	7
Germany	1	1	2	–	1	–	5
FRG	1	2	–	–	1	–	4
Spain	–	2	1	1	–	–	4
Korea	–	–	–	–	2	–	2
Soviet Union	–	–	1	–	–	1	2
United States	–	–	1	–	–	1	2
New Zealand	1	–	–	–	–	–	1
Zimbabwe	–	–	–	1	–	–	1
Czechoslovakia	–	–	–	–	1	–	1
Denmark	–	1	–	–	–	–	1
Japan	–	1	–	–	–	–	1
Belgium	–	–	1	–	–	–	1
	18	18	19 [1]	5	5	5	70

[1] Two bronzes in 1908

Ice Hockey

The game was introduced in 1920 as part of the Summer Games. The tournament was won by Canada, the first of a run of six victories only interrupted by Great Britain in 1936. The record number of wins is eight by the Soviet Union/EUN between 1956 and 1992. However, in 1994 they did not win a medal for the first time since they entered in 1956. In the early days, the Canadians were always represented by a club side, not a national one, so that the first Olympic champions were actually the Winnipeg Falcons. Since 1948 the tournament has been decided on a championship format and not, as previously, on a knock-out basis — thus there is no Olympic final as such. The game has been the centre of much bitter argument about amateur/professional status, and in 1972 Canada withdrew in protest against alleged 'professionalism' of the Eastern European teams in particular. Happily, they returned in 1980. In 1994, professionals were allowed to compete, and in 1998, the National Hockey League, in Canada and the United States, suspended its season for the first time ever, to allow 125 of its players to compete for nine national teams. The major surprise of the 1998 tournament was that neither the United States nor Canadian teams gained a medal. The latter were beaten in a semi-final by the Czech Republic in the first ever Olympic game decided by a penalty shoot-out.

In 1948 there was a strange situation when two teams turned up to represent the United States, one from the Amateur Hockey Association (AHA) and the other picked by the US Olympic Committee (USOC). The AHA, while not affiliated to the USOC, was a member of the International Ice Hockey Federation (IIHF), the governing body of most of the other teams present in St Moritz. The IHF threatened to withdraw all the other teams if the AHA team did not play, while the USOC threatened to withdraw the whole Olympic team if the AHA team did play. Initially the IIOC barred both teams, but then agreed to allow the AHA team to compete. They eventually finished fourth, but a year later were disqualified for non-affiliation to the Olympic movement. Strangely the USOC hockey team members marched in the opening ceremony.

Six Soviet players have won a record three gold medals, but only goalminder Vladislaw Tretyak, 1972–84, also won a silver. Richard 'Bibi' Torriani (SUI) won a bronze in 1928 and another in 1948, for a record 20-year span. The oldest gold medallist was Carl Erhardt (GBR) in 1936 on the day after his 39th birthday. The youngest was John Kilpatrick (GBR) in 1936, aged 18 years and 224 days, while the youngest medallist was Torriani (SUI) at 16 years and 141 days in 1928. The oldest medallist was Erhardt. The first brothers to win gold were Herbert, Hugh and Roger Plaxton along with Frank and Joseph Sullivan in the 1928 Canadian team. The only twins were Boris and Yevgeni Maiorov (URS) in 1964. The only known father and son gold medallists were Bill and David Christian (USA) who won in 1960 and 1980 respectively. Another distinction for Bill is that he and his brother, Roger, were one of two sets of brothers (the other was Bill and Bob Cleary), who helped the USA to win its first ice hockey gold in 1960. Pavel and Valeri Bure, who won silver medals in the Russian team in 1998, are the sons of Vladimir Bure (URS) who won a silver and two bronze medals in swimming at Munich in 1972.

The highest score and aggregate in Olympic ice hockey was the 33–0 victory by Canada over Switzerland in 1924. In that tournament the Canadians scored 110 goals in five matches with only three against. In the 1980 tournament the American goalminder, James Craig, stopped 163 of 178 shots (91.6 per cent), including 39 in the match against the Soviet Union. When the Czechs won the 1948 silver medal a member of the team was 1954 Wimbledon tennis champion, Jaroslav Drobny. Vladimir Ruzicka of the Czech Republic, who won a gold medal in 1998, had won silver in the Czechoslovakian team 14 years previously.

ICE HOCKEY MEDALS

	Men			Women			
	G	S	B	G	S	B	Total
Canada	6	4	2	–	1	–	13
Soviet Union	8	1	1	–	–	–	10
United States	2	6	1	1	–	–	10
Czechoslovakia	–	4	4	–	–	–	8
Sweden	1	2	4	–	–	–	7
Finland	–	1	2	–	–	1	4
Great Britain	1	–	1	–	–	–	2
Switzerland	–	–	2	–	–	–	2
Czech Republic	1	–	–	–	–	–	1
Russia	–	1	–	–	–	–	1
FRG	–	–	1	–	–	–	1
Germany	–	–	1	–	–	–	1
	19	19	19	1	1	1	60

A women's tournament was instituted in 1998. The highest score, margin of victory, and aggregate came when Canada beat Japan 13–0. The youngest gold medallist/medallist was Angela Ruggerio (USA), aged 18 years and 45 days. The oldest gold medallist was Lisa Brown-Miller (USA) at 31 years and 93 days. The oldest medallist was France St Louis, in the silver medal Canadian team when 39 years and 123 days. Cammi Granato of the winning USA squad did considerably better than her father, Tony, who was a member of the seventh placed American team at Calgary in 1988.

Ice Skating

See separate entries for *Figure Skating, Speed Skating and Short-Track Speed Skating*

Innsbruck 1964
IX Winter Games (29 January–9 February)

Attended by representatives of 36 countries, comprising 1091 competitors, of which 200 were women.

Awarded to Innsbruck in 1959 these Games were the most successful yet with over one million spectators attending a then record 34 events. Among them were lugeing and a second ski jump. However, weather again was a problem, and snow had to be transported to some venues by the Austrian Army. During practices before the Games began there were two tragic deaths, of a British tobogganist and an Australian skier. The official opening by the Austrian President, Dr Adolf Schärf, took place at the Bergisel ski jump in front of 60 000 people. The last relay runner who lit the flame was a skier, Joseph Rieder, and the oath was taken by a bobsledder, Paul Aste. Mongolia and India competed for the first time, while Korea was split into North and South teams. South Africa was now banned from the Olympics. An innovation was the use of computers officially to aid judging as well as provide electronic timing.

The Games were dominated by the Soviet Union but, for the first time, Switzerland failed to gain a single medal. Lydia Skoblikova (URS), a teacher from Siberia, won all four women's speed skating events, to give her a total of six gold medals in two Games, a record for the sport. The Soviet husband and wife skating pair, Ludmila Belousova and Oleg Protopopov, brought a new concept, classical ballet, to the sport. The silver medal went for the second consecutive occasion to Marika Kilius and Hansjürgen Bäumler (GER), but two years later they were disqualified owing to professional activities which had then come to light. In 1987 they were reinstated by the IOC. The women's individual skating title went to Sjoukje Dijkstra, The Netherland's first ever Winter Games gold medal.

The first sisters to win gold medals at the same Games were Marielle and Christine Goitschel (FRA) who swapped first and second places in the Alpine slalom events. The reintroduced bobsleigh events were won, for the first time, by countries which did not possess bob runs of their own. Also, the victory by Tony Nash and Robin Dixon (GBR) in the 2-man bob was the first by a 'lowland' country, and owed much to a replacement bolt supplied by an Italian adversary, Eugenio Monti. He was later awarded the Pierre de Coubertin Fair Play Trophy for this action. Klaudia Boyarskikh (URS) won three gold medals in Nordic skiing, while Sixten Jernberg (SWE) brought his total to a record nine medals in three Games. A demonstration of German curling was also held.

The oldest gold medallist was Sixten Jernberg, winning his fourth gold medal two days after his 35th birthday. The youngest was Manfred Stengl (AUT), aged 17 years and 310 days in the 2-man luge, with Marielle Goitschel (FRA) the youngest female winner in the giant slalom, aged 18 years and 128 days. The oldest female champion was Alevtina Koltschina (URS) in the Nordic relay at 33 years and 88 days. Scott Allen (USA) was the youngest medallist with his bronze in the men's figure skating just two days short of his 15th birthday, while the oldest was Eugenio Monti (ITA), aged 36 years and 15 days.

1964 MEDALS (WINTER)

	G	S	B
Soviet Union	11	8	6
Austria	4	5	3
Norway	3	6	6
Finland	3	4	3
France	3	4	–
Sweden	3	3	1
Germany	3	3	3
United States	1	2	3
Canada	1	–	2
The Netherlands	1	1	–
Great Britain	1	–	–
Italy	–	1	3
North Korea (PRK)	–	1	–
Czechoslovakia	–	–	1

Innsbruck 1976
XII Winter Games (4–15 February)

Attended by representatives of 37 countries, comprising 1123 competitors, of which 231 were women.

These Games were originally awarded to Denver, Colorado, in 1970, but two years later a State referendum decided against providing the necessary finance. So, in February 1973, Innsbruck became the first centre to be awarded the Winter Games for a second time. Most facilities were still available from 1964, and 'only' $44 million was required to refurbish and update. The Games were opened by the President of Austria, Dr Rudolf Kirchschläger, and two Olympic flames were lit, by Christl Haas, 1964 gold medal skier, and Josef Feistmantl, 1964 gold medal luger. The oath was taken by Werner Delle-Karth, a bobsledder. A total of 1.5 million spectators watched the

37-event schedule. There were also 600 million television viewers around the world. Unfortunately, an influenza outbreak affected some of the competitors. Two of the smallest States in the world, Andorra and San Marino, made their Winter Games debuts.

The outstanding competitor was Rosi Mittermaier (FRG) who, by winning the downhill and slalom races, and taking second place in the giant slalom, set up the best series of performances ever by a female Alpine skier. She failed by a mere 0.13sec, in the giant slalom, to match the male record of three golds held by Anton Sailer and Jean-Claude Killy. In taking the men's downhill on the Patscherkofel course, Austria's Franz Klammer achieved the then highest speed recorded in an Olympic downhill race, 102.828km/h (63.894mph). In Nordic skiing Galina Kulakova (URS) was disqualified from third place in the 5000m event when a banned drug was found present in a nasal spray she was using to combat influenza, but she was allowed to compete in other events and won a gold and another bronze. Her team-mate, Raisa Smetanina, won two golds and a silver to be the most successful Nordic skier. Particular attention, and some ridicule, was given to Bill Koch (USA) who used his newly developed 'skating' style of skiing. Rather more attention, and less ridicule, came when he won a silver medal in the 30km race, the only Nordic skiing medal ever won by an American. However, the greatest tally of medals at these Games was two gold and two bronze by Tatyana Averina (URS) in speed skating. Preventing a clean sweep of those titles by the Soviet women was Sheila Young (USA) who took the 500m title, and later in the year won her second world cycling championship.

In figure skating the 'jilted' Irina Rodnina (URS) successfully defended her pairs skating title, but this time with a different partner, her new husband, Alexander Zaitsev. The men's champion, John Curry (GBR), brought balletic art to his event just as the Russian pairs had in 1964 and 1968. His Italian/American coach, Carlo Fassi, became the first to train both individual champions at a single Games when Dorothy Hamill (USA) won the women's title. In the new ice dancing event Soviet couples were placed first, second and fourth. All five luge and bobsled events were won by GDR competitors.

The oldest gold medallist was Meinhard Nehmer (GDR) in the 2-man bob, aged 35 years and 25 days, and the youngest was skater Hamill, aged 19 years and 201 days. The youngest male gold medallist was Boris Aleksandrov (URS) in the champion ice hockey team, aged 20 years and 93 days, while the oldest female champion was Galina Kulakova (URS) in the Nordic relay, aged 33 years and 289 days. Toni Innauer (AUT) won a silver in ski jumping, aged 17 years and 320 days, while the oldest medallist was Marjatta Kajosmaa (FIN) with a Nordic relay silver nine days after her 38th birthday. The oldest competitor at these Games was 46-year-old Carl Erik Eriksson (SWE) in the bob events, while the youngest was figure skater Yelena Voderzova (URS), only three months away from her 13th birthday.

1976 MEDALS (WINTER)

	G	S	B
Soviet Union	13	6	8
GDR	7	5	7
United States	3	3	4
Norway	3	3	1
FRG	2	5	3
Finland	2	4	1
Austria	2	2	2
Switzerland	1	3	1
The Netherlands	1	2	3
Italy	1	2	1
Canada	1	1	1
Great Britain	1	–	–
Czechoslovakia	–	1	–
Lichtenstein	–	–	2
Sweden	–	–	2
France	–	–	1

International Olympic Committee (IOC)

The IOC was inaugurated on 23 June 1894 under the presidency of Demetrius Vikelas of Greece, with Baron de Coubertin as its first Secretary-General. On 23 June 1994 the IOC celebrated its centenary, noting that the advances of Olympianism had extended competition to all continents, and given access for all races, religions and languages. Its headquarters are in Lausanne, Switzerland. The IOC co-opts and elects its members, and they are the IOC's representatives in their respective countries, and not delegates from those countries. The Executive Board consists of the President, four Vice-Presidents and six other members. At the time of writing, January 2000, after a number of resignations and expulsions following a bribery scandal to do with the selection of certain host cities, there were 113 members of the IOC. Presidents of the organisation are listed below.

1894–1896	Demetrius Vikelas (Greece)
1896–1925	Baron Pierre de Coubertin (France)
1925–1942	Count Henri de Baillet-Latour (Belgium)
1942–1952	J. Sigfrid Edström (Sweden)
1952–1972	Avery Brundage (USA)
1972–1980	Lord Killanin (Ireland)
1980	Juan Antonio Samaranch (Spain)

Jeu De Paume

A medal sport only at London in 1908, held at Queen's Club, Kensington, it was also a demonstration sport at Amsterdam in 1928. The winner in London was Jay Gould Jr, son of the American railroad tycoon of the same name, who had tried to corner the gold market in 1869, causing the infamous 'Black Friday' panic.

Judo

This sport was introduced in 1964 and appropriately the first gold medal was won by Japan's Takehide Nakatani in the lightweight class. However, one of the greatest upsets to a nation's sporting pride occurred in Tokyo's Nippon Budokan Hall in 1964 when the giant Dutchman Anton Geesink (1.98m, 6ft 6in) beat the Japanese favourite for the Open category title in front of 15 000 home supporters. Another Dutchman, Willem Ruska, is the only man to win two gold medals at a single Games, in the over 93kg and Open classes in 1972. Hiroshi Saito (JPN) and Peter Seisenbacher (AUT) are the only men to successfully defend their titles, both in 1984 and 1988. Angelo Parisi won a record four medals, with a bronze in 1972 representing Great Britain, and then gold and two silvers in 1980 and 1984 representing France. The winning of medals for two different countries at the Olympic Games is rare, but not uncommon. Parisi was born in Italy, moved to Great Britain as a child, became a citizen, then married a French girl in 1973 and changed his nationality again. Robert Van de Walle (BEL) competed in a record five Olympic judo competitions between 1976 and 1992.

The oldest gold medallist was Ruska when he won the 1972 Open class, aged 32 years and 11 days, whilst the youngest was Antal Kovács (HUN) in the 1992 light-heavyweight division, aged 20 years and 61 days. The oldest medallist was Arthur Schnabel (FRG) with a bronze in the 1984 Open class, aged 35 years and 329 days, and the youngest medallist was Amiran Totikashvili (URS) with a bronze in the 1988 extra-lightweight class at 19 years and 66 days. The fastest throw in Olympic competition was 4sec by Akio Kaminaga (JPN) against Thomas Ong (PHI) in 1964.

JUDO MEDALS

	Men			Women			
	G	S	B	G	S	B	Total
Japan	18	5	8	1	5	3	40
Soviet Union	7	5	14	–	–	1	27
France	5	3	12	3	–	3	26
Korea	5	7	8	2	2	1	25
Cuba	1	3	2	2	2	5	15
Great Britain	–	5	7	–	1	2	15
The Netherlands	3	–	4	–	–	3	10
GDR	1	2	6	–	–	–	9
Germany	1	1	6	–	–	1	9
Poland	3	2	2	–	1	–	8
FRG	1	4	3	–	–	–	8
Hungary	1	2	4	1	–	–	8
Brazil	2	1	5	–	–	–	8
United States	–	3	5	–	–	–	8
China	–	–	–	2	–	4	6
Italy	1	2	1	–	1	1	6
Spain	–	1	–	2	–	2	5
Belgium	1	–	2	–	1	1	5
Austria	2	–	1	–	–	–	3
Switzerland	1	1	1	–	–	–	3
Canada	–	1	2	–	–	–	3
Mongolia	–	1	2	–	–	–	3
North Korea (PRK)	–	–	1	1	–	–	2
Bulgaria	–	1	1	–	–	–	2
Israel	–	–	1	–	1	–	2
Romania	–	–	2	–	–	–	2
Yugoslavia	–	–	2	–	–	–	2
Egypt	–	1	–	–	–	–	1
Uzbekistan	–	1	–	–	–	–	1
Australia	–	–	1	–	–	–	1
Czechoslovakia	–	–	1	–	–	–	1
Georgia	–	–	1	–	–	–	1
Iceland	–	–	1	–	–	–	1
Turkey	–	–	–	–	–	1	1
	53	52 [1]	106	14	14	28	267

[1] 1972 silver withheld due to disqualification

The youngest female gold medallist was Kye Sun (KOR), aged 16 years and 359 days winning the 48kg class in 1996, while the oldest was Miriam Blasco Sotoi (ESP) at 28 years and 232 days in 1992. The oldest medallist was Laetitia Meignan (FRA), aged 32 years and 33 days at Barcelona, and the youngest was Ryoko Tamura (JPN) at 16 years and 331 days, also in 1992.

The biggest of many big men in Olympic judo was Jong Gil Pak (PRK) who was 2.13m (7ft) tall and weighed 163kg (359lb) in the 1976 Games. In 1972 the Mongolian lightweight silver medallist, Bakhaavaa Buidaa, became the first competitor ever disqualified for failing a dope test in any Olympic judo competition. An amusing sideline was provided by the 1976 lightweight gold medal winner, Hector Rodriguez (CUB), who said that he took up the sport as a child in order to defend himself against his six older brothers.

Women's events were contested as a demonstration sport in Seoul, and were added to the official programme in 1992. In 1996 a total limit of 400 competitors for the sport was imposed.

Korfball

A demonstration event in 1920 and 1928, it is related to basketball and handball, and originated in Holland in 1902.

Lacrosse

Held at St Louis in 1904 and London in 1908, both were won by Canada. In 1904 a Mohawk Indian team, representing Canada, won the bronze, but in 1908 only two teams competed. The highest score was when Canada beat Great Britain 14–10 in 1908. Demonstrations were held in 1928, 1932 and 1948.

Lake Placid 1932
III Winter Games (4–15 February)

Attended by representatives of 17 countries, comprising 306 competitors, of which 32 were women.

Snow had to be brought over to the United States from Canada by large trucks for some of the venues at Lake Placid, and a thaw caused the 4-man bob event to be held after the official closing ceremony on 13 February. The Games were opened by the Governor of New York State, Franklin D. Roosevelt, who became President of the United States the following year. Eleanor, his formidable wife, took a ride down the bob course. The oath was taken by Jack Shea, who won the 500m speed skating gold later in the day. An Olympic first was achieved in the opening ceremony by the British contingent when their flag was carried by a woman, skater Mollie Phillips.

Innovatively, figure skating was held indoors, and drew large crowds, and three speed skating events for women were given demonstration status — 28 years later such events were on the programme proper. Demonstrations were also given of curling and dog sled racing, the latter won by Emile St Goddard of Canada.

Not surprisingly the Scandinavians swept the Nordic skiing, but an upset occurred in the speed skating where the Americans and Canadians dominated. It is arguable whether this was more to do with the abilities of the North Americans than with the change of rules that the organising committee had invoked. Instead of the more usual European system of competition in pairs, with the fastest times deciding the medal places, American rules were in force. Under these, mass start races were held, similar to track running, with heats and finals. Lack of familiarity with the tactics employed, often quite physical, put the Europeans at a distinct disadvantage. Indeed, Finland's four-time gold medallist Clas Thunberg did not even bother to appear at Lake Placid. The Canadians won the ice hockey title for the fourth consecutive time, but only on goal average after three periods of overtime against the United States in the final game.

In figure skating the peerless Sonja Henie (NOR) easily retained her title, but triple champion Gillis Grafström (SWE), now 38, was the victim of an unfortunate accident. During the compulsory figures he collided with a badly positioned movie camera and fell, suffering a mild concussion. This may well have cost him an unprecedented fourth title. The oldest competitor was Joseph Savage (USA), aged 52 years and 144 days in the pairs skating. The winners of that title, Pierre and Andrée Brunet (FRA), became the first pair to win both as an unmarried (1928) and married couple. In so doing Andrée was the oldest female gold medal winner in Lake Placid, aged 30 years and 149 days. They later coached American gold medallists Carol Heiss (1960) and Hayes (1956) and David (1960) Jenkins. In the women's individual event, Cecilia Colledge was Great Britain's youngest ever Olympic competitor, at any sport, aged 11 years and 73 days. She was also the youngest ever competitor in the Olympic Winter Games.

History of a different kind was made by Eddie Eagan (USA) in the 4-man bob as a late and virtually untried draftee. As part of the winning team he became the only man to win gold medals in both Summer and Winter celebrations, as he was a 1920 boxing champion. The 2-man bob was won by brothers Curtis and Hubert Stevens (USA), and a third brother, Paul, won a silver medal in the 4-man event. The oldest gold medallist at Lake Placid was Eagan's bob team-mate, Jay O'Brien aged, 48 years and 359 days, while Sonja Henie was again the youngest, now aged 19 years and 308 days. The youngest male champion was ice hockey player Albert Duncansson (CAN), aged 20 years and 134 days. O'Brien is still the oldest person to win a Winter Olympics gold medal.

1932 MEDALS (WINTER)

	G	S	B
Untied States	6	4	2
Norway	3	4	3
Sweden	1	2	–
Canada	1	1	5
Finland	1	1	1
Austria	1	1	–
France	1	–	–
Switzerland	–	1	–
Germany	–	–	2
Hungary	–	–	1

Lake Placid 1980
XII Winter Games (13–24 February)

Attended by representatives of 37 countries, comprising 1072 competitors, of which 233 were women.

Lake Placid had been applying for the Games unsuccessfully since 1962 when they were finally rewarded in 1974. Most of the facilities used in 1932 had to be rebuilt, and new ones constructed, so that the budget for these Games was nearly 80 times the $1.1 million spent in 1932. Some complaints were voiced about the 'village', a building later to be used as a penal institution, but as a report noted, 'at least security would not be a problem'. Once the Games were under way the accommodation was found to be quite suitable and acceptable. One pre-Games worry which turned into a major problem was transport for the spectators and press. At times it was virtually impossible to reach and/or return from venues. The official opening was undertaken by Walter Mondale, the Vice-President of the United States. The last relay runner was Dr Charles Morgan Kerr, a psychiatrist, and the oath was taken, with outstanding foresight, by speed skater Eric Heiden. The People's Republic of China and Cyprus made their debuts in the Winter Games.

The aforementioned Eric Heiden (USA) stole all the headlines by gaining an unprecedented sweep of all five speed skating gold medals, all in Olympic record times. His sister, Beth, also won a bronze in the women's events. Her team-mate Leah Poulos-Mueller won two silver medals but could not match her husband Peter's gold performance of 1976. In Nordic skiing Nikolai Simyatov (URS) won three golds in one Games, while team-mate Galina Kulakova, now over 37, raised her record total of medals over four Games to eight. Ulrich Wehling (GDR) won his third consecutive gold medal in the Nordic combination, and Alexander Tikhonov (URS) won a fourth consecutive gold in the biathlon relay. The closest ever result in Olympic Nordic skiing came in the men's 15km cross-country event when Thomas Wassberg (SWE) beat Juha Mieto (FIN) by 0.01sec. Eight years previously the unlucky Finn had lost a bronze medal by only 0.06sec. However, he did win a gold in the 1976 relay.

Slalom specialist Ingemar Stenmark (SWE) won both of his races to became the most successful male Alpine skier at these Games, but Hanni Wenzel from tiny Liechtenstein won both women's slaloms and the silver medal in the downhill. Her brother, Andreas, added a silver to put their country in sixth place on the unofficial medal table. Another sister, Petra, was also in the team of seven. In winning the 90m ski jump Jouko Törmänen (FIN) made the longest jump attained to that time in Olympic competition when he cleared 117m (383ft). In the 70m event there was an unfortunate incident when after nine competitors had taken their jumps the judges ruled that conditions were too dangerous. The start point was moved lower down, to reduce take-off speed, and the competition begun again. Irina Rodnina (URS) equalled the record of three gold medals by a figure skater when she and her husband, Alexander Zaitsev, retained the pairs title. By successfully defending the men's singles for Great Britain, Robin Cousins, won his country's only medal of these Games. The bobsledding was a virtual replay of the 1976 rivalry between the Swiss and GDR teams. A member of the American 12th-placed 4-man bob was Willie Davenport, who had competed in the Summer Games between 1964 and 1976 and had won the 110m hurdles in 1968. By far the most popular win was that of the United States ice hockey team over the Soviet Union (their first defeat since 1964) on the way to the final. The celebrations which followed were described on American television as the biggest since the end of World War II. In the final they then beat Finland.

The oldest gold medallist was Meinhard Nehmer (GDR) in the 4-man bob, aged 39 years and 42 days, and the youngest was his team-mate, Karin Enke who won the 500m speed skating title, aged 18 years and 240 days. The youngest male winner was Mike Ramsey of the victorious USA ice hockey team, aged 19 years and 83 days. The oldest female champion was Irina Rodnina (URS), aged 30 years and 159 days. Special mention must be made of Marina Tcherkasova (URS), a silver medallist in pair skating only 93 days past her 15th birthday.

1980 MEDALS (WINTER)

	G	S	B
Soviet Union	10	6	6
GDR	9	7	7
United States	6	4	2
Austria	3	2	2
Sweden	3	–	1
Liechtenstein	2	2	–
Finland	1	5	3
Norway	1	3	6
The Netherlands	1	2	1
Switzerland	1	1	3
Great Britain	1	–	–
FRG	–	2	3
Italy	–	2	–
Canada	–	1	1
Hungary	–	1	–
Japan	–	1	–
Bulgaria	–	–	1
Czechoslovakia	–	–	1
France	–	–	1

Lausanne

In 1915 it was agreed that the administrative headquarters of the IOC were to be set up in Lausanne, Switzerland, a town popular with Baron de Coubertin. In 1922 he and the IOC moved into a house in the centre of the town. By 1968 the premises had become too small, and the Chateau de Vidy, on the outskirts, was made available by the Town Council as the headquarters of the IOC. Lausanne also houses the ultra modern-Olympic museum, on the Quai d'Ouchy.

Lillehammer 1994
XVII Winter Games (12–27 February)

Attended by representatives of 67 countries, comprising 1736 competitors of which 519 were women.

It was during the 1988 Olympic Games at Seoul, in September, that the IOC decided to award these Games to Lillehammer, a town of 23 000 people some 180km (111 miles) north of Oslo. Three other cities had made bids but the Norwegian town, which had lost out to Albertville in the 1992 vote, won the IOC's approval this time. This was the first Winter Games not held in the same year as a Summer celebration. Lillehammer held one of the most successful Games, Summer or Winter, of all time, with excellent weather, eye-catching facilities, firm and deep snow, good organisation, and enthusiastic but non-chauvinistic spectators. The only adverse variables were extremely cold temperatures, often below 20°C, and the high cost of food and drink.

A spectacular opening ceremony, embodying traditional themes such as the mythical Vetter people, involved actress Liv Ullmann and Kon-Tiki anthropologist Thor Heyerdahl. The Games were officially opened by King Harald V, himself a former Olympian. The torch was brought into the stadium by Stein Gruben, who leaped from the ski jump before handing it to Catherine Nottingnes. She, in turn, passed it to Crown Prince Haakon, who lit the flame. The oath was taken by triple gold medallist skier Vegard Ulvang. There was a minute's silence for the plight of Sarajevo, a former Olympic site.

The record number of countries, including 14 first-timers, was boosted by the break-up of the former Soviet Union, and led to a then record 22 countries winning medals. In ice hockey and figure skating, professionals were allowed to compete. In the latter, stricter rules were in force governing skimpy clothing, and there were a number of controversial judging decisions which drew strong criticisms. Prior to the Games, excessive media interest had been generated by the vicious attack on US skater Nancy Kerrigan, and the alleged involvement of her team-mate Tonya Harding.

A reported 83 per cent sale of event tickets was evidenced by enormous crowds, particularly at the Nordic skiing despite the intense cold. There were a number of new events including aerials in the freestyle skiing, and men's 500m and women's 1000m in the short-track speed skating. A reported $295 million was paid by CBS for the American television rights.

The most successful competitor at Lillehammer was Manuela di Centa (ITA) who won five medals (two gold, two silver, one bronze) in cross-country skiing, equalling a single Games best-ever total. However, fellow Nordic skier Lyubov Yegorova (RUS) won three golds and one silver, thus equalling the Winter Games record total of six gold medals. In bobsledding, Gustave Weder (SUI) became the only man to successfully defend the 2-man title, while Wolfgang Höppe (GER), was uniquely a medallist in four Games. Alpine skier Vreni Schneider (SUI) was the first woman to total three gold medals in her sport, as well as setting an all-time record of five medals. Alberto Tomba (ITA) won medals at three consecutive Games in Alpine skiing. This sport also featured some very small margins of victory. Remarkably, for the first time ever, no Alpine nation gained a medal in the men's downhill race.

American speed skaters, Bonnie Blair (with a record third consecutive 500m title) and Dan Jansen (a very popular emotional winner after a series of disasters in the previous three Games) could not take the spotlight away from Norway's Johann Olav Koss. He won three gold medals, all in world record times. The ice hockey competition witnessed shockingly bad results from the United States and, even more surprisingly, Russia, and resulted in the first ever win by Sweden.

The youngest ever gold medallist at a Winter Games was Kim Yoon-mi (KOR), in the short-track skating women's relay, aged 13 years and 83 days. She was also the youngest ever female Olympic champion in either Winter or Summer Games. The youngest male gold medallist at these Games was Maurizio Carnino (ITA) in the short-track relay, aged 18 years and 356 days. The winner of the women's figure skating, Oksana Baiul (UKR) was the youngest, at 16 years and 101 days, to win that title since Sonja Henie (NOR) in 1928. The oldest gold medallist/medallist was Maurilio De Zolt (ITA) in the Nordic relay, aged 43 years and 150 days, in his fifth Games. The oldest female medallist was Marja-Liisa Kirvesniemi (FIN) at 38 years and 167 days, in her record-equalling sixth Games.

Lillehammer was also the scene for the greatest sibling performance in a Winter Games, by the four Huber brothers of Italy. Wilfried and Norbert won gold and silver, separately, in the luge pairs; Gunther got a bronze in the 2-man bob; Arnold placed fourth in the luge singles.

At the end of these Games it was estimated that, excluding multi-participation by athletes, some 85 000 competitors had attended the Modern Games since 1896.

1994 MEDALS (WINTER)

	G	S	B
Russia	11	8	4
Norway	10	11	5
Germany	9	7	8
Italy	7	5	8
United States	6	5	2
Korea	4	1	1
Canada	3	6	4
Switzerland	3	4	2
Austria	2	3	4
Sweden	2	1	–
Japan	1	2	2
Kazakhstan	1	2	–
Ukraine	1	–	1
Uzbekistan	1	–	–
Belarus	–	2	–
Finland	–	1	5
France	–	1	4
The Netherlands	–	1	3
China	–	1	2
Slovenia	–	–	3
Great Britain	–	–	2
Australia	–	–	1

London 1908
IV Olympic Games (27 April–31 October)

Attended by representatives of 22 countries, comprising 2035 competitors, of which 36 were women.

Originally awarded to Rome the IV Games were reallocated to London when the Italian authorities informed the IOC during the Interim Games that they would have to withdraw due to financial problems. London formally accepted on 19 November 1906. Nevertheless, they were the most successful held up to that point and set the pattern for future Games. Drawing on the expertise of many British sporting governing bodies, like the Amateur Swimming Association (founded 1869), and the Amateur Athletic Association (founded 1880), the organising committee under Lord Desborough went to work. A 68 000 capacity stadium was built in West London for a reported cost of £40,000. (That stated 'capacity' was apparently well-exceeded on a number of occasions.) It contained an athletics track of three laps to the mile, inside a 660yd banked concrete cycle track. On the grass infield stood a giant (330ft × 50ft, 100m × 15.24m) pool for the swimming events. Rowing was held at Henley, on the River Thames; tennis was held at the All-England Club, Wimbledon; yachting at Ryde, Isle of Wight; and the new sport of motor boating was on Southampton Water. The main competitions took place in July, although the overall programme lasted from April to October. There were 21 sports in all including four ice skating events. There was also a demonstration sport, bicycle polo, in which Ireland beat Germany 3–1.

Entries were only by nations, as opposed to individuals. This tended to emphasise the nationalism that undoubtedly caused some of the disputes and marred this first truly international sporting occasion. These problems started during the formal opening, by King Edward VII, at what later became known as the White City stadium on 13 July. Sweden and the United States were upset that their flags had been inadvertently missed from those flying around the stadium. Then Ralph Rose, the American flag-bearer, and eventual winner of the shot, refused to dip the Stars and Stripes to King Edward in the march past. The Finnish team would not march behind the flag of Czarist Russia and came in without any banner. Later, things got worse as complaints came from all sides, but especially from US officials. They complained about 'fixed' heats, illegal coaching, rule breaking and British chauvinism. The weather was also rather foul, even by British standards, and badly affected cycling and tennis in particular.

All the rancour came to a head in the 400m event final, in which three of the four finalists were Americans. Prior to the race, officials had been tipped off regarding an American 'plot', after someone overheard them planning how to impede and beat the British favourite, Lieutenant Wyndham Halswelle. After the event, the race was declared void and a re-run, with strings delineating the lanes, was ordered for the next day, whilst the winner of the disputed race, John Carpenter, was disqualified. The other Americans refused to appear and Halswelle gained the gold medal in the only walk-over in Games history. One of the runners involved was John Taylor who, as a member of the winning medley relay team, became the first black man to win an Olympic gold medal. A more imaginative resolution to a problem, apparently, came in the 110m hurdles. The favourite, Forrest Smithson, an American student of theology, protested against the official decision to run the final on a Sunday, and then proceeded to break the world record in 15.0sec, supposedly carrying a bible in his left hand. While uplifting, the only 'evidence' of this story is a photograph that was obviously staged after the event.

Finally the bitterness reached such a level that it was thought necessary to produce a booklet entitled Replies to Criticism of the Olympic Games, which, owing to its rather pompous tone, did little to alleviate the situation. One result of all this was the decision that future control of competitions should be in the hands of the various international governing bodies of the sports and not left solely to the host country.

The previous year the IOC had decided that medals should be awarded for the top three places in all events. There were many excellent performances throughout the Games, despite all the problems. The ubiquitous Ray Ewry, now 33 years old, won his record-breaking ninth and 10th gold medals in the standing jumps, while John Flanagan, one of the so-called Irish-American 'Whales', won his third hammer title. Middle distance runner Mel Sheppard (USA) was a triple gold medallist, as did British swimmer

Henry Taylor. Charles Daniels (USA) won the 100m freestyle to add to his three titles from the last two Games, and set a record of four individual event swimming gold medals that has been equalled, but not beaten, since. The Hungarian swimmer Zoltán von Halmay increased his total medal haul to nine since 1900, a total unsurpassed in the sport until 1972.

The introduction of skating events gave the opportunity to Russia to win its first Olympic title, courtesy of Nikolai Panin (actually Kolomenkin) who, four years later, was a member of the fourth-placed revolver shooting team. Another Olympic first came in the London shooting programme when Oscar and Alfred Swahn of Sweden became the first father and son to win gold medals, with Oscar being the oldest gold medallist at these Games, aged 60 years and 265 days. The youngest champion was Daniel Carroll (AUS), in rugby aged 16 years and 245 days, while the youngest female gold medallist was Gladys Eastlake-Smith (GBR) in tennis, aged 24 years and 273 days. The oldest female champion was archer Queenie Newall (GBR), aged 53 years and 275 days.

Undoubtedly the most famous event in the IV Games was the marathon. Originally, the distance was to be about 25 miles (40km), but the start was moved to Windsor Castle, an exact 26 miles (41.8km). Then, at the request of Princess Mary, it was moved again to start beneath the windows of the royal nursery in the Castle grounds, making a final distance of 26 miles 385yd (42.195km). This arbitrarily arrived at distance was later (1924) accepted worldwide as the standard marathon distance. The race itself was run in intensely hot and humid conditions, quite the opposite of most of the preceding weather, and was watched by an estimated 250 000 people. The little Italian Dorando Pietri reached the stadium first in a state of near collapse. It has been suggested that his gargling with wine during the race did not react well with the heat. He fell five times on the last part-lap of the track. Overzealous officials, reputedly including the famous author Sir Arthur Conan Doyle, helped him over the finish line, thus leading to his disqualification. On behalf of the second finisher, Irish-born Johnny Hayes, the Americans lodged a protest which was upheld, and the Italian was disqualified. The wave of public sympathy found expression in the gift of Queen Alexandra to Pietri of a special gold cup.

Great Britain won the greatest number of medals overall, but the United States, as always, was well in front in the centrepiece of the Games, the track and field events. Two sportsmen, Ivan Osiier (DEN) a fencer, and Magnus Konow (NOR) a yachtsman, though unplaced in their events, began Olympic careers which continued until the next Games in London in 1948, setting a record-breaking span for Olympic competition of 40 years. Colonel Joshua Millner, winner of the 1000yd free rifle, aged at least 58 years and 237 days, was Great Britain's oldest ever Olympic gold medallist. The youngest British winner in 1908 was William Foster, in the 4 × 200m swimming relay, six days past his 18th birthday.

1908 MEDALS

	G	S	B
Great Britain	56	50	39
United States	23	12	12
Sweden	8	6	11
France	5	5	9
Germany	3	5	5
Hungary	3	4	2
Canada	3	3	10
Norway	2	3	3
Italy	2	2	–
Belgium	1	5	2
Australia [1]	1	2	1
Russia	1	2	–
Finland	1	1	3
South Africa	1	1	–
Greece	–	3	1
Denmark	–	2	3
Czechoslovakia	–	–	2
The Netherlands	–	–	2
Austria	–	–	1
New Zealand [1]	–	–	1

[1] Australia and New Zealand combined as Australasia

London 1948
XIV Olympic Games (29 July–14 August)

Attended by representatives of 59 countries, comprising 4099 competitors, of which 385 were women.

In 1936 the XII Games were awarded to Tokyo, to take place 24 August–8 September 1940. When the Sino-Japanese war began in 1938, the Games were transferred to Helsinki, but the Soviet invasion of Finland cancelled these plans. In June 1939, a very optimistic IOC awarded the XIII Games, for 1944, to London, over competing claims from Detroit, Lausanne and Rome. A postal vote of IOC members called by the President, Sigfrid Edström of Sweden, in 1946, awarded the XIV Games to London. In the meantime, Baron de Coubertin had died, in 1937, and his heart was buried at Olympia in Greece.

Organised by the British Olympic Association, under the Presidency of Lord Burghley, the 1948 Olympics were an austere Games — after six years of war Britain still had rationing of food and clothing. Housing was in short supply due to wartime destruction, and competitors were housed at RAF and Army camps (for men) and colleges (for women). A temporary running track was laid at the 83 000-capacity Wembley Stadium, the home of British football. Other existing buildings were adapted. Rowing was held at Henley, on the River Thames, and the yachting was at Torbay, Devon. The total expenditure amounted to no more than £600,000, and final accounts suggested that a profit of over £10,000 was made. The Games were opened by King George VI. Not surprisingly,

Germany and Japan were not invited, but a record 59 countries attended. These included the first entries by countries under Communist governments. Some of the hottest weather for years occurred on the opening days, but later it rained. Photo-finish equipment, as used on race courses, was used for the track events, but only to decide places. The first proper television coverage of the Games occurred with pictures beamed into an estimated 80 000 black and white receivers within transmission range from Wembley.

The undoubted star of the Games was Francina 'Fanny' Blankers-Koen (NED) who won four gold medals, a record for a woman. At the time, 30 years of age, and a mother of two children, she had finished in sixth place in the 1936 high jump. In 1948 she held seven world records including those in the high and long jumps, neither of which she contested in London. The gap between her and the second woman in the 200m, 0.7sec, remains the largest margin of victory ever achieved in an Olympic sprint, by men or women. In the high jump Dorothy Tyler (née Odam) (GBR) placed second again, 12 years after her first silver medal. Both times she had cleared the same height as the winner. Bob Mathias (USA) became the youngest ever male Olympic individual athletics champion when he won the decathlon, aged 17 years and 263 days. He retained the title in 1952, became a movie actor, and later was elected as a US Congressman. Another athlete to catch the eye was Emil Zátopek (TCH), not so much by his easy win in the 10 000m, but by his remarkable last 300m sprint to narrowly lose the 5000m. An American, Harrison Dillard, acknowledged as the world's best high hurdler, had fallen in the US trials and failed to make their team in his best event. In London he won the 100m, and won another gold in the relay. Two of the debuting countries made their marks early in the Games. Duncan White of Ceylon (now Sri Lanka) gained the only medal his country has ever won with a silver in the 400m hurdles. Jamaica made an even bigger impact by collecting a gold, two silvers and had two other finalists in the 200m, 400m, and 800m. The marathon provided its usual drama when Etienne Gailly, a Belgian paratrooper, entered the stadium first but, exhausted, was passed by two runners prior to the tape.

An outstanding competitor in the modern pentathlon was Willie Grut of Sweden who won three disciplines of the five-sport event, and placed fifth and eighth in the others, to win by a large margin. He was the son of the designer of the 1912 Olympic stadium. Another exceptional champion was South African boxer George Hunter, who not only won the light-heavyweight title, but also the Val Barker Trophy as the best stylist in the whole competition. However, lack of experienced referees and judges resulted in much criticism of the boxing tournament. There were also problems at Herne Hill stadium where some of the cycling events finished in very poor light due to the lack of floodlighting. There was an unfortunate turn of events in the equestrian competitions where the team dressage contest was won by the Swedes. The following year they were disqualified, and their

medals taken away, when it was learned that one of their number, Gehnäll Persson, was not a commissioned officer, as the rules then required.

In fencing Ilona Elek (HUN) retained her 1936 title even though she was now over 41 years of age. Her sister, Margit, placed sixth. The 1932 champion, Ellen Müller-Preis (AUT) gained the bronze medal. An even more outstanding veteran was 40-year-old Heikki Savolainen, the famous Finnish gymnast who, in his fourth Olympics, won his first gold medal, on the pommel horse.

The soccer gold medallists, Sweden, were involved in one of the strangest goals in the history of the sport, in their semi-final against Denmark. The Swedish centre-forward, Gunnar Nordahl, (one of three brothers in the team), leapt into the Danish goalnet to avoid being offside during a Swedish attack. At the end of the move his inside-left headed the ball into the goal, where in the absence of the Danish keeper it was caught by Nordahl. Yachting witnessed the end of a long Olympic career when Ralph Craig, the 1912 dou-

1948 MEDALS (SUMMER)

	G	S	B
United States	38	27	19
Sweden	16	11	17
France	10	6	13
Hungary	10	5	12
Italy	8	12	9
Finland	8	7	5
Turkey	6	4	2
Czechoslovakia	6	2	3
Switzerland	5	10	5
Denmark	5	7	8
The Netherlands	5	2	9
Great Britain	3	14	6
Argentina	3	3	1
Australia	2	6	5
Belgium	2	2	3
Egypt	2	2	1
Mexico	2	1	2
South Africa	2	1	1
Norway	1	3	3
Jamaica	1	2	–
Austria	1	–	3
India	1	–	–
Peru	1	–	–
Yugoslavia	–	2	–
Canada	–	1	2
Portugal	–	1	1
Uruguay	–	1	1
Ceylon (now Sri Lanka)	–	1	–
Cuba	–	1	–
Spain	–	1	–
Trinidad and Tobago	–	1	–
Korea	–	–	2
Panama	–	–	2
Brazil	–	–	1
Iran	–	–	1
Poland	–	–	1
Puerto Rico	–	–	1

ble sprint champion, reappeared in the American yachting team. Although he carried the US flag in the opening ceremony he did not actually compete. Torbay was also the start of another exceptional career with the appearance of Durward Knowles competing for Great Britain. He competed in yachting events for the Bahamas in the next six Games, and made it an eighth time in 1988. A rare occurence in the yachting was the victory of father/son combination Paul and Hilary Smart (USA) in the Star class. At the Empire Pool, site of the swimming competitions, US competitors won 12 of the 15 events there, excluding water polo. One of the few non-American champions was Greta Andersen (DEN) in the 100m freestyle, who, 16 years later, set a female record for swimming the English Channel. In diving, Vicki Draves (USA) won both titles, then a unique achievement.

The oldest gold medallist in London was Paul Smart (USA) in yachting, aged 56 years and 212 days, and the youngest was Thelma Kalama (USA) in the swimming sprint relay for women, aged 17 years and 135 days. Bob Mathias, the decathlon champion, was the youngest male champion, while the oldest female winner was fencer Ilona Elek (HUN), aged 41 years and 77 days.

Longest

The longest race ever held at the Olympic Games, in any sport, was the cycling road race in 1912, which measured 320km (198.8 miles). The longest equestrian event ever held at the Games was the 55km (34.1 miles) distance riding discipline at Stockholm in 1912. Athletics and Nordic skiing both share the upper limit of 50km (31 miles); in athletics it is a walk and in skiing, a cross-country event. The furthest a swimming race has ever been is 4000m (2.48 miles) in 1900, while in rowing there was a 3000m (1.86 miles) race in 1906 for coxed 16-man naval rowing boats. The longest yachting event seems to have been the 12m class race in 1908 which was over a 41.8km (26 mile) course.

Los Angeles 1932
X Olympic Games (30 July–14 August)

Attended by representatives of 37 countries, comprising 1408 competitors, of which 127 were women.

As early as 1920 the US delegation to the IOC, led by William May Garland, had applied for either the 1924 or 1928 Games to be held in Los Angeles. Despite trepidations felt over the memory of the 1904 'farce' at St Louis, in 1923 Los Angeles was awarded the 1932 Games. Against further worries of distance and cost of travel were set the advantages of favourable weather and competitive conditions. The announcement by the organising committee that they would subsidize transportation, housing and feeding costs helped greatly at a time of the Depression and did much to offset the critics. One source of income was from a new three cent

postage stamp, which depicted a runner, for which the model was the anchor man of the 1924 gold medal relay team, Alfred Leconey. The concept of an Olympic 'village' came to fruition with the construction of 550 specially designed small houses for male competitors in the Baldwin Hills area. It was strictly guarded by cowboys who 'rode the fences' around the perimeter and the strict rule preventing women in the village barred the Finnish team's lady cook. Female competitors were put up separately in the Chapman Park Hotel on Wilshire Boulevard. Despite the strictures of Prohibition, the French team were allowed to bring in wine for their own consumption. After journeys often lasting two weeks the foreigners found excellent weather and facilities awaiting them.

The main stadium was the Los Angeles Coliseum which had begun construction in 1921 and opened two years later. In 1930 it had been enlarged to hold 101 000-seated spectators, and the track had a new crushed peat running surface. Also there was the 10 000-seat swimming stadium, the State Armory where fencing took place, the Olympic Auditorium, seating 10 000 to watch boxing, wrestling and weightlifting events, and a specially built wooden track erected in the famous Pasadena Rose Bowl for the cycling. Long Beach harbour was the venue for yachting, and the Long Beach Marine stadium hosted the rowing. The Games were formally opened by the Vice-President of the United States, Charles Curtis, on behalf of President Herbert Hoover who was in the middle of an electioneering tour. The oath on behalf of the competitors was taken by an American fencer Lieutenant George Calnan of the US Navy, who died the following April when the dirigible *Akron* crashed in the Pacific Ocean. Although the number of teams and the total number of competitors were lower than at Amsterdam, there were two countries making their Olympic debuts, Columbia and China, both with sole representatives, neither of whom achieved any success. However, another small team, Ireland, with only eight men, finished well up the medal table with two gold medals.

At these Games new ideas included the use of photo-finish equipment, the Kirby Two-Eyed Camera, for track races. Although it could accurately provide times to one-hundredth of a second it was only used to decide close finishes. Another innovation was the three-tiered victory stand, with medal awarding ceremonies involving the raising of national flags taking place at the end of each day's events. In boxing the system of having the referee in the ring with the boxers was introduced into the Games for the first time, although it did not settle all arguments in that sport.

As with all such international gatherings there were some unfortunate incidents, but in the main they were of minor importance. Prior to the arrival of teams there was a major 'scandal' with the banning of the great Finnish runner, Paavo Nurmi, under charges of professionalism. He was accused of accepting unduly large expenses on a German tour. Despite rigorous protests on his behalf, the Finnish Federation finally accepted the ruling although he had already been selected for the marathon and indeed arrived with the team in Los Angeles. It seems fair to suggest that he would have finished a remarkable career with another gold medal. Once the Games were underway, the Finns were involved in another incident when the runners in the 3000m steeplechase ran an extra lap due to a miscalculation by the lap counter. Happily the error did not appear to have altered the final medal placings.

Another minor irritant was the American habit of announcing all the field event results only in imperial units of measurement, much to the annoyance and bafflement of the foreign competitors and spectators. But there were two more serious occurrences, one on the track and one in the swimming pool. The first was when the eventual winner, Lauri Lehtinen (FIN) deliberately blocked the American, Ralph Hill, twice in the final stages of the race, a not uncommon practice in Europe, but one which drew loud booing from the basically partisan crowd. They were quickly quietened by the announcer, Bill Henry, whose words 'Remember please, these people are our guests' have entered Olympic lore. The second incident was of a more serious nature when the Brazilian water polo team, after losing 7–3 to Germany, lost their tempers and insulted the referee. They were disqualified from the tournament. On the brighter side was the performance of the outstanding individual of the Games, Mildred 'Babe' Didrikson. (Surname also spelt the Swedish way Didriksen.) Much to her annoyance she was only allowed to enter three events. She set Olympic records in each of them, winning the javelin and 80m hurdles, and gaining a silver in the high jump. In the high jump there was a strange judgement made, although Didrikson cleared the same height as her team-mate, Jean Shiley, and then tied in a jump-off, the judges decided that her 'Western Roll' style of jump had been performed illegally, with her head preceding her body over the bar, and illogically they placed her second. Thus she is the only athlete to win medals in individual running, jumping and throwing events. She later became the world's greatest female golfer under her married name of Zaharias.

Another unusual thing occurred in the 400m hurdles when Irishman Bob Tisdall, who reportedly spent most of the preceding days in bed recuperating from a long and tiring journey, won the gold medal in a time superior to the world record. However, because he knocked down the last hurdle, the world record was given to the runner-up, Glenn Hardin (USA). Remarkably, the top four finishers were all gold medallists in the event — Tisdall (1932), Hardin (1936), Taylor (1924) and Burghley (1928).

In the 200m final Ralph Metcalfe was inadvertently made to start about 1.5m (5ft) before the correct place, thus almost certainly costing him a silver medal. As Americans had placed 1-2-3 Metcalfe, later a US Congressman, declined the offered re-run. The Indian hockey team, while not quite as invincible in previous years, set a record score by defeating the United States by 24–1, with Roop Singh scoring 12 goals. Similarly, in the water polo competition, Hungary beat Japan with a record score of 18–0. Nevertheless, the Japanese were particularly noteworthy in swimming,

highlighted by their superb 4 × 200m team breaking the world record by a remarkable 37.8sec.

The oldest gold medallist at Los Angeles was yachtsman Pierpoint Davis (USA), aged 47 years and 224 days, while the youngest was 1500m freestyle champion Kusuo Kitamura (JPN), aged 14 years and 309 days. The youngest female champion was Claire Dennis (AUS) who won the 200m breaststroke, aged 16 years and 117 days. The oldest female winner was Lillian Copeland (USA) in the discus, aged 27 years and 251 days. The youngest medallist was diver Katharine Rawls (USA) 58 days past her 14th birthday. The oldest medallist was Hiram Tuttle (USA) in the dressage, aged 49 years and 231 days. As demonstration sports the hosts provided American football and lacrosse. During the closing ceremony the President of the IOC, Count Henri de Baillet-Latour, presented Olympic Merit Awards for Alpinism to Franz and Toni Schmid (GER) for the first climb of the north face of the Matterhorn. Despite all the economic and organisational misgivings the X Games were a great success, attended by a total of 1.25 million spectators, and resulted in a profit of about $1 million.

One last innovation at these Games was the use of two sentences, attributed to Baron de Coubertin, but actually based on words used by the Bishop of Central Pennsylvania, Ethelbert Talbot, in a sermon at St Paul's Cathedral, London on 19 July 1908. Displayed on the scoreboard at every opening ceremony since 1932, the words are: 'The most important thing in the

1932 MEDALS (SUMMER)

	G	S	B
United States	41	32	30
Italy	12	12	12
France	10	5	4
Sweden	9	5	9
Japan	7	7	4
Hungary	6	4	5
Finland	5	8	12
Germany	3	12	5
Great Britain	4	7	5
Australia	3	1	1
Argentina	3	1	–
Canada	2	5	8
The Netherlands	2	5	–
Poland	2	1	4
South Africa	2	–	3
Ireland	2	–	–
Czechoslovakia	1	2	1
Austria	1	1	3
India	1	–	–
Denmark	–	3	3
Mexico	–	2	–
Latvia	–	1	–
New Zealand	–	1	–
Switzerland	–	1	–
Philippines	–	–	3
Spain	–	–	1
Uruguay	–	–	1

Olympic Games is not to win but to take part, just as the most important thing in life is not the triumph but the struggle. The essential thing is not to have conquered but to have fought well.'

Los Angeles 1984
XXIII Olympic Games (28 July–12 August)

Attended by representatives of 140 countries, comprising 6797 competitors, of which 1567 were women.

The IOC awarded the Games to Los Angeles in 1978, only after protracted negotiations about the financial guarantees usually required from a host city. Various innovations to protect the city from a Montreal-like deficit were implemented — not least, widespread sponsorship by private corporations. Television rights alone amounted to $287 million, one of the largest television audiences in history, some 2500 million, watched the Games. The great bulk came from the ABC network for US rights. The programme was expanded to 221 events, including an extra 12 for women, while baseball and tennis were demonstration sports. The Memorial Coliseum, main site for the 1932 Games, was fully refurbished and had a seating capacity of 92 607. Many other venues, often famous in their own right, were utilized. There were complaints that some of these venues were too far-flung, but the overall good weather and the enthusiasm, at times overwhelming, of the American crowds offset most problems.

The one major disaster suffered by these Games was the last-minute boycott by the Soviet Union, which announced its non-participation on the very day, 8 May 1984, that the Olympic flame arrived in the United States to begin a nationwide torch relay. Within a week or so most of the Soviet bloc had also pulled out, with the notable exception of Romania. Additionally, but not surprisingly, Iran and Libya did not appear. However, of 159 invitations sent out, 140 countries accepted, beating the Munich record. Nevertheless, a number of sports were very seriously affected, although standards were still generally high. In particular, canoeing, fencing, gymnastics, weightlifting, wrestling and women's athletics were diminished, both in numbers and quality.

The Games were formally opened by President Ronald Reagan, the first incumbent to ever do so. The final runner on the torch relay was Gina Hemphill, a granddaughter of the great Olympian Jesse Owens. Interestingly she had also run the first leg on American soil, jointly with Jim Thorpe's grandson, Bill. Some years after the Games she married Henry Tillman who won the heavyweight boxing title at Los Angeles. In the stadium she handed over the torch to 1960 Olympic decathlon champion, Rafer Johnson, who by means of a gantry lit the flame on the top of the stadium peristyle. Apparently in rehearsals, Johnson had developed a leg injury, and 1976 champion Bruce Jenner, one of the Olympic flag's escorts, stood by in case he had to replace Johnson. The oath

was taken, by the 1976 400m hurdle champion Edwin Moses, who went on to win a second gold medal. There followed a three-hour Hollywood-style extravaganza featuring, among other things, marching bands and 85 pianos, which was produced by film producer David Wolper.

Smog and traffic congestion did not materialize to anything like the degree predicted; one unfortunate phenomenon, however, was the orgy of American chauvinism displayed — especially by the media. Attendances at all sports were quite remarkable, with a final attendance figure of 5.7 million, and a highest single figure, 101 799, for the final of the soccer tournament (France beat Brazil 2–0) in the famed Rose Bowl at Pasadena. One particular feature of these Games was the tremendous outlay made on security comprising some 7000 personnel and ancillary equipment costing as much as $100 million.

The first gold medal of the Games was won by shooter Xu Haifeng with China's first ever Olympic title. Aided enormously by the absence of Soviet and East German opposition, the United States gained by far the lion's share of the medals. Leading their gold rush was sprinter/jumper Carl Lewis, who mirrored Jesse Owens's feat of 1936, with four gold medals in the 100m, 200m, long jump and relay. Another athlete, Valerie Brisco-Hooks, and five swimmers, all won three golds each. However, the most successful competitors were gymnasts Ecaterina Szabó (ROM) with four golds and a silver and China's Li Ning with three golds, two silvers and a bronze.

The introduction of consolation finals in swimming, for non-qualifiers to the regular finals, led to the unusual situation of an Olympic record being set in the men's 400m freestyle 'B' final, faster than the gold medallist had attained. The judo open champion Yasuhiro Yamashita (JPN) extended his winning streak to 198, despite being handicapped by a foot injury. A number of families were particularly successful: twins Mark and David Schultz (USA), and Lou and Ed Banach (USA) all won wrestling gold medals; William Buchan (USA) and his son William Jr won yachting titles, but not together; British husband and wife medal winners, Gary (silver, 4 × 400m) and Kathy Cook (bronze, 400m and 4 × 100m); Al Joyner (USA) and his sister Jackie won gold (triple jump) and silver (heptathlon) medals respectively; brothers Carmine and Giuseppe Abbagnale (ITA) won the coxed pairs rowing event.

In the dressage event, 48 year old Reiner Klimke (FRG) won two gold medals in his fourth Games over a 20-year period, equalling his countryman Hans Günter Winkler's equestrian record of five golds and seven medals. One of the few negative things at Los Angeles was the disqualification for doping offences of 12 competitors from weightlifting, wrestling, volleyball and athletics. Probably the most well-known of these was Martti Vainio (FIN) who finished second in the 10 000m on the track.

The oldest gold medallist at Los Angeles was William Buchan (USA) in the Star yachting, aged 49 years and 91 days. The youngest was Romanian gymnast Simona Pauca in the team event, aged 14 years and 317 days, who won the individual beam title four days later. The youngest male champion was Perica Bukic (YUG) in water polo, aged 17 years and 264 days, while the oldest female gold medallist was Linda Thom (CAN) winning the women's pistol, aged 40 years and 212 days. The oldest female medallist was the lady who finished third in that competition, Patricia Dench (AUS) at 52 years and 143 days. The oldest male medallist was another shooter Ragnar Skanåker (SWE), aged 50 years and 52 days. At the

1984 MEDALS (SUMMER)

	G	S	B
United States	83	61	30
Romania	20	16	17
FRG	17	19	23
China	15	8	9
Italy	14	6	12
Canada	10	18	16
Japan	10	8	14
New Zealand	8	1	2
Yugoslavia	7	4	7
Great Britain	5	11	21
France	5	7	16
The Netherlands	5	2	6
Australia	4	8	12
Finland	4	2	6
Sweden	2	11	6
Mexico	2	3	1
Morocco	2	–	–
Brazil	1	5	2
Spain	1	2	2
Belgium	1	1	2
Austria	1	1	1
Kenya	1	–	2
Portugal	1	–	2
Pakistan	1	–	–
Switzerland	–	4	4
Denmark	–	3	3
Jamaica	–	1	2
Norway	–	1	2
Greece	–	1	1
Nigeria	–	1	1
Puerto Rico	–	1	1
Colombia	–	1	–
Egypt	–	1	–
Ireland	–	1	–
Ivory Coast	–	1	–
Peru	–	1	–
Syria	–	1	–
Thailand	–	1	–
Turkey	–	–	3
Venezuela	–	–	3
Algeria	–	–	2
Cameroon	–	–	1
Dominican Republic	–	–	1
Iceland	–	–	1
Chinese Taipei	–	–	1
Zambia	–	–	1

other end of the scale was Belgian coxswain, Philippe Cuelenaere, the youngest competitor at Los Angeles, a month short of his 13th birthday.

At the end of the Games, after another closing extravaganza featuring one of the greatest firework displays ever seen, the organisers reported a profit of $215 million, prompting the suggestion that perhaps the pendulum had swung too far the other way since Montreal. The whole thing was a triumphant vindication of the leadership of Peter Ueberroth, President of the Los Angeles Olympic Organizing Committee. Coincidentally, Ueberroth was born on the very day, 2 September 1937, that Baron de Coubertin had died. A sour note was added some time later when it was reported that a number of drug test samples had been unaccountably lost.

Lugeing (Tobogganing)

In 1928 and 1948 there were one-man skeleton sled races held on the famous Cresta Run at St Moritz. In those events the contestants laid face down. Luge racing, in which contestants lie back, was introduced in 1964. The most successful luger has been Georg Hackl (GER), with three golds and a silver between 1988–98. Hackl is the only man to successfully defend the singles title, which he has done twice. However, the pair of Stefan Krausse and Jan Behrendt (GDR/GER) also won four medals (two gold, one silver, one bronze) 1988–98. The most successful woman was Steffi Martin-Walter (GDR) with two golds in 1984 and 1988.

The oldest gold medallist was Paul Hildgartner (ITA), aged 31 years and 249 days in the 1984 singles, while the youngest was Manfred Stengl (AUT) in the 2-man in 1964, aged 17 years and 310 days. The youngest female winner was Ortrun Enderlein (GER), aged 20 years and 65 days in 1964, and the oldest was Silke Krausshaar (GER) in 1998, aged 27 years and 124 days. The youngest medallist has been Ute Ruhrold (GDR), aged 17 years and 60 days gaining the silver in 1972. The oldest medallist in luge was Fritz Nachmann (FRG) in 1968, aged 38 years and 186 days, but John Crammond (GBR) was 41 years and 213 days when he took the bronze in the 1948 skeleton event. The oldest female medallist was Angelika Neuner (AUT), aged 28 years and 50 days taking the bronze in 1998. Anne Abernathy of the US Virgin Islands was the oldest ever female Olympic luger at the 1998 Games, aged 44 years and 305 days. She may well have been the oldest luger, male or female, ever to compete at the Games. Probably the heaviest winner of a luge title was Hans Stanggassinger (FRG) in the 2-man of 1984 at a weight of 111kg (244lb).

The Heaton brothers (USA) deserve mention for their exploits on the skeleton sleds as well as on bobs. Jennison won the 1928 skeleton event and a silver in the 5-man bob that year. Brother John was second in

LUGEING (TOBOGANNING) MEDALS (including 1928 and 1948 skeleton sled events)

	Men			Women			
	G	S	B	G	S	B	Total
GDR	9	3	5	4	5	3	29
Germany	6	2	3	2	3	1	17
Austria	2	4	3	1	1	3	14
Italy	4	4	3	2	–	–	13
FRG	1	3	3	–	1	2	10
Soviet Union	–	2	2	1	–	1	6
United States	1	3	1	–	–	–	5
Great Britain	–	–	2	–	–	–	2
	23 1	21	22	10	10	10	96

1 Two golds in the 1972 2-man event

the 1928 skeleton, won a bronze in the 1932 2-man bob and then returned in 1948, in his 40th year, to win another skeleton silver. Seventh in that 1948 competition was Lt.-Col. James Coats (GBR), holder of the Military Cross, and at 53 years and 297 days, the oldest ever competitor in the Winter Olympic Games. In 2002 there will be two skeleton sled events, one each for men and women.

The smallest winning margin was in the women's singles in 1998, when Silke Krausshaar (GER) beat team-mate Barbara Niederhuber by 0.002sec. The closest in the men's contests was in the 1994 men's singles when Georg Hackl (GER) beat Markus Prock (AUT) in the second successive Games, by only 0.013sec. In contrast, Ortrun Enderlein (GDR) won the inaugural women's event in 1964 by the remarkable margin of 2.75sec. At the following Games in 1968 a scandal shook the Games when the first, second and fourth placed women from the GDR were all disqualified for illegally heating the runners of their sleds. The leading woman was Enderlein. The greatest speed attained (average for a single run) was 99.54km/h (61.85mph) by Georg Hackl (GER) in 1992, but speeds in excess of 130km/h (80.77mph) have been reached briefly. The equivalent fastest by a female luger (average for a single run) was 88.31km/h (54.87mph) by Angelika Neuner (AUT) in 1992. Optimum speeds in the female event have been in excess of 125km/h (77.67mph).

Mascots

The various symbols and emblems used to publicise the Olympic Games over the years have generally been very successful. In 1932 there was an unofficial live mascot, a dog named Smoky, but it was only in 1968 that the first official Olympic mascot made its appearance. For the Mexico City Games it was a Red Jaguar, selected because of its cultural and geographical associations. However, it was not given a name, and was not marketed with any particular enthusiasm. Since then, however, the mascot has become an institution.

Summer		
Name	Name	Character
1968	–	Red Jaguar
1972	Waldi	Dachshund
1976	Amik	Beaver
1980	Misha	Bear
1984	Sam	Eagle
1988	Hodori/Hosuni	Tigers
1992	Cobi	Dog
1996	Izzy	Cartoon
2000	Olly	Kookaburra
2000	Syd	Platypus
2000	Millie	Anteater
Winter		
1968	Schuss	Man
1972	–	
1976	Schneemanner	Snowman
1980	Roni	Raccoon
1984	Vucko	Wolf
1988	Hidy/Howdy	Polar bears
1992	Magique	Man/Star
1994	Haakon/Kristin	Children
1998	The Snowlets	Owls

Medal Winners, by Nation 1896–1998

These totals include all first, second and third places, including those events no longer on the current (2000) schedule. The 1906 Games, which were officially staged by the International Olympic Committee (IOC), have also been included.

Note: Medals won in 1896, 1900, 1904, 1908 and 1912 by mixed teams from two countries have been counted twice, for both countries involved. The Unified teams of 1992 have been included in the Soviet Union figures. Medals won by IOP designated competitors in 1992 have been included in Yugoslavia figures.

This unique table indicates a country's position in the medal tables three ways. Mainly it shows its position overall, but also gives that for the Summer and Winter Games respectively.

Overall		G	S	B	Total	G	S	B	Total	Total
			Summer				Winter			
1	United States	833	634	548	2015 (1)	59	59	41	159 (3)	2174
2	Soviet Union [1]	485	395	354	1234 (2)	87	63	67	217 (2)	1451
3	Great Britain	177	235	225	637 (3)	7	4	13	24 (18)	661
4	Germany [2]	151	181	184	516 (5)	46	38	32	116 (6)	632
5	France	176	181	206	563 (4)	18	17	26	61 (=12)	624
6	Sweden	134	152	173	459 (6)	39	28	35	102 (8)	561
7	Italy	166	136	142	444 (7)	27	27	23	77 (11)	521
8	GDR [3]	153	130	127	410 (9)	39	36	35	110 (7)	520
9	Hungary	142	128	155	425 (8)	-	2	4	6 (22)	431
10	Finland	99	80	113	292 (11)	38	49	48	135 (5)	427
11	Norway	46	40	38	124 (25)	83	87	69	239 (1)	363
12	Japan	93	89	98	280 (12)	8	9	12	29 (16)	309
=13	Australia	87	85	122	294 (10)	–	–	2	4(=31)	296
=13	Canada	49	77	91	217 (15)	25	24	30	79 (10)	296
15	Switzerland	46	68	60	174 (19)	29	31	32	92 (9)	266
16	The Netherlands	49	57	81	187 (17)	19	23	19	61 (=12)	248
=17	Romania	63	77	99	239 (13)	–	–	1	1 (=36)	240
=17	FRG [4]	56	64	80	200 (16)	11	16	13	40 (15)	240
19	Poland	50	67	110	227 (14)	1	1	2	4 (=25)	231
20	Austria	19	31	34	84 (29)	39	53	53	145 (4)	229
21	Bulgaria	43	76	63	182 (18)	1	–	1	2 (=31)	184
22	China	52	63	49	164 (20)	–	10	4	14 (20)	178
23	Czechoslovakia [5]	49	50	50	149 (22)	2	8	16	26 (17)	175
24	Denmark	39	60	57	156 (21)	–	1	–	1 (=36)	157
25	Korea	38	42	46	126 (24)	9	3	4	16 (19)	142
26	Belgium	37	50	48	135 (23)	1	1	3	5 (=23)	140
27	Greece	28	42	44	114 (26)	–	–	–	–	114
28	Russia [6]	26	25	19	70 (31)	21	14	7	42 (14)	112
29	Cuba	45	33	31	109 (27)	–	–	–	–	109
30	Yugoslavia	27	31	32	90 (28)	–	3	1	4 (=25)	94
31	New Zealand	30	12	29	71 (30)	–	1	–	1 (=36)	72
32	Spain	22	25	17	64 (32)	1	–	1	2 (=31)	66
33	Turkey	30	16	13	59 (33)	–	–	–	–	59
34	South Africa	19	18	21	58 (34)	–	–	–	–	58
35	Brazil	12	13	29	54 (35)	–	–	–	–	54
36	Argentina	13	21	16	50 (36)	–	–	–	–	50
37	Kenya	14	17	16	47 (37)	–	–	–	–	47
38	Mexico	9	13	19	41 (38)	–	–	–	–	41
39	Iran	5	13	18	36 (39)	–	–	–	–	36
40	Jamaica	5	16	11	32 (40)	–	–	–	–	32
41	North Korea (PRK)	8	6	12	26 (41)	–	1	1	2 (=31)	28
42	Ukraine	9	2	12	23 (=42)	1	1	1	3 (=28)	26
43	Estonia	7	6	10	23 (=42)	–	–	–	–	23
=44	Ireland	8	5	6	19 (44)	–	–	–	–	19
=44	Belarus	1	6	8	15 (=47)	–	2	2	4 (=25)	19
46	Egypt	6	6	6	18 (45)	–	–	–	–	18
=47	Ethiopia	8	1	7	16 (46)	–	–	–	–	16
=47	Kazakhstan	3	4	4	11 (=52)	1	2	2	5 (=23)	16
49	Portugal	3	4	8	15 (=47)	–	–	–	–	15
=50	Czech Republic [5]	4	3	4	11 (=52)	1	1	1	3 (=28)	14
=50	Nigeria	2	5	7	14 (=50)	–	–	–	–	14
=50	Mongolia	–	5	9	14 (=50)	–	–	–	–	14
53	India	8	1	4	13 (=51)	–	–	–	–	13
54	Morocco	4	2	5	11 (=52)	–	–	–	–	11
=55	Indonesia	3	4	3	10 (=55)	–	–	–	–	10
=55	Pakistan	3	3	4	10 (=55)	–	–	–	–	10
=57	Liechtenstein	–	–	–	–	2	2	5	9 (21)	9
=57	Uruguay	2	1	6	9 (=57)	–	–	–	–	9
=57	Trinidad and Tobago	1	2	6	9 (=57)	–	–	–	–	9
=57	Philippines	–	2	7	9 (=57)	–	–	–	–	9
=61	Venezuela	1	2	5	8 (=60)	–	–	–	–	8
=61	Chile		6	2	8 (=60)	–	–	–	–	8

continued

Overall		Summer				Winter				Total
		G	S	B	Total	G	S	B	Total	Total
=63	Algeria	3	–	4	7 (=62)	–	–	–	–	7
=63	Latvia	–	5	2	7 (=62)	–	–	–	–	7
=63	Slovenia	–	2	2	4 (=71)	–	–	3	3 (=28)	7
=66	Uganda	1	3	2	6 (=64)	–	–	–	–	6
=66	Tunisia	1	2	3	6 (=64)	–	–	–	–	6
=66	Thailand	1	1	4	6 (=64)	–	–	–	–	6
=66	Colombia	–	2	4	6 (=64)	–	–	–	–	6
=66	Puerto Rico	–	1	5	6 (=64)	–	–	–	–	6
=71	Croatia	1	2	2	5 (=69)	–	–	–	–	5
=71	Chinese Taipei	–	3	2	5 (=69)	–	–	–	–	5
=73	Peru	1	3	–	4 (=71)	–	–	–	–	4
=73	Luxembourg	1	1	–	2 (=81)	–	2	–	2 (=31)	4
=73	Bahamas	1	1	2	4 (=71)	–	–	–	–	4
=73	Namibia	–	4	–	4 (=71)	–	–	–	–	4
=73	Lebanon	–	2	2	4 (=71)	–	–	–	–	4
=73	Ghana	–	1	3	4 (=71)	–	–	–	–	4
=79	Slovakia [5]	1	1	1	3 (=77)	–	–	–	–	3
=79	Uzbekistan	–	1	1	2 (=81)	1	–	–	1 (=36)	3
=79	Lithuania	1	–	2	3 (=77)	–	–	–	–	3
=79	Israel	–	1	2	3 (=77)	–	–	–	–	3
=79	Malaysia	–	1	2	3 (=77)	–	–	–	–	3
=84	Armenia	1	1	–	2 (=81)	–	–	–	–	2
=84	Costa Rica	1	1	–	2 (=81)	–	–	–	–	2
=84	Syria	1	1	–	2 (=81)	–	–	–	–	2
=84	Surinam	1	–	1	2 (=81)	–	–	–	–	2
=84	Tanzania	–	2	–	2 (=81)	–	–	–	–	2
=84	Cameroon	–	1	1	2 (=81)	–	–	–	–	2
=84	Haiti	–	1	1	2 (=81)	–	–	–	–	2
=84	Iceland	–	1	1	2 (=81)	–	–	–	–	2
=84	Moldova	–	1	1	2 (=81)	–	–	–	–	2
=84	Zambia	–	1	1	2 (=81)	–	–	–	–	2
=84	Georgia	–	–	2	2 (=81)	–	–	–	–	2
=84	Panama	–	–	2	2 (=81)	–	–	–	–	2
=96	Burundi	1	–	–	1 (=95)	–	–	–	–	1
=96	Ecuador	1	–	–	1 (=95)	–	–	–	–	1
=96	Hong Kong	1	–	–	1 (=95)	–	–	–	–	1
=96	Zimbabwe	1	–	–	1 (=95)	–	–	–	–	1
=96	Azerbaijan	–	1	–	1 (=95)	–	–	–	–	1
=96	Ivory Coast	–	1	–	1 (=95)	–	–	–	–	1
=96	Netherlands Antilles	–	1	–	1 (=95)	–	–	–	–	1
=96	Senegal	–	1	–	1 (=95)	–	–	–	–	1
=96	Singapore	–	1	–	1 (=95)	–	–	–	–	1
=96	Sri Lanka	–	1	–	1 (=95)	–	–	–	–	1
=96	Tonga	–	1	–	1 (=95)	–	–	–	–	1
=96	Virgin Islands	–	1	–	1 (=95)	–	–	–	–	1
=96	Barbados	–	–	1	1 (=95)	–	–	–	–	1
=96	Bermuda	–	–	1	1 (=95)	–	–	–	–	1
=96	Djibouti	–	–	1	1 (=95)	–	–	–	–	1
=96	Dominican Republic	–	–	1	1 (=95)	–	–	–	–	1
=96	Guyana	–	–	1	1 (=95)	–	–	–	–	1
=96	Iraq	–	–	1	1 (=95)	–	–	–	–	1
=96	Mozambique	–	–	1	1 (=95)	–	–	–	–	1
=96	Niger Republic	–	–	1	1 (=95)	–	–	–	–	1
=96	Qatar	–	–	1	1 (=95)	–	–	–	–	1

[1] Including Unified Team of 1992
[2] Germany 1896–64, 1992–98
[3] GDR, East Germany, 1968–88
[4] FRG, West Germany, 1968–88
[5] Includes Bohemia
[6] Includes Czarist Russia

MEDALS, MOST BY INDIVIDUALS (SUMMER GAMES ONLY)

Men

15	Nikolai Andrianov (URS)	1972–80	Gymnastics
13	Edoardo Mangiarotti (ITA)	1936–60	Fencing
13	Takashi Ono (JPN)	1952–64	Gymnastics
13	Boris Shakhlin (URS)	1956–64	Gymnastics
12	Sawao Kato (JPN)	1968–76	Gymnastics
12	Paavo Nurmi (FIN)	1920–28	Athletics
11	Matt Biondi (USA)	1984–92	Swimming
11	Viktor Chukarin (URS)	1952–56	Gymnastics
11	Carl Osburn (USA)	1912–24	Shooting
11	Mark Spitz (USA)	1968–72	Swimming
10	Alexander Dityatin (URS)	1976–80	Gymnastics
10	Ray Ewry (USA)	1900–08	Athletics
10	Aladár Gerevich (HUN)	1932–60	Fencing
10	Akinori Nakayama (JPN)	1968–72	Gymnastics
10	Carl Lewis (USA)	1984–96	Athletics
10	Vitali Scherbo (EUN/BLR)	1992–96	Gymnastics
9	Zoltán von Halmay (HUN)	1900–08	Swimming
9	Alfred Swahn (SWE)	1908–24	Shooting
9	Giulio Gaudini (ITA)	1928–36	Fencing
9	Eizo Kenmotsu (JPN)	1968–76	Gymnastics
9	Heikki Savolainen (FIN)	1928–52	Gymnastics
9	Martin Sheridan (USA)	1904–08	Athletics
9	Yuri Titov (URS)	1956–64	Gymnastics
9	Mitsuo Tsukahara (JPN)	1968–76	Gymnastics
9	Hubert van Innis (BEL)	1900–20	Archery
9	Mikhail Voronin (URS)	1968–72	Gymnastics

Women

18	Larissa Latynina (URS)	1956–64	Gymnastics
11	Vera Cáslavská (TCH)	1960–68	Gymnastics
10	Polina Astakhova (URS)	1956–64	Gymnastics
10	Agnes Keleti (HUN)	1952–56	Gymnastics
9	Nadia Comaneci (ROM)	1976–80	Gymnastics
9	Ludmila Turischeva (URS)	1968–76	Gymnastics
8	Shirley Babashoff (USA)	1972–76	Swimming
8	Kornelia Ender (GDR)	1972–76	Swimming
8	Dawn Fraser (AUS)	1956–64	Swimming
8	Margit Korondi (HUN)	1952–56	Gymnastics
8	Sofia Muratova (URS)	1956–60	Gymnastics
7	Maria Gorokhovskaya (URS)	1952	Gymnastics
7	Karin Janz (GDR)	1968–72	Gymnastics
7	Ildikó Ujlakiné-Rejtó (HUN)	1960–76	Fencing
7	Shirley Strickland (AUS)	1948–56	Athletics
7	Irena Szewinska (POL)	1964–76	Athletics
7	Merlene Ottey (JAM)	1980–96	Athletics

MEDALS, MOST BY INDIVIDUALS (WINTER GAMES ONLY)

Men

12	Bjørn Dæhlie (NOR)	1992–98	Nordic Skiing
9	Sixten Jernberg (SWE)	1956–64	Nordic Skiing
7	Clas Thunberg (FIN)	1924–28	Speed Skating
7	Ivar Ballangrud (NOR)	1928–36	Speed Skating
7	Veikko Hakulinen (FIN)	1952–60	Nordic Skiing
7	Eero Mäntyranta (FIN)	1960–68	Nordic Skiing
7	Bogdan Musiol (GDR/GER)	1980–92	Bobsledding
7	Vladimir Smirnov (URS/EUN/KZK)	1988–98	Nordic Skiing

MEDALS, MOST BY INDIVIDUALS (WINTER GAMES ONLY) continued

Women

10	Raisa Smetanina (URS/EUN)	1976–92	Nordic Skiing
9	Lyubov Yegorova (RUS/EUN)	1992–94	Nordic Skiing
8	Galina Kulakova (URS)	1968–76	Nordic Skiing
8	Karin Kania-Enke (GDR)	1980–88	Speed Skating
8	Marja-Liisa Hämäläinen-Kirvesniemi (FIN)	1980–98	Nordic Skiing
8	Gunda Niemann-Stirnemann (GDR/GER)	1992–98	Speed Skating
7	Andrea Mitscherlich-Schöne-Ehrlich (GDR)	1976–88	Speed Skating
7	Manuela Di Centa (ITA)	1988–98	Nordic Skiing
7	Larissa Lazutina (RUS/EUN)	1992–98	Nordic Skiing
7	Yelena Valbe (RUS/EUN)	1992–98	Nordic Skiing

Media

During the first modern Games at Athens in 1896 there was very little coverage in the world's press. Throughout its 100-plus year history the Games have constantly been written off and rubbished by some of the media, prophets of doom who predicted their demise, especially at the time of boycotts and financial and drugs scandals. Despite this the Games have gone from strength to strength and indeed there has been tremendous coverage of each celebration. Thus, at Atlanta in 1996 there were over 17 000 representatives of the world media, far in excess of the number of competitors, and at the Winter Games at Nagano in 1998 there were over 10 000.

The Games at Berlin in 1936 witnessed the first major radio coverage of the event, with broadcasts going to some 40 countries. At those Games there was limited television coverage with a closed circuit system to special halls, operated by the Reich Rundfunkgesellschaft, and watched by a reported 150 000 people at 28 venues around Berlin. By 1996 television pictures were beamed to some 220 countries, with a global cumulative audience of 19.6 billion, and it has been estimated nine out of 10 people in the developed world watched some part of the Atlanta Games.

The money from television rights has now become the prime source of income for the IOC, and the host countries. In August 1995 the American television company NBC paid $1.27 billion for the exclusive US rights to the Games at Sydney in 2000, and the Winter Games at Salt Lake City in 2002. A few months later they paid $2.3 billion for the US rights to the Games of 2004, 2006 and 2008.

Melbourne 1956

XVI Summer Games (22 November–8 December)
(also at Stockholm, Sweden 10–17 June)

Attended by representatives of 67 countries, comprising 3184 competitors, of which 371 were women. (At Stockholm there were representatives of 29 countries, comprising 158 competitors, of which 13 were women.)

In 1949 the IOC had decided on Melbourne by only one vote, and they were disquieted, to say the least, by first the apparent tardiness in finishing facilities, and second the inability of the Australians to hold the equestrian events. (This was due to their stringent animal quarantine laws.) Thus for the first and only time, contrary to the Olympic Charter, a sport was detached from the main Games and held elsewhere, in Stockholm. Except for the cross-country section of the three-day event, the venue was the 1912 Olympic Stadium. The host country won three of the six titles, but there was strong criticism and accusations of chauvinism by the judges in the dressage competition. Also the above-mentioned cross-country was thought to be too dangerous in the existing wet conditions.

The Games 'proper', the only celebration so far in the Southern Hemisphere, opened in Melbourne under a cloud of international ill-will, occasioned by the Soviet invasion of Hungary, and the French and British intervention in the Suez Canal dispute between Israel and Egypt. The Netherlands, Spain and Switzerland withdrew because of the former, and Egypt and Lebanon because of the latter. This time, mainland China withdrew because of the presence of Taiwan. Perhaps surprisingly the Hungarians did compete, and with good effect. West and East Germany entered a combined team, and continued to do so until the 1968 Games. In addition to Taiwan, Olympic debuts were made by teams from Ethiopia, Fiji, Kenya, Liberia, Uganda, Malaya and North Borneo (the two latter now combined as Malaysia). Cambodia's appearance in the Stockholm events was its Olympic debut. HRH The Duke of Edinburgh opened the Games at the Melbourne Cricket Ground, the main venue. The final torch bearer was a 19-year-old Australian miler, Ron Clarke, destined to be one of the world's greatest runners.

The distance runs in Melbourne were dominated by the Soviet sailor Vladimir Kuts, with record-breaking victories at 5000m and 10 000m. Ireland won its first gold medal since 1932, when Ronnie Delaney took the 1500m with an exceptionally fast last 300m. In the sprints both Bobby-Joe Morow (USA) and Betty Cuthbert (AUS) gained three gold medals, including the relays. Teamed with Cuthbert in the 4 × 100m was Shirley de la Hunty (née Strickland), who ended her three Games career with an unbeaten total of seven medals (three gold, one silver, three bronze). A photo-finish picture, which was not unearthed for many years after the event, indicates that she was also third, not fourth, in the 200m in 1948. She made no official claim and the result remains as it was. Frenchman Alain Mimoun, who had previously finished second to Emil Zátopek (TCH) in three Olympic races, won the marathon with Zátopek in sixth place. Mimoun was the oldest man to win the marathon only a month short of his 36th birthday. The 50km walk was won by Norman Read, representing his adopted country, New Zealand. As a former English junior mile walk champion Read had watched the 1952 Games as a spectator (sitting next to the author).

Another English-born competitor, Murray Rose (AUS), was the first male swimmer to win two individual freestyle events since 1924. He also won a third gold medal in the relay. Pat McCormick (USA) achieved a unique double 'double' retaining both her diving titles from Helsinki. Boxing, too, had its record-breaker when László Papp did his bit to raise Hungarian spirits by gaining an unprecedented third gold medal at boxing. Not surprisingly bad feelings erupted in the water polo semi-final between Hungary and the Soviet Union. By a nice touch of irony the referee was from the perennially neutral Sweden. With Hungary leading 4–0 he ended the game as it had degenerated into a 'boxing match under water'. However, by beating Yugoslavia in the soccer final on the last day, 8 December, the Soviet Union went into history as the winners of the latest gold medal ever won in an Olympic year.

John Kelly Jr (USA), the son of the 1920 gold medallist, won a bronze in the single sculls as Vyacheslav Ivanov (URS) gained the first of his record three consecutive titles. At the shooting range Gerald Ouellette (CAN) won the prone small bore rifle competition with a world record 'maximum' of 600, only to have the record, but not the gold medal, disallowed because the range was found to be 1.5m short of the international distance of 50m.

The oldest gold medallist in the 1956 Games, albeit in his case at Stockholm, was Henri St. Cyr (SWE) in dressage, aged 54 years and 93 days, while the youngest was Sandra Morgan (AUS) in the 4 × 100m freestyle relay, aged 14 years and 183 days. The youngest male winner was Murray Rose (AUS), aged 17 years and 332 days, while the oldest female champion was Hungarian gymnast, Agnes Keleti at 35 years and 331 days. Although not even a medallist, Gunhild Larking, a beautiful Swedish high jumper, undoubtedly had more photographs taken of her than any of the more successful competitors. Actually a member of the combined Germany team, Wolfgang Behrendt, winner of the boxing bantamweight title, was the GDR's first gold medallist.

At the closing ceremony for the first time the athletes entered en masse, signifying the friendship of the Games. The idea for this had come from an Australian-born Chinese boy, John Wing, in a letter to the chairman of the organising committee, the Hon. W. S. Kent-Hughes. A happy postscript to these Games occurred in Prague in March 1957 when the American hammer winner, Harold Connolly, married Olga Fikotová, the Czech Olympic discus champion.

The best man at this 'Olympic' wedding was, appropriately, Emil Zátopek.

1956 MEDALS (SUMMER)

	G	S	B
Soviet Union	37	29	32
United States	32	25	17
Australia	13	8	14
Hungary	9	10	7
Italy	8	8	9
Sweden	8	5	6
Germany	6	13	7
Great Britain	6	7	11
Romania	5	3	5
Japan	4	10	5
France	4	4	6
Turkey	3	2	2
Finland	3	1	11
Iran	2	2	1
Canada	2	1	3
New Zealand	2	–	–
Poland	1	4	4
Czechoslovakia	1	4	1
Bulgaria	1	3	1
Denmark	1	2	1
Ireland	1	1	3
Norway	1	–	2
Mexico	1	–	1
Brazil	1	–	–
India	1	–	–
Yugoslavia	–	3	–
Chile	–	2	2
Belgium	–	2	–
Argentina	–	1	1
Korea	–	1	1
Iceland	–	1	–
Pakistan	–	1	–
South Africa	–	–	4
Austria	–	–	2
Bahamas	–	–	1
Greece	–	–	1
Switzerland	–	–	1
Uruguay	–	–	1

Member Countries

For member countries of the IOC, see under *Participation, by country.*

Mexico City 1968
XIX Olympic Games (12–27 October)

Attended by representatives of 112 countries, comprising 5530 competitors, of which 781 were women.

From 1963, when these Games were awarded to Mexico City, there was a gradually increasing furore about the effects of its altitude, 2240m (7347ft) above sea level, on competitors in events which required endurance. Some medical authorities even forecast possible deaths. This extreme view was, thankfully, overly pessimistic, but many cases of severe exhaustion occurred. When Australian distance runner Ron Clarke developed serious heart problems in 1981, there was speculation that his condition had been aggravated by his efforts in Mexico City in 1968. Certainly standards were low in events that required over three minutes of continuous effort. However, the same conditions contributed to some startling performances in the 'explosive' events. Outstanding was the 8.90m (29ft 2½in) long jump by Bob Beamon (USA) — a performance of 21st-century quality. The world records set in that long jump, and in the 4 × 400m relay, lasted for over 22 years.

The thin air was not the only complaint raised prior to these Games. Some felt that the traditional 'mañana' attitude attributed to the Mexicans would result in incomplete facilities. In fact all were ready in good time. There was a threat of a boycott by Black African nations over the re-admission of South Africa earlier in the year. After 40 countries had indicated that they would withhold their teams the IOC reversed its decision and South Africa was barred again, permanently. In August the Soviet Union and its allies invaded Czechoslovakia, and international tension mounted. A few weeks before the Games began serious student riots erupted at the University of Mexico which were ruthlessly suppressed with dozens killed and hundreds injured. Some of the foreign press sports reporters became 'war' correspondents for their newspapers. In America there was a move to get black athletes to boycott the US team to protest the alleged bad treatment of blacks in general in the United States. When this appeared to get little support, the organisers implied that some sort of dramatic demonstration would be held at the Games. Despite all these problems, President Gustavo Diaz Ordaz declared the Games open to a record number of teams and athletes. Enriqueta Basilio, a hurdler, became the first woman to light the Olympic flame in the stadium.

Due to conditions the distance running events were dominated by athletes who lived and trained at high altitude, such as the Kenyans and Ethiopians. Exceptional performances abounded in the sprints and jumps. Beamon's jump was beyond the limits of the measuring device in use at the pit, and a steel tape had to be used. In the triple jump the existing Olympic record was beaten by seven men, and the world mark was improved on five occasions. The high jump winner, Dick Fosbury (USA), used the 'flop' style which he popularised and was to revolutionise the event. Al Oerter (USA) won his record fourth consecutive discus title, and Wyomia Tyus (USA) was the first sprinter successfully to defend an Olympic 100m crown, other than Archie Hahn (USA) in the 1906 Intercalated Games. The men's 100m final was unique, up to that time, in that all eight finalists were black. A more heralded expression of black power was the demonstration by the Black Power supporters, Tommie Smith and John Carlos (USA), in the 200m victory ceremony. The Americans, who had come first and third respectively, raised black-gloved, clenched

fists, with heads bowed, during the playing of the American anthem. For this action they were suspended and expelled from the Olympic village. Some old-timers noted that their action was no more, no less, insulting than that of the numerous medallists who had given the Nazi salute in 1936. The marathon was won, for the third consecutive time, by an Ethiopian, but this time by Mamo Wolde, after two-time champion Abebe Bikila withdrew at 17km. Tragically, Bikila was paralysed in a car accident the following year, and died in 1973 at the age of 41.

Most medals were won, as usual, by gymnasts. Although Mikhail Voronin (URS) won seven medals (two gold, four silver, one bronze), the star of the sport was Vera Cáslavská (TCH) with four golds and two silvers. Her floor exercise routine to the music of the *Mexican Hat Dance*, was immensely popular. Soon after her events were over, but still during the Games, she married her countryman, Josef Odlozil, the 1964 1500m silver medallist. Incidentally, Voronin's wife, Sinaida, won a gold, a silver, and two bronze medals in the Soviet women's gymnastic team. The outstanding swimmers were Charles Hickcox (USA) with three gold and a silver, and Debbie Meyer (USA), who won three individual events. Six other swimmers won two gold medals each, including an 18-year-old American named Mark Spitz. Mexico's first ever swimming gold medal was won by Felipe Muñoz in the 200m breaststroke. He was nicknamed 'Tibio', which means lukewarm in English. This was no reflection an his determination, but was the result of his father coming from a town named Aguascalientes ('hot water'), and his mother from Rio Frio ('cold river').

Although eliminated in the fencing, Janice Romary (USA) became the first woman to compete in six consecutive Games and because of this also became the first woman to carry the flag for the United States in a Games opening ceremony. The 5.5m class yachting, held at the resort city of Acapulco, produced the unique result of triple gold medal siblings. The Swedish brothers, Ulf, Peter and Jörgen Sundelin crewed *Wasa IV* to an easy victory. Behind them, skippering the second placed Swiss boat *Toucan*, was Louis Noverraz at 66 years and 154 days, the oldest medallist at these Games.

The oldest gold medallist was Josef Neckarmann (FRG) in the dressage team, aged 56 years and 141 days, while the youngest was Günther Tiersch (GDR), cox of the winning eight, aged 14 years and 172 days. The oldest female champion was Liselott Linsenhoff (FRG), also in the dressage team, aged 41 years and 58 days, while the youngest female gold medallist was swimmer Susan Pedersen (USA) in the medley relay the day after her 15th birthday. The oldest competitor at Mexico City was Roberto Soundy, a trapshooter from El Salvador, aged 68 years and 229 days, and the same country had the youngest male competitor in Ruben Guerrero, a medley relay swimmer, aged 13 years and 351 days. However, the youngest competitor of all was Liana Vicens, of Puerto Rico, only 11 years and 328 days in the women's 100m breaststroke. The oldest woman was

Britain's Lorna Johnstone, who was 13th in the dressage at 66 years and 51 days.

For the first time since they had entered the hockey competition in 1928 India failed to reach the final. In soccer, Hungary won for a record third time, the surprise bronze medallist was Japan. They were the first, and to date only, Asian team to win a soccer medal, and the first non-European team to do so for 40 years.

1968 MEDALS (SUMMER)

	G	S	B
United States	45	28	34
Soviet Union	29	32	30
Japan	11	7	7
Hungary	10	10	12
GDR	9	9	7
France	7	3	5
Czechoslovakia	7	2	4
FRG	5	11	10
Australia	5	7	5
Great Britain	5	5	3
Poland	5	2	11
Romania	4	6	5
Italy	3	4	9
Kenya	3	4	2
Mexico	3	3	3
Yugoslavia	3	3	2
The Netherlands	3	3	1
Bulgaria	2	4	3
Iran	2	1	2
Sweden	2	1	1
Turkey	2	–	–
Denmark	1	4	3
Canada	1	3	1
Finland	1	2	1
Ethiopia	1	1	–
Norway	1	1	–
New Zealand	1	–	2
Tunisia	1	–	1
Pakistan	1	–	–
Venezuela	1	–	–
Cuba	–	4	–
Austria	–	2	2
Switzerland	–	1	4
Mongolia	–	1	3
Brazil	–	1	2
Belgium	–	1	1
Korea	–	1	1
Uganda	–	1	1
Cameroon	–	1	–
Jamaica	–	1	–
Argentina	–	–	2
Greece	–	–	1
India	–	–	1
Chinese Taipei	–	–	1

Military Patrol

A demonstration sport, held at four Winter Games, it is considered to be the forerunner of the official biathlon contests introduced in 1960. Switzerland won in 1924 and 1948, Norway in 1928, and Italy took the 1936 title.

Modern Pentathlon

The five events constituting the modern pentathlon are: riding (formerly over an 800m course, now a 12-fence show jumping test); fencing (with épée); swimming (formerly 300m freestyle, now 200m); shooting; cross-country running (formerly 4000m, now 3000m). Shooting until 1992 was with a rapid-fire pistol over 25m, but at Atlanta it was an air pistol over 10m. Also at Atlanta the team event was eliminated and the individual competition was completed in one day. In recent years there have been suggestions that the Triathlon should replace the modern pentathlon in future Games, due to the fact that the latter is not practised in as many countries as the IOC would like. (*See* Triathlon.) However, in 2000 a modern pentathlon event for women has been added.

The order of events has differed over the years, as has the points system. Prior to 1956 competitors were given points according to their placings in each event, i.e. one point for first place, two points for second, etc. Since 1956 points have been allocated according to an international scoring table. It is difficult therefore to compare performers under the two systems, but it is generally accepted that the margin of victory by Willie Grut (SWE) in 1948 was the greatest ever. In that competition, Grut, later the Secretary-General of the sport's governing body Union Internationale de Pentathlon Moderne (UIPM), placed first in riding, fencing and swimming, fifth in shooting, and eighth in running.

The most gold medals have been won by András Balczó (HUN) with three in 1960 (team), 1968 (team) and 1972 (individual). Only Lars Hall (SWE) has won two individual gold medals, in 1952 and 1956. Pavel Lednev (URS) won a record seven medals (two gold, two silver, three bronze) between 1968 and 1980. He was also the oldest gold medallist/medallist in 1980, aged 37 years and 121 days, while the youngest gold medallist/medallist was Aládar Kovacsi (HUN) in 1952, aged 19 years and 227 days. Peter Macken of Australia competed in record five Olympic contests 1960–76.

Gustaf Dyrssen (SWE), who won the gold medal in 1920, and a silver in 1924, and Sven Thofelt (SWE), who won the gold in 1928, both won silver medals as members of the 1936 Swedish épée fencing team. Thofelt also won a bronze in the fencing team event in 1948, while his son competed in the 1960 modern pentathlon. Dyrssen later became Sweden's IOC representative, and Thofelt became president of the UIPM.

George Patton (USA), later the famous World War II General, was fifth in 1912, with results that indicated he was not very good at shooting. Two men have scored maximums of 200 hits in shooting: Charles Leonard (USA) in 1936 and George Horvath (SWE) in 1980. The fastest time ever recorded in the 300m swimming event was 3min 10.47sec by Gintaras Staskevicius (LTU) in 1992. The other three disciplines are either not measurable or comparable. However, it is noteworthy that the fastest time recorded for the 4000m cross-country run is 12min 09.50sec by Adrian Parker (GBR) in 1976.

One of the biggest scandals in Olympic history occurred in the fencing segment of the 1976 competition when Boris Onischenko (URS), previous winner of a gold and two silver medals, was disqualified for using an illegal weapon. It transpired that he had tampered with his épée so that it registered a hit even when contact with an opponent had not taken place. The incident has caused speculation about whether he had used the implement in the 1972 Games, where his fencing victory over Jim Fox cost the Briton the individual bronze medal. By coincidence Onischenko was fencing against Fox when the Montreal incident came to light.

MODERN PENTATHLON MEDALS

	G	S	B	Total
Sweden	9	7	5	21
Hungary	8	7	4	19
Soviet Union	5	6	6	17
United States	-	5	3	8
Italy	2	2	3	7
Finland	–	1	4	5
Poland	3	–	–	3
Germany	1	–	1	2
Great Britain	1	–	1	2
Czechoslovakia	-	1	1	2
France	–	–	2	2
Kazakhstan	1	–	–	1
Russia	–	1	–	1
	30	30	30	90

Montreal 1976
XXI Olympic Games (17 July–1 August)

Attended by representatives of 92 countries, comprising 6028 competitors, of which 1247 were women.

When the Games were initially awarded to Montreal, mainly due to the efforts of Mayor Jean Drapeau, it was estimated that they would cost $310 million. Because of planning errors, strikes, slowdowns and, it has been suggested, widespread corruption, the final bill amounted to $1400 million — the stadium alone cost $485 million, and the projected 160m (439ft) high tower and suspended roof was never completed. In 1994 it was stated that the total debt remaining to the citizens of Quebec was $304 million. After the Munich disaster security arrangements involving 16 000 police and soldiers cost $100 million. Six months before it seemed that the main facilities would not be finished in time, but by the official opening pronounced by Queen Elizabeth II, all that was necessary was ready. The expected record number of entries was well down due to a last minute boycott by

20 third world countries, mainly African nations, protesting against the inclusion of New Zealand, whose rugby union team had visited South Africa. Also withdrawing was Taiwan because Canada refused to recognise them under the title of Republic of China, a situation which owed much, it was suggested, to Canada's grain-trading relations with mainland China. The withdrawals, most only two days prior to the start of competitions, caused some problems with seeding arrangements, and particularly affected the quality of boxing and some running events.

Efforts had been made by the IOC to prune the programme, and to this ended the 50km walk, tandem cycling, canoeing slalom, the free rifle and three swimming events had been eliminated. However, with the addition of women's basketball and handball, four canoeing races and seven rowing events, of which six were for women, the total number of gold medals available was now 198 — three more than at Munich. The torch was brought into the stadium by two 15-year-olds, a girl and a boy, Sandra Henderson of English descent and Stephane Prefontaine of French stock, each with a hand on the torch, signifying Canada's joint heritage. In true storybook fashion the pair were married some years later.

The star of Munich, gymnast Olga Korbut (URS), was at Montreal, but she was overshadowed by a 14-year-old Romanian, Nadia Comaneci, who scored the first-ever maximum 10.00 marks achieved at the Olympics on the first day, and ended the Games with a total of seven maximums, having drawn a world-record crowd for gymnastics of 18 000 to the finals of the women's events. Nelli Kim (URS) also scored two maximums. The men's individual champion, Nikolai Andrianov (URS) won the most medals at Montreal with four golds, two silver and a bronze. In the swimming pool, Kornelia Ender (GDR) and John Naber (USA) each won four golds and a silver, with Ender and her team-mates only failing to win two of the 13 women's swimming titles. The American men did better, only losing one of their 13 events — David Wilkie won Britain's first men's swimming gold since 1908. Incidentally, Ender later married her team-mate, backstroke swimmer Roland Matthes, giving them a family total of eight gold, six silver and two bronze medals from three Games. In highboard diving the Austrian-born Italian, Klaus Dibiasi, competing in his fourth Games, became the first diver to gain three consecutive gold medals. A member of the Hungarian water polo team, which won their country's record sixth victory in the sport, was István Szivós, whose father had been in the winning 1952 and 1956 teams.

In the main stadium Lasse Virén, the latest 'Flying Finn', completed his double 'double' by successfully defending his 5000m and 10 000m titles. He attempted to emulate Zátopek's 1952 feat but finished fifth in the marathon. The Cuban Alberto Juantorena, nicknamed El Caballo — 'The Horse'— won a rare 400m/800m double (only America's Paul Pilgrim had previously achieved it in the 1906 Games). Irena Szewinska (POL), now aged 30, won the 400m in her fourth games, to equal the record total of seven medals in athletics. The winner of the men's javelin with a new world record, Miklós Németh (HUN), was the son of the 1948 hammer winner. They remain the only father and son in track and field to win gold medals.

Three sets of brothers did very well in the rowing events. Frank and Alf Hansen (NOR) won the double sculls, while the Landvoigt twins, Jörg and Bernd (GDR) took the coxless pairs. Another set of GDR twins, Walter and Ullrich Diessner, were in the silver medal coxed four crew. Elsewhere the Flying Dutchman class yachting was won by another set of brothers, Jörg and Eckart Diesch (FRG). In women's fencing Yelena Novikova-Belova (URS) won her record fourth gold medal in the team contest, while Hungary's Ildikó Uljakiné-Retjö set an all-medal record of seven, comprising two gold, three silver and two bronze collected at five Games. America's Margaret Murdock became the first woman to win a shooting medal, and was unlucky not to win the gold. Initially she was declared the winner of the small-bore rifle (three positions) event, but an error was discovered which gave her a tie with her team-mate, Lanny Bassham. A closer examination of targets then relegated her down a place. Although unplaced, show jumpers Raimondo and Piero d'Inzeo (ITA) set an unprecedented record by competing in their eighth Games 1948–76. Alwin Schockemöhle (FRG) became only the third rider in Games history to win the jumping title without any faults.

The new Olympic sport of women's basketball produced the tallest known woman ever to compete in the Games. She was Iuliana Semenova (URS) who was unofficially 2.18m (7ft 2in) tall (See Heaviest and Tallest) and weighed 129kg (284lb). Her team won the title, and she is one of tallest, including men, to win an Olympic gold medal. In weightlifting two Bulgarians and a Pole, all medallists, were later disqualified for failing dope tests. A far greater scandal occurred in the modern pentathlon when one of the favourites, Boris Onischenko (URS), was discovered to have tampered with his épée in the fencing segment of the competition. His disqualification eliminated the Soviet team and the team gold medal went to Great Britain. The revenge basketball match between the USA and USSR never materialized as the Soviets were beaten by Yugoslavia in the semifinals. Thus the United States regained the title, making their Olympic match record — played 70, won 69.

The oldest gold medallist at Montreal was Harry Boldt (FRG) in the winning dressage team, aged 46 years and 157 days. The youngest was gymnast Nadia Comaneci who won her first gold medal, aged 14 years and 252 days. The youngest male champion/medallist was Brian Goodell (USA), aged 17 years and 109 days when he won the 1500m freestyle, while the oldest female gold medallist was Ivanka Khristova (BUL) in the shot, aged 34 years and 255 days. The youngest female medallist was Canadian swimmer, Robin Corsiglia, in the medley relay, aged 13 years and 341 days. The oldest medallist was Australian three-day eventer Bill Roycroft,

aged 61 years and 131 days. One of the youngest competitors ever in the Olympics was Spanish swimmer Antonia Real, aged 12 years and 310 days. At these Games Canada gained the unhappy distinction of being the only host country of a Summer Olympics not to win a single gold medal.

1976 MEDALS (SUMMER)

	G	S	B
Soviet Union	49	41	35
GDR	40	25	25
United States	34	35	25
FRG	10	12	17
Japan	9	6	10
Poland	7	6	13
Bulgaria	6	9	7
Cuba	6	4	3
Romania	4	9	14
Hungary	4	5	13
Finland	4	2	–
Sweden	4	1	–
Great Britain	3	5	5
Italy	2	7	4
France	2	3	4
Yugoslavia	2	3	3
Czechoslovakia	2	2	4
New Zealand	2	1	1
Korea	1	1	4
Switzerland	1	1	2
Jamaica	1	1	–
North Korea (PRK)	1	1	–
Norway	1	1	–
Denmark	1	–	2
Mexico	1	–	1
Trinidad and Tobago	1	–	–
Canada	–	5	6
Belgium	–	3	3
The Netherlands	–	2	3
Portugal	–	2	–
Spain	–	2	–
Australia	–	1	4
Iran	–	1	1
Mongolia	–	1	–
Venezuela	–	1	–
Brazil	–	–	2
Austria	–	–	1
Bermuda	–	–	1
Pakistan	–	–	1
Puerto Rico	–	–	1
Thailand	–	–	1

Moscow 1980
XXII Olympic Games (19 July–3 August)

Attended by representatives of 80 countries, comprising 5217 competitors, of which 1124 were women.

There had been only a little dissent when the IOC awarded these Games to Moscow in 1974. Tsarist Russia had competed in 1900 and from 1906 to 1912.

Athletes from Lithuania, Estonia and Latvia, which had been provinces of Russia prior to 1918 and were taken over by the Soviet Union in 1940, had competed independently between 1920 and 1936. The Soviet Union had entered the Olympics in force in 1952, and was now the second highest medal scorer of all time — a remarkable achievement. However, in December 1979 the Soviet Union invaded Afghanistan, and much of the non-Communist world, led by the United States, tried to impose a boycott on the Games — although not, it should be noted, on trade or other economic activity. Not all countries supported the boycott, although sports within those countries sometimes did. Because a number of countries which were unlikely to go to Moscow anyway for financial reasons found it politic to 'jump on the bandwagon', it is difficult to complete a list of boycotting nations. The most reliable estimate is 45–50, of which the most important in sporting terms were the United States, the Federal Republic of Germany and Japan. When the Games were officially opened by Leonid Brezhnev, President of the USSR, there were eight first-time entries, not including Zimbabwe which had previously competed as Rhodesia.

Facilities in Moscow were excellent, including the 103 000-capacity Lenin stadium, and large crowds attended most sports. It must be stated that though, in the main, the Soviet spectators were very knowledgeable, they left something to be desired in their treatment of foreign competitors, particularly those from other Eastern bloc countries. New competitions, such as women's hockey, two extra judo classes, one extra weightlifting class, and various reintroduced events brought the total of gold medals available to a record 203 (barring ties). The heroine of Montreal, Nadia Comaneci (ROM), returned but was no longer the force she had been, and for the first time for many years the star of gymnastics was a male, Alexander Dityatin (URS). He won the greatest number of medals, eight, ever won by a competitor at any sport at one Games, and was also awarded a 10.00 in the horse vault, the first maximum ever by a male gymnast in the Olympics. His team-mate, Nikolai Andrianov, brought his total of medals to a male record of 15, in three Games. This total has only ever been exceeded by Larissa Latynina, also a Soviet gymnast.

East African athletes dominated the distance runs, led by Miruts Yifter (ETH) with a 5000m/10 000m double. The 100m was the closest for 28 years with Great Britain's Alan Wells given the verdict over Silvio Leonard of Cuba. Two other Britons each won the 'wrong' event, Steve Ovett and Sebastian Coe taking the 800m and 1500m respectively. Waldemar Cierpinski (GDR) became only the second man to successfully defend the marathon title, although he was over a minute slower than in 1976. In the triple jump Viktor Saneyev (URS) ended his remarkable career with a silver to add to his three gold medals since 1968. By repeating her Montreal gold medals in the 200m and relay Barbel Wöckel (GDR) equalled

the female track and field record of four. In that relay Ludmila Maslakova of the silver medal Soviet team was running in her fourth consecutive relay final since 1968. Although only winning the pentathlon silver medal Olga Rukavishnikova (URS) theoretically held the world record, albeit for only 0.4sec, as she finished first in the last discipline of 800m. That gave her the shortest reign of any world record holder ever.

Once more the GDR women dominated the swimming events, winning 26 of the available 35 medals. Highest medal scorers were Caren Metschuck with three golds and a silver, and Ines Diers with two golds, two silvers and a bronze. More unusually their team-mate Rica Reinisch won three gold medals all in world record times. The inaugural women's hockey competition resulted in Zimbabwe gaining a gold medal in its debut at the Games, while India was back to its former winning ways by taking a record eighth title in the men's competition. In the yachting events held at Tallinn, the capital of Estonia, the Finn class dinghy event was won appropriately enough by a Finn, Esko Rechardt.

Vladimir Parfenovich (URS) was the first canoeist to win three gold medals at the same Games, and the Cuban heavyweight, Teofilo Stevenson, became the only boxer to win the same event in three Games. Note that the great Hungarian, László Papp, had won three golds at two different weights. In rowing the Landvoigt twins, Jörg and Bernd (GDR) retained their coxless pairs title by beating the Soviet Pimenov twins, Yuri and Nikolai. The other GDR twins, Ullrich and Walter Diessner, went one better than four years ago and won gold medals in the coxed fours. Yet another pair of twins won titles in wrestling when Anatoli and Sergei Beloglasov (URS) won the 52kg and 57kg freestyle events respectively.

The oldest gold medallist at Moscow, or rather Tallinn, was Valentin Mankin (URS) in the Star yachting, in his fourth Games, aged 41 years and 346 days, while the youngest champion at these Games was swimmer Rica Reinisch (GDR) winning the first of her three golds, aged 15 years and 105 days. The oldest female winner was Anthea Stewart (ZIM) at 35 years and 253 days in the hockey, while the youngest male gold medallist was the Hungarian backstroker Sándor Wladár, seven days after his 17th birthday. The youngest medallist was Zirvard Emirzyan (URS) with a silver in women's diving, aged 14 years and 52 days, while the oldest medallist was Petre Rosca (ROM) in the dressage at 57 years and 283 days. The youngest competitor of all was Polish gymnast Anita Jokiel, aged 13 years and 232 days. In the same competition was Myong Hui Choe of North Korea, the smallest competitor of all at 1.35m (4ft 5in) tall and weighing 25kg (55lb). At the other end of the scale was Soviet basketball player Vladimir Tkachenko, standing 2.20m (7ft 2½in) tall, and Greco-Roman wrestler Roman Codreanu (ROM) who weighed 170kg (374lb). Despite the unfillable losses and gaps caused by the boycott, the standard of performances was very high throughout the Games.

1980 MEDALS (SUMMER)

	G	S	B
Soviet Union	80	69	46
GDR	47	37	42
Bulgaria	8	16	17
Cuba	8	7	5
Italy	8	3	4
Hungary	7	10	15
Romania	6	6	13
France	6	5	3
Great Britain	5	7	9
Poland	3	14	15
Sweden	3	3	6
Finland	3	1	4
Czechoslovakia	2	3	9
Yugoslavia	2	3	4
Australia	2	2	5
Denmark	2	1	2
Brazil	2	–	2
Ethiopia	2	–	2
Switzerland	2	–	–
Spain	1	3	2
Austria	1	2	1
Greece	1	–	2
Belgium	1	–	–
India	1	–	–
Zimbabwe	1	–	–
North Korea (PRK)	–	3	2
Mongolia	–	2	2
Tanzania	–	2	–
Mexico	–	1	3
The Netherlands	–	1	2
Ireland	–	1	1
Uganda	–	1	–
Venezuela	–	1	–
Jamaica	–	–	3
Guyana	–	–	1
Lebanon	–	–	1

Motor Boating

A medal sport only held at London in 1908, when only one boat finished in each of the three classes. The competitions were held over a distance of 40 miles. Thomas Thornycroft (GBR) was in the crew of two of the winning boats, winning his second, aged 44 years and 281 days. He was a reserve for the 1952 British Olympic yachting team when in his 71st year.

Motto

The Olympic motto, Citius, Altius, Fortius (faster, higher, stronger), was a Latin phrase noted by Father Henri Didon, of Paris, which was apparently carved over the entrance to his school. His use of the words to illustrate the sporting achievements of the scholars of another college in 1895, was noted by de Coubertin, who instituted them at the 1924 Games.

Munich 1972
XX Olympic Games (26 August–10 September)

Attended by representatives of 121 countries, comprising 7123 competitors, of which 1058 were women.

Awarded the Games in 1966, Munich built a magnificent complex on the rubble of World War II bombings. Total costs were estimated at $650 million. Just prior to the opening day the IOC expelled Rhodesia under intense pressure from Black African nations. A number of new electronic devices were used in the duration of the Games, including a triangulation device to measure distances in the athletics throwing events. Archery and men's handball returned to the Olympic programme, and there were additions to other sports, making a total of 195 gold medals available. The Soviet Union took over a quarter of them. It became the most widely covered sports occasion in history with over 4000 representatives of the world's media on hand. When the German President Gustav Heinemann opened the Games in a colourful ceremony there was a television audience estimated at an all-time viewing record of 1000 million. The oath was taken by athlete Heidi Schüller, the first woman ever to do so. The record number of countries taking part included first-timers Albania, Dahomey (later Benin), Lesotho, Malawi, Upper Volta (later Burkina Faso), Somalia, Swaziland, Togo and North Korea (South Korea sent a separate team).

The first week was dominated by swimmer Mark Spitz (USA) who smashed all records for a single Games by winning seven gold medals, four individual and three relays, and there were world records in each of his events. With his medals from Mexico City he had a total of nine golds, one silver and a bronze. His female equivalent, Shane Gould (AUS), won three golds, a silver and a bronze, swimming in 12 races, itself a record for a female swimmer in the Games. The closest win in Olympic history came in the men's 400m medley when Gunnar Larsson (SWE) was given the decision over Tim McKee (USA) by 0.002 of a second. This decision led to a change in the rules so that, in the future times and places would be decided in hundredths. Valeri Borzov (URS) became the first European to win a men's sprint double on the track. In 1994 he became the IOC member for the Ukraine. Ulrike Meyfarth (FRG) equalled the world high jump record to win the gold medal, aged 16 years and 123 days, the youngest ever individual athletics champion. In hockey, for the first time since 1920, a team, from outside the Indian sub-continent — Germany — won the title. However, the outstanding attraction of the first few days was gymnast Olga Korbut (URS) whose gamine qualities stole the show from her more illustrious colleague, Ludmilla Tourischeva (who later married sprint champion Borzov). Virtually overnight, with blanket media coverage, Korbut became a 'superstar', although she only finished seventh in the all-around competition.

On the morning of 5 September all the euphoria evaporated when a band of eight Arab terrorists broke into the Israeli team headquarters at 31 Connollystrasse in the Olympic village. Two Israelis were killed immediately, and nine others held hostage, as German police and the world's press surrounded the area. After lengthy negotiations the terrorists and their hostages were allowed to go to the airport, where an abortive rescue attempt resulted in the murder of all nine Israelis and the death of some of their captors. The following morning the Games were suspended for a memorial service in a packed stadium, but with the agreement of most of the parties involved, including the Israeli officials, competitions were resumed later in the day. The overall feeling seemed to be that the Games should go on, although a number of individuals, notably from The Netherlands, Norway and the Philippines decided to withdraw. The Israeli team returned home immediately.

The Games continued with the United States suffering an unusual number of misfortunes and reverses. Two prospective medallists had missed the 100m second round heats due to a misreading, by their coach, of the starting time. The world 1500m record-holder, Jim Ryun, did not get seeded as his entry performance, a fast mile time, was mistakenly submitted as a slow 1500m time. Then, to add to his misfortunes, he fell in his heat and was eliminated. A pre-Games banning of the poles used by the American vaulters probably ended a 13 Games winning streak. Their gold and silver medallists in the 400m were banned from further competition for a 'Black Power' protest which meant that the United States, the favourites, could not field a 4 × 400m relay team. Since 1920, teams from the USA had always won a medal. In swimming, Rick DeMont was disqualified after winning the 400m freestyle when a dope test proved positive. If the USA team officials had notified the IOC beforehand that he had to take a certain drug, containing the prohibited substance, to alleviate an asthma condition he would have retained his title. Then, to cap it all, the American basketball team were controversially defeated by the Soviet Union, ending a remarkable 63 consecutive victories in the Games since 1936. Another incident, with a happier conclusion, occurred when the 800m champion, Dave Wottle, in his excitement at the victory ceremony forgot to remove his lucky cap during the American national anthem. He was very embarrassed and proffered apologies to everyone who would listen.

On the track Kipchoge Keino (KEN) added the 3000m steeplechase title to the 1500m that he had won four years earlier. This made him the first runner since James Lightbody (USA) in 1904 to win Olympic titles at the two distances. Lasse Virén (FIN) won the 5000m/10 000m double, setting a world record in the latter despite falling over early in the race, and America's Frank Shorter won the marathon in the city of his birth. Romanian discus thrower Lia Manoliu competed in her record sixth Games (placing ninth with a performance superior to that which won her the gold medal in Mexico City). In the women's pentathlon, silver medallist Heide Rosendahl (FRG), theoretically held the Olympic and world records for the event for 1.12sec, the difference between her winning time in the last discipline, the 200m, and that of the eventual overall champion Mary Peters (GBR).

By winning the five-sport modern pentathlon individual title, Hungary's András Balczó brought his total medal haul since 1960 to an event record of three golds and two silvers. For the second consecutive Games the three medallists in skeet shooting all achieved the same score, the tie being broken by shooting another 25-bird round. Double cycling gold medallist from 1968, Daniel Morelon (FRA), added a third by retaining the sprint title, and Alexander Medved (URS) won his third wrestling title in a row (and his 10th world championship) after a disputed decision over the giant American Chris Taylor. Taylor, reportedly weighing 182kg (401lb) or more, was the heaviest known man to have competed in the Olympic Games. Among serious doping disqualifications at these Games were those of Bakhaavaa Buidaa who had won a wrestling silver medal for Mongolia, Jaime Huelamo (ESP) the bronze medallist in the cycling road race, and the four Dutchmen who had gained third place in the cycling team race.

The oldest gold medallist at Munich was Hans Günter Winkler (FRG), aged 46 years and 49 days in the show-jumping team, and the youngest Deana Deardurff (USA), aged 15 years and 118 days in the swimming medley relay. The oldest female champion was Liselott Linsenhoff (FRG) in the dressage at 45 years and 13 days, and she was also the first woman to win an individual equestrian event. In that competition Great Britain's Lorna Johnstone set a record as the oldest ever female competitor in the Olympics when she reached the last 12 five days past her 70th birthday. A bronze medallist in this event was Maud Van Rosen (SWE), the oldest female medallist at these Games at 46 years and 258 days. The youngest male gold medallist at Munich was Uwe Benter (FRG), cox of the winning fours at 16 years and 276 days, although it should be noted that the unfortunate Rick DeMont was 143 days younger. The youngest medallist was swimmer Kornelia Ender (GDR) at 13 years and 308 days.

The tallest competitor at the Games, and the tallest medallist ever in the Olympics, was Tom Burleson (USA) the 2.23m (7ft 4in) basketball player. One of the runners in the torch relay bringing the Olympic flame to Munich was Edgar Fried, a former Secretary-General of the Austrian Olympic Committee, who had been in the original torch relay in 1936, and repeated that feat again, in his 78th year. At the end of the XX Games a record 48 countries had won at least one medal.

1972 MEDALS (SUMMER)

	G	S	B
Soviet Union	50	27	22
United States	33	31	30
GDR	20	23	23
FRG	13	11	16
Japan	13	8	8
Australia	8	7	2
Poland	7	5	9
Hungary	6	13	16
Bulgaria	6	10	5
Italy	5	3	10
Sweden	4	6	6
Great Britain	4	5	9
Romania	3	6	7
Cuba	3	1	4
Finland	3	1	4
The Netherlands	3	1	1
France	2	4	7
Czechoslovakia	2	4	2
Kenya	2	3	4
Yugoslavia	2	1	2
Norway	2	1	1
North Korea (PRK)	1	1	3
New Zealand	1	1	1
Uganda	1	1	–
Denmark	1	–	–
Switzerland	–	3	–
Canada	–	2	3
Iran	–	2	1
Belgium	–	2	–
Greece	–	2	–
Austria	–	1	2
Colombia	–	1	2
Argentina	–	1	–
Korea	–	1	–
Lebanon	–	1	–
Mexico	–	1	–
Mongolia	–	1	–
Pakistan	–	1	–
Tunisia	–	1	–
Turkey	–	1	–
Brazil	–	–	2
Ethiopia	–	–	2
Ghana	–	–	1
India	–	–	1
Jamaica	–	–	1
Niger Republic	–	–	1
Nigeria	–	–	1
Spain	–	–	1

Nagano 1998
XVIII Winter Games (7–22 February)

Attended by representatives of 72 countries, comprising 2177 competitors, of which 787 were women

Nagano in Japan was awarded these Games in 1991 winning the IOC vote against Val d'Aosta (Italy), Jaca (Spain), Ostersund (Sweden) and Salt Lake City (USA). It was the most southerly venue ever for a Winter Games. In 1994 CBS paid a record $375 million for the US television rights, while the European Broadcasting Union (EBU) paid another record $72 million for the European rights. Curling, snowboarding and women's ice hockey not only made their Olympic debuts but brought the number of events to a record 68. There were a record number of competitors from a record number of countries. Making their Winter Games debuts were Kenya, Uruguay and Venezuela. The 10 300 media representatives was yet another record for a Winter celebration.

The Games were officially opened by Emporer Akihito, whose father had done the honours at Sapporo in 1972. Part of the opening ceremony consisted of a multi-continental concert, via television satellite, with Beethoven's Ninth Symphony *Ode to Joy* conducted by the reknowned Seiji Ozawa. The Olympic flame was lit by Midori Ito, the 1992 figure skating silver medallist, after the torch had been run up the steps to the cauldron by Hiromi Suzuki, the women's world marathon champion. The oath on behalf of the competitors was taken by Kenji Ogiwara, who had won gold in the 1992 Nordic combination.

Bad weather caused serious disruption to the Alpine skiing events with the programme losing five days of competition and the organisers had to reschedule an unprecedented three events for the same day. The weather also caused severe transportation problems. Many competitors were badly affected by a flu epidemic. Nevertheless, there was a very high standard of competition. In Alpine skiing Katja Seizinger (GER) was the most successful with two gold medals and a bronze, while the biggest surprise was the poor showing of the Swiss skiers. The Austrian, Hermann Maier, suffered a bad fall in the downhill race, but returned to win golds in the giant slalom and the super giant slalom. In the Nordic events Larissa Lazutina (RUS) became the most bemedalled competitor at the Games with three golds, one silver and a bronze, her total of five equalling the record for medals at a single Winter Games. Even more of a record breaker was Norway's Bjørn Dæhlie, whose three golds and a silver, raised his total medal tally to a record eight golds and 12 medals overall, 1992–98.

The youngest gold medallist/medallist at Nagano was Tara Lipinski (USA) who won the women's figure skating, aged 15 years and 255days, the youngest ever to win that title. The youngest male champion, and medallist, was Kim Dong-sung (KOR) who took the 1000m short track speed skating event aged eight days past his 18th birthday. The oldest gold medallist was Patrik Loertscher, a member of the Swiss curling team at 37 years and 333 days, while the oldest female champion was Jan Betker of the winning Canadian curling team, aged 37 years and 211 days. A member of the Danish silver medal women's curling team, Jane Bidstrup, was 42 years and 178 days old, while Paul Savage (CAN) won a silver in the men's curling at 50 years and 235 days. Both Bidstrup and Savage are the oldest ever medallists, respectively, in Winter Games history.

Perhaps the most startling of upsets was the failure of the teams from the United States or Canada, which included the legendary Wayne Gretzky (CAN), to win medals in men's ice hockey. An agreement had been reached to allow players from the National Hockey League (NHL) in Canada and the United States to attend. The NHL suspended its season to allow players to compete for their national teams and 125 such players were present in nine of the teams. In snowboarding there was a minor furore when the winner of the men's slalom event, Ross Rebagliati of Canada, was initially disqualified after a doping test. After an appeal he was reinstated.

1998 MEDALS (WINTER)

	G	S	B
Germany	12	9	8
Norway	10	10	5
Russia	9	6	3
Canada	6	5	4
United States	6	3	4
The Netherlands	5	4	2
Japan	5	1	4
Austria	3	5	9
Korea	3	1	2
Italy	2	6	2
Finland	2	4	6
Switzerland	2	2	3
France	2	1	5
Czech Republic	1	1	1
Bulgaria	1	–	–
China	–	6	2
Sweden	–	2	1
Denmark	–	1	–
Ukraine	–	1	–
Belarus	–	–	2
Kazakhstan	–	–	2
Australia	–	–	1
Belgium	–	–	1
Great Britain	–	–	1

Nordic Combination

The event was the 'blue riband' of Nordic skiing in the early Games. The all-round title, comprising a cross-country race and a jump, was won three successive times by Ulrich Wehling (GDR) 1972–80. The oldest winner and medallist was Simon Slåttvik (NOR) who won the title in 1952, aged 34 years and 209 days. The youngest champion was Wehling in 1972, aged 19 years and 212 days, and the youngest medallist was Stefan Kreiner (AUT) with a team bronze in 1992, aged 18 years and 110 days. Up until 1952 the cross-country segment was held first, but at Oslo the order of events was reversed, and has remained so. In 2002 there will be a 'sprint' race.

NORDIC COMBINATION MEDALS

	G	S	B	Total
Norway	11	7	6	24
Finland	1	7	1	9
GDR	3	–	4	7
Switzerland	1	2	1	4
Austria	–	1	3	4
FRG	2	1	–	3
Japan	2	1	–	3
France	1	1	1	3
Soviet Union	–	1	2	3
Germany	1	–	1	2
Sweden	–	1	1	2
Poland	–	–	1	1
Russia	–	–	1	1
	22	22	22	66

Nordic Skiing
(See also *Nordic Combination, Biathlon and Ski-jumping*)

Nordic or cross-country skiing was the first form of skiing in the Olympics. Bjørn Dæhlie (NOR) won a record 12 medals, 1992–98, comprising of another record eight golds and four silvers. The most successful female competitor was Raisa Smetanina (URS/EUN) with four golds, five silvers and a bronze (a female record total of ten medals) between 1976 and 1992. Only Sixten Jernberg (SWE), 1956–64, and Dæhlie have won individual titles in three successive Games, Jernberg doing it over an eight-year period. Lyubov Yegorova (RUS/EUN) equalled the women's Winter Games record of six gold medals with three golds and two silvers in 1992 and three golds and one silver in 1994. Yegorova and team-mate Yelena Valbe, both in 1992, and Larissa Lazutina (RUS) in 1998, have all set a female record of five medals in a single Games. Marja-Liisa Hämäläinen (later Kirvesniemi) of Finland won a record three individual gold medals at one Games in 1984. She competed in a record six Games, 1976–94, during which she raced a total of 185km (115 miles), winning an additional two bronzes. Her husband Harri Kirvesniemi (FIN) has also competed in six Games 1980–98, winning six bronze medals, during this period he raced an unmatched record of 450km (279 miles). Dæhlie raced 345km (214 miles) in his three Games.

The oldest gold medallist/medallist was Maurilio De Zolt (ITA), aged 43 years and 150 days in the 1994 relay, and the youngest champion was Gunde Svan (SWE) who won the 15km race in 1984, aged 22 years and 32 days. The youngest medallist was Ivar Formo (NOR) in the 1972 relay, aged 20 years and 234 days. The oldest female gold medallist was Smetanina as a member of the 1992 relay team, aged 39 years and 354 days. She is also the only competitor to win medals in five Games. The youngest female champion was Carola Anding (GDR) aged, 19 years and 54 days in

NORDIC SKIING MEDALS

	Men			Women			
	G	S	B	G	S	B	Total
Soviet Union	11	8	12	17	16	13	77
Norway	23	22	11	2	7	7	72
Finland	11	13	19	8	9	10	70
Sweden	18	13	12	3	2	2	50
Italy	2	5	5	3	4	4	23
Russia	–	–	–	8	3	2	13
Czechoslovakia	–	–	1	–	1	3	5
GDR	–	1	–	2	–	1	4
Kazakhstan	1	2	1	–	–	–	4
Switzerland	–	–	3	–	–	–	3
Austria	–	1	1	–	–	–	2
Czech Republic	–	–	–	–	1	1	2
Bulgaria	–	–	1	–	–	–	1
United States	–	1	–	–	–	–	1
	66	66	66	43	43	43	327

the 1980 relay, while the youngest female medallist was Marjo Matikainen (FIN) in the 1984 relay, aged 19 years and 12 days. In 1994 a brother and sister won medals when Giorgio Vanzetta (ITA) took gold in the 4 × 10km relay and Bice gained a bronze in the 4 × 5km. The 1928 50km race was won by Per-Erik Hedlund (SWE) with a remarkable margin of 13min 27sec over the second man, whereas in the 1980 15km a mere 0.01sec separated first and second. Certain races are designated as freestyle events, i.e., the 'skating' technique may be used. Otherwise only the classical stride and glide is allowed. The surprising silver medal won by Bill Koch (USA) in the 1976 50km was credited to his development of the former style.

Oldest Competitors/Winners

The oldest ever competitor at the Olympic Games was Oscar Swahn of Sweden who was in the shooting contests in 1928 at the age of 72 years and 279 days (when he won a silver medal in a team event). He had won a gold medal eight years earlier, at Antwerp, in the running deer team, to become the oldest ever gold medallist seven days short of his 65th birthday. (His son, Alfred, also won gold in the team.) He actually qualified for the 1924 Games in his 77th year but illness prevented him making the trip. In 1904 Revd Galen Spencer (USA) had won an archery team gold just two days past his 64th birthday, while a fellow American, Samuel Duvall, won a team silver at 68 years and 194 days. The oldest winner of an individual event was Joshua 'Jerry' Millner (GBR) who was four days past his 61st birthday winning the free rifle (1000yd) event at London in 1908. The oldest woman to compete in the Games was Great Britain's Lorna Johnstone, who was four days past her 70th birthday when she took part in the dressage competition at Munich in 1972. The oldest female gold medallist was Queenie Newall (GBR), who won the archery contest in 1908 at 53 years and 277 days.

In October 1994 Hjalmari Kivenheimo (FIN), silver medallist in the 1912 gymnastics team competition, died aged 105 years and 34 days, and was the greatest known age ever reached by an Olympic medallist. Not a medallist, but Dirk Janssen, of The Netherlands, also a gymnast, in 1908, held the Olympian longevity record when he died in November 1986 aged 105 years and 114 days.

Olympic Oath

Instituted in 1920, at the opening ceremony a representative of the host country, usually a veteran of previous Games, mounts the rostrum, holds a corner of their national flag and, with the flag bearers of all the other countries drawn up in a semi-circle, pronounces the oath: 'In the name of all competitors, I promise that we shall take part in these Olympic Games, respecting and abiding by the rules which govern them, in the true spirit of sportsmanship, for the glory of sport and the honour of our teams'. (A similar oath is taken on behalf of all the judges.)

The following have taken the Olympic oath on behalf of the athletes.

Summer

1920	Victor Boin	Fencer
1924	Georges André	Athlete
1928	Harry Denis	Footballer
1932	George Calnan	Fencer
1936	Rudolf Ismayr	Weightlifter
1948	Donald Finlay	Athlete
1952	Heikki Savolainen	Gymnast
1956	John Landy	Athlete
	Henri St Cyr	Equestrian (Stockholm)
1960	Adolfo Consolini	Athlete
1964	Takashi Ono	Gymnast
1968	Pablo Garrido	Athlete
1972	Heidi Schüller	Athlete

Summer *continued*

1976	Pierre St Jean	Weightlifter
1980	Nikolai Andrianov	Gymnast
1984	Edwin Moses	Athlete
1988	Huh Jae/Son Mi-na	Basketballer/ Handballer
1992	Luis Doreste Blanco	Yachtsman
1996	Teresa Edwards	Basketballer

Winter

1924	Camille Mandrillon	Military Patrol
1928	Hans Eidenbenz	Skier
1932	Jack Shea	Speed skater
1936	Wilhelm Bogner	Skier
1948	Richard Torriani	Ice hockey player
1952	Torbjörn Falkanger	Ski jumper
1956	Guiliana Chenal- Minuzzo	Skier
1960	Carol Heiss	Figure skater
1964	Paul Aste	Bobsledder
1968	Leo Lacroix	Skier
1972	Keichi Suzuki	Speed skater
1976	Werner Delle-Karth	Bobsledder
1980	Eric Heiden	Speed skater
1984	Bojan Krizaj	Skier
1988	Pierre Harvey	Skier
1992	Surya Bonaly	Figure skater
1994	Vegard Ulvang	Skier
1998	Kenji Ogiwara	Skier

Openings

The Olympic Games traditionally are opened by a member of the reigning Royal Family or a senior representative of the national government of the host country.

Summer

1896	King George I
1900	–
1904	David Francis (President of the World's Fair)
1906	King George I
1908	King Edward VII
1912	King Gustaf V
1920	King Albert
1924	President Gaston Doumergue
1928	HRH Prince Hendrik
1932	Vice-President Charles Curtis
1936	Chancellor Adolf Hitler
1948	King George VI
1952	President Juho Paasikivi
1956	HRH The Duke of Edinburgh King Gustav VI (Stockholm)
1960	President Giovanni Gronchi
1964	Emperor Hirohito
1968	President Gustavo Diaz Ordaz
1972	President Gustav Heinemann
1976	HM Queen Elizabeth II
1980	President Leonid Brezhnev
1984	President Ronald Reagan

Summer *continued*

1988	President Rok Tae-woo
1992	King Juan Carlos
1996	President William Clinton

Winter

1924	Under-Secretary Gaston Vidal
1928	President Edmund Schulthess
1932	Governor Franklin D. Roosevelt
1936	Chancellor Adolf Hitler
1948	President Enrico Celio
1952	HRH Princess Ragnhild
1956	President Giovanni Gronchi
1960	Vice-President Richard Nixon
1964	President Adolf Schärf
1968	President Charles de Gaulle
1972	Emperor Hirohito
1976	President Rudolf Kirchschläger
1980	Vice-President Walter Mondale
1984	President Mika Spiljak
1988	Governor-General Jeanne Sauvé
1992	President Francois Mitterand
1994	King Harald V
1998	Emperor Akihito

Oslo 1952
VI Winter Games (14–25 February)

Attended by representatives of 30 countries, comprising 732 competitors, of which 109 were women.

A feature of these Games were the enormous crowds at all venues, including a record for any Olympic event at the ski jumping at Holmenkollen, estimated at 150 000. An innovation was the Olympic flame coming, not from Olympia, but from Morgedal in southern Norway, home of Sondre Nordheim, the father of modern skiing. The last relay 'runner' who brought the flame into the Bislett Stadium was Eigil Nansen, the grandson of the reknowned Polar explorer Fridtjof Nansen. The oath was taken by ski jumper Torbjörn Falkanger. All entrants from Commonwealth countries wore black armbands as the opening day coincided with the funeral of Great Britain's King George VI. As King Haakon and the Crown Prince were in London for this, the Games were opened by HRH Princess Ragnhild. Back in the Olympic fold were Germany and Japan, and for the first time in the Winter Games entries included Portugal and New Zealand.

Bad weather conditions necessitated the start of some of the competitions, with the women's giant slalom and the 2-man bob, the day before the opening ceremony. Of the three Alpine events, the giant slalom and downhill races were held some 120km from Oslo, at Norefjell. In the men's giant slalom Stein Eriksen (NOR) became the first ever winner of an Alpine skiing event from a Nordic country. This did not happen again until 1980. The star of the Games was Hjalmar Andersen of the host country who won three speed skating gold medals. In winning the women's figure skating title Jeanette Altwegg won Great Britain's first skating gold medal since Madge Syers in 1908. Instead of turning professional, as did most of her predecessors and successors, she went to work at the famed village for orphan children, Pestalozzi in Switzerland. The men's title went to defending champion Dick Button (USA) with some of the most remarkable jumps ever seen in competition. Finishing sixth, was Carlo Fassi (ITA), later to coach Olympic champions Peggy Fleming (USA), Dorothy Hamill (USA), John Curry (GBR) and Robin Cousins (GBR).

The basic running abilities required by cross-country skiers were highlighted in the Nordic skiing when the 18km gold medal was won by Hallgeir Brenden (NOR), who in following years won two national steeplechase titles. Also in the silver Norwegian relay team with him was Martin Stokken, who had placed fourth in the 1948 Olympic 10 000m in London. By competing again at Helsinki he became one of the few men to compete in a Winter and Summer Games in the same year. For the first time there was a Nordic ski race for women, dominated by Finland with four of the top five places. Bandy, a distant relative of ice hockey, was played as a demonstration sport and won by Sweden.

The oldest gold medallist at Oslo was Franz Kemser in the German 4-man bob, aged 41 years and 103 days, and the youngest was slalom winner Andrea Mead-Lawrence (USA), aged 19 years and 301 days. The youngest male winner was Robert Dickson (CAN) in ice hockey, aged 20 years and 308 days, while the oldest female champion was Lydia Wideman (FIN) in the 10km cross-country, aged 31 years and 282 days. The youngest medallist was skater Tenley Albright (USA) with a silver, aged 16 years and 217 days. Albert Madorin (SUI) won a bronze in the 4-man bob, aged 46 years and 342 days.

1952 MEDALS (WINTER)

	G	S	B
Norway	7	3	6
United States	4	6	1
Finland	3	4	2
Germany	3	2	2
Austria	2	4	2
Canada	1	–	1
Italy	1	–	1
Great Britain	1	–	–
The Netherlands	–	3	–
Sweden	–	–	4
Switzerland	–	–	2
France	–	–	1
Hungary	–	–	1

Paris 1900
II Olympic Games (20 May–28 October)

Attended by representatives of 25 countries, comprising 1225 competitors, of which 19 were women.

Despite strong Greek pressure for the exclusive rights to organise future Games, Baron de Coubertin won agreement to hold the 1900 Games in Paris, but made a serious mistake in making it part of the Fifth Universal Exposition also being held there. The Games became merely a sideshow to the fair. Numerous internal rivalries within French sport left many of the sports without experienced officials or adequate venues. The track and field events were held on uneven turf at Croix-Catelan, in the Bois de Boulogne, where it is reported that the jumpers had to dig their own pits. Many of the competitors, especially the Americans, had never run on a grass track before. Generally there were few spectators, and even these were nearly reduced in number when the 1896 discus champion threw the implement into the crowd on all three throws. Cricket, croquet and golf made their appearance and amid the general confusion many competitors, even medal winners, were not aware until much later that they had been competing at the Olympic Games.

France, the host country, had a record-sized team numbering 884, the largest ever entered for the Games. The Americans were still represented by colleges and clubs, and the decision to have competition on Sunday upset many of those whose colleges were church controlled. Thus the long jump world record holder, Myer Prinstein, a Russian-born Jew but under the aegis of the University of Syracuse, a strong Methodist institution, gained a silver medal with his Saturday qualifying round jump (such performances then counted for medals), but had to withdraw from the Sunday final. The eventual winner, Alvin Kraenzlein (USA), set a record of four individual gold medals, a feat never surpassed in track and field at one Games. Also much in evidence was America's Ray Ewry, the standing jump expert, at the start of his fabulous Olympic career, with three gold medals here. Behind him in those standing jumps was countryman, Irving Baxter. He had already won the regular high jump and the pole vault, and reputedly became the first athlete of American Indian ancestry to win at the Olympic Games. Athlete Norman Pritchard (GBR), usually, but mistakenly, shown as from India, won two silvers in the 200m flat and 200m hurdles, and later became an actor in Hollywood films.

Women were allowed to compete for the first time, but not in the major sports, and the first female Olympic competitor (only recently researched) was Helen, Countess de Pourtalès (SUI), in the 1–2 ton yachting in May. The first individual champion was Charlotte Cooper (GBR) who won the tennis singles on 7 July. A unique record was set in the coxed pairs rowing final, in which a small French boy was drafted in at the last moment to cox the winning Dutch crew. His name was never recorded and he disappeared without trace afterwards, but he was no more than 10 years old, and possibly as young as seven, in either case the youngest ever Olympic gold medallist. The oldest gold medallist in 1900 was French-born Count Hermann de Pourtalès (SUI) in the 1–2 ton class yachting, aged 53 years and 55 days. The youngest female champion was Margaret Abbott (USA) in golf, aged 20 years and 110 days, while the oldest was 31-year-old Helen, Countess de Pourtalès, a crew member for her father.

Press coverage was barely apparent, with many of the events not mentioned at all, and for years afterwards there was much confusion as to the names and nationalities of even the medallists. Thus it was the first Olympic medals won by Canada, a gold and bronze gained by George Orton, were not 'discovered' for some years, as Orton had been entered by his American university and was billed as an American. Even more recently it has been found that the winner of the marathon, Michel Théato (FRA), was actually a Luxembourgeois — in this case the medal tables have not been altered.

1900 MEDALS

	G	S	B
France	27	39	34
United States	19	15	15
Great Britain	17	9	12
Switzerland	6	3	1
Belgium	5	5	3
Germany	3	2	2
Australia	2	–	4
Denmark	2	3	2
Italy	2	2	–
The Netherlands	1	1	4
Hungary	1	2	2
Cuba	1	1	–
Canada	1	–	1
Sweden	1	–	1
Austria	–	3	3
Norway	–	2	3
Czechoslovakia	–	1	2

Paris 1924
VIII Olympic Games (4 May–27 July)

Attended by representatives of 44 countries, comprising 3092 competitors, of which 136 were women.

Originally scheduled for Amsterdam, de Coubertin requested that the Games be transferred to Paris in the hope that the bad image acquired in 1900 could be eradicated. The IOC had taken steps to impose its authority on the staging of the Olympics so that never again could a host country add events as it wished. The Colombes stadium with a 500m track built in 1909, was enlarged to hold 60 000 spectators. An Olympic village had been proposed but the idea was not carried through, although competitors were housed in huts scattered around the main site. Four of the five 'enemy' countries in the war were included in the record number of nations accepting invitations, but Germany was still not present due to the particularly frosty relations between them and France. Among the newcomers were Ireland, competing sepa-

rately from Great Britain for the first time, Romania and Poland. Polish sportsmen had competed previously but always in the teams of other countries. The Games were formally opened by President Gaston Doumergue, and were attended by well over 600 000 spectators in total. However, the chauvinism of the French supporters was outrageous at times. The weather was good, in fact sometimes too good. For the 10 000m cross-country event it was reported to be over 40°C and over half of the starters did not finish.

Despite, for the first time, all sports being organised by their international governing bodies and the instigation of Juries of Appeal, there were still many complaints of unfair decisions, notably in boxing. The newly instituted Olympic motto, Citius, Altius, Fortius (faster, higher, stronger) originally composed by Father Henri Didon in 1895, was taken to heart. Numerous records were set, sometimes unexpectedly. The long jump was won by William DeHart Hubbard (USA), with 7.44m. Another American, Robert LeGendre, had been left out of that event but entered in the athletic pentathlon in which he broke the world long jump record with 7.76m on the way to winning a bronze medal. Hubbard was the first black athlete to win a gold medal in an individual, as opposed to a team event.

The track events were dominated by the resurgent Finns with their outstanding stars Paavo Nurmi and Ville Ritola. Nurmi won a then record five gold medals, and American-based Ritola four golds and two silvers. The remarkable Nurmi won the 1500m and 5000m title within 90 minutes on the same day, a unique performance. His other victories came in the 3000m team race and the 10 000m cross-country individual and team events. In this latter event, run in record high temperatures, only 15 of the 38 starters finished, as Nurmi beat Ritola by well over a minute. The statue of him which stands outside Helsinki stadium was sculpted in 1925 to commemorate his Paris triumphs. It is interesting to note that the only viable opposition to the 'Flying Finns' came from Edvin Wide of Sweden who was actually born in Finland. Two Britons scored upset wins when Harold Abrahams became the first European to win an Olympic sprint title, and Eric Liddell set a world record by taking the 400m crown. Abrahams, who was coached by Sam Mussabini who had also trained Reggie Walker to victory in 1908, later recollected that there were no victory ceremonies and that he received his gold medal in the post some time later. Third in that 100m final was New Zealand's Arthur Porritt, who later became Governor-General of his country. The Oscar-winning film Chariots of Fire was made in 1981 with a not too accurate account of the period leading up to the achievements of Abrahams and Liddell. Kasutoshi Naito, who placed third in the freestyle wrestling featherweight class, became the first Asian to win an Olympic medal.

A double was achieved by Harold Osborn (USA) who won the decathlon title and the high jump. In that latter event, Osborn's habit of pressing the bar back against the uprights with his hand as he jumped using the western roll technique led to a change in the event's rules. The rules in another event resulted in a strange set of circumstances when the third finisher in the 400m hurdles was credited with a new Olympic record (also bettering the world mark). This happened because the winner, Frank Morgan Taylor (USA), had knocked down a hurdle, while the second finisher, Charles Brookins (USA), was disqualified for leaving his lane. Thus the eventual silver medallist, third finisher Erik Vilén (FIN) claimed the record. In fourth place was Georges André (FRA) who had taken the oath at the opening ceremony, and who had won a silver medal in the 1908 high jump.

In the pool Johnny Weissmuller (USA) won three golds in freestyle swimming and a bronze at water polo. After more medals four years later he turned to films and in the 1930s he became the most famous screen *Tarzan* of them all. His team-mate in Paris, Gertrude Ederle, who had become the youngest person ever to set a world record in 1919 at the age of 12 years and 298 days, won a gold in the relay, and two years later became the first woman to swim the English Channel. Incidentally, this Games was the first to introduce lane dividers in the pool. In rowing, another American to gain fame elsewhere was Benjamin Spock, as part of the winning eights, who later was reknown as a best-selling writer and paediatrician. France came into her own in the fencing and cycling events. In the former Roger Ducret won three golds and one silver, while in the latter, Armand Blanchonnet won the 188km (117 miles) road race by a near-record margin of over nine minutes. A pointer to the future came in the soccer final which was won by Uruguay, the first South American country to enter the Olympic football competition.

Now aged 45 Alfred Swahn (SWE) won his ninth shooting medal in four Games. His father, the incredible Oscar, had been picked for the team, but almost 77 was too ill. However, he and Alfred won a family total of six golds, four silvers and five bronzes. The American shooter Carl Osburn gained another silver to raise his individual total since 1912 to 11, comprising of five gold, four silver and two bronze. Tennis made its last appearance for 64 years, and had an all-star entry with all titles won by Wimbledon champions. One of them, Norris Williams, who partnered Hazel Wightman in the mixed doubles, had been a survivor of the *Titanic* disaster in 1912. Rugby also disappeared from the Games, leaving the United States as reigning Olympic champions.

The oldest gold medallist at Paris was Allen Whitty (GBR), in the running deer shooting, aged 58 years and 78 days. The youngest winner at Paris was featherweight boxer Jackie Fields (USA) at 16 years and 162 days. The youngest female winner was 400m freestyle champion Martha Norelius (USA) at 14 years and 177 days (recent research confirming her as two years younger than originally thought). The oldest female gold medallist was Hazel Wightman (USA) in tennis, aged 37 years and 213 days. The United States won the major share of the medals at Paris, but a record number of 30 countries shared in the total.

1924 MEDALS (SUMMER)

	G	S	B
United States	45	27	27
Finland	14	13	10
France	13	15	10
Great Britain	9	13	12
Italy	8	3	5
Switzerland	7	8	10
Norway	5	2	3
Sweden	4	13	12
The Netherlands	4	1	5
Belgium	3	7	3
Australia	3	1	
Denmark	2	5	
Hungary	2	3	
Yugoslavia	2	–	–
Czechoslovakia	1	4	5
Argentina	1	3	2
Estonia	1	1	4
South Africa	1	1	1
Uruguay	1	–	–
Austria	–	3	1
Canada	–	3	1
Poland	–	1	1
Haiti	–	–	1
Japan	–	–	1
New Zealand	–	–	1
Portugal	–	–	1
Romania	–	–	1

Participation, by Country

(The three-character country abbreviations used here are those used officially by the IOC. Individual sports governing bodies sometimes use different abbreviations at other times.)

		Summer Games		Winter Games	
Country		Debut	Number attended	Debut	Number attended
AFG	Afghanistan	1936	10	–	
AHO	Netherlands Antilles	1952	10	1988	2
ALB	Albania	1972	3	–	
ALG	Algeria	1964	8	1992	1

continued

	Country	Summer Games Debut	Number attended	Winter Games Debut	Number attended
AND	Andorra	1976	6	1976	7
ANG	Angola	1980	4	–	
ANT	Antigua/Barbuda	1976	5	–	
ARG	Argentina	1920	17	1908	14
ARM	Armenia	1996	1	1994	2
ARU	Aruba	1988	3	–	
ASA	American Samoa	1988	3	1994	1
AUS	Australia [1]	1896	24	1936	14
AUT	Austria [2]	1896	23	1924	18
AZE	Azerbaijan	1996	1	1998	1
BAH	Bahamas	1952	11	–	
BAN	Bangladesh	1984	4	–	
BAR	Barbados [10]	1960	8	–	
BDI	Burundi	1996	1	–	
BEL	Belgium	1900	22	1920	17
BEN	Benin (ex Dahomey)	1972	6	–	
BER	Bermuda	1936	13	1992	3
BHU	Bhutan	1984	4	–	
BIZ	Belize (ex British Honduras)	1968	7	–	
BLR	Belarus	1996	1	1994	2
BOH	Bohemia [3]	–		–	
BOL	Bolivia	1936	9	1956	5
BOT	Botswana	1980	5	–	
BRA	Brazil	1920	17	1992	3
BRN	Bahrain	1984	4	–	
BRU	Brunei	1996	1	–	
BSH	Bosnia-Herzegovina	1992	2	1994	2
BUL	Bulgaria	1896	15	1936	15
BUR	Burkina Faso (ex Upper Volta)	1972	4	–	
CAF	Central African Republic	1968	5	–	
CAM	Cambodia [4]	1956	4	–	
CAN	Canada	1900	22	1920	19
CAY	Cayman Islands	1976	5	–	
CGO	Congo	1964	7	–	
CHA	Chad	1964	7	–	
CHI	Chile	1896	18	1948	12
CHN	China	1932	8	1980	6
CIV	Ivory Coast	1964	8	–	
CMR	Cameroon	1964	9	–	
COK	Cook Islands	1988	3	–	
COL	Colombia	1932	14	–	
COM	Comoros Isands	1996	1	–	
CPV	Cape Verde Islands	1996	1	–	
CRC	Costa Rica	1936	10	1984	3
CRO	Croatia	1992	2	1992	2
CUB	Cuba	1900	15	–	
CYP	Cyprus	1980	5	1980	6
CZE	Czech Republic [3]	1996	1	1994	2
DEN	Denmark	1896	23	1948	9
DJI	Djibouti	1984	4	–	
DMA	Dominica	1996	1	–	
DOM	Dominican Republic	1964	9	–	
ECU	Ecuador	1924	9	–	
EGY	Egypt [5]	1906	18	1984	1
ESA	El Salvador	1968	6	–	
ESP	Spain	1900	18	1936	15
EST	Estonia [6]	1920	7	1928	5

continued

	Country	Summer Games Debut	Number attended	Winter Games Debut	Number attended
ETH	Ethiopia	1956	8	–	
FIJ	Fiji	1956	9	1988	2
FIN	Finland	1906	21	1920	19
FRA	France	1896	24	1920	19
FRG	Federal Republic of Germany [7]	1968	5	1968	6
GAB	Gabon	1972	5	–	
GAM	Gambia	1984	4	–	
GBR	Great Britain	1896	24	1908	20
GDR	German Democratic Republic [7]	1968	5	1968	6
GEO	Georgia	1996	1	1994	2
GEQ	Equatorial Guinea	1984	4	–	
GER	Germany [8]	1896	15	1908	11
GHA	Ghana (Ex Gold Coast)	1952	9	–	
GNB	Guinea-Bissau	1996	1	–	
GRE	Greece	1896	24	1936	14
GRN	Grenada	1984	4	–	
GUA	Guatemala	1952	9	1988	1
GUI	Guinea	1968	6	–	
GUM	Guam	1988	3	1988	1
GUY	Guyana (ex British Guiana)	1948	12	–	
HAI	Haiti	1900	11	–	
HKG	Hong Kong	1952	11	–	
HON	Honduras	1968	6	1992	1
HUN	Hungary	1896	22	1924	18
INA	Indonesia	1952	10	–	
IND	India	1920	18	1964	5
IRI	Iran	1948	11	1956	5
IRL	Ireland [9]	1924	16	1992	2
IRQ	Iraq	1948	9	–	
ISL	Iceland	1908	16	1948	13
ISR	Israel	1952	11	1994	2
ISV	Virgin Islands	1968	7	1984	5
ITA	Italy	1900	22	1924	18
IVB	British Virgin Islands	1984	4	–	
JAM	Jamaica [10]	1948	13	1988	4
JOR	Jordan	1980	5	–	
JPN	Japan	1912	17	1928	15
KEN	Kenya	1956	9	1998	1
KGZ	Kyrghyzstan	1996	1	1994	2
KOR	Korea [11]	1948	12	1948	13
KSA	Saudi Arabia	1972	6	–	
KUW	Kuwait	1968	8	–	
KZK	Kazakhstan	1996	1	1994	2
LAO	Laos	1980	4	–	
LAT	Latvia [6]	1924	6	1924	6
LBA	Libya	1968	6	–	
LBR	Liberia	1956	7	–	
LCA	St Lucia	1996	1	–	
LES	Lesotho	1972	6	–	
LIB	Lebanon	1948	12	1948	12
LIE	Liechtenstein	1936	12	1936	14
LTU	Lithuania [6]	1924	4	1928	4
LUX	Luxembourg	1912	18	1928	6
MAD	Madagascar	1964	7	–	
MAR	Morocco	1960	9	1968	4
MAS	Malaysia [12]	1956	10	–	

		Summer Games		Winter Games	
	Country	Debut	Number attended	Debut	Number attended
MAW	Malawi	1972	5	–	
MDA	Moldova	1996	1	1994	2
MDV	Maldives	1988	3	–	
MEX	Mexico	1924	17	1928	5
MGL	Mongolia	1964	8	1964	9
MKD	Macedonia	1996	1	1998	1
MLI	Mali	1964	8	–	
MLT	Malta	1928	11	–	
MON	Monaco	1920	15	1984	5
MOZ	Mozambique	1980	5	–	
MRI	Mauritius	1984	4	–	
MTN	Mauritania	1984	4	–	
MYA	Myanmar (ex Burma)	1948	12	–	
NAM	Namibia	1992	2	–	
NAU	Nauru	1996	1	–	
NCA	Nicaragua	1968	7	–	
NED	The Netherlands	1900	22	1928	16
NEP	Nepal	1964	8	–	
NGR	Nigeria	1952	11	–	
NIG	Niger Republic	1964	7	–	
NOR	Norway	1900	22	1920	19
NZL	New Zealand	1908	20	1952	11
OMA	Oman	1984	4	–	
PAK	Pakistan	1948	12	–	
PAN	Panama	1928	12	–	
PAR	Paraguay	1968	7	–	
PER	Peru	1936	13	–	
PHI	Philippines	1924	16	1972	3
PLE	Palestine	1996	1	–	
PNG	Papua New Guinea	1976	5	–	
POL	Poland	1924	16	1924	18
POR	Portugal	1912	19	1952	4
PRK	Democratic People's Republic of Korea [11]	1972	5	1964	6
PUR	Puerto Rico	1948	13	1984	5
QAT	Qatar	1984	4	–	
ROM	Romania	1924	15	1928	16
RSA	South Africa [13]	1904	15	1960	3
RUS	Russia [14]	1900	4	1908	3
RWA	Rwanda	1984	4	–	
SAM	Western Samoa	1984	4	–	
SAR	Saar [15]	1952	1	–	
SEN	Senegal	1964	9	1984	3
SEY	Republic of Seychelles	1980	4	–	
SIN	Singapore	1948	12	–	
SKN	St Kitts and Nevis	1996	1	–	
SLE	Sierra Leone	1968	6	–	
SLO	Slovenia	1992	2	1992	3
SMR	San Marino	1960	8	1976	5
SOL	Solomon Islands	1984	4	–	
SOM	Somalia	1972	4	–	
SRI	Sri Lanka (ex Ceylon)	1948	12	–	
STP	São Tomé and Príncipe	1996	1	–	
SUD	Sudan	1960	7	–	
SUI	Switzerland [16]	1896	24	1920	19
SUR	Surinam	1968	7	–	
SVK	Slovakia	1996	1	1994	2
SWE	Sweden	1896	23	1908	20

continued

	Country	Summer Games Debut	Number attended	Winter Games Debut	Number attended
SWZ	Swaziland	1972	5	1992	1
SYR	Syria	1948	8	–	
TAN	Tanzania	1964	8	–	
TCH	Czechoslovakia [3]	1900	20	1920	17
TGA	Tonga	1984	4	–	
THA	Thailand	1952	11	–	
TJK	Tadjikistan	1996	1	–	
TKM	Turkmenistan	1996	1	–	
TOG	Togo	1972	5	–	
TPE	Chinese Taipei (ex Formosa/Taiwan)	1956	9	1972	7
TRI	Trinidad and Tobago [10]	1948	13	1994	2
TUN	Tunisia	1960	9	–	
TUR	Turkey	1908	17	1936	12
UAE	United Arab Emirates	1984	4	–	
UGA	Uganda	1956	10	–	
UKR	Ukraine	1996	1	1994	2
URS	Soviet Union [17]	1952	10	1956	10
URU	Uruguay	1924	16	1998	1
USA	United States	1896	23	1908	20
UZB	Uzbekistan	1996	1	1994	2
VAN	Vanuatu	1988	3	–	
VEN	Venezuela	1948	13	1998	1
VIE	Vietnam [18]	1952	10	–	
VIN	St Vincent and Grenadines	1988	3	–	
YEM	Yemen [19]	1992	2	–	
YUG	Yugoslavia [20]	1912	19	1924	15
ZAI	Zaire	1968	5	–	
ZAM	Zambia (ex North Rhodesia)	1964	8	–	
ZIM	Zimbabwe (ex Rhodesia)	1928	8	–	

[1]   Australia and New Zealand combined as Australasia 1908–12
[2]   Not invited in 1920
[3]   Czechoslovakia was represented by Bohemia up to 1912
[4]   Provisional recognition of current regime in Cambodia
[5]   As United Arab Republic 1960–68
[6]   Annexed by the Soviet Union in 1940; Independent again from 1992
[7]   Separate teams 1968–88; GDR part of combined German team 1956–64
[8]   Not invited 1920, 1924 and 1948
[9]   Part of Great Britain until 1924
[10] Jamaica, Barbados and Trinidad and Tobago combined as Antilles in 1960
[11] Country partitioned in 1945, and separate regimes established in 1948
[12] Prior to 1964 Malaya and North Borneo (later Sabah) competed separately. In 1964 they combined with Sarawak and Singapore. In 1965 Singapore left the Federation
[13] Not invited 1960–88
[14] As Czarist Russia 1900–12; Separate entity again in 1994
[15] Independent 1947–57, then incorporated into Germany
[16] Switzerland only attended Stockholm in 1956
[17] A combined team of the National Olympic Committees (NOCs) of the former Soviet republics (excluding the Baltic States) competed in the 1992 Summer and Winter Games as the Unified Team (EUN) or Commonwealth of Independent States (CIS)
[18] From 1952–72 only a South Vietnamese team competed
[19] The Republic of Yemen was formed in 1960 of the Yemen Arab Republic (which competed 1984–88) and the Yemen People's Democratic Republic (which competed in 1988)
[20] Representatives of the Yugoslavia Serbs competed as Independent Olympic Participants (IOP) in the 1992 Games. In 1912 Serbia had competed as a separate entity

Pelota Basque

It was a demonstration sport at Paris in 1924, with teams from Spain and France. It was seen again at Mexico City in 1968, and at Barcelona in 1992.

Polo

A medal sport on five occasions. Only Sir John Wodehouse (GBR), the 3rd Earl of Kimberley, won a silver (1908) and a gold (1920). The oldest gold medallist was Manuel Andrada (ARG) in 1936, aged 46 years and 211 days, and the youngest was his team-mate Roberto Cavanagh, aged 21 years and 269 days. The biggest winning margin was 16–2 by Argentina v Spain and Great Britain v France, both in 1924, and by Mexico v Hungary in 1936. In 1900, in a remarkable display of unchauvinistic behaviour, there was an American in the British gold medal team, an American and a Spaniard in the British silver medal team, and a Briton in the French bronze team.

Press

See under *Media*

Rackets

Rackets has only been a medal sport at London in 1908, with all competitors from Great Britain. The most successful were Evan Noel and American-born John Jacob Astor. Noel won the singles gold and a bronze in the doubles, while Astor won a gold in the doubles and a bronze in the singles. Later he became an MP, and in 1956, he was made Baron Astor of Hever.

Roller Hockey

This was demonstrated for the first time at Barcelona in 1992.

Rome 1960
XVII Olympic Games (25 August–11 September)

Attended by representatives of 83 countries, comprising 5346 competitors, of which 610 were women.

After withdrawing as hosts of the 1908 Games, they finally returned to Rome. Home city of the Emperor Theodosius, who reputedly had ended the Ancient Games 1567 years before. A number of old Roman sites were utilized as well as a brand-new 90 000 capacity stadium. The Baths of Caracalla housed the gymnastics and the Basilica di Massenzio had the wrestling competitions. The marathon began at the Capitol Hill and finished on Appian Way, near the Arch of Constantine. It was the first time that an Olympic marathon had not started or finished in the main Olympic stadium. Yachting was held in the bay of Naples under the shadow of Mt Vesuvius. The Games were opened by the President of Italy, Giovanni Gronchi, before 90 000 spectators. The oath was taken by the 1948 discus champion Adolfo Consolini. Barbados (as part of the Antilles team), Morocco, Sudan, San Marino and Tunisia made their debuts. Nationalist China protested, but competed, when they were told by the IOC to appear under the name of Taiwan and not China. These Games were the first to have worldwide television coverage.

The extreme heat undoubtedly caused upsets but did nothing to hinder the successes of the Australasians in the middle distance running events. Peter Snell (NZL) won the 800m, Herb Elliott (AUS) won the 1500m by a record margin of 2.8sec in world-record time, and Murray Halberg (NZL), handi-capped by a withered arm, won the 5000m. An unknown runner, Abebe Bikila, won the marathon barefoot and signalled the entry of Ethiopia on to the world distance running scene. The team from Taiwan was cheered up somewhat when their decathlete Chuan-Kwang Yang had a tremendous battle with Rafer Johnson (USA), his team-mate at the University of Southern California, and only lost the gold medal narrowly. The stadium was captivated by sprinter Wilma Rudolph (USA) who won three gold medals. She was one of 19 children and had suffered from polio as a child. Sisters Irina and Tamara Press (URS) won the 80m hurdles and shot respectively, while their countrywoman, Ludmila Shevtsova, won the first 800m event for women since 1928.

In the swimming pool only one of the 15 events not won by either Australia or the United States went to Anita Lonsbrough (GBR). The outstanding swimmer was America's Christine von Saltza, a descendant of Prussian/Swedish nobility, with three golds and a sil-ver. The standard was very high with Olympic records broken in every event. An unfortunate incident occurred in the men's 100m freestyle when Lance Larson (USA) was timed at 0.1sec faster than John Devitt (AUS) but was placed second to him despite slow-motion film indicating that the American was first. In future Games, full electronic timing was used. Only the second Royal gold medal in Olympic history was won by Crown Prince Constantine (later King Constantine II of Greece) in the Dragon class yacht-ing. It is reported that he received the traditional win-ner's ducking, being pushed into the water by his mother, Queen Frederika. In the Flying Dutchman class Peder Lunde Jr (NOR) became the third genera-tion of his family to win a medal, equalling his grand-father's gold of 1924, but going one better than his mother and father in 1952. Paul Elvstrøm (DEN) won his fourth consecutive individual gold medal in dinghy sailing, the first sportsman from any sport to achieve this distinction. The canoeing, on Lake

Albano, had a particularly distinguished spectator, as the Pope apparently watched some of the competitions from his summer palace. In boxing the light-welterweight silver medallist, Clement 'Ike' Quartey (GHA) was the first black African to win an Olympic medal.

The most medals won in Rome were the seven (four gold, two silver, one bronze) gained by gymnast Boris Shakhlin (URS). Aladár Gerevich (HUN) at 50 years and 178 days the oldest champion in Rome, won his sixth team sabre gold medal in as many Games, a feat

1960 MEDALS (SUMMER)

	G	S	B
Soviet Union	43	29	31
United States	34	21	16
Italy	13	10	13
Germany	12	19	11
Australia	8	8	6
Turkey	7	2	–
Hungary	6	8	7
Japan	4	7	7
Poland	4	6	11
Czechoslovakia	3	2	3
Romania	3	1	6
Great Britain	2	6	12
Denmark	2	3	1
New Zealand	2	–	1
Bulgaria	1	3	3
Sweden	1	2	3
Finland	1	1	3
Austria	1	1	–
Yugoslavia	1	1	–
Pakistan	1	–	1
Ethiopia	1	–	–
Greece	1	–	–
Norway	1	–	–
Switzerland	–	3	3
France	–	2	3
Belgium	–	2	2
Iran	–	1	3
The Netherlands	–	1	2
South Africa	–	1	2
Argentina	–	1	1
Egypt (UAR)	–	1	1
Canada	–	1	–
Ghana	–	1	–
India	–	1	–
Morocco	–	1	–
Portugal	–	1	–
Singapore	–	1	–
Chinese Taipei	–	1	–
Brazil	–	–	2
Jamaica [1]	–	–	2
Barbados [1]	–	–	1
Iraq	–	–	1
Mexico	–	–	1
Spain	–	–	1
Venezuela	–	–	1

[1] Double counted as part of the Antilles team

unsurpassed by any other Olympic competitor. In the foil and épée events Edoardo Mangiarotti (ITA) brought his total of fencing medals to a record 13 (six gold, five silver, two bronze) in five Games, 1936–60. The light-heavyweight boxing title went to Cassius Clay (USA), who as Muhammad Ali amassed the greatest amount ever earned by a sportsman, $68 million, when he turned professional after the Games. In football, Yugoslavia won the gold medal after three consecutive runner-up placings. The first loss by India in Olympic hockey since they entered the competition in 1928 occurred when Pakistan beat them 1–0 in the final.

The youngest gold medallist was Klaus Zerta, cox of the German coxed pairs, aged 13 years and 283 days, and the youngest female champion was swimmer Carolyn Wood (USA) in the freestyle relay, aged 14 years and 260 days. The oldest female winner was discus champion Nina Ponomaryeva (URS) at 31 years and 131 days. She had achieved further fame, or notoriety, in 1956 when it was alleged that she stole hats from an Oxford Street store, while on a trip to London for an international match, which was thereby cancelled. The oldest medallist was yachtsman Manfred Metzger (SUI) at 55 years and 104 days, while the oldest female medallist was Italian fencer Welleda Cesari at 40 years and 201 days.

A tragic note was struck by the collapse and death of cyclist Knut Jensen (DEN), originally diagnosed as due to the excessive heat, but later revealed as a drug overdose. At the end of the Games a then record 44 countries had shared in the medals.

Roque

A variation of croquet, played on a hard-surfaced court. Only a medal sport at St Louis in 1904 with all competitors from the United States. The gold medallist, Charles Jacobus, was aged 45 years and 41 days.

Rowing

Rowing for men was first held in the 1900 Games over a 1750m course on the river Seine in Paris. In 1904 the course measured 3219m (2 miles), in 1908 it was 2414m (1.5 miles) and in 1948 1883m (1 mile 300 yards). Women's rowing was introduced in 1976 over a 1000m course, but since 1988 both men and women race over a standard 2000m (1.24 miles) course. Even though in recent Games rowing has been held on still water, as opposed to flowing rivers as in the past, water and weather conditions vary too much to allow official Olympic records. However, it is worthy of note that the fastest average speed achieved by a men's eights over the full course was 21.85km/h (13.57mph) when the Canadian crew clocked 5min 29.53sec in 1992. In a 1992 heat the Romanian crew averaged 22.77km/h (14.14mph) for the first 500m. The 1992 Canadian women's eights won the final in 6min 02.62sec, averaging 19.85km/h (12.33mph). The

1988 GDR women's crew averaged 20.65 km/h (12.83mph) for the first 500m in a repêchage. The narrowest winning margin in an Olympic final was 0.1sec in the 1924 pairs, although the 1932 coxed fours may actually have been closer. Since automatic timing was introduced the smallest margin has been 0.14sec in the 1992 men's eights.

One of the first winning crews in the Games, the 1900 German fours, contained three brothers, Oskar, Gustav and Carl Gossler, the latter as coxswain. This was the beginning of a tradition of sibling participation and success which reached a landmark at Moscow in 1980 when the Landvoigt twins (GDR) beat the Pimenov twins (URS) in the coxless pairs final, causing problems at the medal ceremony. Similarly, in the 1992 coxed pairs, Jonathan and Greg Searle of Great Britain beat the Italian defending champions, Carmine and Giuseppe Abbagnale. When the latter pair won in 1988, their younger brother Agostino also won a gold in the quadruple sculls event. Fathers and sons have had great success in the sport, but usually independently of each other. The most famous are: the Beresfords (GBR), Julius with a silver in 1912, and Jack with five medals in the next five Games; the Costellos (USA), Paul winning three golds in the 1920s and son, Bernard, a silver in 1956; the Kellys (USA), John Sr winning three gold medals and John Jr a bronze in 1956; the Nickalls (GBR) with Guy Sr winning a gold in the 1908 eights and Guy Jr gaining two silvers in the 1920 and 1928 crews. However, the Burnells (GBR), Charles (1908) and Richard (1948), are the only father and son in Olympic rowing to both win gold medals.

Steve Redgrave (GBR) won a record four successive gold medals 1984–96. Jack Beresford (GBR) won three gold medals and two silvers for a record five medals 1920–36, and also a record of medals at five Games. Vyacheslav Ivanov (URS) and Pertti Karppinen (FIN) are the only men to win three individual golds. Ivanov

ROWING MEDALS

	Men			Women			
	G	S	B	G	S	B	Total
United States	28	21	17	1	7	2	76
GDR	20	4	7	13	3	1	48
Soviet Union	11	14	6	1	6	5	43
Germany	16	11	9	3	1	2	42
Great Britain	19	15	7	–	–	–	41
Italy	13	11	9	–	–	–	33
Canada	4	8	9	4	4	3	32
France	4	14	11	–	–	1	30
Romania	2	4	2	10	6	5	29
Switzerland	6	7	9	–	–	–	22
Australia	6	5	6	1	–	2	20
The Netherlands	5	5	6	–	1	2	19
Denmark	4	3	6	–	–	2	15
FRG	4	4	4	–	–	2	14
Norway	1	5	6	–	–	–	12
Czechoslovakia	2	2	7	–	–	–	11
New Zealand	3	2	5	–	–	1	11
Poland	–	1	9	–	1	–	11
Bulgaria	–	–	1	2	3	4	10
Belgium	–	6	1	–	1	1	9
Finland	3	–	3	–	–	–	6
Austria	–	3	2	–	–	–	5
Yugoslavia	1	1	3	–	–	–	5
Greece	1	2	1	–	–	–	4
Argentina	1	1	2	–	–	–	4
China	–	–	–	–	2	2	4
Uruguay	–	1	3	–	–	–	4
Hungary	–	1	2	–	–	–	3
Belarus	–	–	–	1	–	1	2
Slovenia	–	–	2	–	–	–	2
Russia	–	–	2	–	–	–	2
Sweden	–	2	–	–	–	–	2
Spain	–	1	–	–	–	–	1
Ukraine	–	–	–	–	1	–	1
	154	154	157	36	36	36	573

had an unfortunate experience after his first title win in Melbourne. He excitedly threw his medal into the air and lost it in the waters of Lake Wendouree. It was never recovered and later the IOC gave him a replacement. John Kelly (USA) won gold medals in both the single and double sculls in 1920 within an hour.

The oldest gold medallist was Róbert Zimonyi who coxed the United States eights in 1964, aged 46 years and 180 days. In 1948 he had won a bronze coxing a pair from his native Hungary. The oldest oarsman to win a gold medal was Guy Nickalls (GBR) in the 1908 eights, aged 41 years and 261 days. His compatriot Julius Beresford won his silver medal, aged 44 years and 20 days. The youngest gold medal oarsman was Giliante D'Este (ITA) in 1928, aged 18 years and 141days, while the youngest medallist oarsman was Australian Walter Howell in 1956 at 16 years and 346 days. The youngest gold medallist was the unknown French boy who coxed the winning Dutch pair in 1900. Believed to have been under 10 years of age, he was recruited at the last moment out of the spectators to replace Hermanus Brockmann, their cox in the heats, who was considered to be too heavy. Incidentally, Brockmann coxed the Dutch fours to a silver medal and the eights to a bronze. Of the many other young winning coxes over the years, the youngest known for certain was another French boy, Noël Vandernotte, in the 1936 pairs and fours, aged 12 years and 232 days. The latter crew included his father and uncle.

In women's rowing, the youngest gold medal oarswoman was Andrea Kurth (GDR) in 1976, aged 18 years and 298 days, while the youngest medallist was Rodica Puscatu (ROM) at 18 years and 83 days in 1980. The youngest female coxswain of a winning crew was Sabine Hess (GDR) in the 1976 coxed fours, aged 17 years and 297 days, and Lynn Silliman was 17 years and 92 days old when she coxed the USA eights to a bronze in 1976. The oldest female gold medallist oarswoman was Marioara Popescu (ROM) in 1996, aged 33 years and 262 days, and the oldest to win a medal was Valentina Skrabatun (BLR) in 1996 when five days past her 38th birthday.

The US oarsman, Conn Findlay, winner of two golds and a bronze in coxed pairs 1956–64, also won a yachting bronze medal in 1976 in the Tempest class. In 1996 several changes to the programme included the deletion of men's coxed pairs and fours, and women's coxless fours. New events include men's and women's lightweight double sculls and men's lightweight coxless fours.

Royalty

In 1896 two princes of the Greek royal house escorted the marathon winner into the stadium at Athens. Since then a number of members of the royal families in Europe have actually competed, now and again with great success, in the Olympic Games. The first winner of a gold medal was Crown Prince Olav of Norway, later King Olav V, who was a member of the winning crew of the 6m yachting class in 1928. His son, Crown Prince Harald, later King Harald V, competed in the same sport from 1964–72, gaining his best placing of eighth in the 5.5m class in 1964. The only other royal winner was the then Prince Constantine of Greece, later King Constantine II, who won gold in the Dragon class in 1960. His brother-in-law, Juan Carlos of Spain, was in the 1972 yachting, while his niece, Princess Christina competed in the 1988 Tornado class, and his nephew, Prince Felipe, placed sixth in the Soling class of 1992.

Great Britain's Princess Anne finished 24th in the three-day equestrian event in 1976. Her husband-to-be, Captain Mark Phillips had been a member of the gold medal winning three-day team in 1972. In the Winter Games, Prince Albert of Monaco has competed in the 2-man and 4-man bob events between 1988 and 1998.

Rugby Union

A medal sport on four occasions: at Paris in 1900, London in 1908, Antwerp in 1920 and Paris again in 1924. Only six countries competed in the four tournaments held — Australia, France, Germany, Great Britain, Romania and the United States. The 1908 title was won by Australia while the Wallabies were on their first tour of Great Britain. In the final they beat Cornwall, the English County champions. Five American players won two gold medals in 1920 and 1924: Charles Doe, John O'Neil, Colby Slater, John Patrick and Rudolph Scholz. Additionally, Daniel Carroll became the only Olympian to win gold medals for different countries when he won his second gold with the 1920 USA team, having been on the 1908 Australian squad when only 16 years and 245 days. Thus he is the youngest ever rugby international, although 'purists' have never considered the Olympic matches to be 'full' internationals. The highest score was when France beat Romania 61–3 in 1924. In 1920 sprint relay gold medallist Morris Kirksey, also runner-up in the 100m, won another gold in the winning US rugby team. It always comes as a shock to enthusiasts to realise that the United States are the reigning Olympic rugby champions. Before their Paris victory, they had played in Great Britain and were beaten by the Harlequins and Blackheath club teams.

Salt Lake City 2002
XIX Winter Games (9–24 February)

There were nine original applicants. After four previous bids, the first being in 1966 for the 1972 Games, Salt Lake City was finally chosen by the IOC in June 1995. At the end of 1998 there was a scandal about several IOC members having taken bribes relating to the selection of various Games venues. Salt Lake City was one of the places involved, and a number of local and international officials resigned. With the addition of ten extra events there will be a record total of 78 events contested.

Sapporo 1972
XI Winter Games (3–13 February)

Attended by representatives of 35 countries, comprising 1006 competitors, of which 206 were women.

The Games finally came to Sapporo 32 years after they were first awarded to the city but cancelled due to World War II. It was the most populous city, with one million inhabitants, ever to host the Winter Games. Some $555 million was spent on facilities over a five-year period, not least for the enormous number of media personnel who outnumbered competitors by two to one. Arguments between the IOC and sponsored skiers, which had caused problems in 1968, came to a head and resulted in Austria's star skier, Karl Schranz, being expelled. Although there was a list of 40 competitors apparently under threat of suspension, only he was banned. This led to an initial threat of withdrawal by the Austrian team, but at Schranz's urging this was averted. Another aspect of the amateur/professional debate was highlighted by Canada's refusal to compete at ice hockey due to the state-sponsored players from the Eastern bloc. Their call for 'open' Olympic ice hockey was ignored.

The Games were formally opened by Emperor Hirohito. The flame was delivered by Hideki Takada, a speed skater, and Keichi Suzuki also a speed skater, took the oath. Teams from Taiwan and the Philippines competed for the first time. First ever Winter gold medals were won by Poland (ski jumping), Spain (slalom) and Japan (ski jumping). In the latter event, on the 70m hill, Japan had a grand slam of all three medals. To win his title, Spanish skier Francisco Fernandez-Ochoa beat the Italian cousins Gustav and Roland Thöni. The women's slalom was won by Barbara Cochran (USA) by the smallest margin ever (0.02sec), in an Olympic Alpine event. Her sister, Marilyn, and brother, Bob, were also in the USA team.

Galina Kulakova (URS) won three gold medals in Nordic skiing, and this total was matched in the speed skating by Ard Schenk (NED). The Dutchman might have had more but he fell in the 500m event and finished 34th out of 37 competitors. East Germany (GDR) returned to total domination of the luge competitions. The women's event was won by Anna-Maria Müller, one of the three women who had been disqualified for heating their runners at the previous Games. Austria's Trixi Schuba took the women's figure skating title despite a comparatively poor (seventh placed) free skating segment. Her compulsory figures were excellent and at the time the two segments scored on a 50–50 basis. Soon after the Games this method was changed in favour of free skating ability. Irina Rodnina and Alexei Ulanov (URS) won the pairs, it was Ulanov's 'affaire de coeur' with Ludmila Smirnova, a silver medallist with Andrei Suraikin, that titillated the skating world. Later they married and competed internationally as partners, but never with the success they had attained with their original partners.

The oldest gold medallist was Jean Wicki (SUI) in the 4-man bob, aged 38 years and 239 days. The youngest was Anne Henning (USA) who won the 500m speed skating title, aged 16 years and 157 days. The oldest female winner was Christina Baas-Kaiser (NED) with her 3000m speed skating victory at 33 years and 268 days, and the youngest male champion was Wojciech Fortuna (POL) who won the small hill (90m) ski jump, aged 19 years and 189 days. The youngest medallist was skater Manuela Gross (GDR), bronze in the pairs, aged 15 years and 10 days. In all, medals were won by a record 17 countries, with 14 of them gaining gold.

1972 MEDALS (WINTER)

	G	S	B
Soviet Union	8	5	3
GDR	4	3	7
Switzerland	4	3	3
The Netherlands	4	3	2
United States	3	2	3
FRG	3	1	1
Norway	2	5	5
Italy	2	2	1
Austria	1	2	2
Sweden	1	1	2
Japan	1	1	1
Czechoslovakia	1	–	2
Poland	1	–	–
Spain	1	–	–
Finland	–	4	1
France	–	1	2
Canada	–	1	–

Sarajevo 1984
XIV Winter Games (8–19 February)

Attended by representatives of 49 countries, comprising 1274 competitors, of which 274 were women.

The first Winter Games held in Eastern Europe was awarded to Sarajevo in 1978. With a population of 500 000 it was the second largest city to host the Winter Games, and was previously only famous as the site of the assassination of Archduke Ferdinand on 28 June 1914, an act which historians argue contributed to the start of World War I. There were a record 49 countries attending, including debuts by the British Virgin Islands, Egypt, Costa Rica, Puerto Rico and Senegal. The Games were opened by Mika Spiljak, the President of the Presidency of the Socialist Federal Republic of Yugoslavia. The flame was lit by Sandra Dubravcic after running up 94 steps in the Kosovo stadium. She later placed 10th in the women's figure skating. The oath was taken by skier Bojan Krizaj, later seventh in the slalom. Preliminary rounds of the ice hockey tournament started the day before the opening ceremony. Prior to the Games much had been made of the wolf mascot, Vucko, being depicted with its claws crossed — as though hoping for the best.

In fact, although the weather caused various problems, the enthusiasm of the organisers and the local populace overcame most difficulties. Even the transport system worked. One of the few things that did cause hackles to rise was outside the control of the host city. This was the highly questionable, or at the least confusing, judging of the figure skating — a problem not unique to Sarajevo in recent years. One 'cause celebre' just prior to the Games was the banning of the two defending champions in the men's and women's slalom races, Ingemar Stenmark (SWE) and Hanni Wenzel (LIE) as professionals. There was only one new event in the programme, a 20km Nordic skiing race for women.

For the first time the GDR won more gold medals than the Soviet Union, although not total medals. However, in the men's luge, GDR who had won seven gold, two silver and four bronze medals in the last four Games, only took a single bronze. The outstanding competitor, unusually, was a female Nordic skier, Marja-Liisa Hämäläinen (FIN), who won all three individual events and a bronze in the relay. Great Britain's Jayne Torvill and Christopher Dean gained the most media attention with their superb ice dancing. Their artistic interpretation of Ravel's *Bolero* was awarded an unprecedented nine perfect 6.0, with another three for technical merit. The women's singles winner, Katarina Witt (GDR), was trained by Jutta Müller, who had not only coached her daughter, Gabriele Seyfert, to a silver in 1968, but had also been the driving force behind the 1980 champion, Anett Pötzsch.

Alpine skiers from the United States made a major impact with three titles. Bill Johnson, hardly a retiring personality, proved he was as good as he had been saying he was, to anyone and everyone who would listen, by winning the first Olympic downhill title by an American, in a record average speed of 104.532km/h (64.593mph). His team-mates, twins Phil and Steve Mahre, took the gold and silver medals in the slalom. By winning the women's downhill, Michaela Figini (SUI) became the youngest ever Alpine skiing gold medallist, aged 17 years and 314 days, as well as being the youngest champion at Sarajevo. In Alpine skiing only one skier, Perrine Pelen (FRA), won more than one medal, and few begrudged the silver gained by Jure Franko in the giant slalom, the first Winter Games medal ever by Yugoslavia.

In speed skating Tomas Gustafson (SWE) and Igor Malkov (URS) swapped medals over 5000m and 10 000m, in two of the closest races ever skated in the Games, over such distances. The Swede won the shorter race by 0.02 sec and the Soviet won the longer by 0.05sec. The Soviet ice hockey team equalled Canada's record with its sixth gold medal. Just prior to the Games another ice hockey eligibility controversy had arisen with the decision that an amateur for Olympic purposes was someone who had not played in the National Hockey League in North America. One other bone of contention had been resolved

before competitions began when the revolutionary rocket-shaped Soviet bobs were banned. The 90m ski jump was won by a young Finn, Matti Nykänen, by a record margin of 18.5 points, but he was to make a far greater impression four years later.

The oldest gold medallist at Sarajevo was the Soviet ice hockey goalminder Vladislav Tretyak, in his fourth Games, aged 31 years and 299 days. The youngest was Michaela Figini (SUI). The youngest male champion was speed skater Igor Malkov (URS) just nine days past his 19th birthday, while the oldest female gold medallist was Marja-Liisa Hämäläinen (FIN), aged 28 years and 161 days. The oldest competitor was Carl-Erik Eriksson (SWE) at 53 years and 289 days, competing in his record sixth successive Olympic bobsleigh competition. The youngest was Babette Preussler (GDR) in pair skating, aged 15 years and 143 days. One of the victorious German pair in the luge, Hans Stanggassinger, had another distinction. He was reportedly the heaviest champion, weighing 111kg (244lb).

1984 MEDALS (WINTER)

	G	S	B
GDR	9	9	6
Soviet Union	6	10	9
United States	4	4	–
Finland	4	3	6
Sweden	4	2	2
Norway	3	2	4
Switzerland	2	2	1
Canada	2	1	1
FRG	2	1	1
Italy	2	–	–
Great Britain	1	–	–
Czechoslovakia	–	2	4
France	–	1	2
Japan	–	1	–
Yugoslavia	–	1	–
Liechtenstein	–	–	2
Austria	–	–	1

Seoul 1988
XXIV Olympic Games (17 September–2 October)

Attended by representatives of 159 countries, comprising 8465 competitors of which 2186 were women.

The capital of Korea, Seoul, has one of the largest populations of any city on earth — an estimated 9 000 000. Nearly all facilities for the Games were in situ by the end of 1986 when the Asian Games were held there. Most major installations are part of the sports complex on the banks of the Han River, and include a 90 000-spectator stadium. Once again the programme was expanded, with the reintroduction of tennis for the first time since 1924, the addition of table tennis, and the inclusion of a number of extra events, which brought the total to a record 237. Baseball, tae kwon do and women's judo were demonstration sports. American television companies offered incredible sums (up to $750 million) for the US rights, providing the major sporting finals took place during the American prime time viewing. That would have required that athletics finals be held between 9.00–11.00am Korean time. This was opposed by the International Amateur Athletic Federation, and indeed by the IOC, although some compromise was finally agreed. The income from television sources was still immense, NBC acquiring the American rights alone for $300 million. There were an estimated 16 000 media personnel at these Games.

Prior to the opening ceremony the most tenacious problem was the claim from North Korea to host half the Games. Against IOC rules, but with their blessing, some sports were offered to them, but they continued to be intransigent. They finally refused to attend and attempted to get the Eastern bloc to support them. However, only the hard line Communist countries backed them, and the only other absentees were: Albania, Cuba, Ethiopia, Madagascar, Nicaragua and the Seychelles. There were a number of first-timers including: American Samoa, Aruba, Burkina Faso (which had competed as Upper Volta in 1972), Cook Islands, Guam, Maldives, St Vincent and Grenadines, Vanuatu and the Democratic Republic of Yemen. Also attending was Brunei, but only with an official, so that the officially claimed figure of 160 countries participating is not correct.

The opening ceremony began on the Han River and transferred to the main stadium. The President of Korea, Roh Tae-woo, declared the Games open, and the oath was taken jointly by Huh Jae, a basketball player, and Son Mi-na, a handball player. One unusual feature of the ceremony was that as the Korean alphabet begins with the letter 'G', the traditional first team, Greece, was then followed by Gabon and Ghana. A more entertaining occurrence in the march-past was the inclusion in the Thailand contingent of the reigning Miss Universe, Porntip 'Pui' Nakirunkanot, a beautiful Thai woman which delighted the spectators. Because the original 1920 Olympic flag had been fading away, a new one, made of Korean silk, had been presented to the IOC by the Seoul Organising Committee and was flown for the first time on the 17 September 1988. The torch was carried for part of the distance on the track by 76-year-old Sohn Kee-chung (better known as Kitei Son), the 1936 marathon champion — a Korean who had been forced to run for Japan, the occupying power at the time. He passed it to the final runner, a female athlete, Lim Chun-ae. The torch was raised to the top of the cauldron tower , and the flame was lit by three representatives of Science, Art and Sport (Ching Sun-man , Kim Won-tuk and Sohn Mi-chung). It is feared that some of the pigeons which had been released during part of the ceremony, and

had perched on the cauldron, were caught in the rush of the flame.

The athlete who gained most attention at these Games was undoubtedly the Canadian sprinter, Ben Johnson, initially for the best of reasons and then for the worst. Having looked somewhat out of form in the preliminary rounds of the 100m, he blasted away in the final to destroy a talented field, including arch-rival, Carl Lewis, and recorded an almost unbelievable world record of 9.79sec. Three days later it was revealed that he had failed a drug test and was disqualified, with Lewis moving up to the gold medal with a very respectable 9.92sec. Another nine competitors, from weightlifting (four), modern pentathlon (two), judo, wrestling and shooting were disqualified for drug-related offences. Although African men won everything on the track over 400m, the outstanding athlete at the Games was a woman, Florence Griffith-Joyner (USA), wife of the 1984 triple jump winner, who won three golds and a silver in the sprints and relays, running a total of 11 races. Her sister-in-law, Jackie Joyner-Kersee won the heptathlon, as expected, and the long jump. Continuing the Olympic tradition of successful families, Viktor Bryzgin (4 × 100m) and his wife Olga Bryzgina (400m, 4 × 400m) both won gold medals. In rowing, Carmine and Giuseppe Abbagnale (ITA) retained their coxed pair title from 1984, and a third brother, Agostino, was a member of the winning quadruple sculls crew.

The most successful competitor in Seoul was Kristin Otto (GDR) who not only won six gold medals (a record by any woman, in any sport, at any Games), but also became the first swimmer to win titles at three different strokes at the same Games. America's Matt Biondi, saddled before the Games with an impossible Mark Spitz-like scenario, nevertheless ended the Games with seven medals (five gold, one silver, one bronze). Vladimir Salnikov (URS) became the only swimmer to regain a title eight years after winning it the first time. Greg Louganis (USA) gained the first double 'double' by a male diver when he successfully defended his two titles from Los Angeles, despite hitting his head on the board during a dive in the springboard preliminaries. Also in the pool Anthony Nesty of Surinam became the first black and the first South American to win a swimming gold medal by taking the 100m butterfly. Similarly, Kenny Monday (USA) was the first black American to win a wrestling gold.

A number of 'old-timers' reappeared on the Olympic scene. Fifty-two-year-old Reiner Klimke (FRG) won his sixth dressage gold medal, and his eighth medal in five Games, over a 24 year period. These are all records for his sport. His horse *Ahlerich* also set a record. One of Klimke's compatriots in the winning team was Ann-Kathrin Linsenhoff — remarkably her mother had been his team-mate in the gold medal team of 1968. Great Britain's David Broome returned after three Games out as a 'professional', 28 years after he first competed. The yachting events, held at Pusan, had two of the greatest Olympians of all time. Quadruple gold medallist Paul

Elvstrøm (DEN), partnered by his daughter Trine, was competing in a record-equalling eighth Games, over a 40-year span. This was matched by yachtsman Durward Knowles (BAH), a 1964 gold medallist, also in his eighth celebration over a similar span.

1988 MEDALS (SUMMER)

	G	S	B
Soviet Union	55	31	46
GDR	37	35	30
United States	36	31	27
Korea	12	10	11
FRG	11	14	15
Hungary	11	6	6
Bulgaria	10	12	13
Romania	7	11	6
France	6	4	6
Italy	6	4	4
China	5	11	12
Great Britain	5	10	9
Kenya	5	2	2
Japan	4	3	7
Australia	3	6	5
Yugoslavia	3	4	5
Czechoslovakia	3	3	2
New Zealand	3	2	8
Canada	3	2	5
Poland	2	5	9
Norway	2	3	–
The Netherlands	2	2	5
Denmark	2	1	1
Brazil	1	2	3
Finland	1	1	2
Spain	1	1	2
Turkey	1	1	–
Morocco	1	–	2
Austria	1	–	–
Portugal	1	–	–
Surinam	1	–	–
Sweden	–	4	7
Switzerland	–	2	2
Jamaica	–	2	–
Argentina	–	1	1
Chile	–	1	–
Costa Rica	–	1	–
Indonesia	–	1	–
Iran	–	1	–
Netherlands Antilles	–	1	–
Peru	–	1	–
Senegal	–	1	–
Virgin Islands	–	1	–
Belgium	–	–	2
Mexico	–	–	2
Colombia	–	–	1
Djibouti	–	–	1
Greece	–	–	1
Mongolia	–	–	1
Pakistan	–	–	1
Philippines	–	–	1
Thailand	–	–	1

By winning the silver medal in women's sprint cycling, the GDR's Christa Röthenburger-Luding became the first competitor in Olympic history to win medals at a Summer and Winter celebration in the same year. She had won a speed skating gold and silver at Calgary. Because of a record number of entries in boxing, two rings were used simultaneously. Not surprisingly this caused some confusion. Also, not for the first time, the boxing competitions witnessed some 'bizarre', often home-town, decisions. One of the most scandalous decisions in Olympic boxing history occurred when Roy Jones (USA) was judged to have lost his light-middleweight bout against Park Si-hun of Korea. Pointedly, the Association Internationale de Boxe Amateur (AIBA) awarded Jones the Val Barker Cup as the best stylist at the Games. There were other disputed decisions and some of the judges were suspended. One of the Korean boxers, Byun Jong-il, refused to leave the ring after the decision went against him in his bantamweight bout, and remained there, a solitary figure, for over an hour.

The oldest gold medallist at Seoul was Reiner Klimke, aged 52 years and 255 days. The youngest was swimmer Krisztina Egerszegi (HUN) at 14 years and 41 days. The oldest female champion was hockey player Elspeth Clement (AUS), aged 32 years and 103 days, while the youngest male winner was Soviet cyclist Dmitri Nelyubin, aged 17 years and 229 days. The oldest medallist at Seoul was Romanian cox Ladislau Lovrenski, aged 56 years and 65 days days. The youngest male medallist was Xiong Ni (CHN) with a silver in diving, aged 14 years and 247 days. The oldest competitor was Durward Knowles (BAH) in Star class yachting, aged 70 years and 331 days, while the youngest was swimmer Nadia Cruz of Angola, aged 13 years and 73 days. The oldest female competitor was Inoue Kikuko (JPN) in the dressage, aged 63 years and 297 days.

Thus, despite threats of boycotts, of North Korean terror and student riots, the Games on the whole went very well. The good humour, flexibility and courtesy of the hosts overcame most minor problems. A record 52 countries won medals, and some time after the Games ended it was reported that a record profit of $288 million had been made.

Shooting

Baron de Coubertin, the founder of the modern Olympic Games, was a pistol shot of note in his youth, and this undoubtedly led to the sport being included in the first Games held in 1896. The first champion was Pantelis Karasevdas (GRE) who won the free rifle event over 200m on 9 April 1896. The number of events has varied considerably, especially in the early celebrations of the Games, from 21 in 1920 to only two in 1932. There were none at all in 1928. Since 1952 there has been some standardisation. In 1984 three events for women were introduced, with another added in 1988, and two more for 2000. In 1996 mixed competition in the skeet and trap events was abolished, and at the same time double trap events for men and women were inaugurated. New regulations were introduced in 1988, in accordance with International Shooting Union rules. The leading eight competitors at the end of the designated number of rounds take part in a final shoot-out round with the target subdivided into tenths of a point for rifle and pistol shooting. For trap and skeet each of the leading competitors has 25 extra shots.

The most successful competitor has been Carl Osburn (USA) who won a record 11 medals (five gold, four silver, two bronze) between 1912 and 1924. Six other men have won five gold medals: Konrad Stäheli (SUI) 1900–06; Louis Richardet (SUI) 1900–06; Alfred Lane (USA) 1912–20; Ole Lilloe-Olsen (NOR) 1920–24; Morris Fisher (USA) 1920–24; Willis Lee (USA) all in 1920, a record for the sport. However, the only man to win three individual gold medals at one Games was Gudbrand Skatteboe (NOR) in 1906. Lloyd Spooner (USA) competed in 12 events at the 1920 Games, a record in any sport in Olympic history. Lars Jorgen Madsen (DEN) won gold medals over a record 20-year span, 1900–20. Ragnar Skanåker (SWE) 1972–96, won four medals (one gold, two silver, one bronze) over a 24-year period, in the free pistol event. The most successful female shooter has been Marina Logvinenko-Dobrancheva (URS/EUN/RUS) who won two golds, one silver and two bronzes 1988–96.

Women first competed in men's events, in 1968 when three countries, Mexico, Peru and Poland, entered one each. Eulalia Rolinska (POL) and Gladys de Seminario (PER) were the first to compete, finishing 22nd and 31st respectively in the small-bore rifle, prone event. The first medallist was Margaret Murdock (USA) in the 1976 small-bore rifle, three positions. Initially listed the winner, an error was discovered which placed Murdock equal with her teammate, Lanny Bassham. Then, on the count-back rule, she was placed second, to the embarrassment of Bassham, who pulled her up to the top of the victory rostrum at the medal ceremony. The only woman to win an Olympic mixed shooting event is Zhang Shan (CHN) in the 1992 skeet contest and scored a maximum possible 200 in the preliminary round.

The oldest gold medallist in Olympic history, in any sport, was the remarkable Oscar Swahn (SWE) in the 1912 running deer team, aged 64 years and 258 days (his son, Alfred, was also in the team). At Antwerp in 1920 he became the oldest medallist (72 years and 280 days) and, indeed, the oldest competitor at any sport in the Olympics ever, when he was again a member of the Swedish running deer silver medal team. He qualified for the 1924 Games in his 77th year, but illness prevented him from competing. He died three years later. However, it should be noted that very recent research has discovered that the winner of the 1908 free rifle (1000yd) event, Joshua 'Jerry' Millner (GBR) was some years older than originally thought, and at four days past his 61st birthday was the oldest ever Olympic gold medallist in an individual event. The youngest winner of a shooting gold medal was Konstantin Lukachik of the Unified Team in the 1992 free pistol, aged 16 years and 312 days. The oldest female champion was Linda Thom (CAN), aged 40 years and 212 days when winning the sport pistol in 1984. The youngest woman to win a gold was Kim Rhode (USA) in the Double Trap event in 1996 seven days after her 17th birthday. The youngest medallists were Marcus Dinwiddie (USA), silver in the 1924 small-bore rifle, prone event, and Ulrike Holmer (FRG), silver in the 1984 standard rifle, both at 16 years and 301 days.

John and Sumner Paine (USA) were the first brothers to win gold medals at the Olympic Games, in 1896, while the first twins to do so were Vilhelm and Eric Carlberg (SWE) in 1912. Károly Takács (HUN) was a European pistol champion in the 1930s using his right hand. In 1938, while on army training, a grenade blew up in his hand destroying his right arm. After the war he won the rapid fire pistol event with his left hand at the 1948 and 1952 Games. The 1960 rapid fire pistol champion, William McMillan (USA), competed in his record sixth Games in 1976. Walter Winans (USA), who had won a gold medal in the 1908 running deer event, became the only man to win medals in both sport and artistic events at the same Games in 1912 when he gained a silver in shooting and a gold at sculpture. Winans was born in Russia to Dutch-American parents, and lived most of his life in England — he never set foot in America.

Gerald Ouellette (CAN) won the 1956 small-bore, prone gold medal with a world record maximum possible score of 600, but it was not accepted as such as the range was found to be 1.5m short of the regulation 50m distance. Miroslav Varga (TCH) also scored 600 in the 1988 event. When Li Ho Jun (PRK) won the same event in 1972 with a score of 599 he was asked how he concentrated so well. He answered that he pretended that he was 'aiming at a capitalist'. Francois La Fortune Jr (BEL) competed in a record seven Games, 1952–76 over a 24-year period and his father, Francois Sr, competed over a 36-year span, 1924–60. Philip Neame (GBR) is the only holder of the Victoria Cross to win an Olympic gold medal (1924 running deer, team).

One of the oddest occurrences in Olympic shooting was in the 1976 trap shooting event, when 65-year-old Paul Cerutti of Monaco was disqualified for using drugs, even though he had finished 43rd out of 44 competitors. He is the oldest competitor ever penalised in this way.

SHOOTING MEDALS

	Men [1]			Women			
	G	S	B	G	S	B	Total
United States	42	25	20	3	1	1	92
Soviet Union	18	16	15	4	1	3	57
Sweden	13	23	19	–	–	–	55
Great Britain	13	14	18	–	–	–	45
France	13	16	13	–	–	–	42
Norway	16	9	11	–	–	–	36
Switzerland	11	11	12	–	–	–	34
Italy	8	4	10	–	1	–	23
Greece	5	7	7	–	–	–	19
China	4	4	4	3	1	1	17
Finland	3	5	9	–	–	–	17
Denmark	3	8	5	–	–	–	16
GDR	3	8	5	–	–	–	16
Germany	6	4	3	–	2	–	15
Hungary	6	3	6	–	–	–	15
Romania	5	4	4	–	–	–	13
Bulgaria	1	2	3	–	4	2	12
FRG	3	2	3	1	2	–	11
Poland	2	2	3	1	1	2	11
Canada	3	3	2	1	–	–	9
Czechoslovakia	4	3	2	–	–	–	9
Belgium	2	3	3	–	–	–	8
Yugoslavia	1	–	1	2	1	3	8
Russia	2	1	1	1	1	1	7
Austria	1	2	4	–	–	–	7
Japan	1	1	3	–	1	–	6
Australia	2	–	1	–	–	2	5
Brazil	1	1	1	–	–	–	3
Korea	1	1	–	1	–	–	3
Peru	1	2	–	–	–	–	3
Kazakhstan	–	2	1	–	–	–	3
Colombia	–	2	–	–	–	–	2
The Netherlands	–	1	1	–	–	–	2
Spain	–	1	1	–	–	–	2
North Korea (PRK)	1	–	–	–	–	–	1
Argentina	–	1	–	–	–	–	1
Belarus	–	1	–	–	–	–	1
Chile	–	1	–	–	–	–	1
Latvia	–	1	–	–	–	–	1
Mexico	–	1	–	–	–	–	1
Portugal	–	1	–	–	–	–	1
South Africa	–	1	–	–	–	–	1
Cuba	–	–	1	–	–	–	1
Czech Republic	–	–	1	–	–	–	1
Haiti	–	–	1	–	–	–	1
New Zealand	–	–	1	–	–	–	1
Mongolia	–	–	–	–	–	1	1
Slovenia	–	–	1	–	–	–	1
Venezuela	–	–	1	–	–	–	1
	195	197	197	17 [2]	16	16	638

[1] Including female medallists prior to 1984
[2] Including female winner of 1992 open skeet competition

Short-Track Speed Skating

In 1988 short-track speed skating was a demonstration sport, and in 1992 it became a medal sport with two events each for men and women. In 1994 an extra two events were added. So far the only person to gain a medal in both styles of speed skating is Eric Flaim (USA) with silvers in the 1988 1500m and the 1994 short-track relay. The most successful competitor has been Chun Lee-kyung (KOR) with a record four gold medals and a bronze, 1994–98, while the best by a man has been by Kim Ki-hoon (KOR) with three golds 1992–4. The youngest ever winner of a Winter Games gold medal was Kim Yoon-mi (KOR) in the 1998 women's relay, aged 13 years and 83 days. She was also the youngest ever female Olympic winner in either Winter or Summer Games. The oldest champion in short-track was Cathy Turner (USA) who won the 1994 500m title, aged 31 years and 320 days. The youngest male gold medallist was Jae Kun Song (KOR), aged 18 years and 7 days in the 1992 relay, only one day younger than countryman Kim Dong-sung who won the 1000m individual event in 1998. The oldest was Jae's team-mate, Ji Soo Mo, aged 30 years and 264 days. It is noteworthy that the average age of the winning Korean women's relay team in 1994 was about 15¾ years. In 2002 there will be two extra events at 1500m for both men and women.

OLYMPIC RECORDS

Men

500m	43.45sec	Chae Ji-hoon (Kor)	1994
1000m	1min 30.76sec	Kim Ki-hoon (Kor)	1992
5000m relay	7min 11.74sec	Italy	1994

Women

500m	45.98sec	Cathy Turner (USA)	1994
1000m	1min 36.87sec	Chun Lee-kyung (Kor)	1994
3000m relay	4min 26.64sec	Korea	1994

Sisters

The first sisters to take part in Olympic competition were Marion and Georgina Jones (USA) in the 1900 tennis events. Marion finished third in the singles, and was fourth in the mixed doubles. Georgina was eliminated in the first round of both contests. The most successful sisters in Olympic competition have been Irina and Tamara Press (URS) in athletics. Irina won the 80m hurdles title in 1960 and the pentathlon in 1964. Tamara won the shot in 1960 and 1964, the discus silver in 1960 and the discus gold in 1964. However, there have been questions asked since they disappeared from competition when sex tests were introduced in 1966. (*See also* Twins).

Skiing

See separate entries for *Alpine Skiing*, *Freestyle Skiing*, and *Nordic Skiing*.

Ski-Jumping

First contested in 1924 with one hill. In 1964 two hills (70m and 90m) were introduced, which were changed to 90m and 120m in 1992. The controversial 'V' style was introduced by Jan Boklöv (SWE) in 1988, and was initially frowned on, and penalised, by the judges. However, by 1994 virtually all the competitors were using it. The most successful jumper has been Matti Nykänen (FIN) with four golds and one silver medal in 1984 and 1988, including three golds in one Games. However, his successes include the team competition, introduced in 1988. Prior to him, the most successful had been Birger Ruud (NOR) with two golds and a silver medal between 1932 and 1948. He also came fourth in the Alpine combination event of 1936, winning the downhill segment. His brother, Sigmund, won a silver in 1928, while a third brother, Asbjørn, was seventh in 1948. In 1994 Jens Weissflog (GER) became only the

SHORT-TRACK SPEED SKATING MEDALS

	Men			Women			
	G	S	B	G	S	B	Total
Korea	5	2	1	4	–	3	15
Canada	1	2	2	2	2	1	10
China	–	2	1	–	3	–	8
United States	–	1	–	2	1	2	6
Japan	1	–	2	–	–	–	3
Italy	1	1	–	–	–	–	2
Australia	–	–	1	–	–	–	1
Great Britain	–	–	1	–	–	–	1
North Korea (PRK)	–	–	–	–	–	1	1
Soviet Union	–	–	–	–	–	1	1
	8	8	8	8	8	8	48

third man to win at two Games, in his case, with a ten-year gap, having competed in four Games.

The longest jump achieved in Olympic competition was 137m (449ft) by both Takanobu Okabe and Masahiko 'Happy' Harada, of the winning Japanese team, on the 120m hill at Nagano in 1998. The longest jump ever on the 90m hill was 118.5m (388ft) by Matti Nykänen (FIN) in 1988. The oldest gold medallist was Masahiko Harada in 1998, aged 29 years and 284 days, while the youngest gold medallist was Toni Nieminen (FIN) in the 1992 team event, aged 16 years and 259 days, the youngest ever Winter Games winner. The oldest was Birger Ruud in 1948, aged 36 years and 168 days. Sepp Bradl (AUT), the first man ever to jump over 100m (328ft), competed over a period of 20 years, 1936–56, but never won a medal.

SKI-JUMPING MEDALS

	G	S	B	Total
Norway	8	9	7	24
Finland	10	5	3	18
Austria	3	6	8	17
Japan	3	4	2	9
GDR	2	3	2	7
Czechoslovakia	1	2	4	7
Germany	3	1	2	6
Sweden	–	1	1	2
Yugoslavia	–	1	1	2
Poland	1	–	–	1
Soviet Union	1	–	–	1
Switzerland	–	1	–	1
United States	–	–	1	1
	32	33 [1]	31	96

[1] Tie for silver in 1980 70m event

Smallest

The smallest ever Olympic champion is gymnast Lu Li (CHN) who won the gold medal in the asymmetrical bars event at Barcelona in 1992. She stood only 1.36m (4ft 5½in) tall and weighed 36kg (79lb). The 1920 springboard diving champion, Aileen Riggin (USA), weighed less 31.5kg (70lb) but was taller. Perhaps the smallest ever competitor in the Games was the North Korean gymnast Choe Myong-hui, at Moscow in 1980. She was only 1.35m (4ft 5in) tall and weighed a mere 25kg (55lb).

Snowboarding

This sport evolved in the middle 1960s, and made its debut at the Olympic Games in 1998. There are two events, the giant slalom, and the halfpipe, which is a freestyle discipline down a 120m U-shaped course, of which a series of leaps, twists, rotations and flips are performed. The first winner of an Olympic title, the men's giant slalom was Ross Rebagliati of Canada, initially disqualified after testing positive for marijuana allegedly a much-used substance by the sport's devotees. On appeal he was reinstated.

The youngest gold medallist was Karine Ruby (FRA) who won the women's giant slalom, aged 20 years and 43 days. The youngest male champion was Gian Simmen (SUI) in the halfpipe, aged 20 years and 358 days. The oldest gold medallist was Rebagliati at 26 years and 210 days, while the oldest female winner was Nicola Thost (GER) in the halfpipe, aged 20 years and 285 days. The youngest medallist was Ross Powers (USA) who won the halfpipe bronze two days after his 19th birthday, and the oldest medallist was Brigitte Koeck (AUT) with a bronze in the giant slalom, aged 27 years and 274 days. The oldest male medallist was Thomas Prugger (ITA) with a silver in the giant slalom in 1998, aged 27 years and 109 days.

SNOWBOARDING MEDALS

	Men			Women			
	G	S	B	G	S	B	Total
Germany	–	–	–	1	1	–	2
Switzerland	1	–	1	–	–	–	2
Norway	–	1	–	–	1	–	2
United States	–	–	1	–	–	1	2
Canada	1	–	–	–	–	–	1
France	–	–	–	1	–	–	1
Italy	–	1	–	–	–	–	1
Austria	–	–	–	–	–	1	1
	2	2	2	2	2	2	12

Soccer (Football)

Some sources refer to two exhibition matches at Athens in the first Games of 1896, where two Greek towns had played an eliminator match. The winner, Smyrna, was then defeated by a Danish side 15–0. However, the Swedish Olympic expert Ture Widlund, after considerable research, considers these reports to be spurious. Although sometimes considered unofficial, the tournaments of 1900, 1904 and 1906 are usually counted in medal tables. Therefore soccer was the first team game to be included in the Olympics. The first goal was scored by Great Britain (represented by Upton Park Football Club) versus France (4–0) in 1900. The 1904 tournament only had three entries, one Canadian and two American teams, while in 1906 a Danish team beat Greece (represented by Smyrna). In that latter team were five Britons named Whittal, of which three were one set of brothers and the other two another set, the two lots being cousins. This must be some sort of Olympic record for siblings, and a family.

With the founding of Fédération Internationale Football Association (FIFA) in 1904, Olympic soccer came under their control, and from 1908 the competition grew in stature. In 1920, Egypt, the first non-European country (except the North Americans of 1904) entered, and by 1924 there were 22 countries competing. The tournaments were won by Uruguay who surprisingly never took part in Olympic soccer again. Two years after their Amsterdam victory, Uruguay won the inaugural World Cup of 1930 with nine of their Olympic team playing. Only three other players, all Italian, have been in both Olympic (1936) and World Cup (1938) winning sides.

There was considerable disillusionment with the interpretation of the term 'amateur' as applied to soccer at the Games, similar to the troubles in ice hockey.

These arguments about pseudo-amateurs were exacerbated with the entry of the Eastern European powers into the game after 1948. Great Britain, after three gold medals in the early days, did not enter in 1924 and 1928 due to disagreements between the Football Association (FA) and FIFA about broken time payments to amateurs re-entered Olympic competition in 1936, but after a series of poor results, Great Britain has not taken part since 1972. In 1952, as entries increased, qualifying rounds were introduced to decide on final 16 teams. In 1984 professionals were allowed to take part, but only those who had not yet participated in World Cup competition were eligible. Out of the 26 players, 23 must be under the age of 23 years.

The highest team score in Olympic soccer was the 17–1 defeat of France by Denmark in 1908, during which the Danish centre-forward Sophus Nielsen scored a record 10 goals. This mark was equalled by Gottfried Fuchs for Germany when they beat Russia 16–0 in 1912. The most goals scored by an individual in one tournament is 12 by Ferenc Bene (HUN) in 1964. The most scored in Olympic competition is 13 by Sophus Nielsen (DEN) 1908–12, and by Antal Dunai (HUN) 1968–72. The highest score in a final since the institution of 'proper' tournaments in 1908 has been the 4–2 defeat of Denmark by Great Britain in 1912. France's victory in 1984 was the first win by a Western European side since the outstanding Swedish team of 1948, and the first medal since the Swedish bronze of four years later. The 1968 final ended with only 18 players on the field, as three Bulgarians and a Hungarian had been sent off.

There has only been one draw in an Olympic final. That was in 1928 between Uruguay and Argentina (1–1), and the replay was won by the defending champions Uruguay, 2–1. Hungary and Great Britain are the only countries to win on three occasions. Hungary won in Helsinki in 1952 was virtually the same team

HIGHEST SCORING INDIVIDUALS IN OLYMPIC TOURNAMENTS

1908	10	Sophus Nielsen (DEN)
1912	10	Gottfried Fuchs (GER)
1920	7	Herbert Karlsson (SWE)
1924	8	Pedro Petrone (URU)
1928	11	Domingo Tarasconi (ARG)
1936	7	Annibale Frossi (ITA)
1948	7	Gunnar Nordahl (SWE) and Karl Aage Hansen (DEN)
1952	7	Branko Zebec (YUG) and Rajko Mitic (YUG)
1956	4	Dimiter Milanov (BUL) and Neville d'Souza (IND)
1960	7	Milan Galic (YUG) and Borivoje Kostic (YUG)
1964	12	Ferenc Bene (HUN)
1968	7	Kunishige Kamamoto (JPN)
1972	9	Kazimiercz Deyna (POL)
1976	6	Andrzej Szarmach (POL)
1980	5	Sergei Andreyev (URS)
1984	5	Borislav Cvetkovic (YUG), Stjepan Deveric (YUG) and Daniel Xuereb (FRA)
1988	7	Romario Farias (BRA)
1992	7	Andrzej Juskowiak (POL)
1996	6	Hernan Crespo (ARG) and Bebeto (BRA)

that 16 months later inflicted the first home defeat on England's professionals at Wembley stadium. The most successful player has been Dezsö Nowák (HUN) who added gold medals in 1964 and 1968 to the bronze he won in 1960. Of the ten other players to win two gold medals only Arthur Berry and Vivian Woodward (both GBR) were not Uruguayans. Two of those latter, Antonio and Santos Urdinaran, became the first brothers to win soccer gold medals in 1924. This feat was surpassed by the Nordahl brothers of Sweden, Bertil, Knut and Gunnar, in 1948. In 1908 two Danish brothers had gained silver medals in a team which included mathematician Harald Bohr, the brother of the famous nuclear physicist, Niels.

The oldest gold medallist was Rostislav Václavícek (TCH), aged 33 years and 239 days in the 1980 final. The youngest was Celestine Babayaro (NGR) in the 1996 winning team, aged 17 years and 340 days. The youngest medallist was Osei Kuffour (GHA) in 1992 at 15 years and 339 days, and the oldest Fyodor Cherenkov (URS), aged 41 years and 92 days in 1980.

A women's competition was instituted in 1996, which proved popular with both media and fans. There were 76 481 spectators for the final when the USA beat China 2–1, reportedly one of the largest crowd to watch any women-only sporting event. The greatest aggregate was when China beat Denmark 5–1, with China's score the highest achieved. The greatest winning margin was that match plus when Norway beat Japan 4–0. Linda Medalen (NOR), Pretinha (BRA) and Ann Kristin Aarønes (NOR) all scored a record four goals. The youngest gold medallist/medallist was Cindy Parlow (USA), aged 18 years and 85 days. The oldest gold medallist was her team-mate Carin Gabarra who was 31 years and 205 days, and the oldest medallist was Heidi Støre (NOR) with a bronze, aged 33 years and 28 days. Twins Anne and Nina Andersen of Norway, won bronze medals in 1996.

One of the most remarkable goals in Olympic football involved the Swedish centre-forward Gunnar Nordahl in the 1948 semi-final against Denmark. Unexpectedly caught offside by a quick reversal of play, Nordahl realised that his team were attacking again. With lightning presence of mind he leapt into the back of the Danish goal, taking himself off the field of play, and duly caught the goal scoring header from

SOCCER MEDALS

| | Men | | | Women | | | |
	G	S	B	G	S	B	Total
Hungary	3	1	1	–	–	–	5
Soviet Union	2	–	3	–	–	–	5
Denmark	1	3	1	–	–	–	5
Yugoslavia	1	3	1	–	–	–	5
Great Britain	3	–	–	–	–	–	3
Poland	1	2	–	–	–	–	3
GDR	1	1	1	–	–	–	3
United States	–	1	1	1	–	–	3
Sweden	1	–	2	–	–	–	3
Brazil	–	2	1	–	–	–	3
The Netherlands	–	–	3	–	–	–	3
Uruguay	2	–	–	–	–	–	2
Czechoslovakia	1	1	–	–	–	–	2
France	1	1	–	–	–	–	2
Spain	1	1	–	–	–	–	2
Belgium	1	–	1	–	–	–	2
Italy	1	–	1	–	–	–	2
Argentina	–	2	–	–	–	–	2
Austria	–	1	–	–	1	–	2
Bulgaria	–	1	1	–	–	–	2
Greece	–	1	1	–	–	–	2
Norway	–	–	1	–	–	1	2
Nigeria Canada	1	–	–	–	–	–	1
Switzerland	–	1	–	–	–	–	1
FRG	–	–	1	–	–	–	1
Germany	–	–	1	–	–	–	1
Ghana	–	–	1	–	–	–	1
Japan	–	–	1	–	–	-	1
	21	22	23 [1]	1	1	1	69

[1] Third place tie in 1972

his team-mate Henry Carlsson with the goalkeeper on the ground five metres away. In the 1920 final between Belgium and Czechoslovakia the latter team walked off the field in protest against the referee, before half-time when they were 2–0 down. The match was abandoned and the Czechs disqualified. The 1936 tournament resulted in many incidents, not least the withdrawal of the Peruvian team when its win over Austria in the second round was ordered to be re-played. Austria went on to reach the final.

After many years in the doldrums Olympic soccer had a revival in 1980 when the 56 games of the tournament, played in Moscow, Leningrad, Minsk and Kiev, attracted nearly two million spectators — over a third of all spectators for the 1980 Games. This revival was reinforced, somewhat surprisingly, in Los Angeles in 1984, when nearly 1.5 million watched the matches, including a record 101 799 audience for the final.

Softball

Invented as an indoor version of baseball in 1887, it didn't become known as softball until 1920. Originally a 10-a-side game, it is now played with nine-per-side, and is governed by the International Softball Federation (ISF), formed in 1950. Pitching is done underarm, and there are fast-pitch and slow-pitch forms. A game lasts for seven innings. The fast-pitch variety for women was introduced as an official Olympic medal sport in 1996 — surprisingly never having been a demonstration sport — with eight teams.

The highest score achieved by a team is 10 attained by the USA v Puerto Rico (10–0), China v Puerto Rico (10–0), Australia v Japan (10–0), and Chinese Taipei v Puerto Rico (10–2). This latter match totalled the highest aggregate of 12.

The youngest gold medallist/medallist was Christa Lee Williams (USA), aged 18 years and 173 days, while the oldest champion was her team-mate Dorothy Richardson at 34 years and 312 days. The oldest medallist was Jocelyn Lester in the Australian bronze medal team, aged 38 years and 130 days.

SOFTBALL MEDALS

	G	S	B	Total
United States	1	–	–	1
China	–	1	–	1
Australia	–	–	1	1
	1	1	1	3

Speed

The fastest speed achieved by an athlete without mechanical aid at the Olympic Games is 43.56km/h (27.06mph), by 1996 100m champion Donovan Bailey (CAN), recorded reaching his peak speed at 60m in the stadium at Atlanta. The fastest of all Olympians are the bobsledders, who have been recorded at 143km/h (88.8mph). Downhill skiers and lugers attain 120km/h (74.56mph) at times.

The fastest Summer Games Olympians were Daniel Morelon and Pierre Trentin (FRA) when they attained a speed of 73.24km/h (45.50mph) in their 1968 cycling tandem event, clocking 9.83sec for the last 200m of their race. The fastest individual cyclist was Gary Niewand (AUS) in 1996 when he clocked 10.219sec for 200m — 71.08km/h (44.16mph). The fastest female cyclist was Michelle Ferris (AUS), also at Atlanta, with 11.212sec — 64.21km/h (39.90mph). Speed skater, Ids Postma (NED), set a record 1min 10.64sec for 1000m at Nagano in 1998, which is an average of 50.96km/h (31.66mph), while on the women's side, Marianne Timmer (NED) did 500m in 38.21sec to average 47.10km/h (29.27mph). (*See also* Speed Skiing.)

Speed Skating

The sport was introduced into the Olympics in 1924, with the first official events for women in 1960. There have been two major controversies over the years. In 1928, the 10km event was cancelled by the Norwegian referee due to bad weather. That caused much ill-feeling in the American camp because at the time Irving Jaffee (USA) was the surprise leader and as all the best skaters had competed the medal positions seemed assured. Despite vigorous protests by all nationalities no medals were awarded. The other occasion was in 1932 when the American 'mass start' system was used, for the only time in Olympic competition. This undoubtedly gave the Americans and Canadians a tremendous advantage as the Europeans were completely unfamiliar with the tactics involved and only two medals were won by European skaters. In 1998, the 500m events were decided on the aggregate of two runs — interestingly, both male and female winners at Nagano would have won under the old system of one race. A new type of skate, the clap skate, was used at Nagano, and the Dutch introduced aerodynamic silicon 'stripes' on their racing suits.

Lydia Skoblikova (URS) won a record six gold medals in 1960 and 1964, which is also a record for any sport in the Winter Games for either a male or female competitor. The most by a man is five by Clas Thunberg (FIN) in 1924 and 1928, and by Eric Heiden (USA) with all five in 1980. There have been five events for men since 1976, while a fifth event was added for women in 1988. The most medals won is eight by Karin Enke-Kania (GDR) with three golds, four silvers and a bronze between 1980 and 1988, and by Gunda Niemann-Stirnemann (GDR/GER) also with three golds, four silvers and a bronze between 1992 and 1996 — in both cases a Winter Games record for individual events. The most by a male skater is seven by Thunberg, who added a silver and a bronze to his golds, and by Ivar Ballangrud (NOR) who won four golds, two silvers and a bronze between 1928 and 1936. Skoblikova won her four golds in 1964 on four successive days. In 1994 Bonnie Blair (USA)

OLYMPIC RECORDS

Men

500m	35.59sec	Hiroyasu Shimizu (JPN)	1998
1000m	1min 10.64sec	Ids Postma (NED)	1998
1500m	1min 47.87sec	Adne Søndrål (NOR)	1998
5000m	6min 22.20sec	Gianni Romme (NED)	1998
10 000m	13min 15.33sec	Gianni Romme (NED)	1998

Women

500m	38.21sec	Catriona LeMay-Doan (CAN)	1998
1000m	1min 16.51sec	Marianne Timmer (NED)	1998
1500m	1min 57.88sec	Marianne Timmer (NED)	1998
3000m	4min 07.29sec	Gunda Niemann-Stirnemann (GER)	1998
5000m	6min 59.61sec	Claudia Pechstein (GER)	1998

SPEED SKATING MEDALS

	Men			Women			
	G	S	B	G	S	B	Total
Norway	24	28	23	1	–	1	77
Soviet Union	12	10	9	12	7	10	60
The Netherlands	9	17	15	9	4	4	58
United States	14	7	3	8	9	7	48
GDR	2	1	2	6	11	7	29
Germany	2	–	-	7	9	7	25
Finland	6	6	7	1	2	1	24
Canada	2	3	7	1	3	1	17
Sweden	7	4	5	–	–	–	16
Japan	1	2	5	–	–	3	11
Austria	–	1	2	1	1	1	6
Russia	1	1	1	1	1	–	5
FRG	2	–	–	1	–	–	3
China	–	–	–	–	2	1	3
Poland	–	–	–	–	1	1	2
Belarus	–	1	–	–	–	–	1
Korea	–	1	–	–	–	–	1
North Korea (PRK)	–	–	–	–	1	–	1
Belgium	–	–	1	–	–	–	1
Kazakhstan	–	–	–	–	–	1	1
	82	82	80	48	51	46	389

won the same title (500m) for the third consecutive time.

The oldest gold medallist was Clas Thunberg, aged 35 years and 315 days in the 1928 1500m. The youngest winner was Anne Henning (USA) in the 500m in 1952, aged 16 years and 157 days. The youngest male champion was Igor Malkov (URS) winning the 10km in 1984, aged 19 years and 9 days, while the oldest woman was Christina Baas-Kaiser (NED) who won the 3000m title in 1972, aged 33 years and 268 days. The youngest ever medallist was Andrea Mitscherlich (later Schöne and Ehrlich) (GDR) winning the 3000m silver in 1976 when only 15 years and 69 days. The youngest male medallist was Alv Gjestvang (NOR) in 1956, aged 18 years and 147 days. The oldest medallist was Julius Skutnabb (FIN) in 1928 at 38 years and 246 days, while the oldest female medallist was Eevi Huttunen (FIN) in the 1960 3000m, aged 37 years and 184 days. Frank Stack (CAN) competed over a 20-year period between 1932 and 1952 and when he was 46 won the bronze in 1932, while Colin Coates (AUS) also competed for 20 years, in six Games 1968–88, but his best placing was 6th in the 10km in 1976.

A number of speed skaters have found a happy affinity with cycle racing. One of the most successful at both roles has been Sheila Young (USA), who won the 500m Olympic skating title in 1976 and the world amateur sprint cycle championship in 1973 and 1976. However, Christa Rothenburger-Luding (GDR) possibly surpassed that in 1988. Having won the 1984 Olympic 500m gold and the 1986 world cycling sprint title in 1986, she then won the skating 1000m at Calgary and gained a cycling silver in Seoul, to become the first competitor to win medals at Summer and Winter games in the same year. This achievement can no longer be equalled. Eric Flaim (USA) who had won a silver in the 1988 speed skating 1500m, became the first to also gain a medal at short track skating in 1994 with another silver in the relay.

Speed Skiing

A demonstration sport at Albertville in 1992, when world records were set in both men's, 229.299km/h (142.479mph) by Mickaël Prufer (FRA), and women's, 219.245km/h (136.232mph) by Tarja Mulari (FIN), events. Second in the men's competition was Philippe Goitschel (FRA) nephew of the sisters who had won golds in the 1964 Alpine events. Davina Galica (GBR) competed in the women's event 28 years after her first Olympic appearance as an Alpine skier, aged 47 years and 189 days.

Sports

Only five sports have been on the programme of every Modern Games since 1896 — cycling, fencing, gymnastics, swimming and athletics. Rowing should have been included, but although actually on the 1896 programme of events, rough seas caused its cancellation. To become an Olympic sport, recognised by the IOC but not necessarily contested at the Games, it must be widely practised in 75 countries on four continents (men's sports), and in 40 countries on three continents (women's sports). For the Winter Games a sport must be widely practised in 25 countries on three continents.

Squaw Valley 1960
VIII Winter Games (18–28 February)

Attended by representatives of 30 countries, comprising 665 competitors, of which 144 were women.

When the IOC voted narrowly, 32–30, to give the Games to Squaw Valley, California USA, instead of Innsbruck, virtually nothing existed at the site. Due to the efforts of Alexander Cushing, who owned most of the area, it became the first purpose-built Winter Games venue. Despite initial delays everything was ready for the official opening, under the direction of Walt Disney. The formal opening was by Richard Nixon, then Vice-President of the United States. The last relay runner was Ken Henry, the 500m speed skating champion of 1952, and the oath was taken by figure skater Carol Heiss, who went on to win the women's title.

There were a number of protests and problems. Bobsledding was dropped as the organisers would not accept the cost of building a run for what they considered would be a small number entries. Artificial obstacles were built into the downhill runs to make them more difficult, and concern was expressed over the altitude (over 1900m, 6230ft) at which the Nordic skiing events were held. East and West Germany competed as one entity, with agreement reached on the popular theme from Beethoven's *Ninth Symphony* played for any victory ceremonies, instead of their respective national anthems. A team from South Africa appeared, for the first time in the Winter Games — they were banned thereafter until 1992. The biathlon and speed skating for women made Olympics debuts. The biathlon event had been a demonstration sport on four previous occasions.

The speed skating times in general were excellent, with Knut Johannesen (NOR) beating the 10 000m world record by 46.0sec, the greatest margin achieved this century. Yevgeni Grishin (URS) equalled his own world mark to become the first man to successfully defend the 500m title. Helga Haase (GER) was the first ever women's Olympic champion in speed skating when she won the 500m. In figure skating, David Jenkins kept the men's title in the family as his brother, Hayes, had won in 1956, and made the family even more Olympian by marrying the Squaw Valley women's champion, Carol Heiss, two months later.

There was a first in Nordic skiing when Georg Thoma, a German postman from the Black Forest region who was often forced to deliver mail on skis in bad weather, achieved the first victory by a non-Scandinavian in the sport. The winner of the inaugural biathlon, Klas Lestander (SWE), was only 15th in the cross-country segment of the contest, but scored a maximum possible 20 in the shooting. The Soviet Union's women dominated the 10 000m race, taking the top four places, but they lost the relay, a virtual certainty, when the first woman fell and broke a ski. A protest was made against the first Swedish woman who was accused of deliberate fouling, but it was not upheld.

In Alpine skiing metallic skis were used in the Games for the first time. The medals were more widespread than usual, with no skier winning more than one event, and only Penny Pitou (USA) won more than one medal, with two silvers. The outstanding competitor was Anne Heggtveit (CAN) who won the women's slalom by a margin of 3.3sec only ever bettered by the 1936 combination winner, Christl Cranz (GER).

The oldest gold medallist was Veikko Hakulinen (FIN) in the Nordic relay, aged 35 years and 52 days, and the youngest Heidi Biebl (GER), the downhill champion three days past her 19th birthday. The youngest male champion was American ice hockey player Thomas Williams, aged 19 years and 317 days. The oldest female gold medallist was Sonja Ruthström (SWE) in the Nordic relay, aged 29 years and 94 days. The youngest medallist was skier Gertaud Hecher (AUT) with a downhill bronze, aged 16 years and 145 days.

1960 MEDALS (WINTER)

	G	S	B
Soviet Union	7	5	9
Germany	4	3	1
United States	3	4	3
Norway	3	3	–
Sweden	3	2	2
Finland	2	3	3
Canada	2	1	1
Switzerland	2	–	–
Austria	1	2	3
France	1	–	2
The Netherlands	–	1	1
Poland	–	1	1
Czechoslovakia	–	1	–
Italy	–	–	1

St Louis 1904
III Olympic Games (1 July–23 November)

Attended by representatives of 13 countries, comprising 687 competitors, of which six were women.

For a time the third celebration seemed likely to go to Great Britain, and then to Philadelphia, whilst de Coubertin had favoured New York. The IOC finally designated Chicago for these Games, but at the request of President Theodore Roosevelt, also president of the US Olympic Committee, the venue was changed to St Louis to coincide with the World's Fair, held to celebrate the centenary of the Louisiana Purchase. Once again, the Games became merely a sideshow. Held in the centre of the North American continent the problems of distance and travel meant that there were few overseas entrants. Indeed, even de Coubertin did not attend. Hence 85 per cent of the competitors were from the host country, and, not surprisingly, they won 84 per cent of the medals. In fact the Games were a virtual college and club tournament with the New York Athletic Club beating the Chicago Athletic Association for the track and field team title (a points table was actually published). In swimming New York beat Germany and Hungary overall.

In such circumstances the Games degenerated into something of a farce, so that the cycling events, which had no foreign entrants at all and included a number professional riders, were initially refused official Olympic status. However, recent scholarship suggests that they should be included in medal tables and results. So the unique achievement of Marcus Hurley in winning four cycling events should now be given due credit. Gymnast Anton Heida (USA) won five golds and one silver to be the most successful at these Games.

Under the rather loose controls imposed on most sports some strange things happened. In the 400m track race no heats were held and all 13 entrants ran in the final. Rowing events were held over a 2.4km (1.5 mile) course which entailed making a turn. The swim-

ming events were held over imperial distances, while the athletics track (in the grounds of Washington University, St Louis) measured one-third of a mile in circumference (536m) and had a 220yd straightaway, which was quite an innovation for the visiting Europeans. In the track and field programme only two events went to non-Americans. The French-Canadian policeman, Etienne Desmarteau, won the 25.4kg (56lb) weight throw. He unfortunately died the following year of typhoid and a park was named after him in his home-town of Montreal. The 10-event all-round competition, a forerunner of the decathlon, was won by Thomas Kiely, who like the silver medallist in the 2500m steeplechase, John Daly, was an Irishman. However, as Ireland at the time was part of the United Kingdom, they represented the Great Britain team, despite attempts by 'historical revisionists' to make it otherwise. The unfortunate Myer Prinstein redressed his grievance of four years previously by taking the long jump title as well as winning the hop, step and jump. He also placed fifth in both the 60m and 400m finals. The ever liberal Prinstein was representing the Greater New York Irish Athletic Association.

The 200m final, held on a straightaway (i.e. no turns), was won by Archie Hahn, with all three of his opponents given a one yard (0.99m) handicap under the rules then governing false starts. Joseph Stadler won a silver medal in the standing high jump, while George Poage won bronzes in the 200m and 400m hurdle races. The significance of their performances was that they became the first black men to win medals in the Olympics. Despite the lack of foreign opposition, the standard in many sports was very high, and the triple victories of Archie Hahn, Harry Hillman, James Lightbody, Ray Ewry and swimmer Charles Daniels were outstanding. Daniels in winning the 220yd, 440yd and mile freestyle events was the prototype of the American swimmers who were to dominate Olympic freestyle swimming for many years.

There was a scandal in the marathon when the first man out of the stadium, Fred Lorz (USA), was the first man back, looking remarkably fresh. It later transpired that he had received a lift in a car after suffering a cramp, and when the car itself broke down near the stadium he resumed running, as a joke he claimed. He was banned for life (but was competing again after only a year) and the title was awarded to British-born American Thomas Hicks who had finished in a daze due to being administered strychnine by his coaches as a stimulant — a practice then common and allowable. In ninth place was Len Tau (SAF), in St Louis as part of a World's Fair exhibit, the first black African distance runner to compete in the Olympics.

The youngest gold medallist was golfer Robert Hunter (USA), aged 17 years and 301 days, while the oldest was the Revd Galen Spencer (USA), an archer, aged 64 years and 2 days. Another American archer, Samuel Duvall, won a silver medal, aged 68 years and 194 days — the oldest American medallist ever. The oldest female champion was Lida Howell (USA) in archery, aged 45 years and 25 days. The youngest medallist was another archer, Henry Richardson (USA), aged 15 years and 124 days. Another American, Frank Kungler, won a silver in wrestling, a bronze in tug-of-war, and two bronzes in weightlifting, to become the only Olympian to win medals at three different sports at a single Games.

A final insult to the Games were the Anthropology Days during which competitions were held, parodying the regular Olympic events, for aboriginal peoples, such as American Indians, African pygmies, Patagonians, Ainus from Japan, and the like. Finally in November, with the association football competition won by a Canadian college over two American teams, the III Olympic Games came to an end, and many in Europe wondered if the fledgling movement would recover.

1904 MEDALS

	G	S	B
United States	80	84	78
Germany	4	4	5
Canada	4	1	1
Cuba	4	–	–
Austria	2	1	1
Hungary	2	1	1
Great Britain	1	1	–
Greece	1	–	1
Switzerland	1	–	1
France	–	1	–

St Moritz 1928
II Winter Games (11–19 February)

Attended by representatives of 25 countries, comprising 495 competitors, of which 27 were women.

The decision that the same country should host both Summer and Winter editions of the Games had been abandoned in 1928, although the principle was still thought to be a sound one. The Games were officially declared open by the President of Switzerland, Edmund Schulthess, and the oath was taken by Hans Eidenbenz, a skier. Japan, The Netherlands, Romania and Mexico were making their debuts at the Winter Games. Unseasonal weather threatened the programme. On one day the temperature varied by over 20°C from morning to afternoon. One of the speed skating events had to be cancelled and in the bobsled there were only two runs instead of four.

The cancellation of the 10 000m skating event by the Norwegian referee, particularly caused bad feeling among the American team, as Irving Jaffee (USA) was the surprise leader and seemed likely to retain that lead. Despite vigorous protests by all nationalities no medals were awarded. At Lake Placid four years later Jaffee won the gold medal in the 10 000m skating event. In the other events Clas Thunberg (FIN) added two more golds to his 1924 haul to amass a total of five

golds, one silver and one bronze, a record for the sport. There was a unique occurrence in the 500m in which two men tied for first place and three men for third, with no silver medals awarded. The skeleton toboggan race conducted on the famous Cresta Run, and brothers Jennison and John Heaton (USA) gained the gold and silver respectively.

The bobsled, for the first and only time composed of 5-man teams, went to the United States. The driver, William Fiske, was aged only 16 years and 260 days, and was then the youngest ever male Winter gold medallist. Also in the team was the oldest gold medallist at these Games, Nion Tucker, aged 42 years and 182 days. The youngest was Sonja Henie (NOR) taking the first of her three figure skating titles, aged 15 years and 316 days. She was the 'star' of the Games with her interpretation of *The Dying Swan*, which began a whole new era for the sport. The youngest medallist at these Games was Thomas Doe Jr (USA) in the bob, aged 15 years and 129 days, while the oldest was his team-mate Jay O'Brien at 44 years and 361 days. Pair skating witnessed the last appearance of the 1920 champions, Ludowika and Walter Jakobsson (FIN), who were placed fifth, their ages totalling 89 years. In men's skating Gillis Grafström (SWE) obtained his third consecutive gold medal.

In ski-jumping the defending champion, Jacob Tullin-Thams (NOR), was nearly killed crashing at the end of a 73m jump on a hill designed for jumps of considerably less distance. A true Olympian, he reappeared in 1936 to gain a silver medal in yachting. Johan Grøttumsbråten (NOR) won the 18km race and the Nordic combination title to match Thunberg's two wins. As was becoming a habit the Canadians easily won the ice hockey tournament scoring a total of 38 goals for and none against. The only demonstration event was a military patrol.

1928 MEDALS (WINTER)

	G	S	B
Norway	6	4	5
United States	2	2	2
Sweden	2	2	1
Finland	2	1	1
Canada	1	–	–
France	1	–	–
Austria	–	3	1
Belgium	–	–	1
Czechoslovakia	–	–	1
Germany	–	–	1
Great Britain	–	–	1
Switzerland	–	–	1

St Moritz 1948
V Winter Games (30 January–8 February)

Attended by representatives of 28 countries, comprising 713 competitors, of which 77 were women.

In 1936 the Winter Games of 1940 were initially awarded to Sapporo, Japan, but as a consequence of the Sino-Japanese conflict they were reallocated to St Moritz. Due to some disagreements the IOC transferred them again in June 1939 to Garmisch-Partenkirchen, Germany, at the same time deciding that the 1944 meeting should be held at Cortina d'Ampezzo, Italy. The Second World War then upset these plans and in 1946 a postal vote of IOC members relocated the 1948 Games in St Moritz as neutral Switzerland had been virtually untouched by the war. Chile, Denmark, Iceland, Korea and Lebanon competed for the first time in the Winter Games, but Germany and Japan were not invited, although Italy was. The oath was taken by ice hockey player Richard Torriani on behalf of the competitors, and Swiss President Enrico Celio formally opened the Games. There were now six Alpine events which attracted larger fields than the Nordic disciplines. Poor weather affected some of the competitions, and there were a number of disputes.

The most medals were won by Henri Oreiller (FRA) with gold in the downhill (by a record margin of 4.1sec), and Alpine combination, with a bronze in the slalom. Alpine skier Gretchen Fraser (USA) gained the first skiing title ever won by a non-European. In Nordic skiing the Swedes broke the Norwegian monopoly. They had the three medals and fifth place in the 18km, first two and fifth in the 50km, and won the 4 × 10km relay by a margin of nearly nine minutes. They also won their first ever speed skating title when Ake Seyffarth took the 10km event. The American figure skaters brought a new concept to figure skating as Dick Button gained an easy victory.

The ice hockey competition was the cause of a major argument as two American teams appeared in St Moritz. One represented the Amateur Hockey Association (AHA) and the other was picked by the US Olympic Committee (USOC). The AHA, while not affiliated to the USOC, was a member of the International Ice Hockey Federation (IIHF), who were the governing body of most of the other teams at the Games, and threatened to withdraw all the other teams if the AHA team were not allowed to play. The USOC in turn threatened to withdraw its whole Olympic team if it did. Initially the IOC decided to bar both teams, but then agreed with the Swiss organisers and the IIHF to allow the AHA team to compete. However, the USOC team members marched in the opening ceremony. The AHA team eventually finished fourth, but a year later the AHA was disqualified for non-affiliation to the Olympic movement. The Canadians won the title once again, but only just. The title was decided on goal average, with the Czechs taking the silver. Richard 'Bibi' Torriani who was part of the bronze medal ice hockey team, had also won another bronze 20 years earlier when he was just past his 16th birthday.

The US bobsleds were sabotaged prior to the competitions, but it did not prevent them from winning a gold and two bronzes. They have never won an Olympic bob event since. In the skeleton toboggan,

which was only held when the Games were at St Moritz, on the Cresta Run, John Heaton (USA) won his second silver medal, 20 years after his first. The gold medal went to Nino Bibbia of Italy who was a master of the Cresta Run and went on to win many titles and championships over the next quarter of a century.

The great Norwegian ski jumper Birger Ruud, nearly 37-years-old and a survivor of a wartime concentration camp, ended his Olympic career with a silver medal to add to his golds from 1932 and 1936. He and his brother, Sigmund (silver 1928), had made the event a family tradition since 1928. A third brother, Asbjørn, was also in the 1948 team.

A record 13 countries shared the medals, with Italy and Belgium winning their first ever Winter Games titles. There were two demonstration events: military patrol, and a winter pentathlon. This latter consisted of 10km cross-country skiing, pistol shooting, downhill skiing, fencing and horse riding. No medals were awarded, but in second place was Captain Willie Grut (SWE) of whom much more was to be heard six months later, at the London Games.

The oldest gold medallist was Francis Tyler, in the US 4-man bob, aged 43 years and 58 days, while the youngest was skater Dick Button (USA), aged 18 years and 202 days. The youngest female champion was skater Barbara-Ann Scott (CAN), aged 19 years and 273 days, while the oldest female winner was Gretchen Fraser (USA) in the slalom, aged 28 years and 360 days. The youngest medallist was skater Suzanne Morrow (CAN) with a pairs bronze, aged 17 years and 55 days, while the oldest was bobsledder Max Houben (BEL) at 49 years and 278 days.

1948 MEDALS (WINTER)

	G	S	B
Norway	4	3	3
Sweden	4	3	3
Switzerland	3	4	3
United States	3	4	2
France	2	1	2
Canada	2	–	1
Austria	1	3	4
Finland	1	3	2
Belgium	1	1	–
Italy	1	–	–
Czechoslovakia	–	1	–
Hungary	–	1	–
Great Britain	–	–	2

Stadiums

The largest main stadium used in the Olympics has been the Melbourne Cricket Ground in 1956, which had its capacity increased to 104 000 for the Games. This was closely followed by the Lenin stadium in Moscow in 1980, which had a capacity of 103 000 at the time. The Berlin stadium in 1936 actually held 100 000, and not 110 000 as was reported by some sources, and the Los Angeles Coliseum, used for the 1932 Games, could then seat 101 000. For the 2000 Games, Sydney's stadium will hold an 'Olympic record' of 110 000 spectators.

Stamps

The first Olympic stamps were issued on 6 April 1896 in Greece to raise funds for the I Games, and to publicise the occasion. There were 12 stamps in the set, designed by Professor Gillieron and engraved by Eduard Mouchon, and were produced by the French Government Printing Office for the Greek Post Office. The designs included ancient boxers, the stadium, and Myron's famous statue of 'The Discus Thrower'. As Greece was still using the Julian calendar, the cancelling postmark was dated 25 March. The first issue of Olympic stamps to use representations of modern sportsmen was that for the 1928 Games at Amsterdam. The first Winter Games to stimulate an issue of stamps was that at Lake Placid in 1932. After World War II many countries began to produce stamps with an Olympic theme, sometimes to commemorate them, but usually to raise funds for future participation. In 1980, in connection with the Games at Moscow, the Soviet Union produced a record of 74 stamps for the occasion. Well over 100 countries have issued stamps relating to the Games.

Stockholm 1912
V Olympic Games (5 May–22 July)

Attended by representatives of 28 countries, comprising 2547 competitors, of which 57 were women.

Stockholm finally attained the honour that Sweden had wanted from the very beginning, to host the Olympic Games. Torben Grut designed and built a 31 000 capacity stadium, with a 383m (407yd) track laid out under the direction of Charles Perry, the Englishman responsible for the 1896 and 1908 tracks. Baron de Coubertin had insisted that the number of sports be cut, and now with only 14 there were high standards of performance and sportsmanship, with few arguments or protests. Boxing was not held, the last time that it has been left out of the Olympic programme. The Games were opened officially by King Gustaf V. One of the rare complaints at these Games was from the Finns, again about competing under the Russian flag. Indeed, the triple gold medallist Kolehmainen stated that he almost wished he had not won rather than see the hated flag raised for his victories.

Various innovations included the first use of electrical timing equipment for the running events. Baron de Coubertin had asked for a new event, the modern pentathlon, to be introduced, which consisted of five disciplines. It was dominated by the Swedes but in fifth place was Lieutenant George S. Patton (USA), later to become a controversial World War II general.

The American team lived on the liner that had brought them across the Atlantic. This was the Games in which the first of the 'Flying Finns', Hannes Kolehmainen, made his appearance, winning the 5000m, 10 000m and 12 000m cross-country. Thus began a domination which lasted into the 1940s. Kolehmainen's race with Jean Bouin of France in the 5000m was one of the most enthralling races ever seen to that time, with the Finn winning by a stride in 14min 36.6sec, improving the world record by a margin of 24.6sec. Other track stars were Ted Meredith (USA), gold medallist in the 800m in a new world time, and Ralph Craig (USA) who took both sprints. Under current rules, he would not have won as he was responsible for three of the seven false starts to the race. He reappeared at the Games, as a reserve yachtsman, 36 years later, at London, when he was given the honour of carrying the USA team flag.

In the swimming pool the first of the great Hawaiian competitors, Duke Kahanamoku, won the 100m freestyle. The son of Hawaiian royalty, he received his first name as a mark of respect for the Duke of Edinburgh, Queen Victoria's second son, who was visiting the islands at the time of his birth. He competed in three more Games before becoming a movie star. There was only one cycling event, but it was unique in that it was the longest road race ever held in the Games. It was won by Rudolph Lewis (SAF), who took the 320km (198 miles) event in just short of 10¾ hours. A great impetus was given to the game of soccer at these Olympics, with 25 000 spectators present to see Great Britain beat Denmark 4–2 in the final. Gymnastics, like wrestling, was held outdoors and gained new status.

In wrestling, problems were caused by the extreme length of some of the bouts. In the light-heavyweight final the judges called a halt after the bout had gone on for nine hours and gave both wrestlers a silver medal, with no gold awarded. Even this was surpassed in the middleweight category where the tussle for the silver medal between Alfred Asikainen (FIN) and Martin Klein, an Estonian representing Russia, went on for 11hr 40min, a record for the sport. Klein finally triumphed. The first known twins to win Olympic gold medals were the Carlberg brothers, Vilhelm (three) and Eric (two), in shooting, while an another sibling combination came in the 6m class yachting when the French winner *Mac Miche* was crewed by the three Thubé brothers.

However, the star of the Games was undoubtedly Jim Thorpe. Of Irish, French, but mainly American Indian ancestry, Thorpe won both the athletic pentathlon (a discontinued event since 1924) as well as the decathlon, with consummate ease. Additionally, he was fourth in the individual high jump and seventh in the long jump. Presenting him with his medals King Gustav V called him 'the greatest athlete in the world'. Thorpe reportedly replied 'Thanks King'. Six months later, a sportswriter for the Worcester Telegram in Massachusetts, Roy Johnson, reported that Thorpe had played minor baseball for money. Owing to the violent amateur/professional dichotomy of the time, perhaps reinforced by American anti-Indian prejudice, Thorpe's medals were taken back and his performances removed from Olympic annals. It seems almost certain that he was ignorant of the amateur laws of the time, and the amount of money involved was very small. Twenty years after his death in 1953 the American Athletic Union reinstated him as an amateur, but the IOC stubbornly refused all entreaties on his behalf. It has been suggested that his cause was not helped by the fact that the President of the IOC from 1952–72 was Avery Brundage, a team-mate of Thorpe's in 1912 who had placed fifth (or sixth depending on your view) in the pentathlon. To their credit, the runners-up to Thorpe, Hugo Wieslander (SWE) and Ferdinand Bie (NOR) initially refused to accept the gold medals when they were sent them, although their names were inscribed in Olympic annals as winners of the events. Finally, in October 1982 Thorpe, the man who had been voted in 1950 as the greatest athlete of the first half-century, was pardoned by the IOC and the medals presented to his family. The amended result still stands and two people are considered as winners.

The oldest gold medallist at these Games was the ubiquitous Oscar Swahn (SWE) now, aged 64 years and 258 days, while team-mate, diver Greta Johansson, was the youngest, aged 17 years and 186 days. Only 40 days older was Isabella Moore (GBR) in the winning freestyle swimming relay team, who became Great Britain's youngest ever female gold medallist. The youngest male champion was fencer Nedo Nadi (ITA), aged 18 years and 30 days. British tennis player Edith Hannam was the oldest female gold medallist, aged 33 years and 171 days. The youngest medallist was swimmer Grete Rosenberg (GER) in the relay at 15 years and 280 days.

At the Stockholm Games the Olympic movement finally 'came of age' and the marvellous efforts of the organising committee under Viktor Balck, later deservedly President of the IOC, must take much of the credit. The only unfortunate incident at the Games was the collapse and death of Francisco Lazzaro (POR) during the marathon. Ironically it was the first Games that his country had attended. Another new country was Japan, and the Games were beginning to achieve the wide-world support originally envisaged for them.

1912 MEDALS

	G	S	B
United States [1]	25	19	18
Sweden	24	24	16
Great Britain	10	15	16
Finland	9	8	9
France	7	4	3
Germany	5	13	7
South Africa	4	2	–
Norway	4	1	5
Hungary	3	2	3
Canada	3	2	2
Italy	3	1	2
Australia [2]	2	2	2
Belgium	2	1	3
Denmark	1	6	5
Greece	1	–	1
New Zealand [2]	1	–	1
Switzerland	1	–	–
Russia	–	2	3
Austria	–	2	2
The Netherlands	–	–	3

[1] Adjusted by the reinstatement of Jim Thorpe in 1982
[2] Australia and New Zealand combined as Australasia

Stockholm 1956

In 1956, due to Australian quarantine regulations, the equestrian events of the Melbourne Olympic Games were held in the city of Stockholm, Sweden. For data and medals *see* Melbourne 1956.

Superlatives

MOST GOLDS (SUMMER)

Men	10	Ray Ewry (USA)	1900–08	Athletics
Women	9	Larissa Latynina (URS)	1956–64	Gymnastics
Men, in one Games	7	Mark Spitz (USA)	1972	Swimming
Women, in one Games	6	Kristin Otto (GDR)	1988	Swimming

MOST MEDALS (SUMMER)

Men	15	Nikolai Andrianov (URS)	1972–80	Gymnastics
Women	18	Larissa Latynina (URS)	1956–64	Gymnastics
Men, in one Games	8	Alexander Dityatin (URS)	1980	Gymnastics
Women, in one Games	7	Maria Gorokhovskaya (URS)	1952	Gymnastics

MOST GOLDS (WINTER)

Men	8	Bjørn Dæhlie (NOR)	1992–98	Nordic Skiing
Women	6	Lydia Skoblikova (URS)	1960–64	Speed Skating
	6	Lyubov Yegorova (RUS/EUN)	1992–94	Nordic Skiing
Men, in one Games	5	Eric Heiden (USA)	1980	Speed Skating
Women, in one Games	4	Lydia Skoblikova (URS)	1964	Speed Skating

MOST MEDALS (WINTER)

Men	12	Bjørn Dæhlie (NOR)	1992–98	Nordic Skiing
Women	10	Raisa Smetanina (URS)	1976–92	Nordic Skiing
Men, in one Games	5	Clas Thunberg (FIN)	1924	Speed Skating
	5	Roald Larsen (NOR)	1924	Speed Skating
	5	Eric Heiden (USA)	1980	Speed Skating
Women, in one Games	5	Lyubov Yegorova (RUS/EUN)	1992	Nordic Skiing
	5	Yelena Valbe (RUS/EUN)	1992	Nordic Skiing
	5	Manuela di Centa (ITA)	1994	Nordic Skiing
	5	Larissa Lazutina (RUS)	1998	Nordic Skiing

AGE RECORDS (SUMMER)

Oldest

Male Gold	64 years and 258 days	Oscar Swahn (SWE)	1912	Shooting
Female Gold	53 years and 277 days	Queenie Newall (GBR)	1908	Archery
Male Medal	72 years and 280 days	Oscar Swahn (SWE)	1920	Shooting
Female Medal	53 years and 277 days	Queenie Newall (GBR)	1908	Archery

Youngest

Male Gold	7–10 years	Unknown boy (FRA)	1900	Rowing
Female Gold	13 years and 268 days	Marjorie Gestring (USA)	1936	Diving
Male Medallist	7–10 years	Unknown boy (FRA)	1900	Rowing
Female Medallist	11 years and 302 days	Luigina Giavotti (ITA)	1928	Gymnastics

Oldest Competitor

Male	72 years and 280 days	Oscar Swahn (SWE)	1920	Shooting
Female	70 years and 5 days	Lorna Johnstone (GBR)	1972	Equestrianism

Youngest Competitor

Male	7-10 years	Unknown boy (FRA)	1900	Rowing
Female	11 years and 328 days	Liana Vicens (PUR)	1968	Swimming

AGE RECORDS (WINTER)

Oldest

Male Gold	48 years and 359 days	Jay O'Brien (USA)	1932	Bobsledding
Female Gold	39 years and 354 days	Raisa Smetanina (RUS/EUN)	1992	Nordic Skiing
Male Medal	50 years and 235 days	Paul Savage (CAN)	1998	Curling
Female Medal	42 years and 178 days	Jane Bidstrup (DEN)	1998	Curling

Youngest

Male Gold	16 years and 259 days	Toni Nieminen (FIN)	1992	Ski Jumping
Female Gold	13 years and 83 days	Kim Yoon-mi (KOR)	1994	Short-Track Speed Skating
Male Medal	14 years and 363 days	Scott Allen (USA)	1964	Figure Skating
Female Medal	13 years and 83 days	Kim Yoon-mi (KOR)	1994	Short-Track Speed Skating

Oldest Competitor

Male	53 years and 297 days	James Coats (GBR)	1948	Tobogganing
Female	45 years and 318 days	Edwina Chamier (CAN)	1936	Skiing

Youngest Competitor

Male	12 years and 110 days	Jan Hoffmann (GDR)	1968	Figure Skating
Female	11 years and 73 days	Cecilia Colledge (GBR)	1932	Figure Skating

MOST GAMES/LONGEST SPAN (SUMMER) — MEN

9 Games	Hubert Raudaschl (AUT)	1964–96	Yachting
40 years	Ivan Osiier (DEN)	1908–48	Fencing
40 years	Magnus Konow (NOR)	1908–48	Yachting
40 years	Durward Knowles (GBR/BAH)	1948–88	Yachting
40 years	Paul Elvstrøm (DEN)	1948–88	Yachting

MOST GAMES/LONGEST SPAN (SUMMER) — WOMEN

7 Games	Kerstin Palm (SWE)	1964–88	Fencing
28 years	Anne Newberry-Ransehousen (USA)	1960–88	Equestrianism
	Christilot Hanson-Boylen (CAN)	1964–92	Equestrianism

MOST GAMES/LONGEST SPAN (WINTER) — MEN

6 Games	Colin Coates (AUS)	1968–88	Speed Skating
6 Games	Carl-Erik Eriksson (SWE)	1964–84	Bobsledding
20 years	John Heaton (USA)	1928–48	Tobogganing
20 years	Max Houben (BEL)	1928–48	Bobsledding
20 years	Richard Torriani (SUI)	1928–48	Ice Hockey
20 years	Frank Stack (CAN)	1932–52	Speed Skating
20 years	Stanislaw Marusarz (POL)	1932–52	Nordic Skiing
20 years	James Bickford (USA)	1936–56	Bobsledding
20 years	Sepp Bradl (AUT)	1936–56	Ski Jumping
20 years	Carl-Erik Eriksson (SWE)	1964–84	Bobsledding
20 years	Colin Coates (AUS)	1968–88	Speed Skating

MOST GAMES/LONGEST SPAN (WINTER) — WOMEN

6 Games	Marja-Liisa Hämäläinen-Kirvesniemi (FIN)	1976–94	Nordic Skiing
18 years	Marja-Liisa Hämäläinen-Kirvesniemi (FIN)	1976–94	Nordic Skiing

Swimming

(See also *Synchronized Swimming, Diving,*
and *Water Polo*)

The sport has been an integral part of the Games since 1896 when the swimming was held in the Bay of Zea near Piraeus. The first champion was Alfréd Hajós (né Guttmann) (HUN) who won the 100m freestyle in freezing water. The first female champion (women's events were introduced in 1912) was Australia's Fanny Durack, also in the 100m freestyle. The first Olympic competition in a pool was in 1908, in a 100m-long tank constructed inside the track at the stadium (later called the White City), London. The first 50m pool was outdoors in 1924 (Paris), and the first one indoors was at Wembley, London in 1948. Emil Rausch (GER), in 1904, was the last person to win an Olympic title using the side-stroke technique.

The most successful swimmer was Mark Spitz (USA) with nine gold medals plus a silver and a bronze in 1968 and 1972. His seven golds at one Games (1972) is unmatched in any sport. The most individual event golds won is five by Krisztina Egerszegi (HUN) 1988–96. Kristin Otto (GDR) tally of six golds at Seoul set female records for most all-time and most at a single Games. Otto is also the only swimmer to win Olympic titles in three different strokes — freestyle, backstroke and butterfly. Dawn Fraser (AUS) in the 100m freestyle, and Krisztina Egerszegi (HUN) in the 200m backstroke, are the only swimmers, male or female, to win the same event three times. Matt Biondi (USA) equalled the record of 11 medals by Spitz, but his comprised of eight golds, two silvers and a bronze 1984–92. Three women have won a record eight medals: Fraser 1956–64 and Kornelia Ender (GDR) 1972–76, both with four golds and four silvers; and Shirley Babashoff (USA) who won two gold and six silver medals in 1972 and 1976. Both Spitz and Babashoff set an endurance record of sorts in 1972 and 1976 respectively by taking part in 13 races within eight days.

The first swimmer to defend successfully an Olympic swimming title was Charles Daniels (USA) in the 100m freestyle in 1908. The first woman to do so was Martha Norelius (USA) in 1928 in the 400m freestyle. She was born in Sweden and her father, Charles, had been a member of the 1906 Swedish Olympic swimming team, while an uncle, Benkt, had won gold in the 1912 gymnastics. Later, her first hus-band was the 1928 Canadian silver medallist oarsman Joseph Wright. Particularly noteworthy is the nine gold medals in nine attempts by the American 4 × 100m medley relay team 1960–96 — they didn't compete in 1980 due to the boycott. In 1996 Claudia Poll (CRC) won the 200m freestyle to gain her country's first ever swimming gold medal. Costa Rica's only other swimming medal, a silver in the same event, was won by Poll's sister, Silvia, in 1988. Also in 1996 Michelle Smith (IRL) not only became the first Irish swimmer to reach an Olympic final, but won three

gold medals and a bronze. Gary Hall Jr (USA) won a gold and two silvers in 1996 — his father had won two silvers and a bronze 1968–76.

The oldest gold medallist was Cecil Healy (AUS) in the 1912 800m relay team, aged 30 years and 229 days. The oldest female champion/medallist was Ursula Happe (GER) in the 1956 200m breaststroke, aged 30 years and 41 days. The oldest medallist was William Henry (GBR), a last-minute replacement in the 1906 relay, aged 46 years and 301 days. The youngest gold medallist was Kyoko Iwasaki (JPN) in the 1992 women's 200m breaststroke in 1964 at 14 years and 6 days. The youngest male champion/medallist was Kusuo Kitamura (JPN) in the 1500m in 1932, aged 14 years and 309 days, while the youngest known individual event medallist in any sport at the Games was Inge Sörensen (DEN), aged 12 years and 24 days winning a bronze in the 200m breaststroke of 1936.

The first dead heat in Games swimming came in the 1984 women's 100m freestyle final when Carrie Steinseifer and Nancy Hogshead (both USA) gained a gold medal each. Also in those Games there was a strange situation when the winner of the 400m freestyle 'B' final, Thomas Fahrner (FRG), set an Olympic record faster than the winner of the 'A' final. The closest to a dead heat in the men's events was in the 1972 400m medley when Gunnar Larsson (SWE) was given the decision over Tim McKee (USA). The margin was 0.002 of a second or about three millimetres. Happily timings and placings are now decided to hundredths only, and the above would now be given as a dead heat. Another controversial decision occurred in the 1960 100m freestyle when Lance Larson (USA) was timed (manually and by the unofficial automatic system) faster than John Devitt (AUS), but the judges placed the Australian first — and that is how the result remained despite protests. In 1968 poolside touch panels were introduced.

In the 1912 100m freestyle competition the three best American swimmers missed the semi-finals because they had been told that there would not be any. Following protests it was agreed that if they were timed, in a special race, faster than the slowest qualifiers from those semis then they would go forward to the final. The outstanding Hawaiian swimmer, Duke Kahanamoku, was so incensed that he broke the world record, and then won the final. At the next Games, in 1920, the final was re-swum after the Australian, William Herald, complained that he was impeded by Norman Ross (USA) — this was before lane dividers were used. The winner of the original race and the re-swim, once again was Duke Kahanamoku (USA). His first swim of 60.4sec was recognised as a world record, even after he recorded a slower time in the re-swim. Kahanamoku, the first of the great Hawaiian swimmers, was born into the Hawaiian royal family, and was named 'Duke' after the Duke of Edinburgh, Queen Victoria's second son, who was visiting the islands at the time. He was a pioneer of surfing, and made many movies in Hollywood. He was the oldest individual event champion in 1920 when five days past his 30th birthday, and remained so until 1956 when Ursula Happe (GDR), 36 days older, won the 200m breaststroke. Duke's brother, Sam, won a bronze in the 1924 100m freestyle.

Hollywood has attracted a number of Olympian swimmers: Romanian-born Johnny Weissmuller (USA) who won five gold medals 1924–28 and then became the most famous *Tarzan* of them all; Clarence 'Buster' Crabbe (USA), the 1932 400m champion, played *Flash Gordon* and *Buck Rogers* in children's serials; Aileen Riggin (USA), the 1920 diving champion, and Eleanor Holm (USA), the 1932 backstroke champion, both took their good looks into movies. Holm was also in a *Tarzan* movie, in 1938, as *Jane* to the hero played by 1936 decathlon champion, Glenn Morris.

Gertrude Ederle (USA) and Greta Andersen (DEN), gold medallists in 1924 and 1948 respectively, both later set English Channel swimming records. As a matter of interest, the first Olympian to swim the English Channel, in 1934, was Edward Temme (GBR), who was in the fourth-placed British water polo team in 1928. Mexico's first ever swimming gold medallist, Felipe Muñoz who won the 1968 200m breaststroke, was nicknamed 'Tibio' which means 'lukewarm' in English. This a result of his father coming from Aguascalientes ('hot water') and his mother from Rio Frio ('cold river'). A change to the rules for 1992 allowed female swimmers to wear two-piece costumes in competition, but only a few competitors took advantage of this at the time, most notably the Italians.

OLYMPIC RECORDS

Men

50m freestyle	21.91sec	Alexander Popov (EUN)	1992
100m freestyle	48.63sec	Matt Biondi (USA)	1988
200m freestyle	1min 46.70sec	Yevgeni Sadovyi (EUN)	1992
400m freestyle	3min 45.00sec	Yevgeni Sadovyi (EUN)	1992
1500m freestyle	14min 43.38sec	Kieren Perkins (AUS)	1992
4 × 100m freestyle	3min 15.41sec	United States	1996
4 × 200m freestyle	7min 11.95sec	Unified Team	1992
100m breaststroke	1min 00.60sec	Fred Deburghgraeve (BEL)	1996
200m breaststroke	2min 10.16sec	Mike Barrowman (USA)	1992
100m backstroke	53.86sec [1]	Jeff Rouse (USA)	1992
200m backstroke	1min 58.47sec	Martin Lopez-Zubero (ESP)	1992
100m butterfly	52.27sec	Denis Pankratov (RUS)	1996
200m butterfly	1min 56.26sec	Mel Stewart (USA)	1992
200m medley	1min 59.91sec	Attila Czene (HUN)	1996
400m medley	4min 14.23sec	Tamás Darnyi (HUN)	1992
4 × 100m medley	3min 34.84sec	United States	1996

[1] First leg in medley relay

Women

50m freestyle	24.79sec	Yang Wenyi (CHN)	1992
100m freestyle	54.50sec	Jingyi Le (CHN)	1996
200m freestyle	1min 57.65sec	Heike Friedrich (GDR)	1988
400m freestyle	4min 03.85sec	Janet Evans (USA)	1988
800m freestyle	8min 20.20sec	Janet Evans (USA)	1988
4 × 100m freestyle	3min 39.29sec	United States	1996
4 × 200m freestyle	7min 59.87sec	United States	1996
100m breaststroke	1min 07.02sec	Penny Heyns (RSA)	1996
200m breaststroke	2min 25.41sec	Penny Heyns (RSA)	1996
100m backstroke	1min 00.68sec	Krisztina Egerzegi (HUN)	1992
200m backstroke	2min 07.06sec	Krisztina Egerzegi (HUN)	1992
100m butterfly	58.62sec	Qian Hong (CHN)	1992
200m butterfly	2min 06.90sec	Mary Meagher (USA)	1984
200m medley	2min 11.65sec	Li Lin (CHN)	1992
400m medley	4min 36.29sec	Petra Schneider (GDR)	1980
4 × 100m medley	4min 02.54sec	United States	1992

YOUGEST & OLDEST MEDALLISTS BY EVENT

Men

50m freestyle	G	20 years and 157 days	Alexander Popov (RUS)	1992
		24 years and 252 days	Alexander Popov (RUS)	1996
	M	19 years and 166 days	Charles Davies (USA)	1904 [1]
		27 years and 298 days	Tom Jager (USA)	1992
100m freestyle	G	15 years and 297 days	Yasuji Miyazaki (JPN)	1932
		30 years and 5 days	Duke Kahanamoku (USA)	1920
	M	15 years and 297 days	Yasuji Miyazaki (JPN)	1932
		33 years and 330 days	Duke Kahanamoku (USA)	1924
200m freestyle	G	18 years and 342 days	Mike Wenden (AUS)	1968
		22 years and 201 days	Mark Spitz (USA)	1972
	M	18 years and 219 days	Antti Kasvio (FIN)	1992
		24 years and 72 days	Andrei Krylov (URS)	1980
400m freestyle	G	16 years and 134 days	Otto Scheff (AUT)	1906
		24 years and 118 days	Norman Ross (USA)	1920
	M	16 years and 134 days	Otto Scheff (AUT)	1906
		34 years and 61 days	John Jarvis (GBR)	1906
1500m freestyle	G	14 years and 309 days	Kusuo Kitamura (JPN)	1932
		28 years and 127 days	Vladimir Salnikov (URS)	1988
	M	14 years and 309 days	Kusuo Kitamura (JPN)	1932
		34 years and 59 days	John Jarvis (GBR)	1906
4 × 100m freestyle	G	18 years and 167 days	Don Schollander (USA)	1964
		27 years and 297 days	Tom Jager (USA)	1992
	M	16 years and 338 days	Peter Bruch (GDR)	1972
		27 years and 321 days	Dirk Richter (GDR)	1992
4 × 200m freestyle	G	15 years and 299 days	Yasuji Mizayaki (JPN)	1932
		30 years and 229 days	Cecil Healy (AUS)	1912
	M	15 years and 299 days	Yasuji Miyazaki (JPN)	1932
		46 years and 301 days	William Henry (GBR)	1906 [2]
100m breaststroke	G	21 years and 73 days	Nobutaka Taguchi (JPN)	1972
		24 years and 117 days	Adrian Moorhouse (GBR)	1988
	M	18 years and 93 days	John Hencken (USA)	1972
		26 years and 156 days	Mark Warnecke (GER)	1996
200m breaststroke	G	17 years and 226 days	Ian O'Brien (AUS)	1964
		28 years and 286 days	Yoshiyuki Tsoruta (JPN)	1932
	M	16 years and 245 days	Reizo Koike (JPN)	1932
		38 years and 25 days	William Robinson (GBR)	1908
100m backstroke	G	16 years and 173 days	Warren Kealoha (USA)	1920
		26 years and 172 days	Jeff Rouse (USA)	1996
	M	16 years and 173 days	Warren Kealoha (USA)	1920
		28 years and 15 days	Herbert Haresnape (GBR)	1908
200m backstroke	G	17 years and 7 days	Sándor Wladár (HUN)	1980
		23 years and 119 days	Brad Bridgewater (USA)	1996
	M	17 years and 7 days	Sándor Wladár (HUN)	1980
		24 years and 185 days	Frank Baltrusch (GDR)	1988
100m butterfly	G	19 years and 48 days	Matt Vogel (USA)	1976
		27 years and 235 days	Pablo Morales (USA)	1992
	M	18 years and 254 days	Mark Spitz (USA)	1968
		27 years and 235 days	Pablo Morales (USA)	1992
200m butterfly	G	17 years and 345 days	Jon Sieben (AUS)	1984
		24 years and 97 days	Michael Gross (FRG)	1988
	M	16 years and 275 days	Neville Hayes (AUS)	1960
		27 years and 324 days	György Tumpek (HUN)	1956
200m medley	G	20 years and 105 days	Alex Baumann (CAN)	1984
		25 years and 58 days	Tamás Darnyi (HUN)	1992
	M	18 years and 41 days	Attila Czene (HUN)	1992
		25 years and 58 days	Tamás Darnyi (HUN)	1992

continued

400m medley	G	17 years and 18 days	Richard Roth (USA)	1964	
		25 years and 54 days	Tamás Darnyi (HUN)	1992	
	M	16 years and 166 days	András Hargitay (HUN)	1972	
		25 years and 349 days	Eric Namesnik (USA)	1996	
4 × 100m medley	G	18 years and 2 days	Neil Brooks (AUS)	1980	
		27 years and 239 days	Pablo Morales (USA)	1992	
	M	16 years and 274 days	Neville Hayes (AUS)	1960	
		30 years and 94 days	Horst-Günter Gregor (GDR)	1968	

Women

50m freestyle	G	20 years and 202 days	Yang Wenyi (CHN)	1992	
		23 years and 162 days	Amy Van Dyken (USA)	1996	
	M	15 years and 252 days	Katrin Meissner (GDR)	1988	
		29 years and 86 days	Angel Martino (USA)	1996	
100m freestyle	G	16 years and 162 days	Sandra Nielson (USA)	1972	
		27 years and 39 days	Dawn Fraser (AUS)	1964	
	M	14 years and 112 days	Franziska Van Almsick (GER)	1992	
		27 years and 136 days	Frances Schroth (USA)	1920	
200m freestyle	G	15 years and 283 days	Shane Gould (AUS)	1972	
		21 years and 17 days	Barbara Krause (GDR)	1980	
	M	14 years and 113 days	Franziska Van Almsick (GER)	1992	
		26 years and 212 days	Dagmar Hase (GER)	1996	
400m freestyle	G	15 years and 281 days	Shane Gould (AUS)	1972	
		22 years and 219 days	Dagmar Hase (GER)	1992	
	M	14 years and 156 days	Sylvia Ruuska (USA)	1956	
		27 years and 139 days	Frances Schroth (USA)	1920	[3]
800m freestyle	G	15 years and 190 days	Keena Rothhammer (USA)	1972	
		20 years and 337 days	Janet Evans (USA)	1992	
	M	15 years and 70 days	Maria Teresa Ramirez (MEX)	1968	
		26 years and 216 days	Dagmar Hase (GER)	1996	
4 × 100m freestyle	G	14 years and 96 days	Lilian 'Pokey' Watson (USA)	1964	
		29 years and 88 days	Angel Martino (USA)	1996	
	M	13 years and 310 days	Kornelia Ender (GDR)	1972	
		29 years and 88 days	Angel Martino (USA)	1996	
4 × 200m freestyle	G	18 years and 135 days	Christina Teuscher (USA)	1996	
		27 years and 129 days	Sheila Taormina (USA)	1996	
	M	16 years and 152 days	Emma Johnson (AUS)	1996	
		27 years and 129 days	Sheila Taormina (USA)	1996	
100m breaststroke	G	18 years and 61 days	Petra Van Staveren (NED)	1984	
		24 years and 85 days	Tonya Dangalakova (BUL)	1988	
	M	14 years and 266 days	Amanda Beard (USA)	1996	
		24 years and 85 days	Tonya Dangalakova (BUL)	1988	
200m breaststroke	G	14 years and 6 days	Kyoko Iwasaki (JPN)	1992	
		30 years and 41 days	Ursula Happe (GER)	1956	
	M	12 years and 24 days	Inge Sörensen (DEN)	1936	
		30 years and 41 days	Ursula Happe (GER)	1956	
100m backstroke	G	15 years and 62 days	Beth Botsford (USA)	1996	
		23 years and 259 days	Karen Harup (DEN)	1948	
	M	14 years and 38 days	Krisztina Egerszegi (HUN)	1988	
		25 years and 135 days	Whitney Hedgepeth (USA)	1996	
200m backstroke	G	14 years and 41 days	Krisztina Egerszegi (HUN)	1988	
		21 years and 344 days	Krisztina Egerszegi (HUN)	1996	
	M	14 years and 41 days	Krisztina Egerszegi (HUN)	1988	
		25 years and 138 days	Whitney Hedgepeth (USA)	1996	
100m butterfly	G	15 years and 342 days	Sharon Stouder (USA)	1964	
		23 years and 159 days	Amy Van Dyken (USA)	1996	
	M	15 years and 75 days	Andrea Pollack (GDR)	1976	
		29 years and 89 days	Angel Martino (USA)	1996	

continued

200m butterfly	G	15 years and 72 days	Andrea Pollack (GDR)	1976
		22 years and 274 days	Kathleen Nord (GDR)	1988
	M	15 years and 72 days	Andrea Pollack (GDR)	1976
		23 years and 334 days	Mary Meagher (USA)	1988
200m medley	G	15 years and 279 days	Shane Gould (AUS)	1972
		21 years and 295 days	Lin Li (CHN)	1992
	M	13 years and 308 days	Kornelia Ender (GDR)	1972
		25 years and 289 days	Lin Li (CHN)	1996
400m medley	G	17 years and 29 days	Gail Neall (AUS)	1972
		21 years and 200 days	Tracey Caulkins (USA)	1984
	M	16 years and 99 days	Sabine Steinbach (GDR)	1968
		21 years and 339 days	Krisztina Egerszegi (HUN)	1996
4 × 100m medley	G	14 years and 269 days	Amanda Beard (USA)	1996
		29 years and 90 days	Angel Martino (USA)	1996
	M	13 years and 314 days	Kornelia Ender (GDR)	1972
		29 years and 90 days	Angel Martino (USA)	1996

[1] 50 yards
[2] 4 × 250m
[3] 300m

SWIMMING MEDALS

(Excluding diving, synchronized swimming and water polo)

	Men			Women			
	G	S	B	G	S	B	Total
United States	103	79	51	75	51	42	401
Australia [1]	25	22	32	15	15	15	124
GDR	6	7	5	32	25	17	92
Soviet Union	14	17	18	4	7	9	69
Great Britain	10	13	14	4	9	12	62
Germany	9	11	12	3	12	15	62
Hungary	14	14	11	9	6	5	59
Japan	12	17	11	3	1	1	45
Canada	6	7	8	1	6	10	38
The Netherlands	–	–	2	9	13	12	36
Sweden	7	10	10	–	2	2	31
FRG	3	4	7	–	1	7	22
France	2	5	9	–	1	3	20
China	–	–	–	5	11	3	19
Denmark	–	2	1	2	3	3	11
Austria	2	3	5	–	–	1	11
Russia	4	2	2	–	–	–	8
Greece	1	4	3	–	–	–	8
Brazil	–	3	5	–	–	–	8
New Zealand [1]	3	1	2	–	–	1	7
South Africa	–	–	–	3	–	4	7
Italy	–	–	4	–	1	2	7
Ireland	–	–	–	3	–	1	4
Belgium	1	1	1	–	–	1	4
Finland	–	1	3	–	–	–	4
Bulgaria	–	–	–	1	1	1	3
Poland	–	1	1	–	–	1	3
Romania	–	–	–	–	1	2	3
Spain	1	–	2	–	–	–	3
Argentina	1	–	–	–	1	–	2
Costa Rica	–	–	–	1	1	–	2
Yugoslavia	–	–	–	1	1	–	2
Mexico	1	–	–	–	–	1	2
Surinam	1	–	1	–	–	–	2

continued

	Men			Women			
	G	S	B	G	S	B	Total
Cuba	–	1	1	–	–	–	2
Philippines	–	–	2	–	–	–	2
Switzerland	–	–	1	–	–	–	1
Venezuela	–	–	1	–	–	–	1
	226 [1]	225	225	171 [2]	169	171 [3]	1187

[1] Double counting of Australia/New Zealand relay team in 1912
[2] Two golds in 1984 100m freestyle
[3] Two bronzes in 1988 50m freestyle

Sydney 2000
XXVII Olympic Games (15 September–1 October)

In 1994 Sydney, Australia was awarded the first Games of the second millennium. It beat bids from Beijing, Brasilia, Istanbul, Manchester, and tentatively, Berlin. There are 28 sports on the programme, including, new to the Games, tae kwon do (with four classes each for men and women), triathlon and synchronized diving. Additionally, for the first time, there will be modern pentathlon, weightlifting and water polo for women. In all there will be a record total of 300 medal events, including 23 new events for women. It was announced in August 1995 that NBC paid a staggering $1.27 billion for the US televeision rights for Sydney ($705 million) and for the Winter Games of 2002. Over 10 000 competitors from some 200 countries are expected.

The main stadium will be the largest ever at the Games with a capacity for 110 000 spectators, and it is expected that the torch relay will be the longest ever, over a distance of 60 852km (31 811 miles).

Synchronised Diving

Will be held for the first time at the Games at Sydney in 2000. There will be separate pairs events for men and women.

Synchronized Swimming

Introduced in the Games in 1984, there were solo and duet events until 1996. At Atlanta they were replaced by a single team event, consisting of eight women. Also, compulsory figures were replaced with a technical programme. The most successful women have been Tracie Ruiz-Conforto (USA) and Carolyn Waldo (CAN) both with two gold and one silver 1984–88. The youngest gold medallist was Tammy Cleland (USA) in the 1996, aged 20 years and 281 days, while the youngest medallist was Valerie Hould-Marchand (CAN) with a silver in 1996, aged 16 years and 65 days. The oldest champions were Karen and

Sarah Josephson (USA) in the 1992 duet, aged 28 years and 210 days. The latter are among the most successful twins ever in Olympic swimming with their gold medal in 1992 to add to the silver from 1988. In 1992 the second place went to another set of twins, Penny and Vicky Vilagos of Canada, who are the oldest medallists at 29 years and 112 days. In the 1992 solo event a mistake by a judge deprived Sylvie Frechette (CAN) from sharing the gold medal. In December 1993 the result was revised. In 2000 the duet event has been reinstated.

SYNCHRONIZED SWIMMING MEDALS

	G	S	B	Total
United States	5	2	–	7
Canada	3	4	–	7
Japan	–	–	7	7
	8 [1]	6	7	21

[1] Tie for gold in 1992

Table Tennis

Recognised as an Olympic sport by the IOC in 1977, table tennis was first included in the 1988 Seoul Games as a medal sport, never having been a demonstration sport. There are 64 men and 32 women, selected by an agreed international formula, competing in men's and women's singles and doubles events.

The most successful player has been Deng Yaping (CHN), only 1.50m (4ft 11in) tall, who successfully retained her singles and doubles titles from 1992 to 1996, thus totalling four gold medals in women's events. The most successful male was Guoliang Liu (CHN) with two golds in 1996, but Yoo Nam-kyu (KOR) has won four medals comprising a gold and three bronzes 1988–96.

The youngest gold medallist was Hyun Jung-hwa (KOR) in the 1988 women's doubles, aged 18 years and 360 days, while the youngest male champion was Yoo Nam-kyu (KOR) winning the 1988 singles, aged 20 years and 119 days. The oldest gold medallist was Jan-Ove Waldner (SWE) winning the 1992 men's singles,

TABLE TENNIS MEDALS

| | Men | | | Women | | | |
	G	S	B	G	S	B	Total
China	4	2	1	5	5	2	19
Korea	1	1	5	1	–	3	11
Sweden	1	–	1	–	–	–	2
Germany	–	1	1	–	–	–	2
Yugoslavia	–	1	–	–	–	1	2
North Korea (PRK)	–	–	–	–	–	2	2
France	–	1	–	–	–	–	1
Chinese Taipei	–	–	–	–	1	–	1
	6	6	8 [1]	6	6	8 [1]	40

[1] Two bronze medals in 1992

aged 26 years and 308 days, while the oldest female champion was Hong Qiao (CHN) in the 1996 women's doubles, aged 27 years and 251 days. The youngest female medallist as Jasna Fazlic (YUG) in the 1988 women's doubles, aged 17 years and 285 days, and the youngest male medallist was Zoran Primorac (YUG) in 1988 at 19 years and 143 days. The oldest female medallist was Yunping Giao (CHN) in the 1996 doubles, aged 27 years and 320 days, and the oldest male medal winner was Wang Tao (CHN) who took silver in the 1996 singles, aged 28 years and 232 days.

Tae Kwon Do

A demonstration sport at Seoul in 1988 and Barcelona in 1992, it will be a medal sport at Sydney in the 2000 Games. The following weight categories will apply: 58kg, 68kg, 80kg and over 80kg for men; and 49kg, 57kg, 67kg and over 67kg for women.

Tallest

The tallest person ever to win an Olympic medal was Tom Burleson (USA) in the silver medal team at Munich in 1972. He was 2.23m (7ft 4in) tall. A member of the 1988 winning Soviet basketball team, Arvidas Sabonis, who also won a bronze in the Lithuanian team in 1992, was reported to be as tall, but was 2.21m (7ft 3in), and is the tallest ever Olympic gold medallist. Probably the tallest ever gold medal winner of an individual athletics event at the Games was Walt Davis (USA) who was 2.04m (6ft 8¼in) when he won the 1952 high jump title.

The tallest female gold medallist was the Soviet basketball player Iuliana Semenova in the winning 1976 and 1980 teams. Although officially given as 2.10m (perhaps a misprint), closer investigation indicates that her correct height was 2.18m (7ft 2in).

The tallest competitor in the Winter Games was Sam Guss (AUS) who competed in the 1984 Alpine events at Sarajevo. He was 2.08m (6ft 10in) tall.

Television
(See also *Media*)

The first live international coverage of the Games came from Rome in 1960, with the Tokyo 1964 pictures the first to be sent by satellite. Live colour television pictures were first broadcast from Mexico City in 1968.

The major providers of television income to the IOC and host cities have been the American networks, whose rivalry has pushed the sums involved ever upwards, as the following table of the winners of US television rights shows.

Summer	$(million)		Winter	$ (million)	
1960	CBS	0.394	1960	CBS	0.050
1964	NBC	1.5	1964	ABC	0.597
1968	ABC	4.5	1968	ABC	2.5
1972	ABC	7.5	1972	NBC	6.4
1976	ABC	25.0	1976	ABC	10.0
1980	NBC	87.0	1980	ABC	15.5
1984	ABC	225.0	1984	ABC	91.5
1988	NBC	300.0	1988	ABC	309.0
1992	NBC	401.0	1992	CBS	243.0
1996	NBC	456.0	1994	CBS	300.0
2000	NBC	705.0	1998	CBS	375.0
2004	NBC	793.0	2002	NBC	545.0
2008	NBC	894.0	2006	NBC	613.0

Tennis

The inclusion of tennis in the Games was suspended from 1924 until 1988, although it was a demonstration sport in 1968 and 1984. The first gold medallist was Irish-born John Pius Boland (GBR) in the 1896 singles. He happened to be in Athens, visiting the famous German archaeologist Heinrich Schliemann, and entered the Games at the last minute. The women's singles champion in 1900, Charlotte Cooper (GBR), was until recently thought to be the first woman to win an Olympic title in any sport (*see* Women). In the early years a number of medal winning pairs were composed of players from two countries, thus Boland combined with a German to win the first doubles title. The most successful player was Max Decugis (FRA) with a total of six medals comprising four golds, one silver and a bronze between 1900 and 1920. Britain's Kitty McKane won a record total for a woman of five (one gold, two silvers and two bronzes) in 1920 and 1924.

The oldest gold medallist was George Hillyard (GBR) in the 1908 men's doubles, aged 44 years and 160 days. The oldest female champion was Winifred McNair (GBR), aged 43 years and 14 days in the women's doubles of 1920. She was also the oldest British female competitor to win a gold medal in any sport. The youngest gold medallist/medallist in tennis was Jennifer Capriati (USA), winner of the 1992 singles, aged 16 years and 132 days, while the youngest male champion was Fritz Traun (GER), Boland's partner in 1896, aged 20 years and 13 days. The youngest male medallist was Max Decugis (FRA) in 1900, aged 17 years and 290 days. Six years later, he and his wife, Marie, won the mixed title, becoming the first married couple to win gold medals in the Olympic Games. Brothers Reggie and Laurie Doherty (GBR) added the 1900 Olympic title to the eight Wimbledon doubles championships they won. Steffi Graf (FRG), in 1988, is the only Grand Slam winner to win an Olympic title.

Many of the greatest names in tennis have played in the Games and there have been 31 gold medal winners who also were successful at Wimbledon. One of the most remarkable of these was Swiss-born Norris Williams (USA), who survived the sinking of the *Titanic* in 1912 by swimming in icy water for over an hour. He won the Croix de Guerre and the Legion d'Honneur in the First World War, a Wimbledon title in 1920, an Olympic gold medal in 1924 (mixed doubles), and died aged 77.

Both 1996 singles winners had fathers who were ex-Olympians: Andre Agassi's father, Emanoul Aghassian, boxed for Iran 1948–52; Lindsay Davenport's father, Winthrop Davenport, played volleyball for the United States in 1968. Additionally, Indian bronze medallist Leander Paes's father won a bronze medal at hockey in 1972.

Tobogganing

See under *Lugeing*

TENNIS MEDALS

	Men [1]			Women			
	G	S	B	G	S	B	Total
Great Britain	11	9	11	5	5	5	46
United States	7	5	6	7	–	3	28
France	6	5	5	2	2	1	21
Greece	–	4	2	1	1	1	9
Germany	3	1	2	–	2	–	8
Czechoslovakia [2]	1	–	5	–	1	1	8
Spain	–	3	–	–	2	2	7
Sweden	–	2	4	–	–	1	7
South Africa	3	2	–	–	–	–	5
Australia	1	–	1	–	–	2	4
FRG	–	–	–	1	–	1	2
Japan	–	2	–	–	–	–	2
Argentina	–	–	1	–	1	–	2
Czech Republic	–	–	–	–	1	1	2
Croatia	–	–	2	–	–	–	2
Soviet Union	–	–	1	–	–	1	2
Switzerland	1	–	–	–	–	–	1
Austria	–	1	–	–	–	–	1
Denmark	–	–	–	–	1	–	1
Bulgaria	–	–	–	–	–	1	1
Hungary	–	–	1	–	–	–	1
India	–	–	1	–	–	–	1
Italy	–	–	1	–	–	–	1
The Netherlands	–	–	1	–	–	–	1
New Zealand	–	–	1	–	–	–	1
Norway	–	–	–	–	–	1	1
	33	34	45	16	16	21	165 [3]

[1] Includes mixed doubles
[2] Includes Bohemia
[3] Two-country pairs counted as two medals

Ray Ewry
The exercises he did after contracting polio as a child strengthened Ray Ewry's legs so well that he won a record 10 gold medals in the now defunct standing jumps, 1900-1908.

Aladár Gerevich
Hungarian-born Aladár Gerevich is regarded as the greatest ever fencer with a sabre, winning a total of ten Olympic medals, of which seven were gold, over a remarkable period of 28 years, 1932-60.

Sixten Jernberg
In 1956 at Cortina d'Ampezzo, at the start of a fabulous Olympic career, Sixten Jernberg (SWE) went on to amass nine skiing medals, including four golds.

Sonja Henie
Seen here practising at St Moritz for the games of 1928, Sonja Henie (NOR) was unbeatable from 1926 to her retirement in 1936, winning three Olympic golds, ten World and six European championships.

Dawn Fraser
Three times Olympic 100m freestyle champion, Dawn Fraser (AUS), won eight medals at three Olympic Games. She also set 27 world records in individual events.

**Ville Ritola/
Paavo Nurmi**
Two of the greatest ever
Finnish distance runners,
Ville Ritola and Paavo
Nurmi, who dominated
the Olympic distance runs
in the 1920s.

Cassius Clay
The 1960 light-heavyweight medal ceremony, with Cassius Clay (USA)
(later Muhammad Ali) the champion, silver medallist Zbigniew
Pietrzykowski (POL) (*right*), and the two bronze medallists Guilio Saraudi
(ITA) (*far left*) and Tony Madigan (AUS)

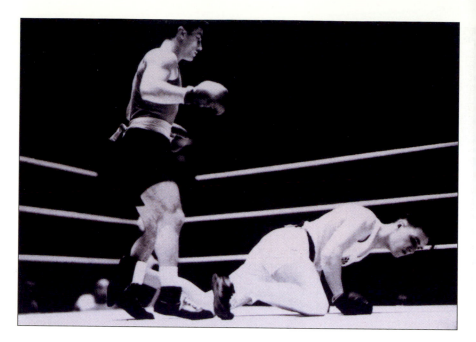

László Papp
One of triple gold medallist László Papp's many Olympic victories. Although the Hungarian authorities frowned on professional boxing, he eventually became a European champion.

Fanny Blankers-Koen
Dutchwoman Fanny Blankers-Koen was recently voted the greatest female athlete of the century – not least for her four gold medals in the 1948 Games. Here she wins the 100m from Great Britain's Dorothy Manley (*far left*) and Shirley Strickland (AUS) (*middle*).

Jesse Owens
A famous photograph of Jesse Owens (USA), the winner of four gold medals at the 1936 Games at Berlin. It shows all the power and grace which delighted the fans, much to the annoyance of German authorities.

Nadia Comaneci
Nadia Comaneci (ROM) was the first gymnast to score a perfect 10 in Olympic competition, one of them on the beam. After moving to the United States at the end of her career, she married American gymnast Bart Conner.

Olga Korbut
Although not the best Soviet gymnast, Olga Korbut's gamine charm made her the star of the gymnastics at Munich in 1972, and by 1976, shown here when she was captain of the Soviet team, she was past her best.

Barcelona
The tremendous fireworks display at the opening of the 1992 Olympic Games at Barcelona, the birthplace of the IOC President, Juan Antonio Samaranch.

Bjørn Dæhlie
Seen here in the 50km in 1998, Bjørn Dæhlie (NOR) added
three golds and a silver at Nagano to bring his total from
three Games to a remarkable eight gold and four silver medals.

Jean-Claude Killy
Triple gold medallist Jean-Claude Killy (FRA) won his titles on home
ground Grenoble, in 1968. He later became co-president of the
Organising Committee for the 1992 Games at Albertville.

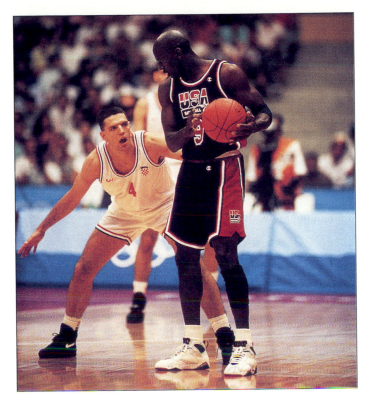

Michael Jordan
One of the stars on the 1992 American 'Dream Team', Michael Jordan is almost disdainful of Croatian Drazen Petrovic in the final, which the United States won 117-85.

Pinsent/Redgrave
Great Britain's Matthew Pinsent and Steve Redgrave won the 1992 coxless pairs, and for good measure, did it again in 1996. Redgrave will be trying for a record fifth consecutive rowing gold at Sydney.

Michael Johnson
Michael Johnson (USA) after his fabulous clocking of
19.32sec winning the 1996 200m event – a record time that
experts consider will last well into the new century.

Dorando Pietri
The famous picture of Dorando Pietri (ITA) being assisted over the line in the 1908
marathon, after falling five times on the track. He was disqualified, but the ending made
him one of the most famous runners of all time.

Rodnina/Zaitsev
Irina Rodnina (URS), the greatest pairs skater ever, seen here with her partner and husband, Alexander Zaitsev, won three Olympic pairs titles (the first with a different partner), and 10 world championships (six with her husband).

Mark Spitz
By winning seven swimming gold medals in one Games, at Munich in 1972, Mark Spitz (USA) set a record unmatched by any other sportsman. In all of them, including the relay events, new world records were set. He had won two gold medals, a silver and a bronze four years previously at Mexico City.

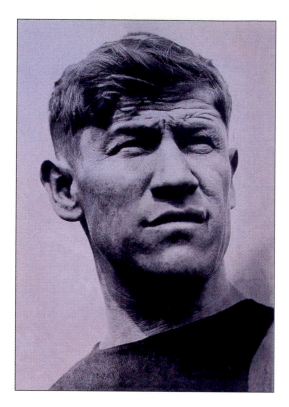

Jim Thorpe
After Jim Thorpe (USA) had won the decathlon and athletics pentathlon at Stockholm in 1912, the King of Sweden called him 'The greatest athlete in the world'. He was also one of the best American football players of his era.

Naim Suleymanoglu
Born Naim Suleimanov in Bulgaria of Turkish stock, weightlifter Naim Suleymanoglu's change of nationality was 'bought' by Turkey. Gratefully he repaid them by winning the 1988 and 1992 Olympic featherweight titles.

Eric Heiden
A picture of power on the line in the 1980 Games, Eric Heiden (USA) won all five events, in Olympic record times. His sister, Beth, won a bronze medal at the same Games.

Teofilo Stevenson
Three-time Olympic heavyweight champion, Cuba's Teofilo Stevenson was undoubtedly the greatest heavyweight boxer never to win a world professional title – the Cuban government would not allow him to fight professionally.

(Left)
Kristin Otto
Kristin Otto's unique haul of six swimming gold medals at the 1988 Games encompassed three different strokes. She was the last of the great East German swimmers who dominated their sport from the mid-1970s to the end of the 1980s.

(Below)
Mark Todd
Mark Todd (NZL) on his great horse *Charisma* winning the three-day event in 1984. They successfully defended it four years later.

(Right)
Steve Batchelor
Steve Batchelor celebrates his winning goal for Great Britain against West Germany in the 1988 hockey final.

(Below)
Carl Lewis
With Carl Lewis (USA) taking the baton on the anchor leg of the sprint relay in 1984, it wasn't a question of whether his team would win, but what time would they clock. It was 37.38sec – a new world record.

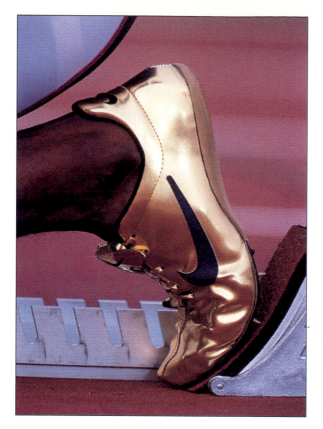

Shoe
The golden shoes worn by Michael Johnson (USA) at Atlanta anticipated his two winning performances at those Games, which were enhanced by a superlative 200m world record.

(Below and Opposite Bottom)
Homebush
Homebush Stadium, Sydney, the focal point for the 2000 Games. It will be the largest ever Olympic main stadium, seating 110,000 spectators.

Emil Zátopek
Perhaps the greatest of all distance runners, Emil Zátopek of Czechoslovakia. His records have been broken. But it is unlikely that anyone will ever match his 5km, 10km and marathon treble of 1952.

Torvill/Dean
Jayne Torvill and Christopher Dean (GBR), arguably the finest ice dancers of all time. In addition to their legendary 1984 Olympic triumph they also won four World championships.

Tokyo 1964
XVIII Olympic Games (10–24 October)

Attended by representatives of 93 countries, comprising 5140 competitors, of which 683 were women.

Asia's first Games witnessed large crowds and a tremendous assault on the record books. Vast sums, estimated to be as much as $3 billion, were spent not only on the stadiums but also on transport facilities. Teams from 14 countries made their first appearance at the Games, but South Africa no longer received an invitation. Also missing were Indonesia and North Korea, whose athletes, having competed in the previous year's unsanctioned GANEFO Games (Games of the New Emergent Forces), were banned. Emperor Hiriohito performed the formal opening, and the flame was brought into the stadium by a young runner who had been born near Hiroshima on the day the atomic bomb had been dropped in 1945. The Olympic flag was raised to the top of a flagpole which measured 15.21m (50ft 6¾in), the distance reached in the triple jump by Mikio Oda in 1928 when he won Japan's first Olympic gold medal. The growth of the Games can be highlighted by distance runner Ron Clarke's remark after failing to gain the gold medal over 10 000m. Having dropped all the known opposition he looked over his shoulder and saw 'an Ethiopian, a North African Arab and an American Indian'. This latter, Billy Mills, a part-Sioux Marine officer, was America's first ever winner at the distance. In the marathon, Abebe Bikila (ETH), only six weeks after having his appendix removed — and this time wearing shoes — became the first man to retain the title, and Peter Snell (NZL) won the rare 800m/1500m double. The winner of the 100m, Bob Hayes, ran a phenomenal last leg in the 4 × 100m relay, to regain the title that the USA had lost in Rome for the first time in 40 years. There is a story told that one of the beaten teams denounced the USA team to the effect that all they had was Hayes. This was met by the now famous rejoinder, 'Man, that's all we needed'. Great Britain won its first ever gold in women's athletics when Mary Rand took the long jump and her roommate Ann Packer added the 800m gold.

At the much admired pool, Australia and the United States won all the titles but one. That was the women's 200m breaststroke, the event which had also prevented a clean sweep by the two swimming superpowers in Rome. Here it was won by Galina Prozumenshchikova (later Stepanova), the Soviet Union's first ever swimming gold medallist. She won a further two silver and two bronze at the next two Games. Don Schollander (USA) became the first swimmer to win four golds in a single Games. Close behind him came Sharon Stouder (USA) with three gold and a silver in the women's events. Australia's Dawn Fraser, just past her 27th birthday, won her third consecutive 100m title, then an achievement in swimming, and added a relay silver to take her total haul to eight medals, a record for a female swimmer. Another competitor to complete a triple was Soviet

rower Vyacheslav Ivanov by winning the single sculls once again. An unusual thing occurred in the eights where the cox of the winning American crew, Róbert Zimonyi, aged 46, had been cox of the third placed Hungarian pairs in 1948. In water polo, the Hungarian veteran Deszö Gyarmati won his third gold medal, his fifth medal in as many Games.

The most medals were won by a gymnast Larissa Latynina (URS) with two golds, two silvers and two bronzes. Her team-mate Boris Shakhlin brought his total of golds since 1956 to seven, of which a record six were in individual events. In weightlifting, Norbert Schemansky (USA) won a bronze to add to his previous gold, silver and bronze since 1948, giving him a record for his sport of four medals. Unusually, wrestler Imre Polyák (HUN) finally won gold in his fourth Games after an unprecedented three silvers. One of

1964 MEDALS (SUMMER)

	G	S	B
United States	36	26	28
Soviet Union	30	31	35
Japan	16	5	8
Germany	10	22	18
Italy	10	10	7
Hungary	10	7	5
Poland	7	6	10
Australia	6	2	10
Czechoslovakia	5	6	3
Great Britain	4	12	2
Bulgaria	3	5	2
Finland	3	–	2
New Zealand	3	–	2
Romania	2	4	6
The Netherlands	2	4	4
Turkey	2	3	1
Sweden	2	2	4
Denmark	2	1	3
Yugoslavia	2	1	2
Belgium	2	–	1
France	1	8	6
Canada	1	2	1
Switzerland	1	2	1
Bahamas	1	–	–
Ethiopia	1	–	–
India	1	–	–
Korea	–	2	1
Trinidad and Tobago	–	1	2
Tunisia	–	1	1
Argentina	–	1	–
Cuba	–	1	–
Pakistan	–	1	–
Philippines	–	1	–
Iran	–	–	2
Brazil	–	–	1
Ghana	–	–	1
Ireland	–	–	1
Kenya	–	–	1
Mexico	–	–	1
Nigeria	–	–	1
Uruguay	–	–	1

the two new sports (the other being volleyball), judo had been included at the express wish of the host country. It was considered to be a Japanese monopoly, and the whole country suffered a terrible shock when the Open class judo title went to the big (1.98m, 6ft 6in) Dutchman Anton Geesink. Leading the United States basketball team to its sixth consecutive victory was Bill Bradley, a Rhodes scholar and later a member of the US Senate and presidential candidate.

The oldest gold medallist in Tokyo was Australian 5.5m yachtsman William Northam, aged 59 years and 23 days, and the youngest was swimmer Lilian 'Pokey' Watson (USA) aged, 14 years and 96 days in the freestyle relay. The oldest female winner was Katalin Juhász Nagy (HUN), a member of the foil team at 31 years and 328 days, while the youngest male champion was swimmer Richard Roth (USA) in the 400m medley 18 days past his 17th birthday. Teammate 1500m freestyler John Nelson was the youngest male medallist at 16 years and 131 days.

Torch Relay

In the Ancient Games a flame would burn at the altar of the statue of Zeus (one of the Seven Wonders of the World) during the period of the Games. In 1928, at Amsterdam, this was commemorated by a flame burning in the stadium throughout the competitions. The chairman of the organising committee of the Berlin Games in 1936, Carl Diem, had the idea of lighting the Olympic flame at Olympia in Greece, and then bringing it by a series of relay runners, across Europe, to the Olympic stadium in Berlin. It has been done ever since, including transportation by sea and air where necessary. It was inaugurated for the Winter Games in 1952.

Trampolining

In 2000, at Sydney, two events have been added to the gymnastics programme.

Trebles

Frank Kungler (USA) has won medals at three sports at the same Games. At St Louis in 1904 he won a silver in wrestling, a bronze in tug-of-war, and two bronzes in weightlifting. Another excellent treble attempt was by Viggo Jensen (DEN) at Athens in 1896 when he won a gold and silver in weightlifting, a silver and bronze in shooting, and placed fourth in the rope climb. Possibly the greatest treble in Olympic history, albeit all in the same sport, was that by the Czech distance runner, Emil Zátopek, who won the 5000m, 10 000m and marathon at Helsinki in 1952, all within eight days, including running a heat of the shorter distance.

Triathlon

This will be contested at the Games for the first time at Sydney in 2000. There will be contests for men and women, and both will consist of a 1500m swim, a 40km cycle race and a 10km run.

Tug-of-War

This sport was part of the athletics programme 1900–20. Three men won a record two golds and one silver between 1908 and 1920: John Shepherd, Frederick Humphreys and Edwin Mills, all from Great Britain. The oldest gold medallist was Humphreys, aged 42 years and 204 days in 1920, while the youngest was Karl Staaf (SWE), aged 19 years and 101 days in 1900. There were some strange team compositions in the early days: the winning 1900 team was composed of three Swedes and three Danes; the 1904 competition was between American clubs; and the 1908 tournament was between British Police Clubs with London City police beating their colleagues from Liverpool.

TUG-OF-WAR MEDALS

	G	S	B	Total
Great Britain	2	2	1	5
Sweden	2	–	1	3
United States	1	1	1	3
Denmark	1	–	–	1
Germany	1	–	–	1
France	–	1	–	1
Greece	–	1	–	1
The Netherlands	–	1	–	1
Belgium	–	–	1	1
	7 [1]	6	4 [2]	17

[1] Joint Denmark/Sweden team in 1900, counted as two medals
[2] No bronze medals in 1900 or 1912

Turin 2006
XX Winter Games

In June 1999 the Italian city of Turin was selected as the venue for the 2006 Winter Olympics. Other places in contention had been Sion, Klagenfurt, Poprad-Tatry, Zakopane and Helsinki.

Twins

The first twins to win Olympic medals were Eric and Vilhelm Carlberg (SWE) in the 1908 shooting events. Four years later, at Stockholm, they became the first twins to win gold medals, in the duelling pistol 30m team event. The most successful have been the rowing twins, Bernd and Jörg Landvoigt (GDR), who won the coxless pairs in 1976 and 1980. Among women, the most successful are Karen and Sarah Josephson (USA) who won a silver and then gold in the synchronized duet swimming events in 1988 and 1992.

Volleyball
(See also *Beach Volleyball*)

Introduced into the Games in 1964 for men and women, volleyball has been dominated by Soviet teams. Their men's teams have played 51 matches losing only 10 between 1964 and 1992 (when they failed to win a medal for the first time), and their women played 37 matches, losing only five in the same period. The most successful player was Inna Ryskal (URS) with two gold and two silver medals, 1964–76. The best by a male player was two golds and a silver by Yuri Poyarkov (URS) 1964–72. Ryskal has competed in a record four Games in the women's sport, which is matched in the men's game by Katsutoshi Nekoda (JPN), Antonio Moreno (BRA) and Amauri Ribiero (BRA).

The oldest gold medallist was Georgi Mondsolevski (URS), aged 34 years and 274 days in 1968, and the oldest female winner/medallist was Ludmila Buldakova (URS), aged 34 years and 105 days in 1972. The youngest gold medallist was Regla Herrera (CUB) in 1992, aged 17 years and 177 days, and the youngest male champion was Marcelo Negrao (BRA), aged 19 years and 303 days in 1992. The oldest medallist was Bohumil Golián (TCH) winning a bronze in 1968, aged 37 years and 215 days, while the youngest was Yevgeniya Artamonova of the Unified Team in 1992 at 17 years and 22 days. The youngest male medallist was Alexander Savin (URS) in 1976, aged 19 years and 29 days.

In 1996 beach volleyball tournaments for men and women were introduced (*see* beach volleyball).

Water Polo

The first Olympic contest was won by the Osborne Swimming Club, Manchester, representing Great Britain in 1900. Five players have won three gold medals each: George Wilkinson (GBR) 1900, 1908 and 1912; Paul Radmilovic and Charles Smith (both GBR) 1908–20; Dezsö Gyarmati and György Kárpáti (HUN) 1952, 1956 and 1964. Of these Radmilovic, Welsh-born to a Greek father and Irish mother, also won a gold in the 4 × 200m team in 1908. He 1908–28, Gyarmati 1948–64, and Gianni De Magistris (ITA) 1968–84, competed in a record five Olympic tournaments. However, the Hungarian is the most successful player, adding a silver in 1948 and a bronze in 1960. He became one of the few Olympians in any sport to win medals in five Games. Gyarmati also heads a fine Olympic family, as his wife Éva Székely won a gold (1952) and a silver (1956) in the 200m breaststroke, and their daughter, Andrea, won silver and bronze medals in the 1972 backstroke and butterfly events respectively. She then added to the family total of medals by marrying Mihály Hesz (HUN), a canoeist with a gold (1968 K1) and a silver (1964 K1).

The oldest gold medallist was Charles Smith (GBR), aged 41 years and 217 days in 1920, while the youngest was György Kárpáti (HUN) in 1952, aged 17 years and 40 days. The oldest medallist was also Smith, while the youngest was Paul Vasseur (FRA) in 1900, aged 15 years and 305 days. The first brothers to win gold medals in the same team were Ferenc and Alajos Keserü (HUN) in 1932, and they were matched by Tulio and Franco Pandolfini (ITA) in 1948. Georgi

VOLLEYBALL MEDALS

	Men			Women			
	G	S	B	G	S	B	Total
Soviet Union	3	2	1	4	3	–	13
Japan	1	1	1	2	2	1	8
United States	2	–	1	–	1	1	5
Cuba	–	–	1	2	–	–	3
Brazil	1	1	–	–	–	1	3
China	–	–	–	1	1	1	3
Poland	1	–	–	–	–	2	3
The Netherlands	1	1	–	–	–	–	2
GDR	–	1	–	–	1	–	2
Bulgaria	–	1	–	–	–	1	2
Czechoslovakia	–	1	1	–	–	–	2
Italy	–	1	1	–	–	–	2
Peru	–	–	–	–	1	–	1
Argentina	–	–	1	–	–	–	1
Korea	–	–	–	–	–	1	1
North Korea (PRK)	–	–	–	–	–	1	1
Romania	–	–	1	–	–	–	1
Yugoslavia	–	–	1	–	–	–	1
	9	9	9	9	9	9	54

Mshvenieradze (URS) won a gold medal in 1980, going one better than his father Piotr, who had gained a silver (1960) and a bronze (1956). A number of men have won medals at both swimming and water polo, the most notable being Johnny Weissmuller (USA) who gained a bronze in 1924 on the same day that he won two freestyle golds. Tim Shaw (USA) who won a silver medal in the 1976 400m freestyle won another in the 1984 water polo competition.

The highest score by any team was in the 1996 semi-final when Italy beat Hungary 20–18, a match which also set an aggregate record of 38. The biggest margin of victory came when the GDR beat UAE 19–2 in 1968. The most goals scored by an individual in one game is nine, by Zoran Jankovic of Yugoslavia against Japan in 1968, and by Manuel Estiarte for Spain against Brazil in 1984. In the winning Hungarian teams of 1932 and 1936, Olivér Halassy, had had a leg amputated below the knee as a child. In 2000, at Sydney, there will be an inaugural tournament for women.

WATER POLO MEDALS

	G	S	B	Total
Hungary	6	3	3	12
United States	1	4	3	8
Soviet Union	2	2	4	8
Yugoslavia	3	4	–	7
Italy	3	1	2	6
Belgium	–	4	2	6
Great Britain	4	–	–	4
France	1	–	3	4
Germany	1	2	–	3
Sweden	–	1	2	3
Spain	1	1	–	2
The Netherlands	–	–	2	2
Croatia	–	1	–	1
FRG	–	–	1	1
	22	23 1	22 1	67

1   Two bronzes in 1900; two silvers and no bronze in 1904

Water Skiing

A demonstration sport, held at Kiel, Germany in 1972, with 36 competitors from 20 countries, with many of the best skiers in the world. Events were won by Roby Zucchi (ITA), Ricky McCormick (USA), Willy Stähle (NED), Liz Allan-Shetter (USA) and Sylvie Maurial (FRA).

Weightlifting

Two events were held in 1896, consisting of one-arm and two-arm lifts. The first Olympic weightlifting champion was Viggo Jensen (DEN) who won the two-

arm competition from Launceston Eliot (GBR); both had lifted the same weight but the Briton had moved one of his feet. The positions were reversed in the other event. An amusing incident occurred when an attendant was having great trouble moving one of the weights. Prince George of Greece, a member of the organising committee and an immensely big and strong man, bent down and easily lifted it aside. Jensen was one of the first great all-rounders, as he also won silver and bronze medals at pistol and rifle shooting, and placed fourth in the rope climb.

The sport was not included in the Games of 1900, 1908 and 1912. In 1920 the contests were decided in the aggregate of a one-hand snatch, a one-hand jerk, and a two-hands jerk. In 1924, an additional two lifts were included: two-hands press and snatch. Between 1928 and 1972 the result depended on the aggregate of three two-handed lifts: the press, snatch and clean and jerk. In 1976 the press was eliminated, owing to difficulty in judging it correctly, and the total now is for the snatch and the clean and jerk. At the suggestion of the IOC the forerunner of the International Weightlifting Federation (IWF) was formed in 1920 to control the sport.

Only Naim Suleymanoglu (TUR) has won three gold medals, 1988–96, all in the featherweight category. Of the 14 men to win two gold medals, only Tommy Kono (USA), Norair Nurikyan (BUL) and Kakhi Kakhiashvili (EUN/GRE) have won them in different categories. Kono won the 67.5kg (1952) and the 82.5kg (1956); Kakhiashvili won the 91kg (1992) and the 99kg (1996); more unusually Nurikyan moved down from the 60kg (1972) to the 56kg (1976). Norbert Schemansky (USA) has won the most medals with one gold, one silver and two bronzes medals between 1948 and 1964.

The oldest gold medallist was Rudolf Plukfelder (URS) in the 82.5kg class of 1964, aged 36 years and 40 days, while Schemansky was the oldest medallist in 1964, aged 40 years and 141 days. The youngest gold medallist was Zeng Guoqiang (CHN) who won the 52kg class in 1984, aged 19 years and 133 days, and the youngest ever medallist was Andrei Socaci (ROM) who won a 1984 silver in the 67.5kg category, aged 18 years and 43 days. The oldest known competitor was 56-year-old Teunist Jonck (SAF) in 1952. It was originally reported that Mehmet Djemal (TUR), who competed in 1924, was only 13 years of age — this has proved to be untrue. Imre Földi (HUN) competed in five Games, 1960–76. The heaviest weightlifter ever at the Games was Mark Henry (USA) in 1996 when he weighed in at 184.92kg (407.5lbs). The greatest single weight lifted at the Games came in 1996 when super-heavyweight Andrei Chemerkin (RUS) made a clean and jerk of 260kg (573lbs) .

The only brothers to win medals in the same event at the same Games were Yoshinobu and Yoshiyuki Miyake (JPN) who won gold and bronze medals respectively in the 60kg class in 1968. Yoshinobu also won another gold and a silver, but Peter and James George (USA) hold the family record for medals with one gold, three silvers and a bronze between 1948 and

1960. The silver medallist in the 82.5kg class in 1948, Harold Sakata (USA), later gained fame portraying *Oddjob* in the James Bond film *Goldfinger*. Incidentally, the margin of victory (37.5kg) winner in this event, Stanley Stanczyk (USA), was a record for Olympic competition. In the 1988 featherweight class (up to 60kg) Naim Suleymanoglu (TUR) — for whose emigration the Turkish government is reported to have paid $1 million to Bulgaria — set an Olympic record, equalling that of the next weight class.

Disqualification due to use of drugs has affected this sport more than most with the first cases, gold medallist Zbigniew Kaczmarek (POL) and silver medallist Blagoi Blagoyev (BUL), being disqualified in 1976. At the end of 1992 the old weight classes were abolished by the IWF and replaced by new ones, in an attempt to replace any of the old records which may have been set by drug users prior to the introduction of strict controls. At Sydney in 2000 there have been further changes to the weight classes, and the introduction of events for women. The new categories are as follows: 56kg, 62kg, 69kg, 77kg, 85kg, 94kg, 105kg and over 105kg for men; and 48kg, 53kg, 58kg, 63kg, 69kg, 75kg and over 75kg for women.

WEIGHTLIFTING MEDALS

	G	S	B	Total
Soviet Union	44	25	2	71
United States	15	16	10	41
Bulgaria	10	14	7	31
Poland	4	3	19	26
Germany	5	5	11	21
China	6	6	7	19
Hungary	2	7	10	19
France	9	2	4	15
Italy	5	5	5	15
Japan	2	2	8	12
Greece	5	3	3	11
Austria	4	5	2	11
Romania	2	6	3	11
GDR	1	4	6	11
Egypt	5	2	2	9
Iran	1	3	5	9
Czechoslovakia	3	2	3	8
FRG	2	2	3	7
Estonia	1	3	3	7
Great Britain	1	3	3	7
Korea	1	1	4	6
North Korea (PRK)	–	2	3	5
Turkey	4	–	–	4
Cuba	2	1	1	4
Belgium	1	2	1	4
Australia	1	1	2	4
Switzerland	–	2	2	4
Sweden	–	–	4	4
Russia	2	1	–	3
Denmark	1	2	–	3
Finland	1	–	2	3
Trinidad and Tobago	–	1	2	3
The Netherlands	–	–	3	3
Ukraine	1	–	1	2
Canada	–	2	–	2
Argentina	–	1	1	2
Norway	1	–	–	1
Kazakhstan	–	1	–	1
Lebanon	–	1	–	1
Luxembourg	–	1	–	1
Singapore	–	1	–	1
Iraq	–	–	1	1
Chinese Taipei	–	–	1	1
	144 [1]	138	146 [2,3,4]	428

[1] Tie for gold in 1928 and 1936 lightweight class
[2] Four-way tie for bronze in 1896
[3] Triple tie for bronze in 1906 heavyweight class
[4] No bronze in 1992 light-heavyweight class

Winter Games

The first Winter Olympic Games were held at Chamonix, France in 1924. At first it was only called the 'The International Winter Sports Week' in deference to the Scandinavian countries who worried that a Winter Olympic meeting would detract from the importance of their Nordic Games. It was only in 1926 that, retrospectively, it was accorded Olympic status. Prior to this, there had been figure skating in London in 1908, and figure skating and ice hockey at Antwerp in 1920, both times as part of the Summer Games programme.

Winter Pentathlon

A demonstration sport held at St Moritz in 1948 and comprising a 10km cross-country skiing race, a pistol shoot, fencing, downhill skiing and horse-riding over a distance of 3500m. Gustaf Lindh (SWE) came first, with his team-mate, Willie Grut, second. Grut later that year won the modern pentathlon in the Summer Games by a record margin. In sixth-place was Derek Allhusen (GBR) who, 20 years later, in his 55th year won an equestrian gold medal at Mexico City.

Women
Participation in the Olympic Games

In the Ancient Games women were banned, under threat of death, from even attending as spectators. The only exceptions being made for the high priestesses of the most important gods. Nevertheless, it was possible for a woman to gain an Olympic prize — as the owner of a winning chariot. One of the first to win in such a way was Belistike of Macedonia, the owner of the champion two-horse chariot in 268BC. Some women defied the rules and disguised themselves, but were found out and thrown over a cliff on discovery. It is recorded that Pherenice of Rhodes acted as a second to watch her son, Pisidores, win his event. In her excitement she gave herself away, but when it was realised that not only her son, but also her father and brothers had all been Olympic victors, she was pardoned.

The founder of the Modern Games, Baron de Coubertin, was not in favour of women competing at the Games, but in 1900, at Paris, women were allowed in specified events. It has always been thought that the first female Olympic champion was Charlotte Cooper (GBR), the winner of the women's tennis singles at Paris in 1900, but new evidence now gives that honour to Helen, Countess de Pourtalès, a crew member of the Swiss gold medal yacht *Lerina* in the 1-2 ton class at the same Games. She also becomes the first ever female Olympic competitor.

Women's swimming events were included for the first time at Stockholm in 1912, and athletics events at Amsterdam in 1928. Soccer was added and proved very popular, in 1996. By the Sydney Games in 2000, there are 120 events for women, compared to 168 for the men, and another 12 which are mixed. In the Winter Games, female skaters competed from the beginning, and Alpine skiing events began, alongside the men, in 1936. In 1998, there was a women's ice hockey tournament.

Wrestling

Wrestling was the most popular sport in the ancient Games with victors recorded from 708BC. The most famous was Milon of Kroton, a five-time winner. Greco-Roman wrestling was included in the 1896 Games and freestyle in 1904. Basically, holds are unlimited in freestyle, but in the Greco-Roman style holds below the waist are barred. There was no bodyweight limit in Athens and it was won, surprisingly, by

gymnastics triple gold medallist Carl Schuhmann (GER), who was only 1.63m (5ft 4in) tall, and he defeated Games weightlifting champion, Launceston Eliot (GBR), in the preliminaries. Until a time limit was set in 1924 bouts often lasted for remarkable lengths of time. The most extreme was when Martin Klein, an Estonian representing Russia, and Alfred 'Alpo' Asikainen of Finland, in the 1912 Greco-Roman middleweight class, wrestled for 11hrs 40mins. Klein won, but was too exhausted to challenge for the gold medal. In the light-heavyweight final that year, Anders Ahlgren (SWE) and Ivar Böhling (FIN) were declared equal second after nine hours without a decision, and no gold medal was awarded.

Four men have won three gold medals: Carl Westergren (SWE), 1920–32; Ivar Johansson (SWE) 1932–36, Alexander Medved (URS) 1964–72, and Alexander Karelin (URS/EUN/RUS) 1988–96. Karelin is the only man to win three successive titles in the same event, Greco-Roman super-heavyweight. Johansson, 1932, and Kristjan Palusala (EST), 1936, are the only men to win titles in both styles at the same Games, although Kaarle Antila (FIN) had achieved this distinction previously over a two Games period, 1920–24. Wilfried Dietrich (GER/FRG) won most medals with one gold, two silvers and two bronzes at both styles between 1956 and 1968, and competed in a record seven tournaments, in both styles, 1956–72. Dietrich, 1956–72; Mario Tovar Gonzalez (MEX), 1952–68; Khorloo Baianmunkh (MGL), 1964–80; Czeslaw Kwiecinski (POL), 1964–80; and George Mackenzie (GBR), 1908–28, competed at a record five Games in the one style. Mackenzie also competed over a record span of 20 years. Although a number of brothers have each won gold medals, uniquely two pairs of brothers, Ed and

WRESTLING MEDALS

	Freestyle			Greco-Roman			
	G	S	B	G	S	B	Total
Soviet Union	31	17	15	37	19	13	132
United States	44	33	22	2	5	3	109
Finland	8	7	10	19	21	18	83
Sweden	8	10	8	19	16	19	80
Bulgaria	7	16	9	8	14	7	61
Turkey	16	11	6	10	4	3	50
Hungary	3	4	7	15	9	11	49
Japan	16	9	8	4	4	2	43
Romania	1	–	4	6	8	13	32
Germany	1	3	3	4	13	8	32
Korea	4	7	6	4	1	5	27
Iran	4	9	12	–	1	1	27
Poland	–	1	3	5	8	6	23
Italy	1	–	–	5	4	9	19
Great Britain	3	4	10	–	–	–	17
Yugoslavia	1	1	2	3	5	4	16
Czechoslovakia	–	1	3	1	6	4	15
Switzerland	4	4	5	–	–	1	14
France	2	2	3	1	2	2	12
Denmark	–	–	–	2	3	7	12

continued

	Freestyle			Greco-Roman			
	G	S	B	G	S	B	Total
Estonia	2	1	–	3	–	4	10
Russia	3	1	–	1	3	2	10
Canada	–	5	5	–	–	–	10
FRG	–	1	3	1	3	1	9
Greece	–	–	1	1	3	4	9
North Korea (PRK)	3	2	3	–	–	–	8
Cuba	1	–	2	2	1	2	8
Mongolia	–	4	4	–	–	–	8
GDR	–	2	1	2	1	1	7
Austria	–	–	1	1	2	2	6
Egypt (UAR)	–	–	–	1	2	2	5
Norway	–	1	–	2	1	1	5
Ukraine	–	–	2	1	–	1	4
Belgium	–	3	–	–	–	1	4
Belarus	–	–	–	–	2	1	3
Australia	–	1	2	–	–	–	3
Lebanon	–	–	–	–	1	2	3
Armenia	–	1	–	1	–	–	2
Kazakhstan	–	–	1	1	–	–	2
China	–	–	–	–	–	2	2
Azerbaijan	–	1	–	–	–	–	1
Latvia	–	–	–	–	1	–	1
Mexico	–	–	–	–	1	–	1
Syria	–	1	–	–	–	–	1
Georgia	–	–	1	–	–	–	1
India	–	–	1	–	–	–	1
Moldova	–	–	–	–	–	1	1
Pakistan	–	–	1	–	–	–	1
	165	164	167 [1]	163 [2]	165	165	989

[1] Two bronzes in 1920 heavyweight class
[2] No gold in 1912 light-heavyweight class

Lou Banach and Dave and Mark Schultz, all from the United States, won titles in 1984. The only twins to win gold medals were Anatoli and Sergei Beloglazov (URS) in 1980, and Ed and Lou Banach (USA) in 1984. Kustaa and Hermanni Pihlajamäki (FIN), who won three golds, one silver and a bronze between 1924 and 1936, were not brothers, as is often thought, but cousins. A unique situation occurred in the freestyle 82kg class in 1996, when Elmadi Zhabrailov (KZK) beat his brother Lucman representing Moldova. The first black champion was Kenny Monday (USA) in the 1988 freestyle welterweight class.

The oldest gold medallist/medallist was Adolf Lindfors (FIN) in 1920, aged 41 years and 199 days. The youngest champion was Saban Trstena (YUG) in 1984, aged 19 years and 222 days, and the youngest medallist was Nasser Givechi (IRN) in 1952, aged 16 years and 254 days. The heaviest competitor ever in any Olympic event was the 1972 super-heavyweight bronze medallist Chris Taylor (USA) who weighed between 182kg (401lb) and 190kg (419lb). When Osamu Watanabe (JPN) won the 1964 freestyle featherweight title, it was his 186th successive victory in the sport. After gaining the silver medal in the 1920 unlimited class, Nat Pendleton first turned professional, and then went to Hollywood and appeared in many films, usually playing 'dumb ox' roles.

At Sydney in 2000 there will be only eight categories in each discipline, as follows: 48kg, 54kg, 58kg, 63kg, 76kg, 85kg, 97kg and 125kg.

Yachting

The first Olympic regatta should have been on the Bay of Salamis, but it was cancelled due to bad weather. Since 1900 the classes have been changed regularly until very recently when some measure of standardisation was imposed. In each class there are seven races over a prescribed course in which the fastest time wins. Yachts count their six best results. The only event which has been a permanent fixture is the Olympic monotype, i.e. one-man dinghy, albeit represented by different classes of boats prior to 1952 (now the Finn).

The most successful yachtsman is Paul Elvstrøm (DEN) who won four successive Olympic monotype titles from 1948–60 — the first man to achieve such a run in any sport. He competed again in the 1968 Star (fourth), 1972 Soling (13th), 1984 Tornado (fourth), and 1988 Tornado (15th) — in the last two partnering his daughter, Trine. Frances Clytie Rivett-Carnac (GBR) and her husband, Charles, in the winning 7m yacht *Heroine* in 1908, were the first married couple to win gold medals in Olympic yachting, but not in the Games as is sometimes reported. The oldest gold medallist was Everard Endt (USA) in the 1952 6m class, aged 59 years and 112 days, while the oldest in a single-handed event was Léon Huybrechts (BEL), aged 47 years and 215 days in 1924. The oldest female winner and medallist was Virginie Hériot (FRA) in the 1928 8m class, aged 38 years and 16 days. The youngest gold medallist/medallist was Franciscus Hin (NED), in the 1920 12-foot dinghy event with his brother, Johannes, aged 14 years and 163 days. The youngest female champion was Kristine Roug (DEN) in the 1996 Europe class, aged 21 years and 141 days, while the youngest female medallist was Natalia Via Dufresne Perena (ESP), second in the same event in 1992 at 19 years and 54 days. The oldest medallist was Louis Noverraz (SUI) in the 5.5m category in 1968, aged 66 years and 154 days.

Outstanding family achievements have occurred in Olympic yachting. In 1920 four Norwegian brothers, Henrik, Jan, Ole and Kristian Østervold won gold medals in the 12m (1907 rating) class. The full crew of the winning 5.5m in 1968 were brothers Ulf, Jörgen and Peter Sundelin (SWE), and the winning 6m in 1912 was crewed by Amédée, Gaston and Jacques Thubé (FRA). The only twins to win gold were Sumner and Edgar White (USA) in the 5.5m of 1952. The first father and son to win together were Emile and Florimond Cornellie (BEL) in the 6m (1907 rating) in 1920. However, the greatest Olympic yachting family must be the Norwegians Lunde: Eugen won a gold in the 1924 6m class, his son Peder and daughter-in-law, Vibeke, along with Vibeke's brother, won a silver in the 5.5m in 1952, and grandson Peder Jr won a gold in the 1960 Flying Dutchman contest. The winner of the women's sailboard title in 1992, Barbara Kendall (NZL), was the sister of the 1988 men's winner, Bruce Kendall.

Rodney Pattisson and Iain Macdonald-Smith (GBR) scored the lowest number of penalty points (three) ever achieved in Olympic yachting when they won the 1968 Flying Dutchman class with five wins, a second place and a disqualification (finished first) in their seven starts. Their boat *Superdocius* is now in the National Maritime Museum, London. The only boat to win two gold medals in the same Games was *Scotia*, crewed by Lorne Currie and John Gretton of Great Britain, in the 1/2–1 ton and Open classes in 1900. The United States yacht *Llanoria* won the 6m class in 1948 and 1952, skippered both times by Herman Whiton.

In 1948 Magnus Konow (NOR) equalled the longest span of Olympic competition when he took part in the 6m event 40 years after his debut in the 8m class of 1908. He won two golds and a silver in 1912, 1920 and 1936, the only other Games he attended. Durward

Knowles competed in a record eight Games, all in the Star class, from 1948 when he competed for Great Britain. He represented the Bahamas in the next six celebrations, and then again in 1988 (aged 71 he was probably the oldest Olympic yachtsman ever). The aforementioned Paul Elvstrøm (DEN) also made it eight Games in 1988, and both he and Knowles matched the 40-year span record. In 1996 Hubert Raudaschl (AUT) outclassed them all, and competed in his ninth Games, 1964–96, which is a record for any sport. This could have been even more remarkable, as he had been a reserve for the Austrian Olympic team in 1960. Tore Holm (SWE) won medals over a record span of 28 years (1920–48), and, more unusual, Hans Fogh won medals 24 years apart (1960–84), firstly for Denmark and then for Canada.

Harry Melges (USA) won a gold medal in the 1972 Soling class, and then co-skippered the winning US yacht in the 1992 America's Cup. This achievement was matched by Russell Coutts (NZL) who won the 1984 Finn event, and was the skipper of *Black Magic I* which won the America's Cup for New Zealand in 1995. The helmsman of the third placed *Tempest* in 1976 was Dennis Conner (USA), who had won America's Cup for the United States in 1980, lost it in 1983, and regained it in 1987. His Canadian partner, Conn Findlay, had won rowing golds in 1956 and 1964, and then was a crew member of successful America's Cup defender *Courageous* in 1977. A number of other Olympic yachtsmen have also competed, sometimes successfully, in the America's Cup competitions.

In the 1984 Games all 13 members of the United States team won either gold or silver medals, a unique team achievement. The greatest number of boats in an Olympic regatta was the 239 (plus 73 sailboards) at

OLYMPIC YACHTING VENUES

1900	River Seine at Meulan (10-20 tonners at Le Havre)
1908	Cowes, Isle of Wight, and the Clyde, Scotland
1912	Nyhashamn
1920	Ostend
1924	River Seine at Meulan (6m and 8m at Le Havre)
1928	Zuider-Zee
1932	San Pedro Bay
1936	Kiel
1948	Torbay, Devon
1952	Harmaja
1956	Port Phillip Bay
1960	Bay of Naples
1964	Sagami Bay
1968	Acapulco Bay
1972	Kiel
1976	Lake Ontario at Kingston
1980	Tallinn, Estonia
1984	Long Beach
1988	Pusan
1992	Barcelona
1996	Savannah

YACHTING MEDALS

	G	S	B	Total
United States	16	19	16	51
Great Britain	14	12	9	35
Sweden	9	12	9	30
Norway	16	11	2	29
France	12	6	9	27
Denmark	10	8	4	22
The Netherlands	4	5	6	15
New Zealand	6	4	3	13
Spain	9	2	1	12
Soviet Union	4	5	3	12
Australia	3	2	7	12
Brazil	4	1	5	10
Germany	3	3	3	9
Italy	2	1	6	9
Belgium	2	4	2	8
Finland	1	1	6	8
Canada	–	2	6	8
FRG	2	2	3	7
GDR	2	2	2	6
Greece	2	1	1	4
Portugal	–	2	2	4
Switzerland [1]	1	1	1	3
Argentina	–	3	–	3
Austria [1]	–	3		3
Bahamas	1	–	1	2
Ukraine	1	–	1	2
Russia	–	1	1	2
Estonia	–	–	2	2
Hong Kong	1	–	–	1
Poland	1	–	–	1
China	–	1	–	1
Cuba	–	1	–	1
Ireland	–	1	–	1
Japan	–	1	–	1
Netherlands Antilles	–	1	–	1
Virgin Islands	–	1	–	1
Hungary [1]	–	–	1	1
Israel	–	–	1	1
	126	119 [2]	113 [2]	358

[1] It is perhaps worth noting that Austria, Hungary and Switzerland have no direct access to the sea

[2] Some events in the early Games had no silver and/or bronze medals

Atlanta (Savannah) in 1996. The greatest entry in just one event was 56 in the 1996 Laser competition. When Lai Shan Lee (HKG) won the women's sailboard title in 1996 she gained the first, and what is thought to be the last, Olympic gold medal ever for her country. It is understood that Hong Kong will compete at Sydney as a separate entry.

An attempt has been made to bring some method of comparison to the Olympic results, made particularly difficult due to the wide variety of classes and types of boat used over the years. Where classes have been superseded by those of similar type, they have been listed in the same table. Purists may be unhappy but the general reader will find it easier to follow.

Youngest

The youngest competitor, and indeed medallist, in the Olympic Games, except for the unconfirmed report of a an even younger rowing cox in 1920, was gymnast Dimitrios Loundras (GRE) in the bronze medal team in 1896, aged 10 years and 218 days. The youngest female participant was the British skater, Cecilia Colledge, in 1932, aged 11 years and 73 days. (Four years later she won a silver medal.) The youngest female competitor, and medallist, in any Summer Games was Luigina Giavotti (ITA) in the 1928 silver medal gymnastic team at 11 years and 302 days. The youngest to win a medal in an individual event was Inge Sörensen (DEN) in 1936 with a 200m breaststroke bronze, aged 12 years and 24 days, while the youngest male medallist in an individual event was Nils Skoglund (SWE) in the 1920 diving, aged 14 years and 11 days. At Berlin in 1936 diver Marjorie Gestring (USA) became the youngest ever female gold medallist, aged 13 years and 267 days. The youngest male to win an individual event gold medal was swimmer Kusuo Kitamura (JPN) in the 1932 1500m freestyle, aged 14 years and 309 days.

The youngest male competitor in the Winter Games was figure skater Jan Hoffmann (GDR), aged 12 years and 110 days in 1968. (Later, in 1980 he gained a silver medal.) The youngest ever gold medallist/medallist at the Winter Games was Kim Yoon-mi (KOR) in the women's short track speed skating relay in 1994, aged 13 years and 83 days. In 1964 Scott Allen (USA) became the youngest male Winter medallist with a figure skating bronze, aged 14 years and 363 days. The youngest male gold medallist was Finnish ski-jumper Toni Nieminen in 1992, aged 16 years and 259 days.

Medal Tables by Sport and Year

The tables below indicate medallists by sport and year. These tables have been split by summer and winter games with winter medals tables starting with Alpine Skiing on page 234. Over the years the scoring methods for various sports and/or events have changed making comparisons over time difficult. Please also note that the scoring references, i.e. pts, relate to all medallists within a table — due to space constraints the scoring reference has only been included in the gold medallist column.

Abbreviations and Timings:

d.n.a.–data not available	kg–kilograms	m–metres
n.t.a.–no times available	pl–placings	pts–points

FRG refers to West Germany, GDR refers to East Germany

Timed events are indicated in seconds (14.67), minutes (1:14.67) and hours (2hr 1:14.67)

Archery Medals — 1900–20

GOLD	SILVER	BRONZE
1900 *Au cordon doré-50m*		
Henri Hérouin (FRA)	Hubert van Innis (BEL)	Emile Fisseux (FRA)
Au cordon doré-33m		
Hubert van Innis (BEL)	Victor Thibaud (FRA)	Charles Petit (FRA)
Au chapelet-50m		
Eugène Mougin (FRA)	Henri Helle (FRA)	Emile Mercier (FRA)
Au chapelet-33m		
Hubert van Innis (BEL)	Victor Thibaud (FRA)	Charles Petit (FRA)
Sur la perche à la herse		
Emmanuel Foulon (FRA)	Pierre Serrurier (FRA)	Emile Druart Jr (BEL)
Sur la perche à la pyramide		
Emile Grumiaux (FRA)	Auguste Serrurier (FRA)	Louis Glineaux (BEL)
1904 Men		
Double York Round		
Phillip Bryant (USA)	Robert Williams (USA)	William Thompson (USA)
Double American Round		
Phillip Bryant (USA)	Robert Williams (USA)	William Thompson (USA)
Team Round		
Potomac Archers (USA)	Cincinnati Archery Club (USA)	Boston AA (USA)
Women		
Double National Round		
Lida Howell (USA)	Jessie Pollack (USA)	Emma Cooke (USA)
Double Columbia Round		
Lida Howell (USA)	Emma Cooke (USA)	Jessie Pollack (USA)
1908 Men		
York Round		
William Dod (GBR)	Reginald Brooks-King (GBR)	Henry Richardson (USA)
Continental Style		
Eugène Grisot (FRA)	Louis Vernet (FRA)	Gustave Cabaret (FRA)
Women		
National Round		
Queenie Newall (GBR)	Charlotte Dod (GBR)	Beatrice Hill-Lowe (GBR)
1920 *Fixed bird target-small birds-individual*		
Edmond van Moer (BEL)	Louis van de Perck (BEL)	Joseph Hermans (BEL)
Fixed bird target-small birds-team		
Belgium	–	–
Fixed bird target-large birds-individual		
Edouard Cloetens (BEL)	Louis van der Perck (BEL)	Firmin Flamand (BEL)

Fixed bird target-large birds-team
Belgium — —

Moving bird target-28m-individual
Hubert van Innis (BEL)   Léone Quentin (FRA)   —

Moving bird target-team
The Netherlands   Belgium   France

Moving bird target-33m-individual
Hubert van Innis (BEL)   Julien Brulé (FRA)   —

Moving bird target-33m-team
Belgium   France   —

Moving bird target-50m-individual
Julien Brulé (FRA)   Hubert van Innis (BEL)   —

Moving bird target-50m-team
Belgium   France   —

Archery Medals 1972–96

GOLD	SILVER	BRONZE

Double Fita Round (*Maximum possible score 2880 points*)

Men

	GOLD	SILVER	BRONZE
1972	John Williams (USA) 2528pts	Gunnar Jarvil (SWE) 2481	Kyösti Lassonen (FIN) 2467
1976	Darrell Pace (USA) 2571pts	Hiroshi Michinaga (JPN) 2502	Giancarlo Ferrrari (ITA) 2495
1980	Tomi Poikolainen (FIN) 2455pts	Boris Isachenko (URS) 2452	Giancarlo Ferrari (ITA) 2449
1984	Darrell Pace (USA) 2616pts [1]	Richard McKinney (USA) 2564	Hiroshi Yamamoto (JPN) 2563
1988	Jay Barrs (USA) 338pts (2605)	Park Sung-Soo (KOR) 336 (2614)	Vladimir Yecheyev (URS) 335 (2600)
1992[2]	Sebastien Flute (FRA)	Chung Jae-hun (KOR)	Simon Terry (GBR)
1996[2]	Justin Huish (USA)	Magnus Petersson (SWE)	Oh Kyun-moon (KOR)

[1] Olympic record
[2] Due to further rule changes point scores are no longer comparable with previous results

Women

	GOLD	SILVER	BRONZE
1972	Doreen Wilber (USA) 2424pts	Irena Szydlowska (POL) 2407	Emma Gapchenko (URS) 2403
1976	Luann Ryon (USA) 2499pts	Valentina Kovpan (URS) 2460	Zebeniso Rustamova (URS) 2407
1980	Keto Losaberidze (URS) 2491pts	Batalya Butuzova (URS) 2477	Päivi Meriluoto (FIN) 2449
1984	Seo Hyang-soon (KOR) 2568pts	Li Lingjuan (CHN) 2559	Kim Jin-ho (KOR) 2555
1988	Kim Soo-nyung (KOR) 344pts (2683) [1]	Wang Hee-kyung (KOR) 332 (2612)	Yung Young-sook (KOR) 327 (2603)
1992[2]	Cho Youn-jeong (KOR)	Kim Soo-nyung (KOR)	Natalia Valeyeva (EUN)
1996[2]	Kim Kyung-wook (KOR)	He Ying (CHN)	Olena Sadovnycha (UKR)

[1] Olympic record
[2] Due to further rule changes point scores are no longer comparable with previous results

Team-Men

	GOLD	SILVER	BRONZE
1988	Korea	United States	Great Britain
1992	Spain	Finland	Great Britain
1996	United States	Korea	Italy

Team-Women

	GOLD	SILVER	BRONZE
1988	Korea	Indonesia	United States
1992	Korea	China	Unified Team
1996	Korea	Germany	Poland

Athletics Medals

GOLD	SILVER	BRONZE

Men

100 metres

1896 Thomas Burke (USA) 12.0	Fritz Hofmann (GER) 12.2	Alajos Szokolyi (HUN) 12.6
1900 Frank Jarvis (USA) 11.0	Walter Tewksbury (USA) 11.1	Stanley Rowley (AUS) 11.2
1904 Archie Hahn (USA) 11.0	Nathaniel Cartmell (USA) 11.2	William Hogenson (USA) 11.2
1906 Archie Hahn (USA) 11.2	Fay Moulton (USA) 11.3	Nigel Barker (AUS) 11.3
1908 Reginald Walker (RSA) 10.8	James Rector (USA) 10.9	Robert Kerr (CAN) 11.0
1912 Ralph Craig (USA) 10.8	Alvah Meyer (USA) 10.9	Donald Lippincott (USA) 10.9
1920 Charles Paddock (USA) 10.8	Morris Kirksey (USA) 10.8	Harry Edward (GBR) 11.0
1924 Harolds Abrahams (GBR) 10.6	Jackson Scholz (USA) 10.7	Arthur Porritt (NZL) 10.8
1928 Percy Williams (CAN) 10.8	Jack London (GBR) 10.9	Georg Lammers (GER) 10.9
1932 Eddie Tolan (USA) 10.3 (10.38)	Ralph Metcalfe (USA) 10.3 (10.38)	Arthur Jonath (GER) 10.4 (10.50)
1936 Jesse Owens (USA) 10.3	Ralph Metcalfe (USA) 10.4	Martinus Osendarp (NED) 10.5
1948 Harrison Dillard (USA) 10.3	Norwood Ewell (USA) 10.4	Lloyd La Beach (PAN) 10.4
1952 Lindy Remigino (USA) 10.4 (10.79)	Herb McKenley (JAM) 10.4 (10.80)	Emmanuel McDonald Bailey (GBR) 10.4 (10.83)
1956 Bobby Joe Morrow (USA) 10.5 (10.62)	Thane Baker (USA) 10.5 (10.77)	Hector Hogan (AUS) 10.6 (10.77)
1960 Armin Hary (GER) 10.2 (10.32)	David Sime (USA) 10.2 (10.35)	Peter Radford (GBR) 10.3 (10.42)
1964 Bob Hayes (USA) 10.0 (10.06) [1]	Enrique Figuerola (CUB) 10.2 (10.25)	Harry Jerome (CAN) 10.2 (10.27)
1968 James Hines (USA) 9.9 (9.95)	Lennox Miller (JAM) 10.0 (10.04)	Charles Greene (USA) 10.0 (10.07)
1972 Valeri Borzov (URS) 10.14	Robert Taylor (USA) 10.24	Lennox Miller (JAM) 10.33
1976 Hasely Crawford (TRI) 10.06	Don Quarrie (JAM) 10.08	Valeri Borzov (URS) 10.14
1980 Allan Wells (GBR) 10.25	Silvio Leonard (CUB) 10.25	Petar Petrov (BUL) 10.39
1984 Carl Lewis (USA) 9.99	Sam Graddy (USA) 10.19	Ben Johnson (CAN) 10.22
1988 Carl Lewis (USA) 9.92 [2]	Linford Christie (GBR) 9.97	Calvin Smith (USA) 9.99
1992 Linford Christie (GBR) 9.96	Frankie Fredericks (NAM) 10.02	Dennis Mitchell (USA) 10.04
1996 Donovan Bailey (CAN) 9.84	Frankie Fredericks (NAM) 9.89	Ato Boldon (TRI) 9.90

[1] Hayes ran a wind-assisted 9.91 in the semi-final
[2] Ben Johnson (CAN) won in 9.79 but was later disqualified

200 metres

1900 Walter Tewksbury (USA) 22.2	Norman Pritchard (GBR) 22.8	Stanley Rowley (AUS) 22.9
1904[1] Archie Hahn (USA) 21.6	Nathaniel Cartmell (USA) 21.9	William Hogenson (USA) d.n.a.
1908 Robert Kerr (CAN) 22.6	Robert Cloughen (USA) 22.6	Nathaniel Cartmell (USA) 22.7
1912 Ralph Craig (USA) 21.7	Donald Lippincott (USA) 22.1	Willie Applegarth (GBR) 22.0
1920 Allen Woodring (USA) 22.0	Charles Paddock (USA) 22.1	Harry Edward (GBR) 22.2
1924 Jackson Scholz (USA) 21.6	Charles Paddock (USA) 21.7	Eric Liddell (GBR) 21.9
1928 Percy Williams (CAN) 21.8	Walter Rangeley (GBR) 21.9	Helmut Kornig (GER) 21.9 [2]
1932 Eddie Tolan (USA) 21.2 (21.12)	George Simpson (USA) 21.4	Ralph Metcalfe (USA) 21.5 [3]
1936 Jesse Owens (USA) 20.7	Mack Robinson (USA) 21.1	Martinus Osendarp (NED) 21.3
1948 Mel Patton (USA) 21.1	Norwood Ewell (USA) 21.1	Lloyd La Beach (PAN) 21.2
1952 Andrew Stanfield (USA) 20.7 (20.81)	Thane Baker (USA) 20.8 (20.97)	James Gathers (USA) 20.8 (21.08)
1956 Bobby Joe Morrow (USA) 20.6 (20.75)	Andrew Stanfield (USA) 20.7 (20.97)	Thane Baker (USA) 20.9 (21.05)
1960 Livio Berruti (ITA) 20.5 (20.62)	Lester Carney (USA) 20.6 (20.69)	Abdoulaye Seye (FRA) 20.7 (20.83)
1964 Henry Carr (USA) 20.3 (20.36)	Paul Drayton (USA) 20.5 (20.58)	Edwin Roberts (TRI) 20.6 (20.63)
1968 Tommie Smith (USA) 19.8 (19.83)	Peter Norman (AUS) 20.0 (20.06)	John Carlos (USA) 20.0 (20.10)
1972 Valeri Borzov (URS) 20.00	Larry Black (USA) 20.19	Pietro Mennea (ITA) 20.30
1976 Don Quarrie (JAM) 20.23	Millard Hampton (USA) 20.29	Dwayne Evans (USA) 20.43
1980 Pietro Mennea (ITA) 20.19	Allan Wells (GBR) 20.21	Don Quarrie (JAM) 20.29
1984 Carl Lewis (USA) 19.80	Kirk Baptiste (USA) 19.96	Thomas Jefferson (USA) 20.26
1988 Joe DeLoach (USA) 19.75	Carl Lewis (USA) 1979	Robson da Silva (BRA) 20.04

| 1992 | Mike Marsh (USA) 20.01 | Frankie Fredericks (NAM) 20.13 | Michael Bates (USA) 20.38 |
| 1996 | Michael Johnson (USA) 19.32 | Frankie Fredericks (NAM) 19.68 | Ato Boldon (TRI) 19.80 |

1896, 1906 *Event not held*

1 Race over straight course. Hahn's three opponents were all given 1yd handicaps for false starting
2 Awarded bronze medal when Scholz (USA) refused to re-run after tie
3 Metcalfe's lane was later found to be 1.5m too long

400 metres

1896	Thomas Burke (USA) 54.2	Herbert Jamison (USA) 55.2	Fritz Hofmann (GER) 55.6
1900	Maxey Long (USA) 49.4	William Holland (USA) 49.6	Ernst Schultz (DEN) 15m
1904	Harry Hillman (USA) 49.2	Frank Waller (USA) 49.9	Herman Groman (USA) 50.0
1906	Paul Pilgrim (USA) 53.2	Wyndham Halswelle (GBR) 53.8	Nigel Barker (AUS) 54.1
1908[1]	Wyndham Halswelle (GBR) 50.0	–	–
1912	Charles Reidpath (USA) 48.2	Hanns Braun (GER) 48.3	Edward Lingberg (USA 48.4
1920	Bevil Rudd (RSA) 49.6	Guy Butler (GBR) 49.9	Nils Engdahl (SWE) 50.0
1924	Eric Liddell (USA) 47.6	Horatio Fitch (USA) 48.4	Guy Butler (GBR) 48.6
1928	Ray Barbuti (USA) 47.8	James Ball (CAN) 48.0	Joachim Büchner (GER) 48.2
1932	William Carr (USA) 46.2 (46.28)	Ben Eastman (USA) 46.4 (46.50)	Alexander Wilson (CAN) 47.4
1936	Archie Williams (USA) 46.5 (46.66)	Godfrey Brown (GBR) 46.7 (46.68)	James LuValle (USA) 46.8 (46.84)
1948	Arthur Wint (JAM) 46.2	Herb McKenley (JAM 46.4	Mal Whitfield (USA) 46.6
1952	George Rhoden (JAM) 45.9 (46.09)	Herb McKenley (JAM) 45.9 (46.20)	Ollie Matson (USA) 46.8 (46.94)
1956	Charles Jenkins (USA) 46.7 (46.85)	Karl-Friedrich Haas (GER) 46.8 (47.12)	Voitto Hellsten (FIN) 47.0 (47.15) Ardalion Ignatyev (URS) 47.0 (47.15)
1960	Otis Davis (USA) 44.9 (45.07)	Carl Kaufmann (GER) 45.9 (45.08)	Mal Spence (RSA) 45.5 (45.60)
1964	Mike Larrabee (USA) 45.1 (45.15)	Wendell Mottley (TRI) 45.2 (45.24)	Andrzej Badenski (POL) 45.6 (45.64)
1968	Lee Evans (USA) 43.8 (43.86)	Lawrence James (USA) 43.9 (43.97)	Ron Freeman (USA) 44.4 (44.41)
1972	Vince Matthews (USA) 44.66	Wayne Collett (USA) 44.80	Julius Sang (KEN) 44.92
1976	Alberto Juantorena (CUB) 44.26	Fred Newhouse (USA) 44.40	Herman Frazier (USA) 44.95
1980	Viktor Markin (URS) 44.60	Rick Mitchell (AUS) 44.84	Frank Schaffer (GDR) 44.87
1984	Alonzo Babers (USA) 44.27	Gabriel Tiacoh (CIV) 44.54	Antonio McKay (USA) 44.71
1988	Steve Lewis (USA) 43.87	Butch Reynolds (USA) 43.93	Danny Everett (USA) 44.09
1992	Qunicy Watts (USA) 43.50	Steve Lewis (USA) 44.21	Samson Kitur (KEN) 44.24
1996	Michael Johnson (USA) 43.49	Roger Black (GBR) 44.41	Davis Kamoga (UGA) 44.53

1 Re-run ordered after John Carpenter (USA) disqualified in first final. Only Halswelle showed up and 'walked over' for the title

800 metres

1896	Edwin Flack (AUS) 2:11.0	Nándor Dáni (HUN) 2:11.8	Dimitrios Golemis (GRE) 2:28.0
1900	Alfred Tysoe (GBR) 2:01.2	John Cregan (USA) 2:03.0	David Hall (USA) d.n.a.
1904	James Lightbody (USA) 1:56.0	Howard Valentine (USA) 1:56.3	Emil Breitkreutz (USA) 1:56.4
1906	Paul Pilgrim (USA) 2:01.5	James Lightbody (USA) 2:01.6	Wyndham Halswelle (GBR) 2:03.0
1908	Mel Sheppard (USA) 1:52.8	Emilio Lunghi (ITA) 1:54.2	Hanns Braun (GER) 1:55.2
1912	James Meredith (USA) 1:51.9	Mel Sheppard (USA) 1:52.0	Ira Davenport (USA) 1:52.0
1920	Albert Hill (GBR) 1:53.4	Earl Eby (USA) 1:53.6	Bevil Rudd (RSA) 1:54.0
1924	Douglas Lowe (GBR) 1:52.4	Paul Martin (SUI) 1:52.6	Schuyler Enck (USA) 1:53.0
1928	Douglas Lowe (GBR) 1:51.8	Erik Bylehn (SWE) 1:52.8	Hermann Engelhardt (GER) 1:53.2
1932	Thomas Hampson (GBR) 1:49.7	Alexander Wilson (CAN) 1:49.9	Phil Edwards (CAN) 1:51.5
1936	John Woodruff (USA) 1:52.9	Mario Lanzi (ITA) 1:53.3	Phil Edwards (CAN) 1:53.6
1948	Mal Whitfield (USA) 1:49.2	Arthur Wint (JAM) 1:49.5	Marcel Hansenne (FRA) 1:49.8
1952	Mal Whitfield (USA) 1:49.2	Arthur Wint (JAM) 1:49.4	Heinz Ulzheimer (GER) 1:49.7
1956	Tom Courtney (USA) 1:47.7	Derek Johnson (GBR) 1:47.8	Audun Boysen (NOR) 1:48.1
1960	Peter Snell (NZL) 1:46.3	Roger Moens (BEL) 1:46.5	George Kerr (JAM) 1:47.1 [1]
1964	Peter Snell (NZL) 1:45.1	Bill Crothers (CAN) 1:45.6	Wilson Kiprugut (KEN) 1:45.9
1968	Ralph Doubell (AUS) 1:44.3	Wilson Kiprugut (KEN) 1:44.5	Tom Farrell (USA) 1:45.4
1972	Dave Wottle (USA) 1:45.9	Yevgeni Arzhanov (URS) 1:45.9	Mike Boit (KEN) 1:46.0
1976	Alberto Juantorena (CUB) 1:43.5	Ivo Van Damme (BEL) 1:43.9	Richard Wohlhuter (USA) 1:44.1

1980 Steve Ovett (GBR) 1:45.4	Sebastian Coe (GBR) 1:45.9	Nikolai Kirov (URS) 1:46.0
1984 Joachim Cruz (BRA) 1:43.00	Sebastian Coe (GBR) 1:43.64	Earl Jones (USA) 1:43.83
1988 Paul Ereng (KEN) 1:43.45	Joachim Cruz (BRA) 1:43.90	Saïd Aouita (MAR) 1:44.06
1992 William Tanui (KEN) 1:43.66	Nixon Kiprotich (KEN) 1:43.70	Johnny Gray (USA) 1:43.97
1996 Vebjörn Rodal (NOR) 1:42.58	Hezekiel Sepeng (RSA) 1:42.74	Fred Onyancha (KEN) 1:42.79

[1] Kerr was a Jamaican in the combined Antilles team

1500 metres

1896 Edwin Flack (AUS) 4:33.2	Arthur Blake (USA) 4:34.0	Albin Lermusiaux (FRA) 4:36.0
1900 Charles Bennett (GBR) 4:06.2	Henri Deloge (FRA) 4:06.6	John Bray (USA) 4:07.2
1904 James Lightbody (USA) 4:05.4	William Verner (USA) 4:06.8	Lacey Hearn (USA) d.n.a.
1906 James Lightbody (USA) 4:12.0	John McGough (GBR) 4:12.6	Kristian Hellström (SWE) 4:13.4
1908 Mel Sheppard (USA) 4:03.4	Harold Wilson (GBR) 4:03.6	Norman Hallows (GBR) 4:04.0
1912 Arnold Jackson (GBR) 3:56.8 [1]	Abel Kiviat (USA) 3:56.9	Norman Taber (USA) 3:56.9
1920 Albert Hill (GBR) 4:01.8	Philip Baker (GBR) 4:02.4 [1]	Lawrence Shields (USA) 4:03.1
1924 Paavo Nurmi (FIN) 3:53.6	Willy Schärer (SUI) 3:55.0	Henry Stallard (GBR) 3:55.6
1928 Harri Larva (FIN) 3:53.2	Jules Ladoumègue (FRA) 3:53.8	Eino Purje (FIN) 3:56.4
1932 Luigi Beccali (ITA) 3:51.2	John Cornes (GBR) 3:52.6	Phil Edwards (CAN) 3:52.8
1936 Jack Lovelock (NZL) 3:47.8	Glenn Cunningham (USA) 3:48.4	Luigi Beccali (ITA) 3:49.2
1948 Henry Eriksson (SWE) 3:49.8	Lennart Strand (SWE) 3:50.4	Willem Slijkhuis (NED) 3:50.4
1952 Josef Barthel (LUX) 3:45.1	Bob McMillen (USA) 3:45.2	Werner Lueg (GER) 3:45.4
1956 Ron Delany (IRL) 3:41.2	Klaus Richtzenhain (GER) 3:42.0	John Landy (AUS) 3:42.0
1960 Herb Elliott (AUS) 3:35.6	Michel Jazy (FRA) 3:38.4	István Rózsavölgyi (HUN) 3:39.2
1964 Peter Snell (NZL) 3:38.1	Josef Odlozil (TCH) 3:39.6	John Davies (NZL) 3:39.6
1968 Kipchoge Keino (KEN) 3:34.9	Jim Ryun (USA) 3:37.8	Bodo Tümmler (FRG) 3:39.0
1972 Pekka Vasala (FIN) 3:36.3	Kipchoge Keino (KEN) 3:36.8	Rod Dixon (NZL) 3:37.5
1976 John Walker (NZL) 3:39.2	Ivo Van Damme (BEL) 3:39.3	Paul-Heinz Wellmann (FRG) 3:39.3
1980 Sebastian Coe (GBR) 3:38.4	Jürgen Straub (GDR) 3:38.8	Steve Ovett (GBR) 3:39.0
1984 Sebastian Coe (GBR) 3:32.53	Steve Cram (GBR) 3:33.40	José Abascal (ESP) 3:34.30
1988 Peter Rono (KEN) 3:35.96	Peter Elliott (GBR) 3:36.15	Jens-Peter Herold (GDR) 3:36.21
1992 Fermin Cacho (ESP)	Rachid El Basir (MAR) 3:40.62	Mohamed Suleiman (QAT) 3:40.69
1996 Noureddine Morceli (ALG) 3:35.78	Fermin Cacho (ESP) 3:36.40	Stephen Kipkorir (KEN) 3:36.72

[1] Jackson later changed his name to Strode-Jackson, and Baker changed to Noel-Baker

5000 metres

1912 Hannes Kolehmainen (FIN) 14:36.6	Jean Bouin (FRA) 14:36.7	George Hutson (GBR) 15:07.6
1920 Joseph Guillemot (FRA) 14:55.6	Paavo Nurmi (FIN) 15:00.0	Erik Backman (SWE) 15:13.0
1924 Paavo Nurmi (FIN) 14:31.2 [1]	Ville Ritola (FIN) 14:31.4	Edvin Wide (SWE) 15:01.8
1928 Ville Ritola (FIN) 14:38.0	Paavo Nurmi (FIN) 14:40.0	Edvin Wide (SWE) 14:41.2
1932 Lauri Lehtinen (FIN) 14:30.0	Ralph Hill (USA) 14:30.0	Lauri Virtanen (FIN) 14:44.0
1936 Gunnar Höckert (FIN) 14:22.2	Lauri Lehtinen (FIN) 14:25.8	Henry Jonsson (SWE) 14:29.0 [2]
1948 Gaston Rieff (BEL) 14:17.6	Emil Zátopek (TCH) 14:17.8	Willem Slijkhuis (NED) 14:26.8
1952 Emil Zátopek (TCH) 16:06.6	Alain Mimoun (FRA) 14:07.4	Herbert Schade (GER) 14:08.6
1956 Vladimir Kuts (URS) 13:39.6	Gordon Pirie (GBR) 13:50.6	Derek Ibbotson (GBR) 13:54.4
1960 Murray Halberg (NZL) 13:43.4	Hans Grodotzki (GDR) 13:44.6	Kazimierz Zimny (POL) 13:44.8
1964 Bob Schul (USA) 13:48.8	Harald Norpoth (GER) 13:49.6	Bill Dellinger (USA) 13:49.8
1968 Mohamed Gammoudi (TUN) 14:05.0	Kipchoge Keino (KEN) 14:05.2	Naftali Temu (KEN) 14:06.4
1972 Lasse Viren (FIN) 13:26.4	Mohamed Gammoudi (TUN) 13:27.4	Ian Stewart (GBR) 13:27.6
1976 Lasse Viren (FIN) 13:24.8	Dick Quax (NZL) 13:25.2	Klaus-Peter Hildenbrand (FRG) 13:35.4
1980 Miruts Yifter (ETH) 13:21.0	Suleiman Nyambui (TAN) 13:21.6	Kaarlo Maaninka (FIN) 13:22.0
1984 Saïd Aouita (MAR) 13:05.59	Markus Ryffel (SUI) 13:07.54	Antonio Leitao (POR) 13:09.20
1988 John Ngugi (KEN) 13:11.70	Dieter Baumann (FRG) 13:15.52	Hansjörg Kunze (GDR) 13:15.73

1992 Dieter Baumann (GER) 13:12.52   Paul Bitok (KEN) 13:12.71   Fita Bayissa (ETH) 13:13.03
1996 Venuste Niyongabo (BDI)   Paul Bitok (KEN) 13:08.16   Khalid Boulami (MAR) 13:08.37
      13:07.96

1896-1908 *Event not held*

[1] Nurmi won the 5000m only 90 minutes after winning the 1500m
[2] Jonsson later changed his name to Kälarne

10 000m

1906 [1]Henry Hawtrey (GBR) 26:11.8   John Svanberg (SWE) 26:19.4   Edward Dahl (SWE) 26:26.2
1908 [1]Emil Voigt (GBR) 25:11.2   Edward Owen (GBR) 25:24.0   John Svanberg (SWE) 25:37.2
1912 Hannes Kolehmainen (FIN)   Louis Tewanima (USA) 32:06.6   Albin Stenroos (FIN) 32:21.8
      31:20.8
1920 Paavo Nurmi (FIN) 31:45.8   Joseph Guillemot (FRA) 31:47.2   James Wilson (GBR) 31:50.8
1924 Ville Ritola (FIN) 30:23.2   Edvin Wide (SWE) 30:55.2   Eero Berg (FIN) 31:43.0
1928 Paavo Nurmi (FIN) 30:18.8   Ville Ritola (FIN) 30:19.4   Edvin Wide (SWE) 31:00.8
1932 Janusz Kusocinski (POL) 30:11.4   Volmari Iso-Hollo (FIN) 30:12.6   Lauri Virtannen (FIN) 30:35.0
1936 Ilmari Salminen (FIN) 30:15.4   Arvo Askola (FIN) 30:15.6   Volmari Iso-Hollo (FIN) 30:20.2
1948 Emil Zátopek (TCH) 29:59.6   Alain Mimoun (FRA) 30:47.4   Bertil Albertsson (SWE) 30:53.6
1952 Emil Zátopek (TCH) 29:17.0   Alain Mimoun (FRA) 29:32.8   Alexander Anufriyev (URS) 29:48.2
1956 Vladimir Kuts (URS) 28:45.6   József Kovács (HUN) 28:52.4   Allan Lawrence (AUS) 28:53.6
1960 Pyotr Bolotnikov (URS) 28:32.2   Hans Grodotzki (GDR) 28:37.0   David Power (AUS) 28:28.2 [2]
1964 Billy Mills (USA) 28:24.4   Mohamed Gammoudi (TUN)   Ron Clarke (AUS) 28:25.8
                                        28:24.8
1968 Naftali Temu (KEN) 29:27.4   Mamo Wolde (ETH) 29:28.0   Mohamed Gammoudi (TUN)
                                                                    29:34.2
1972 Lasse Viren (FIN) 27:38.4   Emiel Puttemans (BEL) 27:39.6   Miruts Yifter (ETH) 27:41.0
1976 Lasse Viren (FIN) 27:44.4   Carlos Lopes (POR) 27:45.2   Brendan Foster (GBR) 27:54.9
1980 Miruts Yifter (ETH) 27:42.7   Kaarlo Maaninka (FIN) 27:44.3   Mohammed Kedir (ETH) 27:44.7
1984 Alberto Cova (ITA) 27:47.54   Mike McLeod (GBR) 28:06.22 [3]   Mike Musyoki (KEN) 28:06.46
1988 Brahim Boutayeb (MAR) 27:21.46   Salvatore Antibo (ITA) 27:23.55   Kipkemboi Kimeli (KEN) 27:25.16
1992 Khalid Skah (MAR) 27:46.70   Richard Chelimo (KEN) 27:47.72   Adiis Abebe (ETH) 28:00.07
1996 Haile Gebrselassie (ETH)   Paul Tergat (KEN) 27:08.17   Salah Hissou (MAR) 27:24.67
      27:07.34

1896–1908 *Event not held*

[1] Held over 5 miles (8046m)
[2] Recent investigation suggests 28:37.7
[3] Martti Vainio (FIN) finished second but failed a drug test

Marathon

(The length of the marathon was standardised from 1924 at the 1908 distance of 26 miles 385 yards (42,195m.)
(Previously the distances had been: 1896 and 1904 — 40 000m, 1900 — 40 260m, 1906 — 41 860m, 1912 — 40
200m, 1920 — 42 750m)

1896 Spyridon Louis (GRE) 2hr 58:50   Charilaos Vasilakos (GRE)   Gyula Kellner (HUN) 3hr 09:35
                                        3hr 06:03
1900 Michel Theato (FRA) 2hr 59:45 [1]   Emile Champion (FRA) 3hr 04:17   Ernst Fast (SWE) 3hr 36:14
1904 Thomas Hicks (USA) 3hr 28:35   Albert Coray (FRA) 3hr 34:52 [2]   Arthur Newton (USA) 3hr 47:33
1906 William Sherring (CAN)   John Svanberg (SWE) 2hr 58:20.8   William Frank (USA) 3hr 00:46.8
      2hr 51:23.6
1908 [3]John Hayes (USA) 2hr 55:18.4   Charles Hefferon (RSA) 2hr   Joseph Forshaw (USA) 2hr 57:10.4
                                        56:06.0
1912 Kenneth McArthur (RSA)   Christian Gitsham (RSA) 2hr   Gaston Strobino (USA) 2hr 38:42.4
      2hr 36:54.8   37:52.0
1920 Hannes Kolehmainen (FIN) 2hr   Jüri Lossman (EST) 2hr 32:48.6   Valerio Arri (ITA) 2hr 36:32.8
      32:35.8
1924 Albin Stenroos (FIN) 2hr 41:22.6   Romeo Bertini (ITA) 2hr 47:19.6   Clarence DeMar (USA) 2hr 48:14.0
1928 Mohamed El Ouafi (FRA) 2hr   Miguel Plaza (CHI) 2hr 33:23   Martti Marttelin (FIN) 2hr 35:02
      32:57

1932 Juan Carlos Zabala (ARG) 2hr 31:36 | Sam Ferris (GBR) 2hr 31:55 | Armas Toivonen (FIN) 2hr 32:12

1936 Sohn Kee-chung (JPN) 2hr 29:19.2 [4] | Ernest Harper (GBR) 2hr 31:23.2 | Nam Seong-yong (JPN) 2hr 31:42:0 [4]

1948 Delfo Cabrera (ARG) 3hr 34:51.6 | Tom Richards (GBR) 2hr 35:07.6 | Etienne Gailly (BEL) 2hr 35:33.6

1952 Emil Zátopek (TCH) 2hr 23:03.2 | Reinaldo Gorno (ARG) 2hr 25:35.0 | Gustaf Jansson (SWE) 2hr 26:07.0

1956 Alain Mimoun (FRA) 2hr 25:00 | Franjo Mihalic (YUG) 2hr 26:32 | Veikko Karvonen (FIN) 2hr 27:47

1960 Abebe Bikila (ETH) 2hr 15:16.2 | Rhadi Ben Abdesselem (MAR) 2hr 15:41.6 | Barry Magee (NZL) 2hr 17:18.2

1964 Abebe Bikila (ETH) 2hr 12:11.2 | Basil Heatley (GBR) 2hr 16:19.2 | Kokichi Tsuburaya (JPN) 2hr 16:22.8

1968 Mamo Wolde (ETH) 2hr 20:26.4 | Kenji Kimihara (JPN) 2hr 23:31.0 | Michael Ryan (NZL) 2hr 23:45.0

1972 Frank Shorter (USA) 2hr 12:19.8 | Karel Lismont (BEL) 2hr 14:31.8 | Mamo Wolde (ETH) 2hr 15:08.4

1976 Waldemar Cierpinski (GDR) 2hr 09:55.0 | Frank Shorter (USA) 2hr 10:45.8 | Karel Lismont (BEL) 2hr 11:12.6

1980 Waldemar Cierpinski (GDR) 2hr 11:03 | Gerard Nijboer (NED) 2hr 11:20 | Satymkul Dzhumanazarov (URS) 2hr 11:35

1984 Carlos Lopes (POR) 2hr 09:21 | John Treacy (IRL) 2hr 09:56 | Charles Spedding (GBR) 2hr 09:58

1988 Gelindo Bordin (ITA) 2hr 10:32 | Douglas Wakiihuri (KEN) 2hr 10:47 | Ahmed Saleh (DJI) 2hr 10:59

1992 Hwang Young-cho (KOR) 2hr 13:23 | Koichi Morishita (JPN) 2hr 13:45 | Stephan Freigang (GER) 2hr 14:00

1996 Josiah Thugwane (RSA) 2hr 12:36 | Lee Bong-ju (KOR) 2hr 12:39 | Eric Wainaina (KEN) 2hr 12:44

[1] Recently found to be of Luxembourg origin
[2] Usually shown incorrectly
[3] Dorando Pietri (ITA) finished first but was disqualified due to assistance by officials on last lap of the track
[4] Then known as Kitei Son and Shoryu Nan — both from Korea

3000 metres Steeplechase

1900[1] George Orton (CAN) 7:34.4 | Sidney Robinson (GBR) 7:38.0 | Jacques Chastanié (FRA) 7:41.0

1900[2] John Rimmer (GBR) 12:58.4 | Charles Bennett (GBR) 12:58.6 | Sidney Robinson (GBR) 12:58.8

1904[3] James Lightbody (USA) 7:39.6 | John Daly (GBR) 7:40.6 | Arthur Newton (USA) 25m

1908[4] Arthur Russell (GBR) 10:47.8 | Archie Robertson (GBR) 10:48.4 | John Eisele (USA) 11:00.8

1920 Percy Hodge (GBR) 10:00.4 | Patrick Flynn (USA) 100m | Ernesto Ambrosini (ITA) 50m

1924 Ville Ritola (FIN) 9:33.6 | Elias Katz (FIN) 9:44.0 | Paul Bontemps (FRA) 9:45.2

1928 Toivo Loukola (FIN) 9:21.8 | Paavo Nurmi (FIN) 9:31.2 | Ove Andersen (FIN) 9:35.6

1932[5] Volmari Iso-Hollo (FIN) 10:33.4 | Tom Evenson (GBR) 10:46.0 | Joseph McCluskey (USA) 10:46.2

1936 Volmari Iso-Hollo (FIN) 9:03.8 | Kaarlo Tuominen (FIN) 9:06.8 | Alfred Dompert (GER) 9:07.2

1948 Tore Sjöstrand (SWE) 9:04.6 | Erik Elmsäter (SWE) 9:08.2 | Göte Hagström (SWE) 9:11.8

1952 Horace Ashenfelter (USA) 8:45.4 | Vladimir Kazantsev (URS) 8:51.6 | John Disley (GBR) 8:51.8

1956 Chris Brasher (GBR) 8:41.2 | Sándor Rozsnói (HUN) 8:43.6 | Ernst Larsen (NOR) 8:44.0

1960 Zdzslaw Krzyszkowiak (POL) 8:34.2 | Nikolai Sokolov (URS) 8:36.4 | Semyon Rzhischin (URS) 8:42.2

1964 Gaston Roelants (BEL) 8:30.8 | Maurice Herriott (GBR) 8:32.4 | Ivan Belyayev (URS) 8:33.8

1968 Amos Biwott (KEN) 8:51.0 | Benjamin Kogo (KEN) 8:51.6 | George Young (USA) 8:51.8

1972 Kipchoge Keino (KEN) 8:23.6 | Benjamin Jipcho (KEN) 8:24.6 | Tapio Kantanen (FIN) 8:24.8

1976 Anders Garderud (SWE) 8:08.0 | Bronislaw Malinowski (POL) 8:09.1 | Frank Baumgartl (GDR) 8:10.4

1980 Bronislaw Malinowski (POL) 8:09.7 | Filbert Bayi (TAN) 8:12.5 | Eshetu Tura (ETH) 8:13.6

1984 Julius Korir (KEN) 8:11.80 | Joseph Mahmoud (FRA) 8:13.31 | Brian Diemer (USA) 8:14.06

1988 Julius Kariuki (KEN) 8:05.51 | Peter Koech (KEN) 8:06.79 | Mark Rowland (GBR) 8:07.96

1992 Matthew Birir (KEN) 8:08.84 | Patrick Sang (KEN) 8:09.55 | William Mutwol (KEN) 8:10.74

1996 Joseph Keter (KEN) 8:07.12 | Moses Kiptanui (KEN) 8:08.33 | Alessandro Lambruschini (ITA) 8:11.28

1896, 1906, 1912 *Event not held*

[1] 2500m
[2] 4000m
[3] 2590m
[4] 3200m
[5] 3460m in final due to lap scoring error. Iso-Hollo ran 9:14.6 in a heat

110 metres Hurdles

1896	Thomas Curtis (USA) 17.6	Grantley Goulding (GBR) 18.0	− [1]	
1900	Alvin Kraenzlein (USA) 15.4	John McLean (USA) 15.5	Fred Moloney (USA) 15.6	
1904	Frederick Schule (USA) 16.0	Thadeus Shideler (USA) 16.3	Lesley Ashburner (USA) 16.4	
1906	Robert Leavitt (USA) 16.2	Alfred Healey (GBR) 16.2	Vincent Duncker (RSA) 16.3 [2]	
1908	Forrest Smithson (USA) 15.0	John Garrels (USA) 15.7	Arthur Shaw (USA) 15.8	
1912	Frederick Kelly (USA) 15.1	James Wendell (USA) 15.2	Martin Hawkins (USA) 15.3	
1920	Earl Thomson (CAN) 14.8	Harold Barron (USA) 15.1	Frederick Murray (USA) 15.2	
1924	Daniel Kinsey (USA) 15.0	Sydney Atkinson (RSA) 15.0	Sten Pettersson (SWE) 15.4	
1928	Sydney Atkinson (RSA) 14.8	Stephen Anderson (USA) 14.8	John Collier (USA) 15.0	
1932	George Saling (USA) 14.6 (14.57)	Percy Beard (USA) 14.7	Don Finlay (GBR) 14.8	
1936	Forrest Towns (USA) 14.2	Don Finlay (GBR) 14.4	Fred Pollard (USA) 14.4	
1948	William Porter (USA) 13.9	Clyde Scott (USA) 14.1	Craig Dixon (USA) 14.1	
1952	Harrison Dillard (USA) 13.7 (13,91)	Jack Davis (USA) 13.7 (14.00)	Art Barnard (USA) 14.1 (14.40)	
1956	Lee Calhoun (USA) 13.5 (13.70)	Jack Davis (USA) 13.5 (13,73)	Joel Shankle (USA) 14.1 (14.25)	
1960	Lee Calhoun (USA) 13.8 (13.98)	Willie May (USA) 13.8 (13.99)	Hayes Jones (USA) 14.0 (14.17)	
1964	Hayes Jones (USA) 13.6 (13.67)	Blaine Lindgren (USA) 13.7 (13.74)	Anatoli Mikhailov (URS) 13.7 (13.78)	
1968	Willie Davenport (USA) 13.3 (13.33)	Ervin Hall (USA) 13.4 (13.42)	Eddy Ottoz (ITA) 13.4 (13.46)	
1972	Rod Milburn (USA) 13.24	Guy Drut (FRA) 13.34	Tom Hill (USA) 13.48	
1976	Guy Drut (FRA) 13.30	Alejandro Casanas (CUB) 13.33	Willie Davenport (USA) 13.38	
1980	Thomas Munkelt (GDR) 13.39	Alejandro Casanas (CUB) 13.40	Alexander Puchkov (URS) 13.44	
1984	Roger Kingdom (USA) 13.20	Greg Foster (USA) 13.23	Arto Bryggare (FIN) 13.40	
1988	Roger Kingdom (USA) 12.98	Colin Jackson (GBR) 13.28	Tonie Campbell (USA) 13.38	
1992	Mark McKoy (CAN) 13.12	Tony Dees (USA) 13,24	Jack Pierce (USA) 13.26	
1996	Allen Johnson (USA) 12.95	Mark Crear (USA) 13.09	Florian Schwarthoff (GER) 13.17	

[1] There were only two finalists
[2] Recent research suggests that Duncker may have had German nationality at the time

400 metres Hurdles

1900[1]	Walter Tewksbury (USA) 57.6	Henri Tauzin (FRA) 58.3	George Orton (CAN) d.n.a.	
1904[2]	Harry Hillman (USA) 53.0	Frank Waller (USA) 53.2	George Poage (USA) 30m	
1908	Charles Bacon (USA) 55.0	Harry Hillman (USA) 55.3	Leonard Tremeer (GBR) 57.0	
1920	Frank Loomis (USA) 54.0	John Norton (USA) 54.3	August Desch (USA) 54.5	
1924	Morgan Taylor (USA) 52.6 [3]	Erik Vilén (FIN) 53.8	Ivan Riley (USA) 54.2	
1928	Lord Burghley (GBR) 53.4	Frank Cuhel (USA) 53.6	Morgan Taylor (USA) 53.6	
1932	Bob Tisdall (IRL) 51.7 (51.67) [3]	Glenn Hardin (USA) 51.9 (51.85)	Morgan Taylor (USA) 52.0 (51,96)	
1936	Glenn Hardin (USA) 52.4	John Loaring (CAN) 52.7	Miguel White (PHI) 52.8	
1948	Roy Cochran (USA) 51.1	Duncan White (SRI) 51.8	Rune Larsson (SWE) 52.2	
1952	Charlie Moore (USA) 50.8 (51.06)	Yuri Liyuyev (URS) 51.3 (51.51)	John Holland (NZL) 52.2 (52.26)	
1956	Glenn Davis (USA) 50.1 (50.29)	Eddie Southern (USA) 50.8 (50.94)	Josh Culbreath (USA) 51.6 (51.74)	
1960	Glenn Davis (USA) 49.3 (49.51)	Cliff Cushman (USA) 49.6 (49.77)	Dick Howard (USA) 49.7 (49.90)	
1964	Rex Cawley (USA) 49.6	John Cooper (GBR) 50.1	Salvatore Morale (ITA) 50.1	
1968	David Hemery (GBR) 48.1 (48.12)	Gerhard Hennige (FRG) 49.0 (49.02)	John Sherwood (GBR) 49.0 (49.03)	
1972	John Akii-Bua (UGA) 47.82	Ralph Mann (USA) 48.51	David Hemery (GBR) 48.52	
1976	Edwin Moses (USA) 47.64	Mike Shine (USA) 48.69	Yevgeni Gavrilenko (URS) 49.45	
1980	Volker Beck (GDR) 48.70	Vasili Arkhipenko (URS) 48.86	Gary Oakes (GBR) 49.11	
1984	Edwin Moses (USA) 47.75	Danny Harris (USA) 48.13	Harald Schmid (FRG) 48.19	
1988	Andre Phillips (USA) 47.19	Amadou Dia Ba (SEN) 47.23	Edwin Moses (USA) 47.56	
1992	Kevin Young (USA) 46.78	Winthrop Graham (JAM) 47.66	Kriss Akabusi (GBR) 47.82	
1996	Derrick Adkins (USA) 47.54	Samuel Matete (ZAM) 47.78	Calvin Davis (USA) 47.96	

1896, 1906, 1912 *Event not held*

[1] Tenth barrier was a water jump
[2] Hurdles 2ft 6in (76.2cm) high instead of usual 3ft (91.4cm)
[3] Record not allowed because hurdle knocked down

4 × 100 metres Relay

1912	Great Britain 42.4	Sweden 42.6 [1]	−
1920	United States 42.2	France 42.6	Sweden 42.9

1924 United States 41.0	Great Britain 41.2	The Netherlands 41.8
1928 United States 41.0	Germany 41.2	Great Britain 41.8
1932 United States 40.0 (40.10)	Germany 40.9	Italy 41.2
1936 United States 39.8	Italy 41.1	Germany 41.2
1948 United States 40.6 [2]	Great Britain 41.3	Italy 41.5
1952 United States 40.1 (40.26)	Soviet Union 40.3 (40.58)	Hungary 40.5 (40.83)
1956 United States 39.5 (39.60)	Soviet Union 39.8 (39.92)	Germany 40.3 (40.34)
1960 Germany 39.5 (39.66) [3]	Soviet Union 40.1 (40.24)	Great Britain 40.2 (40.32)
1964 United States 39.0 (39.06)	Poland 39.3 (39.36)	France 39.3 (39.36)
1968 United States 38.2 (38.24)	Cuba 38.3 (38.40)	France 38.4 (38.43)
1972 United States 38.19	Soviet Union 38.50	West Germany 38.79
1976 United States 38.33	East Germany 38.66	Soviet Union 38.78
1980 Soviet Union 38.26	Poland 38.33	France 38.53
1984 United States 37.83	Jamaica 38.62	Canada 38.70
1988 Soviet Union 38.19	Great Britain 38.28	France 38.40
1992 United States 37.40	Nigeria 37.98	Cuba 38.00
1996 Canada 37.69	United States 38.05	Brazil 38.41

1896–1908 *Event not held*

[1] Germany finished second but was disqualified
[2] United States originally disqualified but later reinstate
[3] United States finished first (39.60) but was disqualified

4 × 400 metres Relay

1908[1]United States 3:29.4	Germany 3:32.4	Hungary 3:32.5
1912 United States 3:16.6	France 3:20.7	Great Britain 3:23.2
1920 Great Britain 3:22.2	South Africa 3:24.2	France 3:24.8
1924 United States 3:16.0	Sweden 3:17.0	Great Britain 3:17.4
1928 United States 3:14.2	Germany 3: 14.8	Canada 3:15.4
1932 United States 3:08.2 (3:08.14)	Great Britain 3:11.2	Canada 3:12.8
1936 Great Britain 3:09.0	United States 3:11.0	Germany 3:11.8
1948 United states 3:10.4	France 3:14.8	Sweden 3:16.3
1952 Jamaica 3:03.9 (3:04.04)	United States 3:04.0 (3:04.21)	Germany 3:06.6 (3:06.78)
1956 United States 3:04.8 (3:04.81)	Australia 3:06.2 (3:06.19)	Great Britain 3:07.2 (3:07.19)
1960 United States 3:02.2 (3:02.37)	Germany 3:02.7 (3:02.84)	Antilles 3:04.0 (3:04.13) [2]
1964 United States 3:00.7	Great Britain 3:01.6	Trinidad and Tobago 3:01.7
1968 United States 2:56.1 (2:56.16)	Kenya 2:59.6 (2:59.64)	West Germany 3:00.5 (3:00.57)
1972 Kenya 2:59.83	Great Britain 3:00.46	France 3:00.65
1976 United States 2:58.65	Poland 3:01.43	West Germany 3:01.98
1980 Soviet Union 3:01.08	East Germany 3:01.26	Italy 3:04.3
1984 United States 2:57.91	Great Britain 2:59.13	Nigeria 2:59.32
1988 United States 2:56.16	Jamaica 3:00.30	West Germany 3:00.56
1992 United States 2:55.74	Cuba 2:59.51	Great Britain 2:59.73
1996 United States 2:55.99	Great Britain 2:56.60	Jamaica 2:59.42

1896–1906 *Event not held*

[1] Medley relay — 200m, 200m, 400m, 800m
[2] British West Indies team, comprising three from Jamaica and one from Barbados

20 000 metres Road Walk

1956 Leonid Spirin (URS) 1hr 31:27.4	Antonas Mikenas (URS) 1hr 32:03.0	Bruno Junk (URS) 1hr 32:12.0
1960 Vladimir Golubnichi (URS) 1hr 34:07.2	Noel Freeman (AUS) 1hr 34:16.4	Stan Vickers (GBR) 1hr 34:56.4
1964 Ken Matthews (GBR) 1hr 29:34.0	Dieter Lindner (GER) 1hr 31:13.2	Vladimir Golubnichi (URS)1hr 31:59.4
1968 Vladimir Golubnichi (URS) 1hr 33:58.4	José Pedraza (MEX) 1hr 34:00.0	Nikolai Smaga (URS) 1hr 34:03.4
1972 Peter Frenkel (GDR) 1hr 26:42.4	Vladimir Golubnichi (URS) 1hr 26:55.2	Hans Reimann (GDR) 1hr 27:16.6
1976 Daniel Baitista (MEX) 1hr 24:40.6	Hans Reimann (GDR) 1hr 25:13.8	Peter Frenkel (GDR) 1hr 25:29.4

1980 Maurizio Damilano (ITA) 1hr 23:35.5	Pyotr Pochenchuk (URS) 1hr 24:45.4	Roland Wieser (GDR) 1hr 25:58.2
1984 Ernesto Canto (MEX) 1hr 23:13	Raul Gonzalez (MEX) 1hr 23:20	Maurizio Damilano (ITA) 1hr 23:26
1988 Jozef Pribilinec (TCH) 1hr 19:57	Ronald Weigel (GDR) 1hr 20:00	Maurizio Damilano (ITA) 1hr 20:14
1992 Daniel Plaza (ESP) 1hr 21:45	Guillaume Leblanc (CAN) 1hr 22:25	Giovanni de Benedictus (ITA) 1hr 23:11
1996 Jefferson Perez (ECU) 1hr 20:07	Ilya Markov (RUS) 1hr 20:16	Bernardo Segura (MEX) 1hr 20:23

1896-1952 *Event not held*

50 000 metres Road Walk

1932 Thomas Green (GBR) 4hr 50:10	Janis Dalinsh (LAT) 4hr 57:20	Ugo Frigerio (ITA) 4hr 59:06
1936 Harold Whitlock (GBR) 4hr 30:41.1	Arthur Schwab (SUI) 4hr 32:09.2	Adalberts Bubenko (LAT) 4hr 32:42.2
1948 John Ljunggren (SWE) 4hr 41:52	Gaston Godel (SUI) 4hr 48:17	Tebbs Lloyd Johnson (GBR) 4hr 48:31
1952 Giuseppe Dordoni (ITA) 4hr 28:07.8	Josef Dolezal (TCH) 4hr 30:17.8	Antal Tóka (HUN) 4hr 31:27.2
1956 Norman Read (NZL) 4hr 30:42.8	Yevgeni Maskinov (URS) 4hr 32:57.0	John Ljunggren (SWE) 4hr 35:02.0
1960 Don Thompson (GBR) 4hr 25:30.0	John Ljunggren (SWE) 4hr 25:47.0	Abdon Pamich (ITA) 4hr 27:55.4
1964 Abdon Pamich (ITA) 4hr 11:12.4	Paul Nihill (GBR) 4hr 11:31.2	Ingvar Pettersson (SWE) 4hr 14:17.4
1968 Christoph Höhne (GDR) 4hr 20:13.6	Antal Kiss (HUN) 4hr 30:17.0	Larry Young (USA) 4hr 31:55.4
1972 Bernd Kannenberg (FRG) 3hr 56:11.6	Venjamin Soldatenko (URS) 3hr 58:24.0	Larry Young (USA) 4hr 00:46.0
1980 Hartwig Gauder (GDR) 2hr 49:24	Jorge Llopart (ESP) 3hr 51:25	Yevgeni Ivchenko (URS) 3hr 56:32
1984 Raul Gonzalez (MEX) 3hr 47:26	Bo Gustafsson (SWE) 3hr 53:19	Sandro Bellucci (ITA) 3hr 53:45
1988 Vyacheslav Ivanenko (URS) 3hr 38:29	Ronald Weigel (GDR) 3hr 38:56	Hartwig Gauder (GDR) 3hr 39:45
1992 Andrei Perlov (EUN) 3hr 50:13	Carlos Mercenario (MEX) 3hr 52:09	Ronald Weigel (GER) 3hr 53:45
1996 Robert Korzeniowski (POL) 3hr 43:30	Mikhail Shchennikov (RUS) 3hr 43:46	Valentin Massana (ITA) 3hr 44:19

1896–1928, 1976 *Event not held*

High Jump

1896 Ellery Clark (USA) 1.8m	James Connolly (USA) 1.65 Robert Garrett (USA) 1.65	–
1900 Irving Baxter (USA) 1.90m	Patrick Leahy (GBR) 1.78	Lajos Gönczy (HUN) 1.75
1904 Samuel Jones (USA) 1.80m	Garrett Serviss (USA) 1.77	Paul Weinstein (GER) 1.77
1906 Con Leahy (GBR) 1.77m	Lajos Gönczy (HUN) 1.75	Herbert Kerrigan (USA) 1.72 Themistoklis Diakidis (GRE) 1.72
1908 Harry Porter (USA) 1.905m	Con Leahy (GBR) 1.88 István Somodi (HUN) 1.88 Georges André (FRA) 1.88	–
1912 Alma Richards (USA) 1.93m	Hans Liesche (GER) 1.91	George Horine (USA) 1.89
1920 Richmond Landon (USA) 1.94m	Harold Muller (USA) 1.90	Bo Ekelund (SWE) 1.90
1924 Harold Osborn (USA) 1.98m	Leroy Brown (USA) 1.95	Pierre Lewden (FRA) 1.92
1928 Robert King (USA) 1.94m	Ben Hedges (USA) 1.91	Claude Ménard (FRA) 1.91
1932 Duncan MacNaughton (CAN) 1.97m	Robert Van Osdel (USA) 1.97	Simeon Toribio (PHI) 1.97
1936 Cornelius Johnson (USA) 2.03m	David Albritton (USA) 2.00	Delos Thurber (USA) 2.00
1948 John Winter (AUS) 1.98m	Björn Paulsen (NOR) 1.95	George Stanich (USA) 1.95
1952 Walt Davis (USA) 2.04m	Ken Wiesner (USA) 2.01	Jose Telles da Conceicao (BRA) 1.98
1956 Charlie Dumas (USA) 2.12m	Chilla Porter (AUS) 2.10	Igor Kashkarov (URS) 2.08

1960 Robert Shavlakadze (URS) 2.16m	Valeri Brumel (URS) 2.16	John Thomas (USA) 2.14
1964 Valeri Brumel (URS) 2.18m	John Thomas (USA) 2.18	John Rambo (USA) 2.16
1968 Dick Fosbury (USA) 2.24m	Ed Caruthers (USA) 2.22	Valentin Gavrilov (URS) 2.20
1972 Yuri Tarmak (RUS) 2.23m	Stefan Junge (GDR) 2.21	Dwight Stones (USA) 2.21
1976 Jacec Wszola (POL) 2.25m	Greg Joy (CAN) 2.23	Dwight Stones (USA) 2.21
1980 Gerd Wessig (GDR) 2.36m	Jacek Wszola (POL) 2.31	Jörg Freimuth (GDR) 2.31
1984 Dietmar Mögenburg (FRG) 2.35m	Patrik Sjöberg (SWE) 2.33	Zhu Jianhua (CHN) 2.31
1988 Gennadi Avdeyenko (URS) 2.38m	Hollis Conway (USA) 2.36	Rudolf Povarnitsin (URS) 2.36
	Patrik Sjöberg (SWE) 2.36	
1992 Javier Sotomayor (CUB) 2.34m	Patrik Sjöberg (SWE) 2.34	
	Tim Forsythe (AUS) 2.34	
	Artur Partyka (POL) 2.34	
1996 Charles Austin (USA) 2.39m	Artur Partyka (POL) 2.37	Hollis Conway (USA) 2.34
		Steve Smith (GBR) 2.35

Pole Vault

1896 William Hoyt (USA) 3.30m	Albert Tyler (USA) 3.20	Ioannis Theodoropoulos (GRE) 2.60
		Vasilios Xydas (GRE) 2.60
		Evangelos Damaskos (GRE) 2.60
1900 Irving Baxter (USA) 3.30m	Meredith Colkett (USA) 3.25	Carl-Albert Andersen (NOR) 3.20
1904 Charles Dvorak (USA) 3.50m	LeRoy Samse (USA) 3.43	Louis Wilkins (USA) 3.4m
1906 Fernand Gonder (FRA) 3.50m	Bruno Söderstrom (SWE) 3.40	Edward Glover (USA) 3.35
1908 Edward Cooke (USA) 3.70m	–	Edward Archibald (CAN) 3.58
Alfred Gilbert (USA) 3.70m		Bruno Söderstrom (SWE) 3.58
		Charles Jacobs (USA) 3.58
1912 Harry Babcock (USA) 3.95m	Frank Nelson (USA) 3.85	Bertil Uggla (SWE) 3.80
	Marcus Wright (USA) 3.85	William Hapenny (CAN) 3.80
		Frank Murphy (USA) 3.80
1920 Frank Foss (USA) 4.09m	Henry Petersen (DEN) 3.70	Edwin Meyers (USA) 3.60
1924 Lee Barnes (USA) 3.95m	Glenn Graham (USA) 3.95	James Brooker (USA) 3.90
1928 Sabin Carr (USA) 4.20m	William Droegemuller (USA) 4.10	Charles McGinnis (USA) 3.95
1932 William Miller (USA) 4.31m	Shuhei Nishida (JPN) 4.30	George Jefferson (USA) 4.20
1936 Earle Meadows (USA) 4.35m	Shuhei Nishida (JPN) 4.25 [1]	Sueo Oe (JPN) 4.25 [1]
1948 Guinn Smith (USA) 4.30m	Erkki Kataja (FIN) 4.20	Bob Richards (USA) 4.20
1952 Bob Richards (USA) 4.55m	Don Laz (USA) 4.50	Ragnar Lundberg (SWE) 4.20
1956 Bob Richards (USA) 4.56m	Bob Gutowski (USA) 4.53	Georgios Roubanis (GRE) 4.50
1960 Don Bragg (USA) 4.70m	Ron Morris (USA) 4.60	Eeles Landstrom (FIN) 4.55
1964 Fred Hansen (USA) 5.10m	Wolfgang Reinhardt (GER) 5.05	Klaus Lehnertz (GER) 5.00
1968 Bob Seagren (USA) 5.40m	Claus Schiprowski (FRG) 5.40	Wolfgang Nordwig (GDR) 5.40
1972 Wolfgang Nordwig (GDR) 5.50m	Bob Seagren (USA) 5.40	Jan Johnson (USA) 5.35
1976 Tadeusz Slusarski (POL) 5.50m	Antti Kalliomaki (FIN) 5.50	David Roberts (USA) 5.50
1980 Wladislaw Kozakiewicz (POL) 5.78m	Tadeusz Slusarski (POL) 5.65	–
	Konstantin Volkov (URS) 5.65	
1984 Pierre Quinon (FRA) 5.75m	Mike Tully (USA) 5.65	Earl Bell (USA) 5.60
		Thierry Vigneron (FRA) 5.60
1988 Sergei Bubka (URS) 5.90m	Rodion Gataullin (URS) 5.85	Grigori Yegorov (URS) 5.80
1992 Maksim Tarasov (EUN) 5.80m	Igor Trandenkov (EUN) 5.80	Javier Garcia (CUB) 5.75
1996 Jean Galfione (FRA) 5.92m	Igor Trandenkov (RUS) 5.92	Andrei Tivontchik (GER) 5.92

[1] Nishida and Oe refused to jump-off and decided places by lot

Long Jump

1896 Ellery Clark (USA) 6.35m	Robert Garrett (USA) 6.18	James Connolly (USA) 6.11
1900 Alvin Kraenzlein (USA) 7.18m	Myer Prinstein (USA) 7.17	Patrick Leahy (GBR) 6.95
1904 Myer Prinstein (USA) 7.34m	Daniel Frank (USA) 6.89	Robert Stangland (USA) 6.88
1906 Myer Prinstein (USA) 7.20m	Peter O'Connor (GBR) 7.02	Hugo Friend (USA) 6.96
1908 Francis Irons (USA) 7.48m	Daniel Kelly (USA) 7.09	Calvin Bricker (CAN) 7.08
1912 Albert Guttersson (USA) 7.60m	Calvin Bricker (CAN) 7.21	Georg Aberg (SWE) 7.18
1920 William Pettersson (SWE) 7.15m	Carl Johnson (USA) 7.09	Erik Abrahamsson (SWE) 7.08
1924 William DeHart Hubbard (USA) 7.44m	Ed Gourdin (USA) 7.27	Sverre Hansen (NOR) 7.26
1928 Edward Hamm (USA) 7.73m	Silvio Cator (HAI) 7.58	Alfred Bates (USA) 7.40
1932 Ed Gordon (USA) 7.63m	Lambert Redd (USA) 7.60	Chuhei Nambu (JPN) 7.44

1936 Jesse Owens (USA) 8.06m	Luz Long (GER) 7.87	Naoto Tajima (JPN) 7.74
1948 Willie Steele (USA) 7.82m	Theodore Bruce (AUS) 7.55	Herbert Douglas 7.54
1952 Jerome Biffle (USA) 7.57m	Meredith Gourdine (USA) 7.53	Odön Földessy (HUN) 7.30
1956 Greg Bell (USA) 7.83m	John Bennett (USA) 7.68	Jorma Valkama (FIN) 7.48
1960 Ralph Boston (USA) 8.12m	Irvin Roberson (USA) 8.11	Igor Ter-Ovanesian (URS) 8.04
1964 Lynn Davies (GBR) 8.07m	Ralph Boston (USA) 8.03	Igor Ter-Ovanseian (URS) 7.99
1968 Bob Beamon (USA) 8.90m	Klaus Beer (GDR) 8.19	Ralph Boston (USA) 8.16
1972 Randy Williams (USA) 8.24m	Hans Baumgartner (FRG) 8.18	Arnie Robinson (USA) 8.03
1976 Arnie Robinson (USA) 8.35m	Randy Williams (USA) 8.11	Frank Wartenberg (GDR) 8.02
1980 Lutz Dombrowski (GDR) 8.54m	Frank Paschek (GDR) 8.21	Valeri Podluzhni (URS) 8.18
1984 Carl Lewis (USA) 8.54m	Gary Honey (AUS) 8.24	Giovanni Evangeisti (ITA) 8.24
1988 Carl Lewis (USA) 8.72m	Mike Powell (USA) 8.49	Larry Myricks (USA) 8.27
1992 Carl Lewis (USA) 8.67m	Mike Powell (USA) 8.64	Joe Greene (USA) 8.34
1996 Carl Lewis (USA) 8.50m	James Beckford (JAM) 8.29	Joe Greene (USA) 8.24

Triple Jump (Formerly known as the Hop, Step and Jump)

1896[1] James Connolly (USA) 13.71m	Alexandre Tuffere (FRA) 12.70	Ioannis Persakis (GRE) 12.52
1900 Myer Prinstein (USA) 14.47m	James Connolly (USA) 13.97	Lewis Sheldon (USA) 13.64
1904 Myer Prinstein (USA) 14.35m	Frederick Englehardt (USA) 13.90	Robert Stangland (USA) 13.36
1906 Peter O'Connor (GBR) 14.07m	Con Leahy (GBR) 13.98	Thomas Cronan (USA) 13.70
1908 Tim Ahearne (GBR) 14.92m	Garfield McDonald (CAN) 14.76	Edvard Larsen (NOR) 14.39
1912 Gustaf Lindblom (SWE) 14.76m	Georg Aberg (SWE) 14.51	Erik Amlöf (SWE) 14.17
1920 Vilho Tuulos (FIN) 14.50m	Folke Jansson (SWE) 14.48	Erik Amlöf (SWE) 14.27
1924 Anthony Winter (AUS) 15.52m	Luis Brunetto (ARG) 15.42	Vilho Tuulos (FIN) 15.37
1928 Mikio Oda (JPN) 15.21m	Levi Casey (USA) 15.17	Vilho Tuulos (FIN) 15.11
1932 Chuhei Nambu (JPN) 15.72m	Erik Svensson (SWE) 15.32	Kenkichi Oshima (JPN) 15.12
1936 Naoto Tajima (JPN) 16.00m	Masao Harada (JPN) 15.66	John Metcalfe (AUS) 15.50
1948 Arne Ahman (SWE) 15.40m	George Avery (AUS) 15.36	Ruhi Sarialp (TUR) 15.02
1952 Adhemar Ferreira de Silva (BRA) 16.22m	Leonid Shcherbakov (URS) 15.98	Arnoldo Devonish (VEN) 15.52
1956 Adhemar Ferreira da Silva (BRA) 16.35m	Vilhjalmur Einarsson (ISL) 16.26	Vitold Kreyer (URS) 16.02
1960 Jozef Schmidt (POL) 16.81m	Vladimir Goryayev (URS) 16.63	Vitold Kreyer (URS) 16.43
1964 Jozef Schmidt (POL) 16.85m	Oleg Fedoseyev (URS) 16.58	Viktor Kravchenko (URS) 16.57
1968 Viktor Saneyev (URS) 17.39m	Nelson Prudencio (BRA) 17.27	Giuseppe Gentile (ITA) 17.22
1972 Viktor Saneyev (URS) 17.35m	Jörg Drehmel (GDR) 17.31	Nelson Prudencio (BRA) 17.05
1976 Viktor Saneyev (URS) 17.29m	James Butts (USA) 17.18	João de Oliveira (BRA) 16.90
1980 Jaak Uudmae (URS) 17.35m	Viktor Saneyev (URS) 17.24	João de Oliveira (BRA) 17.22
1984 Al Joyner (USA) 17.26m	Mike Conley (USA) 17.18	Keith Connor (GBR) 16.87
1988 Khristo Markov (BUL) 17.61m	Igor Lapshin (URS) 17.52	Alexander Kovalenko (URS) 17.42
1992 Mike Conley (USA) 18.17m	Charles Simkins (USA) 17.60	Frank Rutherford (BAH) 17.36
1996 Kenny Harrison (USA) 18.09m	Jonathan Edwards (GBR) 17.88	Yoelbi Quesada (CUB) 17.44

1 Winner took two hops with his right foot, contrary to present rules

Shot

1896[1] Robert Garrett (USA) 11.22m	Miltiades Gouskos (GRE) 11.15	Georgios Papasideris (GRE) 10.36
1900[1] Richard Sheldon (USA) 14.10m	Josiah McCracken (USA) 12.85	Robert Garrett (USA) 12.37
1904[1] Ralph Rose (USA) 14.81m	Wesley Coe (USA) 14.40	Leon Feuerbach (USA) 13.37
1906 Martin Sheridan (USA) 12.32m	Mihály Dávid (HUN) 11.83	Eric Lemming (SWE) 11.26
1908 Ralph Rose (USA) 14.21m	Dennis Horgan (GBR) 13.61	John Garrels (USA) 13.18
1912 Patrick McDonald (USA) 15.34m	Ralph Rose (USA) 15.25	Lawrence Whitney (USA) 13.93
1920 Ville Pörhöla (FIN) 14.81m	Elmer Niklander (FIN) 14.155	Harry Liversedge (USA) 14.15
1924 Clarence Houser (USA) 14.99m	Glenn Hartranft (USA) 14.89	Ralph Hills (USA) 14.64
1928 John Kuck (USA) 15.87m	Herman Brix (USA) 15.75	Emil Hirschfield (GER) 15.72
1932 Lero Sexton (USA) 16.00m	Harlow Rothert (USA) 15.67	Frantisek Douda (TCH) 15.60
1936 Hans Woellke (GER) 16.20	Sulo Bärlund (FIN) 16.12	Gerhard Stöck (GER) 15.66
1948 Wilbur Thompson (USA) 17.12m	Jim Delaney (USA) 16.68	Jim Fuchs (USA) 16.42
1952 Parry O'Brien (USA) 17.41m	Darrow Hooper (USA) 17.39	Jim Fuchs (USA) 17.06
1956 Parry O'Brien (USA) 18.57m	Bill Nieder (USA) 18.18	Jiri Skobla (TCH) 17.65
1960 Bill Nieder (USA) 19.68m	Parry O'Brien (USA) 19.11	Dallas Long (USA) 19.01
1964 Dallas Long (USA) 20.33m	Randy Matson (USA) 20.20	Vilmos Varju (HUN) 19.39
1968 Randy Matson (USA) 20.54m	George Woods (USA) 20.12	Eduard Gushchin (URS) 20.09

1972	Wladyslaw Komar (POL) 21.18m	George Woods (USA) 21.17	Hartmut Briesenick (GDR) 21.14
1976	Udo Beyer (GDR) 21.05m	Yevgeni Mironov (URS) 21.03	Alexander Baryshnikov (URS) 21.00
1980	Volodomir Kiselyev (URS) 21.25m	Alexander Baryshnikov (URS) 21.08	Udo Beyer (GDR) 21.06
1984	Alessandro Andrei (ITA) 21.26m	Michael Carter (USA) 21.09	Dave Laut (USA) 20.97
1988	Ulf Timmermann (GDR) 22.47m	Randy Barnes (USA) 22.39	Werner Günthör (SUI) 21.99
1992	Mike Stulce (USA) 21.70m	James Doerhring (USA) 20.96	Vyacheslav Lykho (EUN) 20.94
1996	Randy Barnes (USA) 21.62m	John Godina (USA) 20.79	Alexander Bagach (UKR) 20.75

[1] Competition was from a 7ft (2.13m) square

Discus

1896[1]	Robert Garrett (USA) 29.15m	Panoyotis Paraskevopoulos (GRE) 28.95	Sotirios Versis (GRE) 28.78
1900[1]	Rudolf Bauer (HUN) 36.04m	Frantisek Janda-Suk (BOH) 35.25	Richard Sheldon (USA) 34.60
1904[2]	Martin Sheridan (USA) 39.28m	Ralph Rose (USA) 39.28	Nicolaos Georgantas (GRE) 37.68
1906	Martin Sheridan (USA) 41.46m	Nicolaos Georgantas (GRE) 38.06	Werner Järvinen (FIN) 36.82
1908	Martin Sheridan (USA) 40.89m	Merritt Griffin (USA) 40.70	Marquis Horr (USA) 39.44
1912	Armas Taipale (FIN) 45.21m	Richard Byrd (USA) 42.32	James Duncan (USA) 42.28
1920	Elmer Niklander (FIN) 44.68m	Armas Taipale (FIN) 44.19	Augustus Pope (USA) 42.13
1924	Clarence Houser (USA) 46.15m	Vilho Niittymaa (FIN) 44.95	Thomas Lieb (USA) 44.83
1928	Clarence Houser (USA) 47.32m	Antero Kivi (FIN) 47.23	James Corson (USA) 47.10
1932	John Anderson (USA) 49.49m	Henri Laborde (USA) 48.47	Paul Winter (FRA) 47.85
1936	Ken Carpenter (USA) 50.48m	Gordon Dunn (USA) 49.36	Giorgio Oberweger (ITA) 49.23
1948	Adolfo Consolini (ITA) 52.78m	Giuseppe Tosi (ITA) 51.78	Fortune Gordien (USA) 50.77
1952	Sim Iness (USA) 55.03m	Adolfo Consolini (ITA) 53.78	James Dillion (USA) 52.38
1956	Al Oerter (USA) 56.36m	Fortune Gordien (USA) 54.81	Des Koch (USA) 54.40
1960	Al Oerter (USA) 59.18m	Rink Babka (USA) 58.02	Dick Cochran (USA) 57.16
1964	Al Oerter (USA) 61.00m	Ludvik Danek (TCH) 60.52	Dave Weill (USA) 59.49
1968	Al Oerter (USA) 64.78m	Lothar Milde (GDR) 63.08	Ludvik Danek (TCH) 62.92
1972	Ludvik Danek (TCH) 64.40m	Jay Silvester (USA) 63.50	Ricky Bruch (SWE) 63.40
1976	Mac Wilkins (USA) 67.50m	Wolfgang Schmidt (GDR) 66.22	John Powell (USA) 65.70
1980	Viktor Rashchupkin (URS) 66.64m	Imrich Bugár (TCH) 66.38	Luis Delis (CUB) 66.32
1984	Rolf Danneberg (FRG) 66.60m	Mac Wilkins (USA) 66.30	John Powell (USA) 65.46
1988	Jürgen Schult (GDR) 68.82m	Romas Ubartas (URS) 67.48	Rolf Danneberg (FRG) 67.38
1992	Romas Ubartas (LTU) 65.12m	Jürgen Schult (GER) 64.94	Roberto Moya (CUB) 64.12
1996	Lars Riedel (GER) 69.40m	Vladimir Dubrovchik (BLR) 66.60	Vasili Kaptyukh (BLR) 65.80

[1] Competition was from a 2.50m square
[2] First place decided by a throw-off

Hammer

1900[1]	John Flanagan (USA) 49.73m	Truxton Hare (USA) 49.13	Josiah McCracken (USA) 42.46
1904	John Flanagan (USA) 51.23m	John De Witt (USA) 50.26	Ralph Rose (USA) 45.73
1908	John Flanagan (USA) 51.92m	Matt McGrath (USA) 51.18	Con Walsh (CAN) 48.50
1912	Matt McGrath (USA) 54.74m	Duncan Gillis (CAN) 48.39	Clarence Childs (USA) 48.17
1920	Patrick Ryna (USA) 52.87m	Carl Lind (SWE) 48.43	Basil Bennett (USA) 48.25
1924	Fred Tootell (USA) 53.29m	Matt McGrath (USA) 50.84	Malcolm Nokes (GBR) 48.87
1928	Patrick O'Callaghan (IRL) 51.39m	Ossian Skjöld (SWE) 51.29	Edmund Black (USA) 49.03
1932	Patrick O'Callaghan (IRL) 53.92m	Ville Pörhöla (FIN) 52.27	Peter Zaremba (USA) 50.33
1936	Karl Hein (GER) 56.49m	Erwin Blask (GER) 55.04	Fred Warngard (SWE) 54.83
1948	Imre Németh (HUN) 56.07m	Ivan Gubijan (YUG) 54.27	Bob Bennett (USA) 53.73
1952	József Csermák (HUN) 60.34m	Karl Storch (GER) 58.86	Imre Németh (HUN) 57.74
1956	Harold Connolly (USA) 63.19m	Mikhail Krivonosov (URS) 63.03	Anatoli Samotsvetov (URS) 62.56
1960	Vasili Rudenkov (URS) 67.10m	Gyula Zsivótzky (HUN) 65.79	Tadeusz Rut (POL) 65.64
1964	Romuald Klim (URS) 69.74m	Gyula Zsivótzky (HUN) 69.09	Uwe Beyer (GER) 68.09
1968	Gyula Zsivótzky (HUN) 73.36m	Romuald Klim (URS) 73.28	Lázár Lovász (HUN) 69.78
1972	Anatoli Bondarchuk (URS) 75.50m	Jochen Sachse (GDR) 74.96	Vasili Khmelevski (URS) 74.04
1976	Yuri Sedykh (URS) 77.52m	Alexei Spriridonov (URS) 76.08	Anatoli Bondarchuk (URS) 75.48
1980	Yuri Sedykh (URS) 81.80m	Sergei Litvinov (URS) 80.64	Juri Tamm (URS) 78.96
1984	Juha Tiainen (FIN) 78.08m	Karl-Hans Riehm (FRG) 77.98	Klaus Ploghaus (FRG) 76.68
1988	Sergei Litvinov (URS) 84.80m	Yuri Sedykh (URS) 83.76	Juri Tamm (URS) 81.16

1992 Anrei Abduvalyev (EUN) 82.54m	Igor Astapkovich (EUN) 81.96	Igor Nikulin (EUN) 81.38
1996 Balázs Kiss (HUN) 81.24m	Lance Deal (USA) 81.12	Alexander Krykun (UKR) 80.02

1896 and 1906 *Event not held*

1 Competition from a 9ft (2.74m) circle

Javelin

1906 Eric Lemming (SWE) 53.90m	Knut Lindberg (SWE) 45.17	Bruno Söderström (SWE) 44.92
1908 Eric Lemming (SWE) 54.82m	Arne Halse (NOR) 50.57	Otto Nilsson (SWE) 47.09
1912 Eric Lemming (SWE) 60.64m	Juho Saaristo (FIN) 58.66	Mór Kóczán (HUN) 55.50
1920 Jonni Myyrä (FIN) 65.78m	Urho Peltonen (FIN) 63.50	Pekka Johansson (FIN) 63.09
1924 Jonni Myyrä (FIN) 62.96m	Gunnar Lindström (SWE) 60.92	Eugene Oberst (USA) 58.35
1928 Erik Lundkvist (SWE) 66.60m	Béla Szepes (HUN) 65.26	Olva Sunde (NOR) 63.97
1932 Matti Järvinen (FIN) 72.71m	Matti Sippala (FIN) 69.79	Eino Penttila (FIN) 68.69
1936 Gerhard Stöck (GER) 71.84m	Yrjö Nikkanen (FIN) 70.77	Kalervo Toivonen (FIN) 70.72
1948 Tapio Rautavaara (FIN) 69,77m	Steve Seymour (USA) 67.56	József Várszegi (HUN) 67.03
1952 Cyrus Young (USA) 73.78m	Bill Miller (USA) 72.46	Toivo Hyytiäinen (FIN) 71.89
1956 Egil Danielsen (NOR) 85.71m	Janusz Sidlo (POL) 79.98	Viktor Tsibulenko (URS) 79.50
1960 Viktor Tsibulenko (URS) 84.64m	Walter Krüger (GER) 79.36	Gergely Kulcsár (HUN) 78.57
1964 Pauli Nevala (FIN) 82.66m	Gergely Kulcsár (HUN) 82.32	Janis Lusis (URS) 80.57
1968 Janis Lusis (URS) 90.10m	Jorma Kinnunen (FIN) 88.58	Gergely Kulcsár (HUN) 87.06
1972 Klaus Wolfermann (FRG) 90.48m	Janis Lusis (URS) 90.46	Bill Schmidt (USA) 84.42
1976 Miklos Németh (HUN) 94.58m	Hannu Siitonen (FIN) 87.92	Gheorghe Megelea (ROM) 87.16
1980 Dainis Kula (URS) 91.20m	Alexander Makarov (URS) 89.64	Wolfgang Hanisch (GDR) 86.72
1984 Arto Härkonen (FIN) 86.76m	David Ottley (GBR) 85.74	Kenth Eldebrink (SWE) 83.72
1988[1] Tapio Korjus (FIN) 84.28m	Jan Zelezny (TCH) 84.12	Seppo Räty (FIN) 83.26
1992 Jan Zelezny (TCH) 89.66m	Seppo Räty (FIN) 86.60	Steve Backley (GBR) 83.38
1996 Jan Zelezny (CZE) 88.16m	Steve Backley (GBR) 87.44	Seppo Räty (FIN) 86.98

1896–1904 *Event not held*

1 New javelin introduced

Decathlon [1] [2]

1904[3] Thomas Kiely (GBR) 6036pts	Adam Gunn (USA) 5907	Truxton Hare (USA) 5813
1912[4] Hugo Wieslander (SWE) 5965pts	Charles Lomberg (SWE) 5721	Gösta Holmer (SWE) 5768
1920 Helge Lövland (NOR) 5803pts	Brutus Hamilton (USA) 5739	Bertil Ohlsson (SWE) 5639
1924 Harold Osboen (USA) 6476pts	Emerson Norton (USA) 6117	Alexander Klumberg (EST) 6056
1928 Paavo Yrjölä (FIN) 6587pts	Akilles Järvinen (FIN) 6645	Ken Doherty (USA) 6428
1932 Jim Bausch (USA) 6735pts	Akilles Järvinen (FIN) 6879	Wolrad Eberle (GER) 6661
1936 Glenn Morris (USA) 7254pts	Robert Clark (USA) 7063	Jack Parker (USA) 6760
1948 Bob Mathias (USA) 6628pts	Ignace Heinrich (FRA) 6559	Floyd Simmons (USA) 6531
1952 Bob Mathias (USA) 7592pts	Milt Campbell (USA) 6995	Floyd Simmons (USA) 6945
1956 Milt Campbell (USA) 7614pts	Rafer Johnson (USA) 7457	Vasili Kuznetsov (URS) 7337
1960 Rafer Johnson (USA) 7926pts	Yang Chuan-Kwang (TPE) 7839	Vasili Kuznetsov (URS) 7557
1964 Willi Holdorf (GER) 7794pts	Rein Aun (URS) 7744	Hans-Joachim Walde (GER) 7735
1968 Bill Toomey (USA) 8144pts	Hans-Joachim Walde (FRG) 8094	Kurt Bendlin (FRG) 8071
1972 Nikolai Avilov (URS) 8466pts	Leonid Litvinenko (URS) 7970	Ryszard Katus (POL) 7936
1976 Bruce Jenner (USA) 8634pts	Guido Kratschmer (FRG) 8407	Nikolai Avilov (URS) 8378
1980 Daley Thompson (GBR) 8522pts	Yuri Kutsenko (URS) 8369	Sergei Zhelanov (URS) 8135
1984 Daley Thompson (GBR) 8847pts	Jürgen Hingsen (FRG) 8695	Siegfried Wentz (FRG) 8416
1988 Christian Schenk (GDR) 8488pts	Torsten Voss (GDR) 8399	Dave Steen (CAN) 8328
1992 Robert Zmelik (TCH) 8611pts	Antonio Penalver (CUB) 8412	Dave Johnson (USA) 8309
1996 Dan O'Brien (USA) 8824pts	Frank Busemann (GER) 8706	Tomas Dvorak (CZE) 8664

1896–1900, 1906–08 *Event not held*

1 The decathlon consists of 100m, long jump, shot put, high jump, 400m, 110m hurdles, discus, pole vault, javelin and 1500m. The competition occupies two days, although in 1912 it took three days

2 The scores since 1912 given above have been recalculated on the current, 1984, scoring tables, for purposes of comparison. Note that in 1912, 1928, 1932 and 1948 the original medal order would have been different if these tables had been in force

3 Consisted of 100yd, 1 mile, 120yd hurdles, 880yd walk, high jump, long jump, pole vault, shot out hammer and 56lb weight

4 Jim Thorpe (USA) finished first with 6564pts, but was later disqualified for a breach of the then amateur rules. He was reinstated posthumously by the IOC in 1982, but only as joint first

Women

(Women's events first contested in 1928)

100m

1928 Elizabeth Robinson (USA) 12.2	Fanny Rosenfeld (CAN) 12.3	Ethel Smith (CAN) 12.3
1932 Stanislawa Walasiewicz (POL) 11.9	Hilda Strike (CAN) 11.9	Wilhelmina von Bremen (USA) 12.0
1936 Helen Stephens (USA) 11.5	Stanislawa Walalsiewicz (POL) 11.7	Kathe Krauss (GER) 11.9
1948 Fanny Blankers-Koen (NED) 11.9	Dorothy Manley (GBR) 12.2	Shirley Strickland (AUS) 12.2
1952 Marjorie Jackson (AUS) 11.5 (11.67)	Daphne Hasenjager (RSA) 11.8 (12.05)	Shirley Strickland (AUS) 11.9 (12.12)
1956 Betty Cuthbert (AUS) 11.5 (11.82)	Christa Stubnick (GER) 11.7 (11.92)	Marlene Matthews (AUS) 11.7 (11.94)
1960 Wilma Rudolph (USA) 11.0 (11.18)	Dorothy Hyman (GBR) 11.3 (11.43)	Giuseppina Leone (ITA) 11.3 (11.48)
1964 Wyomia Tyus (USA) 11.4 (11.49)	Edith Maguire (USA) 11.6 (11.62)	Ewa Klobukowska (POL) 11.6 (11.64)
1968 Wyomia Tyus (USA) 11.0 (11.08)	Barbara Ferrell (USA) 11.1 (11.15)	Irena Szewinska (POL) 11.1 (11.19)
1972 Renate Stecher (GDR) 11.07	Raelene Boyle (AUS) 11.23	Silvia Chivas (CUB) 11.24
1976 Annegret Richter (FRG) 11.08	Renate Stecher (GDR) 11.13	Inge Helten (FRG) 11.17
1980 Ludmila Kondratyeva (URS) 11.06	Marlies Göhr (GDR) 11.07	Ingrid Auerswald (GDR) 11.14
1984 Evelyn Ashford (USA) 10.97	Alice Brown (USA) 11.13	Merlene Ottey-Page (JAM) 11.16
1988 Florence Griffith-Joyner (USA) 10.54 [1]	Evelyn Ashford (USA) 10.83	Heike Drechsler (GDR) 10.85
1992 Gail Devers (USA) 10.82	Juliet Cuthbert (JAM) 10.83	Irina Privalova (EUN) 10.84
1996 Gail Devers (USA) 10.94	Merlene Ottey (JAM) 10.94	Gwen Torrence (USA 10.96

[1] Final was wind-assisted; 10.62 in preliminary round

200m

1948 Fanny Blankers-Koen (NED) 24.4	Audrey Williamson (GBR) 25.1	Audrey Patterson (USA) 25.2 [1]
1952 Marjorie Jackson (AUS) 23.7 (23.89)	Bertha Brouwer (NED) 24.2 (24.25)	Nadyezda Khnykina (URS) 24.2 (24.37)
1956 Betty Cuthbert (AUS) 23.4 (23.55)	Christa Stubnick (GER) 23.7 (23.89)	Marlene Matthews (AUS) 23.8 (24.10)
1960 Wilma Rudolph (USA) 24.0 (24.13)	Jutta Heine (GER) 24.4 (24.58)	Dorothy Hyman (GBR) 24.7 (24.82)
1964 Edith Maguire (USA) 23.0 (23.05)	Irena Kirszenstein (POL) 23.1 (23.13)	Marilyn Black (AUS) 23.1 (23.18)
1968 Irena Szewinskas (POL) 22.5 (22.58)	Raelene Boyle (AUS) 22.7 (22.74)	Jennifer Lamy (AUS) 22.8 (22.88)
1972 Renate Stecher (GDR) 22.40	Raelene Boyle (AUS) 22.45	Irena Szewinska (POL) 22.74
1976 Bärbel Eckert (GDR) 22.37	Annegret Richter (FRG) 22.39	Renate Stecher (GDR) 22.47
1980 Bärbel Wöckel (GDR) 22.03	Natalya Bochina (URS) 22.19	Merlene Ottey (JAM) 22.20
1984 Valerie Brisco-Hooks (USA) 21.81	Florence Griffith (USA) 22.04	Merlene Ottey-Page (JAM) 22.09
1988 Florence Giffith-Joyner (USA) 21.34	Grace Jackson (JAM) 21.72	Heike Drechsler (GDR) 21.95
1992 Gwen Torrence (USA) 21.81	Juliet Cuthbert (JAM) 22.02	Merlene Ottey (JAM) 22.09
1996 Marie-José Pérec (FRA) 22.12	Merlene Ottey (JAM) 22.24	Mary Onyali (NGR) 22.38

1928–36 *Event not held*

[1] Photo-finish picture indicates that Shirley Strickland (AUS) was third

400m

1964 Betty Cuthbert (AUS) 52.0 (52.01)	Ann Packer (GBR) 52.2 (52.20)	Judith Amoore (AUS) 53.4
1968 Colette Besson (FRA) 52.0 (52.03)	Lillian Board (GBR) 52.1 (52.12)	Natalya Burda (URS) 52.2 (52.25)
1972 Monika Zehrt (GDR) 51.08	Rita Wilden (FRG) 51.21	Kathy Hammond (USA) 51.64
1976 Irena Szewinska (POL) 49.29	Christina Brehmer (GDR) 50.51	Ellen Streidt (GDR) 50.55
1980 Marita Koch (GDR) 48.88	Jarmila Kratochvilová (TCH) 49.46	Christina Lathan (GDR) 49.66
1984 Valerie Brisco-Hooks (USA) 48.83	Chandra Cheeseborough (USA) 49.05	Kathy Cook (GBR) 49.43

1988 Olga Bryzgina (URS) 48.65	Petra Müller (GDR) 49.45	Olga Nazarova (URS) 49.90
1992 Marie-José Pérec (FRA) 48.83	Olga Bryzgina (EUN) 49.05	Ximena Restrepo (COL) 49.64
1996 Marie-José Pérec (FRA) 48.25	Cathy Freeman (AUS) 48.63	Flailat Ogunkoya (NGR) 49.10

1928–60 *Event not held*

800m

1928 Lina Radke (GER) 2:216.8	Kinuye Hitomi (JPN) 2:17.6	Inga Gentzel (SWE) 2:17.8
1960 Ludmila Shevtsova (URS) 2:04.3	Branda Jones (AUS) 2:04.4	Ursula Donath (GER) 2:05.6
1964 Ann Packer (GBR) 2:01.1	Maryvonne Dupureur (FRA)	Marise Chamberlain (NZL) 2:02.8
1968 Madeline Manning (USA) 2:00.9	Ilona Silai (ROM) 2:02.5	Maria Gommers (NED) 2:02.6
1972 Hildegard Falck (FRG) 1:58.6	Niole Sabaite (URS) 1:58.7	Gunhild Hoffmeister (GDR) 1:59.2
1976 Tatyana Kazankina (URS) 1:54.9	Nikolina Shtereva (BUL) 1:55.4	Elfi Zinn (GDR) 1:55.6
1980 Nadyezda Olizarenko (URS) 1:53.5	Olga Mineyeva (URS) 1:54.9	Tatyana Providokhina (URS) 1:55.5
1984 Doina Melinte (ROM) 1:57.60	Kim Gallagher (USA) 1:58.63	Fita Lovin (ROM) 1:58.83
1988 Sigrun Wodars (GSR) 1:56.10	Christine Wachtel (GDR) 1:56.64	Kim Gallagher (USA) 1:56.91
1992 Ellen van Langen (NED) 1:55.54	Lilia Nurutdinova (EUN) 1:55.99	Ana Quirot (CUB) 1:56.80
1996 Svetlana Masterkova (RUS) 1:57.73	Ana Quirot (CUB) 1:58.11	Maria Mutola (MOZ) 1:58.71

1932–56 *Event not held*

1500m

1972 Ludmila Bragina (URS) 4:01.4	Gunhild Hoffmeister (GDR) 4:02.8	Paola Cacchi-Pigni (ITA) 4:02.9
1976 Tatyana Kazankina (URS) 4:05.5	Gunhild Hoffmeister (GDR) 4:06.0	Ulrike Klapezynski (GDR) 4:06.1
1980 Tatyana Kazankina (URS) 3:56.6	Christiane Wartenberg (GDR) 3:57.8	Nadyezda Olizarenko (URS) 3:59.6
1984 Gariella Dorio (ITA) 4:03.25	Doina Melinte (ROM) 4:03.76	Maricica Puica (ROM) 4:04.15
1988 Paula Ivan (ROM) 3:53.96	Laima Baikauskaite (URS) 4:00.24	Tatyana Samolenko (URS) 4:00.30
1992 Hassiba Boulmerka (ALG) 3:55.30	Ludmila Ragacheva (EUN) 3:56.91	Qu Yunxia (CHN) 3:57.08
1996 Svetlana Masterkova (RUS) 4:00.83	Gabriela Szabo (ROM) 4:01.54	Theresia Kiesl (AUT) 4:03.02

1928–68 *Event not held*

3000m (Replaced by 5000m in 1996)

1984 Maricica Puica (ROM) 8:35.96	Wendy Sly (GBR) 8:39.47	Lynn Williams (CAN) 8:42.14
1988 Tatyana Samolenko (URS) 8:26.53	Paula Ivan (ROM) 8:27.15	Yvonne Murray (GBR) 8:29.02
1992 Yelena Romanova (EUN) 8:46.04	Tatyana Dorovskikh (EUN) 8:46.85	Angela Chalmers (CAN) 8:47.22

1928–80 *Event not held*

5000m

1996 Wang Junxia (CHN) 14:59.88	Pauline Konga (KEN) 15:03.49	Roberta Brunet (ITA) 15:07.52

1928–92 *Event not held*

10 000m

1988 Olga Bondarenko (URS) 31:05.21	Liz McColgan (GBR) 31:08.44	Yelena Zhupiyeva (URS) 31:19.82
1992 Derartu Tulu (ETH) 31:06.02	Elana Meyer (RSA) 31:11.75	Lynn Jennings (USA) 31:19.89
1996 Fernanda Ribeiro (POR) 31:01.63	Wang Junxia (CHN) 31:02.58	Gete Wami (ETH) 31:06.65

1928–84 *Event not held*

Marathon

1984 Joan Benoit (USA) 2hr 24:52	Grete Waitz (NOR) 2hr 26:18	Rosa Mota (POR) 2hr 26:57
1988 Rosa Mota (POR) 2hr 25:40	Lisa Martin (AUS) 2hr 25:53	Kathrin Dörre (GDR) 2hr 26:21
1992 Valentina Yegorova (EUN) 2hr 32:41	Yuko Arimori (JPN) 2hr 32:49	Lorraine Moller (NZL) 2hr 33:59
1996 Fatuma Roba (ETH) 2hr 26:05	Valentina Yegorova (RUS) 2hr 28:05	Yuko Arimori (JPN) 2hr 28:39

1928–80 *Event not held*

100 metres Hurdles
(Held over 80 metres Hurdles 1932–68)

1932 Mildred Didrikson (USA) 11.7	Evelyne Hall (USA) 11.7	Marjorie Clark (RSA) 11.8
1936 Trebisonda Valla (ITA) 11.7 (11.75)	Anny Steuer (GER) 11.7 (11.81)	Elizabeth Taylor (CAN) 11.7 (11.81)
1948 Fanny Blankers-Koen (NED) 11.2	Maureen Gardner (GBR) 11.2	Shirley Strickland (AUS) 11.4
1952 Shirley de la Hunty (AUS) 10.8 (11.01)	Maria Golubichnaya (URS) 11.1 (11.24)	Maria Sander (GER) 11.1 (11.38)
1956 Shirley de la Hunty (AUS) 10.7 (10.96)	Gisela Köhler (GER) 10.9 (11.12)	Norma Thrower (AUS) 11.0 (11.25)
1960 Irina Press (URS) 10.8 (10.93)	Carol Quinton (GBR) 10.9 (10.99)	Gisela Birkemeyer (GER) 11.0 (11.13)
1964 Karin Balzer (GER) 10.5 (10.54)	Teresa Ciepla (POL) 10.5 (10.55)	Pam Kilborn (AUS) 10.5 (10.56)
1968 Maureen Caird (AUS) 10.3 (10.39)	Pam Kilborn (AUS) 10.4 (10.46)	Chi Cheng (TPE) 10.4 (10.51)
1972 Annelie Ehrhardt (GDR) 12.59	Valeria Bufanu (ROM) 12.84	Karin Balzer (GDR) 12.90
1976 Johanna Schaller (GDR) 12.77	Tatyana Anisimova (URS) 12.78	Natalya Lebedyeva (URS) 12.80
1980 Vera Komisova (URS) 12.56	Johanna Klier (GDR) 12.63	Lucyna Langer (POL) 12.65
1984 Benita Fitzgerald-Brown (USA) 12.84	Shirley Strong (GBR) 12.88	Kim Turner (USA) 13.06
		Michele Chardonnet (FRA) 13.06
1988 Yordanka Donkova (BUL) 12.38	Gloria Siebert (GDR) 12.61	Claudia Zackiewicz (FRG) 12.75
1992 Paraskevi Patoulidou (GRE) 12.64	LaVonna Martin (USA) 12.69	Yordanka Donkova (BUL) 12.70
1996 Ludmila Engquist (SWE) 12.58	Brigita Bukovec (SLO) 12.59	Patricia Girard-Leno (FRA) 12.65

1928 *Event not held*

400 metres Hurdles

1984 Nawal El Moutawakel (MAR) 54.61	Judi Brown (USA) 55.20	Cristina Cojocaru (ROM) 55.41
1988 Debbie Flintoff-King (AUS) 53.17	Tatyana Ledovskaya (URS) 53.18	Ellen Fiedler (GDR) 53.63
1992 Sally Gunnell (GBR) 53.23	Sandra Farmer-Patrick (USA) 53.69	Janeene Vickers (USA) 54.31
1996 Deon Hemmings (JAM) 52.82	Kim Batten (USA) 53.08	Tonja Buford-Bailey (USA) 53.22

1928–80 *Event not held*

4 × 100 metres Relay

1928 Canada 48.4	United States 48.8	Germany 49.2
1932 United States 47.0 (46.86)	Canada 47.0	Great Britain 47.6
1936 United States 46.9	Great Britain 47.6	Canada 47.8
1948 The Netherlands 47.5	Australia 47.6	Canada 47.8
1952 United States 45.9 (46.14)	Germany 45.9 (46.18)	Great Britain 46.2 (46.41)
1956 Australia 44.5 (44.65)	Great Britain 44.7 (44.70)	United States 44.9 (45.04)
1960 United States 44.5 (44.72)	Germany 44.8 (45.00)	Poland 45.0 (45.19)
1964 Poland 43.6 (43.69)	United States 43.9 (43.92)	Great Britain 44.0 (44.09)
1968 United States 42.8 (42.88)	Cuba 43.3 (43.36)	Soviet Union 43.4 (43.41)
1972 West Germany 42.81	East Germany 42.95	Cuba 43.36
1976 East Germany 42.55	West Germany 42.59	Soviet Union 43.09
1980 East Germany 41.60	Soviet Union 42.10	Great Britain 42.43
1984 United States 41.65	Canada 42.77	Great Britain 43.11
1988 United States 41.98	East Germany 42.09	Soviet Union 42.75
1992 United States 42.11	Unified Team 42.16	Nigeria 42.81
1996 United States 41.95	Bahamas 42.14	Jamaica 42.24

4 × 400 metres Relay

1972 East Germany 3:22.95	United States 3:25.15	West Germany 3:26.51
1976 East Germany 3:19.23	United States 3:22.81	Soviet Union 3:24.24
1980 Soviet Union 3:20.12	East Germany 3:20.35	Great Britain 3:27.5
1984 United States 3:18.29	Canada 3:21.21	West Germany 3:22.98
1988 Soviet Union 3:15.17	United States 3:15.51	East Germany 3:18.29
1992 Unified Team 3:20.20	United States 3:20.92	Great Britain 3:24.23
1996 United States 3:20.91	Nigeria 3:21.04	Germany 3:21.14

1928–68 *Event not held*

10 000 metres Walk
(Will be replaced by a 20 000 metres walk in 2000)

1992 Chen Yueling (CHN) 44:32	Yelena Nikoleyeva (EUN) 44:33	Li Chunxiu (CHN) 44:41
1996 Yelena Nikolayeva (RUS) 41:49	Elisabetta Perrone (ITA) 42:12	Wang Yan (CHN) 42:19

1928–88 *Event not held*

High Jump

1928 Ether Catherwood (CAN) 1.59m	Carolina Gisolf (NED) 1.56	Mildred Wiley (USA) 1.56
1932 Jean Shiley (USA) 1.657m [1]	Mildred Didrikson (USA) 1.657 [1]	Eva Dawes (CAN) 1.60
1936 Ibolya Csák (HUN) 1.60m	Dorothy Odam (GBR) 1.60	Elfriede Kaun (GER) 1.60
1948 Alice Coachman (USA) 1.68m	Dorothy Tyler (GBR) 1.68	Micheline Ostermeyer (FRA) 1.61
1952 Esther Brand (RSA) 1.67m	Sheila Lerwill (GBR) 1.65	Alexandra Chudina (URS) 1.63
1956 Mildred McDaniel (USA) 1.76m	Thelma Hopkins (GBR) 1.67	–
	Maria Pisaryeva (URS) 1.67	
1960 Iolanda Balas (ROM) 1.85m	Jaroslawa Józwiakowska (POL) 1.71	–
	Dorothy Shirley (GBR) 1.71	
1964 Iolanda Balas (ROM) 1.90m	Michelle Brown (AUS) 1.80	Tasia Chenchik (URS) 1.78
1968 Miloslava Rezková (TCH) 1.82m	Antonina Okorokova (URS) 1.80	Valentina Kozyr (URS) 1.80
1972 Ulrike Meyfarth (FRG) 1.92m	Yordanka Bloyeva (BUL) 1.88	Ilona Gusenbauer (AUT) 1.88
1976 Rosemarie Ackermann (GDR) 1.93m	Sara Simeoni (ITA) 1.91	Yordanka Blagoyeva (BUL) 1.91
1980 Sara Simeoni (ITA) 1.97m	Urszula Kielan (POL) 1.94	Jutta Kirst (GDR) 1.94
1984 Ulrike Meyfarth (FRG) 2.02m	Sara Simeoni (ITA) 2.00	Joni Huntley (USA) 1.97
1988 Louise Ritter (USA) 2.03m	Stefka Kostadinova (BUL) 2.01	Tamara Bykova (URS) 1.99
1992 Heike Henkel (GER) 2.02m	Galina Astafei (ROM) 2.00	Ioamnet Quintero (CUB) 1.97
1996 Stefka Kostadinova (BUL) 2.05m	Niki Bakogianni (GRE) 2.03	Inha Babakova (UKR) 2.01

[1] Some sources suggest 1.66m

Pole Vault
(Will be held for first time in 2000)

Long Jump

1948 Olga Gyarmati (HUN) 5.69m	Noëmi Simonetta de Portela (ARG) 5.60	Ann-Britt Leyman (SWE) 5.57
1952 Yvette Williams (NZL) 6.24m	Alexandra Chudina (URS) 6.14	Shirley Cawley (GBR) 5.92
1956 Elzbieta Krzesinska (POL) 6.35m	Willye White (USA) 6.09	Nadyezda Dvalishvili (URS) 6.07
1960 Vera Krepkina (URS) 6.37m	Elzbieta Krzesinska (POL) 6.27	Hildrun Claus (GER) 6.21
1864 Mary Rand (GBR) 6.76m	Irena Kirszenstein (POL) 6.27	Tatyana Schelkanova (URS) 6.42
1968 Niorica Viscopoleanu (ROM) 6.82m	Sheila Sherwood (GBR) 6.68	Tatyana Talysheva (URS) 6.66
1972 Heidemarie Rosendahl (FRG) 6.78m	Diana Yorgova (BUL) 6.77	Eva Suranová (TCH) 6.67
1976 Angela Voigt (GDR) 6.72m	Kathy McMillan (USA) 6.66	Lidia Alfeyeva (URS) 6.60
1980 Tatyana Kolpakova (URS) 7.06m	Brigitte Wujak (GDR) 7.04	Tatyana Skatchko (URS) 7.01
1984 Anisoara Stanciu (ROM) 6.96m	Vali Ionescu (ROM) 6.81	Susan Hearnshaw (GBR) 6.80
1988 Jackie Joyner-Kersee (USA) 7.40m	Heike Drechsler (GDR) 7.22	Galina Chistiakova (URS) 7.11
1992 Heike Drechsler (GDR) 7.14m	Inessa Kravets (EUN) 7.12	Jackie Joyner-Kersee (USA) 7.07
1996 Chioma Ajunwa (NGR) 7.12m	Fiona May (ITA) 7.02	Jackie Joyner-Kersee (USA) 7.00

1928–36 *Event not held*

Triple Jump

1996 Inessa Kravets (UKR) 15.33m	Inna Lasovskaya (RUS) 14.98	Sarka Kasparkova (CZE) 14.98

1928–92 *Event not held*

Shot

1948 Micheline Ostermeyer (FRA) 13.75m	Amelia Piccinini (ITA) 13.09	Ina Schäffer (AUT) 13.08
1952 Galina Zybina (URS) 15.28m	Marianne Werner (GER) 14.57	Klavdia Tochonova (URS) 14.50
1956 Tamara Tyshkevich (URS) 16.59m	Galina Zybina (URS) 15.53	Marianne Werner (GER) 15.61

1960	Tamara Press (URS) 17.32m	Johanna Lüttge (GER) 16.61	Earlene Brown (USA) 16.42
1964	Tamara Press (URS) 18.14m	Renate Garisch (GDR) 17.61	Galina Zybina (URS) 16.42
1968	Margitta Gummel (GDR) 19.61m	Marita Lange (GDR) 18.78	Nadyezda Chizhova (URS) 18.19
1972	Nadyezda Chizhova (URS) 21.03m	Margitta Gummel (GDR) 20.22	Ivanka Khristova (BUL) 19.35
1976	Ivanka Khristova (BUL) 21.16m	Nadyezda Chizhova (URS) 20.96	Helena Fibingerová (TCH) 20.67
1980	Ilona Slupianek (GDR) 22.41m	Svetlana Krachevskaya (URS) 21.42	Margitta Pufe (GDR) 21.20
1984	Claudia Losch (FRG) 20.48m	Mihaela Loghin (ROM) 20.47	Gael Martin (AUS) 19.19
1988	Natalya Lisovskaya (URS) 22.24m	Kathrin Neimke (GDR) 21.07	Li Meisu (CHN) 21.06
1992	Svetlana Krivelyova (EUN) 21.06m	Huang Zhihong (CHN) 20.47	Kathrin Neimke (GER) 19.78
1996	Astrid Kumbernuss (GER) 20.56m	Sui Xinmei (CHN) 19.88	Irina Khudorozhkina (RUS) 19.35

1928–36 *Event not held*

Discus

1928	Helena Konopacka (POL) 39.62m	Lilian Copeland (USA) 37.08	Ruth Svedberg (SWE) 35.92
1932	Lilian Copeland (USA) 40.58m	Ruth Osburn (USA) 40.11	Jadwiga Wajsówna (POL) 38.73
1936	Gisela Mauermayer (GER) 47.63m	Jadwiga Wajsówna (POL) 46.22	Paula Mollenhauer (GER) 39.80
1948	Micheleine Ostermeyer (FRA) 41.92m	Edera Gentile (ITA) 41.17	Jacqueline Mazéas (FRA) 40.47
1952	Nina Romashkova (URS) 51.42m	Elizaveta Bagryantseva (URS) 47.08	Nina Dumbadze (URS) 46.29
1956	Olga Fikotová (TCH) 53.69m	Irina Beglyakova (URS) 52.54	Nina Ponomaryeva (URS) 52.02
1960	Nina Ponomaryeva (URS) 55.10m	Tamara Press (URS) 52.59	Lia Manoliu (ROM) 52.36
1964	Tamara Press (URS) 57.27m	Ingrid Lotz (GER) 57.21	Lia Manoliu (ROM) 56.97
1968	Lia Manoliu (ROM) 58.28m	Liesel Westerman (FRG) 57.76	Jolán Kleiber (HUN) 54.90
1972	Faina Melnik (URS) 66.62m	Argentina Menis (ROM) 65.06	Vasilka Stoyeva (BUL) 64.34
1976	Evelin Sclaak (GDR) 69.00m	Maria Vergova (BUL) 67.30	Gabriele Hinzmann (GDR) 66.84
1980	Evelin Jahl (GDR) 69.96m	Maria Petkova (BUL) 67.90	Tatyana Lesovaya (URS) 67.40
1984	Ria Stalman (NED) 65.36m	Leslie Deniz (USA) 64.86	Florenta Craciunescu (ROM) 63.64
1988	Martina Hellmann (GDR) 72.30m	Diane Gansky (GDR) 71.88	Tsvetanka Khristova (BUL) 69.74
1992	Maritza Marten (CUB) 70.06m	Tsvetanka Khristova (BUL) 67.78	Daniela Costian (AUS) 66.24
1996	Ilke Wyludda (GER) 69.66m	Natalya Sadova (RUS) 66.48	Elya Zvereva (BLR) 65.64

Javelin

1932	Mildred Didrikson (USA) 43.68m	Ellen Braumüller (GER) 43.49	Tilly Fleischer (GER) 43.40
1936	Tilly Fleischer (GER) 45.18m	Louise Krüger (GER) 43.29	Marja Kwasniewska (POL) 41.80
1948	Herma Bauma (AUT) 45.57m	Kaisa Parviainen (FIN) 43.79	Lily Carlstedt (DEN) 42.08
1952	Dana Zátopková (TCH) 50.47m	Alexandra Chudina (URS) 50.01	Yelena Gorchkova (URS) 49.76
1956	Inese Jaunzeme (URS) 53.86m	Marlene Ahrens (CHI) 50.38	Nadyezda Konyayeva (URS) 50.28
1960	Elvira Ozolina (URS) 55.98m	Dana Zátopková (TCH) 53.78	Birute Kalediene (URS) 53.45
1964	Mihaela Penes (ROM) 60.64m	Márta Rudas (HUN) 58.27	Yelena Gorchkova (URS) 57.07
1968	Angéla Németh (HUN) 60.36m	Mihaela Penes (ROM) 59.92	Eva Janko (AUT) 58.04
1972	Ruth Fuchs (GDR) 63.88m	Jacqueline Todten (GDR) 62.54	Kathy Schmidt (USA) 59.94
1976	Ruth Fuchs (GDR) 65.94m	Marion Becker (FRG) 64.70	Kathy Schmidt (USA) 63.96
1980	María Colón (CUB) 68.40m	Saida Gunba (URS) 67.76	Ute Hommola (GDR) 66.56
1984	Tessa Sanderson (GBR) 69.56m	Tiina Lillak (FIN) 69.00	Fatima Whitbread (GBR) 67.14
1988	Petra Felke (GDR) 74.68m	Fatima Whitbread (GBR) 70.32	Beate Koch (GDR) 67.30
1992	Silke Renk (GER) 68.34m	Natalya Shikolenko (EUN) 68.26	Karen Forkel (GER) 66.86
1996	Heli Rantanen (FIN) 67.94m	Louise McPaul (AUS) 65.54	Trine Hattestad (NOR) 64.68

1928 *Event not held*

Pentathlon [1]

1964	Irina Press (URS) 5246pts	Mary Rand (GBR) 5035	Galina Bystrova (URS) 4956
1968	Ingrid Becker (FRG) 5098pts	Liese Prokop (AUT) 4966	Annamaria Tóth (HUN) 4959
1972[2]	Mary Peters (GBR) 4801pts	Heidemarie Rosendahl (FRG) 4791	Burglinde Pollak (GDR) 4768

1976[3] Siegrun Siegl (GDR) 4745pts   Chrstine Laser (GDR) 4745   Burglinde Pollak (GDR) 4740
1980   Nadyezda Tkachenko (URS)   Olga Rukavishnikova (URS) 4937   Olga Kuragina (URS) 4875
      5083pts

1928–60 *Event not held.*

[1]   The pentathlon consisted of 100m hurdles, shot, high jump, long jump and 200m, between 1964 and 1976. In 1980 the 200m was replaced by 800m
[2]   New scoring tables were introduced in May 1971
[3]   Siegl finished ahead of Laser in three events

Heptathlon [4]
(Replaced Pentathlon in 1984)

1984   Glynis Nunn (AUS) 6387pts [5]   Jackie Joyner (USA) 6363   Sabine Everts (FRG) 6388
1988   Jackie Joyner-Kersee (USA)   Sabine John (GDR) 6897   Anke Behmer (GDR) 6858
      7291pts
1992   Jackie Joyner-Kersee (USA)   Irina Belova (EUN) 6845   Sabine Braun (GER) 6649
      7044pts
1996   Ghada Shouaa (SYR) 6780pts   Natasha Sazanovich (BLR) 6563   Denise Lewis (GBR) 6489

[4]   The heptathlon consists of 100m hurdles, high jump, shot, 200m on the first day; long jump, javelin and 800m on the second day
[5]   Recalculated on current tables

Women who have won medals under both their maiden and married names

Becker — Mickler (FRG)
Brehmer — Lathan (GDR)
Eckert — Wöckel (GDR)
Foulds — Paul (GBR)
Joyner — Kersee (USA)
Khnykina — Dvalishvili (URS)
Kirszenstein — Szewinska (POL)
Köhler — Birkemeyer (GDR)
Manning — Jackson (USA)
Odam — Tyler (GBR)
Ponomaryeva — Romashkova (URS)
Richter — Górecka (POL)
Samolenko — Dorovskikh (URS)
Schaller — Klier (GDR)
Schlaak — Jahl (GDR)
Vergova — Petkova (BUL)
Wieczorek — Ciepla (POL)
Zharkova — Maslakaova (URS)

Discontinued Events

	GOLD	SILVER	BRONZE
Men			
60 metres			
1900	Alvin Kraenzlein (USA) 7.0	Walter Tewsbury (USA) 7.1	Stanley Rowley (AUS) 7.2
1904	Archie Hahn (USA) 7.0	William Hogenson (USA) 7.2	Fay Moulton (USA) 7.2
3000 metres Team Race			
1912	United States 9pts	Sweden 13	Great Britain 23
1920	United States 10pts	Great Britain 20	Sweden 24
1924	Finland 8pts	Great Britain 14	United States 25
3 miles Team Race			
1908	Great Britain 6pts	United States 19	France 32
5000 metres Team Race			
1900	Great Britain 26pts	France 29	–
4 miles Team Race			
1904	United States 27pts	United States 28	–

Individual Cross-Country

1912[1] Hannes Kolehmainen (FIN) 45:11.6	Hjalmar Andersson (SWE) 45:44.8	John Eke (SWE) 46:37.6
1920[2] Paavo Nurmi (FIN) 27:15.0	Erick Backman (SWE) 27:27.6	Heikki Liimatainen (FIN 27:37.4
1924[3] Paavo Nurmi (FIN) 32:54.8	Ville Ritola (FIN) 34:19.4	Earle Johnson (USA) 35:21.0

[1] 12 000m
[2] 8000m
[3] 10 000m

Team Cross-Country

1912 Sweden 10pts	Finland 11	Great Britain 49
1920 Finland 10pts	Great Britain 21	Sweden 23
1924 Finland 11pts	United States 14	France 20

200 metres Hurdles

1900 Alvin Kraenzlein (USA) 25.4	Norman Pritchard (GBR) 26.6	Walter Tewksbury (USA) n.t.a.
1904 Harry Hillman (USA) 24.6	Frank Castleman (USA) 24.9	George Poage (USA) n.t.a.

1500 metres Walk

1906 George Bonhag (USA) 7:12.6	Donald Linden (CAN) 7:19.8	Konstantin Spetsiosis (GRE) 7:22.0

3000 metres Walk

1906 György Szantics (HUN) 15:13.2	Hermann Müller (GER) 15:20.0	Georgios Saridakis (GRE) 15:33.0
1920 Ugo Frigerio (ITA) 13:14.2	George Parker (AUS) n.t.a.	Richard Remer (USA) n.t.a.

3500 metres Walk

1908 George Larner (GBR) 14:55.0	Ernest Webb (GBR) 15:07.4	Harry Kerr (NZL) 15:43.4

10 000 metres Walk

1912 George Goulding (CAN) 46:28.4	Ernest Webb (GBR) 46:50.4	Fernando Altimani (ITA) 47:37.6
1920 Ugo Frigerio (ITA) 48:06.2	Joseph Pearman (USA) n.t.a.	Charles Gunn (GBR) n.t.a.
1924 Ugo Frigerio (ITA) 47:49.0	Gordon Goodwin (GBR) 200m	Cecil McMaster (RSA) 300m
1948 John Mikaelsson (SWE) 45:13.2	Ingemar Johansson (SWE) 45:43.8	Fritz Schwab (SUI) 46:00.2
1952 John Mikaelsson (SWE) 45:02.8	Fritz Schwab (SUI) 45:41.0	Bruno Junk (URS) 45:41.2

1928–36 *Event not held*

10 mile Walk

1908 George Larner (GBR) 1hr 15:57.4	Ernest Webb (GBR) 1hr 17:31.0	Edward Spencer (GBR) 1hr 21:20.2

Standing High Jump

1900 Ray Ewry (USA) 1.655m	Irving Baxter (USA) 1.525	Lewis Sheldon (USA) 1.50
1904 Ray Ewry (USA) 1.50m [1]	Joseph Stadler (USA) 1.45	Lawson Robertson (USA) 1.45
1906 Ray Ewry (USA) 1.565m	Martin Sheridan (USA) 1.40	–
	Léon Dupont (BEL) 1.40	
	Lawson Robertson (USA) 1.40	
1908 Ray Ewry (USA) 1.575m	Konstantin Tsiklitiras (GRE) 1.55	–
	John Biller (USA) 1.55	
1912 Platt Adams (USA) 1.63m	Benjamin Adams (USA) 1.60	Konstantin Tsiklitiras (GRE) 1.55

[1] Some reports suggest height was 1.60m

Standing Long Jump

1900 Ray Ewry (USA) 3.21m	Irving Baxter (USA) 3.135	Emile Torchebeouf (FRA) 3.03
1904 Ray Ewry (USA) 3.476m	Charles King (USA) 3.28	John Biller (USA) 3.26
1906 Ray Ewry (USA) 3.30m	Martin Sheridan (USA) 3.095	Lawson Robertson (USA) 3.05
1908 Ray Ewry (USA) 3.335m	Konstantin Tsiklitiras (GRE) 3.23	Martin Sheridan (USA) 3.225
1912 Konstantin Tsiklitiras (GRE) 3.37m	Platt Adams (USA) 3.36	Benjamin Adams (USA) 3.28

Standing Triple Jump

1900 Ray Ewry (USA) 10.58m   Irving Baxter (USA) 9.95   Robert Garrett (USA) 9.50
1904 Ray Ewry (USA) 10.55m   Charles King (USA) 10.16   Joseph Stadler (USA) 9.53

Stone Put (6.40kg)

1906 Nicolaos Georgantas (GRE)   Martin Sheridan (USA) 19.035   Michel Dorizas (GRE) 18.585
      19.925m

Shot (Both Hands)
(Aggregate of throws with right and left hands)

1912 Ralph Rose (USA) 27.70m   Patrick McDonald (USA) 27.53   Elmer Niklander (FIN) 27.14

Discus (Both Hands)
(Aggregate of throws with right and left hands)

1912 Armas Taipale (FIN) 82.86m   Elmer Niklander (FIN) 77.96   Emil Magnusson (SWE) 77.37

Discus (Greek Style)

1906 Werner Järvinen (FIN) 35.17m   Nicolaos Georgantas (GRE)   István Mudin (HUN) 31.91
                       32.80
1908 Martin Sheridan (USA) 38.00m   Marquis Horr (USA) 37.325   Werner Järvinen (FIN) 36.48

Javelin (Both Hands)
(Aggregate of throws with right and left hands)

1912 Juho Saaristo (FIN) 109.42m   Väinö Siikamiemi (FIN) 101.13   Urho Peltonen (FIN) 100.24

Javelin (Free Style)

1908 Eric Lemming (SWE) 54.445m   Michel Dorizas (GRE) 51.36   Arne Halse (NOR) 49.73

56-Pound (25.4kg) Weight Throw

1904 Étienne Desmateau (CAN)   John Flanagan (USA) 10.16   James Mitchell (USA) 10.135
      10.465m
1920 Patrick McDonald (USA) 11.265m   Patrick Ryan (USA) 10.965   Carl Lind (SWE) 10.25

Pentathlon

1906[1] Hjalmar Mellander (SWE) 24pts   István Mudin (HUN) 25   Eric Lemming (SWE) 29
1912[2] Ferdinand Bie (NOR) 16pts[3]   James Donahue (USA) 24   Frank Lukeman (CAN) 24
1920[2] Eero Lehtonen (FIN) 14pts   Everett Bradley (USA) 24   Hugo Lahtinen (FIN) 26
1924[2] Eero Lehtonen (FIN) 14pts   Elemér Somfay (HUN) 16   Robert LeGendre (USA) 18

[1]   Consisted of standing long jump, discus (Greek style), javelin, one-lap (192m) race, Greco-Roman wrestling
[2]   Consisted of long jump, javelin, 200m, discus, 1500m
[3]   Jim Thorpe (USA) finished first with 7 pts but was subsequently disqualified. He was reinstated posthumously in
     1982, but only as joint first

Badminton Medals

GOLD	SILVER	BRONZE

Men

1992 Alan Budi Kusuma (INA)	Ardy Wiranata (INA)	Thomas Stuer-Lauridsen (DEN)
		Hermawan Susanto (INA)
1996 Poul-Erik Hoyer-Larsen (DEN)	Jiong Dong (CHN)	Rashid Sidek (MAS)

1896–1988 *Event not held.*

Women

1992 Susi Susanti (INA)	Bang Soo-hyun (KOR)	Huang Hua (CHN)
		Tang Jiuhong (CHN)
1996 Bang Soo-hyun (KOR)	Mia Audina (INA)	Susi Susanti (INA)

1896–1988 *Event not held*

Men's Team

1992 Korea	Indonesia	Malaysia
		China
1996 Indonesia	Malaysia	Indonesia

1896–1988 *Event not held*

Women's Team

1992 Korea	China	Korea
		China
1996 China	Korea	China

1896–1988 *Event not held*

Mixed Doubles

1996 Korea	Korea	China

Baseball Medals

GOLD	SILVER	BRONZE
1992 Cuba	Taiwan	Japan
1996 Cuba	Japan	United States

1896–1988 *Event not held*

Basketball Medals

GOLD	SILVER	BRONZE

Men

1936 United States	Canada	Mexico
1948 United States	France	Brazil
1952 United States	Soviet Union	Uruguay
1956 United States	Soviet Union	Uruguay
1960 United States	Soviet Union	Brazil
1964 United States	Soviet Union	Brazil
1968 United States	Yugoslavia	Soviet Union
1972 Soviet Union	United States	Cuba
1976 United States	Yugoslavia	Soviet Union
1980 Yugoslavia	Italy	Soviet Union
1984 United States	Spain	Yugoslavia
1988 Soviet Union	Yugoslavia	United States
1992 United States	Croatia	Lithuania
1996 United States	Yugoslavia	Lithuania

1896–1932 *Event not held*

Women

1976 Soviet Union	United States	Bulgaria
1980 Soviet Union	Bulgaria	Yugoslavia
1984 United States	Korea	China
1988 United States	Yugoslavia	Soviet Union
1992 Unified Team	China	United States
1996 United States	Brazil	Australia

1896–1972 *Event not held*

Beach Volleyball Medals

GOLD	SILVER	BRONZE

Men's Team

1996 United States	United States	Canada

Women's Team

1996 Brazil	Brazil	Australia

Boxing Medals

GOLD	SILVER	BRONZE

Light-Flyweight
Weight up to 48kg (105.8lb)

GOLD	SILVER	BRONZE
1968 Francisco Rodriguez (VEN)	Jee Yong-ju (KOR)	Harlan Marbley (USA)
		Hubert Skrzypczak (POL)
1972 György Gedo (HUN)	U Gil Kim (PRK)	Ralph Evans (GBR)
		Enrique Rodriguez (ESP)
1976 Jorge Hernandez (CUB)	Byong Uk Li (PRK)	Payao Pooltarat (THA)
		Orlando Maladonado (PUR)
1980 Shamil Sabirov (URS)	Hipolito Ramos (CUB)	Byong Uk Li (PRK)
		Ismail Moustafov (BUL)
1984 Paul Gonzales (USA)	Saltore Todisco (ITA)	Keith Mwila (ZAM)
		Jose Bolivar (VEN)
1988 Ivailo Hristov (CUB)	Michael Carabajal (USA)	Robert Isaszegi (HUN)
		Leopoldo Serantes (PHI)
1992 Rogelio Marcelo (CUB)	Daniel Bojinov (BUL)	Roel Velasco (PHI)
		Jan Quast (GER)
1996 Daniel Petrov (BUL)	Mansueto Velsco (PHI)	Oleg Kuryukhin (UKR)
		Rafeal Lozano (ESP)

1896–1964 *Event not held*

Flyweight
From 1948 the weight limit has been 51kg/112.5lb. In 1904 it was 105lb/47.6kg. Between 1920 and 1936 112lb/50.8kg

GOLD	SILVER	BRONZE
1904 George Finnegan (USA)	Miles Burke (USA)	– [1]
1920 Frank Di Gennara (USA)	Anders Petersen (DEN)	William Cuthbertson (GBR)
1924 Fidel LaBarba (USA)	James McKenzie (GBR)	Raymond Fee (USA)
1928 Antal Kocsis (HUN)	Armand Appel (FRA)	Carlo Cavagnogli (ITA)
1932 István Enekes (HUN)	Francisco Cabanas (MEX)	Louis Salica (USA)
1936 Willi Kaiser (GER)	Gavino Matta (ITA)	Louis Lauria (USA)
1948 Pascual Perez (ARG)	Spartaco Bandinelli (ITA)	Han Soo-ann (KOR)
1952 Nathan Brooks (USA)	Edgar Basel (GER)	Anatoli Bulakov (URS)
		William Toweel (RSA)
1956 Terence Spinks (GBR)	Mircea Dobrescu (ROM)	John Caldwell (IRL)
		René Libeer (FRA)
1960 Gyula Török (HUN)	Sergei Sivko (URS)	Kyoshi Tanabe (JPN)
		Abdelmoneim Elguindi (EGY)
1964 Fernando Atzori (ITA)	Artur Olech (POL)	Robert Carmody (USA)
		Stanislav Sorokin (URS)
1968 Ricardo Delagdo (MEX)	Artur Olech (POL)	Servilio Oliveira (BRA)
		Leo Rwabwogo (UGA)
1972 Gheorghi Kostadinov (BUL)	Leo Rwabwogo (UGA)	Leszek Blazynski (POL)
		Douglas Rodriguez (CUB)
1976 Leo Randolph (USA)	Ramón Duvalon (CUB)	Leszek Blazynski (POL)
		David Torsyan (URS)
1980 Petar Lessov (BUL)	Viktor Miroschnicheko (URS)	Hugh Russel (IRL)
		Janos Varadi (HUN)
1984 Steve McCrory (USA)	Redzep Redzepovski (YUG)	Eyüp Can (TUR)
		Ibrahim Bilali (KEN)
1988 Kim Kwang-sun (KOR)	Andreas Tew (GDR)	Mario González (MEX)
		Timofey Skriabin (URS)
1992 Choi Chol-su (PRK)	Rául González (CUB)	Timothy Austin (USA)
		István Kovács (HUN)
1996 Maikro Romero (CUB)	Bulat Dzumadilov (KZK)	Albert Pakeyev (RUS)
		Zoltan Lunka (GER)

1896–1900, 1906–12 *Event not held*

[1] No third place

156 Boxing

Bantamweight
From 1948 the weight limit has been 54kg/119lb. In 1904 it was 115lb/52.16kg. In 1908 it was 116lb/52.62kg. Between 1920 and 1936 118lb/53.52kg

1904 Oliver Kirk (USA)	George Finnegan (USA)	– 1
1908 Henry Thomas (GBR)	John Condon (GBR)	William Webb (GBR)
1920 Clarence Walker (RSA)	Christopher Graham (CAN)	James McKenzie (GBR)
1924 William Smith (RSA)	Salvadore Tripoli (USA)	Jean Ces (FRA)
1928 Vittorio Tamagnini (ITA)	John Daley (USA)	Harry Issacs (RSA)
1932 Horace Gwynne (CAN)	Hans Ziglarski (GER)	José Villanueva (PHI)
1936 Ulderico Sergo (ITA)	Jack Wilson (USA)	Fidel Ortiz (MEX)
1948 Tibor Csik (HUN)	Giovanni Zuddas (ITA)	Juan Venegas (PUR)
1952 Pentti Hämäläinen (FIN)	John McNally (IRL)	Gennadi Garbuzov (URS)
		Kang Joon-ho (KOR)
1956 Wolfgang Behrendt (GER)	Soon Chun-song (KOR)	Frederick Gilroy (IRL)
		Claudio Barrientos (CHI)
1960 Oleg Grigoriev (URS)	Primo Zamparini (ITA)	Brunoh Bendig (POL)
		Oliver Taylor (AUS)
1964 Takao Sakurai (JPN)	Shin Cho Chung (KOR)	Juan Fabila Mendoza (MEX)
		Washington Rodriguez (URU)
1968 Valeri Sokolov (URS)	Eridadi Mukwanga (UGA)	Eiji Morioka (JPN)
		Chang Kyou-chull (KOR)
1972 Orlando Martinez (CUB)	Alfonso Zamora (MEX)	George Turpin (GBR)
		Ricardo Carreras (USA)
1976 Yong Jo Gu (PRK)	Charles Mooney (USA)	Patrick Cowdell (GBR)
		Viktor Rybakov (URS)
1980 Juan Hernandez (CUB)	Bernando Pinango (VEN)	Dumitru Cipere (ROM)
		Michael Anthony Parris (GUY)
1984 Maurizio Stecca (ITA)	Hector Lopez (MEX)	Dale Walters (CAN)
		Pedro Nolasco (DOM)
1988 Kennedy McKinney (USA)	Alexandar Hristov (BUL)	Jorge Julio Rocha (COL)
		Phajol Moolsan (THA)
1992 Joel Casamayor (CUB)	Wayne McCullough (IRL)	Li Gwang-sik (PRK)
		Mohamed Achik (MAR)
1996 István Kovács (HUN)	Arnoldo Mesa (CUB)	Raimkul Malkhbekov (RUS)
		Khadpo Vichairachanun (THA)

1896–1900, 1906, 1912 *Event not held*

1 No third place

Featherweight
From 1952 the weight limit has been 57kg/126lb. In 1904 it was 56.70kg/125lb. Between 1908 and 1936 it was 57.15kg/126lb. In 1948 it was 58kg/128lb

1904 Oliver Kirk (USA)	Frank Haller (USA)	Fred Gilmore (USA)
1908 Richard Gunn (GBR)	Charles Morris (GBR)	Hugh Roddin (GBR)
1920 Paul Fritsch (FRA)	Jean Gachet (FRA)	Edoardo Garzena (ITA)
1924 John Fields (USA)	Joseph Salas (USA)	Pedro Quartucci (ARG)
1928 Lambertus van Klaveren (NED)	Victor Peralta (ARG)	Harold Devine (USA)
1932 Carmelo Robeldo (ARG)	Josef Schleinkofer (GER)	Carl Carlsson (SWE)
1936 Oscar Casanovas (ARG)	Charles Cattterall (RSA)	Josef Miner (GER)
1948 Ernesto Foremnti (ITA)	Denis Shepherd (RSA)	Alexei Antkiewicz (POL)
1952 Jan Zachara (TCH)	Sergio Caprari (ITA)	Joseph Ventaja (FRA)
		Leonard Leisching (RSA)
1956 Vladimir Safronov (URS)	Thomas Nicholls (GBR)	Henryk Niedzwiedzki (POL)
		Pentti Hämäläinen (FIN)
1960 Francesco Musso (ITA)	Jerzy Adamski (POL)	William Meyers (RSA)
		Jorma Limmonen (FIN)
1964 Stanislav Stepashkin (URS)	Anthony Villaneuva (PHI)	Charles Brown (USA)
		Heinz Schultz (GER)
1968 Antonio Roldan (MEX)	Albert Robinson (USA)	Philip Waruinge (KEN)
		Ivan Michailov (BUL)
1972 Boris Kuznetsov (URS)	Philip Waruinge (KEN)	Clemente Rojas (COL)
		András Botos (HUN)

1976 Angel Herrera (CUB)	Richard Nowakowski (GDR)	Juan Peredes (MEX)
		Leszek Kosedowski (POL)
1980 Rudi Fink (GDR)	Adolfo Horta (CUB)	Viktor Rybakov (URS)
		Krzysztof Kosedowski (POL)
1984 Meldrick Taylor (USA)	Peter Konyegwachie (NGR)	Turgut Aykac (TUR)
		Omar Peraza (VEN)
1988 Giovanni Parisi (ITA)	Daniel Dumitrescu (ROM)	Lee Jae-hyuk (KOR)
		Abdelhak Achik (MAR)
1992 Andreas Tew (GER)	Faustino Reyes Lopez (ESP)	Hocine Soltani (ALG)
		Ramazi Paliani (EUN)
1996 Somluck Kamsing (THA)	Serafim Todorov (BUL)	Pablo Chacon (ARG)
		Floyd Mayweather (USA)

1896–1900, 1906, 1912 *Event not held*

Lightweight
From 1952 the weight has been 60kg/132lb. In 1904 and between 1920 and 1936 it was 61.24kg/135lb. In 1908 it was 63.50kg/140lb. In 1948 it was 62kg/136.5lb

1904 Harry Springer (USA)	James Eagan (USA)	Russell Van Horn (USA)
1908 Frederick Grace (GBR)	Frederick Spiller (GBR)	Harry Johnson (GBR)
1920 Samuel Mosberg (RSA)	Gotfried Johansen (DEN)	Clarence Newton (CAN)
1924 Hans Nielsen (DEN)	Alfredo Coppello (ARG)	Frederick Boylstein (USA)
1928 Carlo Orlandi (ITA)	Stephen Halaiko (USA)	Gunnar Berggren (SWE)
1932 Lawrence Stevens (RSA)	Thure Ahlqvist (SWE)	Nathan Bor (RSA)
1936 Imre Harangi (HUN)	Nikolai Stepulov (EST)	Erik Agren (SWE)
1948 Gerald Dreyer (USA)	Joseph Vissers (BEL)	Svend Wad (DEN)
1952 Aureliano Bolognesi (ITA)	Alexei Antkiewicz (POL)	Gheorge Fiat (ROM)
		Erkki Pakkanen (FIN)
1956 Richard McTaggart (GBR)	Harry Kurschat (GER)	Anthony Byren (IRL)
		Anatoli Lagetko (URS)
1960 Kazimierz Pazdzior (POL)	Sandro Lopopoli (ITA)	Richard McTaggart (GBR)
		Abel Laudonio (ARG)
1964 Józef Grudzien (POL)	Velikton Barannikov (URS)	Ronald Harris (USA)
		James McCourt (IRL)
1968 Ronald Harris (USA)	Józef Grudzien (POL)	Calistrat Cutov (ROM)
		Zvonimir Vujin (YUG)
1972 Jan Szczepanksi (POL)	László Orban (HUN)	Samuel Mbugna (KEN)
		Alfonso Perez (COL)
1976 Howard Davis (USA)	Simion Cutov (ROM)	Ace Rusevski (YUG)
		Vasili Solomin (URS)
1980 Angel Herrara (CUB)	Viktor Demianenko (URS)	Kazimierz Adach (POL)
		Richard Nowakowski (GDR)
1984 Pernell Whitaker (USA)	Luis Ortiz (PUR)	Martin Mbanga (CMR)
		Chun Chi-sung (KOR)
1988 Andreas Zülow (GDR)	George Cramme (SWE)	Nerguy Enkhbat (MGL)
		Romallis Ellis (USA)
1992 Oscar de la Hoya (CUB)	Marco Rudolph (USA)	Namjil Bayarsaikhan (MGL)
		Hong Sung-sik (KOR)
1996 Hocine Soltani (ALG)	Tontcho Tonchev (BUL)	Terrance Cauthen (USA)
		Leonard Doroftei (ROM)

1896–1900, 1906, 1912 *Event not held*

Light-Welterweight
Weight up to 63.5kg/140lb

1952 Charles Adkins (USA)	Viktor Mednov (URS)	Erkki Mallenius (FIN)
		Bruno Visintin (ITA)
1956 Vladimir Yengibarvan (URS)	Franco Nenci (ITA)	Henry Loubscher (RSA)
		Constantin Dumitrescu (ROM)
1960 Bohumil Nemecek (TCH)	Clement Quartey (GHA)	Quincy Daniels (USA)
		Marian Kasprzyk (POL)
1964 Jerzy Kulej (POL)	Yevgeni Frolov (URS)	Eddie Blay (GHA)
		Habib Galhia (TUN)

1968 Jerzy Kulej (POL)	Enrique Regueiforos (CUB)	Arto Nilsson (FIN)
		James Wallington (USA)
1972 Ray Seales (USA)	Anghel Anghelov (BUL)	Zvonimir Vujin (YUG)
		Issaka Daborg (NGR)
1976 Ray Leonard (USA)	Andres Aldama (CUB)	Vladimir Kolev (BUL)
		Kazimierz Szczerba (POL)
1980 Patrizio Oliva (ITA)	Serik Konakbeyev (URS)	Jose Aguilar (CUB)
		Anthony Willis (GBR)
1984 Jerry Page (USA)	Dhawee Umponmana (THA)	Mircea Fuger (ROM)
		Mirko Puzovic (YUG)
1988 Vycheslav Janovski (URS)	Grahame Cheney (AUS)	Lars Myrberg (SWE)
		Reiner Gies (FRG)
1992 Hector Vinent (CUB)	Marc Leduc (CAN)	Jyri Kjall (FIN)
		Leonard Doroftei (ROM)
1996 Hector Vinent (CUB)	Oktay Urkal (GER)	Bolat Niyazymbetov (KZK)
		Fathi Missaoui (TUN)

1896–1900, 1906–12 *Event not held*

Welterweight
From 1948 the weight limit has been 67kg/148lb. In 1904 it was 65.27kg/147.5lb. Between 1920 and 1936 it was 66.68kg/147lb

1904 Albert Young (USA)	Harry Springer (USA)	Joseph Lydon (USA)
		James Eagan (USA)
1920 Albert Schneider (CAN)	Alexander Ireland (GBR)	Frederick Colberg (USA)
1924 Jean Delarge (BEL)	Héctor Mendez (ARG)	Douglas Lewis (CAN)
1928 Edward Morgan (NZL)	Raul Landini (ARG)	Raymond Smillie (CAN)
1932 Edward Flynn (USA)	Erich Campe (GER)	Bruno Ahlberg (FIN)
1936 Sten Suvio (FIN)	Michael Murach (GER)	Gerhard Petersen (DEN)
1948 Julius Torma (TCH)	Horace Herring (USA)	Alessandro D'Ottavio (ITA)
1952 Zygmunt Chycla (POL)	Sergei Schtsherbakov (URS)	Victor Jörgensen (DEN)
		Günther Heidemann (GER)
1956 Nicholae Lince (ROM)	Frederick Tiedt (IRL)	Kevin Hogarth (AUS)
		Nicholas Gargano (GBR)
1960 Giovanni Benvenutti (ITA)	Yuri Radonyak (URS)	Leszek Drogosz (POL)
		James Lloyd (GBR)
1964 Marian Kasprzyk (POL)	Ritschardas Tamulis (URS)	Pertti Perhonen (FIN)
		Silvano Bertini (ITA)
1968 Manfred Wolfe (GDR)	Joseph Bessala (CMR)	Vladimir Musalinov (URS)
		Mario Guillot (ITA)
1972 Emilio Corea (CUB)	Janos Kajdi (HUN)	Dick Murunga (KEN)
		Jesse Valdez (USA)
1976 Jochen Bachfeld (GDR)	Pedro Gamarro (VEN)	Reinhard Skricek (FRG)
		Victor Zilberman (ROM)
1980 Andrew Aldama (CUB)	John Mugabi (UGA)	Karl-Heinz Krüger (GDR)
1984 Mark Breland (USA)	An Young-su (KOR)	Joni Nyman (FIN)
		Luciano Bruno (ITA)
1988 Robert Wanglia (KEN)	Laurent Boudouani (FRA)	Jan Dydak (POL)
		Kenneth Gould (USA)
1992 Michael Carruth (IRL)	Juan Hernandez (CUB)	Akrom Chenglai (THA)
		Anibal Acevedo (PUR)
1996 Oleg Saitov (RUS)	Juan Hernandez (CUB)	Marian Simion (ROM)
		Daniel Santos (PUR)

1896–1900, 1906–12 *Event not held*

Light-Middleweight
Weight up to 71kg/157lb

1952 László Papp (HUN)	Theunis van Schalkwyk (RSA)	Boris Tishin (URS)
		Eladio Herrera (ARG)
1956 László Papp (HUN)	José Torres (USA)	John McCormack (GBR)
		Zbigniew Pietrzkowski (POL)
1960 Wilbert McClure (USA)	Carmelo Bossi (ITA)	Boris Lagutin (URS)
		William Fisher (GBR)
1964 Boris Lagutin (URS)	Josef Gonzales (FRA)	Nohim Maivegun (NGR)
		Jozef Grzsiak (POL)

1968 Boris Lagutin (URS)	Rolondo Garbey (CUB)	John Baldwin (USA)
		Günther Meier (FRG)
1972 Dieter Kottysch (FRG)	Wieslaw Rudkowski (POL)	Alan Minter (GBR)
		Peter Tiepold (GDR)
1976 Jerzy Rybicki (POL)	Tadiji Kacar (YUG)	Rolando Garbey (CUB)
		Viktor Savchenko (URS)
1980 Armando Martinez (CUB)	Alexander Koshkin (URS)	Jan Franck (TCH)
		Detlef Kastner (GDR)
1984 Frank Tate (USA)	Shawn O'Sullivan (CAN)	Manfred Zielonka (FRG)
		Christophe Tiozzo (FRA)
1988 Park Si-hun (KOR)	Roy Jones (USA)	Richard Woodhall (GBR)
		Raymond Downey (CAN)
1992 Juan Carlos Lemus (CUB)	Orhan Delibas (NED)	György Mizsei (HUN)
		Robin Reid (GBR)
1996 David Reid (USA)	Alfredo Duvergel (CUB)	Karim Tulaganov (UZB)
		Esmouhan Ibraimov (KZK)

1896–1948 *Event not held*

Middleweight
From 1952 the weight has been 75kg/165lb. Betweeen 1904 and 1908 it was 71.68kg/158lb. Between 1920 and 1936 it was 72.57kg/160lb. In 1948 it was 73kg/161lb

1904 Charles Mayer (USA)	Benjamin Spradley (USA)	– [1]
1908 John Douglas (GBR)	Reginald Baker (AUS/NZL)	William Philo (GBR)
1920 Harry Mallin (GBR)	Georges Prud'homme (CAN)	Moe Herscovich (CAN)
1924 Harry Mallin (GBR)	John Elliott (GBR)	Joseph Beecken (BEL)
1928 Piero Toscani (ITA)	Jan Hermandek (TCH)	Léonard Steyaert (BEL)
1932 Carmen Barth (USA)	Amado Azar (ARG)	Ernest Pierce (RSA)
1936 Jean Despeaux (FRA)	Henry Tiller (NOR)	Raúl Villareal (ARG)
1948 László Papp (HUN)	John Wright (GBR)	Ivano Fontana (ITA)
1952 Floyd Patterson (USA)	Vasile Tita (ROM)	Boris Nikolov (URS)
		Stig Sjolin (SWE)
1956 Gennadi Schatkov (URS)	Ramon Tapia (CHI)	Gilbert Chapron (FRA)
		Victor Zalazar (ARG)
1960 Edward Crook (USA)	Tadeusz Walasek (POL)	Ion Monea (ROM)
		Yevgeni Feofanov (URS)
1964 Valeri Popenchenko (URS)	Emil Schultz (GER)	Franco Valle (ITA)
		Tadeusz Walasek (POL)
1968 Christopher Fiinnegan (GBR)	Alexei Kisselyov (URS)	Agustin Zaragoza (MEX)
		Alfred Jones (USA)
1972 Vyatcheslav Lemechev (URS)	Reima Virtanen (FIN)	Prince Armartey (GHA)
		Marvin Johnston (USA)
1976 Michael Spinks (USA)	Rufat Riskiev (URS)	Alec Nastac (ROM)
		Luis Martinez (CUB)
1980 Jose Gomez (CUB)	Viktor Savchenko (URS)	Jerzy Rybicki (POL)
		Valentin Silaghi (ROM)
1984 Shin Joop-sup (KOR)	Virgil Hill (USA)	Mohammed Zaoui (ALG)
		Aristides Gonzales (PUR)
1988 Henry Maske (GDR)	Egerton Marcus (CAN)	Chris Sande (KEN)
		Hussain Shaw Syed (PAK)
1992 Ariel Hernandez (CUB)	Chris Byrd (USA)	Chris Johnson (CAN)
		Lee Seung-bae (KOR)
1996 Ariel Hernandez (CUB)	Malik Beyleroglu (TUR)	Mohamed Bahari (ALG)
		Roshii Wells (USA)

1896–1900, 1906 and **1912** *Event not held*

[1] No third place

Light-Heavyweight
From 1952 the weight limit has been 81kg/178.5lb. Between 1920 and 1936 it was 79.38kg/175lb. In 1948 it was 80kg/186.25lb

1920 Edward Eagan (USA)	Sverre Sörsdal (NOR)	Harold Franks (GBR)
1924 Harry Mitchell (GBR)	Thyge Petersen (DEN)	Sverre Sörsdal (NOR)
1928 Victor Avendano (ARG)	Ernst Pistulla (GER)	Karel Miljon (NED)
1932 David Carstens (RSA)	Gino Rossi (ITA)	Peter Jörgensen (DEN)
1936 Roger Michelot (FRA)	Richard Vogt (GER)	Francisco Risiglione (ARG)

1948 George Hunter (RSA)	Donald Scott (GBR)	Maurio Cla (ARG)
1952 Norvel Lee (USA)	Antonio Pacenza (ARG)	Anotoli Perov (URS)
		Harri Siljander (FIN)
1956 James Boyd (USA)	Gheorghe Negrea (ROM)	Carlos Lucas (CHI)
		Romualdas Murauskas (URS)
1960 Cassius Clay (USA)	Zbigniew Pietrzykowski (POL)	Anthony Madigan (AUS)
		Giulio Saraudi (ITA)
1964 Cosimo Pinto (ITA)	Alexei Kisselyov (URS)	Alexander Nikolov (BUL)
		Zbigniew Pietrzykowski (POL)
1968 Dan Poznyak (URS)	Ion Monea (ROM)	Georgy Stankov (BUL)
		Stanislav Gragan (POL)
1972 Mate Petlov (YUG)	Gilberto Carrillo (CUB)	Issac Ikhouria (NGR)
		Janusz Gortat (POL)
1976 Leon Spinks (USA)	Sixto Soria (CUB)	Costica Danifoiu (ROM)
		Janusz Gortat (POL)
1980 Slobodan Kacar (YUG)	Pavel Skrzecz (POL)	Herbert Bauch (GDR)
		Ricardo Rojas (CUB)
1984 Anton Josipovic (YUG)	Kevin Barry (NZL)	Mustapha Moussa (ALG)
		Evander Holyfield (USA)
1988 Andrew Maynard (USA)	Nourmagomed Chanavazov (URS)	Damir Skaro (YUG)
		Henryk Petrich (POL)
1992 Torsten May (GER)	Rostislav Zaoulitchyni (EUN)	Wojciech Bartnik (POL)
		Zoltan Beres (HUN)
1996 Vasili Jirov (KZK)	Lee Seung-bae (KOR)	Antonio Tarver (USA)
		Thomas Ulrich (GER)

1896–1912 *Event not held*

Heavyweight

From 1984 the weight limit has been 91kg/200.5lb. Between 1904 and 1908 it was over 71.67kg/158lb. Between 1920 and 1936 it was over 79.38kg/175lb. In 1948 it was over 80kg/176.25lb. Between 1952 and 1980 it was over 81kg/178.25lb

1904 Samuel Berger (USA)	Charles Mayer (USA)	William Michaels (USA)
1908 Albert Oldman (GBR)	Sydney Evans (GBR)	Frederick Parks (GBR)
1920 Ronald Lawton (GBR)	Sören Petersen (DEN)	Xavier Eluère (FRA)
1924 Otto von Porat (NOR)	Sören Petersen (DEN)	Alfredo Porzio (ARG)
1928 Arturo Rodriguez Jurado (ARG)	Nils Ramm (SWE)	Jacob Michaelsen (DEN)
1932 Santiago Lovell (ARG)	Luigi Rovati (ITA)	Frederick Feary (USA)
1936 Herbert Runge (GER)	Guillermo Lovell (ARG)	Erling Nilsen (NOR)
1948 Rafael Iglesias (ARG)	Gunnar Nilsson (SWE)	John Arthur (RSA)
1952 Hayes Edward Sanders (USA)	Ingemar Johansson (SWE) [1]	Andries Nieman (RSA)
		Ilkka Koski (FIN)
1956 Peter Rademacher (USA)	Lev Mukhin (URS)	Daniel Bekker (RSA)
		Giacomo Ros (ITA)
1960 Franco de Piccoli (ITA)	Daniel Bekker (RSA)	Josef Nemec (TCH)
		Günther Siegmund (GER)
1964 Joe Frazier (USA)	Hans Huber (GER)	Guiseppe Ros (ITA)
		Vadim Yemeynaov (URS)
1968 George Foreman (USA)	Ionas Tschepulis (URS)	Giorgio Bambini (ITA)
		Joaquim Rocha (MEX)
1972 Teofilio Stevenson (CUB)	Ion Alexe (ROM)	Peter Hussing (FRG)
		Hasse Thomsen (SWE)
1976 Teofilio Stevenson (CUB)	Mircea Simon (ROM)	Johnny Tate (USA)
		Clarence Hill (BER)
1980 Teofilio Stevenson (CUB)	Pyotr Zayev (URS)	Jürgen Fanghanel (GDR)
		István Levai (HUN)
1984 Henry Tillman (USA)	Willie Dewitt (CAN)	Angelo Musone (ITA)
		Arnold Vanderlijde (NED)
1988 Ray Mercer (USA)	Baik Hyun-man (KOR)	Andrzej Golota (POL)
		Arnold Vanderlidje (NED)

1992	Félix Savón (CUB)	David Izonretei (NGR)	David Tua (NZL)
			Arnold Vanderlijde (NED)
1996	Félix Savón (CUB)	David Defiagbon (CAN)	Nates Jones (USA)
			Luan Krasniqui (GER)

1896–1900, 1906, 1912 *Event not held*

[1] Silver medal originally not awarded; Johansson disqualified but reinstated in 1982

Super-Heavyweight
From 1984 the class has been for those over 91kg/200.5lb

1984	Tyrell Biggs (USA)	Francesco Damiani (ITA)	Robert Wells (GBR)
			Salihu Azis (YUG)
1988	Lennox Lewis (CAN)	Riddick Bowe (USA)	Alexander Mirochnitchenko (URS)
			Jasz Zarenkiewicz (POL)
1992	Roberto Balado (CUB)	Richard Igbineghu (NGR)	Brian Nielsen (DEN)
			Svilen Roussinov (BUL)
1996	Vladimir Klichko (UKR)	Paea Wolfgram (TGA)	Alexei Lezin (RUS)
			Duncan Dokwari (NGR)

1896–1980 *Event not held*

Canoeing Medals

GOLD	SILVER	BRONZE

Men

500 Metres Kayak Singles (K1)

1976	Vasile Diba (ROM) 1:46.41	Zoltán Szytanity (HUN) 1:46.95	Rüdiger Helm (GDR) 1:48.30
1980	Vladimir Parfenovich (URS) 1:43.43	John Sumegi (AUS) 1:44.12	Vasile Diba (ROM) 1:44.90
1984	Ian Ferguson (NZL) 1:47.84	Lars-Erik Möberg (SWE) 1:48.18	Bernard Bregeon (FRA) 1:48.41
1988	Zsolt Gyulay (HUN) 1:44.82	Andreas Stähle (GDR) 1:46.38	Paul McDonald (NZL) 1:46.46
1992	Mikko Kolehmainen (FIN) 1:40.34	Zsolt Gyulay (HUN) 1:40.64	Knut Holmann (NOR) 1:40.71
1996	Antonio Rossi (ITA) 1:37.42	Knut Holmann (NOR) 1:38.33	Piotr Markiewicz (POL) 1:38.61

1896–1972 *Event not held*

1000 Metres Kayak Singles (K1)

1936	Gregor Hradetsky (AUT) 4:22.9	Helmut Cämmerer (GER) 4:25.6	Jacob Kraaier (NED) 4:35.1
1948	Gert Fredriksson (SWE) 4:33.2	Johann Kobberup (DEN) 4:39.9	Henri Eberhardt (FRA) 4:41.4
1952	Gert Fredriksson (SWE) 4:07.9	Thorvald Strömberg (FIN) 4:09.7	Louis Gantois (FRA) 4:20.1
1956	Gert Fredriksson (SWE) 4:12.8	Igor Pissaryev (URS) 4:15.3	Lajos Kiss (HUN) 4:16.2
1960	Erik Hansen (DEN) 3:53.00	Imre Szöllösi (HUN) 3:54.02	Gert Fredriksson (SWE) 3:55.89
1964	Rolf Peterson (SWE) 3:57.13	Mihály Hesz (HUN) 3:57.28	Aurel Vernescu (ROM) 4:00.77
1968	Mihály Hesz (HUN) 4:02.63	Alexander Shaparenko (URS) 4:03.58	Erik Hansen (DEN) 4:04.39
1972	Alexander Shaparenko (URS) 3:48.06	Rolf Peterson (SWE) 3:48.35	Géza Csapó (HUN) 3:49.38
1976	Rüdiger Helm (GDR) 3:48.20	Géza Csapó (HUN) 3:48.84	Vasile Diba (ROM) 3:49.65
1980	Rüdiger Helm (GDR) 3:48.77	Alain Lebas (FRA) 3:50.20	Ion Birladeanu (ROM) 3:50.49
1984	Alan Thompson (NZL) 3:45.73	Milan Janic (YUG) 3:46.88	Greg Barton (USA) 3:47.38
1988	Greg Barton (USA) 3:55.27	Grant Davies (AUS) 3:55.28	Andre Wohliebe (GDR) 3:55.55
1992	Clint Robinson (AUS) 3:37.26	Knut Holmann (NOR) 3:37.50	Greg Barton (USA) 3:37.93
1996	Knut Holmann (NOR) 3:25.78	Beniamino Bonomi (ITA) 3:27.07	Clint Robinson (AUS) 3:29.71

1896–1932 *Event not held*

10 000 Metres Kayak Singles (K1)

1936	Ernst Krebs (GER) 46:01.6	Fritz Landertinger (AUT) 46:14.7	Ernest Riedel (USA) 47:23.9
1948	Gert Fredriksson (SWE) 50:47.7	Kurt Wires (FIN) 51:18.2	Ejvind Skabo (NOR) 51:35.4
1952	Thorvald Strömberg (FIN) 47:22.8	Gert Fredriksson (SWE) 47:34.1	Michel Scheuer (GER) 47:54.5
1956	Gert Fredriksson (SWE) 47:43.4	Ferenc Hatlaczky (HUN) 47:53.3	Michel Scheuer (GER) 48.00.3

1896–1932, 1960–96 *Event not held*

500 Metres Kayak Pairs (K2)

1976 East Germany 1:35.87	Soviet Union 1:36.81	Romania 1:37.43
1980 Soviet Union 1:32.38	Spain 1:33.65	East Germany 1:34.00
1984 New Zealand 1:34.21	Sweden 1:35.26	Canada 1:35.41
1988 New Zealand 1:33.98	Soviet Union 1:34.15	Hungary 1:34.32
1992 Germany 1:28.27	Poland 1:29.84	Italy 1:30.00
1996 Germany 1:28.69	Italy 1:28.72	Australia 1:29.40

1896–1972 *Event not held*

1000 Metres Kayak Pairs (K2)

1936 Austria 4:03.8	Germany 4:08.9	The Netherlands 4:12.2
1948 Sweden 4:07.3	Denmark 4:07.5	Finland 4:08.7
1952 Finland 3:51.1	Sweden 3:51.1	Austria 3:51.4
1956 Germany 3:49.6	Soviet Union 3:51.4	Austria 3:55.8
1960 Sweden 3:34.7	Hungary 3:34.91	Poland 3:37.34
1964 Sweden 3:38.4	The Netherlands 3:39.30	Germany 3:40.69
1968 Soviet Union 3:37.54	Hungary 3:38.44	Austria 3:40.71
1972 Soviet Union 3:31.23	Hungary 3:32.00	Poland 3:38.33
1976 Soviet Union 3:29.01	East Germany 3:29.33	Hungary 3:30.56
1980 Soviet Union 3:26.72	Hungary 3:28.49	Spain 3:28.66
1984 Canada 3:24.22	France 3:25.97	Australia 3:26.80
1988 United States 3:32.42	New Zealand 3:32.71	Australia 3:33.76
1992 Germany 3:16.10	Sweden 3:17.70	Poland 3:18.86
1996 Italy 3:09.19	Germany 3:10.51	Bulgaria 3:11.20

1896–1932 *Event not held*

10 000 Metres Kayak Pairs (K2)

1936 Germany 41:45.0	Austria 42:05.4	Sweden 43:06.1
1948 Sweden 46:09.4	Norway 46:44.8	Finland 46:48.2
1952 Finland 44:21.3	Sweden 44:21.7	Hungary 44:26.6
1956 Hungary 43:37.0	Germany 43:40.6	Australia 43:43.2

1896–1932, 1960–96 *Event not held*

1000 Metres Kayak Fours (K4)

1964 Soviet Union 3:14.67	Germany 3:15.39	Romania 3:15.51
1968 Norway 3:14.38	Romania 3:14.81	Hungary 3:15.10
1972 Soviet Union 3:14.38	Romania 3:15.07	Norway 3:15.27
1976 Soviet Union 3:08.69	Spain 3:08.95	East Germany 3:10.76
1980 East Germany 3:13.76	Romania 3:15.35	Bulgaria 3:15.46
1984 New Zealand 3:02.28	Sweden 3:02.81	France 3:03.94
1988 Hungary 3:00.20	Soviet Union 3:01.40	East Germany 3:02.37
1992 Germany 2:54.18	Hungary 2:54.82	Australia 2:56.97
1996 Germany 2:51.52	Hungary 2:53.18	Russia 2:55.99

1896–1972 *Event not held*

500 Metres Canadian Singles (C1)

1976 Alexander Rogov (URS) 1:59.23	John Wood (CAN) 1:59.58	Matija Ljubek (YUG) 1:59.60
1980 Sergei Postrekhin (URS) 1:53.37	Lubomir Lubenov (BUL) 1:53.49	Olaf Heukrodt (GDR) 1:54.38
1984 Larry Cain (CAN) 1:57.01	Henning Jakobsen (DEN) 1:58.45	Costica Olaru (ROM) 1:59.86
1988 Olaf Heukrodt (GDR) 1:56.42	Mikhail Slivinski (URS) 1:57.26	Martin Marinov (BUL) 1:57.27
1992 Nikolai Boukhalov (BUL) 1:51.15	Mikhail Slivinski (EUN) 1:51.40	Olaf Heukrodt (GER) 1:53.00
1996 Martin Doktor (CZE) 1:49.93	Slavomir Knazovicky (SLO) 1:50.51	Imre Pulai (ITA) 1:50.75

1896–1972 *Event not held*

1000 Metres Canadian Singles (C1)

1936 Francis Amyot (CAN) 5:32.1	Bohuslav Karlik (TCH) 5:36.9	Erich Koschik (GER) 5:39.0

1948 Josef Holocek (TCH) 5:42.0	Douglas Bennet (CAN) 5:53.3	Robert Boutigny (FRA) 5:55.9
1952 Josef Holocek (TCH) 4:56.3	János Parti (HUN) 5:03.6	Olavi Ojanpera (FIN) 5:08.5
1956 Leon Rotman (ROM) 5:05.3	István Hernek (HUN) 5:06.2	Gennadi Bukharin (URS) 5:12.7
1960 János Parti (HUN) 4:33.93	Alexander Silayev (URS) 4:34.41	Leon Rotman (ROM) 4:35.87
1964 Jürgen Eschert (GER) 4:35.14	Andrei Igorov (ROM) 4:37.89	Yevgeni Penyayev (URS) 4:38.31
1968 Tibor Tatai (HUN) 4:36.14	Detlef Lewe (FRG) 4:38.31	Vitali Galkov (URS) 4:40.42
1972 Ivan Patzaichin (ROM) 4:08.94	Tamas Wichmann (HUN) 4:12.42	Detlef Lewe (FRG) 4:13.36
1976 Matija Ljubek (YUG) 4:09.51	Vassili Urchenko (URS) 4:12.57	Tamas Wichmann (HUN) 4:14.11
1980 Lubomir Lubenov (BUL) 4:12.38	Sergei Postrekhin (URS) 4:13.53	Eckhard Leue (GDR) 4:15.02
1984 Ulrich Eicke (FRG) 4:06.32	Larry Cain (CAN) 4:08.67	Henning Jakobsen (DEN) 4:09.51
1988 Ivans Klementjevs (URS) 4:12.78	Jörg Schmidt (GDR) 4:15.83	Nikolai Boukhalov (BUL) 4:18.94
1992 Nikolai Boukhalov (BUL) 4:05.92	Ivans Klementjevs (LAT) 4:06.60	Gyorgy Zala (HUN) 4:07.35
1996 Martin Doktor (CZE) 3:54.41	Ivans Klementjevs (LAT) 3:54.95	Gyorgy Zala (HUN) 3:56.36

1896–1932 *Event not held*

10 000 Metres Canadian Singles (C1)

1948 Frantisek Capek (TCH) 62:05.2	Frank Havens (USA) 62:40.4	Norman Lane (CAN) 64:35.3
1952 Frank Havens (USA) 57:41.1	Gabór Novák (HUN) 57:49.2	Alfréd Jindra (TCH) 57:33.1
1956 Leon Rotman (ROM) 56:41.0	János Parti (HUN) 57:11.0	Gennadi Bukharin (URS) 57:14.5

1896–1936, 1960–96 *Event not held*

500 Metres Canadian Pairs (C2)

1976 Soviet Union 1:45.81	Poland 1:47.77	Hungary 1:47.35
1980 Hungary 1:43.39	Romania 1:44.12	Bulgaria 1:44.83
1984 Yugoslavia 1:43.67	Romania 1:45.68	Spain 1:47.71
1988 Soviet Union 1:41.77	Poland 1:43.61	France 1:43.81
1992 Unified Team 1:41.54	Germany 1:41.68	Bulgaria 1:41.94
1996 Hungary 1:40.42	Moldova 1:40.45	Romania 1:41.33

1896–1972 *Event not held*

1000 Metres Canadian Pairs (C2)

1936 Czechoslovakia 4:50.1	Austria 4:53.8	Canada 4:56.7
1948 Czechoslovakia 5:07.1	United States 5:08.2	France 5:15.2
1952 Denmark 4:38.3	Czechoslovakia 4:42.9	Germany 4:48.3
1956 Romania 4:47.4	Soviet Union 4:48.6	Hungary 4:54.3
1960 Soviet Union 4:17.94	Italy 4:20.77	Hungary 4:20.89
1964 Soviet Union 4:04.64	France 4:06.52	Denmark 4:07.48
1968 Romania 4:07.18	Hungary 4:08.77	Soviet Union 4:11.30
1972 Soviet Union 3:52.60	Romania 3:52.63	Bulgaria 3:58.10
1976 Soviet Union 3:52.76	Romania 3:54.28	Hungary 3:55.66
1980 Romania 3:47.65	East Germany 3:49.93	Soviet Union 3:51.28
1984 Romania 3:40.60	Yugoslavia 3:41.56	France 3:48.01
1988 Soviet Union 3:48.36	East Germany 3:51.44	Poland 3:54.33
1992 Germany 3:37.42	Denmark 3:39.26	France 3:39.51
1996 Germany 3:31.87	Romania 3:32.99	Hungary 3:32.51

1896–1932 *Event not held*

10 000 Metres Canadian Pairs (C2)

1936 Czechoslovakia 50:33.5	Canada 51:15.8	Austria 51:28.0
1948 United States 55:55.4	Czechoslovakia 57:38.5	France 58:00.8
1952 France 54:08.3	Canada 54:09.9	Germany 54:28.1
1956 Soviet Union 54:02.4	France 54:48.3	Hungary 55:15.6

1896–1932, 1960–96 *Event not held*

4 × 500 Metres Kayak Singles (K1) Relay

1960 Germany 7:39.43	Hungary 7:44.02	Denmark 7:46.09

1896–1956, 1964–96 *Event not held*

10 000 Metres Folding Kayak Singles (K1)

1936 Gregor Hradetzky (AUT) 50:01.2   Henri Eberhardt (FRA) 50:04.2   Xaver Hörmann (GER) 50:06.5

1896–1932, 1948–96 *Event not held*

10 000 Metres Folding Kayak Pairs (K2)

1936 Sweden 45:48.9   Germany 45:49.2   The Netherlands 46:12.4

1896–1932, 1948–96 *Event not held*

Women

500 Metres Kayak Singles (K1)

1948 Karen Hoff (DEN) 2:31.9	Alide Van de Anker-Doedans (NED) 3:32.8	Fritzi Schwingl (AUT) 2:32.9
1952 Slyvi Saimo (FIN) 2:18.4	Gertrude Liebhart (AUT) 2:18.8	Nina Savina (URS) 2:21.6
1956 Yelisaveta Demntyeva (URS) 2:18.9	Therese Zenz (GDR) 2:19.6	Tove Söby (DEN) 2:22.3
1960 Antonina Seredina (URS) 2:08.8	Therese Zenz (GDR) 2:08.22	Daniele Walkowiak (POL) 2:10.46
1964 Ludmila Khvedosyuk (URS) 2:12.87	Hilde Lauer (ROM) 2:15.35	Marcia Jones (USA) 2:15.68
1968 Ludmila Pinyeva (URS) 2:11.09	Renate Breuer (FRG) 2:12.71	Viorica Dumitru (ROM) 2:13.22
1972 Yulia Ryabchinskaya (URS) 2:03.17	Mieke Jaapies (NED) 2:04.03	Anna Pfeffer (HUN) 2:05.50
1976 Carola Zirzow (GDR) 2:01.05	Tatyana Korshunova (URS) 2:03.07	Klara Rajnai (HUN) 2:05.01
1980 Birgit Fischer (GDR) 1:57.96	Vanya Gheva (BUL) 1:59.48	Antonina Melnikova (URS) 1:59.66
1984 Agneta Andersson (SWE) 1:58.72	Barbara Schuttpelz (FRG) 1:59.93	Annemiek Derckx (NED) 2:00.11
1988 Vania Guecheva (BUL) 1:55.19	Birgit Schmidt (GDR) 1:55.31	Izabella Dylewska (POL) 1:57.38
1992 Birgit Schmidt (GER) 1:51.60	Rita Koban (HUN) 1:51.96	Izabella Dylewska (POL) 1:52.36
1996 Rita Koban (HUN) 1:47.65	Caroline Brunet (CAN) 1:47.89	Josefa Idem (ITA) 1:48.73

1896–1936 *Event not held*

500 Metres Kayak Pairs (K2)

1960 Soviet Union 1:54.76	Germany 1:56.66	Hungary 1:58.22
1964 Germany 1:56.95	United States 1:59.16	Romania 2:00.25
1968 West Germany 1:56.44	Hungary 1:58.60	Soviet Union 1:58.61
1972 Soviet Union 1:53.50	East Germany 1:54.30	Romania 1:55.01
1976 Soviet Union 1:51.15	Hungary 1:51.69	East Germany 1:51.81
1980 East Germany 1:43.88	Soviet Union 1:46.91	Hungary 1:47.95
1984 Sweden 1:45.25	Canada 1:47.13	West Germany 1:47.32
1988 East Germany 1:43.46	Bulgaria 1:44.06	The Netherlands 1:46.00
1992 Germany 1:40.29	Sweden 1:40.41	Hungary 1:40.81
1996 Sweden 1:39.32	Germany 1:39.68	Australia 1:40.64

1896–1956 *Event not held*

500 Metres Kayak Fours (K4)

1984 Romania 1:38.34	Sweden 1:38.87	Canada 1:39.40
1988 East Germany 1:40.78	Hungay 1:41.88	Bulgaria 1:42.63
1992 Hungary 1:38.32	Germany 1:38.47	Sweden 1:39.79
1996 Germany 1:31.07	Switzerland 1:32.70	Sweden 1:32.91

1896–1980 *Event not held*

Slalom Racing

(Not held 1896–1968, 1976–88)

GOLD	SILVER	BRONZE

Men

Kayak Singles (K1)

1972 Siegbert Horn (GDR) 268.56pts	Norbert Sattler (AUT) 270.76	Harald Gimpel (GDR) 277.95
1992 Pierpaolo Ferrazzi (ITA) 106.89pts	Sylvain Curinier (FRA) 107.06	Jochen Lettmann (GER) 108.52

1996 Oliver Fix (GER) 141.22pts   Andraz Vehovar (SLO) 141.65   Thomas Becker (GER) 142.79

Canadian Singles (C1)

1972 Reinhard Eiben (GDR) 315.84pts   Reinhold Kauder (FRG) 327.89   Jamie McEwan (USA) 335.95
1992 Lukas Pollert (CZE) 113.69pts   Gareth Marriott (GBR) 116.48   Jacky Avril (FRA) 117.18
1996 Michel Martikan (SLK) 151.03pts Lukas Pollert (CZE) 151.17   Patrice Estanguet (FRA) 152.84

Canadian Pairs (C2)

1972 East Germany 310.68pts   West Germany 311.90   France 315.10
1992 United States 122.41pts   Czechoslovakia 124.25   France 124.38
1996 France 158.82pts   Czech Republic 160.16   Germany 163.72

Women

Not held 1896-1968, 1976-88

Kayak Singles (K1)

1972 Angelika Bahmann (GDR)   Gisela Grothaus (FRG) 398.15   Magdelena Wunderlich (FRG)
      364.50pts   400.50
1992 Elisabeth Micheler (GER)   Danielle Woodward (AUS) 128.27   Diana Chladek (USA) 131.75
      126.41pts
1996 Stepanka Hilgertova (CZE)   Dana Chladek (USA) 169.49   Myriam Fox-Jerusalmi (FRA)
      169.49pts   171.00

Cycling Medals

GOLD	SILVER	BRONZE

Men

1000 Metres Time Trial

1896[1] Paul Masson (FRA) 24.0	Stamatios Nikolpoulos (GRE) 25.4	Adolf Schmal (AUT) 26.6
1906[1] Francesco Verri (ITA) 22.8	Herbert Crowther (GBR) 22.8	Menjou (FRA) 23.2
1928 Willy Falck-Hansen (DEN) 1:14.4	Gerard Bosch van Drakestein (NED) 1:15.2	Edgar Gray (AUS) 1:15.6
1932 Edgar Gray (AUS) 1:13.0	Jacobus van Egmond (NED) 1:13.3	Charles Rampelberg (FRA) 1:13.4
1936 Arie van Vliet (NED) 1:12.0	Pierre Georget (FRA) 1:12.8	Rudolf Karsch (GER) 1:13.2
1948 Jacques Dupont (FRA) 1:13.5	Pierre Nihant (BEL) 1:14.5	Thomas Godwin (GBR) 1:15.0
1952 Russell Mockridge (AUS) 1:11.1	Marino Morettini (ITA) 1:12.7	Raymond Robinson (RSA) 1:13.0
1956 Leandro Faggin (ITA) 1:09.8	Ladislav Foucek (TCH) 1:11.4	J. Alfred Swift (RSA) 1:11.6
1960 Sante Gaiardoni (ITA) 1:07.27	Dieter Giessler (GER) 1:08.75	Rotislav Vargshkin (URS) 1:08.86
1964 Patrick Sercu (BEL) 1:09.59	Giovanni Pettonella (ITA) 1:10.09	Pierre Trentin (FRA) 1:10.42
1968 Pierre Trentin (FRA) 1:03.91	Niels-Christian Fredborg (DEN) 1:04.61	Janusz Kierkowski (POL) 1:04.63
1972 Niels-Christian Fredborg (DEN) 1:06.44	Daniel Clark (AUS) 1:06.87	Jürgen Schütze (GDR) 1:07.02
1976 Klaus-Jürgen Grunke (GDR) 1:05.93	Michel Vaarten (BEL) 1:07.52	Niels-Christian Fredborg (DEN) 1:07.62
1980 Lothar Thomas (GDR) 1:02.955	Alexander Pantilov (URS) 1:04.845	David Weller (JAM) 1:05.241
1984 Fredy Schmidke (FRG) 1:06.10	Curtis Harnett (CAN) 1:06.44	Fabrice Colas (FRA) 1:06.65
1988 Alexander Kiritchenko (URS) 1:04.499	Martin Vinnicombe (AUS) 1:04.784	Robert Lechner (FRG) 1:05.114
1992 Jose Manuel Moreno (ESP) 1:03.342	Shane Kelly (AUS) 1:04.288	Erin Hartwell (USA) 1:04.753
1996 Florian Rousseau (FRA) 1:02.712	Erin Hartwell (USA) 1:02.940	Takandu Jumonji (JPN) 1:02.261

1908–24 Event not held

[1] Held over 333.33 metres

1000 Metres Sprint

1896[1] Paul Masson (FRA) 4:56.0	Stamatios Nikopoulos (GRE)	Léon Flemeng (RSA)
1900[1] Georges Taillandier (FRA) 2:52.0	Fernand Sanz (FRA)	John Lake (USA)
1906 Francesco Verri (ITA) 1:42.2	Herbert Bouffler (GBR)	Eugène Debougnie (BEL)
1920 Maurice Peeters (NED) 1:38.3	Horace Johnson (GBR)	Harry Ryan (GBR)
1924[2] Lucien Michard (FRA) 12.8	Jacob Meijer (NED)	Jean Cugnot (FRA)
1928 René Beaufrand (FRA) 13.2	Antoine Mazairac (NED)	Willy Falck-Hansen (DEN)

1932 Jacobus van Egmond (NED) 12.6	Louis Chaillot (FRA)	Bruno Pellizzari (ITA)
1936 Toni Merkens (GER) 11.8	Arie van Vliet (NED)	Louis Chaillot (FRA)
1948 Mario Ghella (ITA) 12.0	Reginald Harris (GBR)	Axel Schandorff (DEN)
1952 Enzo Sacchi (ITA) 12.0	Lionel Cox (AUS)	Werner Potzernheim (GER)
1956 Michel Rousseau (FRA) 11.4	Guglielmo Presenti (ITA)	Richard Ploog (AUS)
1960 Sante Gaiardoni (ITA) 11.1	Leo Sterckx (BEL)	Valentina Gasparella (ITA)
1964 Giovanni Petternella (ITA) 13.69	Sergio Bianchetto (ITA)	Daniel Morelon (FRA)
1968 Daniel Morelon (FRA) 10.68	Giordano Turrini (ITA)	Pierre Trentin (FRA)
1972 Daniel Morelon (FRA) 11.25	John Nicholson (AUS)	Omar Pchakadze (URS)
1976 Anton Tkac (TCH) 10.78	Daniel Morelon (FRA)	Hans-Jürgen Geschke (GDR)
1980 Lutz Hesslich (GDR) 11.40	Yave Cahard (FRA)	Sergei Kopylov (URS)
1984 Mark Gorski (USA) 10.49	Nelson Vails (USA)	Tsutomu Sakamoto (JPN)
1988 Lutz Hesslich (GDR)	Nikolai Kovche (URS)	Gary Neiwand (AUS)
1992 Jens Fiedler (GER)	Gary Neiwand (AUS)	Curtis Harnett (CAN)
1996 Jens Fiedler (GER)	Marthy Nothstein (USA)	Curtis Harnett (CAN)

1904, 1908 [3], 1912 *Event not held*

[1] Held over 2000m. In 1900 Taillander's last 200m was 13.0sec
[2] Since 1924 only times over the last 200m of the event have been recorded
[3] There was a 1000m sprint event in the 1908 Games, but it was declared void because the riders exceeded the time limit, in spite of repeated warnings

4000 Metres Individual Pursuit

Note: Bronze medal times are set in a third place race, so can be faster than those set in the race for first and second place

1964 Jiri Daler (TCH) 5:04.75	Giorgio Utsi (ITA) 5:05.96	Preben Isaksson (DEN) 5:01.90
1968 Daniel Rebillard (FRA) 4:41.71	Mogens Frey Jensen (DEN) 4:42.43	Xavier Kurmann (SUI) 4:39.42
1972 Knut Knudsen (NOR) 4:45.74	Xavier Kurmann (SUI) 4:51.96	Hans Lutz (FRG) 4:50.80
1976 Gregor Braun (FRG) 4:47.61	Herman Ponsteen (NED) 4:49.72	Thomas Huschke (GDR) 4:52.71
1980 Robert Dilli-Bundi (SUI) 4:35.66	Alain Bondue (FRA) 4:42.96	Hans-Henrik Orsted (DEN) 4:36.54
1984 Steve Hegg (USA) 4:39.35	Rolf Gölz (FRG) 4:43.82	Leonard Nitz (USA) 4:44.03
1988 Gintaoutas Umaras (URS) 4:32.00	Dean Woods (AUS) 4:35.00	Bernd Dittert (GDR) 4:34.17
1992 Chris Boardman (GBR) [1]	Jens Lehmann (GER) –	Gary Anderson (NZL) 4:31.061
1996 Andrea Collinelli (ITA) 4:20.893	Philippe Ermenault (FRA) 4:22.714	Bradley McGee (AUS) 4:26.121

[1] Lapped Lehmann in final

4000 Metres Team Pursuit

Note: Bronze medal times are set in a third place race, so can be faster than those set in the race for first and second place

1908 [1] Great Britain 2:18.6	Germany 2:28.6	Canada 2:29.6
1920 Italy 5:14.2 [2]	Great Britain 5:13.8	South Africa 5:17.8
1924 Italy 5:15.0	Poland n.t.a.	Belgium n.t.a.
1928 Italy 5:01.8	The Netherlands 5:06.2	Great Britain n.t.a.
1932 Italy 4:53.0	France 4:55.7	Great Britain 4:56.0
1936 France 4:45.0	Italy 4:51.0	Great Britain 4:52.6
1948 France 4:57.8	Italy 5:36.7	Great Britain 4:55.8
1952 Italy 4:46.1	South Africa 4:53.6	Great Britain 4:51.5
1956 Italy 4:37.4	France 4:39.4	Great Britain 4:42.2
1960 Italy 4:30.90	Germany 4:35.78	Soviet Union 4:34.05
1964 Germany 4:35.67	Italy 4:35.74	The Netherlands 4:38.99
1968 Denmark 4:22.44 [3]	West Germany 4:18.94	Italy 4:18.35
1972 West Germany 4:22.14	East Germany 4:25.25	Great Britain 4:23.78
1976 West Germany 4:21.06	Soviet Union 4:27.15	Great Britain 4:22.41
1980 Soviet Union 4:15.70	East Germany 4:19.67	Czechoslovakia [4]
1984 Australia 4:25.99	United States 4:29.85	West Germany 4:25.60
1988 Soviet Union 4:13.31	East Germany 4:14.09	Australia 4:16.02
1992 Germany 4:08.791	Australia 4:10.218	Denmark 4:15.860
1996 France 4:05.930	Russia 4:07.730	Australia n.t.a.

1896–1906, 1912 *Event not held*

[1] Held over 1810.5m
[2] Great Britain finished first but were relegated to second for alleged interference
[3] Federal Republic of Germany (FRG) finished first but were disqualified for illegal assistance. After the Games ended the International Cycling Federation awarded them the silver medal
[4] Italy disqualified in third place

2000 Metres Tandem

1906 Great Britain 2:57.0	Germany 2:57.2	Germany n.t.a.
1908 France 3:07.8	Great Britain n.t.a.	Great Britain n.t.a.
1920 Great Britain 2:94.4	South Africa n.t.a.	The Netherlands n.t.a.
1924[1]France 12.6	Denmark	The Netherlands
1928 The Netherlands 11.8	Great Britain	Germany
1932 France 12.0	Great Britain	Denmark
1936 Germany 11.8	The Netherlands	France
1948 Italy 11.3	Great Britain	France
1952 Australia 11.0	South Africa	Italy
1956 Australia 10.8	Czechoslovakia	Italy
1960 Italy 10.7	Germany	Soviet Union
1964 Italy 10.75	Soviet Union	Germany
1968 France 9.83	The Netherlands	Belgium
1972 Soviet Union 10.52	East Germany	Poland

1896–1904, 1912, 1976–92 *Event not held*

[1] Since 1924 only times over last 200m have been recorded

Individual Points Race

1984 Roger Ilegems (BEL) 37pts	Uwe Messerschmidt (FRG) 15	Jose Youshimatz (MEX)
1988 Dan Frost (DEN) 38pts	Leo Peelen (NED) 26	Marat Ganeyev (URS)
1992 Giovanni Lombardi (ITA) 44pts	Leon van Bon (NED) 43	Cedric Mathy (BEL) 41
1996 Silvio Martinello (ITA) 37pts	Brian Walton (CAN) 29	Stuart O'Grady (AUS) 25

1896–1980 *Event not held*

Team Road Race
(Consisting of the combined times of the best three-four 1912–20-riders from each country in the individual race. In 1956 based on placings)

1912 Sweden 44hr 35:33.6	Great Britain 44hr 44:39.2	United States 44hr 47:55.5
1920 France 19hr 16:43.2	Sweden 19hr 23:10.0	Belgium 19hr 28:44.4
1924 France 19hr 30:14.0	Belgium 19hr 46:55.4	Sweden 19hr 59:41.6
1928 Denmark 15hr 09:14.0	Great Britain 15hr 14:49.0	Sweden 15hr 27:49.0
1932 Italy 7hr 27:15.2	Denmark 7hr 38:50.2	Sweden 7hr 39:12.6
1936 France 7hr 39:16.2	Switzerland 7hr 39:20.4	Belgium 7hr 39:21.0
1948 Belgium 15hr 58:17.4	Great Britain 16hr 03:31.6	France 16hr 08:19.4
1952 Belgium 15hr 20:46.6	Italy 15hr 33:27.3	France 15hr 38:58.1
1956 France 22pts	Great Britain 23	Germany 27

Road Team Time — Trial
Over 100km except in 1964 (108.89km), 1968 (102km), 1980 (101km)

1960 Italy 2hr 14:33.53	Germany 2hr 16:56.31	Soviet Union 2hr 18:41.67
1964 The Netherlands 2hr 26:31.19	Italy 2hr 26:55.39	Sweden 2hr 27:11.52
1968 The Netherlands 2hr 07:49.06	Sweden 2hr 09:26.60	Italy 2hr 10:18.74
1972 Soviet Union 2hr 11:17.8	Poland 2hr 11:47.5	—[1]
1976 Soviet Union 2hr 08:53.0	Poland 2hr 09:13.0	Denmark 2hr 12:20.0
1980 Soviet Union 2hr 01:21.7	East Germany 2hr 02:53.2	Czechoslovakia 2hr 02:53.9
1984 Italy 1hr 58:28.0	Switzerland 2hr 02:38.0	United States 2hr 02:46.0
1988 East Germany 1hr 57:47.7	Poland 1hr 57:54.2	Sweden 1hr 59:47.3
1992 Germany 2hr 01:39	Italy 2hr 02:39	France 2hr 05:25

1896–1908, 1996 *Event not held*

[1] The Netherlands finished in third place but their bronze medal was withdrawn following a drugs test

Road Individual Time Trial
(Held over 52km in 1996)

1996 Miguel Induráin (ESP) 1hr 04:05	Abraham Olano (ESP) 1hr 04:17	Chris Boardman (GBR) 1hr 04:36

1896–1992 *Event not held*

Individual Road Race

1896 Aristidis Konstantinidis (GRE) 3hr 22:31.0	August Goedrich (GER) 3hr 42:18.0	F.Battel (GBR) d.n.a.
1906 Fernand Vast (FRA) 2hr 41:28.0	Maurice Bardonneau (FRA) 2hr 41:28.4	Edmund Lugnet (FRA) 2hr 41:28.6
1912 Rudolph Lewis (RSA) 10hr 42:39.0	Frederick Grubb (GBR) 10hr 51:24.2	Carl Schutte (USA) 10hr 52:38.8
1920 Harry Stenqvist (SWE) 4hr 40:01.8	Henry Kaltenbrun (RSA) 4hr 41:26.6	Fernand Canteloube (FRA) 4hr 42:54.4
1924 Armand Blanchonnet (FRA) 6hr 20:48.0	Henry Hoevenaers (BEL) 6hr 30:27.0	René Hamel (FRA) 6hr 40:51.6
1928 Henry Hansen (DEN) 4hr 47:18.0	Frank Southall (GBR) 4hr 56:06.0	Gösta Carlsson (SWE) 5hr 00:17.0
1932 Attilio Pavesi (ITA) 2hr 28:05.6	Guglielmo Segato (ITA) 2hr 29:21.4	Bernhard Britz (SWE) 2hr 29:45.2
1936 Robert Charpentier (FRA) 2hr 33:05.0	Guy Lapébie (FRA) 2hr 33:05.2	Ernst Nievergeit (SUI) 2hr 33:05.8
1948 José Bevaert (FRA) 5hr 18:12.6	Gerardus Voorting (NED) 5hr 18:16.2	Lode Wouters (BEL) 5hr 18:16.2
1952 André Noyelle (BEL) 5hr 06:03.4	Robert Grondelaers (BEL) 5hr 06:51.2	Edi Ziegler (GER) 5hr 07:47.5
1956 Ercole Baldini (ITA) 5hr 21:17.0	Arnaud Gevre (FRA) 5hr 23:16.0	Alan Jackson (GBR) 5hr 23:16.0
1960 Viktor Kapitonov (URS) 4hr 20:37.0	Livio Trapé (ITA) 4hr 20:37.0	Willy van den Berghen (BEL) 4hr 20:57.0
1964 Mario Zanin (ITA) 4hr 39:51.63	Kjell Rodian (DEN) 4hr 39:51.65	Walter Godefroot (BEL) 4hr 39:51.74
1968 Pierfranco Vianelli (ITA) 4hr 41:25.24	Leif Mortensen (DEN) 4hr 42:49.71	Gösta Pettersson (SWE) 4hr 43:15.24
1972 Hennie Kuiper (NED) 4hr 14:37.0	Kevin Sefton (AUS) 4hr 15:04.0	– [1]
1976 Bernt Johansson (SWE) 4hr 46:52.0	Giuseppe Martinelli (ITA) 4hr 47:23.0	Mieczyslaw Nowicki (POL) 4hr 47:23.0
1980 Sergei Sukhoruchenkov (URS) 4hr 48:28.9	Czeslaw Lang (POL) 4hr 51:26.9	Yuri Barinov (URS) 4hr 51:26.9
1984 Alexi Grewal (USA) 4hr 59:57.0	Steve Bauer (CAN) 4hr 32:25.0	Dag Otto Lauritzen (NOR) 5hr 00:18.0
1988 Olaf Ludwig (GDR) 4hr 32:22.0	Bernd Gröne (FRG) 4hr 32:25.0	Christian Henn (FRG) 4hr 32:46.0
1992 Fabio Casartelli (ITA) 4hr 35:21	Hendrik Dekker (NED) 4hr 35:22	Dainis Ozols (LAT) 4hr 35:24
1996 Pascal Richard (SUI) 4hr 53.56	Rolf Sörensen (DEN) 4hr 53.56	Max Sciandri (GBR) 4hr 53.58

1900–08 *Event not held*

This event has been held over the following distances: 1896—87km; 1906—84km; 1912—329km; 1920—175km; 1924—188km; 1928—168km; 1932 and 1936—100km; 1948—194.63km; 1952—190.4km; 1956—187.73km; 1960—175.38km; 1968—196.2km; 1972—182.4km; 1976—175km; 1980—189km; 1984—190km; 1988—196.8km; 1992—194km; 1996—221km.

[1] Jaime Huelano (ESP) finished third but medal withdrawn following a drug test

Discontinued Events – Men

440 yards Track (402.34m)

1904 Marcus Hurley (USA) 31.8	Burton Downing (USA)	Edward Billingham (USA)

0.33 mile Track (536.45m)

1904 Marcus Hurley (USA) 43.8	Burton Downing (USA)	Edward Billingham (USA)

660 yards Track (603.5m)

1908 Victor Johnson (GBR) 51.2	Emile Demangel (FRA) close	Karl Neumer (GER) 1 length

880 yards Track (804.67m)

1904 Marcus Hurley (USA) 1:09.0	Edward Billingham (USA)	Burton Downing (USA)

1 mile Track (1609.34m)
1904 Marcus Hurley (USA) 2:41.4 — Burton Downing (USA) — Edward Billingham (USA)

2 miles Track (3218.6m)
1904 Burton Downing (USA) 4:57.8 — Oscar Goerke (USA) — Marcus Hurley (USA)

5000m Track
1906 Francesco Verri (ITA) 8:35.0 — Herbert Crowther (GBR) — Fernand Vast (FRA)
1908 Benjamin Jones (GBR) 8:36.2 — Maurice Schilles (FRA) — Andre Auffray (FRA)

5 miles Track (8046.57m)
1904 Charles Schlee (USA) 13:08.2 — George Wiley (USA) — Arthur Andrews (USA)

10 000m Track
1896 Paul Masson (FRA) 17:54.2 — Léon Flameng (FRA) — Adolf Schmal (AUT)

20 000m Track
1906 William Pett (GBR) 29:00.0 — Maurice Bardonneau (FRA) 29:30.0 — Fernand Vast (FRA) 29:32.0
1908 Clarence Kingsbury (GBR) 34:13.6 — Benjamin Jones (GBR) — Joseph Werbrouck (BEL)

25 miles Track (40.225m)
1904 Burton Downing (USA) 1hr 10:55.4 — Arthur Andrews (USA) — George Wiley (USA)

50 000m Track
1920 Henry George (BEL) 1hr 16:43.2 — Cyril Alden (GBR) [1] — Petrus Ikelaar (NED)
1924 Jacobus Willems (NED) 1hr 18:24 — Cyril Alden (GBR) — Frederick Wyld (GBR)
[1] Most eyewitnesses considered that Ikelaar finished second

100km Track
1896 Leon Flameng (FRA) 3hr 08:19.2 — Georgios Kolettis (GRE) 6 laps — − [1]
1908 Charles Bartlett (GBR) 2hr 41:48.6 — Charles Denny (GBR) — Octave Lapize (FRA)
[1] Only two riders finished

12 hours Track
1896 Adolf Schmal (AUT) 314.997km — Frank Keeping (GBR) 314.664km — Georgios Paraskevopoulous (GRE) 313.330km

Discontinued Events –Women

Sprint
1988 Erika Salumäe (URS) — Christa Rothenburger-Luding (GDR) — Connie Young (USA)
1992 Erika Salumäe (EST) — Annett Neumann (GER) — Ingrid Haringa (NED)
1996 Felicia Ballanger (FRA) — Michelle Ferris (AUS) — Ingrid Haringa (NED)

1896–1984 *Event not held*

3000m Individual Pursuit
1992 Petra Rossner (GER) — Kathryn Watt (AUS) — Rebecca Twigg (USA)
1996 Antonella Bellutti (ITA) 3:33.595 — Marion Clignet (FRA) 3:38.571 — Judith Arnt (GER) 3:38.744

1896–1988 *Event not held*

Individual Road Race
1984 Connie Carpenter-Phinney (USA) 2hr 11:14.0 — Rebecca Twigg (USA) 2hr 11:14.0 — Sandra Schumacher (FRG) 2hr 11:14.0
1988 Monique Knol (NED) 2hr 00.52 — Jutta Niehaus (FRG) close — Laima Zilporitee (URS) close
1992 Kathryn Watt (AUS) 2hr 04:02 — Jeannie Longo-Ciprelli (FRA) 2hr 05:02 — Monique Knol (NED) 2hr 05:03

1996 Jeannie Longo-Ciprelli (FRA)
2hr 36:13   Imelda Chiappa (USA) 2hr 36.38   Clara Hughes (CAN) 2hr 36.44

1896–1980 *Event not held*

Event held over 79.2km in 1984; 82km in 1988; 81km in 1992; 104km in 1996

Road Individual Time Trial
(Held over 26km in 1996)

1996 Zulfiya Zabirova (RUS) 36:40   Jeannie Longo-Ciprelli (FRA) 37:00   Clara Hughes (CAN) 37:13

1896–1992 *Event not held*

Points Race

1996 Nathalie Lancien (FRA) 24pts   Ingrid Haringa (NED) 23   Lucy Tyler-Sharman (USA) 17

1896–1992 *Event not held*

Mountain Bike
Men's Cross-Country

1996 Bart Brentjens (NED) 2hr 17:38   Thomas Frischknecht (SUI) 2hr 20:14   Miguel Martinez (FRA) 2hr 20:26

Women's Cross-Country

1996 Paola Pezzo (ITA) 1hr 50:51   Alison Sydor (CAN) 1hr 51:58   Susan DiMattei (USA) 1hr 52:36

Equestrian Medals

GOLD	SILVER	BRONZE
Grand Prix (Jumping)		
1900 Aimé Haegeman (BEL) *Benton II*	Georges van der Poële (BEL) *Windsor Squire*	Louis de Champsavin (FRA) *Terpsichore*
1912 Jean Cariou (FRA) 186pts *Mignon*	Rabod von Kröcher (GER) 186 *Dohna*	Emanuel de Blomaert de Sove (BEL) 185 *Clonmore*
1920 Tommaso Lequio (ITA) 2 faults *Trebecco*	Alessandro Valerio (ITA) 3 *Cento*	Gustaf Lewenhaupt (SWE) 4 *Mon Coeur*
1924 Alphonse Gemuseus (SUI) 3 faults *Lucette*	Tommaso Lequio (ITA) 8.75 *Trebecco*	Adam Krolikiewicz (POL) 10 *Picador*
1928 Frantisek Ventura (TCH) no faults *Eliot*	Pierre Bertrand de Balanda (FRA) 2 *Papillon*	Charles Kuhn (SUI) 4 *Pepita*
1932 Takeichi Nishi (JPN) 8 faults *Uranus*	Harry Chamberlain (USA) 12 *Show Girls*	Clarence von Rosen Jr (SWE) 16 *Empire*
1936 Kurt Hasse (GER) 4 faults *Tora*	Henri Rang (ROM) 4 *Delius*	József von Platthy (HUN) 8 *Sellö*
1948 Humbeto Mariles Cortés (MEX) 6.25 faults *Arete*	Rubén Uriza (MEX) 8 *Harvey*	Jean d'Orgeix (FRA) 8 *Sucre de Pomme*
1952 Pierre Jonquères d'Oriola (FRA) no faults *Ali Baba*	Oscar Cristi (CHI) 4 *Bambi*	Fritz Thiedemann (GER) 8 *Meteor*
1956 Hans Günter Winkler (GER) 4 faults *Halla*	Raimondo d'Inzeo (ITA) 8 *Merano*	Piero d'Inzeo (ITA) 11 *Halla*
1960 Raimondo d'Inzeo (ITA) 4 faults *Halla*	Piero d'Inzeo (ITA) 16 *The Rock*	David Broome (GBR) 23 *Sunslave*
1964 Pierre Jonquères d'Oriola (FRA) 9 faults *Lutteur*	Hermann Schriddle (GER) 12.75 *Dozent*	Peter Robeson (GBR) 16 *Firecrest*
1968 William Steinkraus (USA) 4 faults *Snowbound*	Marian Coakes (GBR) 8 *Stroller*	David Broome (GBR) 12 *Mister Softee*
1972 Graziano Mancinelli (ITA) 8 faults *Ambassador*	Ann Moore (GBR) 8 *Psalm*	Neal Shapiro (USA) 8 *Sloopy*

1976 Alwin Schockemöhle (FRG) no faults *Warwick Rex*	Michael Vaillancourt (CAN) 12 *Branch County*	François Mathy (BEL) 12 *Gai Luron*
1980 Jan Kowalcyzk (POL) 8 faults *Artemor*	Nikolai Korolkov (URS) 9.50 *Espadron*	Joaquim Perez Heras (MEX) 12 *Alymony*
1984 Joe Fargis (USA) 4 faults *Touch of Class*	Conrad Homfeld (USA) 4 *Abdullah*	Heidi Robbiani (SUI) 8 *Jessica V*
1988 Pierre Durand (FRA) 1.25 faults *Jappeloup*	Greg Best (USA) 4 *Gem Twist*	Karsten Huck (FRG) 4 *Nepomuk 8*
1992 Ludger Beerbaum (GER) no faults *Classic Touch*	Piet Raymakers (NED) 0.25 *Ratina Z*	Norman Dello Joio (USA) 4.75 *Irish*
1996 Ulrich Kirchkoff (GER) 1.00 faults *Jus De Pommes*	Willi Melliger (SUI) 4.00 *Calvaro*	Alexandra Ledermann (FRA) 4.00 *Rochet M*

1896, 1904–08 *Event not held*

Grand Prix (Jumping) Team

1912 Sweden 545pts	France 538	Germany 530
1920 Sweden 14 faults	Belgium 16.25	Italy 18.75
1924 Sweden 42.25 faults	Switzerland 50	Portugal 53
1928 Spain 4 faults	Poland 8	Sweden 10
1932 1–	–	–
1936 Germany 44 faults	The Netherlands 51.5	Portugal 56
1948 Mexico 34.25 faults	Spain 56.50	Great Britain 67
1952 Great Britain 40.75 faults	Chile 45.75	United States 52.25
1956 Germany 40 faults	Italy 66	Great Britain 69
1960 Germany 46.50 faults	United States 66	Italy 80.50
1964 Germany 68.50 faults	France 77.75	Italy 88.50
1968 Canada 102.75 faults	France 110.50	West Germany 117.25
1972 West Germany 32 faults	United States 32.25	Italy 48
1976 France 40 faults	West Germany 44	Belgium 63
1980 Soviet Union 16 faults	Poland 32	Mexico 39.25
1984 United States 12 faults	Great Britain 36.75	West Germany 39.25
1988 West Germany 17.25 faults	United States 20.50	France 27.50
1992 The Netherlands 12.00 faults	Austria 16.75	France 24.75
1996 Germany 1.75 faults	United States 12.00	Brazil 17.25

1896–1908 *Event not held*

1 There was a team competition but no nation had three riders complete the course

Grand Prix (Dressage)

1912 Carl Bonde (SWE) 15pts *Emperor*	Gustaf-Adolf Boltenstern Sr (SWE) 21 *Neptun*	Hans von Blixen-Finecke (SWE) 32 *Maggie*
1920 Janne Lundblad (SWE) 27.9375pts *Uno*	Bertil Sandström (SWE) 26.3125 *Sabel*	Hans von Rosen (SWE) 25.1250 *Running Sister* 1
1924 Ernst Linder (SWE) 276.4pts *Piccolomini*	Bertil Sandström (SWE) 275.8 *Sabel*	Xavier Lesage (FRA) 265.8 *Plumard*
1928 Carl von Langen (GER) 237.42pts *Draüfgänger*	Charles Marion (FRA) 231.00 *Linon*	Ragnar Olsson (SWE) 229.78 *Günstling*
1932 Xavier Lesage (FRA) 1031.25pts *Taine*	Charles Marion (FRA) 916.25 *Linon*	Hiram Tuttle (USA) 901.50 *Olympic*
1936 Heinz Pollay (GER) 1760pts *Kronos*	Friedrich Gerhard (GER) 1745.4 *Absinth*	Alois Podhajsky (AUT) 1721.5 *Nero*
1948 Hans Moser (SUI) 492.5pts *Hummer*	André Jousseaume (FRA) 480.0 *Harpagon*	Gustaf-Adolf Boltenstern Jr (SWE) 477.5 *Trumpf*
1952 Henri St Cyr (SWE) 561pts *Master Rufus*	Lis Hartel (DEN) 541.5 *Jubilee*	André Jousseauame (FRA) 541.0 *Harpagon*
1956 Henri St Cyr (SWE) 860pts *Juli*	Lis Hartel (DEN) 850 *Jubilee*	Liselott Linsenhoff (GER) 832 *Adular*
1960 Sergei Filatov (URS) 2144pts *Absent*	Gustav Fischer (SUI) 2087 *Wald*	Josef Neckermann (GER) 2082 *Asbach*
1964 Henri Chammartin (SUI) 1504pts *Woermann*	Harry Boldt (GER) 1503 *Remus*	Sergei Filatov (URS) 1486 *Absent*

1968	Ivan Kizimov (URS) 1572pts *Ikhov*	Josef Neckermann (FRG) 1546 *Mariano*	Reiner Klimke (FRG) 1527 *Dux*
1972	Liselott Linsenhoff (FRG) 1229pts *Piaff*	Yelena Petuchkova (URS) 1185 *Pepel*	Josef Neckermann (FRG) 2082 *Venetia*
1976	Christine Stückelberger (SUI) 1486pts *Granat*	Harry Boldt (FRG) 1435 *Woycek*	Reiner Klimke (FRG) 1395 *Mehmed*
1980	Elisabeth Theuer (AUT) 1370pts *Mon Cherie*	Yuri Kovshov (URS) 1300 *Igrok*	Viktor Ugyumov (URS) 1234 *Shkval*
1984	Reiner Klimke (FRG) 1504pts *Ahlerich*	Anne Grethe Jensen (DEN) 1442 *Martzog*	Otto Hofer (SUI) 1364 *Limandus*
1988	Nicole Uphoff (FRG) 1521pts *Rembrandt*	Margit Otto Crepin (FRA) 1462 *Corlandus*	Christine Stückelberger (SUI) 1417 *Gauguin De Lully*
1992	Nicole Uphoff (FRG) 1626pts *Rembrandt*	Isabell Werth (GER) 1551 *Gigolo*	Klaus Balkenhol (GER) 1515 *Goldstern*
1996	Isabel Werth (GER) 235.09pts *Gigolo*	Anky van Grunsven (NED) 233.02 *Bonfire*	Sven Rothenberger (NED) 224.94 *Weyden*

1896–1908 *Event not held*

[1] Gustaf-Adolf Boltenstern Sr (SWE) finished third with 26.1875pts but was disqualified

Grand Prix (Dressage Team)

1928	Germany 669.72pts	Sweden 650.86	The Netherlands 642.96
1932	France 2828.75pts	Sweden 2678	United States 2576.75
1936	Germany 5074pts	France 4846	Sweden 4660.5
1948[1]	France 1269pts	United States 1256	Portugal 1182
1952	Sweden 1597.5pts	Switzerland 1759	Germany 1501
1956	Sweden 2475pts	Germany 2346	Switzerland 2346
1964	Germany 2558pts	Switzerland 2526	Soviet Union 2311
1968	West Germany 2699pts	Soviet Union 2657	Switzerland 2547
1972	Soviet Union 5095pts	West Germany 5083	Sweden 4849
1976	West Germany 5155pts	Switzerland 4684	United States 4670
1980	Soviet Union 4383pts	Bulgaria 3580	Romania 3346
1984	West Germany 4955pts	Switzerland 4673	Sweden 4630
1988	West Germany 4302pts	Switzerland 4164	Canada 3969
1992	Germany 5224pts	The Netherlands 4742	United States 4643
1996	Germany 5553pts	The Netherlands 5437	United States 5309

1896–1924, 1960 *Event not held*

[1] Sweden were originally declared winners with 1366pts but were subsequently disqulaified one year later

Three-Day Event

1912	Axel Nordlander (SWE) 46.59pts *Lady Artist*	Friedrich von Rochow (GER) 46.42 *Idealist*	Jean Cariou (FRA) 46.32 *Cocotte*
1920	Helmer Mörner (SWE) 1775pts *Germania*	Age Lundström (SWE) 1738.75 *Yrsa*	Ettore Caffaratti (ITA) 1733.75 *Traditore*
1924	Adolf van de Voort van Zijp (NED) 1976pts *Silver Piece*	Fröde Kirkebjerg (DEN) 1853.5 *Meteor*	Sloan Doak (USA) 1845.5 *Pathfinder*
1928	Charles Pahud de Mortanges (NED) 1969.82pts *Marcroix*	Gerard de Kruyff (NED) 1967.26 *Va-t-en*	Bruno Neumann (GER) 1944.42 *Ilja*
1932	Charles Pahud de Mortanges (NED) 1813.83pts *Marcroix*	Earl Thomson (USA) 1811 *Jenny Camp*	Clarence von Rosen Jr (SWE) 1809.42 *Sunnyside Maid*
1936	Ludwig Stubbendorff (GER) 37.7pts *Nurmi*	Earl Thomson (USA) 99.9 *Jenny Camp*	Hans MathiesenLunding (DEN) 102.2 *Jason*
1948	Bernard Chevallier (FRA) +4pts *Aiglonne*	Frank Henry (USA) −21 *Swing Low*	Robert Selfelt (SWE) −25 *Claque*
1952	Hans von Blixen-Finecke (SWE) 28.33 faults *Jubal*	Guy Lefrant (FRA) 54.50 *Verdun*	Wilhelf Büsing (GER) 55.50 *Hubertus*
1956	Petrus Kasenman (SWE) 66.53 faults *Illuster*	August Lütke-Westhues (GER) 84.87 *Trux van Kamax*	Frank Weldon (GBR) 85.48 *Kilbarry*
1960	Lawrence Morgan (AUS) +7.15pts *Salad Days*	Neale Lavis (AUS) −16.50 *Mirrabooka*	Anton Bühler (SUI) −51.21 *Gay Spark*

1964	Mauro Checcoli (ITA) 64.40pts *Surbean*	Carlos Moratorio (ARG) 56.40 *Lochinvar*	Fritz Ligges (GER) 49.20 *Donkosak*
1968	Jean-Jaques Guyon (FRA) 38.86pts *Pitou*	Derek Allhusen (GBR) 41.61 *Lochinvar*	Michael Page (USA) 52.31 *Faster*
1972	Richard Meade (GBR) 57.73pts *Laurieston*	Alessa Argenton (ITA) 43.33 *Woodland*	Jan Jonsson (SWE) 39.67 *Sarajevo*
1976	Edmund Coffin (USA) 114.99pts *Bally-Cor*	Michael Plumb (USA) 125.85 *Better and Better*	Karl Schultz (FRG) 129.45 *Madrigal*
1980	Federico Roman (ITA) 108.60pts *Rossinan*	Alexander Blinov (URS) 120.80 *Galzun*	Yuri Salinikov (URS) 151.60 *Pintset*
1984	Mark Todd (NZL) 51.60pts *Charisma*	Karen Stives (USA) 54.20 *Ben Arthur*	Virginia Holgate (GBR) 56.80 *Priceless*
1988	Mark Todd (NZL) 42.60pts *Charisma*	Ian Stark (GBR) 52.80 *Sir Wattie*	Virginia Leng (GBR) 62.00 *Master Craftsman*
1992	Matthew Ryan (AUS) 70pts *Kibah Tic Toc*	Herbert Blocker (GER) 81.30 *Feine Dame*	Blyth Tait (NZL) 87.60 *Messiah*
1996	Blyth Tait (NZL) 56.80pts *Redy Teddy*	Sally Clark (NZL) 60.40pts *Squirrel Hill*	Kerry Millikin (USA) 73.70 *Out and About*

1896–1908 *Event not held*

Three-Day Event Team

1912	Sweden 139.06pts	Germany 138.48	United States 137.33
1920	Sweden 5057pts	Italy 4375	Belgium 4560
1924	The Netherlands 5297.5pts	Sweden 4743.5	Italy 4512.5
1928	The Netherlands 5865.68pts	Norway 5395.68	Poland 5067.92
1932	United States 5038.08pts	The Netherlands 4689.08	– [1]
1936	Germany 676.75pts	Poland 991.70	Great Britain 9195.90
1948	United States 161.50pts	Sweden 165.00	Mexico 305.25
1952	Sweden 221.49pts	Germany 235.49	United States 587.16
1956	Great Britain 355.48pts	Germany 475.61	Canada 572.72
1960	Australia 128.18pts	Switzerland 386.02	France 515.71
1964	Italy 85.80pts	United States 65.86	Germany 56.73
1968	Great Britain 175.93pts	United States 245.87	Australia 331.26
1972	Great Britain 95.53pts	United States 10.81	West Germany –18.00
1976	United States 441.00pts	West Germany 584.60	Australia 599.54
1980	Soviet Union 457.00pts	Italy 656.20	Mexico 1172.85
1984	United States 186.00pts	Great Britain 189.20	West Germany 234.00
1988	West Germany 225.95pts	Great Britain 256.80	New Zealand 271.20
1992	Australia 288.60pts	New Zealand 290.80	Germany 300.30
1996	Australia 203.85pts	United States 261.10	New Zealand 268.55

1896–1908 *Event not held*

[1] No other teams finished

Discontinued Events

GOLD	SILVER	BRONZE

Equestrian High Jump

| 1900 | Dominique Gardére (FRA) 1.85m *Canéla* Gian Giorgio Trissino (ITA) 1.85m *Oreste* | – | André Moreaux (FRA) 1.70 *Ludlow* |

Equestrian Long Jump

| 1900 | Constant van Langhendonck (BEL) 6.10m *Extra Dry* | Federico Caprilli (ITA) 5.70 *Oreste* | de Bellegarde (FRA) 5.30 *Tolla* |

Figure Riding
(Only open to soldiers below the rank of NCO)

| 1920 | Bouckaert (BEL) 30 500pts | Field (FRA) 29 500 | Finet (BEL) 29 000 |

Figure Riding, Teams

| 1920 | Belgium 87 500pts | France 81 083 | Sweden 59 416 |

Fencing Medals — Individual

GOLD	SILVER	BRONZE

Foil (Men)

Wins are assessed on both wins (2pts) and draws (1pt) so, as in 1928, the winner does not necessarily have the most wins.

GOLD	SILVER	BRONZE
1896 Emile Gravelotte (FRA) 4 wins	Henri Callott (FRA) 3	Perikles Mavromichalis-Pierrakos (GRE) 2
1900 Emile Cost (FRA) 6 wins	Henri Masson (FRA) 5	Jacques Boulenger (FRA) 4
1904 Ramón Fonst (CUB) 3 wins	Albertson Van Zo Post (USA) 2	Charles Tatham (USA) 1
1906 Georges Dillon-Kavanagh (FRA) d.n.a.	Gustav Casmir (GER) d.n.a.	Pierre d'Hugues (FRA) d.n.a.
1912 Nedo Nadi (ITA) 7 wins	Pietro Speciale (ITA) 5	Richard Verderber (AUT) 4
1920 Nedo Nadi (ITA) 10 wins	Philippe Cattiau (FRA) 9	Roger Ducret (FRA) 9
1924 Roger Ducret (FRA) 6 wins	Philippe Cattiau (FRA) 5	Maurice van Damme (BEL) 4
1928 Lucien Gaudin (FRA) 9 wins	Ermin Casmir (GER) 9	Giulio Gaudini (ITA) 9
1932 Gustavo Marzi (ITA) 9 wins	Joseph Lewis (USA) 6	Giulio Bocchino (ITA) 4
1948 Jean Buhan (FRA) 7 wins	Christian d'Oriola (FRA) 5	Lajos Maszlay (HUN) 4
1952 Christian d'Oriola (FRA) 8 wins	Edouard Gardère (FRA) 6	Manlio di Rosa (ITA) 5
1956 Christian d'Oriola (FRA) 6 wins	Giancarlo Bergamini (ITA) 5	Antonio Spallino (ITA) 5
1960 Viktor Zhdanovich (URS) 7 wins	Yuri Sissikin (URS) 4	Albert Axelrod (USA) 3
1964 Egon Franke (POL) 3 wins	Jean-Claude Magnan (FRA) 2	Daniel Revenu (FRA) 1
1968 Ion Drimba (ROM) 4 wins	Jenö Kamuti (HUN) 3	Daniel Revenu (FRA) 3
1972 Witold Woyda (POL) 5 wins	Jenö Kamuti (HUN) 4	Christian Nöel (FRA) 2
1976 Fabio Dal Zotto (ITA) 4 wins	Alexander Romankov (URS) 4	Bernard Talvard (FRA) 3
1980 Vladimir Smirnov (URS) 5 wins	Paskal Jolyot (FRA) 5	Alexander Romankov (URS) 5
1984 Mauro Numa (ITA)	Matthias Behr (FRG)	Stefano Cerioni (ITA)
1988 Stefano Cerioni (ITA)	Udo Wagner (GDR)	Alexander Romankov (URS)
1992 Phillipe Omnes (FRA)	Sergei Goloubiski (EUN)	Elvis Gregory (CUB)
1996 Alessandro Puccini (ITA)	Lionel Plumenail (FRA)	Franck Boidin (FRA)

Épée (Men)

GOLD	SILVER	BRONZE
1900 Ramón Fonst (CUB)	Louis Perrée (FRA)	Léon Sée (FRA)
1904 Ramón Fonst (CUB)	Charles Tatham (USA)	Albertson Van Zo Post (USA)
1906 Georges de la Falaise (FRA) d.n.a.	Georges Dillon-Kavanagh (FRA) d.n.a.	Alexander van Blijenburgh (NED) d.n.a.
1908 Gaston Alibert (FRA) 5 wins	Alexandre Lippmann (FRA) 4	Eugène Olivier (FRA) 4
1912 Paul Anspach (BEL) 6 wins	Ivan Osiier (DEN) 5	Philippe Le Hardy de Beaulieu (BEL) 4
1920 Armand Massard (FRA) 9 wins	Alexandre Lippmann (FRA) 7	Gustave Buchard (FRA) 6
1924 Charles Delporte (BEL) 8 wins	Roger Ducret (FRA) 7	Nils Hellsten (SWE) 7
1928 Lucien Gaudin (FRA) 8 wins	Georges Buchard (FRA) 7	George Calman (USA) 6
1932 Giancarlo Cornaggia-Medici (ITA) 8 wins	Georges Buchard (FRA) 7	Carlo Agostini (ITA) 7
1936 Franco Riccardi (ITA) 5 wins	Saverio Ragno (ITA) 6	Giancarlo Cornaggia-Medici (ITA) 6
1948 Luigi Cantone (ITA) 7 wins	Oswald Zappelli (SUI) 5	Edoardo Mangiarotti (ITA) 5
1952 Edoardo Mangiarotti (ITA) 7 wins	Dario Mangiarotti (ITA) 6	Oswald Zappelli (SUI) 6
1956 Carlo Pavesi (ITA) 5 wins	Giuseppe Delfino (ITA) 5	Edoardo Mangiarotti (ITA) 5
1960 Giuseppe Delfino (ITA) 5 wins	Allan Jay (GBR) 5	Bruno Khabarov (URS) 4
1964 Grigori Kriss (URS) 2 wins	William Hoskyns (GBR) 2	Guram Kostava (URS) 1
1968 Györö Kulcsár (HUN) 4 wins	Grigori Kriss (URS) 4	Gianluigi Saccaro (ITA) 4
1972 Csaba Fenyvesi (HUN) 4 wins	Jacques la Degaillerie (FRA) 3	Györö Kulcsár (HUN) 3
1976 Alexander Pusch (FRG) 3 wins	Jürgen Hehn (FRG) 3	Györö Kulcsár (HUN) 3
1980 Johan Harmenberg (SWE) 4 wins	Ernö Kolczonay (HUN) 3	Philippe Riboud (FRA) 3
1984 Philippe Boisse (FRA)	Björne Väggö (SWE)	Phillippe Riboud (FRA)
1988 Arnd Schitt (FRG)	Philippe Riboud (FRA)	Andrei Chouvalov (URS)
1992 Eric Srecki (FRA)	Pavel Kolobkov (EUN)	Jean-Michel Henry (FRA)
1996 Alexander Beketov (RUS)	Ivan Trevejo Perez (CUB)	Geza Imre (HUN)

1896 *Event not held*

Sabre (Men)

1896	Jean Georgiadis (GRE) 4 wins	Telemachos Karakalos (GRE) 3	Holger Nielsen (DEN) 2
1900	Georges de la Falaise (FRA) d.n.a.	Léon Thiébault (FRA) d.n.a.	Siegfried Flesch (AUT) d.n.a.
1904	Manuel Diaz (CUB) 4 wins	William Grebe (USA) 3	Albertson Van Zo Post (USA) 2
1906	Jean Georgiadis (GRE) d.n.a.	Gustav Casmir (GER) d.n.a.	Federico Cesarano (ITA) d.n.a.
1908	Jeno Fuchs (HUN) 6 wins	Béla Zulavsky (HUN) 6	Vilem Goppold von Lobsdorf (BOH) 4
1912	Jeno Fuchs (HUN) 6 wins	Béla Békéssy (HUN) 5	Ervin Mészaros (HUN) 5
1920	Nedo Nadi (ITA) 11 wins	Aldo Nadi (ITA) 9	Adrianus E. W. de Jong (NED) 7
1924	Sándor Posta (HUN) 5 wins	Roger Ducret (FRA) 5	János Garai (HUN) 5
1928	Odön Tersztyansky (HUN) 9 wins	Attila Petschauer (HUN) 9	Bino Bini (ITA) 8
1932	György Piller (HUN) 8 wins	Giulio Gaudini (ITA) 7	Endre Kabos (HUN) 5
1936	Endre Kabos (HUN) 7 wins	Gustavo Marzi (ITA) 6	Aladár Gerevich (HUN) 6
1948	Aladár Gerevich (HUN) 7 wins	Vincenzo Pinton (ITA) 5	Pál Kovács (HUN) 5
1952	Pál Kovács (HUN) 8 wins	Aladár Gerevich (HUN) 7	Tibor Berczelly (HUN) 5
1956	Rudolf Kárpáti (HUN) 6 wins	Jerzy Pawlowski (POL) 5	Lev Kuznyetsov (URS) 4
1960	Rudolf Kárpáti (HUN) 5 wins	Zoltán Horvath (HUN) 4	Wladimiro Calarese (ITA) 4
1964	Tibor Pézsa (HUN) 2 wins	Claude Arabo (FRA) 2	Umar Mavlikhanov (URS) 1
1968	Jerzy Pawlowski (POL) 4 wins	Mark Rakita (URS) 4	Tribor Pézsa (HUN) 3
1972	Viktor Sidiak (URS) 4 wins	Peter Maroth (HUN) 3	Vladimir Nazilimov (URS) 3
1976	Viktor Krovopouskov (URS) 5 wins	Vladimir Nazlimov (URS) 4	Viktor Sidiak (URS) 3
1980	Viktor Krovopouskov (URS) 5 wins	Mikhail Burtsev (URS) 4	Imre Gedovari (HUN) 3
1984	Jean François Lamour (FRA)	Marco Marin (ITA)	Peter Westbrook (USA)
1988	Jean François Lamour (FRA)	Janusz Olech (POL)	Giovanni Scalzo (ITA)
1992	Bence Szabo (HUN)	Marco Marin (ITA)	Jean François Lamour (FRA)
1996	Sergei Podnyakov (RUS)	Stanislav Sharikov (RUS)	Damien Touya (FRA)

Foil (Women)

1924	Ellen Osiier (DEN) 5 wins	Gladys Davis (GBR) 4	Grete Heckscher (DEN) 3
1928	Helène Mayer (GER) 7 wins	Muriel Freeman (GBR) 6	Olga Oelkers (GER) 4
1932	Ellen Preis (AUT) 9 wins	Heather Guinness (GBR) 8	Erna Bogen (HUN) 7
1936	Ilona Elek (HUN) 6 wins	Helène Mayer (GER) 5	Ellen Preis (AUT) 5
1948	Ilona Elek (HUN) 6 wins	Karen Lachmann (DEN) 5	Ellen Müller-Preis (AUT) 5
1952	Irene Camber (ITA) 5 wins	Ilona Elek (HUN) 5	Karen Lachmann (DEN) 4
1956	Gillian Sheen (GBR) 6 wins	Olga Orban (ROM) 6	Renée Garilhe (FRA) 5
1960	Heidi Schmid (GER) 6 wins	Valentina Rastvorova (URS) 5	Maria Vicol (ROM) 4
1964	Ildikó Ujlaki-Rejtö (HUN) 2 wins	Helga Mees (GER) 2	Antonella Ragno (ITA) 2
1968	Yelena Novikova (URS) 4 wins	Pilar Roldan (EMX) 3	Ildikó Ujlaki-Rejtö (HUN) 3
1972	Antonella Ragno-Lonzi (ITA) 4 wins	Ildikó Bóbis (HUN) 3	Galina Gorokhova (URS)
1976	Ildikó Schwarczenberger (HUN) 4 wins	Maria Collino (ITA) 4	Yelena Novikova-Belova (URS) 3
1980	Pascale Trinquet (FRA) 4 wins	Magda Maros (HUN) 3	Barbara Wysoczanska (POL) 3
1984	Jujie Luan (CHN)	Cornelia Hanisch (FRG)	Dorina Vaccaroni (ITA)
1988	Anja Fichtel (FRG)	Sabine Bau (FRG)	Zita Funkenhauser (FRG)
1992	Giovanna Trillini (ITA)	Wang Huifeng (CHN)	Tatyana Sadovskaya (EUN)
1996	Laura Badea (ROM)	Valentin Vezzali (ITA)	Giovanna Trillini (ITA)

1896–1920 *Event not held*

Épée (Women)

1996	Laura Flessel (FRA)	Valerie Bartlois (FRA)	Györgyi Horvathné-Szalay (HUN)

1896–1992 *Event not held*

Team

GOLD	SILVER	BRONZE

Foil (Men)

GOLD	SILVER	BRONZE
1904 Cuba/United States	United States	— 1
1920 Italy	France	United States
1924 France	Belgium	Hungary
1928 Italy	France	Argentina
1932 France	Italy	United States
1936 Italy	France	Germany
1948 France	Italy	Belgium
1952 France	Italy	Hungary
1956 Italy	France	Germany
1960 Soviet Union	Italy	Germany
1964 Soviet Union	Poland	France
1968 France	Soviet Union	Poland
1972 Poland	Soviet Union	France
1976 West Germany	Italy	France
1980 France	Soviet Union	Poland
1984 Italy	West Germany	France
1988 Soviet Union	West Germany	Hungary
1992 Germany	Cuba	Poland
1996 Russia	Poland	Cuba

1896–1900, 1906–12 *Event not held*

1 No other teams entered

Foil (Women)

GOLD	SILVER	BRONZE
1960 Soviet Union	Hungary	Italy
1964 Hungary	Soviet Union	Germany
1968 Soviet Union	Hungary	Romania
1972 Soviet Union	Hungary	Romania
1976 Soviet Union	France	Hungary
1980 France	Soviet Union	Hungary
1984 West Germany	Romania	France
1988 West Germany	Italy	Hungary
1992 Italy	Germany	Romania
1996 Italy	Romania	Germany

1896–1956 *Event not held*

Sabre (Men)

GOLD	SILVER	BRONZE
1906 Germany	Greece	The Netherlands
1908 Hungary	Italy	Bohemia
1912 Hungary	Austria	The Netherlands
1920 Italy	France	The Netherlands
1924 Italy	Hungary	The Netherlands
1928 Hungary	Italy	Poland
1932 Hungary	Italy	Poland
1936 Hungary	Italy	Germany
1948 Hungary	Italy	United States
1952 Hungary	Italy	France
1956 Hungary	Poland	Soviet Union
1960 Hungary	Poland	Italy
1964 Soviet Union	Italy	Poland
1968 Soviet Union	Italy	Hungary
1972 Italy	Soviet Union	Hungary
1976 Soviet Union	Italy	Romania
1980 Soviet Union	Italy	Hungary
1984 Italy	France	Romania
1988 Hungary	Soviet Union	Italy

1992 Unified Team	Hungary	France
1996 Russia	Hungary	Italy

1896–1904 *Event not held*

Épée (Men)

1906 France	Great Britain	Belgium
1908 France	Great Britain	Belgium
1912 Belgium	Great Britain	The Netherlands
1920 Italy	Belgium	France
1924 France	Belgium	Italy
1928 Italy	France	Portugal
1932 France	Italy	United States
1936 Italy	Sweden	France
1948 France	Italy	Sweden
1952 Italy	Sweden	Switzerland
1956 Italy	Hungary	France
1960 Italy	Great Britain	Soviet Union
1964 Hungary	Italy	France
1968 Hungary	Soviet Union	Poland
1972 Hungary	Switzerland	Soviet Union
1976 Sweden	West Germany	Switzerland
1980 France	Poland	Soviet Union
1984 West Germany	France	Italy
1988 France	West Germany	Soviet Union
1992 Germany	Hungary	Unified Team
1996 Italy	Russia	France

1896–1904 *Event not held*

Épée (Women)

1996 France	Italy	Russia

1896–1992 *Event not held*

Discontinued Events

Foil for Fencing Masters

1896 Léon Pyrgos (GRE)	Jean Perronnet (FRA)	–
1900 Lucien Mérignac (FRA)	Alphonse Kirchhoffer (FRA)	Jean-Baptiste Mimiague (FRA)

Épée for Fencing Masters

1900 Albert Ayat (FRA)	Emile Bougnol (FRA)	Henri Laurent (FRA)
1906 Cyrille Verbrugge (BEL)	Carlo Gandini (ITA)	Ioannis Raissis (GRE)

Épée for Amateurs and Fencing Masters

1900 Albert Ayat (FRA)	Ramón Fonst (CUB)	Léon Sée (FRA)

Sabre for Fencing Masters

1900 Antonio Conte (ITA)	Italo Santelli (ITA) [1]	Milan Neralic (AUT)
1906 Cyrille Verburgge (BEL)	Ioannis Raissis (GRE)	–

[1] Santelli actually lived in Hungary, hence some confusion as to his nationality

Three Cornered Sabre

1906 Gustav Casmir (GER)	George van Rossem (NED)	Péter Tóth (HUN)

Single Sticks

1904 Albertson van Zo Post (USA) [1]	William Grebe (USA)	William O'Connor (USA)

[1] Van Zo Post was an American citizen wrongly reported as competing for Cuba

Football (Soccer) Medals

GOLD	SILVER	BRONZE
Men		
1900 Great Britain	France	Belgium
1904 Canada	United States	United States
1906 Denmark	Greece	Greece
1908 Great Britain	Denmark	The Netherlands
1912 Great Britain	Denmark	The Netherlands
1920 Belgium	Spain	The Netherlands
1924 Uruguay	Switzerland	Sweden
1928 Uruguay	Argentina	Italy
1936 Italy	Austria	Norway
1948 Sweden	Yugoslavia	Denmark
1952 Hungary	Yugoslavia	Denmark
1956 Soviet Union	Yugoslavia	Bulgaria
1960 Yugoslavia	Denmark	Hungary
1964 Hungary	Czechoslovakia	Germany
1968 Hungary	Bulgaria	Japan
1972 Poland	Hungary	East Germany [1]
1976 East Germany	Poland	Soviet Union [1]
1980 Czechoslovakia	East Germany	Soviet Union
1984 France	Brazil	Yugoslavia
1988 Soviet Union	Brazil	West Germany
1992 Spain	Poland	Ghana
1996 Nigeria	Argentina	Brazil

1896, 1932 *Event not held*

[1] Tie declared after extra time played

Women

1996 United States	China	Norway

1896–1992 *Event not held*

Gymnastics Medals

GOLD	SILVER	BRONZE
Men		
Team		
1904 United States/Austria 374.43pts	United States 356.37	United States 349.69
1906 Norway 19.00pts	Denmark 18.00	Italy16.71
1908 Sweden 438pts	Norway 425	Finland 405
1912 Italy 265.75pts	Hungary 227.25	Great Britain 184.50
1920 Italy 359.855pts	Belgium 346.745	France 340.100
1924 Italy 839.058pts	France 820.528	Switzerland 816.661
1928 Switzerland 1718.652pts	Czechoslovakia 1712.250	Yugoslavia 1648.750
1932 Italy 541.850pts	United States 522.275	Finland 509.995
1936 Germany 657.430pts	Switzerland 654.802	Finland 638.468
1948 Finland 1358.3pts	Switzerland 1356.7	Hungary 1330.35
1952 Soviet Union 575.4pts	Switzerland 567.5	Finland 564.2
1956 Soviet Union 568.25	Japan 566.40	Finland 555.95
1960 Japan 575.20pts	Soviet Union 572.70	Italy 559.05
1964 Japan 577.95pts	Soviet Union 575.45	Germany 565.10
1968 Japan 575.90pts	Soviet Union 571.10	East Germany 557.15
1972 Japan 571.25pts	Soviet Union 564.05	East Germany 559.70
1976 Japan 576.85pts	Soviet Union 576.45	East Germany 654.65
1980 Soviet Union 589.60pts	East Germany 581.15	Hungary 575.00
1984 United States 591.40pts	China 590.80	Japan 586.70

1988 Soviet Union 593.350pts   East Germany 588.450   Japan 585.600
1992 Unified Team 585.450pts   China 580.375   Japan 578.250
1996 Russia 576.778pts   China 575.539   Ukraine 571.541

1896–1900 *Event not held*

Individual Combined Exercises

1900	Gustave Sandras (FRA) 302pts	Noël Bas (FRA) 295	Lucien Démanet (FRA) 293
1904[1]	Julius Lenhart (AUT) 69.80pts	Wilhelm Weber (GER) 69.10	Adolf Spinnler (SUI) 67.99
1906[2]	Pierre Paysse (FRA) 97pts	Alberto Braglia (ITA) 95	Georges Charmoille (FRA) 94
1906	Pierre Paysse (FRA) 116pts	Alberto Braglia (ITA) 115	Georges Charmoille (FRA) 113
1908	Alberto Braglia (ITA) 317.0pts	S. Walter Tysal (GBR) 312.0	Louis Ségura (FRA) 297.0
1912	Alberto Braglia (ITA) 135.0pts	Louis Ségura (FRA) 132.5	Adolfo Tunesi (ITA) 131.5
1920	Giorgio Zampori (ITA) 88.35pts	Marco Torres (FRA) 87.62	Jean Gounot (FRA) 87.45
1924	Leon Stukelj (YUG) 110.340pts	Robert Prazák (TCH) 110.323	Bedrich Supcik (TCH) 106.930
1928	Georges Miez (SUI) 247.500pts	Herman Hänggi (SUI) 246.625	Leon Stukelj (YUG) 244.875
1932	Romeo Neri (ITA) 140.625pts	István Pelle (HUN) 134.925	Heikki Savolainen (FIN) 134.575
1936	Alfred Schwarzmann (GER) 113.100pts	Eugen Mack (SUI) 112.334	Konrad Frey (GER) 111.532
1948	Veikko Huhtanen (FIN) 229.7pts	Walter Lehmann (SUI) 229.0	Paavo Aaltonen (FIN) 228.8
1952	Viktor Chukarin (URS) 115.70pts	Grant Shaginyan (URS) 114.95	Josef Stalder (SUI) 114.75
1956	Viktor Chukarin (URS) 114.25pts	Takashi Ono (JPN) 114.20	Yuri Titov (URS) 113.80
1960	Boris Shakhlin (URS) 115.95pts	Takashi Ono (JPN) 115.90	Yuri Titov (URS) 115.60
1964	Yukio Endo (JPN) 115.95pts	Shuji Tsurumi (JPN) 115.40	–
		Viktor Lisitsky (URS) 115.40	
1968	Sawao Kato (JPN) 115.90pts	Mikhail Voronin (URS) 115.85	Akinori Nakayama (JPN) 115.65
1972	Sawao Kato (JPN) 114.650pts	Eizo Kenmotsu (JPN) 114.575	Akinori Nakayama (JPN) 114.325
1976	Nikolai Andrianov (URS) 116.650pts	Sawao Kato (JPN) 115.650	Mitsuo Tsukahara (JPN) 115.375
1980	Alexander Dityatin (URS) 118.650pts	Nikolai Andrianov (URS) 118.225	Stoyan Deltchev (BUL) 118.000
1984	Koji Gushiken (JPN) 118.700pts	Peter Vidmar (USA) 118.675	Li Ning (CHN) 118.575
1988	Vladimir Artemov (URS) 119.125pts	Valeri Lyukhine (URS) 119.025	Dmitri Bilozertchev (URS) 118.975
1992	Vitali Scherbo (EUN) 59.025pts	Grigori Mistyutin (EUN) 58.925	Valeri Belenki (EUN) 58.625
1996	Li Xiaoshuang (CHN) 58.423pts	Alexei Nemov (RUS) 58.374	Vitali Scherbo (BLR) 58.197

1896 *Event not held*

[1] Lenhart was a member of the Philadelphia Club, USA, which won the team event
[2] Two competitions in 1906, one of five events and one of six

Floor Exercises

1932	István Pelle (HUN) 9.60pts	Georges Miez (SUI) 9.47	Mario Lertora (ITA) 9.23
1936	Georges Miez (SUI) 18.666pts	Josef Walter (SUI) 18.5	Konrad Frey (GER) 18.466
			Eugen Mack (SUI) 18.466
1948	Ferenc Pataki (HUN) 38.7pts	János Mogyorosi-Klencs (HUN) 38.4	Zdenek Ruzicka (TCH) 38.1
1952	William Thoresson (SWE) 19.25pts	Tadao Uesako (JPN) 19.15	–
		Jerzy Jokiel (POL) 19.15	
1956	Valentin Muratov (URS) 19.20pts	Nobuyuki Aihara (JPN) 19.10	–
		Viktor Chukharin (URS) 19.10	
1960	Nobuyuki Aihara (JPN) 19.450pts	Yuri Titov (URS) 19.325	Franco Menichelli (ITA) 19.275
1964	Franco Menichelli (ITA) 19.45pts	Viktor Lisitsky (URS) 19.35	–
		Yukio Endo (JPN) 19.35	
1968	Sawao Kato (JPN) 19.475pts	Akinori Nakayama (JPN) 19.400	Takeshi Kato (JPN) 19.275
1972	Nikolai Andrianov (URS) 19.175pts	Akinori Nakayama (JPN) 19.125	Shigeru Kasamatsu (JPN) 19.025
1976	Nikolai Andrianov (URS) 19.450pts	Vladimir Marchenko (URS) 19.425	Peter Kormann (USA) 19.300
1980	Roland Brückner (GDR) 19.750pts	Nikolai Andrianov (URS) 19.725	Alexander Dityatin (URS) 19.700
1984	Li Ning (CHN) 19.925pts	Yun Lou (CHN) 19.775	Koji Sotomura (JPN) 19.700
			Philippe Vatuone (FRA) 19.700
1988	Sergei Kharikov (URS) 19.925pts	Vladimir Artemov (URS) 19.900	Lou Yun (CHN) 19.850
			Yukio Iketani (JPN) 19.850

1992 Li Xiaoshuang (CHN) 9.925pts	Grigori Misyutin (EUN) 9.787	–
	Yukio Iketani (JPN) 9.787	
1996 Ioannis Melissanidis (GRE) 9.950pts	Li Xiaoshuang (CHN) 9.837	Alexei Nemov (RUS) 9.800

1896–1928 *Event not held*

Parallel Bars

1896 Alfred Flatow (GER) d.n.a.	Jules Zutter (SUI)	Hermann Weingärtner (GER)
1904 George Eyser (USA) 44pts	Anton Heida (USA) 43	John Duha (USA) 40
1924 August Güttinger (SUI) 21.63pts	Robert Prazák (TCH) 21.61	Giorgio Zampori (ITA) 21.45
1928 Ladislav Vácha (TCH) 18.83pts	Josip Primozic (YUG) 18.50	Hermann Hänaggi (SUI) 18.08
1932 Romeo Neri (ITA) 18.97pts	István Pelle (HUN) 18.60	Heikki Savolainen (FIN) 18.27
1936 Konrad Frey (GER) 19.067pts	Michael Reusch (SUI) 109.034	Alfred Schwarzmann (GER) 18.967
1948 Michael Reusch (SUI) 39.5pts	Veikkö Huhtanen (FIN) 39.3	Christian Kipfer (SUI) 39.1
		Josef Stalder (SUI) 39.1
1952 Hans Eugster (SUI) 19.65pts	Viktor Chukarin (URS) 19.60	Josef Stalder (SUI) 19.50
1956 Viktor Chukarin (URS) 19.20pts	Masami Kubota (JPN) 19.15	Takashi Ono (JPN) 19.10
		Masao Takemoto (JPN) 19.10
1960 Boris Shakhlin (URS) 19.400pts	Giovanni Carminucci (ITA) 19.375	Takashi Ono (JPN) 19.350
1964 Yukio Endo (JPN) 19.675pts	Shuji Tsurumi (JPN) 19.450	Franco Menichelli (ITA) 19.350
1968 Akinori Nakayama (JPN) 19.475pts	Mikhail Voronin (URS) 19.425	Vladimir Klimenko (URS) 19.225
1972 Sawao Kato (JPN) 19.475pts	Shigeru Kasamatsu (JPN) 19.375	Eizo Kenmotsu (JPN) 19.25
1976 Sawao Kato (JPN) 19.675pts	Nikolai Andrianov (URS) 19.500	Mitsuo Tsukahara (JPN) 19.475
1980 Alexander Tkachev (URS) 19.775pts	Alexander Dityatin (URS) 19.750	Roland Brückner (GDR) 19.650
1984 Bart Conner (USA) 19.950pts	Nobuyuki Kajitani (JPN) 19.925	Mitchell Gaylord (USA) 19.850
1988 Vladimir Artemov (URS) 19.925pts	Valeri Lyukhine (URS) 19.900	Sven Tippelt (GDR) 19.750
1992 Vitali Scherbo (EUN) 9.900pts	Li Jing (CHN) 9.812	Guo Linyao (CHN) 9.800
		Igor Korobchinkski (EUN) 9.800
		Masayuki Matsunaga (JPN) 9.800
1996 Rustam Sharipov (UKR) 9.837pts	Jair Lynch (USA) 9.825	Vitali Scherbo (BLR) 9.800

1900, 1906–20 *Event not held*

Pommel Horse

1896 Jules Zutter (SUI) d.n.a.	Hermann Weingärtner (GER)	Gyula Kakas (HUN)
1904 Anotn Heida (USA) 42pts	George Eyser (USA) 33	William Merz (USA) 29
1924 Josef Wilhelm (SUI) 21.23pts	Jean Gutweiniger (SUI) 21.13	Antoine Rebetez (SUI) 20.73
1928 Hermann Hänggi (SUI) 19.75pts	Georges Miez (SUI) 19.25	Heikki Savolainen (FIN) 18.83
1932 István Pelle (HUN) 19.07pts	Omero Bonoli (ITA) 18.87	Frank Haubold (USA) 18.57
1936 Konrad Frey (GER) 19.333pts	Eugen Mack (SUI) 19.167	Albert Bachmann (SUI) 19.067
1948 Paavo Aaltonen (FIN) 38.7pts	Luigi Zanetti (ITA) 38.3	Guido Figone (ITA) 38.2
Veikkö Huhtanen (FIN) 38.7pts		
Heikki Savolainen (FIN) 38.7pts		
1952 Viktor Chukarin (URS) 19.50pts	Yevgeni Korolkov (URS) 19.40	–
	Grant Shaginyan (URS) 19.40	
1956 Boris Shakhlin (URS) 19.25pts	Takashi Ono (JPN) 19.20	Viktor Chukarin (URS) 19.10
1960 Eugen Ekman (FIN) 19.375pts	–	Shuji Tsurumi (JPN) 19.150
Boris Shakhlin (URS) 19.375pts		
1964 Miroslav Cerar (YUG) 19.525pts	Shuji Tsurumi (JPN) 19.325	Yuri Tsapenko (URS) 19.200
1968 Miroslav Cerar (YUG) 19.325pts	Olli Laiho (FIN) 19.225	Mikhail Voronin (URS) 19.200
1972 Viktor Klimenko (URS) 19.125pts	Sawao Kato (JPN) 19.00	Eizo Kenmotsu (JPN) 18.950
1976 Zoltän Magyar (HUN) 19.700pts	Eizo Kenmotsu (JPN) 19.575	Nikolai Andrianov (URS) 19.525
1980 Zoltän Magyar (HUN) 19.925pts	Alexander Dityatin (URS) 19.800	Michael Nikolay (GDR) 19.775
1984 Li Ning (CHN) 19.950pts	–	Timothy Daggert (USA) 19.825
Peter Vidmar (USA) 19.950		
1988 Lubomir Gueraskov (BUL) 19.950pts	–	–
Zsolt Borkai (HUN) 19.950pts		
Dmitri Bilozertchev (URS) 19.950pts		

1992	Vitali Scherbo (EUN) 9.925pts	–	Andreas Wecker (GER) 9.887
	Pae Gil-su (PRK) 9.925pts		
1996	Lin Donghua (SUI) 9.875pts	Marius Urzica (ROM) 9.825	Alexei Nemov (RUS) 9.787

1900, 1906–20 *Event not held*

Rings

1896	Ioannis Mitropoulos (GRE) d.n.a.	Hermann Weingärtner (GER)	Petros Persakis (GRE)
1904	Herman Glass (USA) 45pts	William Merz (USA) 35	Emil Voight (USA) 32
1924	Franco Martino (ITA) 21.553pts	Robert Prazák (TCH) 21.483	Ladislav Vácha (TCH) 21.430
1928	Leon Skutelj (YUG) 19.25pts	Ladislav Vácha (TCH) 19.17	Emanuel Löffler (TCH) 18.83
1932	George Gulack (USA) 18.97pts	William Denton (USA) 18.60	Giovanni Lattuada (ITA) 18.50
1936	Alois Hudec (TCH) 19.433pts	Leon Skutelj (YUG) 18.867	Matthias Volz (GER) 18.667
1948	Karl Frei (SUI) 39.60pts	Michael Reusch (SUI) 39.10	Zdenek Ruzicka (TCH) 38.30
1952	Grant Shaginyan (URS) 19.75pts	Viktor Chakarin (URS) 19.55	Hans Eugster (SUI) 19.40
			Dimitri Leonkin (URS) 19.40
1956	Albert Azaryan (URS) 19.35pts	Valentin Muratov (URS) 19.15	Masao Takemoto (JPN) 19.10
			Masami Kubota (JPN) 19.10
1960	Albert Azaryan (URS) 19.475pts	Boris Shakhlin (URS) 19.500	Velik Kapsazov (BUL) 19.425
			Takashi Ono (JPN) 19.425
1964	Takuji Hayata (JPN) 19.475pts	Franco Menichelli (ITA) 19.425	Boris Shakhlin (URS) 19.400
1968	Akinori Nakayama (JPN) 19.450pts	Mikhail Voronin (URS) 19.325	Sawao Kato (JPN) 19.225
1972	Akinori Nakayama (JPN) 19.350pts	Mikhail Voronin (URS) 19.325	Mitsuo Tsukahara (JPN) 19.225
1976	Nikolai Andrianov (URS) 19.875pts	Alexander Ditiyatin (URS) 19.550	Danut Grecu (ROM) 19.500
1980	Alexander Ditiyatin (URS) 19.875pts	Alexander Tkachev (URS) 19.725	Jiri Tabak (TCH) 19.600
1984	Koji Gushiken (JPN) 19.850pts	–	Mitchell Gaylord (USA) 19.825
	Li Ning (CHN) 19.850		
1988	Holger Behrendt (GDR) 19.925pts	–	Sven Tippelt (GDR) 19.875
	Dmitri Bilozerchev (URS) 19.925pts		
1992	Vitali Scherbo (EUN) 9.937pts	Li Jing (CHN) 9.875	Li Xiaoshuang (CHN) 9.862
			Andreas Wecker (GER) 9.862
1996	Yuri Chechi (ITA) 9.887pts	Szilveszter Csollany (HUN) 9.812	–
		Dan Burnica (ROM) 9.812	

1900, 1906–20 *Event not held*

Horizontal Bar

1896	Hermann Weingärtner (GER) d.n.a.	Alfred Flatow (GER)	unknown
1904	Anton Heida (USA) 40pts	–	George Eyser (USA) 39
	Edward Henning (USA) 40pts		
1924	Leon Stukelj (YUG) 19.730pts	Jean Gutweniger (SUI) 19.236	André Higelin (FRA) 19.163
1928	Georges Miez (SUI) 19.17pts	Romeo Neri (ITA) 19.00	Eugen Mack (SUI) 18.92
1932	Dallas Bixler (USA) 18.33pts	Heikki Savolainen (FIN) 18.07	Einari Teräsvirta (FIN) 18.07 [1]
1936	Aleksanteri Sarvaala (FIN) 19.367pts	Konrad Frey (GER) 19.267	Alfred Schwarzmann (GER) 19.233
1948	Josef Stalder (SUI) 39.7pts	Walter Lehmann (SUI) 39.4	Veikkö Huhtanen (FIN) 39.2
1952	Jack Günthard (SUI) 19.55pts	Josef Stalder (SUI) 19.50	–
		Alfred Schwarzmann (GER) 19.50	
1956	Takashi Ono (JPN) 19.60pts	Yuri Titov (URS) 19.40	Masao Takemoto (JPN) 19.30
1960	Takashi Ono (JPN) 19.60pts	Masao Takemoto (JPN) 19.525	Boris Shakhlin (URS) 19.475
1964	Boris Shakhlin (URS) 19.625pts	Yuri Titov (URS) 19.55	Miroslav Cerar (YUG) 19.50
1968	Mikhail Voronin (URS) 19.550pts	–	Eizo Kenmotsu (JPN) 19.375
	Akinori Nakayama (JPN) 19.550pts		
1972	Mitsuo Tsukahara (JPN) 19.725pts	Sawao Kato (JPN) 19.525	Shigeru Kasamatsu (JPN) 19.450

1976 Mitsuo Tsukuhara (JPN) 19.675pts	Eizo Kenmotsu (JPN) 19.500	Eberhard Gienger (FRG) 19.475
		Henry Boërio (FRA) 19.475
1980 Stoyan Deltchev (BUL) 19.825pts	Alexander Dityatin (URS) 19.750	Nikolai Andrianov (URS) 19.675
1984 Shinje Morisue (JPN) 20.00pts	Tong Fei (CHN) 19.955	Koji Gushiken (JPN) 19.950
1988 Vladimir Artemov (URS) 19.900pts	–	Holger Behrendt (GDR) 19.800
Valeri Lyukhine (URS) 19.900pts		Marius Germann (ROM) 19.800
1992 Trent Dimas (USA) 9.875pts	Andreas Wecker (GER) 9.837	–
	Grigori Misyutin (EUN) 9.837	
1996 Alexei Nemov (RUS) 9.787pts	Yeo Hong-chul (KOR) 9.756	Vitali Scherbo (BLR) 9.724

1900, 1906–20 *Event not held*

[1] Teräsvirta conceded second place to Savolainen

Horse Vault

1896 Carl Schuhmann (GER) d.n.a.	Jules Zutter (SUI) d.n.a.	–
1904 Anton Heida (USA) 36pts	–	William Merz (USA) 31
George Eyser (USA) 36pts		
1924 Frank Kriz (USA) 9.98pts	Jan Koutny (TCH) 9.97	Bohumil Morkovsky (TCH) 9.93
1928 Eugen Mack (SUI) 9.58pts	Emanuel Löffler (TCH) 9.50	Stane Derganc (YUG) 9.46
1932 Savino Guglielmetti (ITA) 18.03pts	Alfred Jochim (USA) 17.77	Edward Carmichael (USA) 17.53
1936 Alfred Schwarzmann (GER) 19.200pts	Eugen Mack (SUI) 18.967	Matthias Volz (GER) 18.467
1948 Paavo Aaltonen (FIN) 39.10pts	Olavi Rove (FIN) 39.00	János Mogyorosi-Klencs (HUN) 38.50
		Ferenc Pataki (HUN) 38.50
		Leos Sotornik (TCH) 38.50
1952 Viktor Chukarin (URS) 19.20pts	Masao Takemoto (JPN) 19.15	Tadao Uesako (JPN) 19.10
		Takashi Ono (JPN) 19.10
1956 Helmuth Bantz (GER) 18.85pts	–	Yuri Titov (URS) 18.75
Valentin Muratov (URS) 18.85pts		
1960 Takashi Ono (JPN) 19.350pts	–	Vladimir Portnoi (URS) 19.225
Boris Shakhlin (URS) 19.350pts		
1964 Haruhiro Yamashita (JPN) 19.600pts	Viktor Lisitsky (URS) 19.325	Hannu Rantakari (FIN) 19.300
1968 Mikhail Voronin (URS) 19.000pts	Yukio Endo (JPN) 18.950	Sergei Diomidov (URS) 18.925
1972 Klaus Koste (GDR) 18.850pts	Viktor Klimenko (URS) 18.825	Nikolai Andrianov (URS) 18.800
1976 Nikolai Andrianov (URS) 19.450pts	Mitsuo Tsukahara (JPN) 19.375	Hiroshi Kajiyama (JPN) 19.275
1980 Nikolai Andrianov (URS) 19.825pts	Alexander Dityatin (URS) 19.800	Roland Brückner (GDR) 19.775
1984 Lou Yun (CHN) 19.950pts	Li Ning (CHN) 19.825	–
	Koji Gushiken (JPN) 19.825	
	Mitchell Gaylord (USA) 19.825	
	Shinje Morisue (JPN) 19.825	
1988 Lou Yun (CHN) 19.875pts	Sylvio Kroll (GDR) 19.862	Park Jong-hoon (KOR) 19.775
1992 Vitali Scherbo (EUN) 9.856pts	Grigori Misyutin (EUN) 9.781	Yoo Ok-youl (KOR) 9.762
1996 Andreas Wecker (GER) 9.850pts	Krasimir Dounev (BUL) 9.825	Vitali Scherbo (BLR) 9.800
		Fan Bin (CHN) 9.800
		Alexei Nemov (RUS) 9.800

1900, 1906–20 *Event not held*

Women

Team

1928 The Netherlands 316.75pts	Italy 289.00	Great Britain 258.25
1936 Germany 506.50pts	Czechoslovakia 503.60	Hungary 499.00
1948 Czechoslovakia 445.45pts	Hungary 440.55	United States 422.63
1952 Soviet Union 527.03pts	Hungary 520.96	Czecholslovakia 503.32

1956 Soviet Union 444.80pts	Hungary 443.50	Romania 438.20
1960 Soviet Union 382.320pts	Czechoslovakia 373.323	Romania 372.053
1964 Soviet Union 380.890pts	Czechoslovakia 379.989	Japan 377.889
1968 Soviet Union 382.85pts	Czechoslovakia 382.20	East Germany 379.10
1972 Soviet Union 380.50pts	East Germany 376.55	Hungary 368.25
1976 Soviet Union 390.35pts	Romania 387.15	East Germany 385.10
1980 Soviet Union 394.90pts	Romania 393.50	East Germany 392.55
1984 Romania 392.20pts	United States 391.20	China 388.60
1988 Soviet Union 395.475pts	Romania 394.125	East Germany 390.875
1992 Unified Team 395.666pts	Romania 395.079	United States 394.704
1996 United States 389.225pts	Russia 388.404	Romania 388.246

1896–1924, 1932 *Event not held*

Individual Combined Exercises

1952 Maria Gorokhovskaya (URS) 76.78pts	Nina Bocharova (URS) 75.94	Margit Korondi (HUN) 75.82
1956 Larissa Latynina (URS) 74.933pts	Agnes Keleti (HUN) 74.633	Sofia Muratova (URS) 74.466
1960 Larissa Latynina (URS) 77.031pts	Sofia Muratova (URS) 76.696	Polina Astakhova (URS) 76.164
1964 Vera Cáslavská (TCH) 77.564pts	Larissa Laytnina (URS) 76.998	Polina Astakhova (URS) 76.965
1968 Vera Cáslavská (TCH) 78.25pts	Zinaida Voronina (URS) 76.85	Natalya Muchinskaya (URS) 76.75
1972 Ludmila Tourischeva (URS) 77.025pts	Karin Janz (GDR) 76.875	Tamara Lazakovitch (URS) 76.850
1976 Nadia Comaneci (ROM) 79.275pts	Nelli Kim (URS) 78.675	Ludmila Tourischeva (URS) 78.625
1980 Yelena Davydova (URS) 79.150pts	Maxi Gnauck (GDR) 79.075 Nadia Comaneci (ROM) 79.075	–
1984 Mary Lou Retton (USA) 79.175pts	Ecaterina Szabo (ROM) 79.125	Simona Pauca (ROM) 78.675
1988 Yelena Chouchounova (URS) 79.662pts	Daniela Silivas (ROM) 79.637	Svetlana Bogunskaya (URS)79.40
1992 Tatyana Gutsu (EUN) 39.737pts	Shannon Miller (USA) 39.725	Lavinia Milosovici (ROM) 39.687
1996 Lilia Podkopayeva (UKR) 39.255pts	Gina Gogean (ROM) 39.075	Lavinia Milosovici (ROM) 39.067 Simona Amanar (ROM) 39.067

1896–1948 *Event not held*

Asymmetrical Bars

1952 Margit Korondi (HUN) 19.40pts	Maria Gorokhovskaya (URS) 19.26	Agnes Keleti (HUN) 19.16
1956 Agnes Keleti (HUN) 18.966pts	Larissa Latynina (URS) 18.833	Sofia Muratova (URS) 18.800
1960 Polina Astakhova (URS) 19.616pts	Larissa Latynina (URS) 19.416	Tamara Lyukhina (URS) 19.399
1964 Polina Astakhova (URS) 19.332pts	Katalin Makray (HUN) 19.216	Larissa Latynina (URS) 19.199
1968 Vera Cáslavská (TCH) 19.650pts	Karin Janz (GDR) 19.500	Zinaida Voronina (URS) 19.425
1972 Karin Janz (GDR) 19.675pts	Olga Korbut (URS) 19.450 Erika Zuchold (GDR) 19.450	–
1976 Nadia Comaneci (ROM) 20.00pts	Teodora Ungureanu (ROM) 19.800	Marta Egervari (HUN) 19.775
1980 Maxi Gnauck (GDR) 19.875pts	Emila Eberle (ROM) 19.850	Steffi Kräker (GDR) 19.775 Melita Rühn (ROM) 19.775 Maria Filatova (URS) 19.775
1984 Ma Yanhong (CHN) 19.950pts Julianne McNamara (USA) 19.950pts	–	Mary Lou Retton (USA) 19.800
1988 Daniela Silivas (ROM) 20.00pts	Dagmar Kersten (GDR) 19.987	Yelena Chouchounova (URS) 19.962
1992 Lu Li (CHN) 10.000pts	Tatyana Gutsu (EUN) 9.975	Shannon Miller (USA) 9.962
1996 Svetlana Chorkina (RUS) 9.850pts	Wengji Bi (CHN) 9.837 Amy Chow (USA) 9.837	–

1896–1948 *Event not held*

Balance Beam

1952 Nina Bocharova (URS) 19.22pts	Maria Gorokhovskaya (URS) 19.13	Margit Korondi (HUN) 19.02
1956 Agnes Keleti (HUN) 18.80pts	Eva Bosáková (TCH) 18.63 Tamara Manina (URS) 18.63	–

1960 Eva Bosáková (TCH) 19.283pts   Larissa Latynina (URS) 19.233   Sofia Muratova (URS) 19.232
1964 Vera Cáslavská (TCH) 19.449pts   Tamara Manina (URS) 19.399   Larissa Latynina (URS) 19.382
1968 Natalya Kuchinskaya (URS)   Vera Cáslavská (TCH) 19.575   Larissa Petrik (URS) 19.250
      19.650pts
1972 Olga Korbut (URS) 19.575pts   Tamara Lazokovitch (URS) 19.375 Karin Janz (GDR) 18.975
1976 Nadia Comaneci (ROM)   Olga Korbut (URS) 19.725   Teodora Ungureanu (ROM) 19.700
      19.950pts
1980 Nadia Comaneci (ROM)   Yelena Davydova (URS) 19.750   Natalya Shaposhnikova (URS)
      19.800pts   19.725
1984 Simona Pauca (ROM) 19.800pts   –   Kathy Johnson (USA) 19.650
      Ecaterina Szabo (ROM) 19.800
1988 Daniela Silivas (ROM) 19924pts   Yelena Chouchounova (URS)   Gabriela Potorac (ROM) 19.837
                                       19.875   Phoebe Mills (USA) 19.837
1992 Tayana Lyssenko (EUN) 9.975pts   Lu Li (CHN) 9.912   –
                                       Shannon Miller (USA) 9.912
1996 Shannon Miller (USA) 9.862pts   Lilia Podkopayeva (UKR) 9.825   Gina Gogean (ROM) 9.787

1896–1948 *Event not held*

Floor Exercises

1952 Agnes Keleti (HUN) 19.36pts   Maria Gorokhoskaya (URS) 19.20   Margit Korondi (HUN) 19.00
1956 Larissa Altynina (URS) 18.733pts –   Elena Leustean (ROM) 18.70
      Agnes Keleti (HUN) 18.733pts
1960 Larissa Latynina (URS) 19.583pts Polina Astakhova (URS) 19.532   Tamara Lyukhina (URS) 19.449
1964 Larissa Latynina (URS) 19.599pts Polina Astakhova (URS) 19.500   Anikó Jánosi (HUN) 19.300
1968 Larissa Petrik (URS) 19.675pts   –   Natalya Kuchinskaya (URS) 19.650
      Vera Cáslavská (TCH) 19.675pts
1972 Olga Korbut (URS) 19.575pts   Ludmila Tourischeva (URS) 19.550 Tamara Lazakovitch (URS) 19.450
1976 Nelli Kim (URS) 19.850pts   Ludmila Tourischeva (URS) 19.825 Nadia Comaneci (ROM) 19.750
1980 Nelli Kim (URS) 19.875pts   –   Natalya Shaposhnikova (URS)
      Nadia Comaneci (ROM) 19.875pts   19.825
                                                                        Maxi Gnauck (GDR) 19.825
1984 Ecaterina Szabo (ROM) 19.975pts Julianne McNamara (USA) 19.950   Mary Lou Retton (USA) 19.775
1988 Daniela Silivas (ROM) 19.937pts Svetlana Bogunskaya (URS) 19.887 Diana Doudeva (BUL) 19.850
1992 Lavinia Milosovici (ROM)   Henrietta Onodi (HUN) 9.950   Tatyana Gutsu (EUN) 9.912
      10.000pts   Christina Bontas (ROM) 9.912
                                                                        Shannon Miller (USA) 9.912
1996 Lilia Podkopayeva (UKR)   Simona Amanar (ROM) 9.850   Dominique Dawes (USA) 9.837
      9.887pts

1896–1948 *Event not held*

Horse Vault

1952 Yelena Kalinchuk (URS) 19.20pts Maria Gorokhoskaya (URS) 19.19   Galina Minaitscheva (URS) 19.16
1956 Larissa Latynina (URS) 18.833pts Tamara Manina (URS) 18.800   Ann-Sofi Colling (SWE) 18.733
                                                                        Olga Tass (HUN) 18.733
1960 Margarita Nikolayeva (URS)   Sofia Muratova (URS) 19.049   Larissa Latynina (URS) 19.016
      19.316pts
1964 Vera Cáslavská (TCH) 19.483pts   Larissa Latynina (URS) 19.283   –
                                       Birgit Radochla (GER) 19.283
1968 Vera Cáslavská (TCH) 19.775pts   Erika Zuchold (GDR) 19.625   Zinaida Voronina (URS) 19.500
1972 Karin Janz (GDR) 19.525pts   Erika Zuchold (GDR) 19.275   Ludmila Tourischeva (URS) 19.250
1976 Nelli Kim (URS) 19.800pts   Ludmila Tourischeva (URS)   –
                                       19.650
                                       Carola Dombeck (GDR) 19.650
1980 Natalya Shaposhnikova (URS)   Steffi Kräker (GDR) 19.675   Melita Rühn (ROM) 19.650
      19.725pts
1984 Ecaterina Szabo (ROM)   Mary Lou Retton (USA) 19.850   Lavinia Agache (ROM) 19.750
      19.875pts
1988 Svetlana Bogunskaya (URS)   Gabriela Potorac (ROM) 19.830   Daniela Silivas (ROM) 19.818
      19.905pts

1992 Lavinia Milosovici (ROM) 9.925pts	–	Tatyana Lyssenko (EUN) 9.912
Henrietta Onodi (HUN) 9.925pts		
1996 Simona Amanar (ROM) 9.825pts	Mo Huilan (CHN) 9.768	Gina Gogean (ROM) 9.750

1896–1948 *Event not held*

Modern Rhythmnic

1984 Lori Fung (CAN) 57.950pts	Doina Staiculescu (ROM) 57.900	Regina Weber (FRG) 57.700
1988 Marina Lobatch (URS) 60.00pts	Adriana Dounavska (BUL) 59.950	Alexandra Timochenko (URS) 59.875
1992 Aleksandra Timoschenko (EUN) 59.037pts	Carolina Garcia (ESP) 58.100	Oksana Skaldina (EUN) 57.912
1996 Yekaterina Serebryanskaya (UKR) 39.683pts	Yanina Batyrchina (RUS) 39.382	Yelena Vitrichenko (UKR) 39.331

1896–1980 *Event not held*

Rhythmic Team

1996 Spain 38.933pts	Bulgaria 38.866	Russia 38.365

1896–1992 *Event not held*

Discontinued Events

Parallel Bars (Men's Teams)

1896 Germany	Greece	Greece

Horizontal Bars (Men's Teams)

1896 Germany [1]

[1] Walkover

Rope Climbing (Men)

1896 Nicolaos Andriakopoulos (GRE) 23.4sec	Thomas Xenakis (GRE)	– [1]
1904 George Eyser (USA) 7.0sec	Charles Krause (USA) 7.8	Emil Voigt (USA) 9.8
1906 Georgios Aliprantis (GRE) 11.4sec	Béla Erödy (HUN) 13.8	Konstantinos Kozantis (GRE) 13.8
1924 Bedrich Supchik (TCH) 7.2sec	Albert Séguin (FRA) 7.4	August Güttinger (SUI) 7.8 Ladislav Vácha (TCH) 7.8
1932 Raymond Bass (USA) 6.7sec	William Galbraith (USA) 6.8	Thomas Connelly (USA) 7.0

[1] Fritz Hofmann (GER) did not finish

Club Swinging (Men)

1904 Edward Hennig (USA) 13pts	Emil Voigt (USA) 9	Ralph Wilson (USA) 5
1932 George Roth (USA) 8.97pts	Philip Erenberg (USA) 8.90	William Kuhlmeier (USA) 8.63

Tumbling (Men)

1932 Rowland Wolfe (USA) 18.90pts	Edward Gross (USA) 10.67	Willliam Herrmann (USA) 19.37

Nine Event Competition (Men)

1094 Adolf Spinnler (SUI) 43.49pts	Julius Lenhart (AUT) 43.00	Wilhelm Weber (GER) 41.60

Triathlon (Men)
(Comprised 100 yards, long jump and shot putt)

1904 Max Emmerich (USA) 35.70pts	John Grieb (USA) 34.00	William Merz (USA) 33.90

Four Event Competition (Men)

1904 Anton Heida (USA) 161pts	George Eyser (USA) 152	William Merz (USA) 135

Sidehorse Vault (Men)

1924 Albert Séguin (FRA) 10.00pts	Jean Gounot (FRA) 9.93 François Gangloff (FRA) 9.93	–

Swedish System (Men's Teams)

1912 Sweden 937.46pts	Denmark 898.84	Norway 857.21
1920 Sweden 1364pts	Denmark 1325	Belgium 1094

Free System (Men's Teams)

1912 Norway 114.25pts	Finland 109.25	Denmark 106.25
1920[1] Denmark	Norway	–

[1] Only two teams competed

Portable Apparatus (Women's Teams)

1952 Sweden 74.20pts	Soviet Union 73.00	Hungary 71.60
1956 Hungary 75.20pts	Sweden 74.20	Poland 74.00 Soviet Union 74.00

Handball Medals

GOLD	SILVER	BRONZE
Men		
1936[1] Germany	Austria	Switzerland
1972 Yugoslavia	Czechoslovakia	Romania
1976 Soviet Union	Romania	Poland
1980 East Germany	Soviet Union	Romania
1984 Yugoslavia	West Germany	Romania
1988 Soviet Union	Korea	Romania
1992 Unified Team	Sweden	Yugoslavia
1996 Croatia	Sweden	France
		Spain

1896–1932, 1948–68 *Event not held*

[1] Field handball played outdoors

GOLD	SILVER	BRONZE
Women		
1976 Soviet Union	East Germany	Hungary
1980 Soviet Union	Yugoslavia	East Germany
1984 Yugoslavia	Korea	China
1988 Korea	Norway	Soviet Union
1992 Korea	Norway	Unified Team
1996 Denmark	Korea	Hungary

1896–1972 *Event not held*

Hockey Medals

GOLD	SILVER	BRONZE
Men		
1908[1] England	Ireland	Scotland [2] Wales [2]
1920 England [3]	Denmark	Belgium
1928 India	The Netherlands	Germany
1932 India	Japan	United States
1936 India	Germany	The Netherlands
1948 India	Great Britain	The Netherlands
1952 India	The Netherlands	Great Britain
1956 India	Pakistan	Germany
1960 Pakistan	India	Spain

1964 India	Pakistan	Australia
1968 Pakistan	Australia	India
1972 West Germany	Pakistan	India
1976 New Zealand	Australia	Pakistan
1980 India	Spain	Soviet Union
1984 Pakistan	West Germany	Great Britain
1988 Great Britain	West Germany	The Netherlands
1992 Germany	Australia	Pakistan
1996 The Netherlands	Spain	Australia

1896–1906, 1912, 1924 *Event not held*

[1] Great Britain had four teams entered
[2] Tie for third place
[3] Great Britain represented by England team

Women

1980 Zimbabwe	Czechoslovakia	Soviet Union
1984 The Netherlands	West Germany	United States
1988 Australia	Korea	The Netherlands
1992 Spain	Germany	Great Britain
1996 Australia	Korea	The Netherlands

1896–1976 *Event not held*

Judo Medals

GOLD	SILVER	BRONZE

Men

Up to 60kg

1980 Thierry Rey (FRA)	Rafael Carbonell (CUB)	Tibor Kinces (HUN)
		Aramby Emizh (URS)
1984 Shinji Hosokawa (JPN)	Kim Jae-yup (KOR)	Edward Liddie (USA)
		Neil Eckersley (GBR)
1988 Kim Jae-yup (KOR)	Kevin Asano (USA)	Shinji Hosokawa (JPN)
		Amiran Totikachvili (URS)
1992 Nazim Gousseinov (EUN)	Yoon Hyun (KOR)	Tadamori Koshino (JPN)
		Richard Trautmann (GER)
1996 Tadahiro Nomura (JPN)	Girolamo Giovanazzo (ITA)	Doripalam Narmandakh (MGL)

Up to 65kg

1980 Nikolai Solodukhin (URS)	Tsendying Damdin (MGL)	Ilian Nedkov (BUL)
		Janusz Pawlowski (POL)
1984 Yoshiyuki Matsuoka (JPN)	Hwang Jung-oh (KOR)	Josef Reiter (AUT)
		Marc Alexandre (FRA)
1988 Lee Kyeung-keun (KOR)	Janusz Pawlowski (POL)	Bruno Carabeta (FRA)
		Yosuke Yamamoto (JPN)
1992 Rogerio Sampaio (BRA)	Jozsef Csák (HUN)	Udo Quellmalz (GER)
		Israel Hernandez (CUB)
1996 Udo Quellmalz (GER)	Yukimasa Nakamura (JPN)	Israel Plana Hernandez (CUB)
		Henrique Guimares (BRA)

Up to 71kg

1980 Ezio Gamba (ITA)	Neil Adams (GBR)	Karl-Heinz Lehmann (GDR)
		Ravdan Davaadalai (MGL)
1984 Ahn Byeong-keun (KOR)	Ezio Gamba (ITA)	Luis Onmura (BRA)
		Kerrith Brown (GBR)
1988 Marc Alexandre (FRA)	Sven Loll (GDR)	Michael Swain (USA)
		Guergui Tenadze (URS)
1992 Toshihiko Koga (JPN)	Bertalan Hajtós (HUN)	Chung Hoon (KOR)
		Shay Smadga (ISR)
1996 Kenzo Nakamura (JPN)	Kwak Dae-sung (KOR)	James Pedro (USA)
		Christophe Gagliano (FRA)

Up to 78kg

1980 Shota Khabeleri (URS)	Juan Ferrer La Hera (CUB)	Harald Heinke (GDR)
		Bernard Tchoullouyan (FRA)
1984 Frank Weineke (FRG)	Neil Adams (GBR)	Michel Nowak (FRA)
		Mirces Fratica (ROM)
1988 Waldemar Legien (POL)	Frank Wieneke (FRG)	Torsten Brechot (GDR)
		Bachir Varayev (URS)
1992 Hidehiko Yoshida (JPN)	Jason Morris (USA)	Kim Byung-joo (KOR)
		Bertrand Damaisin (FRA)
1996 Djamel Bouras (FRA)	Toshihiko Koga (JPN)	Soso Liparteliani (GEO)
		Cho In-chul (KOR)

Up to 86kg

1980 Jürg Röthlisberger (SUI)	Issac Azcuy Oliva (CUB)	Detlef Ultsich (GDR)
		Alexander Yatskevitch (URS)
1984 Peter Seisenbacher (AUT)	Robert Berland (USA)	Seiki Nose (JPN)
		Walter Carmona (BRA)
1988 Peter Seisenbacher (AUT)	Vladimir Chestakov (URS)	Ben Spijkers (NED)
		Akinobu Osako (JPN)
1992 Waldemar Legien (POL)	Pascal Tayot (FRA)	Hirotaki Okada (JPN)
		Nicolas Gill (CAN)
1996 Jeon Ki-young (KOR)	Armen Bagdasarov (UZB)	Marko Spittka (GER)
		Mark Huizinga (NED)

Up to 95kg

1980 Robert Van de Walle (BEL)	Tengiz Khubuluri (URS)	Dietmar Lorenz (GDR)
		Henk Numan (NED)
1984 Ha Hyoung-zoo (KOR)	Douglas Vieira (BRA)	Bjarni Fridriksson (ISL)
		Gunther Neureuther (FRG)
1988 Aurelio Miguel (BRA)	Marc Meiling (FRG)	Robert Van de Walle (BEL)
		Dennis Stewart (GBR)
1992 Antal Kovacs (HUN)	Ray Stevens (GBR)	Dmitri Sergeyev (EUN)
		Theo Meijer (NED)
1996 Pawel Nastula (POL)	Kim Min-soo (KOR)	Stephane Traineau (FRA)
		Miguel Fernandez (BRA)

Over 95kg

1980 Angelo Parisi (FRA)	Dimitar Zaprianov (BUL)	Vladimir Kocman (CZE)
		Radomir Kovacevic (YUG)
1984 Hitoshi Saito (JPN)	Angelo Parisi (FRA)	Cho Yong-chul (KOR)
		Mark Berger (CAN)
1988 Hitoshi Saito (JPN)	Henry Stöhr (GDR)	Cho Yong-chul (KOR)
		Grigori Veritchev (URS)
1992 David Khakhaliashvili (EUN)	Naoya Ogawa (JPN)	David Douillet (FRA)
		Imre Csösz (HUN)
1996 David Douillet (FRA)	Ernesto Perez (ESP)	Harry van Barneveld (BEL)
		Frank Moeller (GER)

Open Category No Weight Limit

1964 Antonius Geesink (NED)	Akio Kaminaga (JPN)	Theodore Boronovskis (AUS)
		Klaus Glahn (GER)
1972 Willem Ruska (NED)	Vitali Kuznetsov (URS)	Jean-Claude Brondani (FRA)
		Angelo Parisi (GBR)
1976 Haruki Uemura (JPN)	Keith Remfry (GBR)	Shota Chochoshvili (URS)
		Jeaki Cho (KOR)
1980 Dietmar Lorenz (GDR)	Angelo Parisi (FRA)	András Ozsvar (HUN)
		Arthur Mapp (GBR)
1984 Yasuhiro Yamashita (JPN)	Mohamed Rashwan (EGY)	Mihai Cioc (ROM)
		Arthur Schnabel (FRG)

1968, 1988–92 *Event not held*

Previous Winners
Categories changed in 1980

Over 93kg

1964 Isao Inokuma (JPN)	A. Douglas Rogers (CAN)	Parnaoz Chikviladze (URS)
		Anzor Kiknadze (URS)
1972 Willem Ruska (NED)	Klaus Glahn (FRG)	Givi Onashvili (URS)
		Motoki Nishimura (JPN)
1976 Sergei Novrikov (URS)	Gunther Neureuther (FRG)	Sumio Endo (JPN)
		Allen Coage (USA)

1968 *Event not held*

80kg to 93kg

1972 Shoto Chochoshvili (URS)	David Starbrook (GBR)	Chiaki Ishii (BRA)
		Paul Barth (FRG)
1976 Kazuhiro Ninomiya (JPN)	Ramaz Harshiladze (URS)	David Starbrook (GBR)
		Jürg Röthlisberger (SUI)

1964–68 *Event not held*

70kg to 80kg

1964 Isao Okano (JPN)	Wolfgang Hofmann (GER)	James Bergman (USA)
		Eui Tae Kim (KOR)
1972 Shinobu Sekine (JPN)	Oh Seung-lip (KOR)	Brian Jacks (GBR)
		Jean-Paul Coche (FRA)
1976 Isamu Sonoda (JPN)	Valeri Dvoinikov (URS)	Slavko Obadov (URS)
		Park Youngchul (KOR)

1968 *Event not held*

63kg to 70kg

1972 Toyojazu Nomura (JPN)	Anton Zajkowski (POL)	Dietmar Hötger (GDR)
		Anatoli Novikov (URS)
1976 Vladimir Nevzorov (URS)	Koji Kuramoto (JPN)	Partrick Vial (FRA)
		Marian Talaj (POL)

1964–68 *Event not held*

Up to 63kg

1964 Takehide Nakatani (JPN)	Eric Hänni (SUI)	Oleg Stepanov (URS)
		Aron Bogulubov (URS)
1972 Takao Kawaguchi (JPN)	– 1	Kim Yong Ik (PRK)
		Jean Jacques Mounier (FRA)
1976 Hector Rodriguez (CUB)	Chang Eun-kyung (KOR)	Felice Mariani (ITA)
		Jozsef Tuncsik (HUN)

1968 *Event not held*

1 Bakhaavaa Buidaa (MGL) disqualified after positive drug test

Women

Up to 48kg

1992 Cecile Nowak (FRA)	Ryoko Tamura (JPN)	Hulya Senyurt (TUR)
		Amarilis Savon (CUB)
1996 Kye Sun (PRK)	Ryoko Tamura (JPN)	Amarilis Savon (CUB)
		Yolanda Soler (ESP)

1964–88 *Event not held*

Up to 52kg

1992 Almudena Munoz (ESP)	Noriko Mizuguchi (JPN)	Li Zhongyun (CHN)
		Sharon Rendle (GBR)
1996 Marie-Claire Restoux (FRA)	Hyun Sook-hee (KOR)	Legna Verdecia (CUB)
		Noriko Sugawara (JPN)

1964–88 *Event not held*

Up to 56kg

1992 Miriam Blasco (ESP)	Nicola Fairbrother (GBR)	Chiyori Tateno (JPN)
		Driulis Gonzalez (CUB)
1996 Driulis Gonzalez (CUB)	Jung Sae-yong (KOR)	Isabel Fernandez (ESP)
		Liu Chuang (CHN)
1964–88 *Event not held*		

Up to 61kg

1992 Catherine Fleury (FRA)	Yael Arad (ISR)	Zhang Di (CHN)
		Yelena Petrova (EUN)
1996 Yuko Emoto (JPN)	Gella Van De Caveye (BEL)	Jenny Gal (NED)
		Jung Sung-sook (KOR)
1964–88 *Event not held*		

Up to 66kg

1992 Odalis Reve (CUB)	Emanuela Pierantozzi (ITA)	Kate Howey (GBR)
		Heidi Rakels (BEL)
1996 Cho Min-sun (KOR)	Aneta Szczepanska (POL)	Claudia Zwiers (NED)
		Xianbo Wang (CHN)
1964–88 *Event not held*		

Up to 72kg

1992 Kim Mi-jung (KOR)	Yoko Tanabe (JPN)	Laetitia Meignan (FRA)
		Irene de Kok (NED)
1996 Ulla Werbrouck (HUN)	Yoko Tanabe (JPN)	Ylenia Scapin (ITA)
		Diadenis Luna (CUB)
1964–88 *Event not held*		

Over 72kg

1992 Zhuang Xiaoyan (CHN)	Estela Rodriguez (CUB)	Yoko Sakuae (JPN)
		Natalia Lupino (FRA)
1996 Sun Fu-Ming (CHN)	Estela Rodriguez (CUB)	Johanna Hagn (GER)
		Christine Cicot (FRA)
1964–88 *Event not held*		

Modern Pentathlon Medals

GOLD	SILVER	BRONZE
Individual		
1912 Gösta Lilliehöök (SWE) 27pts	Gösta Asbrink (SWE) 28	Georg de Laval (SWE) 30
1920 Gustaf Dyrssen (SWE) 18pts	Erik de Laval (SWE) 23	Gösta Rüno (SWE) 27
1924 Bo Lindman (SWE) 18pts	Gustaf Dyrssen (SWE) 39.5	Bertil Uggla (SWE) 45
1928 Sven Thofelt (SWE) 47pts	Bo Lindman (SWE) 50	Helmuth Kahl (GER) 52
1932 Johan Gabriel Oxenstierna (SWE) 32pts	Bo Lindman (SWE) 35.5	Richard Mayo (USA) 38.5
1936 Gotthard Handrick (SWE) 31.5pts	Charles Leonard (USA) 39.5	Silvano Abba (ITA) 45.5
1948 Willie Grut (SWE) 16pts	George Moore (USA) 47	Gösta Gärdin (SWE) 49
1952 Lars Hall (SWE) 32pts	Gábor Benedek (HUN) 39	István Szondi (HUN) 41
1956 Lars Hall (SWE) 4843pts	Olavi Nannonen (FIN) 4774.5	Väinö Korhonen (FIN) 4750
1960 Ferenc Németh (HUN) 5024pts	Imre Nagy (HUN) 4988	Robert Beck (USA) 4981
1964 Ferenc Török (HUN) 5116pts	Igor Novikov (URS) 5067	Albert Mokeyev (URS) 5039
1968 Björn Ferm (SWE) 4964pts	András Balczó (HUN) 4953	Pavel Lednev (URS) 4795
1972 András Balczó (HUN) 5412pts	Boris Onischenko (URS) 5335	Pavel Lednev (URS) 5328
1976 Janusz Pyciak-Peciak (POL) 5520pts	Pavel Lednev (URS) 5485	Jan Bartu (TCH) 5466
1980 Anatoli Starostin (URS) 5568pts	Tamás Szombathelyi (HUN) 5502	Pavel Lednev (URS) 5282
1984 Daniel Massala (ITA) 5469pts	Svante Rasmuson (SWE) 5456	Carlo Massullo (ITA) 5406
1988 János Martinek (HUN) 5404pts	Carlo Massullo (ITA) 5379	Vakhtang Yagorachvili (URS) 5367
1992 Arkadiusz Skrzypaszek (POL) 5559pts	Attila Mizsér (HUN) 5446	Edouard Zenovka (EUN) 5361

1996 Alexander Parygin (KZK) 5551pts	Eduard Zenovka (RUS) 5530	János Martinek (HUN) 5501

1896–1908 *Event not held*

Team

1952 Hungary 116pts	Sweden 182	Finland 213
1956 Soviet Union 13 690.5pts	United States 13 482	Finland 13 185.5
1960 Hungary 14 863pts	Soviet Union 14 309	United States 14 192
1964 Soviet Union 14 961pts	United States 14 189	Hungary 14 173
1968 Hungary 14 325pts	Soviet Union 14 248	France 13 289 [1]
1972 Soviet Union 15 968pts	Hungary 15 348	Finland 14 812
1976 Great Britain 15 559pts	Czechoslovakia 15 451	Hungary 15 395
1980 Soviet Union 16 126pts	Hungary 15 912	Sweden 15 845
1984 Italy 16 060pts	United States 15 568	France 15 565
1988 Hungary 15 886pts	Italy 15 571	Great Britain 15 276
1992 Poland 16 018pts	Unified Team 15 924	Italy 15 760

1896–1948, 1996 *Event not held*

[1] Sweden finished third in 1968 but were disqualified when a drug test indicated that a member of the team had an excessive level of alcohol

Rowing Medals

GOLD	SILVER	BRONZE

Men

Single Sculls

GOLD	SILVER	BRONZE
1900 Henri Barrelet (FRA) 7:35.6	André Gaudin (FRA) 7:41.6	St George Ashe (GBR) 8:15.6
1904 Frank Greer (USA) 10:08.5	James Juvenal (USA) 2 lengths	Constance Titus (USA) 1 length − 1
1906 Gaston Delaplane (FRA) 5:53.4	Joseph Larran (FRA) 6:07.2	
1908 Harry Blackstaffe (GBR) 9:26.0	Alexander McCulloch (GBR) 1 length	Bernhard von Gaza (GER) d.n.a. Károly Levitsky (HUN) d.n.a.
1912 William Kinnear (GBR) 7:47.6	Polydore Veirman (BEL) 1 length	Everard Butter (CAN) d.n.a. Mikhail Kusik (RUS) d.n.a.
1920 John Kelly (USA) 7:35.0	Jack Beresford (GBR) 7:36.0	Clarence Hadfield d'Arcy (NZL) 7:48.0
1924 Jack Beresford (GBR) 7:49.2	William Garrett-Gilmore (USA) 7:54.0	Josef Schneider (SUI) 8:01.1
1928 Henry Pearce (AUS) 7:11.0	Kenneth Myers (USA) 7:20.8	David Collett (GBR) 7:19.8
1932 Henry Pearce (AUS) 7:44.4	William Miller (USA) 7:45.2	Guillermo Douglas (URU) 8:13.6
1936 Gustav Schäfer (GER) 8:21.5	Josef Hasenöhri (AUT) 8:25.8	Daniel Barrow (USA) 8:28.0
1948 Mervyn Wood (AUS) 7:24.4	Eduardo Risso (URU) 7:38.2	Romolo Catasta (ITA) 7:51.4
1952 Yuri Tyukalov (URS) 8:12.8	Mervyn Wood (AUS) 8:14.5	Teodor Kocerka (POL) 8:19.4
1956 Vyacheslav Ivanov (URS) 8:02.5	Stuart Mackenzie (AUS) 8:07.0	John Kelly (USA) 8:11.8
1960 Vyacheslav Ivanov (URS) 7:13.96	Achim Hill (GER) 7:20.21	Teodor Kocerka (POL) 7:21.26
1964 Vyacheslav Ivanov (URS) 8:22.51	Achim Hill (GER) 8:26.34	Gottfried Kottmann (SUI) 8:29.68
1968 Henri Jan Wienese (NED) 7:47.80	Jochen Meissner (FRG) 7:52.00	Alberto Demiddi (ARG) 7:57.19
1972 Yuri Malishev (URS) 7:10.12	Alberto Demiddi (ARG) 7:11.53	Wolfgang Gueldenpfennig (GDR) 7:14.45
1976 Pertti Karpinnen (FIN) 7:29.03	Peter Kolbe (FRG) 7:31.67	Joachim Dreifke (GDR) 7:38.03
1980 Pertti Karpinnen (FIN) 7:09.61	Vasili Yakusha (URS) 7:11.66	Peter Kersten (GDR) 7:14.88
1984 Pertti Karpinnen (FIN) 7:00.24	Peter Kolbe (FRG) 7:02.19	Robert Mills (CAN) 7:10.38
1988 Thomas Lange (GDR) 6:49.86	Peter Kolbe (FRG) 6:54.77	Eric Verdonk (NZL) 6:58.86
1992 Thomas Lange (GER) 6:51.40	Vaclav Chalupa (CZE) 6:52.93	Kajetan Broniewski (POL) 6:56.82
1996 Xeno Mueller (SUI) 6:44.85	Derek Porter (CAN) 6:47.45	Thomas Lange (GER) 6:47.72

1896 *Event not held*

[1] Only two competitors

Double Sculls

GOLD	SILVER	BRONZE
1904 United States 10:03.2	United States d.n.a.	United States d.n.a.
1920 United States 7:09.0	Italy 7:19.0	France 7:21.0

1924	United States 7:45.0	France 7:54.8	Switzerland d.n.a.
1928	United States 6:41.4	Canada 6:51.0	Austria 6:48.8
1932	United States 7:17.4	Germany 7:22.8	Canada 7:27.6
1936	Great Britain 7:20.8	Germany 7:26.2	Poland 7:36.2
1948	Great Britain 6:51.3	Denmark 6:55.3	Uruguay 7:12.4
1952	Argentina 7:32.2	Soviet Union 7:38.3	Uruguay 7:43.7
1956	Soviet Union 7:10.66	United States 7:13.16	Australia 7:37.4
1960	Czechoslovakia 6:47.50	Soviet Union 6:50.49	Switzerland 6:50.59
1964	Soviet Union 7:10.66	United States 7:13.16	Czechoslovakia 7:14.23
1968	Soviet Union 6:51.82	The Netherlands 6:52.80	United States 6:54.21
1972	Soviet Union 7:01.77	Norway 7:02.58	East Germany 7:05.55
1976	Norway 7:13.20	Great Britain 7:15.26	East Germany 7:17.45
1980	East Germany 6:24.33	Yugoslavia 6:26.34	Czechoslovakia 6:29.07
1984	United States 6:36.87	Belgium 6:38.19	Yugoslavia 6:39.59
1988	The Netherlands 6:21.13	Switzerland 6:22.59	Soviet Union 6:22.87
1992	Australia 6:17.32	Austria 6:18.42	The Netherlands 6:22.82
1996	Italy 6:16.98	Norway 6:18.42	France 6:19.85

1896–1900, 1906–12 *Event not held*

Coxless Quadruple Sculls

1976	East Germany 6:18.65	Soviet Union 6:19.89	Czechoslovakia 6:21.77
1980	East Germany 5:49.81	Soviet Union 5:51.47	Bulgaria 5:52.38
1984	West Germany 5:57.55	Australia 5:57.98	Canada 5:59.07
1988	Italy 5:53.37	Norway 5:55.08	East Germany 5:56.13
1992	Germany 5:45.17	Norway 5:47.09	Italy 5:47.33
1996	Germany 5:56.93	United States 5:59.10	Australia 6:01.65

1896–1972 *Event not held*

Coxless Pairs

1904	United States 10:57.0	United States d.n.a.	United States d.n.a.
1908	Great Britain 9:43.0	Great Britain 2.5 lengths	Canada
			Germany
1924	The Netherlands 8:19.4	France 8:21.6	–
1928	Germany 7:06.4	Great Britain 7:08.08	United States 7:20.4
1932	Great Britain 8:00.0	New Zealand 8:02.4	Poland 8:08.2
1936	Germany 8:16.1	Denmark 8:19.2	Argentina 8:23.0
1948	Great Britain 7:21.11	Switzerland 7:23.9	Italy 7:31.5
1952	United States 8:20.7	Belgium 8:23.5	Switzerland 8:32.7
1956	United States 7:55.4	Soviet Union 8:03.9	Austria 8:11.8
1960	Soviet Union 7:02.01	Austria 7:03.69	Finland 7:03.80
1964	Canada 7:32.94	The Netherlands 7:33.40	Germany 7:38.63
1968	East Germany 7:26.56	United States 7:26.71	Denmark 7:31.84
1972	East Germany 6:53.16	Switzerland 6:57.06	The Netherlands 6:58.70
1976	East Germany 7:23.31	United States 7:26.73	West Germany 7:30.03
1980	East Germany 6:48.01	Soviet Union 6:50.50	Great Britain 6:51.47
1984	Romania 6:45.39	Spain 6:48.47	Norway 6:51.81
1988	Great Britain 6:36.84	Romania 6:38.06	Yugoslavia 6:41.01
1992	Great Britain 6:27.72	Germany 6:32.68	Slovenia 6:33.43
1996	Great Britain 6:20.09	Australia 6:21.02	France 6:22.15

1896–1906, 1912–20 *Event not held*

Coxed Pairs

1900	The Netherlands 7:34.2	France I 7:34.4	France II 7:57.2
1906[1]	Italy I 4:23.0	Italy II 4:30.0	France d.n.a.
1906[2]	Italy 7:32.4	Belgium 8:03.0 [3]	France 8:08.6
1920	Italy 7:56.0	France 7:57.0	Switzerland d.n.a.
1924	Switzerland 8:39.0	Italy 8:39.1	United States 3m
1928	Switzerland 7:42.6	France 7:48.4	Belgium 7:59.4
1932	United States 8:25.8	Poland 8:31.2	France 8:41.2
1936	Germany 8:36.9	Italy 8:49.7	France 8:54.0

1948 Denmark 8:00.5	Italy 8:12.2	Hungary 8:25.2
1952 France 8:28.6	Germany 8:32.1	Denmark 8:34.9
1956 United States 8:26.1	Germany 8:29.2	Soviet Union 8:31.0
1960 Germany 7:29.14	Soviet Union 7:30.17	United States 7:34.58
1964 United States 8:21.23	France 8:23.15	The Netherlands 8:23.42
1968 Italy 8:04.81	The Netherlands 8:06.80	Denmark 8:08.07
1972 East Germany 7:17.25	Czechoslovakia 7:19.57	Romania 7:21.36
1976 East Germany 7:58.99	Soviet Union 8:01.82	Czecholslovakia 8:03.28
1980 East Germany 7:02.54	Soviet Union 7:03.35	Yugoslavia 7:04.92
1984 Italy 7:05.99	Romania 7:11.21	United States 7:12.81
1988 Italy 6:58.79	East Germany 7.00.63	Great Britain 7:01.95
1992 Great Britain 6:49.83	Italy 6:50.98	Romania 6:51.58

1896, 1904, 1908–12 and 1996 *Event not held*

[1] Over 1000m
[2] Over 1600m
[3] Greek cox

Coxless Fours

1904 United States 9:05.8	United States d.n.a.	United States d.n.a.
1908 Great Britain 8:34.0	Great Britain 1.5 lengths	The Netherlands
		Canada
1924 Great Britain 7:08.6	Canada 7:18.0	Switzerland 2 lengths
1928 Great Britain 6:36.0	United States 6:37.0	Italy 6:31.6
1932 Great Britain 6:58.2	Germany 7:03.0	Italy 7:04.0
1936 Germany 7:01.8	Great Britain 7:06.5	Switzerland 7:10.6
1948 Italy 6:39.0	Denmark 6:43.5	United States 6:47.7
1952 Yugoslavia 7:16.0	France 7:18.4	Finland 7:23.3
1956 Canada 7:08.8	United States 7:18.4	France 7:20.9
1960 United States 6:26.26	Italy 6:28.78	Soviet Union 6:29.62
1964 Denmark 6:59.30	Great Britain 7:00.47	United States 7:01.37
1968 East Germany 6:39.18	Hungary 6:41.64	Italy 6:44.01
1972 East Germany 6:24.27	New Zealand 6:25.64	West Germany 6:28.41
1976 East Germany 6:37.42	Norway 6:41.22	Soviet Union 6:42.52
1980 East Germany 6:08.17	Soviet Union 6:11.81	Great Britain 6:16.58
1984 New Zealand 6:03.48	United States 6:06.10	Denmark 6:07.72
1988 East Germany 6:03.11	United States 6:05.53	West Germany 6:06.22
1992 Australia 5:55.04	United States 5:56.68	Slovenia 5:58.24
1996 Australia 6:06.37	France 6:07.03	Great Britain 6:07.78

1896–1900, 1906, 1912–20 *Event not held*

Coxed Fours

1900[1] Germany 5:59.0	The Netherlands 6:33.0	Germany 6:35.0
1900[1] France 7:11.0	France 7:18.0	Germany 7:18.2
1906 Italy 8:13.0	France d.n.a.	France d.n.a
1912 Germany 6:59.4	Great Britain 2 lengths	Norway d.n.a.
		Denmark d.n.a.
1920 Switzerland 6:54.0	United States 6:58.0	Norway 7:02.0
1924 Switzerland 7:18.4	France 7:21.6	United States 1 length
1928 Italy 6:47.8	Switzerland 7:03.4	Poland 7.12.8
1932 Germany 7:19.0	Italy 7:19.2	Poland 7:26.8
1936 Germany 7:16.2	Switzerland 7:24.3	France 7:33.3
1948 United States 6:50.3	Switzerland 6:53.3	Denmark 6:58.6
1952 Czechoslovakia 7:33.4	Switzerland 7:36.5	United States 7:37.0
1956 Italy 7:19.4	Sweden 7:22.4	Finland 7:30.9
1960 Germany 6:39.12	France 6:41.62	Italy 6:43.72
1964 Germany 7:00.44	Italy 7:02.84	The Netherlands 7:06.46
1968 New Zealand 6:45.62	East Germany 6:48.20	Switzerland 6:49.04
1972 West Germany 6:31.85	East Germany 6:33.30	Czechoslovakia 6:35.64
1976 Soviet Union 6:40.22	East Germany 6:42.70	West Germany 6:46.96
1980 East Germany 6:14.51	Soviet Union 6:19.05	Poland 6:22.52
1984 Great Britain 6:18.64	United States 6:20.28	New Zealand 6:23.68

1988 East Germany 6:10.74	Romania 6:13.58	New Zealand 6:15.78
1992 Romania 5:59.37	Germany 6:00.34	Poland 6:03.27

1896, 1904–08, 1996 *Event not held*

[1] Two separate finals were held in 1900

Eights

1900 United States 6:09.8	Belgium 6:13.8	The Netherlands 6:23.0
1904 United States 7:50.0	Canada d.n.a.	–
1908 Great Britain 7:52.0	Belgium 2 lengths	Great Britain
		Canada
1912 Great Britain 6:15.0	Great Britain 6:19.0	Germany d.n.a.
1920 United States 6:02.6	Great Britain 6:05.0	Norway 6:36.0
1924 United States 6:33.4	Canada 6:49.0	Italy 0.75 length
1928 United States 6:03.2	Great Britain 6:05.6	Canada —
1932 United States 6:37.6	Italy 6:37.8	Canada 6:40.4
1936 United States 6:25.4	Italy 6:26.0	Germany 6:26.4
1948 United States 5:56.7	Great Britain 6:06.9	Norway 6:10.3
1952 United States 6:25.9	Soviet Union 6:31.2	Australia 6:33.1
1956 United States 6:35.2	Canada 6:37.1	Australia 6:39.2
1960 Germany 5:57.18	Canada 6:01.52	Czechoslovakia 6:04.84
1964 United States 6:18.23	Germany 6:23.9	Czechoslovakia 6:25.11
1968 West Germany 6:07.00	Australia 6:07.98	Soviet Union 6:09.11
1972 New Zealand 6:08.94	United States 6:11.61	East Germany 6:11.67
1976 East Germany 5:58.29	Great Britain 6:00.82	New Zealand 6:03.51
1980 East Germany 5:49.05	Great Britain 5:51.92	Soviet Union 5:52.66
1984 Canada 5:41.32	United States 5:41.74	Australia 5:42.40
1988 West Germany 5:46.05	Soviet Union 5:48.01	United States 5:48.26
1992 Canada 5:29.53	Romania 5:29.67	Germany 5:31.00
1996 The Netherlands 5:42.74	Germany 5:44.58	Russia 5:45.77

1896, 1906 *Event not held*

Lightweight — Double Sculls

1996 Switzerland 6:23.27	The Netherlands 6:26.48	Australia 6:26.69

1896–1992 *Event not held*

Lightweight — Coxless Fours

1996 Denmark 6:09.58	Canada 6:10.13	United States 6:12.29

1896–1992 Event not held

Women's

Women's rowing was introduced in 1976 over a course of 1000 metres. From 1988 it was over 2000m

Singles Sculls

1976 Christine Scheiblich (GDR) 4:05.56	Joan Lind (USA) 4:06.21	Yelena Antonova (URS) 4:10.24
1980 Sandra Toma (ROM) 3:40.69	Antonina Makhina (URS) 3:41.65	Martina Schröter (GDR) 3:43.54
1984 Valeria Racila (ROM) 3:40.68	Charlotte Geer (USA) 3:43.89	Ann Haesebrouck (BEL) 3:45.72
1988 Jutta Behrednt (GDR) 7:47.19	Anne Marden (USA) 7:50.28	Magdalene Gueorguivea (BUL) 7:53.65
1992 Elisabeta Lipa (ROM) 7:25.54	Annelies Bredael (BEL) 7:26.64	Silken Laumann (CAN) 7:28.85
1996 Yekaterina Khodotovich (BLR) 7:32.21	Silken Laumann (CAN) 7:35.15	Trine Hansen (DEN) 7:37.20

Double Sculls

1976 Bulgaria 3:44.36	East Germany 3:47.86	Soviet Union 3:49.93
1980 Soviet Union 3:16.27	East Germany 3:17.63	Romania 3:18.91

1984 Romania 3:26.75	The Netherlands 3:29.13	Canada 3:29.82
1988 East Germany 7:00.48	Romania 7:04.36	Bulgaria 7:06.03
1992 Germany 6:49.00	Romania 6:51.47	China 6:55.16
1996 Canada 6:56.84	China 6:58.35	The Netherlands 6:58.72

Coxed Quadruple Sculls

1976 East Germany 3:29.99	Soviet Union 3:32.49	Romania 3:32.76
1980 East Germany 3:15.32	Soviet Union 3:15.73	Bulgaria 3:16.10
1984 Romania 3:14.11	United States 3:15.57	Denmark 3:16.02
1988[1] East Germany 6:21.06	Soviet Union 6:23.47	Romania 6:23.81
1992 Germany 6:20.18	Romania 6:24.34	Unified Team 6:25.07
1996 Germany 6:27.44	Ukraine 6:30.36	Canada 6:30.38

[1] Not coxed.

Coxless Pairs

1976 Bulgaria 4:01.22	East Germany 4:01.64	West Germany 4:02.35
1980 East Germany 3:30.49	Poland 3:30.95	Bulgaria 3:32.39
1984 Romania 3:32.60	Canada 3:36.06	West Germany 3:40.50
1988 Romania 7:28.13	Bulgaria 7:31.95	New Zealand 7:35.68
1992 Canada 7:06.22	Germany 7:07.96	United States 7:08.11
1996 Australia 7:01.39	United States 7:01.78	France 7:03.82

Coxed Fours

1976 East Germany 3:45.08	Bulgaria 3:38.24	Soviet Union 3:49.38
1980 East Germany 3:19.27	Bulgaria 3:20.75	Soviet Union 3:20.92
1984 Romania 3:19.30	Canada 3:21.55	Australia 3:23.29
1988 East Germany 6:56.00	China 6:58.78	Romania 7:01.13

1992–96 *Event not held*

Coxless Fours

1992 Canada 6:30.85	United States 6:31.86	Germany 6:32.34

1976–88, 1996 *Event not held*

Eights

1976 East Germany 3:33.32	Soviet Union 3:36.17	United States 3:38.68
1980 East Germany 3:03.32	Soviet Union 3:04.29	Romania 3:05.63
1984 United States 2:59.80	Romania 3:00.87	The Netherlands 3:02.92
1988 East Germany 6:15.17	Romania 6:17.44	China 6:21.83
1992 Canada 6:02.62	Romania 6:06.26	Germany 6:07.80
1996 Romania 6:19.73	Canada 6:24.05	Belarus 6:24.44

Lightweight-Double Sculls

1996 Romania 7:12.78	United States 7:14.65	Australia 7:16.56

1976–92 *Event not held*

Discontinued Events

GOLD	SILVER	BRONZE

Naval Rowing Boats (200m)

1906 Italy 10:45.0	Greece d.n.a.	Greece d.n.a.

Coxed 16-Man Naval Rowing Boats (3000m)

1906 Greece 16:35.0	Greece 17:09.5	Italy d.n.a.

Coxed Fours (Inriggers)

1912 Denmark 7:47.0	Sweden 1 length	Norway d.n.a.

Shooting Medals

GOLD	SILVER	BRONZE

Men

Free Pistol (50 metres)

GOLD	SILVER	BRONZE
1896 Sumner Paine (USA) 442pts	Holger Nielsen (DEN) 280	Nikolaos Morakis (GRE) d.n.a.
1900 Karl Röderer (SUI) 503pts	Achille Paroche (FRA) 466	Konrad Stäheli (SUI) 453
1906 Georgios Orphanidis (GRE) 221pts	Jean Fouconnier (FRA) 219	Aristides Rangavis (GRE) 218
1912 Alfred Lane (USA) 499pts	Peter Dolfen (USA) 474	Charles Stewart (GBR) 470
1920 Karl Frederick (USA) 496pts	Afranio da Costa (BRA) 489	Alfred Lane (USA) 481
1936 Torsten Ullmann (SWE) 559pts	Erich Krempel (GER) 544	Charles des Jammonières (FRA) 540
1948 Edwin Vazquez Cam (PER) 545pts	Rudolf Schnyder (SUI) 539	Torsten Ullmann (SWE) 539
1952 Huelet Benner (USA) 553pts	Angel Léon de Gozalo (ESP) 550	Ambrus Balogh (HUN) 549
1956 Pentti Linnosvuo (FIN) 556pts	Makhmud Oumarov (URS) 556	Offutt Pinion (USA) 551
1960 Alexei Gushkin (URS) 560pts	Makhmud Oumarov (URS) 552	Yoshihisa Yoshikawa (JPN) 552
1964 Väinö Markkanen (FIN) 560pts	Franklin Green (USA) 557	Yoshihisa Yoshikawa (JPN) 554
1968 Grigori Kossykh (URS) 562pts	Heinz Mertel (FRG) 562	Harald Vollmar (GDR) 560
1972 Ragnar Skanåkar (SWE) 567pts	Dan Iuga (ROM) 562	Rudolf Dollinger (AUT) 560
1976 Uwe Potteck (GDR) 573pts	Harald Vollmar (GDR) 567	Rudolf Dollinger (AUT) 560
1980 Alexander Melentyev (URS) 581pts	Harald Vollmar (GDR) 568	Lubcho Diakov (BUL) 565
1984 Xu Haifeng (CHN) 566pts	Ragnar Skanåker (SWE) 565	Wang Yifu (CHN) 564
1988 Sorin Babii (ROM) (566+94) 660pts	Ragnar Skanåker (SWE) (564+93) 657	Igor Bassinki (URS) (570+87) 657
1992 Konstantin Loukachik (EUN) 658pts	Wang Yifu (CHN) 657	Ragnar Skanåker (SWE) 657
1996 Boris Kokoryev (RUS) 666.4pts	Igor Bassinki (BLR) 692.1	Roberto Di Donna (ITA) 661.8

1904, 1908, 1924–32 *Event not held*

Rapid-Fire Pistol

GOLD	SILVER	BRONZE
1896 Jean Phrangoudis (GRE) 344pts	Georgios Orphanidis (GRE) 249	Holger Nielsen (DEN) d.n.a.
1900 Maurice Larrouy (FRA) 58pts	Léon Moreaux (FRA) 57	Eugene Balme (FRA) 57
1906 Maurice Lecoq (FRA) 250pts	Léon Moreaux (FRA) 149	Aristides Rangavis (GRE) 245
1908 Paul van Asbroeck (BEL) 490pts	Réginald Storms (BEL) 487	James Gorman (USA) 485
1912 Alfred Lane (USA) 287pts	Paul Palén (SWE) 286	Johan von Holst (SWE) 283
1920 Guilherme Paraense (BRA) 274pts	Raymond Bracken (USA) 272	Fritz Zulauf (SUI) 269
1924 Paul Bailey (USA) 18pts	Vilhelm Carlberg (SWE) 18	Lennart Hannelius (FIN) 18
1932 Renzo Morigi (ITA) 36pts	Heinz Hax (GER) 36	Domenico Matteucci (ITA) 36
1936 Cornelius van Oyen (GER) 36pts	Heniz Hax (GER) 35	Torsten Ullmann (SWE) 34
1948 Károly Takács (HUN) 580pts	Carlos Diaz Sáenz Valiente (ARG) 571	Sven Lundqvuist (SWE) 569
1952 Károly Takács (HUN) 579pts	Szilárd Kun (HUN) 578	Gheorghe Lichiardopol (ROM) 578
1956 Stefan Petrescu (ROM) 587pts	Evgeni Shcherkasov (URS) 585	Gheorghe Lichiardopol (ROM) 581
1960 William McMillan (USA) 587pts	Penttii Linnosvuo (FIN) 587	Alexander Zabelin (URS) 587
1964 Penttii Linnosvuo (FIN) 592pts	Ion Tripsa (ROM) 591	Lubomir Nacovsky (TCH) 590
1968 Jozef Zapedzki (POL) 593pts	Marcel Rosca (ROM) 591	Renart Suleimanov (URS) 591
1972 Jozef Zapedzki (POL) 593pts	Ladislav Faita (TCH) 594	Victor Torshin (URS) 593
1976 Norbert Klaar (GDR) 597pts	Jürgen Wiefel (GDR) 596	Roberto Ferraris (ITA) 595
1980 Corneliu Ion (ROM) 596pts	Jürgen Wiefel (GDR) 596	Gerhard Petrisch (AUT) 596
1984 Takeo Kamachi (JPN) 595pts	Corneliu Ion (ROM) 593	Rauno Bies (FIN) 591
1988 Afanasi Kouzmine (URS) (598+100) 698pts	Ralf Schumann (GDR) (597+99) 696	Zoltán Kovács (HUN) (594+99) 693
1992 Ralf Schumann (GER) 885pts	Afanasijs Kuzmins (LAT) 882	Vladimir Vokhmyanin (EUN) 882
1996 Ralf Schumann (GER) 698.0pts	Emil Milev (BUL) 692.1	Vladimir Vokhmyanin (KZK) 691.5

1904 and 1928 *Event not held*

Small-Bore Rifle — (Prone) [1]

1908	Arthur Carnell (GBR) 387pts	Harry Humby (GBR) 386	George Barnes (GBR) 385
1912	Frederick Hird (USA) 194pts	William Milne (GBR) 193	Harry Burt (GBR) 192
1920	Lawrence Nuesslein (USA) 391pts	Arthur Rothrock (USA) 386	Dennis Fenton (USA) 385
1924	Pierre Coquelin de Lisle (FRA) 398pts	Marcus Dinwiddie (USA) 396	Josias Hartmann (SUI) 394
1932	Bertil Rönnmark (SWE) 294pts	Gustavo Huet (MEX) 294	Zoltán Hradetsky-Soos (HUN) 293
1936	Willy Rögeberg (NOR) 300pts	Ralph Berzsenyi (HUN) 296	Wladyslaw Karás (POL) 296
1948	Arthur Cook (USA) 599pts	Walter Tomsen (USA) 599	Jonas Jonsson (SWE) 597
1952	Josif Sarbu (ROM) 400pts	Boris Andreyev (URS) 400	Arthur Jackson (USA) 399
1956	Gerald Ouellette (CAN) 600pts [2]	Vasili Borrisov (URS) 599	Gilmour Boa (CAN) 598
1960	Peter Kohnke (GER) 590pts	James Hill (USA) 589	Enrico Pelliccione (VEN) 587
1964	László Hammerl (HUN) 597pts	Lonas Wigger (USA) 597	Tommy Pool (USA) 596
1968	Jan Kurka (TCH) 598pts	László Hammerl (HUN) 598	Ian Ballinger (NZL) 597
1972	Li Ho Jun (PRK) 599pts	Victor Auer (USA) 598	Nicolae Rotaru (ROM) 595
1976	Karlheinz Smieszek (FRG) 599pts	Ulrich Lind (FRG) 597	Gennadi Luschikov (URS) 595
1980	Karoly Varga (HUN) 599pts	Hellfried Helifort (GDR) 599	Petar Zapianov (BUL) 598
1984	Edward Etzel (USA) 599pts	Michel Bury (FRA) 596	Michael Sullivan (GBR) 596
1988	Miroslav Varga (TCH) (600+103.9) 703.9pts	Cha Young-chul (KOR) (598+104.8) 702.8	Attila Zahonyi (HUN) (597+104.9) 701.9
1992	Lee Eun-chul (KOR) 702.5pts	Harlad Stenvaag (NOR) 701.4	Stefan Pletikosic (IOP) 701.1
1996	Christian Klees (GER) 704.8pts	Sergei Belyayev (KZK) 703.3	Jozef Gobci (SLO) 701.9

1896–1904, 1928 *Event not held*

[1] In 1908 and 1912 any position allowed; in 1920 it was a standing position
[2] Range found to be marginally short — record not allowed

Small-Bore Rifle — Three Positions (Prone, Kneeling, Standing)

1952	Erling Kongshaug (NOR) 1164pts	Viho Ylönen (FIN) 1164	Boris Andreyev (URS) 1163
1956	Anatoli Bogdanov (URS) 1172pts	Otakar Horinek (TCH) 1172	Nils Sundberg (SWE) 1167
1960	Viktor Shamburkin (URS) 1149pts	Marat Niyasov (URS) 1145	Klaus Zähringer (GER) 1139
1964	Lones Wigger (USA) 1164pts	Velitchko Khristov (BUL) 1152	László Hammerl (HUN) 1151
1968	Bernd Klingner (FRG) 1157pts	John Writer (USA) 1156	Vitali Parkhimovich (URS) 1154
1972	John Writer (USA) 1166pts	Lanny Bassham (USA) 1157	Werner Lippoldt (GDR) 1153
1976	Lanny Bassham (USA) 1162pts	Margaret Murdock (USA) 1162	Werner Seibold (FRG) 1160
1980	Viktor Vlasov (URS) 1173pts	Bernd Hartstein (GDR) 1166	Sven Johansson (SWE) 1185
1984	Malcolm Cooper (GBR) 1173pts	Daniel Kipkow (SUI) 1163	Alister Allan (GBR) 1162
1988	Malcolm Cooper (GBR) (1180+99.3) 1279.3pts	Alister Allan (GBR) (1181+94.6) 1275.6	Kirill Ivanov (URS) (1173+102.0) 1275.0
1992	Gratchia Petikiane (EUN) 1267.4pts	Robert Foth (USA) 1266.6	Ryohei Koba (JPN) 1265.9
1996	Jean-Pierre Amat (FRA) 1273.9pts	Sergei Belyayev (KZK) 1272.3	Wolfram Waibel (AUT) 1269.6

1896–1948 *Event not held*

Running Game Target

1900	Louis Debray (FRA) 20pts	Pierre Nivet (FRA) 20	Comte de Lambert (FRA) 19
1972	Lakov Zhelezniak (URS) 569pts	Hanspeter Bellingrodt (COL) 565	John Kynoch (GBR) 562
1976	Alexander Gazov (URS) 579pts	Alexander Kedyarov (URS) 576	Jerzy Greszkiewicz (POL) 571
1980	Igor Sokolov (URS) 589pts	Thomas Pfeffer (GDR) 589	Alexander Gasov (URS) 587
1984	Li Yuwei (CHN) 587pts	Helmut Bellingrodt (COL) 584	Shiping Huang (CHN) 581
1988	Tor Heiestad (NOR) (591+98) 689pts	Hunag Shiping (CHN) (589+98) 687	Gennadi Avramenko (URS) (591+95) 686

1896, 1904–68, 1992–96 *Event not held*

10m Running Target

1992	Michael Jakosits (GER) 673pts	Anatoli Asrabayev (EUN) 672	Lubos Racansky (TCH) 670
1996	Ling Yang (CHN) 685.8pts	Xiao Jun (CHN) 679.8	Miroslav Janus (CZE) 678.4

1896–1988 *Event not held*

Olympic Trap Shooting

1900 Roger de Barbarin (FRA) 17pts	René Guyot (FRA) 17	Justinien de Clary (FRA) 17
1906 [1] Gerald Merlin (GBR) 24pts	Ioannis Peridis (GRE) 23	Sidney Merlin (GBR) 21
1906 [2] Sidney Merlin (GBR) 15pts	Anastasios Metaxas (GRE) 13	Gerald Merlin (GBR) 12
1908 Walter Ewing (CAN) 72pts	George Beattie (CAN) 60	Alexander Maunder (GBR) 57
		Anastasios Metaxas (GRE) 57
1912 James Graham (USA) 96pts	Alfred Goeldel-Bronikowen (GER) 94	Harry Blau (URS) 91
1920 Marke Arie (USA) 95pts	Frank Troeh (USA) 93	Frank Wright (USA) 87
1924 Gyula Halasy (HUN) 98pts	Konrad Huber (FIN) 98	Frank Hughes (USA) 97
1952 George Généreux (CAN) 192pts	Knut Holmqvist (SWE) 191	Hans Lijedahl (SWE) 191
1956 Galliano Rossini (ITA) 195pts	Adam Smelczynski (POL) 190	Alessandro Ciceri (ITA) 188
1960 Ion Dumitrescu (ROM) 192pts	Galliano Rossini (ITA) 191	Sergei Kalinin (URS) 190
1964 Ennio Mattarelli (ITA) 198pts	Pavel Senichev (URS) 194	William Morris (USA) 194
1968 Robert Braithwaite (GBR) 198pts	Thomas Garrigus (USA) 196	Kurt Czekalla (GDR) 196
1972 Angelo Scalzone (ITA) 199pts	Michel Carrega (FRA) 198	Silvano Basnagi (ITA) 195
1976 Don Haldeman (USA) 190pts	Armando Marques (POR) 189	Ulbaldesco Baldi (ITA) 189
1980 Luciano Giovanetti (ITA) 198pts	Rustam Yambulatov (URS) 196	Jörg Damme (GDR) 196
1984 Luciano Giovanetti (ITA) 192pts	Francisco Boza (PER) 192	Daniel Carlisle (USA) 192
1988 Dmitri Monakov (URS) (197+25) 222pts	Miloslav Bednarik (TCH) (197+25) 222	Frans Peeters (BEL) (195+24) 219
1992 Petr Hrdilicka (CZE) 219pts	Kazumi Watanabe (JPN) 219	Marco Venturini (ITA) 218
1996 Michael Diamond (AUS) 149pts	Josh Lakatos (USA) 147.0	Lance Bade (USA) 147.0

1896, 1904, 1928–48 Event not held

[1] Single shot
[2] Double shot

Double Trap

1996 Russell Mark (AUS) 189.0pts	Albano Pera (ITA) 183.0	Zhang Bang (CHN) 183.0

1896–1992 Event not held

Skeet Shooting

1968 Yevgeni Petrov (URS) 198pts	Romano Garagnani (ITA) 198	Konrad Wirnhier (FRG) 198
1972 Konrad Wirnhier (FRG) 195pts	Yevgeni Petrov (URS) 195	Michael Buchheim (GDR) 195
1976 Josef Panacek (TCH) 198pts	Eric Swinkels (NED) 198	Wieslaw Gawlikowski (POL) 196
1980 Hans Kjeld Rasmussen (DEN) 196pts	Lars-Goran Carlsson (SWE) 196	Roberto Garcia (CUB) 196
1984 Matthew Dryke (USA) 198pts	Ole Rasmussen (DEN) 196	Luca Scribiani Rossi (ITA) 196
1988 Axel Wegner (GDR) (198+24) 222pts	Alfonso de Iruarrizaga (CHI) (198+23) 221	Jorge Guardiola (ESP) (196+24) 220
1992 Zhang Shan (CHN) 233pts [1]	Juan Jorge Giha (PER) 222	Bruno Rosetti (ITA) 222
1996 Ennio Falco (ITA) 149.0pts	Miroslav Rzeprkowski (POL) 148.0	Andrea Benelli (ITA) 147.0

1896–1964 Event not held

[1] First female to win an Olympic mixed shooting event

Air Pistol

1988 Taniou Kiriakov (BUL) (585+102.9) 687.9pts	Erich Buljung (USA) (590+97.9) 687.9	Xu Haifeng (CHN) (584+100.5) 684.5
1992 Wang Yifu (CHN) 684.8pts	Sergei Pyzhano (EUN) 684.1	Sorin Babii (ROM) 684.1
1996 Roberto di Donna (ITA) 684.2pts	Wang Yifu (CHN) 684.1	Taniu Kiryakov (BUL) 683.8

1896–1964 Event not held

Air Rifle

1984 Philippe Herberle (FRA) 589pts	Andreas Kronthaler (AUT) 587	Barry Dagger (GBR) 587
1988 Goran Maksimovic (YUG) (594+101.6) 695.6pts	Nicolas Berhtelot (FRA) (593+101.2) 694.2	Johann Riederer (FRG) (592+102.0) 694.0

| 1992 | Yuri Fedkine (EUN) 695.3pts | Franck Badiou (FRA) 691.9 | Johann Riederer (GER) 691.7 |
| 1996 | Artem Khadzhibekov (RUS) 695.7pts | Wolfram Waibel (AUT) 695.2 | Jean-Pierre Amat (FRA) 693.1 |

1896–1980 *Event not held*

Discontinued Events

GOLD	SILVER	BRONZE

Free Rifle (Three Positions)

1896	Georgios Orphanidis (GRE) 1583pts	Jean Phrangoudis (GRE)1312	Viggo Jensen (DEN) 1305
1906	Gudbrand Skatteboe (NOR) 977pts	Konrad Stäheli (SUI) 943	Jean Reich (SUI) 933
1908	Albert Helgerud (NOR) 909pts	Harry Simon (USA) 887	Ole Saether (NOR) 883
1912	Paul Colas (FRA) 987pts	Lars Madsen (DEN) 981	Niels Larsen (DEN) 962
1920	Morris Fisher (USA) 996pts	Niels Larsen (DEN) 989	Östen Östensen (NOR) 980
1924	Morris Fisher (USA) 95pts	Carl Osburn (USA) 95	Niels Larsen (DEN) 93
1948	Emil Grunig (SUI) 1120pts	Pauli Janhonen (FIN) 1114	Willy Rögeberg (NOR) 1112
1952	Anatoli Bogdanov (URS) 1123pts	Robert Bürchler (SUI) 1120	Lev Vainschtein (URS) 1109
1956	Vasili Borissov (URS) 1138pts	Allan Erdman (URS) 1137	Vilho Ylönen (FIN) 1128
1960	Hubert Hammerer (AUT) 1129pts	Hans Spillmann (SUI) 1127	Vasili Borissov (URS) 1127
1964	Gary Anderson (USA) 1153pts	Shota Kveliashvili (URS) 1151	Martin Gunnarsson (USA) 1136
1968	Gary Anderson (USA) 1157pts	Vladimir Kornev (URS) 1151	Kurt Müller (SUI) 1148
1972	Lones Wigger (USA) 1155pts	Boris Melnik (URS) 1155	Lajos Papp (HUN) 1149

1900–04, 1928–36 *Event not held*

Free Rifle

1896[1]	Pantelis Karasevdas (GRE) 2320pts	Paulas Pavlidis (GRE) 1978	Nicolaos Tricoupes (GRE) 1718
1906[2]	Marcel de Stadelhofen (SUI) 243pts	Konrad Stäheli (SUI) 238	Léon Moreaux (FRA) 234
1906[3]	Gudbrand Skatteboe (NOR) 339pts	Louis Richardet (SUI) 332	Konrad Stäheli (SUI) 328
1906[4]	Konrad Stäheli (SUI) 340pts	Louis Richardet (SUI) 338	Jean Reich (SUI) 320
1906[5]	Gudbrand Skatteboe (NOR) 324pts	Julius Braathe (NOR) 310	Albert Helgerud (NOR) 305
1908[6]	Jerry Millner (GBR) 98pts	Kellogg Casey (USA) 93	Maurice Blood (GBR) 92

1900–04 *Event not held*

[1] Over 200m
[2] Any position (300m)
[3] Prone (300m)
[4] Kneeling (300m)
[5] Standing (300m)
[6] Over 1000yd

Free Rifle (Team)

1906	Switzerland 4596pts	Norway 4534	France 4511
1908	Norway 5055pts	Sweden 4711	France 4652
1912	Sweden 5655pts	Norway 5605	Denmark 5529
1920	United States 4876pts	Norway 4741	Switzerland 4698
1924	United States 676pts	–	France 646
			Haiti 646

1896–1904 *Event not held*

Military Rifle

1900[1]	Emil Kellenberger (SUI) 930pts	Anders Nielsen (DEN) 921	Ole Östmo (NOR) 917
1900[2]	Lars Madsen (DEN) 305pts	Ole Östmo (NOR) 299	Charles du Verger (BEL) 298
1900[3]	Konrad Stäheli (SUI) 324pts	Emil Kellenberger (SUI) 314	–
		Anders Nielsen (DEN) 314	

1900[4]Achille Paroche (FRA) 332pts	Anders Nielsen (DEN) 330	Ole Östmo (NOR) 329
1906[5]Léon Moreaux (FRA) 187pts	Louis Richardet (SUI) 187	Jean Reich (SUI) 183
1906[6]Louis Richardet (SUI) 238pts	Jean Reich (SUI) 234	Raoul de Boigne (FRA) 232
1912[1]Sándor Prokopp (HUN) 97pts	Carl Osburn (USA) 96	Embret Skogen (NOR) 95
1912[7]Paul Colas (FRA) 94pts	Carl Osburn (USA) 94	Joseph Jackson (USA) 93
1920[4]Otto Olsen (NOR) 60pts	Léon Johnson (FRA) 59	Fritz Kuchen (SUI) 59
1920[2]Carl Osburn (USA) 56pts	Lars Madsen (DEN) 55	Lawrence Nuesslein (USA) 54
1920[8]Hugo Johansson (SWE) 58pts	Mauritz Eriksson (SWE) 56	Lloyd Spooner (USA) 56

1908 *Event not held*

Footnotes follow Military Rifle (Team)

Military Rifle (Team)

1900 Switzerland 4399pts	Norway 4290	France 4278
1908 United States 2531pts	Great Britain 2497	Canada 2439
1912 United States 1687pts	Great Britain 1602	Sweden 1570
1920[2]Denmark 266pts	United States 255	Sweden 255
1920[4]United States 289pts	France 283	Finland 281
1920[8]United States 287pts	South Africa 287	Sweden 287
1920[9]United States 573pts	Norway 565	Switzerland 563

1896, 1904 *Event not held*

[1] Three positions (300m)
[2] Standing (300m)
[3] Kneeling (300m)
[4] Prone (300m)
[5] Standing or kneeling (200m)
[6] Standing or kneeling (300m)
[7] Any position (600m)
[8] Prone (600m)
[9] Prone (300m and 600m)

Small Bore Rifle

1908[1]John Fleming (GBR) 24pts	M. K. Matthews (GBR) 24	W. B. Marsden (GBR) 24
1908[2]William Styles (GBR) 45pts	H. I. Hawkins (GBR) 45	Edward Amoore (GBR) 45
1912[2]Wilhelm Carlberg (SWE) 242pts	Johan von Holst (SWE) 233	Gustaf Ericsson (SWE) 231

[1] Moving target
[2] Disappearing target

Small Bore Rifle (Team)

1908 Great Britain 771pts	Sweden 737	France 710
1912[1]Sweden 925pts	Great Britain 917	United States 881
1912[2]Great Britain 762pts	Sweden 748	United States 744
1920 United States 1899pts	Sweden 1873	Norway 1866

[1] Over 25m
[2] Over 50m

Live Pigeon Shooting

1900 Léon de Lunden (BEL) 21pts	Maurice Faure (FRA) 20	Donald MacIntosh (AUS) 18
		Crittenden Robinson (USA) 18

Clay Pigeons (Team)

1908 Great Britain 407pts	Canada 405	Great Britain 372
1912 United States 532pts	Great Britain 511	Germany 510
1920 United States 547pts	Belgium 503	Sweden 500
1924 United States 363pts	Canada 360	Finland 360

Running Deer Shooting

1908[1]Oscar Swahn (SWE) 25pts	Ted Ranken (GBR) 24	Alexander Rogers (GBR) 24
1908[2]Walter Winans (USA) 46pts	Ted Ranken (GBR) 46	Oscar Swahn (SWE) 38
1912[1]Alfred Swahn (SWE) 41pts	Ake Lundberg (SWE) 41	Nestori Toivonen (FIN) 41
1912[2]Ake Lundeberg (SWE) 79pts	Edvard Benedicks (SWE) 74	Oscar Swahn (SWE) 72

1920[1]Otto Olsen (NOR) 43pts	Alfred Swahn (SWE) 41	Harald Natwig (NOR) 41
1920[2]Ole Lilloe-Olsen (NOR) 82pts	Fredrik Landelius (SWE) 77	Einar Liberg (NOR) 71
1924[1]John Boles (USA) 40pts	Cyril Mackworth-Praed (GBR) 39	Otto Olsen (NOR) 39
1924[2]Ole Lilloe-Olsen (NOR) 76pts	Cyril Mackworth-Praed (GBR) 72	Alfred Swahn (SWE) 72

[1] Single shot
[2] Double shot

Running Deer Shooting (Team)

1908 Sweden 86pts	Great Britain 85	–
1912 Sweden 151pts	United States 132	Finland 123
1920[1]Norway 178pts	Finland 159	United States 158
1920[2]Noray 343pts	Sweden 336	Finland 284
1924[1]Norway 160pts	Sweden 154	United States 158
1924[2]Great Britain 263pts	Norway 262	Sweden 250

[1] Single shot
[2] Double shot

Running Deer Shooting (Single and Double Shot)

1952 John Larsen (NOR) 413pts	Per Olof Sköldberg (SWE) 409	Tauno Mäki (FIN) 407
1956 Vitali Romanenko (URS) 441pts	Per Olof Sköldberg (SWE) 432	Vladimir Sevrugin (URS) 429

Military Revolver

1896 John Paine (USA) 442pts	Sumner Paine (USA) 380	Nikolaos Morakis (GRE) 205
1906 Louis Richardet (SUI) 253pts	Alexandros Theophilakis (GRE) 250	Georgios Skotadis (GRE) 240
1906[1]Jean Fouconnier (FRA) 219pts	Raoul de Boigne (FRA) 219	Hermann Martin (FRA) 215

1900–04 Event not held

[1] Model 1873

Duelling Pistol

1906[1]Léon Moreaux (FRA) 242pts	Cesare Liverziani (ITA) 233	Maurice Lecoq (FRA) 231
1906[2]Konstantinos Skarlatos (GRE) 133pts	Johann von Holst (SWE) 115	Wilhelm Carlberg (SWE) 115

1896–1904 Event not held

[1] Over 20m
[2] Over 25m

Team Event

1900 Switzerland 2271pts	France 2203	The Netherlands 1876
1908 United States 1914pts	Belgium 1863	Great Britain 1817
1912[1]United States 1916pts	Sweden 1849	Great Britain 1804
1912[2]Sweden 1145pts	Russia d.n.a.	Great Britain d.n.a.
1920[1]United States 2372pts	Sweden 2289	Brazil 2264
1920[2]United States 1310pts	Greece 1285	Switzerland 1270

1904–1906 Event not held.

(1) Over 50m
(2) Over 30m

Women

(Introduced in 1984)

Sport Pistol

1984 Linda Thom (CAN) 585pts	Ruby Fox (USA) 585	Patricia Dench (AUS) 583
1988 Nino Saloukvadze (URS) (591+99) 690pts	Tomoko Hasegawa (JPN) (587+99) 686	Jasna Sekaric (YUG) (591+95) 686
1992 Marina Logvinenko (EUN) 684pts	Li Duihong (CHN) 680	Dorzhsuren Munkhbayar (MGL) 679
1996 Li Duihong (CHN) 687.9pts	Diana Yorgova (BUL) 684.8	Marina Logvinenko (RUS) 684.2

Small-Bore Rifle — Three Positions

1984 Wu Xiaoxuan (CHN) 581pts	Ulrike Holmer (FRG) 578	Wanda Jewell (USA) 578
1988 Silvia Sperber (FRG) (590+95.6) 685.6pts	Vessela Letcheva (BUL) (583+100.2) 683.2	Valentina Tcherkasova (URS) (586+95.4) 681.4
1992 Launi Melli (USA) 684.3pts	Nonka Matova (BUL) 682.7	Malgorzata Ksiazkiewicz (POL) 681.5
1996 Alexandra Ivosev (YUG) 686.1pts	Irina Gerasimenok (POL) 680.1	Renata Mauer (POL) 679.8

Air Pistol

1988 Jasna Sekaric (YUG) (389+100.5) 489.5pts	Nino Saloukvadze (URS) (390+97.9) 487.9	Marina Dobrantcheva (URS) (385+100.2) 485.2
1992 Marina Logvinenko (EUN) 486.4pts	Jasna Sekaric (IOP) 486.4	Maria Grusdeva (BUL) 481.6
1996 Olga Klochneva (RUS) 490.1pts	Marina Logvinenko (RUS) 488.5	Maria Grusdeva (BUL) 488.5

1984 *Event not held*

Air Rifle

1984 Pat Spurgin (USA) 393pts	Edith Gufler (ITA) 391	Wu Xianxuan (CHN) 389
1988 Irina Chilova (URS) (395+103.5) 498.5pts	Silvia Sperber (FRG) (393+104.5) 497.5	Anna Maloukhina (URS) (394+101.8) 495.8
1992 Yeo Kab-soon (KOR) 498.2pts	Vesela Letcheva (BUL) 495.3	Aranka Binder (IOP) 495.1
1996 Renata Mauer (POL) 497.6pts	Petra Horneber (GER) 497.4	Alexandra Ivosev (YUG) 497.2

Double Trap

1996 Kim Rhode (USA) 141pts	Susanne Keirmayer (GER) 139	Deserie Huddleston (AUS) 139

1984–92 *Event not held*

Softball Medals

GOLD	SILVER	BRONZE
(Introduced in 1996)		

Women

1996 United States	China	Australia

Swimming Medals

GOLD	SILVER	BRONZE

Men

50 Metres Freestyle

1904[1] Zóltán Halmay (HUN) 28.0	Scott Leary (USA) 28.6	Charles Daniels (USA) n.t.a.
1988 Matti Biondi (USA) 22.14	Thomas Jager (USA) 22.36	Gennadi Prigoda (URS) 22.71
1992 Alexander Popov (EUN) 21.91	Matt Biondi (USA) 22.09	Tom Jager (USA) 22.30
1996 Alexander Popov (RUS) 22.13	Gary Hall Jr (USA) 22.26	Fernando Scherer (BRA) 22.29

1896–1900, 1906–84 *Event not held*

[1] 50yd — race re-swum after judges disagreed on result of first race

100 Metres Freestyle

1896[1] Alfréd Hajós (HUN) 1:22.2	Efstathios Chorophas (GRE) 1:23.0	Otto Herschmann (AUT) d.n.a
1904[2] Zóltán Halmay (HUN) 1:02.8	Charles Daniels (USA) d.n.a.	Scott Leary (USA) d.n.a.
1906 Charles Daniels (USA) 1:13.4	Zóltán Halmay (HUN) 1:14.2	Cecil Healy (AUS) d.n.a.
1908 Charles Daniels (USA) 1:05.6	Zóltán Halmay (HUN) 1:06.2	Harald Julin (SWE) 1:08.0
1912 Duke Kahanamoku (USA) 1:03.4	Cecil Healy (AUS) 1:04.6	Kenneth Huszagh (USA) 1:05.6
1920 Duke Kahanamoku (USA) 1:01.4	Pua Kealoha (USA) 1:02.2	William Harris (USA) 1:03.0
1924 Johnny Weissmuller (USA) 59.0	Duke Kahanamoku (USA) 1:01.4	Sam Kahanamoku (USA) 1:01.8
1928 Johnny Weissmuller (USA) 58.6	István Bárány (HUN) 59.8	Katsuo Takaishi (JPN) 1:00.0
1932 Yasuji Miyazaki (JPN) 58.2	Tatsugo Kawaishi (JPN) 58.6	Albert Schwartz (USA) 58.8

1936 Ferenc Csik (HUN) 57.6	Masanori Yusa (JPN) 57.9	Shigeo Arai (JPN) 58.0
1948 Walter Ris (USA) 57.3	Alan Ford (USA) 57.8	Géza Kádas (HUN) 58.1
1952 Clarke Scholes (USA) 57.4	Hiroshi Suzuki (JPN) 57.4	Göran Larsson (SWE) 58.2
1956 Jon Hendricks (AUS) 55.4	John Devitt (AUS) 55.8	Gary Chapman (AUS) 56.7
1960³John Devitt (AUS) 55.2 (55.16)	Lance Larson (USA) 55.2 (55.10)	Manuel dos Santos (BRA) 55.4
1964 Don Schollander (USA) 53.4	Bobbie McGregor (GBR) 53.5	Hans-Joachim Klein (GER) 54.0
1968 Mike Wenden (AUS) 52.2	Ken Walsh (USA) 52.8	Mark Spitz (USA) 53.0
1972 Mark Spitz (USA) 51.22	Jerry Heidenreich (USA) 51.65	Vladimir Bure (URS) 51.77
1976 Jim Montgomery (USA) 49.99	Jack Babashoff (USA) 50.81	Peter Nocke (FRG) 51.31
1980 Jörg Woithe (GDR) 50.40	Per Holmertz (SWE) 50.91	Per Johansson (SWE) 51.29
1984 Ambrose Gaines (USA) 49.80	Mark Stockwell (AUS) 50.24	Per Johansson (SWE) 50.31
1988 Matt Biondi (USA) 48.63	Chris Jacobs (USA) 49.08	Stephan Caron (FRA) 49.62
1992 Alexander Popov (EUN) 49.02	Gustavo Borges (BRA) 49.43	Stephan Caron (FRA) 49.50
1996 Alexander Popov (RUS) 48.74	Gary Hall Jr (USA) 48.81	Gustavo Borges (BRA) 49.02

1900 *Event not held*

¹ Some confusion exists about the second and third finishers
² 100yd
³ Larson's original manual timing of 55.1 was revised by the judges (Automatic timings shown were unofficial)

200 Metres Freestyle

1900 Frederick Lane (AUS) 2:25.2	Zóltán Halmay (HUN) 2:31.4	Karl Ruberi (AUT) 2:32.0
1904¹Charles Daniels (USA) 2:44.2	Francis Gailey (USA) 2:46.0	Emil Rausch (GER) 2:56.0
1968 Mike Wenden (AUS) 1:55.2	Don Schollander (USA) 1:55.8	John Nelson (USA) 1:58.1
1972 Mark Spitz (USA) 1:52.78	Steven Genter (USA) 1:53.73	Werner Lampe (FRG) 1:53.99
1976 Bruce Furniss (USA) 1:50.29	John Naber (USA) 1:50.50	Jim Montgomery (USA) 1:50.58
1980 Sergei Kopliakov (URS) 1:49.81	Andrei Krylov (URS) 1:50.76	Graeme Brewer (AUS) 1:51.60
1984 Michael Gross (FRG) 1:47.44	Michael Heath (USA) 1:49.10	Thomas Fahrner (FRG) 1:49.69
1988 Duncan Armstrong (AUS) 1:747.25	Anders Holmertz (SWE) 1:47.89	Matt Biondi (USA) 1:47.99
1992 Yevgeni Sadovyi (EUN) 1:46.70	Anders Holmertz (SWE) 1:46.86	Antti Kasvio (FIN) 1:47.63
1996 Danyon Loader (NZL) 1:47.63	Gustavo Borges (BRA) 1:48.08	Daniel Kowalski (AUS) 1:48.25

1896, 1906–64 *Event not held*

¹ 220yd

400 Metres Freestyle

1896¹Paul Neuman (AUT) 8:12.6	Antonios Pepanos (GRE) 30m	Efstathios Choraphas (GRE) d.n.a
1904²Charles Daniels (USA) 6:16.2	Francis Gailey (USA) 6:22.0	Otto Wahle (AUT) 6:39.0
1906 Otto Scheff (AUT) 6:23.8	Henry Taylor (GBR) 6:24.4	John Jarvis (GBR) 6:27.2
1908 Henry Taylor (GBR) 5:36.8	Frank Beaurepaire (AUS) 5:44.2	Otto Scheff (AUT) 5:46.0
1912 George Hodgson (CAN) 5:24.4	John Hatfield (GBR) 5:25.8	Harold Hardwick (AUS) 5:31.2
1920 Norman Ross (USA) 5:26.8	Ludy Langer (USA) 5:29.2	George Vernot (CAN) 5:29.8
1924 Johnny Weissmuller (USA) 5:04.2	Arne Borg (SWE) 5:05.6	Andrew Charlton (AUS) 5:06.6
1928 Alberto Zorilla (ARG) 5:01.6	Andrew Charlton (AUS) 5:03.6	Arne Borg (SWE) 5:04.6
1932 Buster Crabbe (USA) 4:48.4	Jean Taris (FRA) 4:48.5	Tautomu Oyokota (JPN) 4:52.3
1936 Jack Medica (USA) 4:44.5	Shumpei Uto (JPN) 4:45.6	Shozo Makino (JPN) 4:48.1
1948 William Smith (USA) 4:41.0	James McLane (USA) 4:43.4	John Marshall (AUS) 4:47.7
1952 Jean Boiteux (USA) 4:30.7	Ford Konno (USA) 4:31.3	Per-Olof Ostrand (SWE) 4:35.2
1956 Murray Rose (AUS) 4:27.3	Tsuyoshi Yamanaka (JPN) 4:30.4	George Breen (USA) 4:32.5
1960 Murray Rose (AUS) 4:18.3	Tsuyoshi Yamanaka (JPN) 4:21.4	John Konrads (AUS) 4:21.8
1964 Don Schollander (USA) 4:12.2	Frank Wiegand (GER) 4:14.9	Allan Wood (AUS) 4:15.1
1968 Mike Burton (USA) 4:09.0	Ralph Hutton (CAN) 4:11.7	Allan Mosconi (FRA) 4:13.3
1972 Brad Cooper (AUS) 4:00.27	Steven Genter (USA) 4:01.94	Tom McBeen (USA) 4:02.64
1976 Brian Goodell (USA) 3:51.93	Tim Shaw (USA) 3:52.54	Vladimir Raskatov (URS) 3:55.76
1980 Vladimir Salnikov (URS) 3:51.31	Andrei Krylov (URS) 3:53.24	Ivar Stukolkin (URS) 3:55.76
1984 George DiCarlo (USA) 3:51.23	John Mykkkanen (USA) 3:51.49	Justin Lemberg (AUS) 3:51.79
1988 Uwe Dassler (GDR) 3:46.95	Duncan Armstrong (AUS) 3:47.15	Artur Wojdat (POL) 3:47.34
1992 Yevgeni Sadovyi (EUN) 3:45.00	Kieren Perkins (AUS) 3:45.16	Anders Holmertz (SWE) 3:46.77
1996 Danyon Loader (NZL) 3:47.97	Paul Palmer (GBR) 3:49.00	Daniel Kowalski (AUS) 3:48.39

1900 *Event not held*

¹ 500m
² 440yd

1500 Metres Freestyle

1896 [1] Alfréd Hajós (HUN) 18:22.2	Jean Andreou (GRE) 21:03.4	Efstathios Choraphas (GRE) d.n.a.
1900 [2] John Jarvis (GBR) 13:40.2	Otto Wahle (AUT) 14:53.6	Zóltán Halmay (HUN) 15:16.4
1904 [3] Emil Rausch (GER) 27:18.2	Géza Kiss (HUN) 28:28.2	Francis Gailey (USA) 28:54.0
1906 [3] Henry Taylor (GBR) 28:28.0	John Jarvis (GBR) 30:31.0	Otto Scheff (AUT) 30.59.0
1908 Henry Taylor (GBR) 22:48.4	Sydney Battersby (GBR) 22:51.2	Frank Beaurepaire (AUS) 22:56.2
1912 George Hodgson (CAN) 22:00.0	John Hatfield (GBR) 22:39.0	Harold Hardwick (AUS) 23:15.4
1920 Norman Ross (USA) 22:23.2	George Vernot (CAN) 22:36.4	Frank Beaurepaire (AUS) 23:04.0
1924 Andrew Charlton (AUS) 20:06.6	Arne Borg (SWE) 20:41.4	Frank Beaurepaire (AUS) 21:48.4
1928 Arne Borg (SWE) 19:51.8	Andrew Charlton (AUS) 20:02.6	Buster Crabbe (USA) 20:28.8
1932 Kusuo Kitamura (JPN) 19:12.4	Shozo Makino (JPN) 19:14.1	James Christy (USA) 19:39.5
1936 Noboru Terada (JPN) 19:13.7	Jack Medica (USA) 19:34.0	Shumpei Uto (JPN) 19:34.5
1948 James McLane (USA) 19:18.5	John Marshall (AUS) 19:31.3	György Mitro (HUN) 19:43.2
1952 Ford Konno (USA) 18:30.0	Shiro Hasizune (JPN) 18:41.4	Tetsuo Okamoto (JPN) 18:51.3
1956 Murray Rose (AUS) 17:58.9	Tsuyoshi Yamanaka (JPN) 18:00.3	George Breen (USA) 18:08.2
1960 John Konrads (AUS) 17:19.6	Murray Rose (AUS) 17:21.7	George Breen (USA) 17:30.6
1964 Bob Windle (USA) 17:01.7	John Nelson (USA) 17:03.0	Allan Wood (AUS) 17:07.7
1968 Mike Burton (USA) 16:38.9	John Kinsella (USA) 16:57.3	Greg Brough (AUS) 17:04.7
1972 Mike Burton (USA) 15:52.58	Graham Windeatt (AUS) 15:58.48	Doug Northway (USA) 16:09.25
1976 Brian Goodell (USA) 15:02.40	Bobby Hackett (USA) 15:03.91	Steve Holland (AUS) 15:04.66
1980 Vladimir Salnikov (URS) 14:58.27	Alexander Chaev (URS) 15:14.30	Max Metzker (AUS) 15:14.49
1984 Michael O'Brien (USA) 15:05.20	George DiCarlo (USA) 15:10.59	Stefan Pfeiffer (FRG) 15:12.11
1988 Vladimir Salnikov (URS) 15:00.40	Stevan Pfeiffer (FRG) 15:02.69	Uwe Dassler (GDR) 15:06.15
1992 Kieren Perkins (AUS) 14:43.48	Glen Housman (AUS) 14:55.29	Jörg Hoffmann (GER) 15:02.29
1996 Kieren Perkins (AUS) 14:56.40	Daniel Kowalski (AUS) 15:02.43	Graeme Smith (GBR) 15:02.48

[1] 1200m
[2] 1000m
[3] 1 mile

100 Metres Breaststroke

1968 Don McKenzie (USA) 1:07.7	Vladimir Kossinky (URS) 1:08.0	Nikolai Pankin (URS) 1:08.0
1972 Nobutaka Taguchi (JPN) 1:04.94	Tom Bruce (USA) 1:05.43	John Hencken (USA) 1:05.61
1976 John Hencken (USA) 1:03.11	David Wilkie (GBR) 1:03.43	Arvidas Iuozaytis (URS) 1:04.23
1980 Duncan Goodhew (GBR) 1:03.34	Arsen Miskarov (URS) 1:03.92	Peter Evans (AUS) 1:03.96
1984 Steve Lundquist (USA) 1:01.65	Victor Davis (CAN) 1:01.99	Peter Evans (AUS) 1:02.97
1988 Adrian Moorhouse (GBR) 1:02.04	Karoly Guttler (HUN) 1:02.05	Dmitri Volkov (URS) 1:02.20
1992 Nelson Dreibel (USA) 1:01.50	Norbert Rósza (HUN) 1:01.68	Phil Rogers (AUS) 1:01.76
1996 Frederik Deburghgraeve (BEL) 1:00.65	Jeremy Linn (USA) 1:00.77	Mark Warnecke (GER) 1:01.33

1896–1964 *Event not held*

200 Metres Breaststroke

1908 Frederick Holman (GBR) 3:09.2	William Robinson (GBR) 3:12.8	Pontus Hansson (SWE) 3:14.6
1912 Walter Bathe (GER) 3:01.8	Wilhelm Lützow (GER) 3:05.2	Kurt Malisch (GER) 3:08.0
1920 Häken Malmroth (SWE) 3:04.4	Thor Henning (SWE) 3:09.2	Arvo Aaltonen (FIN) 3:12.2
1924 Robert Shelton (USA) 2:56.5	Joseph de Combe (BEL) 2:59.2	William Kirschbaum (USA) 3:01.0
1928 Yoshiyuki Tsuruta (JPN) 2:48.8	Erich Rademacher (GER) 2:50.6	Teofilo Ylidefonzo (PHI) 2:56.4
1932 Yoshiyuki Tsuruta (JPN) 2:45.4	Reizo Koike (JPN) 2:46.4	Teofilo Ylidefonzo (PHI) 2:47.1
1936 Tetsuo Hamuro (JPN) 2:42.5	Erwin Sietas (GER) 2:42.9	Reizo Koike (JPN) 2:44.2
1948 Joseph Verdeur (USA) 2:39.3 [1]	Keith Carter (USA) 2:40.2	Robert Sohl (USA) 2:43.9
1952 John Davies (AUS) 2:34.4 [1]	Bowen Stassforth (USA) 2:34.7	Herbert Klein (GER) 2:35.9
1956 Masaru Furukawa (JPN) 2:34.7 [2]	Masahiro Yoshimura (JPN) 2:36.7	Charis Yunitschev (URS) 2:36.8
1960 William Mulliken (USA) 2:37.4	Yoshihiko Osaki (JPN) 2:38.0	Weiger Mensonides (NED) 2:39.7
1964 Ian O'Brien (AUS) 2:27.8	Georgi Prokopenko (URS) 2:28.2	Chester Jastremski (USA) 2:29.6
1968 Felipe Munoz (MEX) 2:28.7	Vladimir Kossinsky (URS) 2:29.2	Brian Job (USA) 2:29.9
1972 John Hencken (USA) 2:21.55	David Wilkie (GBR) 2:23.67	Nobutaka Taguchi (JPN) 2:23.88
1976 David Wilkie (USA) 2:15.11	John Hencken (USA) 2:17.26	Rick Colella (USA) 2:19.20
1980 Robertas Shulpa (URS) 2;15.85	Alban Vermes (HUN) 2:16.93	Arsen Miskarov (URS) 2:17.28
1984 Victor Davis (CAN) 2:13.34	Glenn Beringen (AUS) 2:15.79	Etienne Dagon (SUI) 2:17.41
1988 József Szabó (HUN) 2:13.52	Nick Gillingham (GBR) 2:14.12	Sergio Lopez (ESP) 2:15.21

1992 Mike Barrowman (USA) 2:10.16	Norbert Rózsa (HUN) 2:11.23	Nick Gillingham (GBR) 2:11.29
1996 Norbert Rózsa (HUN) 2:12.57	Károly Guttler (HUN) 2:13.03	Alexei Korneyev (RUS) 2:13.17

1896–1906 *Event not held*

[1] Used then permissible butterfly stroke
[2] Used then permissible underwater technique

100 Metres Backstroke

1904[1] Walter Brack (GER) 1:16.8	Georg Hoffmann (GER) 1:18.0	Georg Zacharias (GER) 1:19.6
1908 Arno Bieberstein (GER) 1:24.6	Ludvig Dam (DEN) 1:26.6	Herbert Haresnape (GBR) 1:27.0
1912 Harry Hebner (USA) 1:21.2	Otto Fahr (GER) 1:22.4	Paul Kellner (GER) 1:24.0
1920 Warren Kealoha (USA) 1:15.2	Ray Kegeris (USA) 1:16.2	Gérard Blitz (BEL) 1:19.0
1924 Warren Kealoha (USA) 1:13.2	Paul Wyatt (USA) 1:15.4	Károly Bartha (HUN) 1:17.8
1928 George Kojac (USA) 1:08.2	Walter Laufer (USA) 1:10.0	Paul Wyatt (USA) 1:12.0
1932 Masaji Kiyokawa (JPN) 1:08.6	Toshio Irie (JPN) 1:09.8	Kentaro Kawatsu (JPN) 1:10.0
1936 Adolf Kiefer (USA) 1:05.9	Albert Van de Weghe (USA) 1:07.7	Masaji Kiyokawa (JPN) 1:08.4
1948 Allen Stack (USA) 1:06.4	Robert Cowell (USA) 1:06.5	Georges Vallerey (FRA) 1:07.8
1952 Yoshinobu Oyakawa (JPN) 1:05.4	Gilbert Bozon (FRA) 1:06.2	Jack Taylor (USA) 1:06.4
1956 David Thiele (AUS) 1:02.2	John Monckton (AUS) 1:03.2	Frank McKinney (USA) 1:04.5
1960 David Thiele (AUS) 1:01.9	Frank McKinney (USA) 1:02.1	Robert Bennett (USA) 1:02.3
1968 Roland Matthes (GDR) 58.7	Charles Hickox (USA) 1:00.2	Ronnie Mills (USA) 1:00.5
1972 Roland Matthes (GDR) 56.58	Mike Stamm (USA) 57.70	John Murphy (USA) 58.35
1976 John Naber (USA) 55.49	Peter Rocca (USA) 56.34	Roland Matthes (GDR) 57.22
1980 Bengt Baron (SWE) 56.53	Viktor Kuznetsov (URS) 56.99	Vladimir Dolgov (URS) 57.63
1984 Richard Carey (USA) 55.79	David Wilson (USA) 56.35	Mike West (CAN) 56.49
1988 Daichi Suzuki (JPN) 55.05	David Berkoff (USA) 55.18	Igor Polianski (URS) 55.20
1992 Mark Tewksbury (CAN) 53.98	Jeff Rouse (USA) 54.04	David Berkoff (USA) 54.78
1996 Jeff Rouse (USA) 54.10	Rodolfo Cabrera (CUB) 54.98	Neisser Bent (CUB) 55.02

1896–1900, 1906, 1964 *Event not held*

[1] 100yd

200 Metres Backstroke

1900 Ernst Hoppenberg (GER) 2:47.0	Karl Ruberl (AUT) 2:56.0	Johannes Drost (NED) 3:01.0
1964 Jed Graef (USA) 2:10.3	Gary Dilley (USA) 2:10.5	Robert Bennett (USA) 2:13.1
1968 Roland Matthes (GDR) 2:09.6	Mitchell Ivey (USA) 2:10.6	Jack Horsley (USA) 2:10.9
1972 Roland Matthes (GDR) 2:02.82	Mike Stamm (USA) 2:04.09	Mitchell Ivey (USA) 2:04.33
1976 John Naber (USA) 1:59.19	Peter Rocca (USA) 2:00.55	Don Harrigan (USA) 2:01.35
1980 Sándor Wladár (HUN) 2:01.93	Zóltán Verraszto (HUN) 2:02.40	Mark Kerry (AUS) 2:03.14
1984 Richard Carey (USA) 2:00.23	Frederic Delcourt (FRA) 2:01.75	Cameron Henning (CAN) 2:02.37
1988 Igor Polianski (URS) 1:59.37	Frank Baltrausch (GDR) 1:59.50	Paul Kingsman (NZL) 2:00.48
1992 Martin Lopez-Zubero (ESP) 1:58.47	Vladimir Selkov (EUN) 1:58.87	Stefano Battistelli (ITA) 1:59.40
1996 Brad Bridgewater (USA) 1:58.54	Tripp Schwenk (USA) 1:58.99	Emanuele Meris (ITA) 1:59.18

1896, 1904–60 *Event not held*

100 Metres Butterfly

1968 Doug Russell (USA) 55.9	Mark Spitz (USA) 56.4	Ross Wales (USA) 57.2
1972 Mark Spitz (USA) 54.27	Bruce Robertson (CAN) 55.56	Jerry Heidenreich (USA) 55.74
1976 Matt Vogel (USA) 54.35	Joe Bottom (USA) 54.50	Gary Hall (USA) 54.65
1980 Pär Arvidsson (SWE) 54.92	Roger Pyttel (GDR) 54.94	David Lopez (ESP) 55.13
1984 Michael Gross (FRG) 53.08	Pablo Morales (USA) 53.23	Glenn Buchanan (AUS) 53.85
1988 Anthony Nesty (SUR) 53.00	Matt Biondi (USA) 53.01	Andy Jameson (GBR) 53.30
1992 Pablo Morales (USA) 53.32	Rafal Szukala (POL) 53.35	Anthony Nesty (SUR) 53.41
1996 Denis Pankratov (RUS) 52.27	Scott Miller (AUS) 52.53	Vladislav Kulikov (RUS) 52.13

1896–1964 *Event not held*

200 Metres Butterfly

1956 William Yorzyk (USA) 2:19.3	Takashi Ishimoto (JPN) 2:23.8	György Tumpek (HUN) 2:23.9
1960 Mike Troy (USA) 2:12.8	Neville Hayes (AUS) 2:14.6	David Gillanders (USA) 2:15.3

1964 Kevin Berry (AUS) 2:06.6	Carl Robie (USA) 2:07.5	Fred Schmidt (USA) 2:09.3
1968 Carl Robie (USA) 2:08.7	Martyn Woodroffe (GBR) 2:09.0	John Ferris (USA) 2:09.3
1972 Mark Spitz (USA) 2:00.70	Gary Hall (USA) 2:02.86	Robin Backhaus (USA) 2:03.23
1976 Mike Bruner (USA) 1:59.23	Steven Gregg (USA) 1:59.54	William Forrester (USA) 1:59.96
1980 Sergei Fesenko (URS) 1:59.76	Phil Hubble (GBR) 2:01.20	Roger Pyttel (GDR) 2:01.39
1984 Jon Sieben (AUS) 1:57.04	Michael Gross (FRG) 1:57.40	Rafael Castro (VEN) 1:57.51
1988 Michael Gross (FRG) 1:56.94	Benny Nielsen (DEN) 1:58.24	Anthony Mosse (NZL) 1:58.28
1992 Mel Stewart (USA) 1:56.26	Danyon Loader (NZL) 1:57.93	Franck Esposito (FRA) 1:58.51
1996 Denis Pankratov (RUS) 1:56.51	Matt Malchow (USA) 1:57.44	Scott Miller (AUS) 1:57.48

1896–1952 *Event not held*

200 Metres Individual Medley

1968 Charles Hickox (USA) 2:12.0	Greg Buckingham (USA) 2:13.0	John Ferris (USA) 2:13.3
1972 Gunnar Larsson (SWE) 2:07.17	Tim McKee (USA) 2:08.37	Steve Furniss (USA) 2:08.45
1984 Alex Baumann (CAN) 2:01.42	Pablos Morales (USA) 2:03.05	Neil Cochran (GBR) 2:04.38
1988 Tamás Darnyi (HUN) 2:00.17	Patrick Kühl (GDR) 2:01.61	Vadim Yarochtchouk (URS) 2:02.40
1992 Tamás Darnyi (HUN) 2:00.76	Gregory Burgess (USA) 2:00.97	Attila Czene (HUN) 2:01.00
1996 Attila Czene (HUN) 1:59.91	Jani Sievinen (FIN) 2:00.13	Curtis Myden (CAN) 2:01.13

1896–1964, 1976–80 *Event not held*

400 Metres Individual Medley

1964 Richard Roth (USA) 4:45.4	Roy Saari (USA) 4:47.1	Gerhard Hetz (GER) 4:51.0
1968 Charles Hickox (USA) 4:48.4	Gary Hall (USA) 4:48.7	Michael Holthaus (GER) 4:51.4
1972 Gunnar Larsson (SWE) 4:31.98	Tim McKee (USA) 4:31.98	András Hargitay (HUN) 4:32.70
1976 Rod Strachan (USA) 4:23.68	Tim McKee (USA) 4:24.62	Andrei Smirnov (URS) 4:26.90
1980 Alexander Sidorenko (URS) 4:22.89	Sergei Fesenko (URS) 4:23.43	Zóltán Verraszto (HUN) 4:24.24
1984 Alex Baumann (CAN) 4:17.41	Ricardo Prado (BRA) 4:18.45	Robert Woodhouse (AUS) 4:20.50
1988 Tamás Darnyi (HUN) 4:14.75	David Wharton (USA) 4:17.36	Stefano Battistelli (ITA) 4:18.01
1992 Tamás Darnyi (HUN) 4:14.23	Erik Namesnik (USA) 4:15.57	Luca Sacchi (ITA) 4:16.34
1996 Tom Dolan (USA) 4:14.90	Eric Namesnik (USA) 4:15.25	Curtis Myden (CAN) 4:16.28

1896–1960 *Event not held*

4 × 100 Metres Freestyle Relay

1964 United States 3:33.2	Germany 3:37.2	Australia 3:39.1
1968 United States 3:31.7	Soviet Union 3:34.2	Australia 3:34.7
1972 United States 3:26.42	Soviet Union 3:29.72	East Germany 3:32.42
1984 United States 3:19.03	Australia 3:19.68	Sweden 3:22.69
1988 United States 3:16.53	Soviet Union 3:18.33	East Germany 3:19.82
1992 United States 3:16.74	Unified Team 3:17.56	Germany 3:17.90
1996 United States 3:15.41	Russia 3:17.06	Germany 3:17.20

1896–1960, 1976–80 *Event not held*

4 × 200 Metres Freestyle Relay

1906[1] Hungary 16:52.4	Germany 17:16.2	Great Britain n.t.a.
1908 Great Britain 10:55.6	Hungary 10:59.0	United States 11:02.8
1912 Australasia 10:11.6 [2]	United States 10:20.2	Great Britain 10:28.2
1920 United States 10:04.4	Australia 10:25.4	Great Britain 10:37.2
1924 United States 9:53.4	Australia 10:02.2	Sweden 10:06.8
1928 United States 9:36.2	Japan 9:41.4	Canada 9:47.8
1932 Japan 8:58.4	United States 9:10.5	Hungary 9:31.4
1936 Japan 8:51.5	United States 9:03.0	Hungary 9:12.3
1948 United States 8:46.0	Hungary 8:48.4	France 9:08.0
1952 United States 8:31.1	Japan 8:33.5	France 8:45.9
1956 Australia 8:23.6	United States 8:31.5	Soviet Union 8:34.7
1960 United States 8:10.2	Japan 8:13.2	Australia 8:13.8
1964 United States 7:52.1	Germany 7:59.3	Japan 8:03.8
1968 United States 7:35.78	Australia 7:53.7	Soviet Union 8:01.6

1972	United States 7:35.78	West Germany 7:41.69	Soviet Union 7:45.76
1976	United States 7:23.22	Soviet Union 7:27.97	Great Britain 7:32.11
1980	Soviet Union 7:23.50	East Germany 7:28.60	Brazil 7:29.30
1984	United States 7:15.69	West Germany 7:16.73	Great Britain 7:24.78
1988	United States 7:12.51	East Germany 7:13.68	West Germany 7:14.35
1992	Unified Team 7:11.95	Sweden 7:15.31	United States 7:16.23
1996	United States 7:14.84	Sweden 7:17.56	Germany 7:17.71

1896–1904 *Event not held*

[1] 4 × 250m
[2] Composed of three Australians and a New Zealander

4 × 100 Metres Medley Relay

1960	United States 4:05.4	Australia 4:12.0	Japan 4:12.2
1964	United States 3:38.5	Germany 4:01.6	Australia 4:02.3
1968	United States 3:54.9	East Germany 3:57.5	Soviet Union 4:00.7
1972	United States 3:48.16	East Germany 3:52.12	Canada 3:52.26
1976	United States 3:42.22	Canada 3:43.23	West Germany 3:47.29
1980	Australia 3:45.70	Soviet Union 3:45.92	Great Britain 3:47.71
1984	United States 3:39.30	Canada 3:43.23	Australia 3:43.25
1988	United States 3:36.93	Canada 3:39.28	Soviet Union 3:39.96
1992	United States 3:36.93	Unified Team 3:38.56	Canada 3:39.96
1996	United States 3:34.84	Russia 3:37.55	Australia 3:39.56

1896–1956 *Event not held*

Women

50 Metres Freestyle

1988	Kristin Otto (GDR) 25.49	Yang Wenyi (CHN) 25.64	Katrin Meissner (GDR) 25.71
			Jill Sterkel (USA) 25.71
1992	Yang Wenyi (CHN) 24.79	Zhuang Yong (CHN) 25.08	Angel Martino (USA) 25.23
1996	Amy van Dyken (USA) 24.87	Le Jingyi (CHN) 24.90	Sandra Volker (GER) 25.14

1896–1984 *Event not held*

100 Metres Freestyle

1912	Fanny Durack (AUS) 1:22.2	Wilhelmina Wylie (AUS) 1:25.4	Jennie Fletcher (GBR) 1:27.0
1920	Etheda Bleibtrey (USA) 1:13.6	Irene Guest (USA) 1:17.0	Frances Schroth (USA) 1:17.2
1924	Ethel Lackie (USA) 1:12.4	Mariechen Wehselau (USA) 1:12.8	Gertrude Ederle (USA) 1:14.2
1928	Albina Osipowich (USA) 1:11.0	Eleanor Garatti (USA) 1:11.4	Joyce Cooper (GBR) 1:13.6
1932	Helene Madison (USA) 1:06.8	Willemijntje den Ouden (NED) 1:07.8	Eleanor Garatti-Saville (USA) 1:08.2
1936	Henrika Mastenbroek (NED) 1:05.9	Jeanette Campbell (ARG) 1:06.4	Gisela Arendt (GER) 1:06.6
1948	Greta Andersen (DEN) 1:06.3	Ann Curtis (USA) 1:06.5	Marie-Louise Vaessen (NED) 1:07.6
1952	Katalin Szöke (HUN) 1:06.8	Johanna Termeulen (NED) 1:07.0	Judit Temes (HUN) 1:07.1
1956	Dawn Fraser (AUS) 1:02.0	Lorraine Crapp (AUS) 1:02.3	Faith Leech (AUS) 1:05.1
1960	Dawn Fraser (AUS) 1.01.2	Chris von Saltza (USA) 1:02.8	Natalie Steward (GBR) 1:03.1
1964	Dawn Fraser (AUS) 59.5	Sharon Stouder (USA) 59.9	Kathleen Ellis (USA) 1:00.8
1968	Jan Henne (USA) 1:00.0	Susan Pedersen (USA) 1:00.3	Linda Gustavson (USA) 1:00.3
1972	Sandra Neilson (USA) 58.59	Shirley Babashoff (USA) 59.02	Shane Gould (AUS) 59.06
1976	Kornelia Ender (GDR) 55.65	Petra Priemer (GDR) 56.49	Enith Brigitha (NED) 56.65
1980	Barbara Krause (GDR) 54.79	Caren Metschuck (GDR) 55.16	Ines Diers (GDR) 55.65
1984	Carrie Steinsiefer (USA) 55.92	–	Annemarie Verstappen (NED) 56.08
	Nancy Hogshead (USA) 55.92		
1988	Kristin Otto (GDR) 54.93	Zhuang Yong (CHN) 55.47	Catherine Plewinski (FRA) 55.49
1992	Zhuang Yong (CHN) 54.64	Jenny Thompson (USA) 54.84	Franziska van Almsick (GER) 54.94
1996	Le Jingyi (CHN) 54.50	Sandra Volker (GER) 54.88	Angel Martino (USA) 54.93

1896–1908 *Event not held*

200 Metres Fresestyle

1968 Debbie Meyer (USA) 2:10.5	Jan Henne (USA) 2:11.0	Jane Barkman (USA) 2:11.2
1972 Shane Gould (AUS) 2:03.56	Shirley Babashoff (USA) 2:04.33	Keena Rothhammer (USA) 2:04.92
1976 Kornelia Ender (GDR) 1:59.26	Shirley Babashoff (USA) 2:01.22	Enith Brigitha (NED) 2:01.40
1980 Barbara Krause (GDR) 1:58.33	Ines Diers (GDR) 1:59.64	Carmela Schmidt (GDR) 2:01.44
1984 Mary Wayte (USA) 1:59.23	Cynthia Woodhead (USA) 1:59.50	Annemarie Verstappen (NED) 1:59.69
1988 Heike Friedrich (GDR) 1:57.65	Silvia Poll (CRC) 1:58.67	Manuela Stellmach (GDR) 1:59.01
1992 Nicole Haislett (USA) 1:57.90	Franziska van Almsick (GER) 1:58.00	Kirsten Kielglass (GER) 1:59.67
1996 Claudia Poll (CRC) 1:58.16	Franziska van Almsick (GER) 1:58.57	Dagmar Hase (GER) 1:59.56

1896–1964 *Event not held*

400 Metres Freestyle

1920[1]Etheda Bleibtrey (USA) 4:34.0	Margaret Woodbridge (USA) 4:42.8	Frances Schroth (USA) 4:52.0
1924 Martha Norelius (USA) 6:02.2	Helen Wainwright (USA) 6:03.8	Gertrude Ederle (USA) 6:04.8
1928 Martha Norelius (USA) 5:42.8	Marie Braun (NED) 5:57.8	Jospehine McKim (USA) 6:00.2
1932 Helene Madison (USA) 5:28.5	Lenore Kight (USA) 5:28.6	Jennie Maakal (RSA) 5:47.3
1936 Henrika Mastenbroek (NED) 5:26.4	Ragnhild Hveger (DEN) 5:27.5	Lenore Kight-Wingard (USA) 5:29.0
1948 Ann Curtis (USA) 5:17.8	Karen Harup (DEN) 5:21.2	Cathy Gibson (GBR) 5:22.5
1952 Valeria Gyenge (HUN) 5:12.1	Eva Novak (HUN) 5:13.7	Evelyn Kawamoto (USA) 5:14.6
1956 Lorraine Crapp (AUS) 4:54.6	Dawn Fraser (AUS) 5:02.5	Sylvia Ruuska (USA) 5:07.1
1960 Chris von Salza (USA) 4:50.6	Jane Cederquist (SWE) 4:53.9	Catharina Lagerberg (NED) 4:56.9
1964 Virginia Duenkel (USA) 4:43.3	Marilyn Ramenofsky (USA) 4:44.6	Terri Stickles (USA) 4:47.2
1968 Debbie Meyer (USA) 4:31.8	Linda Gustavson (USA) 4:35.5	Karen Moras (AUS) 4:37.0
1972 Shane Gould (AUS) 4:19.04	Novella Calligaris (ITA) 4:22.44	Gudrun Wegner (GDR) 4:23.11
1976 Petra Thuemer (GDR) 4:09.89	Shirley Babashoff (USA) 4:10.46	Shannon Smith (CAN) 4:14.60
1980 Ines Diers (GDR) 4:08.76	Petra Schneider (GDR) 4:09.16	Carmela Schmidt (GDR) 4:10.86
1984 Tiffany Cohen (USA) 4:07.10	Sarah Hardcastle (GBR) 4:10.27	June Croft (GBR) 4:11.49
1988 Janet Evans (USA) 4:03.85	Heike Friedrich (GDR) 4:05.94	Anke Möhring (GDR) 4:06.62
1992 Dagmar Hase (GER) 4:07.18	Janet Evans (USA) 4:07.37	Hayley Lewis (AUS) 4:11.22
1996 Michelle Smith (IRL) 4:07.25	Dagmar Hase (GER) 4:08.30	Kirsten Vlieghuis (NED) 4:08.70

1896–1912 *Event not held*

[1] 300m

800 Metres Freestyle

1968 Debbie Meyer (USA) 9:24.0	Pamela Kruse (USA) 9:35.7	Maria Ramirez (MEX) 9:38.5
1972 Keena Rothhammer (USA) 8:53.68	Shane Gould (AUS) 8:56.39	Novella Calligaris (ITA) 8:57.46
1976 Petra Thuemer (GDR) 8:37.14	Shirley Babashoff (USA) 8:37.59	Wendy Weinberg (USA) 8:42.60
1980 Michelle Ford (AUS) 8:28.9	Ines Diers (GDR) 8:32.55	Heike Dähne (GDR) 8:33.48
1984 Tiffany Cohen (USA) 8:24.95	Michele Richardson (USA) 8:30.73	Sarah Hardcastle (GBR) 8:32.60
1988 Janet Evans (USA) 8:20.20	Astrid Strauss (GDR) 8:22.09	Julie McDonald (AUS) 8:22.93
1992 Janet Evans (USA) 8:25.52	Hayley Lewis (AUS) 8:30.34	Jana Henke (GER) 8:30.99
1996 Brooke Bennett (USA) 8:27.89	Dagmar Hase (GER) 8:29.91	Kirsten Vlieghuis (NED) 8:30.84

1896–1964 *Event not held*

100 Metres Breaststroke

1968 Djurdjica Bjedov (YUG) 1:15.8	Galina Prozumenschchikova (URS) 1:15.9 [1]	Sharon Wichman (USA) 1:16.1
1972 Catherine Carr (USA) 1:13.58	Galina Stepanova (URS) 1:14.99	Beverley Whitfield (AUS) 1:15.73
1976 Hannelore Anke (GDR) 1:11.16	Lubov Rusanova (URS) 1:13.04	Marina Kosheveya (URS) 1:13.30
1980 Ute Geweniger (GDR) 1:10.22	Elvira Vasilkova (URS) 1:10.41	Susanne Nielsson (DEN) 1:11.16
1984 Petra Van Staveren (NED) 1:09.88	Anne Ottenbrite (CAN) 1:10.69	Catherine Poirot (FRA) 1:10.70
1988 Tania Dangalakova (BUL) 1:07.95	Antoaneta Frankeva (BUL) 1:08.74	Silke Hörner (GDR) 1:08.83

1992 Yelena Rudkovskaya (EUN) 1:08.00	Anita Nall (USA) 1:08.17	Samantha Riley (AUS) 1:09.25
1996 Penelope Heyns (RSA) 1:07.73	Amanda Beard (USA) 1:08.09	Samantha Riley (AUS) 1:09.18

1896–1964 *Event not held*

¹ Later Stepanova

200 Metres Breaststroke

1924 Lucy Morton (GBR) 3:33.2	Agnes Geraghty (USA) 3:34.0	Gladys Carson (GBR) 3:35.4
1928 Hilde Schrader (GER) 3:12.6	Mietje Baron (NED) 3:15.2	Lotte Mühe (GER) 3:17.6
1932 Claire Dennis (AUS) 3:06.3	Hideko Maehata (JPN) 3:06.4	Else Jacobsen (DEN) 3:07.1
1936 Hideko Maehata (JPN) 3:03.6	Martha Genenger (GER) 3:04.2	Inge Sörensen (DEN) 3:07.8
1948 Petronella van Vliet (NED) 2:57.2	Nancy Lyons (AUS) 2:57.7	Eva Novák (HUN) 3:00.2
1952 Eva Székely (HUN) 2:51.7 ¹	Eva Novák (HUN) 2:54.4	Helen Gordon (GBR) 2:57.6
1956 Ursula Happe (GER) 2:53.1 ²	Eva Székely (HUN) 2:54.8	Eva-Maria ten Elsen (GER) 2:55.1
1960 Anita Lonsbrough (GBR) 2:49.5	Wiltrud Urselmann (GER) 2:50.0	Barbara Göbel (GER) 2:53.6
1964 Galina Prozumenshchikova (URS) 2:46.4	Claudia Kolb (USA) 2:47.6	Svetlana Babanina (URS) 2:48.6
1968 Sharon Wichman (USA) 2:44.4	Djurdjica Bjedov (YUG) 2:46.4 2:47.0	Galina Prozumenshchikova (URS)
1972 Beverley Whitfield (AUS) 2:41.7	Dana Schoenfield (USA) 2:42.05	Galina Stepanova (URS) 2:42.36
1976 Marina Kosheveya (URS) 2:33.35	Marina Yurchenia (URS) 2:36.08	Lubov Rusanova (URS) 2:36.22
1980 Lina Kachushite (URS) 2:29.54	Svetlana Varganova (URS) 2:29.61	Yulia Bogdanova (URS) 2:32.39
1984 Anne Ottenbrite (CAN) 2:30.38	Susan Rapp (USA) 2:31.15	Ingrid Lempereur (BEL) 2:31.40
1988 Silke Hörner (GDR) 2:26.71	Huang Xiaomin (CHN) 2:27.49	Antoaneta Frankeva (BUL) 2:28.34
1992 Kyoko Iwasaki (JPN) 2:26.65	Li Lin (CHN) 2:26.85	Anita Nall (USA) 2:26.88
1996 Penelope Heyns (RSA) 2:25.41	Amanda Beard (USA) 2:25.75	Agnes Kovacs (HUN) 2:26.57

1896–1920 *Event not held*

¹ Used then permitted butterfly stroke
² Used then permitted underwater technique

100 Metres Backstroke

1924 Sybil Bauer (USA) 1:23.2	Phyllis Harding (GBR) 1:27.4	Aileen Riggin (USA) 1:28.2
1928 Marie Braun (NED) 1:22.0	Ellen King (GBR) 1:22.2	Joyce Cooper (GBR) 1:22.8
1932 Eleanor Holm (USA) 1:19.4	Philomena Mealing (AUS) 1:21.3	Valerie Davies (GBR) 1:22.5
1936 Dina Senff (NED) 1:18.9	Hendrika Mastenbroek (NED) 1:19.2	Alice Bridges (USA) 1:19.4
1948 Karen Harup (DEN) 1:14.4	Suzanne Zimmermann (USA) 1:16.0	Judy Davies (AUS) 1:16.7
1952 Joan Harrison (RSA) 1:14.3	Geertje Wielema (NED) 1:14.5	Jean Stewart (NZL) 1:15.8
1956 Judy Grinham (GBR) 1:12.9	Carin Cone (USA) 1:12.9	Margaret Edwards (GBR) 1:13.1
1960 Lynn Burke (USA) 1:09.3	Natalie Steward (GBR) 1:10.8	Satoko Tanaka (JPN) 1:11.4
1964 Cathy Ferguson (USA) 1:07.7	Cristine Caron (FRA) 1:07.9	Virginia Duenkel (USA) 1:08.0
1968 Kaye Hall (USA) 1:06.2	Elaine Tanner (CAN) 1:06.7	Jane Swaggerty (USA) 1:08.1
1972 Melissa Belote (USA) 1:05.78	Andrea Gyarmati (HUN) 1:06.26	Susie Atwood (USA) 1:06.34
1976 Ulrike Richter (GDR) 1:01.83	Birgit Treiber (GDR) 1:03.41	Nancy Garapick (CAN) 1:03.71
1980 Rica Reinisch (GDR) 1:00.86	Ina Kleber (GDR) 1:02.07	Petra Reidel (GDR) 1:02.64
1984 Theresa Andrews (USA) 1:02.55	Betsy Mitchell (USA) 1:02.63	Jolanda De Rover (NED) 1:02.91
1988 Kristin Otto (GDR) 1:00.89	Krisztina Egerszegi (HUN) 1:01.56	Cornelia Sirch (GDR) 1:01.57
1992 Krysztina Egerszegi (HUN) 1:00.68	Tunde Szabo (HUN) 1:01.14	Lea Loveless (USA) 1:01.13
1996 Beth Botsford (USA) 1:01.19	Whitney Hedgepeth (USA) 1:01.47	Marianne Kriel (RSA) 1:02.12

1896–1920 *Event not held*

200 Metres Backstroke

1968 Lillian Watson (USA) 2:24.8	Elaine Tanner (CAN) 2:27.4	Kaye Hall (USA) 2:28.9
1972 Melissa Belote (USA) 2:19.19	Susie Atwood (USA) 2:20.38	Donna Marie Gurr (CAN) 2:23.22
1976 Ulrike Richter (GDR) 2:13.43	Birgit Treiber (GDR) 2:14.97	Nancy Garapick (CAN) 2:15.60
1980 Rica Reinisch (GDR) 2:11.77	Cornelia Polit (GDR) 2:13.75	Birgit Treiber (GDR) 2:14.14

1984	Jolanda De Rover (NED) 2:12.38	Amy White (USA) 2:13.04	Aneta Patrascoiu (ROM) 2:13.29
1988	Krysztina Egerszegi (HUN) 2:09.29	Kathrin Zimmermann (GDR) 2:10.61	Cornelia Sirch (GDR) 2:11.45
1992	Krysztina Egerszegi (HUN) 2:07.06	Dagmar Hase (GER) 2:09.46	Nicole Stevenson (AUS) 2:10.20
1996	Krysztina Eegrszegi (HUN) 2:07.83	Whitney Hedgepeth (USA) 2:11.98	Cathleen Rund (GER) 2:12.06

1896–1964 *Event not held*

100 Metres Butterfly

1956	Shelley Mann (USA) 1:11.0	Nancy Ramey (USA) 1:11.9	Mary Sears (USA) 1:14.4
1960	Carolyn Schuler (USA) 1:09.5	Marianne Heemskerk (NED) 1:10.4	Janice Andrew (AUS) 1:12.2
1964	Sharon Stouder (USA) 1:04.7	Ada Kok (NED) 1:05.6	Kathleen Ellis (USA) 1:06.0
1968	Lynette McClements (AUS) 1:05.5	Ellie Daniel (USA) 1:05.8	Susan Shields (USA) 1:06.2
1972	Mayumi Aoki (JPN) 1:03.34	Roswitha Beier (GDR) 1:03.61	Andrea Gyarmati (HUN) 1:03.73
1976	Kornelia Ender (GDR) 1:00.13	Andrea Pollack (GDR) 1:00.98	Wendy Bognoli (USA) 1:01.17
1980	Caren Metschuck (GDR) 1:00.42	Andrea Pollack (GDR) 1:00.90	Christiane Knacke (GDR) 1:01.44
1984	Mary Meagher (USA) 59.26	Jenna Johnson (USA) 1:00.19	Karin Seick (FRG) 1:00.36
1988	Kristin Otto (GDR) 59.00	Birte Weigang (GDR) 59.45	Qian Hong (CHN) 59.52
1992	Qian Hong (CHN) 58.62	Chrissy Ahmann-Leighton (USA) 58.74	Catherine Plewinski (FRA) 59.01
1996	Amy van Dyken (USA) 59.1	Liu Limin (CHN) 59.14	Angel Martino (USA) 59.23

1896–1952 *Event not held*

200 Metres Butterfly

1968	Ada Kok (NED) 2:24.7	Helga Lindner (GDR) 2:24.8	Ellie Daniel (USA) 2:25.9
1972	Karen Moe (USA) 2:15.57	Lynn Colella (USA) 2:16.34	Ellie Daniel (USA) 2:26.74
1976	Andrea Pollack (GDR) 2:11.41	Ulrike Tauber (GDR) 2:12.45	Rosemarie Gabriel (GDR) 2:12.86
1980	Ines Geissler (GDR) 2:10.44	Sybille Schönrock (GDR) 2:10.45	Michelle Ford (AUS) 2:11.66
1984	Mary Meagher (USA) 2:06.90	Karen Phillips (AUS) 2:10.56	Ina Beyermann (FRG) 2:11.91
1988	Kathleen Nord (GDR) 2:09.51	Birte Weigang (GDR) 2:09.91	Mary Meagher (USA) 2:10.80
1992	Summer Sanders (USA) 2:08.67	Wang Xiaohong (CHN) 2:09.01	Susan O'Neil (AUS) 2:09.03
1996	Susan O'Neil (AUS) 2:07.76	Petria Thomas (AUS) 2:09.82	Michelle Smith (IRL) 2:09.91

1896–1964 *Event not held*

200 Metres Individual Medley

1968	Claudia Kolb (USA) 2:24.7	Susan Pedersen (USA) 2:28.8	Jan Henne (USA) 2:31.4
1972	Shane Gould (AUS) 2:23.07	Kornelia Ender (GDR) 2:23.59	Lynn Vidali (USA) 2:24.06
1984	Tracy Caulkins (USA) 2:12.64	Nancy Hogshead (USA) 2:15.17	Michele Pearson (AUS) 2:15.92
1988	Daniela Hunger (GDR) 2:12.59	Yelena Dendeberova (URS) 2:13.31	Noemi Ildiko Lung (ROM) 2:14.85
1992	Li Lin (CHN) 2:11.65	Summer Sanders (USA) 2:11.91	Daniela Hunger (GDR) 2:13.62
1996	Michelle Smith (IRL) 2:13.93	Marianne Limpert (CAN) 2:14.35	Lin Li (CHN) 2:14.74

1896–1964, 1976–80 *Event not held*

400 Metres Individual Medley

1964	Donna De Varona (USA) 5:18.7	Sharon Finneran (USA) 5:24.1	Martha Randall (USA) 5:24.1
1968	Claudia Kolb (USA) 5:08.5	Lynn Vidali (USA) 5:22.2	Sabine Steinbach (GDR) 5:25.3
1972	Gail Neall (AUS) 5:02.97	Leslie Cliff (CAN) 5:03.57	Novella Calligaris (ITA) 5:03.99
1976	Ulrike Tauber (GDR) 4:42.77	Cheryl Gibson (CAN) 4:48.10	Becky Smith (CAN) 4:50.48
1980	Petra Schneider (GDR) 4:36.29	Sharron Davies (GBR) 4:46.83	Agnieszka Czopek (POL) 4:48.17
1984	Tracy Caulkins (USA) 4:39.24	Suzanne Landells (AUS) 4:48.30	Petra Zindler (FRG) 4:48.57
1988	Janet Evans (USA) 4:37.76	Noemi Ildiko Lung (ROM) 4:39.46	Daniela Hunger (GDR) 4:39.76
1992	Krysztina Egerszegi (HUN) 4:36.54	Li Lin (CHN) 4:36.73	Summer Sanders (USA) 4:37.58
1996	Michelle Smith (IRL) 4:39.18	Allison Wagner (USA) 4:42.03	Krysztina Egerszegi (HUN) 4:42.53

1896–1960 *Event not held*

4 × 100 Metres Freestyle Relay

1912 Great Britain 5:52.8	Germany 6:04.6	Austria 6:17.0
1920 United States 5:11.6	Great Britain 5:40.8	Sweden 5:43.6
1924 United States 4:58.8	Great Britain 5:17.0	Sweden 5:35.6
1928 United States 4:47.6	Great Britain 5:02.8	South Africa 5:13.4
1932 United States 4:38.0	The Netherlands 4:47.5	Great Britain 4:52.4
1936 The Netherlands 4:36.0	Germany 4:36.8	United States 4:40.2
1948 United States 4:29.2	Denmark 4:29.6	The Netherlands 4:31.6
1952 Hungary 4:24.4	The Netherlands 4:29.0	United States 4:30.1
1956 Australia 4:17.1	United States 4:19.2	South Africa 4:25.7
1960 United States 4:08.9	Australia 4:11.3	Germany 4:19.7
1964 United States 4:03.8	Australia 4:06.9	The Netherlands 4:12.0
1968 United States 4:02.5	East Germany 4:05.7	Canada 4:07.2
1972 United States 3:55.19	East Germany 3:55.55	West Germany 3:57.93
1976 United States 3:44.82	East Germany 3:45.50	Canada 3:48.81
1980 East Germany 3:42.71	Sweden 3:48.93	The Netherlands 3:49.51
1984 United States 3:43.43	The Netherlands 3:44.40	West Germany 3:45.56
1988 East Germany 3:40.63	The Netherlands 3:43.39	United States 3:44.25
1992 United States 3:39.46	China 3:40.12	Germany 3:41.60
1996 United States 3:39.29	China 3:40.48	Germany 3:41.48

1896–1908 *Event not held*

4 × 200 Metres Freestyle Relay

1996 United States 7:59.87	Germany 8:01.55	Australia 8:05.47

1896–1992 *Event not held*

4 × 100 Metres Medley Relay

1960 United States 4:41.1	Australia 4:45.9	Germany 4:47.6
1964 United States 4:33.9	The Netherlands 4:37.0	Soviet Union 4:39.2
1968 United States 4:28.3	Australia 4:30.0	West Germany 4:36.4
1972 United States 4:20.75	East Germany 4:24.91	West Germany 4:26.46
1976 East Germany 4:06.95	United States 4:14.55	Canada 4:15.22
1980 East Germany 4:06.67	Great Britain 4:12.24	Soviet Union 4:13.61
1984 United States 4:08.34	West Germany 4:11.97	Canada 4:12.98
1988 East Germany 4:03.74	United States 4:07.90	Canada 4:10.49
1992 United States 4:02.54	Germany 4:05.19	Unified Team 4:06.44
1996 United States 4:02.88	Australia 4:05.08	China 4:07.34

1896–1956 *Event not held*

Diving Medals

GOLD	SILVER	BRONZE

Men

Springboard Diving

1908 Albert Turner (GER) 85.5pts	Kurt Behrens (GER) 85.3	George Giadzik (USA) 80.8 Gottlob Walz (GER) 80.8
1912 Paul Günther (GER) 79.23pts	Hans Luber (GER) 76.78	Kurt Behrens (GER) 73.73
1920 Louis Kuehn (USA) 675.4pts	Clarence Pinkston (USA) 655.3	Louis Balbach (USA) 649.5
1924 Albert White (USA) 696.4pts	Pete Desjardins (USA) 693.2	Clarence Pinkston (USA) 653
1928 Pete Desjardins (USA) 185.04pts	Michael Galitzen (USA) 174.06	Farid Simaika (EGY) 172.46
1932 Michael Galitzen (USA) 161.38pts	Harold Smith (USA) 158.54	Richard Degener (USA) 151.82
1936 Richard Degener (USA) 163.57pts	Marshall Wayne (USA) 159.56	Al Greene (USA) 146.29
1948 Bruce Harlan (USA) 163.64pts	Miller Anderson (USA) 157.29	Samuel Lee (USA) 145.52
1952 David Browning (USA) 205.29pts	Miller Anderson (USA) 199.84	Robert Clotworthy (USA) 184.92
1956 Robert Clotworthy (USA) 159.56pts	Donald Harper (USA) 156.23	Joaquin Capilla Pérez (MEX) 162.30
1960 Gary Tobian (USA) 170.00pts	Samuel Hall (USA) 167.08	Juan Botella (MEX) 162.30
1964 Kenneth Sitzberger (USA) 159.90pts	Francis Gorman (USA) 157.63	Larry Andreasen (USA) 143.77

1968 Bernard Wrightson (USA) 170.15pts Klaus Dibiasi (ITA) 159.74 James Henry (USA) 158.09
1972 Vladimir Vasin (URS) 594.09pts F. Giorgio Cagnotto (ITA) 591.63 Craig Lincoln (USA) 577.29
1976 Philip Boggs (USA) 619.05pts F. Giorgio Cagnotto (ITA) 570.48 Alexander Kosenkov (URS) 567.24
1980 Alexander Portnov (URS) Carlos Giron (MEX) 892.140 F. Giorgio Cagnotto (ITA) 871.500
      905.025pts
1984 Greg Louganis (USA) 754.41pts Tan Liangde (CHN) 662.31 Ronald Merriott (USA) 661.32
1988 Greg Louganis (USA) 730.80pts Tan Liangde (CHN) 704.88 Li Deliang (CHN) 665.28
1992 Mark Lenzi (USA) 676.530pts Tan Liangde (CHN) 645.570 Dmitri Sautin (EUN) 627.780
1996 Ni Xiong (CHN) 701.46pts Yu Zhoucheng (CHN) 690.93 Mark Lenzi (USA) 686.49

1896–1906 *Event not held*

Highboard Diving

1904[1] George Shelton (USA) 12.66pts Georg Hoffmann (GER) 11.66 Frank Kehoe (USA) 11.33
                                                                   Alfred Braunschweiger (GER) 11.33
1906 Gottlob Walz (GER) 156.00pts Georg Hoffmann (GER) 150.20 Otto Satzinger (AUT) 147.40
1908 Hajalmar Johansson (SWE) 83.75pts Karl Malmström (SWE) 78.73 Arvid Spangberg (SWE) 74.00
1912 Erik Adlerz (SWE) 73.94pts Albert Zürner (GER) 72.60 Gustaf Blomgren (SWE) 69.56
1920 Clarence Pinkston (USA) 100.67pts Erik Adlerz (SWE) 99.08 Haig Prieste (USA) 93.73
1924 Albert White (USA) 97.46pts David Fall (USA) 97.30 Clarence Pinkston (USA) 94.60
1928 Pete Desjardins (USA) 98.74pts Farid Simiaka (EGY) 99.58 Michael Galitzen (USA) 92.34
1932 Harold Smith (USA) 124.80pts Michael Galitzen (USA) 124.28 Frank Kurtz (USA) 121.98
1936 Marshall Wayne (USA) 113.58pts Elbert Root (USA) 110.60 Hermann Stork (GER) 110.31
1948 Samuel Lee (USA) 130.05pts Bruce Harlan (USA) 122.30 Joaquin Capilla Pérez (MEX)
                                                                   113.52
1952 Samuel Lee (USA) 156.28pts Joaquin Capilla Pérez (MEX) Günther Haase (GER) 141.31
                                   145.21
1956 Joaquin Capilla Pérez (MEX) Gary Tobian (USA) 152.41 Richard Connor (USA) 149.79
      152.44pts
1960 Robert Webster (USA) 165.56pts Gary Tobian (USA) 165.25 Brian Phelps (GBR) 157.13
1964 Robert Webster (USA) 148.58pts Klaus Dibiasi (ITA) 147.54 Thomas Gompf (USA) 153.93
1968 Klaus Dibiasi (ITA) 164.18pts Alvaro Gaxiola (MEX) 154.49 Edwin Young (USA) 153.93
1972 Klaus Dibiasi (ITA) 504.12pts Richard Rydze (USA) 480.75 F. Giorgio Cagnotto (ITA) 475.83
1976 Klaus Dibaisi (ITA) 600.51pts Greg Louganis (USA) 576.99 Vladimir Aleynik (URS) 548.61
1980 Falk Hoffmann (GDR) 835.650pts Vladimir Aleynik (URS) 819.705 David Ambartsumyan (URS)
                                                                   817.440
1984 Greg Louganis (USA) 710.91pts Bruce Kimball (USA) 643.50 Li Kongzheng (CHN) 638.28
1988 Greg Louganis (USA) 638.61pts Ni Xiong (CHN) 637.47 Jesus Mena (MEX) 594.39
1992 Sun Shunwei (CHN) 677.310pts Scott Donie (USA) 633.630 Ni Xiong (CHN) 600.150
1996 Dmitri Sautin (RUS) 692.34pts Jan Hempel (GER) 663.27 Hailiang Xiao (CHN) 658.20

1896–1900 *Event not held*

[1] Combined springboard and highboard event

Women

Springboard Diving

1920 Aileen Riggin (USA) 539.9pts Helen Wainwright (USA) 534.8 Thelma Payne (USA) 534.1
1924 Elizabeth Becker (USA) 474.5pts Aileen Riggin (USA) 460.4 Caroline Fletcher (USA) 434.4
1928 Helen Meany (USA) 78.62pts Dorothy Poynton (USA) 75.62 Georgia Coleman (USA) 73.78
1932 Georgia Coleman (USA) 87.52pts Katherine Rawls (USA) 82.56 Jane Fauntz (USA) 82.12
1936 Majorie Gestring (USA) 89.27pts Katherine Rawls (USA) 88.35 Dorothy Poynton-Hill (USA) 82.36
1948 Victoria Draves (USA) 108.74pts Zoe Ann Olsen (USA) 108.23 Patricia Elsener (USA) 101.30
1952 Patricia McCormick (USA) Madeleine Moreau (FRA) 139.34 Zoe Ann Jensen (USA) 127.57
      147.30pts
1956 Patricia McCormick (USA) Jeanne Stunyo (USA) 125.89 Irene MacDonald (CAN) 121.40
      142.36pts
1960 Ingrid Krämer (GER) 155.81pts Paula Myers-Pope (USA) 141.24 Elizabeth Ferris (GBR) 139.09
1964 Ingrid Krämer-Engel (GER) Jeanne Collier (USA) 138.36 Mary Willard (USA) 138.18
      145.00pts

1968 Sue Gossick (USA) 150.77pts	Tamara Pogozheva (URS) 145.30	Keala O'Sullivan (USA) 145.23
1972 Micki King (USA) 450.03pts	Ulrika Knape (SWE) 434.19	Marina Janicke (GDR) 430.92
1976 Jennifer Chandler (USA) 506.19pts	Christa Kohler (GDR) 469.41	Cynthia McIngvale (USA) 466.83
1980 Irina Kalinina (URS) 725.910pts	Martina Proeber (GDR) 698.895	Karin Guthke (GDR 685.245
1984 Sylvie Bernier (CAN) 530.70pts	Kelly McCormick (USA) 527.46	Christina Seufert (USA) 517.62
1988 Gao Min (CHN) 580.23pts	Li Qing (CHN) 534.33	Kelly Anne McCormick (USA) 533.19
1992 Gao Min (CHN) 572.400pts	Irina Laschko (EUN) 514.140	Brita Baldus (GER) 503.070
1996 Fu Mingxia (CHN) 547.68pts	Irina Laschko (RUS) 512.19	Annie Pelletier (CAN) 509.64

1896–1912 *Event not held*

Highboard Diving

1912 Greta Johnson (SWE) 39.9pts	Lisa Regnell (SWE) 36.0	Isabelle White (GBR) 34.0
1920 Stefani Fryland-Clausen (DEN) 34.6pts	Eileen Armstrong (GBR) 33.3	Eva Ollivier (SWE) 33.3
1924 Caroline Smith (USA) 10.5pts	Elizabeth Becker (USA) 11.0	Hjördis Töpel (SWE) 15.5
1928 Elizabeth Pinkston (USA) 31.6pts	Georgia Coleman (USA) 30.6	Lala Sjöqvist (SWE) 29.2
1932 Dorothy Poynton (USA) 40.26pts	Georgia Coleman (USA) 35.56	Marion Roper (USA) 35.22
1936 Dorothy Poynton-Hill (USA) 33.93pts	Velma Dunn (USA) 33.63	Käthe Köhler (GER) 33.43
1948 Victoria Draves (USA) 68.87pts	Patricia Elsener (USA) 66.28	Birte Christoffersen (DEN) 66.04
1952 Patricia McCormick (USA) 79.37pts	Paula Myers (USA) 71.63	Juno Irwin (USA) 70.49
1956 Patricia McCormick (USA) 84.85pts	Juno Irwin (USA) 81.64	Paula Myers (USA) 81.58
1960 Ingrid Krämer (GER) 91.28pts	Paula Myers-Pope (USA) 88.94	Ninel Krutova (URS) 86.99
1964 Lesley Bush (USA) 99.80pts	Ingrid Krämer-Engel (GER) 98.45	Galina Alekseyeva (URS) 97.60
1968 Milena Duchkova (TCH) 109.59pts	Natalia Lobanova (URS) 105.14	Ann Peterson (USA) 101.11
1972 Ulrika Knape (SWE) 390.00pts	Milena Duchkova (TCH) 370.92	Marina Janicke (GDR) 360.54
1976 Yelena Vaytsekhovskaya (URS) 406.59pts	Ulrika Knape (SWE) 402.60	Deborah Wilson (USA) 401.07
1980 Martina Jäschke (GDR) 596.250pts	Servard Emirzyan (URS) 576.465	Liana Tsotadze (URS) 575.925
1984 Zhou Jihong (CHN) 435.51pts	Michele Mitchell (USA) 431.19	Wendy Wyland (USA) 422.07
1988 Xu Yanmei (CHN) 445.20pts	Michele Mitchell (USA) 436.95	Wendy Williams (USA) 400.44
1992 Fu Mingxia (CHN) 461.430pts	Yelena Mirochina (EUN) 411.630	Mary Ellen Clark (USA) 401.910
1996 Fu Mingxia (CHN) 521.58pts	Annika Walter (GER) 429.22	Mary Ellen Clark (USA) 472.95

1896–1908 *Event not held*

Synchronised Swimming Medals

	GOLD	SILVER	BRONZE
Solo			
1984	Tracie Ruiz (USA) 198.467pts	Carolyn Waldo (CAN) 195.300	Miwako Motoyoshi (JPN) 187.050
1988	Carolyn Waldo (CAN) 200.150pts	Tracie Ruiz-Conforto (USA) 197.633	Miwako Motoyoshi (JPN) 191.850
1992	Kristen Babb-Sprague (USA) 191.848pts	Fumiko Okuno (JPN) 187.056	Sylvia Frechette (CAN)

1896–1980 *Event not held*

	GOLD	SILVER	BRONZE
Duet			
1984	United States 195.584pts	Canada 194.234	Japan 187.992
1988	Canada 197.717pts	United States 197.284	Japan 190.159
1992	United States 192.175pts	Canada 189.394	Japan 186.868
1996	United States 99.720pts	Canada 98.367	Japan 97.753

1896–1980 *Event not held*

Dicscontinued Events

GOLD	SILVER	BRONZE

100 Metres Freestyle (Sailors)

GOLD	SILVER	BRONZE
1896 Ioannis Maloknis (GRE) 2:20.4	Spiridon Khasapis (GRE) n.t.a.	Dimitrios Drivas (GRE) n.t.a.

200 Metres Obstacle Event

1900 Frederick Lane (AUS) 2:38.4	Otto Wahle (AUT) 2:40.0	Peter Kemp (GBR) 2:47.4

400 Metres Breaststroke

1904 Georg Zacharias (GER) 7:23.6	Walter Brack (GER) 20m	Jamison Hardy (USA) d.n.a.
1912 Walter Bathe (GER) 6:29.6	Thor Henning (SWE) 6:35.6	Percy Courtman (GBR) 6:36.4
1920 Hakan Malmroth (SWE) 6:31.8	Thor Henning (SWE) 6:45.2	Arvo Aaltonen (FIN) 6:48.0

880 Yards Freestyle

1904 Emil Rausch (GER) 13:11.4	Francis Gailey (USA) 13:23.4	Géza Kiss (HUN) n.t.a.

4000 Metres Freestyle

1900 John Jarvis (GBR) 58:24.0	Zoltán Halmay (HUN) 1:08:55.4	Louis Martin (FRA) 1:13.08.4

Underwater Swimming

1900 Charles de Vendeville (FRA) 188.4	André Six (FRA) 185.4	Peder Lykkeberg (DEN) 147.0

Plunge for Distance

1904 Paul Dickey (USA) 19.05m	Edgar Adams (USA) 17.53	Leo Goodwin (USA) 17.37

200 Metres Team Swimming

1900 Germany 32pts	France 51	France 61

4 × 50 Yards Relay

1904 United States (New York AC) 2:04.6	United States (Chicago AC) n.t.a.	United States (Missouri AC) n.t.a.

Plain High Diving

1912 Erik Adlerz (SWE) 40.0pts	Hjalmar Johansson (SWE) 39.3	John Jansson (SWE) 39.1
1920 Arvid Wallmann (SWE) 183.5pts	Nils Skoglund (SWE) 183.0	John Jansson (SWE) 175.0
1924 Richmond Eve (AUS) 160.0pts	John Jansson (SWE) 157.0	Harold Clarke (GBR) 158.0

Water Polo Medals

GOLD	SILVER	BRONZE
1900[1] Great Britain	Belgium	France
1904[1] United States	United States	United States
1908 Great Britain	Belgium	Sweden
1912 Great Britain	Sweden	Belgium
1920 Great Britain	Belgium	Sweden
1924 France	Belgium	United States
1928 Germany	Hungary	France
1932 Hungary	Germany	United States
1936 Hungary	Germany	Belgium
1948 Italy	Hungary	The Netherlands
1952 Hungary	Yugoslavia	Italy
1956 Hungary	Yugoslavia	Soviet Union
1960 Italy	Soviet Union	Hungary
1964 Hungary	Yugoslavia	Soviet Union
1968 Yugoslavia	Soviet Union	Hungary
1972 Soviet Union	Hungary	United States
1976 Hungary	Italy	The Netherlands

1980 Soviet Union	Yugoslavia	Hungary
1984 Yugoslavia	United States	West Germany
1988 Yugoslavia	United States	Soviet Union
1992 Italy	Spain	Unified Team
1996 Spain	Croatia	Italy

1896, 1906 *Event not held*

[1] Entries were from clubs not international teams

Table Tennis Medals

(Introduced in 1988)

GOLD	SILVER	BRONZE

Men

Singles

1988 Yoo Nam-kyu (KOR)	Kim Ki-taik (KOR)	Erik Lindh (SWE)
1992 Jan-Ove Waldner (SWE)	Jean-Philippe Gatien (FRA)	Ma Wenge (CHN)
		Kim Taek-soo (KOR)
1996 Liu Guoliang (CHN)	Wang Tao (CHN)	Jörg Rosskoff (GER)

Doubles

1988 China	Yugoslavia	Korea
1992 China	Germany	Korea
		Korea
1996 China	China	Korea

Women

Singles

1988 Chen Jing (CHN)	Li Huifen (CHN)	Jiao Zhimin (CHN)
1992 Deng Yaping (CHN)	Qiao Hong (CHN)	Hyung Jung-hwa (KOR)
		Li Bun-hui (PRK)
1996 Deng Yaping (CHN)	Chen Jung (TAI)	Qiao Hong (CHN)

Doubles

1988 Korea	China	Yugoslavia
1992 China	China	Korea
		Korea
1996 China	China	Korea

Tennis Medals

GOLD	SILVER	BRONZE

Men

Singles

1896[1] John Boland (GBR)	Dionysios Kasdaglis (GRE)	Momcilló Tapavica (HUN)
		Konstantinos Paspatis (GRE)
1900[1] Hugh Doherty (GBR)	Harold Mahoney (GBR)	Reginald Doherty (GBR)
		Arthur Norris (GBR)
1904[1] Beals Wright (USA)	Robert LeRoy (USA)	Edgar Leonard (USA)
		Alphonzo Bell (USA)
1906 Max Décugis (FRA)	Maurice Germot (FRA)	Zdenek Zemla (BOH)
1908 Josiah Ritchie (GBR)	Otto Froitzheim (GER)	Wilberforce Eaves (GBR)
1908[2] Wentworth Gore (GBR)	George Caridia (GBR)	Josiah Ritchie (GBR)
1912 Charles Winslow (RSA)	Harold Kitson (RSA)	Oscar Kreuzer (GER)
1912[2] André Gobert (FRA)	Charles Dixon (GBR)	Anthony Wilding (NZL)
1920 Louis Raymond (RSA)	Ichiya Kumagae (JPN)	Charles Winslow (GBR)

1924 Vincent Reynolds (USA)	Henri Cochet (FRA)	Umberto De Morpurgo (ITA)
1988[1] Miloslav Mecir (TCH)	Tim Mayotte (USA)	Stefan Edberg (SWE)
		Brad Gilbert (USA)
1992[1] Marc Rosset (SUI)	Jordi Arrese (ESP)	Goran Ivanisevic (CRO)
		Andrei Cherkasov (EUN)
1996 Andre Agassi (USA)	Sergi Bruguera (ESP)	Leander Paes (IND)

1928–84 *Event not held*

[1] Two bronze medals
[2] Indoor tournaments

Doubles

1896 Great Britain/Germany	Greece	Great Britain/Australia
1900[1] Great Britain	United States/France	France
		Great Britain
1904[1] United States	United States	United States
		United States
1906 France	Greece	Bohemia
1908 Great Britain	Great Britain	Great Britain
1908[2] Great Britain	Great Britain	Sweden
1912 South Africa	Austria	France
1912[2] France	Sweden	Great Britain
1920 Great Britain	Japan	France
1924 United States	France	France
1988[1] United States	Spain	Czechoslovakia
		Sweden
1992[1] Germany	South Africa	Croatia
		Argentina
1996 Australia	Great Britain	Germany

1928–84 *Event not held*

[1] Two bronze medals
[2] Indoor tournaments

Women

Singles

1900[1] Charlotte Cooper (GBR)	Hélène Prévost (FRA)	Marion Jones (USA)
		Hedwiga Rosenbaumova (BOH)
1906 Esmee Simiriotou (GRE)	Sophia Marinou (GRE)	Euphrosine Paspati (GRE)
1908 Dorothea Chambers (GBR)	Dorothy Boothby (GBR)	Joan Winch (GBR)
1908[2] Gwen Eastlake-Smith (GBR)	Angela Greene (GBR)	Märtha Adlerstrahle (SWE)
1912 Marguerite Broquedis (FRA)	Dora Köring (GER)	Molla Bjurstedt (NOR)
1912[2] Ethel Hannam (GBR)	Thora Castenschoid (DEN)	Mabel Parton (GBR)
1920 Suzanne Lenglen (FRA)	Dorothy Holman (GBR)	Kitty McKane (GBR)
1924 Helen Wills (USA)	Julie Vlasto (FRA)	Kitty McKane (GBR)
1988[1] Steffi Graf (FRG)	Gabriela Sabatini (ARG)	Zina Garrison (USA)
		Manuela Maleyeva (BUL)
1992[1] Jennifer Capriati (USA)	Steffi Graf (GER)	Mary-Jo Fernandez (USA)
		Arantxa Sanchez-Vicario (ESP)
1996 Lindsay Davenport (USA)	Arantxa Sanchez-Vicario (ESP)	Jana Novotna (CZE)

1928–84 *Event not held*

[1] Two bronze medals
[2] Indoor tournaments

Doubles

1920 Great Britain	Great Britain	France
1924 United States	Great Britain	Great Britain
1988[1] United States	Czechoslovakia	Australia
		West Germany

1992[1] United States	Spain	Australia Unified Team
1996 United States	Czech Republic	Spain

1928–84 *Event not held*

[1] Two bronze medals

Mixed Doubles

1900 Great Britain	France/Great Britain	Bohemia/Great Britain United States/Great Britain
1906 France	Greece	Greece
1912 Germany	Sweden	France
1912[2] Great Britain	Great Britain	Sweden
1920 France	Great Britain	Czechoslovakia
1924 United States	United States	The Netherlands

1928–96 *Event not held*

[1] Two bronze medals
[2] Indoor tournament

Volleyball Medals

GOLD	SILVER	BRONZE
Men		
1964 Soviet Union	Czechoslovakia	Japan
1968 Soviet Union	Japan	Czechoslovakia
1972 Japan	East Germany	Soviet Union
1976 Poland	Soviet Union	Cuba
1980 Soviet Union	Bulgaria	Romania
1984 United States	Brazil	Italy
1988 United States	Soviet Union	Argentina
1992 Brazil	The Nethelrands	United States
1996 The Netherlands	Italy	Yugoslavia

1896–1960 *Event not held*

Women		
1964 Japan	Soviet Union	Poland
1968 Soviet Union	Japan	Poland
1972 Soviet Union	Japan	North Korea
1976 Japan	Soviet Union	South Korea
1980 Soviet Union	East Germany	Bulgaria
1984 China	United States	Japan
1988 Soviet Union	Peru	China
1992 Cuba	Unified Team	United States
1996 Cuba	China	Brazil

1896–1960 *Event not held*

Weightlifting Medals

GOLD	SILVER	BRONZE
Flyweight (Up to 52kg 1972–92; up to 54kg 1996)		
1972 Zygmunt Smalcerz (POL) 337.5kg	Lajos Szücs (HUN) 330	Sándor Holczreitzer (HUN) 327.5
1976 Alexander Voronin (URS) 242.5kg	György Köszegi (HUN) 237.5	Mohammad Nassiri (IRN) 235
1980 Kanybek Osmonoliev (URS) 245kg	Bong Chol Ho (PRK) 245	Gyond Si Han (PRK) 245
1984 Zeng Guoqiang (CHN) 235kg	Zhou Peishujn (CHN) 235	Kazushito Manabe (JPN) 232.5
1988 Sevdalin Marinov (BUL) 270kg	Chun Byung-kwan (KOR) 260	He Zhuogiang (CHN) 257.5

| 1992 | Ivan Ivanov (BUL) 265kg | Lin Qisheng (CHN) 262.5 | Traian Ciharean (ROM) 252.5 |
| 1996 | Halil Mutlu (TUR) 287.5kg | Zhang Xiangsen (CHN) 280.0 | Sevdalin Minchev (BUL) 277.5 |

1896–1968 *Event not held*

Bantamweight *(Up to 56kg 1948–92; up to 59kg 1996)*

1948	Joseph de Pietro (USA) 307.5kg	Julian Creus (GBR) 297.5	Richard Tom (GBR) 295
1952	Ivan Udolov (URS) 315kg	Mahmoud Namdjou (IRN) 307.5	Ali Mirzai (IRN) 300
1956	Charles Vinci (USA) 342.5kg	Vladimir Stogov (URS) 337.5	Mahmoud Namdjou (IRN) 332.5
1960	Charles Vinci (USA) 345kg	Yoshinobu Miyake (JPN) 337.5	Esmail Khan (IRN) 330
1964	Alexei Vakhonin (URS) 357.5kg	Imre Földi (HUN) 355	Shiro Ichinoseki (JPN) 347.5
1968	Mohammed Nassiri (IRN) 367.5kg	Imre Földi (HUN) 367.5	Henryk Trebicki (POL) 357.5
1972	Imre Földi (HUN) 377.5kg	Mohammed Nassiri (IRN) 370	Gennadi Chetin (URS) 367.5
1976	Norair Nurikyan (BUL) 262.5kg	Grzegorz Cziura (POL) 252.5	Kenkichi Ando (JPN) 250
1980	Daniel Nunez (CUB) 275kg	Yurik Sarkasian (URS) 270	Tadeusz Demboncyzk (POL) 265
1984	Wu Shude (CHN) 267.5kg	Lai Runming (CHN) 265	Masahiro Kotaka (JPN) 252.5
1988	Oksen Mirzoyan (URS) 292.5kg [1]	He Yingqiang (CHN) 287.5	Liu Shoubin (CHN) 267.5
1992	Chun Byung-kwan (KOR) 287.5kg	Liu Shoubin (CHN) 277.5	Luo Jianming (CHN) 277.5
1996	Tang Ningsheng (CHN) 307.5kg	Leonidas Sabanis (GRE) 305.0	Nikolay Pechalov (BUL) 302.5

1896–1936 *Event not held*

[1] Mitko Grablev (BUL) finished in first place with 297.5kg, but was subsequently disqualified

Featherweight *(Up to 60kg 1920–92; up to 64kg 1996)*

1920	Frans de Haes (BEL) 220kg	Alfred Schmidt (EST) 212.5	Eugène Ryther (SUI) 210
1924	[1] Pierino Gabetti (ITA) 402.5kg	Andreas Stadler (AUT) 385	Arthur Reinmann (SUI) 382.5
1928	Franz Andrysek (AUT) 287.5kg	Pierino Gabetti (ITA) 282.5	Hans Wölpert (GER) 282.5
1932	Raymond Suvigny (FRA) 287.5kg	Hans Wölpert (GER) 282.5	Anthony Terlazzo (USA) 280
1936	Anthony Terlazzo (USA) 312.5kg	Saleh Mohammed Soliman (EGY) 305	Ibrahim Shams (EGY) 300
1948	Mahmoud Fayad (EGY) 332.5kg	Rodney Wilkes (TRI) 317.5	Jaffar Salmassi (IRN) 312.5
1952	Rafael Chimishkyan (URS) 337.5kg	Nikolai Saksonov (URS) 332.5	Rodney Wilkes (TRI) 332.5
1956	Isaac Berger (USA) 352.5kg	Yevgeni Minayev (URS) 342.5	Marian Zielinski (POL) 335
1960	Yevgeni Minayev (URS) 372.5kg	Isaac Berger (USA) 362.5	Sebastiano Mannironi (ITA) 352.5
1964	Yoshinobu Miyake (JPN) 397.5kg	Isaac Berger (USA) 382.5	Mieczyslaw Nowak (POL) 377.5
1968	Yoshinobu Miyake (JPN) 392.5kg	Dito Shanidze (URS) 387.5	Yoshiyuki Miyake (JPN) 385
1972	Norair Nurikyan (BUL) 402.5kg	Dito Shanidze (URS) 400	Janos Benedek (HUN) 390
1976	Nikolai Kolesnikov (URS) 285kg	Georgi Todorov (BUL) 280	Kuzumasa Hirai (JPN) 275
1980	Viktor Mazin (URS) 290kg	Stefan Dimitrov (BUL) 287.5	Marek Seweryn (POL) 282.5
1984	Chen Weiqiang (CHN) 282.5kg	Gelu Radu (ROM) 280	Tsai Wen-Yee (TPE) 272.5
1988	Naim Suleymanoglu (TUR) 342.5kg	Stefan Topourov (BUL) 312.5	Ye Huanming (CHN) 287.5
1992	Naim Suleymanoglu (TUR) 320kg	Nikolai Peshalov (BUL) 305	He Yingqiang (CHN) 295
1996	Naim Suleymanoglu (TUR) 357.5kg	Valerios Leonidis (GRE) 332.5	Jiangang Xiao (CHN) 322.5

[1] Aggregate of 5 lifts

Lightweight *(Up to 67.5kg 1920–92; up to 70kg 1996)*

1920	Alfred Neuland (EST) 257.5kg	Louis Williquet (BEL) 240	Florimond Rooms (BEL) 230
1924	[1] Edmond Décottignies (FRA) 440kg	Anton Zwerina (AUT) 427.5	Bohumil Durdis (TCH) 425
1928	[2] Kurt Helbig (GER) 322.5kg Hans Haas (AUT) 322.5kg	–	Fernand Arnout (FRA) 302.5
1932	René Duverger (FRA) 325kg	Hans Haas (AUT) 307.5	Gastone Pierini (ITA) 302.5
1936	[2] Anwar Mohammed Mesbah (EGY) 342.5kg Robert Fein (AUT) 342.5kg	–	Karl Jensen (GER) 327.5
1948	Ibrahim Shams (EGY) 360kg	Attia Hamouda (EGY) 360	James Halliday (GBR) 340
1952	Tommy Kono (USA) 362.5kg	Yevgeni Lopatin (URS) 350	Verne Barberis (AUS) 350

1956 Igor Rybak (URS) 380kg	Ravil Khabutdinov (URS) 372.5	Kim Chang-hee (KOR) 370
1960 Viktor Bushuyev (URS) 397.5kg	Howe-Liang Tan (SIN) 380	Abdul Wahid Aziz (IRQ) 380
1964 Waldemar Baszanowksi (POL) 432.5kg	Vladimir Kaplunov (URS) 432.5	Marian Zielinski (POL) 420
1968 Waldemar Baszanowski (POL) 437.5kg	Parviz Jalayer (IRN) 422.5	Marian Zielinski (POL) 420
1972 Mukharbi Kirzhinov (URS) 460kg	Miaden Koutchev (BUL) 450	Zbigniev Kaczmarek (POL) 437.5
1976[3]Pyotr Korol (URS) 305kg	Daniel Senet (FRA) 300	Kazimierz Czarnecki (POL) 295
1980 Yanko Rusev (BUL) 342.5kg	Joachim Kunz (GDR) 335	Mintcho Pachov (BUL) 325
1984 Yao Jingyuan (CHN) 320kg	Andrei Socaci (ROM) 312.5	Journi Gronman (FIN) 312.5
1988 Joachim Kunz (GDR) 340kg	Israil Militossian (URS) 337.5	Li Jinhe (CHN) 325
1992 Israil Militossian (EUN) 337.5kg	Yoto Yotov (BUL) 327.5	Andreas Behm (GER) 320
1996 Zhang Xugang (CHN) 357.5kg	Kim Myong-nam (PRK) 345.0	Attila Feri (HUN) 340.0

1896–1912 *Event not held*

[1] Aggregate of five lifts
[2] Tie-breaker rule relating to bodyweight not yet introduced
[3] Zbigniev Kaczmarek (POL) finished in first place with 307.5kg but was subsequently disqualified

Middleweight (Up to 75kg 1920–92; up to 76kg 1996)

1920 Henri Gance (FRA) 245kg	Pietro Bianchi (ITA) 237.5 [1]	Albert Pettersson (SWE) 237.5
1924[2]Carlo Galimberti (ITA) 492.5kg	Alfred Neuland (EST) 455	Jaan Kikas (EST) 450
1928 Roger Francois (FRA) 335kg	Carlo Galimberti (ITA) 332.5	August Scheffer (NED) 327.5
1932 Rudolf Ismayr (GER) 345kg	Carlo Galimberti (ITA) 340	Karl Hipfinger (AUT) 337.5
1936 Khadr El Thouni (EGY) 387.5kg	Rudolf Ismayr (GER) 352.5	Adolf Wagner (GER) 352.5
1948 Frank Spellman (USA) 390kg	Peter George (USA) 412.5	Kim Sung-jip (KOR) 380
1952 Peter George (USA) 400kg	Gérard Gratton (CAN) 390	Kim Sung-jip (KOR) 382.5
1956 Fyodor Bogdanovski (URS) 420kg	Peter George (USA) 412.5	Ermanno Pignatti (ITA) 382.5
1960 Alexander Kurinov (URS) 437.5kg	Tommy Kono (USA) 427.5	Gyözö Veres (HUN) 405
1964 Hans Zdrazila (TCH) 445kg	Viktor Kurentsov (URS) 440	Masashi Ouchi (JPN) 437.5
1968 Viktor Kurentsov (URS) 475kg	Masashi Ouchi (JPN) 455	Károly Bakos (HUN) 440
1972 Yordan Bikov (BUL) 485kg	Mohamed Trabulsi (LIB) 472.5	Anselmo Silvino (ITA) 470
1976 Yordan Bikov (BUL) 335kg	Vartan Militosyan (URS) 330	Peter Wenzel (GDR) 327.5
1980 Asen Zlatev (BUL) 360kg	Alexander Pervy (URS) 357.5	Nedeltcho Kolev (BUL) 345
1984 Karl-Heinz Radschinsky (FRG) 340kg	Jacques Demers (CAN) 335	Dragomir Cioroslan (ROM) 332.5
1988 Borislav Guidikov (BUL) 375kg	Ingo Steinhöfel (GDR) 360	Alexander Varbanov (BUL) 357.5
1992 Fedor Kassapu (EUN) 357.5kg	Pablo Lara (CUB) 357.5	Kim Myong-nam (PRK) 352.5
1996 Pablo Lara (CUB) 367.5kg	Yoto Yotov (BUL) 360.0	Jon Chol-ho (PRK) 357.5

1896–1912 *Event not held*

[1] Bianchi and Pettersson drew lots for the silver medal
[2] Aggregate of five lifts

Light-Heavyweight (Up to 82.5kg 1920–92; up to 83kg 1996)

1920 Ernest Cadine (FRA) 290kg	Fritz Hünenberger (SUI) 275	Erik Pettersson (SWE) 272.5
1924[1]Charles Rigoulot (FRA) 502.5kg	Fritz Hünenberger (SUI) 490	Leopold Friedrich (AUT) 490
1928 Said Nosseir (EGY) 355kg	Louis Hostin (FRA) 352.5	Johannes Verheijen (NED) 337.5
1932 Louis Hostin (FRA) 372.5kg	Svend Olsen (DEN) 360	Henry Duey (USA) 330
1936 Louis Hostin (FRA) 372.5kg	Eugen Deutsch (GER) 365	Ibrahim Wasif (EGY) 360
1948 Stanley Stanczyk (USA) 417.5kg	Harold Sakata (USA) 380	Gösta Magnussen (SWE) 375
1952 Trofim Lomakin (URS) 417.5kg	Stanley Stanczyk (USA) 415	Arkadi Vorobyev (URS) 407.5
1956 Tommy Kono (USA) 447.5kg	Vassili Stepanov (URS) 427.5	James George (USA) 417.5
1960 Ireneusz Palinski (POL) 442.5kg	James George (USA) 430	Jan Bochenek (POL) 420
1964 Rudolf Plukfelder (URS) 475kg	Géza Tóth (HUN) 467.5	Gyözö Veres (HUN) 467.5
1968 Boris Selitsky (URS) 485kg	Vladimir Belyayev (URS) 485	Norbert Ozimek (POL) 472.5
1972 Leif Jenssen (NOR) 507.5kg	Norbert Ozimek (POL) 497.5	György Horváth (HUN) 495
1976[2]Valeri Shary (URS) 365kg	Trendachil Stoichev (BUL) 360	Peter Baczako (HUN) 345
1980 Yurik Vardanyan (URS) 400kg	Blagoi Blagoyev (BUL) 372.5	Dusan Poliacik (TCH) 367.5
1984 Petre Becheru (ROM) 355kg	Robert Kabbas (AUS) 342.5	Ryoji Isaoka (JPN) 340
1988 Israil Arsamokov (URS) 377.5kg	István Messzi (HUN) 370	Lee Hyung-kun (KOR) 367.5

1992 Pyrros Dimas (GRE) 370kg	Krzysztof Siemion (POL) 370	– 3
1996 Pyrros Dimas (GRE) 392.5kg	Marc Huster (GER) 382.5	Andrzej Cofalik (POL) 372.5

1896–1912 *Event not held*

1 Aggregate of five lifts
2 Blagoi Blagoyev (BUL) finished in second place with 362.5kg but was subsequently disqualified
3 Ibraghim Samadov (EUN) placed third but disqualified. No bronze medal awarded

Middle Heavyweight (Up to 90kg 1952–92; up to 91kg 1996)

1952 Norbert Schemansky (USA) 445kg	Grigori Nowak (URS) 410	Lennox Kilgour (TRI) 402.5
1956 Arkadi Vorobyev (URS) 462.5kg	David Sheppard (USA) 442.5	Jean Debuf (FRA) 425
1960 Arkadi Vorobyev (URS) 472.5kg	Trofim Lomakin (URS) 457.5	Louis Martin (GBR) 445
1964 Vladimir Golovanov (URS) 487.5kg	Louis Martin (GBR) 475	Ireneusz Palinski (POL) 467.5
1968 Kaarlo Kanganiemi (FIN) 517.5kg	Jan Talts (URS) 507.5	Marek Golab (POL) 495
1972 Andon Nikolov (BUL) 525kg	Atanas Chopov (BUL) 517.5	Hans Bettembourg (SWE) 512.5
1976 David Rigert (URS) 382.5kg	Lee James (USA) 362.5	Atanas Chopov (BUL) 360
1980 Péter Baczakó (HUN) 377.5kg	Rumen Alexandrov (BUL) 375	Frank Mantek (GDR) 375
1984 Nicu Vlad (ROM) 392.5kg	Dumitru Petre (ROM) 360	David Mercer (GBR) 352.5
1988 Anatoli Khrapati (URS) 412.5kg	Nail Moukhamediarov (URS) 400	Slawomir Zawada (POL) 400
1992 Kakhi Kakhiashvili (EUN) 412.5kg	Sergei Syrtsov (EUN) 412.5	Serguisz Wolczaniecki (POL) 392.5
1996 Alexei Petrov (RUS) 402.5kg	Leonidas Kokas (GRE) 390.0	Oliver Caruso (GER) 390.0

1896–1948 *Event not held*

Up to 100kg (1980–92; up to 99kg 1996)

1980 Ota Zaremba (TCH) 395kg	Igor Nikitin (URS) 392.5	Alberto Blanco (CUB) 385
1984 Rolf Milser (FRG) 385kg	Vasile Gropa (ROM) 382.5	Pekka Niemi (FIN) 367.5
1988 Pavel Kuznetsov (URS) 425kg	Nicu Vlad (ROM) 402.5 1	Peter Immesberger (FRG) 367.5
1992 Viktor Tregubov (EUN) 410kg	Timur Taimazov (EUN) 402.5	Waldemar Malak (POL) 400
1996 Khaki Kakhiashvili (GRE) 420.0kg	Anatoli Khrapati (KZK) 410.0	Denis Gotfrid (UKR) 402.5

1896–1976 *Event not held*

1 Andor Szanyi (HUN) finished second with 407.5kg, but was subsequently disqualified

Heavyweight (1920–48 class over 82.5kg; 1952–68 class over 90kg; 1972–92 class up to 110kg; 1996 up to 108kg)

1896 1 Launceston Eliot (GBR) 71kg	Viggo Jensen (DEN) 57.2	Alexandros Nikolopoulos (GRE) 57.2
1896 2 Viggo Jensen (DEN) 111.5kg	Launceston Eliot (GBR) 111.5	Sotirios Versis (GRE) 90
1904 3 Oscar Osthoff (USA) 48pts	Frederick Winters (USA) 45	Frank Kungler (USA) 10
1904 2 Perikles Kaklousis (GRE) 111.5kg	Oscar Osthoff (USA) 84.36	Frank Kungler (USA) 79.83
1906 1 Josef Steinbach (AUT) 76.55kg	Tullio Camilotti (ITA) 73.75	Heinrich Schneidereit (GER) 70.75
1906 2 Dimitrios Tofalos (GRE) 142.5kg	Josef Steinbach (AUT) 136.5	Alexandre Maspoli (FRA) 129.5 Heinrich Rondl (GER) 129.5 Heinrich Schneidereit (GER) 129.5
1920 Filippo Bottino (ITA) 270kg	Joseph Alzin (LUX) 225	Louis Bernot (FRA) 250
1924 4 Giuseppe Tonani (ITA) 517.5kg	Franz Aigner (AUT) 515	Harald Tammer (EST) 497.5
1928 Josef Strassberger (GER) 372.5kg	Arnold Luhaäär (EST) 360	Jaroslav Skobla (TCH) 375.5
1932 Jaroslav Skobla (TCH) 380kg	Václav Psenicka (TCH) 377.5	Josef Strassberger (GER) 377.5
1936 Josef Manger (GER) 410kg	Václav Psenicka (TCH) 402.5	Arnold Luhaäär (EST) 400
1948 John Davis (USA) 452.2kg	Norbert Schemansky (USA) 425	Abraham Charité (NED) 412.5
1952 John Davis (USA) 460kg	James Bradford (USA) 437.5	Humberto Selvetti (ARG) 432.5
1956 Paul Anderson (USA) 500kg	Humberto Selvetti (ARG) 500	Alberto Pigaiani (ITA) 452.5
1960 Yuri Vlasov (URS) 537.5k	James Bradford (USA) 512.5	Norbert Schemansky (USA) 500
1964 Leonid Zhabotinsky (URS) 572.5kg	Yuri Vlasov (URS) 570	Norbert Schemansky (USA) 537.5
1968 Leonid Zhabotinsky (URS) 572.5kg	Serge Reding (BEL) 555	Joseph Dube (USA) 555

1972 Jan Talts (URS) 580kg	Alexandre Kraitchev (BUL) 562.5	Stefan Grützner (GDR) 555
1976[5] Yuri Zaitsev (URS) 385kg	Krastio Semerdiev (BUL) 385	Tadeusz Rutkowski (POL) 377.5
1980 Leonid Taranenko (URS) 422.5kg	Valentin Christov (BUL) 385	György Szalai (HUN) 390
1984 Norberto Oberburger (ITA) 390kg	Stefan Tasnadi (ROM) 380	Guy Carlton (USA) 377.5
1988 Yuri Zakharevich (URS) 455kg	József Jacsó (HUN) 427.5	Ronny Weller (GDR) 425
1992 Ronny Weller (GER) 432.5kg	Artur Akoyev (EUN) 430	Stefan Botev (BUL) 417.5
1996 Timur Taimazov (UKR) 430.0kg	Sergei Syrtsov (RUS) 420.0	Nicu Vlad (ROM) 420.0

1900, 1908–12 *Event not held*

[1] One-hand lift
[2] Two-hand lift
[3] Dumbell lift
[4] Aggregate of five lifts
[5] Valentin Christov (BUL) finished in first place with 400kg, but was subsequently disqualified

Super-Heavyweight *(Over 110kg 1972–92; over 108kg 1996)*

1972 Vasili Alexeyev (URS) 640kg	Rudolf Mang (FRG) 610	Gerd Bonk (GDR) 572.5
1976 Vasili Alexeyev (URS) 440kg	Gerd Bonk (GDR) 405	Helmut Losch (GDR) 387.5
1980 Sultan Rakhmanov (URS) 440kg	Jürgen Heuser (GDR) 410	Tadeusz Rutkowski (POL) 407.5
1984 Dinko Lukin (AUS) 412.5kg	Mario Martinez (USA) 410	Manfred Nerlinger (FRG) 397.5
1988 Alexander Kurlovich (URS) 462.5kg	Manfred Nerlinger (FRG) 430	Martin Zawieja (FRG) 415
1992 Alexander Kurlovich (EUN) 450kg	Leonid Taranenko (EUN) 425	Manfred Nerlinger (GER) 412.5
1996 Andrei Chemerkin (RUS) 457.5kg	Ronny Weller (GER) 455.0	Stefan Botev (AUS) 455.0

1896–1968 *Event not held*

Wrestling Medals

The contemporary descriptions of some bodyweight classes have varied during the history of the games. Current descriptions are used

GOLD	SILVER	BRONZE

Free-Style —Light Flyweight *(Weight up to 48kg)*

1904 Robert Curry (USA)	John Heim (USA)	Gustav Thiefenthaler (USA)
1972 Roman Dmitriev (URS)	Ognian Nikolov (BUL)	Ebrahim Javadpour (IRN)
1976 Khassan Issaev (BUL)	Roman Dmitriev (URS)	Akira Kudo (JPN)
1980 Claudio Pollio (ITA)	Se Hong Jang (PRK)	Sergei Kornilayev (URS)
1984 Robert Weaver (USA)	Takashi Irie (JPN)	Son Gab-do (KOR)
1988 Takashi Kobaysahi (JPN)	Ivan Tozorov (BUL)	Sergei Karemtchakov (URS)
1992 Kim Il (PRK)	Kim Jong-shin (KOR)	Vougar Oroudzhov (EUN)
1996 Kim Il (PRK)	Armen Mkrchyan (ARM)	Alexis Vila (CUB)

1896–1900, 1906–68 *Event not held*

Free-Style — Flyweight *(1904 weight up to 52.16kg (115lb). From 1948 weight up to 52kg)*

1904 George Mehnert (USA)	Gustave Bauer (USA)	William Nelson (USA)
1948 Lennart Viitala (FIN)	Halit Balamir (TUR)	Thure Johansson (SWE)
1952 Hasan Gemici (TUR)	Yushu Kitano (JPN)	Mahmoud Mollaghessemi (IRN)
1956 Mirian Tslkalamanidze (URS)	Mohamad-Ali Khojastenpour (IRN)	Hüseyin Akbas (TUR)
1960 Ahmet Bilek (TUR)	Masayuki Matsubara (JPN)	Mohamad Saifpour Saidabadi (IRN)
1964 Yoshikatsu Yoshida (JPN)	Chang Chang-sun (KOR)	Said Aliaakbar Haydari (IRN)
1968 Shigeo Nakata (JPN)	Richard Sanders (USA)	Surenjav Sukhbaatar (MGL)
1972 Kiyomi Kato (JPN)	Arsen Alakhverdyev (URS)	Hyong Kim Gwong (PRK)
1976 Yuji Takada (JPN)	Alexander Ivanov (URS)	Jeon Hae-sup (KOR)
1980 Anatoli Beloglazov (URS)	Wladyslaw Stecyk (POL)	Nermedin Selimov (BUL)
1984 Saban Trstena (YUG)	Kim Jong-kyu (KOR)	Yuji Takada (JPN)
1988 Mitsuru Sato (JPN)	Saban Trstena (YUG)	Vladimir Togouzov (URS)
1992 Li Hak-son (PRK)	Larry Lee Jones (USA)	Valentin Jordanov (BUL)
1996 Valentin Jordanov (BUL)	Namik Abdullayev (AZE)	Maulen Mamirov (KZK)

1896–1900, 1906–36 *Event not held*

Free-Style — Bantamweight (Weight 1904 125lb (56.70kg); 1908 119lb (54kg); 1924-36 56kg; from 1948 57kg)

1904 Isidor Niflot (USA)	August Wester (USA)	Zenon Strebler (USA)
1908 George Mehnert (USA)	William Press (GBR)	Aubert Coté (CAN)
1924 Kustaa Pihlajamaki (FIN)	Kaarlo Mäkinen (FIN)	Bryant Hines (USA)
1928 Kaarlo Mäkinen (FIN)	Edmond Spapen (BEL)	James Trifunov (CAN)
1932 Robert Pearce (USA)	Odön Zombori (HUN)	Aatos Jaskari (FIN)
1936 Odön Zombori (HUN)	Ross Flood (USA)	Johannes Herbert (GER)
1948 Nasuk Akar (TUR)	Gerald Leeman (USA)	Charles Kouyov (FRA)
1952 Shohachi Ishii (JPN)	Rashid Mamedbekov (URS)	Kha-Shaba Jadav (IND)
1956 Mustafa Dagistanli (TUR)	Mohamad Yaghoubi (IRN)	Mikhail Chakhov (URS)
1960 Terrence McCann (USA)	Nejdet Zalev (BUL)	Tadeusz Trojanowski (POL)
1964 Yojiro Uetake (JPN)	Hüseyin Akbas (TUR)	Aidyn Ibragimov (URS)
1968 Yojiro Uetake (JPN)	Donald Behm (USA)	Abutaleb Gorgori (IRN)
1972 Hideaki Yanagide (JPN)	Richard Sanders (USA)	László Klinga (HUN)
1976 Vladimir Yumin (URS)	Hans-Dieter Brüchert (GDR)	Masao Arai (JPN)
1980 Sergei Beloglazov (URS)	Li Ho Pyong (PRK)	Dugarsuren Ouinbold (MGL)
1984 Hideyaki Tomiyama (JPN)	Barry Davis (USA)	Kim Eui-kon (KOR)
1988 Sergei Beloglazov (URS)	Askari Mohammadian (IRN)	No Kyung-sun (KOR)
1992 Alejandro Puerto Diaz (CUB)	Sergei Smal (EUN)	Kim Yong-sik (PRK)
1996 Kendall Cross (USA)	Giga Sissaouri (CAN)	Ri Yong-sam (PRK)

1896–1900, 1906, 1912–20 *Event not held*

Free-Style — Featherweight (Weight: 1904, 61.24kg (135lb); 1908, 60.3kg (133lb) ; 1920, 60kg; 1924-36 61kg; 1948–68 63kg; 1972–96, 62kg)

1904 Benjamin Bradshaw (USA)	Theodore McLear (USA)	Charles Clapper (USA)
1908 George Dole (USA)	James Slim (GBR)	William McKie (GBR)
1920 Charles Ackerly (USA)	Samuel Gerson (USA)	P. W. Bernard (GBR)
1924 Robin Reed (USA)	Chester Newton (USA)	Katsutoshi Naito (JPN)
1928 Allie Morrison (USA)	Kustaa Pihlajamäki (FIN)	Hans Minder (SUI)
1932 Hermanni Pihlajamäki (FIN)	Edgar Nemir (USA)	Einar Karlsson (SWE)
1936 Kustaa Pihlajamäki (FIN)	Francis Millard (USA)	Gösta Jönsson (SWE)
1948 Gazanfer Bilge (TUR)	Ivar Sjölin (SWE)	Adolf Müller (SUI)
1952 Bayram Sit (TUR)	Nasser Givétchi (IRN)	Josiah Henson (USA)
1956 Shozo Sasahara (JPN)	Joseph Mewis (BEL)	Erkki Penttilä (FIN)
1960 Mustafa Dagistanli (TUR)	Stantcho Ivanov (BUL)	Vladimir Rubashbili (URS)
1964 Osamu Watanabe (JPN)	Stantcho Ivanov (BUL)	Nodar Khokhashvili (URS)
1968 Masaaki Kaneko (JPN)	Enyu Todorov (BUL)	Shamseddin Seyed-Abbassi (IRN)
1972 Zagalav Abdulbekov (URS)	Vehbi Akdag (TUR)	Ivan Krastev (BUL)
1976 Yang Jung-mo (KOR)	Zeveg Oidov (MGL)	Gene Davis (USA)
1980 Magomedgasan Abushev (URS)	Mikho Doukov (BUL)	Georges Hadiioannidis (GRE)
1984 Randy Lewis (USA)	Kosei Akaishi (JPN)	Lee Jeung-keun (KOR)
1988 John Smith (USA)	Stepan Sarkissian (URS)	Simeon Chterev (BUL)
1992 John Smith (USA)	Askari Mohammadian (IRN)	Lazaro Reinoso (CUB)
1996 Thomas Brands (USA)	Jang Jae-sung (KOR)	Elbrus Tedeyev (UKR)

1896–1900, 1906, 1912 *Event not held*

Free-Style — Lightweight (Weight: 1904, 65.77kg (145lb); 1908, 66.60kg (146.75lb); 1920 67.5kg; 1924–36, 66kg; 1948–60, 67kg; 1964–68, 70kg ; 1972–96 68kg)

1904 Otton Roehm (USA)	Rudolph Tesing (USA)	Albert Zirkel (USA)
1908 George de Relwyskow (GBR)	William Wood (GBR)	Albert Gingell (GBR)
1920 Kalle Anttila (FIN)	Gottfried Svensson (SWE)	Peter Wright (GBR)
1924 Russell Vis (USA)	Volmart Wickström (FIN)	Arvo Haavisto (FIN)
1928 Osvald Käpp (EST)	Charles Pacome (FRA)	Eino Leino (FIN)
1932 Charles Pacome (FRA)	Károly Kápáti (HUN)	Gustaf Klarén (SWE)
1936 Károly Kápáti (HUN)	Wolfgang Ehrl (GER)	Hermanni Pihlajamäki (FIN)
1948 Celál Atik (TUR)	Gösta Frandfors (SWE)	Hermanni Pihilajamäki (FIN)
1952 Olle Anderberg (SWE)	Thomas Evans (USA)	Djahanbakte Tovfighe (IRN)
1956 Emamali Habibi (IRN)	Shigeru Kasahara (JPN)	Alimberg Bestayev (URS)
1960 Shelby Wilson (USA)	Viktor Sinyavskiy (URS)	Enyu Dimov (BUL)
1964 Enyu Valtschev (BUL) [1]	Klaus-Jürgen Rost (GER)	Iwao Horiuchi (JPN)

1968 Abdollah Movahed Ardabili (IRN)	Enyu Valtschev (BUL) [1]	Sereeter Danzandarjaa (MGL)
1972 Dan Gable (USA)	Kikuo Wada (JPN)	Ruslan Ashuraliev (URS)
1976 Pavel Pinigin (URS)	Lloyd Keaser (USA)	Yasaburo Sagawara (JPN)
1980 Saipulla Absaidov (URS)	Ivan Yankov (BUL)	Saban Sejdi (YUG)
1984 You In-tak (KOR)	Andrew Rein (USA)	Jukka Rauhala (FIN)
1988 Arsen Fadzayev (URS)	Park Jang-soon (KOR)	Nate Carr (USA)
1992 Arsen Fadzayev (EUN)	Valentin Getzov (BUL)	Kosei Akaishi (JPN)
1996 Vadim Bogiyev (RUS)	Townsend Saunders (USA)	Zaza Zazirov (UKR)

1896–1900, 1906, 1912 *Event not held*

[1] Valtschev competed as Dimov in 1960

Free-Style — Welterweight *(Weight: 1904, 71.67kg (158lb); 1924–36, 72kg; 1948–60, 73kg; 1972–96 74kg)*

1904 Charles Erikson (USA)	William Beckmann (USA)	Jerry Winholtz (USA)
1924 Hermann Gehri (SUI)	Eino Leino (FIN)	Otto Müller (SUI)
1928 Arvo Haavisto (FIN)	Lloyd Appleton (USA)	Maurice Letchford (CAN)
1932 Jack van Bebber (USA)	Daniel MacDonald (CAN)	Eino Leino (FIN)
1936 Frank Lewis (USA)	Ture Andersson (SWE)	Joseph Schleimer (CAN)
1948 Yasar Dogu (TUR)	Richard Garrard (AUS)	Leland Merrill (USA)
1952 William Smith (USA)	Per Berlin (SWE)	Abdullah Modjtabavi (IRN)
1956 Mitsuo Ikeda (JPN)	Ibrahim Zengin (TUR)	Vakhtang Balavadze (URS)
1960 Douglas Blubaugh (USA)	Ismail Ogan (TUR)	Mohammed Bashir (PAK)
1964 Ismail Ogan (TUR)	Guliko Sagaradze (URS)	Mohamad-Ali Sanatkaran (IRN)
1968 Mahmut Atalay (TUR)	Daniel Robin (FRA)	Dagvasuren Purev (MGL)
1972 Wayne Wells (USA)	Jan Karlsson (SWE)	Adolf Seger (FRG)
1976 Jiichiro Date (JPN)	Mansour Barzegar (IRN)	Stanley Dziedzic (USA)
1980 Valentin Raitchev (URS)	Jamtsying Davaajav (MGL)	Dan Karabin (TCH)
1984 David Schultz (USA)	Martin Knosp (FRG)	Saban Sejdi (YUG)
1988 Kenneth Monday (USA)	Adlan Varayev (URS)	Rakhmad Sofiadi (BUL)
1992 Park Jang-soon (KOR)	Kenneth Monday (USA)	Amir Khadem (IRN)
1996 Buvaisa Saityev (RUS)	Park Jang-soon (KOR)	Taykuo Ota (JPN)

1896–1906, 1912 *Event not held*

Free-Style — Middleweight *(Weight: 1908, 73kg (161lb); 1920, 75kg (165.25lb); 1924–60, 79kg; 1964–68, 87kg; 1972–96 82kg)*

1908 Stanley Bacon (GBR)	George de Relwyskow (GBR)	Frederick Beck (GBR)
1920 Eino Reino (FIN)	Väinö Penttala (FIN)	Charles Johnson (USA)
1924 Fritz Hagmann (SUI)	Pierre Ollivier (BEL)	Vilho Pekkala (FIN)
1928 Ernst Kyburz (SUI)	Donald Stockton (CAN)	Samuel Rabin (GBR)
1932 Ivar Johansson (SWE)	Kyösti Luukko (FIN)	József Tunyogi (HUN)
1936 Emile Poilvé (FRA)	Richard Voliva (USA)	Ahmet Kirecci (TUR)
1948 Glen Brand (USA)	Adil Candemir (TUR)	Erik Lindén (SWE)
1952 David Tsimakuridze (URS)	Gholam Reza Takhti (IRN)	György Gurics (HUN)
1956 Nikola Stantchev (BUL)	Daniel Hodge (USA)	Georgi Skhirtladze (URS)
1960 Hasan Güngör (TUR)	Georgi Skhirtladze (URS)	Hans Antonsson (SWE)
1964 Prodan Gardshev (BUL)	Hasan Güngör (TUR)	Daniel Brand (USA)
1968 Boris Mikhailovich Gurevich (URS)	Munkbat Jigjid (MGL)	Prodan Gradshev (BUL)
1972 Leven Tediashvili (URS)	John Peterson (USA)	Vasile Jorga (ROM)
1976 John Peterson (USA)	Viktor Novoshilev (URS)	Adolf Seger (FRG)
1980 Ismail Abilov (BUL)	Magomedhan Aratsilov (URS)	István Kovács (HUN)
1984 Mark Schultz (USA)	Hideyuki Nagashima (JPN)	Chris Rinke (CAN)
1988 Han Myung-woo (KOR)	Necmi Gencalp (TUR)	Josef Lohyna (TCH)
1992 Kevin Jackson (USA)	Elmadi Zhabraylov (EUN)	Razul Khadem Azghadi (IRN)
1996 Khadshimurad Magomedov (RUS)	Yang Hyun-mo (KOR)	Amir Khadem Azghadi (IRN)

1896–1906, 1912 *Event not held*

Free-Style — Light-Heavyweight *(Weight: 1920, 82.5kg; 1924–60, 87kg; 1964–68, 97kg; 1972–96 90kg)*

1920 Anders Larsson (SWE)	Charles Courant (SUI)	Walter Maurer (USA)
1924 John Spellman (USA)	Rudolf Svensson (SWE)	Charles Courant (FRA)
1928 Thure Sjöstedt (SWE)	Anton Bögli (SUI)	Henri Lefebre (FRA)

1932	Peter Mehringer (USA)	Thure Sjöstedt (SWE)	Eddie Scarf (AUS)
1936	Knut Fridell (SWE)	August Neo (EST)	Erich Siebert (GER)
1948	Henry Wittenberg (USA)	Fritz Stöckli (SUI)	Bengt Fahlkvist (SWE)
1952	Wiking Palm (SWE)	Henry Wittenberg (USA)	Adil Atan (TUR)
1956	Gholam Reza Tahkti (IRN)	Boris Kulayev (URS)	Peter Blair (USA)
1960	Ismet Atli (TUR)	Gholam Reza Tahkti (IRN)	Anatoli Albul (URS)
1964	Alexander Medved (URS)	Ahmet Ayik (TUR)	Said Mustafafov (BUL)
1968	Ahmet Ayik (TUR)	Shota Lomidze (URS)	József Csatári (HUN)
1972	Ben Peterson (USA)	Gennadi Strakhov (URS)	Károly Bajkó (HUN)
1976	Levan Tediashvili (URS)	Ben Peterson (USA)	Stelica Morcov (ROM)
1980	Sanasar Oganesyan (URS)	Uwe Neupert (GDR)	Aleksandr Cichon (POL)
1984	Ed Banach (USA)	Akira Ota (JPN)	Noel Loban (GBR)
1988	Makharbek Khadartsev (URS)	Akira Ota (JPN)	Kim Tae-woo (KOR)
1992	Makharbek Khadartsev (EUN)	Kenan Simsek (TUR)	Christopher Campbell (USA)
1996	Rasul Khadem Azghadi (IRN)	Makharbek Khadartsev (RUS)	Eldari Kurtanidze (GEO)

1896–1912 *Event not held*

Free-Style — Heavyweight *(Weight: 1904, over 71.6kg (158lb); 1908, over 73kg; 1920, over 82.5kg; 1924–60, over 87kg; 1964–68, over 97kg; 1972–96 up to 100kg)*

1904	Bernhuff Hansen (USA)	Frank Kungler (USA)	Fred Warmbold (USA)
1908	George O'Kelly (GBR)	Jacob Gundersen (NOR)	Edmond Barrett (GBR)
1920	Robert Roth (SUI)	Nathan Pendleton (USA)	Ernst Nilsson (SWE)
			Frederick Meyer (USA) [1]
1924	Harry Steele (USA)	Henry Wernli (SUI)	Andrew McDonald (GBR) [1]
1928	Johan Richthoff (SWE)	Aukusti Sihovlla (FIN)	Edmond Dame (FRA)
1932	Johan Richthoff (SWE)	John Riley (USA)	Nikolaus Hirschl (AUT)
1936	Kristjan Palusalu (EST)	Josef Klapuch (TCH)	Hjalmar Nyström (FIN)
1948	Gyula Bóbis (HUN)	Bertil Antonsson (SWE)	Joseph Armstrong (AUS)
1952	Arsen Mekokishvili (URS)	Bertil Antonsson (SWE)	Kenneth Richmond (GBR)
1956	Hamit Kaplan (TUR)	Hussein Mekhmedov (BUL)	Taisto Kangasniemi (FIN)
1960	Wilfried Dietrich (GER)	Hamit Kaplan (TUR)	Savkus Dzarassov (URS)
1964	Alexander Ivanitsky (URS)	Liutvi Djiber (BUL)	Hamit Kaplan (TUR)
1968	Alexander Medved (URS)	Osman Duraliev (BUL)	Wilfried Dietrich (FRG)
1972	Ivan Yaragin (URS)	Khorloo Baianmunkh (MGL)	József Csatári (HUN)
1976	Ivan Yaragin (URS)	Russell Helickson (USA)	Dimo Kostov (BUL)
1980	Ilya Mate (URS)	Slavtcho Tchervenkov (BUL)	Julius Strnisko (TCH)
1984	Lou Banach (USA)	Joseph Atiyeh (SYR)	Vasile Pascasu (ROM)
1988	Vasile Pascasu (ROM)	Leri Khabelov (URS)	William Scherr (USA)
1992	Leri Khabelov (EUN)	Heiko Balz (GER)	Ali Kayali (TUR)
1996	Kurt Angle (USA)	Abbas Jadidi (IRN)	Arwat Sabejew (GER)

1896–1900, 1906, 1912 *Event not held*

[1] Tie for third place

Free-Style — Super-Heavyweight *(Weight over 100kg)*

1972	Alexander Medved (URS)	Osman Duraliev (BUL)	Chris Taylor (USA)
1976	Soslan Andiev (URS)	Jozsef Balla (HUN)	Ladislau Simon (ROM)
1980	Soslan Andiev (URS)	Jozsef Balla (HUN)	Adam Sandurski (POL)
1984	Bruce Baumgartner (USA)	Bob Molle (CAN)	Ayhan Taskin (TUR)
1988	David Gobedjichvili (URS)	Bruce Baumgartner (USA)	Andreas Schröder (GDR)
1992	Bruce Baumgartner (USA)	Jeff Thue (CAN)	David Gobedjhichvili (EUN)
1996	Mahmut Demir (TUR)	Alexei Medvedev (BUL)	Bruce Baumgartner (USA)

1896–1968 *Event not held*

Greco-Roman — Light Flyweight *(Weight up to 48kg)*

1972	Gheorghe Berceanu (ROM)	Rahim Ahabadi (IRN)	Stefan Anghelov (BUL)
1976	Alexei Shumanov (URS)	Gheorghe Berceanu (ROM)	Stefan Anghelov (BUL)
1980	Zaksylik Ushkempirov (URS)	Constantin Alexandru (ROM)	Ferenc Seres (HUN)
1984	Vincenzo Maenza (ITA)	Markus Scherer (FRG)	Ikuzo Saito (JPN)
1988	Vincenzo Maenza (ITA)	Andrzej Glab (POL)	Bratan Tzenov (BUL)

| 1992 | Oleg Kutcherenko (EUN) | Vincenzo Maenza (ITA) | Wiber Sanchez (CUB) |
| 1996 | Sim Kwon-ho (KOR) | Alexander Pavlov (BLR) | Zafar Gulyov (RUS) |

1896–1968 *Event not held*

Greco-Roman — Flyweight *(Weight up to 52kg)*

1948	Pietro Lombardi (ITA)	Kenan Olcay (TUR)	Reino Kangasmäki (FIN)
1952	Boris Maksimovich Gurevich (URS)	Iganzio Fabra (ITA)	Leo Honkala (FIN)
1956	Nikolai Solovyov (URS)	Ignazio Fabra (ITA)	Durum Ali Egribas (TUR)
1960	Dumitru Pirvulescu (ROM)	Osman Sayed (UAR)	Mohamad Paziraye (IRN)
1964	Tsutomu Hanahara (JPN)	Angel Kerezov (BUL)	Dumitru Pirvulescu (ROM)
1968	Petar Kirov (BUL)	Vladimir Bakulin (URS)	Miroslav Zeman (TCH)
1972	Petar Kirov (BUL)	Koichiro Hirayama (JPN)	Giuseppe Bognanni (ITA)
1976	Vitali Konstantinov (URS)	Nicu Ginga (ROM)	Koichiro Kirayama (JPN)
1980	Vakhtang Blagidze (URS)	Lajos Racz (HUN)	Mladen Mladenov (BUL)
1984	Atsuji Miyahama (JPN)	Daniel Aceves (MEX)	Bang Dae-du (KOR)
1988	Jon Ronningen (NOR)	Atsuji Miyahama (JPN)	Lee Jae-suk (KOR)
1992	Jon Ronningen (NOR)	Alfred Ter-Mkrttchian (EUN)	Min Kyung-kap (KOR)
1996	Arman Nazaryan (ARM)	Brandon Paulson (USA)	Andrei Kalashnikov (UKR)

1896–1936 *Event not held*

Greco-Roman — Bantamweight *(Weight: 1924–28, 58kg; 1932–36, 56kg; since 1948, 57kg)*

1924	Eduard Pütsep (EST)	Anselm Ahlfors (FIN)	Väinö Ikonen (FIN)
1928	Kurt Leucht (GER)	Jindrich Maudr (TCH)	Giovanni Gozzi (ITA)
1932	Jakob Brendel (GER)	Marcello Nizzola (ITA)	Louis François (FRA)
1936	Márton Lörincz (HUN)	Egon Svensson (SWE)	Jakob Brendel (GER)
1948	Kurt Pettersén (SWE)	Aly Mahmoud Hassan (EGY)	Habil Kaya (TUR)
1952	Imre Hódos (HUN)	Zakaria Chihab (LIB)	Artem Teryan (URS)
1956	Konstantin Vyrupayev (URS)	Evdin Vesterby (SWE)	Francisco Horvat (ROM)
1960	Oleg Karavayev (URS)	Ion Cernea (ROM)	Petrov Dinko (BUL)
1964	Masamitsu Ichiguchi (JPN)	Vladen Trostiansky (URS)	Ion Cernea (ROM)
1968	János Varga (HUN)	Ion Baciu (ROM)	Ivan Kochergin (URS)
1972	Rustem Kazakov (URS)	Hans-Jürgen Veil (FRG)	Risto Björlin (FIN)
1976	Pertti Ukkola (FIN)	Iván Frgic (YUG)	Farhat Mustafin (URS)
1980	Shamil Serikov (URS)	Jozef Lipien (POL)	Benni Ljungbeck (SWE)
1984	Pasquale Passarelli (FRG)	Masaki Eto (JPN)	Haralambos Holidis (GRE)
1988	Andras Sike (HUN)	Stoyan Balov (BUL)	Haralambos Holidis (GRE)
1992	An Han-bong (KOR)	Rifat Yildiz (GER)	Sheng Zetian (CHN)
1996	Yovei Melnichenko (KZK)	Denis Hall (USA)	Sheng Zetian (CHN)

1896–1920 *Event not held*

Greco-Roman — Featherweight *(Weight: 1912–20, 60kg; 1924–28, 1932–36, 61kg; 1948–60, 62kg; 1964–68, 63kg; 1972–96 62kg)*

1912	Kaarlo Koskelo (FIN)	Georg Gerstacker (GER)	Otto Lasanen (FIN)
1920	Oskari Friman (FIN)	Hekki Kähkönen (FIN)	Fridtjof Svensson (SWE)
1924	Kalle Antila (FIN)	Aleksanteri Toivola (FIN)	Erik Malmberg (SWE)
1928	Voldemar Väli (EST)	Erik Malmberg (SWE)	Giacomo Quaglia (ITA)
1932	Giovanni Gozzi (ITA)	Wolfgang Ehrl (GER)	Lauri Koskela (FIN)
1936	Yasar Erkan (TUR)	Aarne Reini (FIN)	Einar Karlsson (SWE)
1948	Mehmet Oktav (TUR)	Olle Anderberg (SWE)	Ferenc Tóth (HUN)
1952	Yakov Punkin (URS)	Imre Polyák (HUN)	Abdel Rashed (EGY)
1956	Rauno Mäkinen (FIN)	Imre Polyák (HUN)	Roman Dzneladze (URS)
1960	Muzahir Sille (TUR)	Imre Polyák (HUN)	Konstantin Vyrupayev (URS)
1964	Imre Polyák (HUN)	Roman Rurua (URS)	Branko Marttinovic (YUG)
1968	Roman Rurua (URS)	Hideo Fujimoto (JPN)	Simeon Popescu (ROM)
1972	Gheorghi Markov (BUL)	Heniz-Helmut Wehling (GDR)	Kazimierz Lipien (POL)
1976	Kazimierz Lipien (POL)	Nelson Davidian (URS)	László Réczi (HUN)
1980	Stilianos Migiakis (GRE)	István Tóth (HUN)	Boris Kramorenko (URS)
1984	Kim Weon-kee (KOR)	Kent-Olle Johansson (SWE)	Hugo Dietsche (SUI)

1988 Kamandar Madjidov (URS)	Jivko Vanguelov (BUL)	An Dae-hyun (KOR)
1992 Akif Pirim (TUR)	Sergei Martynov (EUN)	Juan Maren (CUB)
1996 Wlodzimierz Zawadzki (POL)	Juan Delis (CUB)	Akif Pirim (TUR)

1896–1920 *Event not held*

Greco-Roman — Lightweight (Note:The weight limit for this event has been: 1906, 75kg; 1908, 66.6kg; 1912–28, 67.5kg; 1932–36, 66kg; 1948–60, 67kg; 1964–68, 70kg; since 1972, 68kg)

1906 Rudolf Watzl (AUT)	Karl Karlsen (DEN)	Ferenc Holuban (HUN)
1908 Enrico Porro (ITA)	Nikolav Orlov (URS0	Avid Lindén-Linko (FIN)
1912 Eemil Wäre (FIN)	Gustaf Malmström (SWE)	Edvin Matiasson (SWE)
1920 Eemil Wäre (FIN)	Taavi Tamminen (FIN)	Fritjof Andersen (NOR)
1924 Oskari Friman (FIN)	Lajos Keresztes (HUN)	Kalle Westerlund (FIN)
1928 Lajos Keresztes (HUN)	Eduard Sperling (GER)	Eduard Westerlund (FIN)
1932 Erik Malmberg (SWE)	Abraham Kurland (DEN)	Eduard Sperling (GER)
1936 Lauri Koskela (FIN)	Josef Herda (TCH)	Voldemar Väli (EST)
1948 Gustaf Freij (SWE)	Aage Eriksen (NOR)	Károly Ferencz (HUN)
1952 Shazam Safim (URS)	Gustaf Freij (SWE)	Mikulás Athanasov (TCH)
1956 Kyösti Lentonen (FIN)	Riza Dogan (TUR)	Gyula Tóth (HUN)
1960 Avtandil Koridza (URS)	Branislav Martinovic (YUG)	Gustaf Freij (SWE)
1964 Kazim Avvaz (TUR)	Valeriu Bularca (ROM)	David Gvantseladze (URS)
1968 Munji Mumemura (JPN)	Stevan Horvat (YUG)	Petros Galaktopoulos (GRE)
1972 Shamii Khisamutdinov (URS)	Stoyan Apostolov (BUL)	Gian Matteo Ranzi (ITA)
1976 Suren Nalbandyan (URS)	Stefan Rusu (ROM)	Heinz-Helmut Wehling (GDR)
1980 Stefan Rusu (ROM)	Andrzej Supron (POL)	Lars-Erik Skiold (SWE)
1984 Vlado Lisjak (YUG)	Tapio Sipila (FIN)	James Martinez (USA)
1988 Levon Djoulfalakian (URS)	Kim Sung-moon (KOR)	Tapio Sipila (FIN)
1992 Attila Repka (HUN)	Islam Dougutchyev (EUN)	Rodney Smith (USA)
1996 Ryzsard Wolny (POL)	Ghani Yalouz (FRA)	Alexander Tretyakov (RUS)

1896–1904 *Event not held*

Greco-Roman — Welterweight (Weight: 1932–36, 72kg; 1948–60, 73kg; 1964–68, 78kg; 1972–96 74kg)

1932 Ivar Johansson (SWE)	Väinö Kajander (FIN)	Ercole Gallegatti (ITA)
1936 Rudolf Svedberg (SWE)	Fritz Schäfer (GER)	Eino Virtanen (FIN)
1948 Gösta Andersson (SWE)	Miklós Szilvási (HUN)	Henrik Hansen (DEN)
1952 Miklós Szilvási (HUN)	Gösta Andersson (SWE)	Khalil Taha (LIB)
1956 Mithat Bayrak (TUR)	Vladimir Maneyev (URS)	Per Berlin (SWE)
1960 Mithat Bayrak (TUR)	Günther Maritschnigg (GER)	René Schiermeyer (FRA)
1964 Anatoli Kolesov (URS)	Cyril Todorov (BUL)	Bertil Nyström (SWE)
1968 Rudolf Vesper (GDR)	Daniel Robin (FRA)	Károly Bajkó (HUN)
1972 Vitezslav Macha (TCH)	Petros Galaktopoulos (GRE)	Jan Karlsson (SWE)
1976 Anatoli Kykov (URS)	Vitezslav Macha (TCH)	Karlhienz Helbing (FRG)
1980 Ferenc Kocsis (HUN)	Anatoli Bykov (URS)	Mikko Huhtala (FIN)
1984 Jonko Salomaki (FIN)	Roger Tallroth (SWE)	Stefan Rusu (ROM)
1988 Kim Young-nam (KOR)	Daoulet Tourlykhanov (URS)	Jozef Tracz (POL)
1992 Mnatsakan Iskandaryan (EUN)	Jozef Tracz (POL)	Torbjörn Kornbakk (SWE)
1996 Feliberto Aguilera (CUB)	Marko Asell (FIN)	Jozef Tracz (POL)

1896–1928 *Event not held*

Greco-Roman — Middleweight (Weight: 1906, 85kg; 1908, 73kg; 1912–28, 75kg; 1932–60, 79kg; 1964–68, 87kg; 1972–96 82kg)

1906 Verner Weckman (FIN)	Rudolf Lindmayer (AUT)	Robert Bebrens (USA)
1908 Frithiof Mårtensson (SWE)	Mauritz Andersson (SWE)	Anders Andersen (DEN)
1912 Claes Johansson (SWE)	Martin Klein (URS)	Alfred Asikainen (FIN)
1920 Carl Westergren (SWE)	Artur Lindfors (FIN)	Matti Perttilä (FIN)
1924 Eduard Westerlund (SWE)	Artur Lindfors (FIN)	Roman Steinberg (EST)
1928 Väinö Kokkinen (FIN)	László Papp (HUN)	Albert Kusnetz (EST)
1932 Väinö Kokkinen (FIN)	Jean Földeák (GER)	Axel Cadier (SWE)
1936 Ivar Johansson (SWE)	Ludwig Schweikert (GER)	József Palotás (HUN)
1948 Axel Grönberg (SWE)	Muhlis Tayfur (TUR)	Ercole Gallegatti (ITA)

1952 Axel Grönberg (SWE)	Kalervo Rauhala (FIN)	Nikolai Belov (URS)
1956 Givi Kartiziya (URS)	Dimiter Dobrev (BUL)	Rune Jansson (SWE)
1960 Dimiter Dobrev (BUL)	Lothar Metz (GER)	Ion Taranu (ROM)
1964 Branislav Simic (YUG)	Jiri Kormanik (TCH)	Lothar Metz (GER)
1968 Lothar Metz (GDR)	Valentin Olenik (URS0	Branislav Simic (YUG)
1972 Csaba Hegedus (HUN)	Anatoli Nazarenko (URS)	Milan Nenadic (YUG)
1976 Momir Petkovic (YUG)	Vladimir Cheboksarov (URS)	Ivan Kolev (BUL)
1980 Gennadi Korban (URS)	Jan Polgowicz (POL)	Pavel Pavlov (BUL)
1984 Ion Draica (ROM)	Dimitrios Thanapoulos (GRE)	Soren Claeson (SWE)
1988 Mikhail Mamiachvili (URS)	Tibor Komaromi (HUN)	Kim Sang-kyu (KOR)
1992 Peter Farkas (HUN)	Piotr Stepien (POL)	Daoulet Tourlykhanov (EUN)
1996 Hamza Yerlikaya (TUR)	Thomas Zander (GER)	Valeri Tsilent (BLR)

1896–1904 *Event not held*

Greco-Roman — Light-Heavyweight *(Weight: 1908, 93kg; 1912–28, 82.5kg; 1932–60, 87kg; 1964–68, 97kg; 1972–96 90kg)*

1908 Verner Weckman (FIN)	Yrjö Saarala (FIN)	Carl Jensen (DEN)
1912 – [1]	Anders Ahlgren (SWE)	Béla Varga (HUN)
	Ivor Böhling (FIN)	
1920 Claes Johansson (SWE)	Edil Rosenqvist (SWE)	Johannes Eriksen (DEN)
1924 Carl Westergren (SWE)	Rudolf Svensson (SWE)	Onni Pellinen (FIN)
1928 Ibrahim Moustafa (EGY)	Adolf Rieger (GER)	Onni Pellinen (FIN)
1932 Rudolf Svensson (SWE)	Onni Pellinen (FIN)	Mario Gruppioni (ITA)
1936 Axel Cadier (SWE)	Edwins Bietags (LAT)	August Néo (EST)
1948 Karl-Erik Nilsson (SWE)	Kaelpo Gröndahl (FIN)	Ibrahim Orabi (EGY)
1952 Kaelpo Gröndahl (FIN)	Shalva Shikhladze (URS)	Karl-Erik Nilsson (SWE)
1956 Valentin Nikolayev (URS)	Petko Sirakov (BUL)	Karl-Erik Nilsson (SWE)
1960 Tevfik Kis (TUR)	Krali Bimbalov (BUL)	Givi Kartoziya (URS)
1964 Boyan Radev (BUL)	Per Svensson (SWE)	Heinz Kiehl (GER)
1968 Boyan Radev (BUL)	Nikolai Yakovenko (URS)	Nicolae Martinescu (ROM)
1972 Valeri Rezantsky (URS)	Josip Corak (YUG)	Czeslaw Kwiecinski (POL)
1976 Valeri Rezantsky (URS)	Stoyan Ivanov (BUL)	Czeslaw Kwiecinski (POL)
1980 Norbert Nottny (HUN)	Igor Kanygin (URS)	Petre Disu (ROM)
1984 Steven Fraser (USA)	Ilie Matei (ROM)	Frank Andersson (SWE)
1988 Atanas Komchev (BUL)	Harri Koskela (FIN)	Vladimir Popov (URS)
1992 Maik Bullmann (GER)	Hakki Basar (TUR)	Gogui Kogouachvili (EUN)
1996 Vyachetslav Oleynik (UKR)	Jacek Fafinski (POL)	Maik Bullmann (GER)

1896–1906 *Event not held*

[1] Ahlgren and Böhling declared equal second after 9 hours of wrestling

Greco-Roman — Heavyweight *(Weight: 1896, open; 1906, over 85kg; 1908, over 93kg; 1912–28, over 82.5kg; 1932–60, over 81kg; 1964–68, over 91kg; 1972–96 up to 100kg)*

1896 Carl Schuhmann (GER)	Georgios Tsitas (GRE)	Stephanos Christopoulos (GRE)
1906 Sören Jensen (DEN)	Henri Baur (AUT)	Marcel Dubois (BEL)
1908 Richard Weisz (HUN)	Alexander Petrov (RUS)	Sören Jensen (DEN)
1912 Yrjö Saarela (FIN)	Johan Olin (FIN)	Sören Jensen (DEN)
1920 Adolf Lindfors (FIN)	Poul Hansen (DEN)	Martti Nieminen (FIN)
1924 Henri Deglane (FRA)	Edil Rosenqvist (FIN)	Raymund Badó (HUN)
1928 Rudolf Svensson (SWE)	Hjalmar Nyström (FIN)	Georg Gehring (GER)
1932 Carl Westergren (SWE)	Josef Urban (TCH)	Nikolaus Hirschl (AUT)
1936 Kristjan Palusalu (EST)	John Nyman (SWE)	Kurt Hornfischer (GER)
1948 Ahmet Kireçci (TUR)	Tor Nilsson (SWE)	Guido Fantoni (ITA)
1952 Johannes Kotkas (URS)	Josef Ruzicka (TCH)	Tauno Kovanen (FIN)
1956 Anatoli Parfenov (URS)	Wilfried Dietrich (GER)	Adelmo Bulgarelli (ITA)
1960 Ivan Bogdan (URS)	Wilfried Dietrich (GER)	Bohumil Kubat (TCH)
1964 István Kozma (HUN)	Anatoli Roschin (URS)	Wilfried Dietrich (GER)
1968 István Kozma (HUN)	Anatoli Roschin (URS)	Petr Kment (TCH)
1972 Nicolae Martinescu (ROM)	Nikolai Yakovenko (URS)	Ferenc Kiss (HUN)
1976 Nikolai Bolboshin (URS)	Kamen Goranov (BUL)	Andrzej Skrzylewski (POL)

1980 Gheorghi Raikov (BUL)	Roman Bierla (POL)	Vasile Andrei (ROM)
1984 Vasile Andrei (ROM)	Greg Gibson (USA)	Jozef Tertelje (YUG)
1988 Andrzej Wronski (POL)	Gerhard Himmel (FRG)	Dennis Koslowski (USA)
1992 Hector Milian (CUB)	Dennis Koslowski (USA)	Sergei Demyashkevich (EUN)
1996 Andreas Wronski (POL)	Sergei Lishvan (BLR)	Mikael Ljungberg (SWE)

1900–04 *Event not held*

Greco-Roman — Super-Heavyweight (Weight over 100kg; Since 1988 a maximum of 130kg has been imposed)

1972 Anatoli Roschin (URS)	Alexandre Tomov (BUL)	Victor Dolipschi (ROM)
1976 Alexander Kolchinsky (URS)	Alexandre Tomov (BUL)	Roman Codreanu (ROM)
1980 Alexander Kolchinsky (URS)	Alexandre Tomov (BUL)	Hassan Bchara (LIB)
1984 Jeffrey Blatnick (USA)	Refik Memisevic (YUG)	Victor Dolipschi (ROM)
1988 Alexander Karelin (URS)	Ranguel Guerovski (BUL)	Tomas Johansson (SWE)
1992 Alexander Karelin (URS)	Tomas Johansson (SWE)	Ioan Grigoras (ROM)
1996 Alexander Karelin (URS)	Matt Ghaffari (USA)	Sergei Moureiko (MDA)

1896–1968 *Event not held*

Discontinued Event

Greco-Roman All-around

1906 Sören Jensen (DEN)	Verner Weckmann (FIN)	Rudolf Watzl (AUT)

Yachting Medals

GOLD	SILVER	BRONZE

Men

Olympic Monotype

1920[1] The Netherlands (Franciscus Hin) (Johannes Hin)	The Netherlands (Arnoud van der Biesen) (Petrus Beukers)	–
1924[2] Léon Huybrechts (BEL)	Henrik Robert (NOR)	Hans Dittmar (FIN)
1928[3] Sven Thorell (SWE)	Henrik Robert (NOR)	Bertil Broman (FIN)
1932[4] Jacques Lebrun (FRA)	Adriaan Maas (NED)	Santiago Cansino (ESP)
1936[5] Daniel Kagchelland (NED)	Werner Krogmann (GER)	Peter Scott (GBR)
1948[6] Paul Elvström (DEN)	Ralph Evans (USA)	Jacobus de Jong (NED)
1952[7] Paul Elvström (DEN)	Charles Currey (GBR)	Rickard Sarby (SWE)
1956 Paul Elvström (DEN)	André Nelis (BEL)	John Marvin (USA)
1960 Paul Elvström (DEN)	Alexander Chuchelov (URS)	André Nelis (BEL)
1964 Willi Kuhweide (GER)	Peter Barrett (USA)	Henning Wird (DEN)
1968 Valentin Mankin (URS)	Hubert Raudaschl (AUT)	Fabio Albarelli (ITA)
1972 Serge Maury (FRA)	Ilias Hatzipavlis (GRE)	Viktor Potapov (URS)
1976 Jochen Schümann (GDR)	Andrei Balashov (URS)	John Bertrand (AUS)
1980 Esko Rechardt (FIN)	Wolfgang Mayrhofer (AUT)	Andrei Balashov (URS)
1984 Russell Coutts (NZL)	John Bertrand (AUS)	Terry Neilson (CAN)
1988 José Luis Doreste (ESP)	Peter Holmberg (ISV)	John Cutler (NZL)
1992 José Maria van der Ploeg (ESP)	Brian Ledbetter (USA)	Craig Monk (NZL)
1996 Mateusz Kuznierewicz (POL)	Sebastian Godefroid (BEL)	Roy Heiner (NED)

1896–1912 *Event not held*

[1] 12-foot dinghy (note two-handled), no bronze medal
[2] Meulan class, 12-foot dinghy
[3] International 12-foot class
[4] Snowbird class
[5] International Olympia class
[6] Firefly class
[7] 1952–96 Finn class

Sailboard Class

1984[1] Steve Van Den Berg (NED)	Randall Steele (USA)	Bruce Kendall (NZL)
1988[2] Bruce Kendall (NZL)	Jan Boersma (AHO)	Michael Gebhardt (USA)

| 1992[2] Franck David (FRA) | Michael Gebhardt (USA) | Lars Kleppich (AUS) |
| 1996[3] Nikolas Kaklamanakis (GRE) | Carlos Espinola (ARG) | Gal Fridman (ISR) |

1896–1980 *Event not held*

[1] Windglider
[2] Lechner
[3] Mistral

International Soling

1972	United States	Sweden	Canada
1976	Denmark	United States	East Germany
1980	Denmark	Soviet Union	Greece
1984	United States	Brazil	Canada
1988	East Germany	United States	Denmark
1992	Denmark	United States	Great Britain
1996	Germany	Russia	United States

1896–1968 *Event not held*

International 470

1976	West Germany	Spain	Australia
1980	Brazil	East Germany	Finland
1984	Spain	United States	France
1988	France	Soviet Union	United States
1992	Spain	United States	Estonia
1996	Ukraine	Great Britain	Portugal

1896–1972 *Event not held*

International Tornado

1976	Great Britain	United States	West Germany
1980	Brazil	Denmark	Sweden
1984	New Zealand	United States	Australia
1988	France	New Zealand	Brazil
1992	France	United States	Australia
1996	Spain	Australia	Brazil

1896–1972 *Event not held*

International Star

1932	United States	Great Britain	Sweden
1936	Germany	Sweden	The Netherlands
1948	United States	Cuba	The Netherlands
1952	Italy	United States	Portugal
1956	United States	Italy	Bahamas
1960	Soviet Union	Portugal	United States
1964	Bahamas	United States	Sweden
1968	United States	Norway	Italy
1972	Australia	Sweden	West Germany
1980	Soviet Union	Austria	Italy
1984	United States	West Germany	Italy
1988	Great Britain	United States	Brazil
1992	United States	New Zealand	Canada
1996	Brazil	Sweden	Australia

1896–1928, 1976 *Event not held*

Flying Dutchman

1956[1]	New Zealand	Australia	Great Britain
1960	Norway	Denmark	Germany
1964	New Zealand	Great Britain	United States
1968	Great Britain	West Germany	Brazil

1972	Great Britain	France	West Germany
1976	West Germany	Great Britain	Brazil
1980	Spain	Ireland	Hungary
1984	United States	Canada	Great Britain
1988	Denmark	Norway	Canada
1992	Spain	United States	Denmark

1896–1952, 1996 *Event not held*

[1] Sharpie class

Laser

1996	Robert Scheldt (BRA)	Ben Ainslie (GBR)	Per Moberg (NOR)

1896–1992 *Event not held*

Women

Sailboard Class

1992[1]	Barbara-Anne Kendall (NZL)	Zhang Xiaodong (CHN)	Dorien de Vries (NED)
1996[2]	Lai-Shan Lee (HKG)	Barbara Kendall (NZL)	Alessandra Sensini (ITA)

1896–1988 *Event not held*

[1] Lechner
[2] Mistral

International 470

1988	United States	Sweden	Soviet Union
1992	Spain	New Zealand	United States
1996	Spain	Japan	Ukraine

1896–1984 *Event not held*

Europe Class

1992	Linda Andersen (NOR)	Natalia Dufresne (ESP)	Julia Trotman (USA)
1996	Kristine Roug (DEN)	Margit Matthijsse (NED)	Courtney Becker-Dey (USA)

1896–1988 *Event not held*

Discontinued Events

Swallow

1948	Great Britain	Portugal	United States

International Tempest

1972	Soviet Union	Great Britain	United States
1976	Sweden	Soviet Union	United States

Dragon

1948	Norway	Sweden	Denmark
1952	Norway	Sweden	Germany
1956	Sweden	Denmark	Great Britain
1960	Greeece	Argentina	Italy
1964	Denmark	Germany	United States
1968	United States	Denmark	East Germany
1972	Australia	East Germany	United States

30 Square Metres

1920	Sweden	–	–

40 Square Metres

1920	Sweden	–	–

5.5 Metres

1952 United States	Norway	Sweden
1956 Sweden	Great Britain	Australia
1960 United States	Denmark	Switzerland
1964 Australia	Sweden	United States
1968 Sweden	Switzerland	Great Britain

6 Metres

1908 Great Britain	Belgium	France
1912 France	Denmark	Sweden
1920 Norway	Belgium	–
1924 Norway	Denmark	The Netherlands
1928 Norway	Denmark	Estonia
1932 Sweden	United States	Canada
1936 Great Britain	Norway	Sweden
1948 United States	Argentina	Sweden
1952 United States	Norway	Finland

6 Metres (1907 Rating)

1920 Belgium	Norway	Norway

6.5 Metres

1920 The Netherlands	France	–

7. Metres

1908 Great Britain	–	–
1920 Great Britain	–	–

1912 *Event not held*

8 Metres

1908 Great Britain	Sweden	Great Britain
1912 Norway	Sweden	Finland
1920 Norway	Norway	Belgium
1924 Norway	Great Britain	France
1928 France	The Netherlands	Sweden
1932 United States	Canada	–
1936 Italy	Norway	Germany

8 Metres (1907 Rating)

1920 Norway	Norway	–

10 Metres

1912 Sweden	Finland	Russia

10 Metres (1907 Rating)

1920 Norway	–	–

10 Metres (1919 Rating)

1920 Norway	–	–

12 Metres

1908 Great Britain	Great Britain	–
1912 Norway	Sweden	Finland

12 Metres (1907 Rating)

1920 Norway	–	–

12 Metres (1919 Rating)
1920 Norway — —

0.5 Ton Class
1900 France France France

0.5–1 Ton Class
1900 France Great Britain France

1–2 Ton Class
1900 Switzerland France France

2–3 Ton Class
1900 Great Britain France France

3–10 Ton Class
1900 France The Netherlands France
Great Britain

10–20 Ton Class
1900 France France Great Britain

Open Class
1900 Great Britain Germany France

Over 20 Ton Class
1900 Great Britain Great Britain United States

Discontinued Sports — Medals

Cricket

GOLD	SILVER	BRONZE
1906 Great Britain	France	—

Croquet

GOLD	SILVER	BRONZE
Simple à la Boule		
1900 Aumoitte (FRA)	Johin (FRA)	Waydelich (FRA)
Simple à deux boules		
1900 Waydelich (FRA)	Vignerot (FRA)	Sautereau (FRA)
Doubles		
1900 France	—	—

Golf

GOLD	SILVER	BRONZE
Men — Singles		
1900 Charles Sands (USA)	Walter Rutherford (GBR)	David Robertson (GBR)
1904 George Lyon (CAN)	Chandler Egan (USA)	Burt McKinnie (USA)
Men — Team		
1904 United States	United States	—
Women — Singles		
1900 Margaret Abbott (USA)	Pauline Whittier (USA)	Daria Pratt (USA)

Jeu De Paume

GOLD	SILVER	BRONZE
1908 Jay Gould (USA)	Eustace Mills (GBR)	Neville Lytton (GBR)

Lacrosse

GOLD	SILVER	BRONZE
1904 Canada	United States	Canada
1908 Canada	Great Britain	–

Motorboating

GOLD	SILVER	BRONZE
Open Class		
1908 France	–	–
60 Foot Class		
1908 Great Britain	–	–
8 Metre Class		
1908 Great Britain	–	–

Polo

GOLD	SILVER	BRONZE
1900 Great Britain	Great Britain	France
1908 Great Britain	Great Britain	Great Britain
1920 Great Britain	Spain	United States
1924 Argentina	United States	Great Britain
1936 Argentina	Great Britain	Mexico

Roque

GOLD	SILVER	BRONZE
1904 Charles Jacobus (USA)	Smith Streeter (USA)	Charles Brown (USA)

Rackets

GOLD	SILVER	BRONZE
Singles		
1908 Evan Noel (GBR)	Henry Leaf (GBR)	John Jacob Astor (GBR)
Doubles		
1908 Great Britain	Great Britain	Great Britain

Rugby Union

GOLD	SILVER	BRONZE
1900 France	Germany	Great Britain
1908 Australia	Great Britain	–
1920 United States	France	–
1924 United States	France	Romania

Tug-of-War

GOLD	SILVER	BRONZE
1900 Sweden/Denmark [1]	France	–
1904 United States	United States	United States
1906 Germany	Greece	Sweden

1908 Great Britain	Great Britain	Great Britain
1912 Sweden	Great Britain	–
1920 Great Britain	The Netherlands	Belgium

1896 *Event not held*

1 Combined team

Alpine Skiing Medals

GOLD	SILVER	BRONZE

Men

Downhill

1948 Henri Oreiller (FRA) 2:55.0	Franz Gabl (AUT) 2:59.1	Karl Molitor (SUI) 3:00.3
		Rolf Olinger (SUI) 3:00.3
1952 Zeno Colò (ITA) 2:30.8	Othmar Schneider (AUT) 2:32.0	Christian Pravda (AUT) 2:32.4
1956 Anton Sailer (FRA) 2:52.2	Raymond Fellay (SUI) 2:55.7	Andreas Molterer (AUT) 2:56.2
1960 Jean Vuarnet (FRA) 2:06.0	Hans-Peter Lanig (GER) 2:06.5	Guy Périllat (FRA) 2:06.9
1964 Egon Zimmerman (AUT) 2:18.16	Léo Lacroix (FRA) 2:18.90	Wolfgang Bartels (GER)2:19.48
1968 Jean-Claude Killy (FRA) 1:59.85	Guy Périllat (FRA) 1:59.93	Jean-Daniel Dätwyler (SUI) 2:00.32
1972 Bernhard Russi (SUI) 1:51.43	Roland Collombin (SUI) 1:52.07	Heinrich Messner (AUT) 1:52.40
1976 Franz Klammer (AUT) 1:45.73	Bernhard Russi (SUI) 1:46.06	Herbert Plank (ITA) 1:46.59
1980 Leonhard Stock (AUT) 1:45.50	Peter Wirnsberger (AUT) 1:46.12	Steve Podborski (CAN) 1:46.62
1984 Bill Johnson (USA) 1:45.59	Peter Müller (SUI) 1:45.86	Anton Steiner (AUT) 1:45.95
1988 Pirmin Zurbriggen (AUT) 1:59.63	Peter Müller (SUI) 2:00.14	Franck Piccard (FRA) 2:01.24
1992 Patrick Ortlieb (AUT) 1:50.37	Franck Piccard (FRA) 1:50.42	Günther Mader (AUT) 1:50.47
1994 Tommy Moe (USA) 1:45.75	Kjetil-André Aamodt (NOR) 1:45.79	Ed Podivinsky (CAN) 1:45.87
1998 Jean Luc Cretier (FRA) 1:50.11	Lasse Kjus (NOR) 1:50.51	Hannes Trink (AUT) 1:50.63

1924–36 *Event not held*

Slalom

1948 Edi Reinalter (SUI) 2:10.3	James Couttret (FRA) 2:10.8	Henri Oreiller (FRA) 2:12.8
1952 Othmar Schneider (AUT) 2:00.0	Stein Eriksen (NOR) 2:01.2	Guttorm Berge (NOR) 2:01.7
1956 Anton Sailer (FRA) 3:14.7	Chiharu Igaya (JPN) 3:18.7	Stig Sollander (SWE) 3:20.2
1960 Ernst Hinterseer (AUT) 2:08.9	Matthias Leitner (AUT) 2:10.3	Charles Bozon (FRA) 2:10.4
1964 Josef Stiegler (AUT) 2:21.13	William Kidd (USA) 2:21.27	James Hengu (USA) 2:21.52
1968 Jean-Claude Killy (FRA) 1:39.73	Herbert Huber (AUT) 1:39.82	Alfred Matt (AUT) 1:40.09
1972 Francisco Fernández Ochoa (ESP) 1:49.27	Gustavo Thöni (ITA) 1:50.28	Rolando Thöni (ITA) 1:50.30
1976 Piero Gros (ITA) 2:03.29	Gustavo Thöni (ITA) 2:03.73	Willy Frommelt (LIE) 2:04.28
1980 Ingemar Stenmark (SWE) 1:44.26	Phil Mahre (USA) 1:44.76	Jacques Lüthy (SUI) 1:45.06
1984 Phil Mahre (USA) 1:39.21	Steve Mahre (USA) 1:39.62	Didier Bouvet (FRA) 1:40.20
1988 Alberto Tomba (ITA) 1:39.47	Frank Wörndl (FRG) 1:39.53	Paul Frommelt (LIE) 1:39.84
1992 Finn Christian Jagge (NOR) 1:44.39	Alberto Tomba (ITA) 1:44.67	Michael Tritscher (AUT) 1:44.85
1994 Thomas Stangassinger (AUT) 2:02.02	Alberto Tomba (ITA) 2:02.17	Jure Kosir (SLO) 2:02.5
1998 Hans Petter Buraas (NOR) 1:49.31	Ole Christian Furuseth (NOR) 1:50.64	Thomas Sykora (AUT) 1:50.68

1924–36 *Event not held*

Giant Slalom

1952 Stein Eriksen (NOR) 2:25.0	Christian Pravda (AUT) 2:26.9	Toni Spiss (AUT) 2:28.8
1956 Anton Sailer (AUT) 3:00.1	Andreas Molterer (AUT) 3:06.3	Walter Schuster (AUT) 3:07.2
1960 Roger Staub (SUI) 1:48.3	Josef Stiegler (AUT) 1:48.7	Ernst Hinterseer (AUT) 1:49.1
1964 François Bonlieu (FRA) 1:46.71	Karl Schranz (AUT) 1:47.09	Josef Steigler (AUT) 1:48.05
1968 Jean-Claude Killy (FRA) 3:29.28	Willy Favre (SUI) 3:31.50	Heinrich Messner (AUT) 3:31.83
1972 Gustavo Thöni (ITA) 3:02.62	Edmund Bruggmann (SUI) 3:10.75	Werner Mattle (SUI) 3:10.99
1976 Heini Hemmi (SUI) 3:26.97	Ernst Good (SUI) 3:27.17	Ingemar Stenmark (SWE) 3:27.41

1980 Ingemar Stenmark (SWE) 2:40.74	Andreas Wenzel (LIE) 2:41.49	Hans Enn (AUT) 2:42.51
1984 Max Julen (SUI) 2:41.18	Jure Franko (YUG) 2:41.41	Andreas Wenzel (LIE)
1988 Alberto Tomba (ITA) 2:06.37	Hubert Strolz (AUT) 2:07.41	Pirmin Zurbriggen (SUI) 2:08.39
1992 Alberto Tomba (ITA) 2:06.98	Marc Girardelli (LUX) 2:07.30	Kjetil-André Aamodt (NOR) 2:07.82
1994 Markus Wasmeier (GER) 2:52.46	Urs Kälin (SUI) 2:52.48	Christian Mayer (AUT) 2:52.58
1998 Hans-Petter Buraas (NOR) 1:49.31	Ole Christian Furuseth (NOR) 1:50.64	Thomas Sykora (AUT) 1:50.68

1924–48 *Event not held*

Super Giant Slalom

1988 Franck Piccard (FRA) 1:39.66	Helmut Mayer (AUT) 1:40.96	Lars-Börje Eriksson (SWE) 1:41.08
1992 Kjetil-André Aamodt (NOR) 1:13.04	Marc Girardelli (LUX) 1:13.77	Jan Einar Thorsen (NOR) 1:13.83
1994 Markus Wasmeier (GER) 1:32.53	Tommy Moe (USA) 1:32.61	Kjetil-André Aamodt (NOR) 1:32.93
1998 Hermann Maier (AUT) 1:34.82	Hans Knauss (AUT) 1:35.43 Didier Cuche (SUI) 1:35.43	–

1924–84 *Event not held*

Alpine Combination (Downhill and Slalom)

1936 Franz Pfnür (GER) 99.25pts	Gustav Lantschner (GER) 96.26	Emile Allais (FRA) 94.69
1948 Henri Orellier (FRA) 3.27pts	Karl Molitor (SUI) 6.44	James Couttet (FRA) 6.95
1988 Hubert Strolz (AUT) 36.55pts	Bernhard Gstrein (AUT) 43.45	Paul Accola (SUI) 48.24
1992 Josef Polig (ITA) 14.58pts	Gianfranco Martin (ITA) 14.90	Steve Locher (SUI) 18.16
1994 Lasse Kjus (NOR) 3:17.53	Kjetil-André Aamodt (NOR) 3:18.55	Harald Strand Nielsen (NOR) 3:19.14
1998 Mario Reiter (AUT) 3:08.06	Lasse Kjus (NOR) 3:08.65	Christian Mayer (AUT) 3:10.11

1924–32, 1952–84 *Event not held*

Women

Downhill

1948 Hedy Schlunegger (SUI) 2:28.3	Trude Beiser (AUT) 2:29.1	Resi Hammerer (AUT) 2:30.2
1952 Trude Jochum-Beiser (AUT) 1:47.1	Annemarie Buchner (GER) 1:48.0	Giuliana Minuzzo (ITA) 1:49.0
1956 Madeleine Berthod (SUI) 1:40.7	Frieda Dänzer (SUI) 1:45.4	Lucile Wheeler (CAN) 1:45.9
1960 Heidi Beibl (GER) 1:37.6	Penelope Pitou (USA) 1:38.6	Traudl Hecher (AUT) 1:38.9
1964 Christl Haas (AUT) 1:55.39	Edith Zimmerman (AUT) 1:56.42	Traudl Hecher (AUT) 1:56.66
1968 Olga Pall (AUT) 1:40.87	Isabelle Mir (FRA) 1:41.33	Christl Haas (AUT) 1:41.41
1972 Marie-Thérèse Nadig (SUI) 1:36.68	Annemarie Pröll (AUT) 1:37.00	Susan Corrock (USA) 1:37.68
1976 Rosi Mittermaier (FRG) 1:46.16	Brigitte Totschnig (AUT) 1:46.68	Cindy Nelson (USA) 1:47.50
1980 Annemarie Moser-Pröll (AUT) 1:37.52	Hanni Wenzel (LIE) 1:38.22	Marie-Thérèse Nadig (SUI) 1:38.36
1984 Michela Figini (SUI) 1:13.36	Maria Walliser (SUI) 1:13.41	Olga Charvátová (TCH) 1:13.53
1988 Marina Kiehl (FRG) 1:25.86	Brigitte Oertli (SUI) 1:26.61	Karen Percy (CAN) 1:26.62
1992 Kerin Lee-Gartner (CAN) 1:52.55	Hilary Lindh (USA) 1:52.61	Veronika Wallinger (AUT) 1:52.64
1994 Katja Seizinger (GER) 1:35.93	Picabo Street (USA) 1:36.59	Isolde Kostner (ITA) 1:36.05
1998 Katja Seizinger (GER) 1:28.89	Pernilla Wiberg (SWE) 1:29.18	Florence Masnada (FRA) 1:29.37

1924–36 *Event not held*

Slalom

1948 Gretchen Fraser (USA) 1:57.2	Antoinette Meyer (SUI) 1:57.7	Erika Mahringer (AUT) 1:58.0
1952 Andrea Mead-Lawrence (USA) 2:10.6	Ossi Reichert (GER) 2:11.4	Annemarie Buchner (GER) 2:13.3
1956 Renée Colliard (SUI) 1:52.3	Regina Schöpf (AUT) 1:55.4	Yevgeniya Sidorova (URS) 1:56.7
1960 Anne Heggtveit (CAN) 1:49.6	Betsy Snite (USA) 1:52.9	Barbi Henneberger (GER) 1:56.6

1964 Christine Goitschel (FRA) 1:29.86	Marielle Goitschel (FRA) 1:30.77	Jean Saubert (USA) 1:31.36
1968 Marielle Goitschel (FRA) 1:25.86	Nancy Greene (CAN) 1:26.15	Annie Famose (FRA) 1:27.89
1972 Barbara Cochran (USA) 1:31.24	Danièlle Debernard (FRA) 1:31.26	Florence Steurer (FRA) 1:32.69
1976 Rosi Mittermaier (FRG) 1:30.54	Claudia Giordani (ITA) 1:30.87	Hanni Wenzel (LIE) 1:32.20
1980 Hanni Wenzel (LIE) 1;25.09	Christa Kinshofer (FRG) 1:26.50	Erika Hess (SUI) 1:27.89
1984 Paolette Magoin (ITA) 1:36.47	Perrine Pelen (FRA) 1:37.38	Ursula Konsett (LIE) 1:37.50
1988 Vreni Schneider (SUI) 1:36.69	Mateja Svet (YUG) 1:38.37	Christa Kinshofer-Güthlein (FRG) 1:38.40
1992 Petra Kronberger (AUT) 1:32.68	Annelise Coberger (NZL) 1:33.10	Blanca Fernández-Ochoa (ESP) 1:33.35
1994 Vreni Schneider (SUI) 1:56.01	Elfi Eder (AUT) 1:56.36	Katja Koren (SLO) 1:56.61
1998 Hilde Gerg (GER) 1:32.40	Deboarah Compagnoni (ITA) 1:32.46	Zali Steggall (AUS) 1:32.67

1924–36 *Event not held*

Giant Slalom

1952 Andrea Mead-Lawrence (USA) 2:06.8	Dagmar Rom (AUT) 2:09.0	Annemarie Buchner (GER) 2:10.0
1956 Ossi Reichert (GER) 1:56.5	Josefine Frandl (AUT) 1:57.8	Dorothea Hochleitner (AUT) 1:58.2
1960 Yvonne Rüegg (SUI) 1:39.9	Penelope Pitou (USA) 1:40.0	Giuliana Chenal-Minuzzo (ITA) 1:40.2
1964 Marielle Goitschel (FRA) 1:52.24	Christine Goitschel (FRA) 1:53.11 Jean Saubert (USA) 1:53.11	–
1968 Nancy Greene (CAN) 1:51.97	Annie Famose (FRA) 1:54.61	Fernande Bochatay (SUI) 1:54.74
1972 Marie-Thérèse Nadig (SUI) 1:29.90	Annemarie Pröll (AUT) 1:30.75	Wiltrud Drexel (AUT) 1:32.35
1976 Kathy Kreiner (CAN) 1:29.13	Rosi Mittermaier (FRG) 1:29.25	Danièlle Debernard (FRA) 1:29.95
1980 Hanni Wenzel (LIE) 2:41.66	Irene Epple (FRG) 2:42.12	Perrine Pelen (FRA) 2:42.41
1984 Debbie Armstrong (USA) 2:20.98	Christin Cooper (USA) 2:21.38	Perrine Pelen (FRA) 2:21.40
1988 Vreni Schneider (SUI) 2:06.49	Christa Kinshofer-Güthlein (FRG) 2:07.42	Maria Walliser (SUI) 2:07.72
1992 Pernilla Wiberg (SWE) 2:12.74	Diann Roffe (USA) 2:13.71 Anita Wachter (AUT) 2:13.71	–
1994 Deborah Compagnoni (ITA) 2:30.47	Martina Ertl (GER) 2:32.19	Vreni Schneider (SUI) 2:32.97
1998 Deborah Compagnoni (ITA) 2:50.59	Alexandra Meissnitzer (AUT) 2:52.39	Katja Seizinger (GER) 2:52.61

1924–48 *Event not held*

Super Giant Slalom

1988 Sigrid Wolf (AUT) 1:19.03	Michela Figini (SUI) 1:20.03	Karen Percy (CAN) 1:20.29
1992 Deborah Compagnoni (ITA) 1:21.22	Carole Merle (FRA) 1:22.63	Katja Seizinger (GER) 1:23.19
1994 Diann Roffe (USA) 1:22.15	Svetlana Gladischeva (RUS) 1:22.44	Isolde Kostner (ITA) 1:22.45
1998 Picabo Street (USA) 1:18.02	Michaela Dorfmeister (AUT) 1:18.03	Alexandra Meissnitzer (AUT) 1:18.09

1924–84 *Event not held*

Alpine Combination (Downhill and Slalom)

1936 Christel Cranz (GER) 97.06pts	Käthe Grasegger (GER) 95.26	Laila Schou Nilsen (NOR) 93.48
1948 Trude Beiser (AUT) 6.58pts	Gretchen Fraser (USA) 6.95	Erika Mahringer (AUT) 7.04
1988 Anita Wachter (AUT) 29.25pts	Brigitte Oertli (SUI) 29.48	Maria Walliser (SUI) 51.28
1992 Petra Kronberger (AUT) 2.55pts	Anita Wachter (AUT) 19.39	Florence Masnada (FRA) 21.38
1994 Pernilla Wiberg (SWE) 3:05.16	Vreni Schneider (SUI) 3:05.29	Alenka Dovzan (SLO) 3:06.64
1998 Katja Seizinger (GER) 2:40.74	Martina Ertl (GER) 2:40.92	Hilde Gerg (GER) 2:41.50

1924–32, 1952–84 *Event not held*

Bobsledding Results

GOLD	SILVER	BRONZE

2-Man Bob

GOLD	SILVER	BRONZE
1932 United States I 8:14.14	Switzerland II 8:16.28	United States II 8:29.15
1936 United States I 5:29.29	Switzerland II 5:30.64	United States II 5:33.96
1948 Switzerland II 5:29.2	Switzerland I 5:30.4	United States II 5:35.3
1952 Germany I 5:24.54	United States I 5:26.89	Switzerland I 5:27.71
1956 Italy I 5:39.14	Italy II 5:31.45	Switzerland I 5:37.46
1964 Great Britain I 4:21.90	Italy II 4:22.02	Italy I 4:22.63
1968 Italy I 4:41.54 [1]	West Germany I 4:41.54	Romania 4:44.46
1972 West Germany II 4:47.07	West Germany I 4:58.84	Switzerland I 4:59.33
1976 East Germany II 3:44.42	West Germany I 3:44.99	Switzerland I 3:45.70
1980 Switzerland II 4:09.36	East Germany II 4:10.93	East Germany I 4:11.08
1984 East Germany II 3:28.56	East Germany I 3:26.04	Soviet Union II 3:26.16
1988 Soviet Union I 3:53.48	East Germany I 3:54.19	East Germany II 3:54.64
1992 Switzerland I 4:03.26	Germany I 4:03.55	Germany II 4:03.63
1994 Switzerland I 3:30.81	Switzerland II 3:30.86	Italy I 3:31.01
1998 Italy I 3:37.24	–	Germany I 3:37.89
Canada I 3:27.24		

1924–28, 1960 *Event not held*

[1] Italy had faster single run

4-Man Bob

GOLD	SILVER	BRONZE
1924 Switzerland I 5:45.54	Great Britain II 5:48.83	Belgium I 6:02.29 [3]
1928[1] United States II 3:20.5[3]	United States I 3:21.0 [3]	Germany II 3:21.9 [3]
1932 United States I 7:53.68	United States II 7:55.70	Germany I 8:00.04
1936 Switzerland II 5:19.85	Switzerland I 5:22.73	Great Britain I 5:23.41
1948 United States II 5:20.1	Belgium 5:21.3	United States I 5:21.5
1952 Germany I 5:07.84	United States I 5:10.48	Switzerland I 5:11.70
1956 Switzerland I 5:10.44	Italy II 5:12.10	United States I 5:12.39
1964 Canada 4:14.46	Austria 4:15.48	Italy II 4:15.60
1968[1] Italy I 2:17.39	Austria I 2:17.48	Switzerland I 2:18.04
1972 Switzerland I 4:43.07	Italy I 4:43.83	West Germany I 4:43.92
1976 East Germany I 3:40.43	Switzerland II 3:40.89	West Germany I 3:41.37
1980 East Germany I 3:59.92	Switzerland I 4:00.87	East Germany II 4:00.97
1984 East Germany I 3:20.22	East Germany II 3:20.78	Switzerland I 3:21.39
1988 Switzerland I 3:47.51	East Germany I 3:47.58	Soviet Union II 3:48.26
1992 Austria I 3:53.90	Germany I 3:53.92	Switzerland I 3:54.13
1994 Germany II 3:27.78	Switzerland I 3:27.84	Germany I 3:28.01
1998[2] Germany II 2:39.41	Switzerland I 2:40.01	Great Britain I 2:40.06
		France 2:40.06

1960 *Event not held*

[1] Only two runs
[2] Only three runs
[3] Five man teams (allowed until 1932)

Curling Medals

GOLD	SILVER	BRONZE

Men

GOLD	SILVER	BRONZE
1998 Switzerland	Canada	Norway

1924–94 *Event not held*

Women

GOLD	SILVER	BRONZE
1998 Canada	Denmark	Sweden

1924–94 *Event not held*

Figure Skating Medals

GOLD	SILVER	BRONZE

Men

	GOLD	SILVER	BRONZE
1908[1]	Nikolai Panin (URS) 219pts	Arthur Cumming (GBR) 164	George Hall-Say (GBR) 104
1908	Ulrich Salchow (SWE) 1886.5pts	Richard Johansson (SWE) 1826.0	Per Thorén (SWE) 1787.0
1920	Gillis Grafström (SWE) 2838.5pts	Andreas Krogh (NOR) 2634	Martin Stixrud (NOR) 2561.5
1924	Gillis Grafström (SWE) 2757.2pts	Willy Böckl (AUT) 2518.75	Georges Gautschi (SUI) 2233.5
1932	Karl Schäfer (AUT) 2602.0pts	Gillis Grafström (SWE) 2514.5	Montgomery Wilson (CAN) 2448.3
1936	Karl Schäfer (AUT) 2959.0pts	Ernst Baier (GER) 2805.3	Felix Kaspar (AUT) 2801.0
1948	Richard Button (USA) 1720pts	Hans Gerschwiler (SUI) 1630.1	Edi Rada (AUT) 1603.2
1952	Richard Button (USA) 1730.3pts	Helmut Seibt (AUT) 1621.3	James Grogan (USA) 1627.4
1956	Hayes Alan Jenkins (USA) 1497.95pts	Ronald Robertson (USA) 1492.1	David Jenkins (USA) 1465.41
1960	David Jenkins (USA) 1440.2pts	Karol Divin (TCH) 141.3	Donald Jackson (CAN) 1401.0
1964	Manfred Schnelldorfer (GER) 1916.9pts	Alain Calmar (FRA) 1876.5	Scott Allen (USA) 1873.6
1968	Wolfgang Schwarz (AUT) 1894.1pts	Tim Woods (USA) 1891.6	Patrick Péra (FRA) 1864.5
1972	Ondrej Nepela (TCH) 2739.1pts	Sergei Tchetveroukhin (URS) 2672.4	Patrick Péra (FRA) 2653.1
1976	John Curry (GBR) 192.74pts	Vladimir Kovalyev (URS) 187.64	Toller Cranston (CAN) 187.38
1980	Robin Cousins (GBR) 189.48pts [2]	Jan Hoffmann (GDR) 189.72 (2)	Charles Tickner (USA) 187.06
1984	Scott Hamilton (USA) 3.4pl	Brian Orser (CAN) 5.6	Jozef Sabovtchik (TCH) 7.4
1988	Brian Boitano (USA) 3.0pl	Brian Orser (CAN) 4.2	Viktor Petrenko (URS) 7.8
1992	Viktor Petrenko (EUN) 1.5pl	Paul Wylie (USA) 3.5	Petr Barna (TCH) 4.0
1994	Alexei Urmanov (RUS) 1.5pl	Elvis Stojko (CAN) 3.0	Philippe Candeloro (FRA) 6.5
1998	Ilya Kulik (RUS) 1.5pl	Elvis Stojko (CAN) 4.0	Philippe Candeloro (FRA) 4.5

1912 *Event not held*

[1] Special figures competition
[2] Majority of judges in favour of Cousins. Since then, all medals decided by judges' placements

Women

	GOLD	SILVER	BRONZE
1908	Madge Syers (GBR) 1262.5pts	Elsa Rendschmidt (GER) 1055.0	Dorothy Greenhough-Smith (GBR) 960.0
1920	Magda Mauroy-Julin (SWE) 913.5pts	Svea Norén (SWE) 887.75	Theresa Weld (USA) 898.0
1924	Herma Planck-Szabó (AUT) 2094.25pts	Beatrix Loughran (USA) 1959.0	Ethel Muckelt (GBR) 1750.50
1928	Sonja Henie (NOR) 2452.25pts	Fritzi Berger (AUT) 2248.50	Beatrix Loughran (USA) 2254.50
1932	Sonja Henie (NOR) 2302.5pts	Fritzi Berger (AUT) 2167.1	Maribel Vinson (USA) 2158.5
1936	Sonja Henie (NOR) 2971.4pts	Cecilia Colledge (GBR) 2926.8	Vivi-Anne Hultén (SWE) 2763.2
1948	Barbara-Ann Scott (CAN) 1467.7pts	Eva Pawlik (AUT) 1418.3	Jeanette Altwegg (GBR) 1405.5
1952	Jeanette Altwegg (GBR) 1455.8pts	Tenley Albright (USA) 1432.2	Jacqueline du Bief (FRA) 1422.0
1956	Tenley Albright (USA) 1866.30pts	Carol Heiss (USA) 1848.24	Ingrid Wendl (AUT) 1753.91
1960	Carol Heiss (USA) 1490.1pts	Sjoukje Dijkstra (NED) 1424.8	Barbara Roles (USA) 1414.8
1964	Sjoukje Dijkstra (NED) 20.18.5pts	Regine Heitzer (AUT) 1945.5	Petra Burka (CAN) 1940.0
1968	Peggy Fleming (USA) 1970.5pts	Gabrielle Seyfert (GDR) 1882.3	Hana Maskova (TCH) 1828.8
1972	Beatrix Schuba (AUT) 2751.5pts	Karen Magnussen (CAN) 2763.2	Janet Lynn (USA) 2663.1
1976	Dorothy Hamill (USA) 193.80pts	Dianne De Leeuw (NED) 190.24	Christine Errath (GDR) 188.16
1980	Anett Pötzsch (GDR) 189.00pts	Linda Fratianne (USA) 188.30	Dagmar Lurz (FRG) 183.04
1984	Katarina Witt (GDR) 3.2pl	Rosalyn Sumners (USA) 4.6	Kira Ivanova (URS) 9.2
1988	Katarina Witt (GDR) 4.2pl	Elizabeth Manley (CAN) 4.6	Debra Thomas (USA) 6.0
1992	Kristi Yamaguchi (USA) 1.5pl	Midori Ito (JPN) 4.0	Nancy Kerrigan (USA) 4.0
1994	Oksana Baiul (UKR) 2.0pl	Nancy Kerrigan (USA) 2.5	Lu Chen (CHN) 5.0
1998	Tara Lipinski (USA) 2.0pl	Michelle Kwan (USA) 2.5	Lu Chen (CHN) 5.0

1912 *Event not held*

Pairs

1908 Germany 56.0pts	Great Britain 51.5	Great Britain 48.0
1920 Finland 80.75pts	Norway 72.75	Great Britain 66.25
1924 Austria 74.50pts	Finland 71.75	France 69.25
1928 France 100.50pts	Austria 99.25	Austria 93.25
1932 France 76.7pts	United States 77.5	Hungary 76.4
1936 Germany 103.0pts	Austria 102.7	Hungary 97.6
1948 Belgium 123.5pts	Hungary 122.2	Canada 121.0
1952 Germany 102.6pts	United States 100.6	Hungary 97.4
1956 Austria 101.8pts	Canada 101.9	Hungary 99.3
1960 Canada 80.4pts	Germany 76.8	United States 76.2
1964[1] Soviet Union 104.4pts	Germany 103.6	Canada 98.5
1968 Soviet Union 315.2pts	Soviet Union 312.3	West Germany 304.4
1972 Soviet Union 420.4pts	Soviet Union 419.4	East Germany 411.8
1976 Soviet Union 140.54pts	East Germany 136.35	East Germany 134.57
1980 Soviet Union 147.26pts	Soviet Union 143.80	East Germany 140.52
1984 Soviet Union 1.4pl	United States 2.8	Soviet Union 3.8
1988 Soviet Union 1.4pl	Soviet Union 2.8	United States 4.2
1992 Unified Team 1.5pl	Unified Team 3.0	Canada 4.5
1994 Russia 1.5pl	Russia 3.0	Canada 4.5
1998 Russia 2.0pl	Russia 3.5	Germany 6.0

1912 *Event not held*

1 Marika Kilius/Hansjürgen Bäumler (GER) finished second, were subsequently disqualified, then reinstated

Ice Dance

1976 Soviet Union 209.92pts	Soviet Union 204.88	United States 202.64
1980 Soviet Union 205.48pts	Hungary 204.52	Soviet Union 201.86
1984 Great Britain 2.0pl	Soviet Union 4.0	Soviet Union 7.0
1988 Soviet Union 2.0pl	Soviet Union 4.0	Canada 6.0
1992 Unified Team 2.0pts	France 4.4	Unified Team 5.6
1994 Russia 3.4pts	Russia 3.8	Great Britain 4.8
1998 Russia 2.0pts	Russia 4.0	France 7.0

1908–72 *Event not held*

Freestyle Skiing Medals

GOLD	SILVER	BRONZE

Men

Moguls

1992 Edgar Grospiron (FRA) 25.81pts	Olivier Allamand (FRA) 24.87	Nelson Carmichael (USA) 24.82
1994 Jean-Luc Brassard (CAN) 27.74pts	Sergei Shoupletsov (RUS) 26.90	Edgar Grospiron (FRA) 26.64
1998 Jonny Moseley (USA) 26.93pts	Janne Lahtela (FIN) 26.01	Sami Mustonen (FIN) 25.76

1924–88 *Event not held*

Aerials

1994 Andreas Schönbächler (SUI) 234.67pts	Phillippe Laroche (CAN) 228.23	Lloyd Langlois (CAN)222.44
1998 Eric Bergoust (USA) 255.64pts	Sebastien Foucras (FRA) 248.79	Dmitri Daschinsky (BLR) 240.79

1924–92 *Event not held*

Women

Moguls

1992 Donna Weinbrecht (USA) 23.69pts	Yelizaveta Kozhevnikova (EUN) 23.50	Stine Lise Hattestad (NOR) 23.04
1994 Stine Lise Hattestad (NOR) 25.97pts	Elizabeth McIntyre (USA) 25.89	Yelizaveta Kozhevnikova (EUN) 25.81
1998 Tae Satoya (JPN) 25.06	Tatyana Mittermayer (GER) 24.62	Kari Traa (NOR) 24.09

1924–88 *Event not held*

Aerials

1994 Lina Cheryasova (UZB) 166.84pts	Marie Lindgren (SWE) 165.88	Hilde Synnøve Lid (NOR) 164.13
1998 Nikki Stone (USA) 193.00pts	Xu Nannan (CHN) 186.97	Colette Brand (SUI) 171.83

1924–92 *Event not held*

Ice Hockey Medals

	GOLD	SILVER	BRONZE
Men			
1920	Canada	United States	Czechoslovakia
1924	Canada	United States	Great Britain
1928	Canada	Sweden	Switzerland
1932	Canada	United States	Germany
1936	Great Britain	Canada	United States
1948	Canada	Czechoslovakia	Switzerland
1952	Canada	United States	Sweden
1956	Soviet Union	United States	Canada
1960	United States	Canada	Soviet Union
1964	Soviet Union	Sweden	Czechoslovakia
1968	Soviet Union	Czechoslovakia	Canada
1972	Soviet Union	United States	Czechoslovakia
1976	Soviet Union	Czechoslovakia	West Germany [1]
1980	United States	Soviet Union	Sweden
1984	Soviet Union	Czechoslovakia	Sweden
1988	Soviet Union	Finland	Sweden
1992	Unified Team	Canada	Czechoslovakia
1994	Sweden	Canada	Finland
1998	Czech Republic	Russia	Finland

[1] Three-way tie for bronze with the USA and Finland, decided on goal average

Women

1998 United States		Canada	Finland

1924–94 *Event not held*

Lugeing Medals

	GOLD	SILVER	BRONZE
Men			
Singles			
1964	Thomas Köhler (GER) 3:26.77	Klaus Bonsack (GER) 3:27.04	Hans Plenk (GER) 3:30.15
1968	Manfred Schmid (AUT) 2:52.48	Thomas Köhler (GDR) 2:52.66	Klaus Bonsack (GDR) 2:55.33
1972	Wolfgang Scheidel (GDR) 3:27.58	Harald Ehrig (GDR) 3:28.39	Wolfram Fiedler (GDR) 3:28.73
1976	Detlef Günther (GDR) 3:27.688	Josef Fendt (FRG) 3:28.196	Hans Rinn (GDR) 3:28.574
1980	Bernhard Glass (GDR) 2:54.796	Paul Hildgartner (ITA) 2:55.372	Anton Winkler (FRG) 2:56.545
1984	Paul Hildgartner (ITA) 3:04.258	Sergei Danilin (URS) 3:04.962	Valeri Dudin (URS) 3:05.012
1988	Jens Müller (GDR) 3:05.548	Georg Hackl (FRG) 3:05.916	Yuri Khartchenko (URS) 3:06.274
1992	Georg Hackl (GER) 3:02.363	Markus Prock (AUT) 3:02.669	Markus Schmidt (AUT) 3:02.942
1994	Georg Hackl (GER) 3:21.571	Markus Prock (AUT) 3:21.584	Armin Zöggeler (ITA) 3:21.833
1998	Georg Hackl (GER) 3:18.436	Armin Zöggeler (ITA) 3:18.939	Jens Müller (GER) 3:19.093

1924–60 *Event not held*

2-Man

1964	Austria 1:41.62	Austria 1:41.91	Italy 1:42.87
1968	East Germany 1:35.85	Austria 1:36.34	West Germany 1:37.29
1972	Italy 1:28.35	–	East Germany 1:29.16
	East Germany 1:28.35		
1976	East Germany 1:25.604	West Germany 1:25.889	Austria 1:25.919
1980	East Germany 1:19.331	Italy 1:19.606	Austria 1:19.795

1984 West Germany 1:23.620	Soviet Union 1:23.660	East Germany 1:23.887
1988 East Germany 1:31.940	East Germany 1:32.039	West Germany 1:32.274
1992 Germany 1:32.053	Germany 1:32.239	Italy 1:32.298
1994 Italy 1:36.720	Italy II 1:36.769	Germany 1:36.945
1998 Germany 1:41.105	United States I 1:41.127	United States II 1:41.217

1924–960 *Event not held*

Women

Singles

1964 Ortrun Enderlein (GER) 3:24.67	Ilse Geisler (GER) 3:27.42	Helene Thurner (AUT) 3:29.06
1968 Erica Lechner (ITA) 2:28.66	Christa Schmuck (FRG) 2:29.37	Angelika Dünhaupt (FRG) 2:29.56
1972 Anna-Maria Müller (GDR) 2:59.18	Ute Rührold (GDR) 2:59.49	Margit Schumann (GDR) 2:59.54
1976 Margit Schumann (GDR) 2:50.621	Ute Rührold (GDR) 2:50.846	Elisabeth Demleitner (FRG) 2:51.056
1980 Vera Sosulya (URS) 2:36.537	Melitta Sollmann (GDR) 2:37.657	Ingrida Amantova (URS) 2:37.817
1984 Steffi Martin (GDR) 2:46.570	Bettine Schmidt (GDR) 2:46.873	Ute Weiss (GDR) 2:47.248
1988 Steffi Martin-Walter (GDR) 3:03.973	Ute Weiss-Oberhoffner (GDR) 3:04.105	Cerstin Schmidt (GDR) 3:04.181
1992 Doris Neuner (AUT) 3:06.696	Angelika Neuner (AUT) 3:06.769	Susi Erdmann (GER) 3:07.115
1998 Slike Krashaar (GER) 3:23.779	Barbara Niedernhuber (GER) 3:23.781	Angelika Neuner (AUT) 3:24.253

1924–60 *Evert not held*

Discontinued Events

Tobogganing — Skeleton Sled

1928[1]Earl of Northesk (GBR) 3:05.1	Jennison Heaton (USA) 3:01.8	John Heaton (USA) 3:02.8
1948[2]John Crammond (GBR) 5:25.1	Nino Bibbia (ITA) 5:23.2	John Heaton (USA) 5:24.6

[1] Aggregate of three runs
[2] Aggregate of six runs

Nordic Skiing Medals

GOLD	SILVER	BRONZE

Men

10 000 Metres Classical

1992 Vegard Ulvang (NOR) 27:36.0	Marco Alberello (ITA) 27:55.2	Christer Majbäck (SWE) 27:56.4
1994 Bjørn Dæhlie (NOR) 24:20.1	Vladimir Smirnov (KZK) 24:38.3	Marco Alberello (ITA) 24:42.3
1998 Bjørn Dæhlie (NOR) 27:24.5	Markus Gander (AUT) 27:32.5	Mika Myllylä (FIN) 27:40.1

1924–88 *Event not held*

15 000 Metres Classical

1924[1]Thorleif Haug (NOR) 1hr 23:07.0	Johan Gröttumsbraaten (NOR) 1hr 15.51.0	Tipani Niku (FIN) 1hr 26:26.0
1928[2]Johan Gröttumsbraaten (NOR) 1hr 37:01.0	Ole Hegge (NOR) 1hr 39:01.0	Reidar Ödegaard (NOR) 1hr 40:11.0
1932[3]Sven Utterström (SWE) 1hr 23.07.0	Axel Wikström (SWE) 1hr 25:07.0	Veli Saarinen (FIN) 1hr 25:24.0
1936[1]Erik-August Larsson (SWE) 1hr 14:38.0	Oddbjörn Hagen (NOR) 1hr 15:33.0	Pekka Niemi (FIN) 1hr 16:59.0
1948[1]Martin Lundström (SWE) 1hr 13:50.0	Nils Östensson (SWE) 1hr 14:22.0	Gunnar Eriksson (SWE)1hr 16:06.6
1952[1]Hallgeir Brenden (NOR) 1hr 1:34.0	Tapio Mäkelä (FIN) 1hr 2:09.0	Paavo Lonkila (FIN) 1hr 2:20.0
1956 Hallgeir Brenden (NOR) 49:39.0	Sixten Jernberg (SWE) 50:14.0	Pavel Koltschin (URS) 50:17.0
1960 Haakon Brusveen (NOR) 51:55.5	Sixten Jernberg (SWE) 51:58.6	Veikko Hakulinen (FIN) 52:03.0
1964 Eero Mäntyranta (FIN) 50:54.1	Harald Grönningen (NOR) 51:34.8	Sixten Jernberg (SWE) 51:42.2

1968 Harald Grönningen (NOR) 47:54.2	Eero Mäntyranta (FIN) 47:56.1	Gunnar Larsson (SWE) 48:33.7
1972 Sven-Ake Lundback (SWE) 45:28.24	Fedor Simsachov (URS) 46:00.84	Ivar Koivisto (FIN) 44:19.25
1976 Nikolai Bayukov (URS) 43:58.47	Yevgeni Belyayev (URS) 44:01.10	Arto Koivisto (FIN) 44:19.25
1980 Thomas Wassberg (SWE) 41:25.63	Juha Mieto (FIN) 41:57.64	Ove Aunli (NOR) 452:28.62
1984 Gunde Swan (SWE) 41:25.6	Aki Karvonen (FIN) 41:34.9	Harri Kirvesniemi (FIN) 41:45.6
1988 Michael Deviatyarov (URS) 41:18.9	Pal Mikkelsplass (NOR) 41:33.4	Vladimir Smirnov (URS) 41:48.5

Event discontinued after 1988

1 Distance was 18km
2 Distance was 19.7km
3 Distance was 18.2km

15 000 Metres Pursuit 1

1992 Bjørn Dæhlie (NOR) 1hr 05:37.9	Vegard Ulvang (NOR) 1hr 06:31.3	Giorgio Vanzetta (ITA) 1hr 06:31.2
1994 Bjørn Dæhlie (NOR) 1hr 00:08.8	Vladimir Smirnov (KZK) 1hr 00:38.0	Silvio Fauner (ITA) 1hr 01:48.6
1998 Thomas Alsgaard (NOR) 1hr 07:01.7	Bjørn Dæhlie (NOR) 1hr 07:02.8	Vladimir Smirnov (URS) 1hr 07:31.5

1924–88 Event not held

1 Contestants' times are added to those achieved in 10km classical race

30 000 Metres Classical

1956 Veikko Hakulinen (FIN) 1hr 44:06.0	Sixten Jernberg (SWE) 1hr 44:30.0	Pavel Koltschin (URS) 1hr 45:45.0
1960 Sixten Jernberg (SWE) 1hr 56:03.9	Rolf Rämgard (SWE) 1hr 51:16.9	Nikolai Anikin (URS) 1hr 52:28.2
1964 Eero Mäntyranta (FIN) 1hr 30:50.7	Harald Grönningen (NOR) 1hr 32:02.3	Igor Voronchikin (URS) 1hr 32:15.8
1968 Franco Nones (ITA) 1hr 35:29.2	Odd Martinsen (NOR) 1hr 36:28.9	Eero Mäntyranta (FIN) 1hr 36:55.3
1972 Vyacheslav Vedenine (URS) 1hr 36:31.2	Paal Tyldum (NOR) 1hr 37:25.3	Johs Harviken (NOR) 1hr 37:32.4
1976 Sergei Savelyev (URS) 1hr 30:29.38	William Koch (USA) 1hr 30:57.84	Ivan Garanin (URS) 1hr 31:09.29
1980 Nikolai Simyatov (URS) 1hr 27:02.80	Vassili Rochev (URS) 1hr 27:34.22	Ivan Lebanov (BUL) 1hr 28:03.87
1984 Nikolai Simyatov (URS) 1hr 28:56.3	Alexander Zavialov (URS) 1hr 24:35.1	Gunde Svan (SWE) 1hr 29:35.7
1988 Alexei Prokurorov (URS) 1hr 24:26.3	Vladimir Smirnov (URS) 1hr 24:35.1	Vegard Ulvang (NOR) 1hr 25:11.6
1992 Vegard Ulvang (NOR) 1hr 22:27.8	Bjørn Dæhlie (NOR) 1hr 23:14.0	Terje Langli (NOR) 1hr 23:42.5
1994 Thomas Alsgaard (NOR) 1hr 12:26.4	Bjørn Dæhlie (NOR) 1hr 13:13.6	Mika Myllylä (FIN) 1hr 14:14.0
1998 Mika Myllylä (FIN) 1hr 33:55.8	Erling Jeune (NOR) 1hr 35:27.1	Silvio Fauner (ITA) 1hr 36:08.5

1924–52 Event not held

50 000 Metres Freestyle

1924 Thorleif Haug (NOR) 3hr 44:32.0	Thoralf Strömstad (NOR) 3hr 46:23.0	Johan Gröttumsbraaten (NOR) 3hr 47:46.0
1928 Per Erik Hedlund (SWE) 4hr 52:03.0	Gustaf Jonsson (SWE) 5hr 05:30.0	Volger Andersson (SWE) 5hr 05:46.0
1932 Veli Saarinen (FIN) 4hr 28:00.0	Väinö Likkanen (FIN) 4hr 28:20.0	Arne Rustadstuen (NOR) 4hr 31:53.0
1936 Elis Wiklung (SWE) 3hr 30:11.1	Axel Wikström (SWE) 3hr 33:20.0	Nils-Joel Englund (SWE) 3hr 34:10.0

1948 Nils Karlsson (SWE) 3hr 47:48.0	Harald Eriksson (SWE) 3hr 52:20.0	Benjamin Vanninen (FIN) 3hr 38:28.0
1952 Veikko Hakulinen (FIN) 3hr 33:33.0	Eero Kolehmainen (FIN) 3hr 38:11.0	Magnar Estenstad (NOR) 3hr 57:28.0
1956 Sixten Jernberg (SWE) 2hr 50:27.0	Veikko Hakulinen (FIN) 2hr 51:45.0	Fedor Terentyev (URS) 2hr 53:32.0
1960 Kalevi Hämäläinen (FIN) 2hr 59:06.3	Veikko Hakulinen (FIN) 2hr 59:26.7	Rolf Rämgard (SWE) 3hr 02:46.7
1964 Sixten Jernberg (SWE) 2hr 43:52.6	Assar Rönnlund (SWE) 2hr 44:58.2	Arto Tiainen (FIN) 2hr 45:30.4
1968 Olle Ellefsäter (NOR) 2hr 28:45.8	Vyacheslav Vedenine (URS) 2hr 29:02.5	Josef Haas (SUI) 2hr 29:14.8
1972 Paal Tyldrum (NOR) 2hr 43:14.75	Magne Myrmo (NOR) 2hr 43:29.45	Vyacheslav Vedenine (URS) 2hr 44:00.19
1976 Ivar Formo (NOR) 2hr 37:30.50	Gert-Dietmar Klause (GDR) 2hr 38:13.21	Benny Södergren (SWE) 2hr 39:39.21
1980 Nikolai Simyatov (URS) 2hr 27:24.60	Juha Mieto (FIN) 2hr 30:20.52	Alexander Savyalov (URS) 2hr 30:51.52
1984 Thomas Wassberg (SWE) 2hr 15:55.8	Gunde Svan (SWE) 2hr 16:00.7	Aki Karvonen (FIN) 2hr 17:04.7
1988 Gunde Svan (SWE) 2hr 04:30.9	Maurilio De Zolt (ITA) 2hr 05:36.4	Andy Grünenfelder (SUI) 2hr 06:01.9
1992 Bjørn Dæhlie (NOR) 2hr 03:41.5	Maurilio De Zolt (ITA) 2hr 04:39.1	Giorgio Vanzetta (ITA) 2hr 06:42.1
1994 Vladimir Smirnov (KZK) 2hr 07:20.0	Myka Myllylä (FIN) 2hr 08:41.9	Sture Sivertsen (NOR) 2hr 08:49.0
1998 Bjørn Dæhlie (NOR) 2hr 05:08.2	Niklas Jonsson (SWE) 2hr 05:16.3	Christian Hoffmann (AUT) 2hr 06:01.8

4 × 10 000 Metres Relay

1936 Finland 2hr 41:33.0	Norway 2hr 41:39.0	Sweden 2hr 43:03.0
1948 Sweden 2hr 32:08.0	Finland 2hr 41:06.0	Norway 2hr 44:33.0
1952 Finland 2hr 20:16.0	Norway 2hr 23:13.0	Sweden 2hr 24:13.0
1956 Soviet Union 2hr 15:30.0	Finland 2hr 16:31.0	Sweden 2hr 17:42.0
1960 Finland 2hr 18:45.6	Norway 2hr 18:46.4	Soviet Union 2hr 21:21.6
1964 Sweden 2hr 18:34.6	Finland 2hr 18:42.4	Soviet Union 2hr 18:46.9
1968 Norway 2hr 08:33.5	Sweden 2hr 10:13.2	Finland 2hr 10:56.7
1972 Soviet Union 2hr 04:47.94	Norway 2hr 04:57.6	Switzerland 2hr 07:00.06
1976 Finland 2hr 07:59.72	Norway 2hr 09:58.36	Soviet Union 2hr 10:51.46
1980 Soviet Union 1hr 57:03.6	Norway 1hr 58:45.77	Finland 2hr 00:00.18
1984 Sweden 1hr 55:06.3	Soviet Union 1hr 55:16.5	Finland 1hr 56:31.4
1988 Sweden 1hr 43:58.6	Soviet Union 1hr 44:11.3	Czechoslovakia 1hr 45:22.7
1992 Norway 1hr 39:26.0	Italy 1hr 40:52.7	Finland 1hr 41:22.9
1994 Italy 1hr 41:15.0	Norway 1hr 41:15.4	Finland 1hr 42:15.6
1998 Norway 1hr 40:55.7	Italy 1hr 40:55.9	Finland 1hr 42:15.5

1924–32 *Event not held*

Women

5000 Metres Classical

1964 Klaudia Boyarskikh (URS) 17:50.5	Mirja Lehtonen (FIN) 17:52.9	Alevtina Koltschina (URS) 18:08.4
1968 Toini Gustafsson (SWE) 16:45.2	Galina Kulakova (URS) 16:48.4	Alevtina Koltschina (URS) 16:51.6
1972 Galina Kulakova (URS) 17:00.50	Marjatta Kajosmaa (FIN) 17:05.50	Helena Sikolova (TCH) 17:07.32
1976 Helena Takalo (FIN) 15:48.69	Raisa Smetanina (URS) 15:49.73	Nina Baldycheva (URS) 16:12.82 [1]
1980 Raisa Smetanina (URS) 15:06.92	Hikka Riihivuori (FIN) 15:11.96	Kvetoslava Jeriová (TCH) 15:23.44
1984 Marja-Liisa Hämäläinen (FIN) 17:04.0	Berit Aunli (NOR) 17:41.1	Kvetoslava Jeriová (TCH) 17:18.3
1988 Marjo Matikainen (FIN) 15:04.0	Tamara Tikhonova (URS) 15:05.3	Vida Ventsene (URS) 15:11.1

1992 Marjut Lukkarinen (FIN) 14:13.8 Lyubov Yegorova (EUN) 14:14.7 Yelena Valbe (EUN) 14:22.7
1994 Lyubov Yegorova (RUS) 14:08.8 Manuela di Centa (ITA) 14:28.3 Marja-Liisa Kirvesniemi (FIN)
    14:36.0
1998 Larissa Lazutina (RUS) 17:37.9 Katerina Neumannova (CZE) Bente Martinsen (NOR) 17:49.4
    17:42.7

1924–60 *Event not held*

1 Galina Kulakova (URS) finished third but was disqualified

10 000 Metres Classical

1952 Lydia Wideman (FIN) 41:40.0 Mirja Hietamies (FIN) 42:39.0 Siiri Rantanen (FIN) 42:50.0
1956 Lyubov Kozyryeva (URS) 38:11.0 Radya Yeroschina (URS) 38:16.0 Sonja Edström (SWE) 38:23.0
1960 Maria Gusakova (URS) 39:46.6 Lyubov Baranova-Kozyryeva Radya Yeroschina (URS) 40:06.0
    (URS) 40:04.2
1964 Klaudia Boyarskikh (URS) 40:24.3 Yevdokia Mekshilo (URS) 40:26.6 Maria Gusakova (URS) 40:46.6
1968 Toini Gustafsson (SWE) 36:46.5 Berit Mördre (NOR) 37:54.6 Inger Aufles (NOR) 37:59.9
1972 Galina Kulakova (URS) 34:17.8 Alevtina Olunina (URS) 34:54.1 Marjatta Kajosmaa (FIN) 34:56.5
1976 Raisa Smetanina (URS) 30:13.41 Helena Takalo (FIN) 30:14.28 Galina Kulalkova (URS) 30:38.61
1980 Barbara Petzold (GDR) 30:31.54 Hilkka Riihivuori (FIN) 30:35.05 Helena Takalo (FIN) 30:45.25
1984 Marja-Liisa Hämäläinen (FIN) Raisa Smetanina (URS) 32:02.9 Brit Petersen (NOR) 32:12.7
    31:44.2
1988 Vida Ventsene (URS) 30:08.3 Raisa Smetanina (URS) 30:17.0 Marjo Matikainen (FIN) 30:20.5

1924–48 *Event not held, discontinued after 1988*

10 000 Metres Pursuit

1992 Lyubov Yegorova (EUN) 40:07.7 Stefania Belmondo (ITA) 40:31.8 Yelena Välbe (EUN) 40:51.7
1994 Lyubov Yegorova (RUS) 41:38.9 Manuela di Centa (ITA) 41:46.7 Stefania Belmondo (ITA) 42:21.1
1998 Larissa Lazutina (RUS) 46:06.9 Olga Danilova (RUS) 46:13.4 Katerina Neumannova (CZE)
    46:14.2

1924–88 *Event not held*

15 000 Metres Classical

1992 Lyubov Yegorova (EUN) 40:07.7 Stefania Belmondo (ITA) 40:31.8 Yelena Välbe (EUN) 40:51.7
1994 Lyubov Yegorova (RUS) 41:38.9 Manuela di Centa (ITA) 41:46.7 Stefania Belmondo (ITA) 42:21.1
1998 Olga Danilova (RUS) 46:55.4 Larissa Lazutina (RUS) 47:01.0 Anita Moen-Guidon (NOR)
    47:52.6

1924–88 *Event not held*

30 000 Metres Freestyle

1984 Marja-Liisa Hämäläinen (FIN) Raisa Smetanina (URS) 1hr Anne Jahren (NOR) 1hr 03:13.06
    1hr 01:45.0 02:26.7
1988 Tamara Tikhonova (URS) Anfissa Reztsov (URS) 56:12.8 Raisa Smetanina (URS) 57:22.1
    55:53.6
1992 Stefania Belmondo (ITA) 1hr Lyubov Yegorova (EUN) 1hr Yelena Välbe (EUN) 1hr 24:13.9
    22:30.1 22:52.0
1994 Manuela di Centa (ITA) 1hr Marit Wold (NOR) 1hr 25:57.8 Marja-Liisa Hämäläinen (FIN) 1hr
    25:41.6 26:13.6
1998 Yulia Chepalova (RUS) 1hr Stefania Belmondo (ITA) 1hr Larissa Lazutina (RUS) 1hr 23:15.7
    22:01.5 22:11.7

1924–80 *Event not held*
1984–88 *Distance 20km; after 1988 30km*

4 × 5000 Metres Relay 1

1956 Finland 1hr 09:01.0 Soviet Union 1hr 09:28.0 Sweden 1hr 09:48.0
1960 Sweden 1hr 04:21.4 Soviet Union 1hr 05:02.6 Finland 1hr 06:27.5
1964 Soviet Union 59:20.2 Sweden 1hr 01:27.0 Finland 1hr 02:45.1
1968 Norway 57:30.0 Sweden 57:51.0 Soviet Union 58:13.6
1972 Soviet Union 48:46.15 Finland 49:19.37 Norway 49:51.49
1976 Soviet Union 1hr 07:49.75 Finland 1hr 08:36.57 East Germany 1hr 09:57.95
1980 East Germany 1hr 02:11.10 Soviet Union 1hr 03:18.30 Norway 1hr 04:13.50
1984 Norway 1hr 06:49.7 Czechoslovakia 1hr 01:33.0 Finland 1hr 07:36.7

1988	Soviet Union 59:51.1	Norway 1hr 01:33.0	Finland 1hr 01:53.8
1992	Unified Team 59:34.8	Norway 59:56.4	Italy 1hr 00:25.9
1994	Russia 57:12.5	Norway 57:42.6	Italy 58:42.6
1998	Russia 55:33.5	Norway 55:38.0	Italy 56:53.3

1924–52 *Event not held*

[1] Over three stages prior to 1976

Biathlon Medals

	GOLD	SILVER	BRONZE
Men			

10 000 Metres

1980	Frank Ulrich (GDR) 32:10.69	Vladimir Alikin (URS) 32:53.10	Anatoli Alyabiev (URS) 33:09.16
1984	Eirik Kvalfoss (NOR) 30:53.8	Peter Angerer (FRG) 31:02.4	Matthias Jacob (GDR) 31:10.5
1988	Frank-Peter Roetsch (GDR) 25:08.1	Valeri Medvedtsev (URS) 25:23.7	Sergei Tchepikov (URS) 25:29.4
1992	Mark Kirchner (GER) 26:02.3	Ricco Gross (GER) 26:18.0	Harri Eloranta (FIN) 26:26.6
1994	Sergei Chepikov (RUS) 28:07.0	Ricco Gross (GER) 28:13.0	Sergei Tarasov (RUS) 28:27.4
1998	Ole Björndalen (NOR) 27:16.2	Frode Andersson (NOR) 28:17.8	Ville Raikkonen (FIN) 28:21.7

1924–76 *Event not held*

20 000 Metres

1960	Klas Lestander (SWE) 1hr 33:21.6	Antii Tyrväinen (FIN) 1hr 33:57.7	Alexander Privalov (URS) 1hr 34:54.2
1964	Vladimir Melyanin (URS) 1hr 20:26.8	Alexander Privalov (URS) 1hr 23:42.5	Olav Jordet (NOR) 1hr 24:38.8
1968	Magnar Solberg (NOR) 1hr 13:45.9	Alexander Tikhonov (URS) 1hr 14:40.4	Vladimir Gundartsev (URS) 1hr 18:27.4
1972	Magnar Solberg (NOR) 1hr 15:55.5	Hans-Jörg Knauthe (GDR) 1hr 16:07.6	Lars Arvidsson (SWE) 1hr 16:27.03
1976	Nikolai Kruglov (URS) 1hr 14:12.26	Heikki Ikola (FIN) 1hr 15:54.10	Alexander Elizarov (URS) 1hr 16:05.57
1980	Anatoli Alyabiev (URS) 1hr 08:16.31	Frank Ullrich (GDR) 1hr 13:21.4	Eberhard Rösch (GDR) 1hr 11:11.73
1984	Peter Angerer (FRG) 1hr 11:52.7	Frank-Peter Roetsch (GDR) 1hr 13:21.4	Eirik Kvalfoss (NOR) 1hr 14:02.4
1988	Frank-Peter Roetsch (GDR) 56:33.3	Valeri Medvedtsev (URS) 56:54.6	Johann Pasler (ITA) 57:10.1
1992	Yevgeni Redkine (EUN) 57:34.4	Mark Kirchner (GER) 57:40.8	Mikael Löfgren (SWE) 57:59.4
1994	Sergei Tarasov (RUS) 57:25.3	Frank Luck (GER) 57:28.7	Sven Fischer (GER) 57:41.9
1998	Halvard Hanevold (NOR) 56:16.4	Pier Carrara (ITA) 56:21.9	Alexei Aidarov (BLR) 56:46.5

1924–56 *Event not held*

Biathlon Relay (4 × 7500 Metres)

1968	Soviet Union 2hr 13:02.4	Norway 2hr 14:50.2	Sweden 2hr 17:26.3
1972	Soviet Union 1hr 51:44.92	Finland 1hr 54:37.22	East Germany 1hr 54:57.67
1976	Soviet Union 1hr 57:55.64	Finland 2hr 01:45.58	East Germany 2hr 04:08.61
1980	Soviet Union 1hr 34:03.27	East Germany 1hr 34:56.99	West Germany 1hr 37:30.26
1984	Soviet Union 1hr 38:51.7	Norway 1hr 39:03.9	West Germany 1hr 39:05.1
1988	Soviet Union 1hr 22:30.0	West Germany 1hr 23:37.4	Italy 1hr 23:51.5
1992	Germany 1hr 24:43.5	Unified Team 1hr 25:06.3	Sweden 1hr 25:38.2
1994	Germany 1hr 30:22.1	Russia 1hr 31:23.6	France 1hr 32:31.3
1998	Germany 1hr 21:36.2	Norway 1hr 21:56.3	Russia 1hr 22:19.3

1924–64 *Event not held*

Women

7500 Metres

1992 Anfissa Reztsova (EUN) 24:29.2	Antje Misersky (GER) 24:45.1	Yelena Belova (EUN) 24:50.8
1994 Myriam Bédard (CAN) 26:08.8	Svetlana Paramygina (BLR) 26:09.9	Valentina Tserbe (UKR) 26:10.0
1998 Galina Kukleva (RUS) 23:08.0	Ursula Disl (GER) 23:08.7	Katrin Apel (GER) 23:32.4

1924–88 Event not held

15 000 Metres

1992 Antje Misersky (GER) 51:47.2	Svetlana Paramygina (EUN) 51:58.5	Myriam Bédard (CAN) 52:15.0
1994 Myriam Bédard (CAN) 52:06.6	Anne Briand (FRA) 52:53.3	Ursula Disl (GER) 53:15.3
1994 Ekaterina Dafovska (BUL) 54:52.0	Yelena Petrova (UKR) 55:09.8	Ursula Disl (GER) 55:17.9

1924–64 Event not held

Biathlon Relay (4 × 7500 Metres)

1992[1] France 1hr 15:55.6	Germany 1hr 16:18.4	Unified Team 1hr 16:54.6
1994 Russia 1hr 47:19.5	Germany 1hr 51:16.5	France 1hr 52:28.1
1998 Germany 1hr 40:13.6	Russia 1hr 40:25.2	Norway 1hr 40:37.3

1924–1988 Event not held

[1] Only three per team

Nordic Combination Medals

GOLD	SILVER	BRONZE

Individual [1]

GOLD	SILVER	BRONZE
1924[2] Thorleif Haug (NOR)	Thoralf Strömstad (NOR)	Johan Gröttumsbraaten (NOR)
1928[2] Johan Gröttumsbraaten (NOR)	Hans Vinjarengen (NOR)	John Snersrud (NOR)
1932 Johan Gröttumsbraaten (NOR) 446.0pts	Ole Stenen (NOR) 436.05	Hans Vinjarengen (NOR) 434.60
1936 Oddbjörn Hagen (NOR) 430.30pts	Olaf Hoffsbakken (NOR) 419.80	Sverre Brodahl (NOR) 408.10
1948 Heikki Hasu (FIN) 448.80pts	Martti Huhtala (FIN) 433.65	Sven Israelsson (SWE) 433.40
1952 Simon Slattvik (NOR) 431.621pts	Heikki Hasu (FIN) 447.50	Sverre Stenersen (NOR) 436.355
1956 Sverre Stenersen (NOR) 455.0pts	Bengt Eriksson (SWE) 437.4	Franciszek Gron-Gasienica (POL) 436.8
1960 Georg Thoma (GER) 457.952pts	Tormod Knutsen (NOR) 453.000	Nikolai Gusakow (URS) 452.000
1964 Tormod Knutsen (NOR) 469.28pts	Nikolai Kiselyev (URS) 453.04	Georg Thoma (GER) 452.88
1968 Frantz Keller (FRG) 449.04pts	Alois Kälin (SUI) 447.94	Andreas Kunz (GDR) 444.10
1972 Ulrich Wehling (GDR) 413.34pts	Rauno Miettinen (FIN) 405.55	Karl-Heinz Luck (GDR) 398.80
1976 Ulrich Wehling (GDR) 423.39pts	Urban Hettich (FRG) 418.90	Konrad Winkler (GDR) 417.47
1980 Ulrich Wehling (GDR) 432.20pts	Jouko Karjalainen (FIN) 429.50	Konrad Winkler (GDR) 425.32
1984 Tom Sandberg (NOR) 422.595pts	Jouko Karjalainen (FIN) 416.900	Jukka Ylipulli (FIN) 410.825
1988 Hippolyt Kempt (SUI)	Klaus Sulzenbacher (AUT)	Allar Levandi (URS)
1992 Fabrice Guy (FRA)	Sylvain Guillaume (FRA)	Klaus Sulzenbacher (AUT)
1994 Fred Børre Lunberg (NOR)	Takanori Kono (JPN)	Bjarte Engen Vik (NOR)
1998 Bjarte Engen Vik (NOR)	Samppa Lajunen (FIN)	Valeri Stolyarov (RUS)

[1] 1924–52 Distance was 18km; since then 15km
[2] 1942–28 scoring on a different basis to that from 1932 onwards

Team

GOLD	SILVER	BRONZE
1988 West Germany	Switzerland	Austria
1992 Japan	Norway	Austria
1994 Japan	Norway	Switzerland
1998 Norway	Finland	France

1924–84 Event not held

Ski-Jumping Medals

GOLD	SILVER	BRONZE

Normal Hill (1924–88 70m; from 1992 90m)

GOLD	SILVER	BRONZE
1924[1] Jacob Tullin Thams (NOR) 18 960pts	Narve Bonna (NOR) 18 689	Anders Haugen (USA) 17 916
1928 Alf Andersen (NOR) 19 208pts	Sigmund Ruud (NOR) 18 542	Rudolf Burkert (TCH) 17 937
1932 Birger Ruud (NOR) 228.1pts	Hans Beck (NOR) 227.0	Kaare Wahlberg (NOR) 219.5
1936 Birger Ruud (NOR) 232.0pts	Sven Eriksson (SWE) 230.5	Reidar Andersen (NOR) 228.9
1948 Petter Hugsted (NOR) 228.1pts	Birger Ruud (NOR) 226.6	Thorleif Schjeldrup (NOR) 225.1
1952 Arnfinn Bergmann (NOR) 226.0pts	Torbjörn Falkangar (NOR) 221.5	Karl Holmström (SWE) 219.5
1956 Antti Hyvärinen (FIN) 229.9pts	Aulis Kallakorpi (FIN) 225.0	Harry Glass (GER) 224.5
1960 Helmut Recknagel (GER) 227.2pts	Niilio Halonen (FIN) 222.6	Otto Leodolter (AUT) 219.4
1964 Veikko Kankkonen (FIN) 229.9pts	Toralf Engan (NOR) 226.3	Torgeir Brandtzäg (NOR) 222.9
1968 Jiri Taska (TCH) 216.5pts	Reinhold Bachler (AUT) 214.2	Baldur Preiml (AUT) 212.6
1972 Yukio Kasaya (JPN) 244.2pts	Akitsuga Konno (JPN) 234.8	Seiji Aochi (JPN) 229.5
1976 Hans-Georg Aschenbach (GDR) 252.0pts	Jochen Danneberg (GDR) 246.2	Karl Schnabl (AUT) 242.0
1980 Toni Innauer (AUT) 266.3pts	Manfred Dekker (GDR) 249.2 Hirokazu Yagi (JPN) 249.2	–
1984 Jens Weissflog (GDR) 215.2pts	Matti Nykänen (FIN) 214.0	Jari Puikkonen (FIN) 212.8
1988 Matti Nykänen (FIN) 229.1pts	Pavel Ploc (TCH) 212.1	Jiri Malec (TCH) 211.8
1992 Ernst Vettori (AUT) 222.8pts	Martin Höllwarth (AUT) 218.1	Toni Nieminen (FIN) 217.0
1994 Espen Bredesen (NOR) 282.0pts	Lasse Ottesen (NOR) 268.0	Dieter Thoma (GER) 260.5
1998 Jani Soininen (FIN) 234.5pts	Kazuyoshi Funaki (JPN) 233.5	Andreas Wiidhoelz (AUT) 232.5

[1] Originally Thorleif Haug (NOR) was placed third due to incorrect calculations at the time. The error was corrected in 1974

Large Hill (1964–88 90m; from 1992 120m)

GOLD	SILVER	BRONZE
1964 Toralf Engan (NOR) 230.7pts	Veikko Kankkonen (FIN) 228.9	Torgeir Brandtzaeg (NOR) 227.2
1968 Vladimir Belousov (URS) 231.3pts	Jiri Raska (TCH) 229.4	Lars Grini (NOR) 214.3
1972 Wojciech Fortuna (POL) 219.9pts	Walter Steiner (SUI) 219.8	Rainer Schmidt (GDR) 219.3
1976 Karl Schnabl (AUT) 234.8pts	Toni Innauer (AUT) 232.9	Henry Glass (GDR) 221.7
1980 Jouko Törmäinen (FIN) 271.0pts	Hubert Neuper (AUT) 262.4	Jari Puikkonen (FIN) 248.5
1984 Matti Nykäinen (FIN) 232.2pts	Jens Weissflog (GDR) 213.7	Pavel Ploc (TCH) 202.9
1988 Matti Nykäinen (FIN) 224.0pts	Erik Johnsen (NOR) 207.9	Matjaz Debelak (YUG) 207.7
1992 Toni Nieminen (FIN) 239.5pts	Martin Höllwarth (AUT) 227.3	Heinz Kuttin (AUT) 214.8
1994 Jens Weissflog (GER) 274.5pts	Espen Bredesen (NOR) 266.5	Andreas Goldberger (AUT) 255.0
1998 Kazuyoshi Funaki (JPN) 272.3pts	Jani Soininen (FIN) 260.8	Mashiko Harada (JPN) 258.3

1924–60 *Event not held*

Large Hill — Team

GOLD	SILVER	BRONZE
1988 Finland 634.4pts	Yugoslavia 625.5	Norway 596.1
1992 Finland 644.4pts	Austria 642.9	Czechoslovakia 620.1
1994 Germany 970.1pts	Japan 956.9	Austria 918.9
1998 Japan 933.0pts	Germany 897.4	Austria 881.5

1924–84 *Event not held*

Snowboarding Medals

(Introduced in 1998)

	GOLD	SILVER	BRONZE

Men

Halfpipe

| 1998 | Gian Simmen (SUI) 85.2pts | Daniel Franck (NOR) 82.4 | Ross Powers (USA) 82.1 |

Giant Slalom

| 1998 | Ross Rebagliati (CAN) 2:03.96 | Thomas Prugger (ITA) 2:03.98 | Ueli Kestenholz (SUI) 2:04.08 |

Women

Halfpipe

| 1998 | Nicola Thost (GER) 74.6pts | Stine Brun Kjeldaas (NOR) 74.2 | Shannon Dunn (USA) 72.8 |

Giant Slalom

| 1998 | Karine Ruby (FRA) 2:17.34 | Heidi Renoth (GER) 2:19.17 | Brigitte Koeck (AUT) 2:19.42 |

Speed Skating Medals

	GOLD	SILVER	BRONZE

Men

500 Metres

1924	Charles Jewtraw (USA) 44.0	Oskar Olsen (NOR) 44.2	Roald Larsen (NOR) 44.8
			Clas Thunberg (FIN) 44.8
1928	Clas Thunberg (FIN) 43.4	–	John Farrrell (USA) 43.6
	Bernt Evensen (NOR) 43.4	–	Roald Larsen (NOR) 43.6
			Jaako Friman (FIN) 43.6
1932	John Shea (USA) 43.4	Bernt Evensen (NOR) 5m	Alexander Hurd (CAN) 8m
1936	Ivar Ballandgrud (NOR) 43.4	Georg Krog (NOR) 43.5	Leo Friesinger (USA) 44.0
1948	Finn Helgesen (NOR) 43.1	Kenneth Bartholomew (USA) 43.2	–
		Thomas Byberg (NOR) 43.2	
		Robert Fitzgerald (USA) 43.2	
1952	Kenneth Henry (USA) 43.2	Donald McDermott (USA) 43.9	Arne Johansen (NOR) 44.0
			Gordon Audley (CAN) 44.0
1956	Yevgeni Grishin (URS) 40.2	Rafael Gratsch (URS) 40.8	Alv Gjestvang (NOR) 41.0
1960	Yevgeni Grishin (URS) 40.2	William Disney (USA) 40.3	Rafael Gratsch (URS) 40.4
1964	Richard McDermott (USA) 40.1	Yevgeni Grishin (URS) 40.6	–
		Vladimir Orlov (URS) 40.6	
		Alv Gjestvang (NOR) 40.6	
1968	Erhard Keller (FRG) 40.3	Richard McDermott (USA) 40.5	–
		Magne Thomassen (NOR) 40.5	
1972	Erhard Keller (FRG) 39.44	Hasse Börjes (SWE) 39.69	Valeri Muratov (URS) 39.80
1976	Yevgeni Kulikov (URS) 39.17	Valeri Muratov (URS) 39.25	Daniel Immerfall (USA) 39.54
1980	Eric Heiden (USA) 38.03	Yevgeni Kulikov (URS) 38.37	Lieuwe de Boer (NED) 38.48
1984	Sergei Fokitchev (URS) 38.19	Yoshihiro Kitazawa (JPN) 38.30	Gaétan Boucher (CAN) 38.39
1988	Uwe-Jens Mey (GDR) 36.45	Jan Ykema (NED) 36.76	Akira Kuriowa (JPN) 36.77
1992	Uwe-Jens Mey (GER) 37.14	Toshiyuki Kuriowa (JPN) 37.18	Junichi Inoue (JPN) 37.26
1994	Alexander Golubyev (RUS) 36.33	Sergei Klevchenya (RUS) 36.39	Manabu Horii (JPN) 36.53
1998	Hiroyasu Shimizu (JPN) 1:11.35	Jeremy Wotherspoon (CAN) 1:11.84	Kevin Overland (CAN) 1:11.86

1000 Metres

1976	Peter Mueller (USA) 1:19.32	Jörn Didriksen (NOR) 1:20.45	Valeri Muratov (URS) 1:20.57
1980	Eric Heiden (USA) 1:15.18	Gaétan Boucher (CAN) 1:16.68	Frode Rönning (NOR) 1:16.91
			Vladimir Lobanov (URS) 1:16.91
1984	Gaétan Boucher (CAN) 1:15.80	Sergei Khlebnikov (URS) 1:16.63	Kai Arne Engelstad (NOR) 1:16.75
1988	Nikolai Gulyayev (URS) 1:13.03	Uwe-Jens Mey (GDR) 1:13.11	Igor Gelezovsky (URS) 1:13.19

1992 Olaf Zinke (GER) 1:14.85   Kim Moon-Yan (KOR) 1:14.86   Yukinori Miyabe (JPN) 1:14.92
1994 Dan Jansen (USA) 1:12.43   Igor Zhelezovsky (BLS) 1:12.72 Sergei Klevchenya (RUS) 1:12.85
1998 Ids Postma (NED) 1:10.64   Jan Bos (NED) 1:10.71   Hiroyasu Shimizu (JPN) 1:11.00

1924–1972 *Event not held*

1500 Metres

1924 Clas Thunberg (FIN) 2:20.8   Roald Larsen (NOR) 2:20.0   Sigurd Moen (NOR) 2:25.6
1928 Clas Thunberg (FIN) 2:21.1   Bernt Evensen (NOR) 2:21.9   Ivar Ballangrud (NOR) 2:22.6
1932 John Shea (USA) 2:57.5   Alexander Hurd (CAN) 5m   William Logan (CAN) 6m
1936 Charles Mathiesen (NOR) 2:19.2   Ivar Ballangrud (NOR) 2:20.2   Birger Wasenius (FIN) 2:20.9
1948 Sverre Farstad (NOR) 2:17.6   Ake Seyffarth (SWE) 2:18.1   Odd Lundberg (NOR) 2:18.9
1952 Hjalmar Andersen (NOR) 2:20.4   Willem van der Voort (NED)   Roald Aas (NOR) 2:21.6
                                       2:20.6
1956 Yevgeni Grishin (URS) 2:08.6   –   Tiovo Salonen (FIN) 2:09.4
     Yuri Mikhailov (URS) 2:08.6
1960 Roald Aas (NOR) 2:10.4   –   Boris Stenin (URS) 2:11.5
     Yevgeni Grishin (URS) 2:10.4
1964 Ants Antson (URS) 2:10.3   Cornelis Verkerk (NED) 2:10.6   Villy Haugen (NOR) 2:11.25
1968 Cornelis Verkerk (NED) 2:03.4   Ard Schenk (NED) 2:05.0   –
                                       Ivar Eriksen (NOR) 2:05.0
1972 Ard Schenk (NED) 2:02.96   Roar Grönvold (NOR) 2:04.26   Göran Claeson (SWE) 2:05.89
1976 Jan Egil Storholt (NOR) 1:59.38   Yuri Kondakov (URS) 1:59.97   Hans Van Helden (NED) 2:00.87
1980 Eric Heiden (USA) 1:55.44   Kai Stenshjemmet (NOR) 1:56.81 Terje Andersen (NOR) 1:56.92
1984 Gaétan Boucher (CAN) 1:58.36   Sergei Khlebnikov (URS) 1:58.83 Oleg Bogyev (URS) 1:58.89
1988 André Hoffmann (GDR) 1:52.06   Eric Flaim (USA) 1:52.12   Michael Hadschieff (AUT) 1:52.31
1992 Johann-Olav Koss (NOR) 1:54.81   Adne Sønderal (NOR) 1:54.85   Leo Visser (NED) 1:54.90
1994 Johann-Olav Koss (NOR) 1:51.29   Rintje Ritsma (NED) 1:51.99   Flako Zandstra (NED) 1:52.38
1998 Adne Sønderal (NOR) 1:47.87   Ids Postma (NED) 1:48.13   Rintje Ritsma (NED) 1:48.52

5000 Metres

1924 Clas Thunberg (FIN) 8:39.0   Julius Skutnabb (FIN) 8:48.4   Roald Larsen (NOR) 2:00.87
1928 Ivar Ballangrud (NOR) 8:50.5   Julius Skutnabb (FIN) 8:59.1   Bernt Evensen (NOR) 9:01.1
1932 Irving Jaffee (USA) 9:40.8   Edward Murphy (USA) 2m   William Logan (CAN) 4m
1936 Ivar Ballangrud (NOR) 8:19.6   Birger Wasenius (FIN) 8:23.3   Antero Ojala (FIN) 8:30.1
1948 Reidar Liaklev (NOR) 8:29.4   Odd Lundberg (NOR) 8:32.7   Göthe Hedlund (SWE) 8:34.8
1952 Hjalmar Andersen (NOR) 8:10.6   Kees Broekman (NED) 8:21.6   Sverre Haugli (NOR) 8:22.4
1956 Boris Schilkov (URS) 7:48.7   Sigvard Ericsson (SWE) 7:56.7   Oleg Gontscharenko (URS) 7:57.5
1960 Viktor Kositschkin (URS) 7:51.3   Knut Johannesen (NOR) 8:00.8   Jan Pesman (NED) 8:05.1
1964 Knut Johannesen (NOR) 7:38.4   Per Moe (NOR) 7:38.6   Anton Maier (NOR) 7:42.0
1968 Anton Maier (NOR) 7:22.4   Cornelis Verkerk (NED) 7:23.2   Petrus Nottet (NED) 7:25.5
1972 Ard Schenk (NED) 7:23.6   Roar Grönvald (NOR) 7:28.18   Sten Stensen (NOR) 7:33.39
1976 Sten Stensen (NOR) 7:24.48   Piet Kleine (NED) 7:26.47   Hans Van Helden (NED) 7:26.54
1980 Eric Heiden (USA) 7:02.29   Kai Stenshjammet (NOR) 7:03.28 Tom Oxholm (NOR) 7:05.59
1984 Tomas Gustafson (SWE) 7:12.28   Igor Malkov (URS) 7:12.30   René Schöfisch (GDR) 7:17.49
1988 Tomas Gustafson (SWE) 6:44.63   Leendert Visser (NED) 6:44.98   Gerard Kemkers (NED) 6:45.92
1992 Geir Karlstad (NOR) 6:59.97   Falko Zandstra (NED) 7:02.28   Leo Visser (NED) 7:04.96
1994 Johann-Olav Koss (NOR) 6:34.96   Kjell Storelid (NOR) 6:42.68   Rintje Ritsma (NED) 6:43.94
1998 Gianni Romme (NED) 6:22.20   Rintje Ritsma (NED) 6:28.24   Bart Veldkamp (BEL) 6:28.31

10 000 Metres

1924 Julius Skutnabb (FIN) 18:04.8   Clas Thunberg (FIN) 18:97.8   Roald Larsen (NOR) 18:12.2
1932 Irving Jaffee (USA) 19:13.6   Ivar Ballangrud (NOR) 5m   Frank Stack (CAN) 6m
1936 Ivar Ballangrud (NOR) 17:24.3   Birger Wasenius (FIN) 17:28.2   Max Stiepl (AUT) 17:30.0
1948 Ake Seyffarth (SWE) 17:26.3   Lauri Parkkinen (FIN) 17:36.0   Pentti Lammio (FIN) 17:42.7
1952 Hjalmar Andersen (NOR) 16:45.8   Kees Broekman (NED) 17:10.6   Carl-Erik Asplund (SWE) 17:16.6
1956 Sigvard Ericsson (SWE) 16:35.9   Knut Johannesen (NOR) 16:36.9   Oleg Gontscharenko (URS) 16:42.3
1960 Knut Johannesen (NOR) 15:46.6   Viktor Kositschkin (URS) 15:49.2 Kjell Bäckman (SWE) 16:14.2
1964 Jonny Nilsson (SWE) 15:50.1   Anton Maier (NOR) 16:06.0   Knut Johannesen (NOR) 16:06.3
1968 Johnny Höglin (SWE) 15:23.6   Anton Maier (NOR) 15:23.9   Orjan Sandler (SWE) 15:31.8
1972 Ard Schenk (NED) 15:01.35   Cornelis Verkerk (NED) 15:04.70 Sten Stensen (NOR) 15:07.08

1976 Piet Kleine (NED) 14:50.59	Sten Stensen (NOR) 14:53.30	Hans Van Helden (NED) 15:02.02
1980 Eric Heiden (USA) 14:28.13	Piet Kleine (NED) 14:36.03	Tom Oxholm (NOR) 14:36.60
1984 Igor Malkov (URS) 14:39.90	Tomas Gustafson (SWE) 14:39.95	René Schöfisch (GDR) 14:46.91
1988 Tomas Gustafson (SWE) 13:48.20	Michael Hadschieff (AUT) 13:56.11	Leendert Visser (NED) 14:00.55
1992 Bart Veldkamp (NED) 14:12.12	Johann-Olav Koss (NOR) 14:14.58	Geir Karlstad (NOR) 14:18.13
1994 Johann-Olav Koss (NOR) 13:30.55	Kjell Storelid (NOR) 13:49.25	Bart Veldkamp (NED) 13:56.73
1998 Gianni Romme (NED) 13:15.33	Bob de Jong (NED) 13:25.76	Rintje Ritsma (NED) 13:28.19

1928 *Event abandoned*

Women *(Introduced in 1960)*

500 Metres

1960 Helga Haase (GER) 45.9	Natalya Donchenko (URS) 46.0	Jeanne Ashworth (USA) 46.1
1964 Lydia Skoblikova (URS) 45.0	Irina Yegorova (URS) 45.4	Tatyana Sidorova (URS) 45.5
1968 Ludmila Titova (URS) 46.1	Mary Meyers (USA) 46.3 Dianne Holum (USA) 46.3 Jennifer Fish (USA) 46.3	–
1972 Anne Henning (USA) 43.33	Vera Krasnova (URS) 44.01	Ludmila Titova (URS) 44.45
1976 Sheila Young (USA) 42.76	Catherine Priestner (CAN) 43.12	Tatyana Averina (URS) 43.17
1980 Karin Enke (GDR) 41.78	Leah Poulos-Mueller (USA) 42.26	Natalya Petruseva (URS) 42.42
1984 Christa Rothenburger (GDR) 41.02	Karin Enke (GDR) 41.28	Natalya Chive (URS) 41.50
1988 Bonnie Blair (USA) 39.10	Christa Rothenburger (GDR) 39.12	Karin Enke-Kania (GDR) 39.24
1992 Bonnie Blair (USA) 40.33	Ye Qiaobo (CHN) 40.51	Christa Rothenburger-Luding (GER) 40.57
1994 Bonnie Blair (USA) 39.25	Susan Auch (CAN) 39.61	Franziska Schenk (GER) 39.70
1998 Catriona LeMay Doan (CAN) 1:16.60	Susan Auch (CAN) 1:16.93	Tomomi Okazaki (JPN) 1:17.10

1000 Metres

1960 Klara Guseva (URS) 1:34.1	Helga Haase (GER) 1:34.3	Tamara Rylova (URS) 1:34.8
1964 Lydia Skoblikova (URS) 1:33.2	Irina Yegorova (URS) 1:34.3	Kaija Mustonen (FIN) 1:34.8
1968 Carolina Geijssen (NED) 1:32.6	Ludmila Titova (URS) 1:32.9	Dianne Holum (USA) 1:33.4
1972 Monika Pflug (FRG) 1:31.40	Atje Keulen-Deelstra (NED) 1:31.61	Anne Henning (USA) 1:31.62
1976 Tatyana Averina (URS) 1:28.43	Leah Poulos (USA) 1:28.57	Sheila Young (USA) 1:29.14
1980 Natalya Petruseva (URS) 1:24.10	Leah Poulos-Mueller (USA) 1:25.41	Sylvia Albrecht (GDR) 1:26.46
1984 Karin Enke (GDR) 1:21.61	Andrea Schöne (GDR) 1:22.83	Natalya Petruseva (URS) 1:23.21
1988 Christa Rothenburger (GDR) 1:17.65	Karin Enke-Kania (GDR) 1:17.70	Bonnie Blair (USA) 1:18.31
1992 Bonnie Blair (USA) 1:21.90	Ye Qiaobo (CHN) 1:21.92	Monique Garbrecht (GER) 1:22.10
1994 Bonnie Blair (USA) 1:18.74	Anke Baier (GER) 1:20.12	Ye Qiaobo (CHN) 1:20.22
1998 Marianne Timmer (NED) 1:16.51	Christine Witty (USA) 1:16.79	Catriona LeMay Doan (CAN) 1:17.37

1500 Metres

1960 Lydia Skoblikova (URS) 2:25.2	Elvira Seroczynska (POL) 2:25.7	Helena Pilejeyk (POL) 2:27.1
1964 Lydia Skoblikova (URS) 2:22.6	Kaija Mustonen (FIN) 2:25.5	Berta Kolokoltseva (URS) 2:27.1
1968 Kaija Mustonen (FIN) 2:22.4	Carolina Geijssen (NED) 2:22.7	Christina Kaiser (NED) 2:24.5
1972 Dianne Holum (USA) 2:20.85	Christina Baas-Kaiser (NED) 2:21.05	Atje Keulen-Deelstra (NED) 2:22.05
1976 Galina Stepanskaya (URS) 2:16.58	Sheila Young (USA) 2:17.06	Tatyana Averina (URS) 2:17.96
1980 Annie Borckink (NED) 2:10.95	Ria Visser (NED) 2:12.35	Sabine Becker (GDR) 2:12.38
1984 Karin Enke (GDR) 2:03.42	Andrea Schöne (GDR) 2:05.29	Natalya Petruseva (URS) 2:05.78
1988 Yvonne Van Gennip (NED) 2:00.68	Karin Enke-Kania (GDR) 2:00.82	Andrea Schöne-Ehrig (GDR) 2:01.49

1992 Jacqueline Börner (GER) 2:05.87	Gunda Niemann (GER) 2:05.92	Seiko Hashimoto (JPN) 2:06.88
1994 Emese Hunyady (AUT) 2:02.19	Svetlana Fedotkin (RUS) 2:02.69	Gunda Niemann (GER) 2:03.41
1998 Marianne Timmer (NED) 1:57.58	Gunda Niemann-Stirnemann (GER) 1:58.86	Christine Witty (USA) 1:58.97

3000 Metres

1960 Lydia Skoblikova (URS) 5:14.3	Valentina Stenina (URS) 5:16.9	Eevi Huttunen (FIN) 5:21.0
1964 Lydia Skoblikova (URS) 5:14.9	Valentina Stenina (URS) 5:18.5	–
	Han Pil-hwa (PRK) 5:18.5	
1968 Johanna Schut (NED) 4:56.2	Kaija Mustonen (FIN) 5:01.0	Christina Kaiser (NED) 5:01.3
1972 Christina Baas-Kaiser (NED) 4:52.14	Dianne Holum (USA) 4:58.67	Atje Keulen-Deelstra (NED) 4:59.91
1976 Tayana Averina (URS) 4:45.19	Andrea Mitscherlich (GDR) 4:45.23	Lisbeth Korsmo (NOR) 4:45.24
1980 Bjørg Eva Jensen (NOR) 4:32.13	Sabine Becker (GDR) 4:32.79	Beth Heiden (USA) 4:33.77
1984 Andrea Mitscherlich-Schöne (GDR) 4:24.79	Karin Enke (GDR) 4:26.33	Gabi Schönbrunn (GDR) 4:33.13
1988 Yvonne Van Gennip (NED) 4:11.94	Andrea Schöne-Ehrig (GDR) 4:12.09	Gabi Schönbrunn-Zange (GDR) 4:16.92
1992 Gunda Niemann (GER) 4:19.90	Heike Warnicke (GER) 4:22.88	Emese Hunyadi (AUT) 4:24.64
1994 Svetlana Bazhanova (RUS) 4:17.43	Emese Hunyadi (AUT) 4:18.14	Claudia Pechstein (GER) 4:18.34
1998 Gunda Niemann-Stirnemann (GER) 4:07.29	Claudia Pechstein (GER) 4:08.47	Anna Friesinger (GER) 4:09.44

5000 Metres

1988 Yvonne Van Gennip (NED) 7:14.13	Andrea Schöne-Ehrig (GDR) 7:17.2	Gabi Schönbrunn-Zange (GDR) 7:21.61
1992 Gunda Niemann (GER) 7:31.57	Heike Warnicke (GER) 7:37.59	Claudia Pechstein (GER) 7:39.80
1994 Claudia Pechstein (GER) 7:14.37	Gunda Neimann (GER) 7:14.88	Hiromi Yamamoto (JPN) 7:19.68
1998 Claudia Pechstein (GER) 6:59.61	Gunda Niemann-Stirnemann (GER) 6:59.65	Lyudmila Prokasheva (KZK) 7:11.14

1960–84 Event not held

Discontinued Event

Men

All-Round Championship (Aggregate of placings in 500m, 1500m, 5000m and 10 000m)

1924 Clas Thunberg (FIN) 5.5pts	Roald Larsen (NOR) 9.5	Julius Skutnabb (FIN) 11

Short-Track Speed Skating Medals

GOLD	SILVER	BRONZE

Men

500 Metres

1994 Chae Ji-hoon (KOR) 43.45	Mirko Vuillermin (ITA) 43.47	Nicky Gooch (GBR) 43.68
1998 Takafuni Nishitani (JPN) 42.862	An Yulong (CHN) 43.022	Hitoshi Uematsu (JPN) 43.713

1924–92 Event not held

1000 Metres

1992 Kim Ki-hoon (KOR) 1:30.76	Frederic Blackburn (CAN) 1:31.11	Lee Joon-ho (KOR) 1:31.16
1994 Kim Ki-hoon (KOR) 1:34.57	Chae Ji-hoon (KOR) 1:34.92	Marc Gagnon (CAN) 1:33.03[1]
1998 Kim Dong-sung (KOR) 1:32.375	Li Jiajun (CHN) 1:32.428	Eric Bedard (CAN) 1:32.661

1924–88 Event not held

[1] As no other finisher in 'A' final, the winner of the 'B' final was placed third

5000 Metres Relay

1992 South Korea 7:14.02	Canada 7:14.06	Japan 7:18.18
1994 Italy 7:11.74	United States 7:13.37	Australia 7:13.68
1998 Canada 7:32.075	Korea 7:06.776	China 7:11.559

1924–88 *Event not held*

Women

500 Metres

1992 Cathy Turner (USA) 47.04	Li Yan (CHN) 47.08	Hwang Ok-sil (PRK) 47.23
1994 Cathy Turner (USA) 45.98	Zhang Yanmei (CHN) 46.44	Amy Peterson (USA) 46.76
1998 Annie Perreault (CAN) 46.568	Yang Yang S (CHN) 46.627	Lee Kyung-chun (KOR) 46.335 [1]

1924–88 *Event not held*

[1] Isabelle Charest (CAN) disqualified so the winner of the 'B' final was placed third

1000 Metres

1994 Chun Lee-kyung (KOR) 1:36.87	Nathalie Lambert (CAN) 1:36.97	Kim So-hee (KOR) 1:37.09
1998 Chun Lee-kyung (KOR) 1:42.776	Yang Yang S (CHN) 1:43.343	Won Hye-kyung (KOR) 1:43.361

1924–92 *Event not held*

3000 Metres Relay

1992 Canada 4:36.62	United States 4:37.85	Unified Team 4:42.69
1994 Korea 4:26.64	Canada 4:32.04	United States 4:39.34
1998 Korea 4:16.260	China 4:16.383	Canada 4:21.205

1924–88 *Event not held*

International Sporting Organisations

Olympic Games International Olympic Committee (IOC)
Château de Vidy, C.P. 356, 1007 Lausanne, Switzerland
Tel: (41-21) 621 6111 Fax: (41-21) 621 6216

Archery
Fédération Internationale de Tir à l'Arc (FITA)
Avenue de Cour 135, 1007 Lausanne, Switzerland
Tel: (41.21) 614 3050 Fax: (41.21) 614 3055

Athletics
International Amateur Athletic Federation (IAAF)
17, rue Princesse Florestine, B.P. 359, 98007 Monte Carlo, Monaco Cédex
Tel: (377) 93-10 8888 Fax: (377) 93-15 9515

Badminton
International Badminton Federation (IBF)
Manor Park Place, Rutherford Way, Cheltenham, Gloucestershire GL51 9TU, United Kingdom
Tel: (44) (0)1242-234904 Fax: (44) (0)1242-221030

Baseball
International Baseball Federation (IBA)
Avenue Mon-Repos 24, 1005 Lausanne 5, Switzerland
Tel: (41-21) 318 8240 Fax: (41-21) 318 8241

Basketball
Fédération Internationale de Basketball (FIBA)
Boschetsrieder Str. 67, 81379 Münich, Germany
Tel: (49-89) 748 1580 Fax: (49-89) 748 15833

Biathlon
International Biathlon Union (IBU)
Airport Center — Kasernenstrasse 1, Postfach 1, 5073 Wals Himmelreich, Austria
Tel: (43-662) 85 5050 Fax: (43-662) 85 50508

Bobsledding
Fédération Internationale de Bobsleigh et de Tobogganing (FIBT)
Via Piranesi 44B, 20137 Milan, Italy
Tel: (39-02) 757 3319 Fax: (39-02) 757 3384

Boxing
Association Internationale de Boxe Amateur (AIBA)
P.O. Box 76343, Atlanta, GA 30358, USA
Tel: (770) 455 8350 Fax: (770) 454 6467

Canoeing
Fédération Internationale de Canoë (FIC)
Dózsa György út 1-3, 1143 Budapest, Hungary
Tel: (36-1) 363 4832 Fax: (36-1) 221 4130

Curling
World Curling Federation (WCF)
81 King Street, Edinburgh EH3 6RN, United Kingdom
Tel: (44) (0) 131-556 4884 Fax: (44) (0) 131-556 9400

Cycling
Union Cycliste Internationale (UCI)
Route de Chavannes 37, 1007 Lausanne, Switzerland
Tel: (41-21) 622 0580 Fax: (41-21) 622 0588

Equestrianism
Fédération Equestre Internationale (FEI)
Avenue Mon-Repos 24, C.P. 157, 1000 Lausanne 5, Switzerland
Tel: (41-21) 310 4747 Fax: (41-21) 310 4760

Fencing
Fédération Internationale d'Escrime (FIE)
Avenue Mon-Repos 24, C.P. 128, 1000 Lausanne 5, Switzerland
Tel: (41-21) 320 3151 Fax: (41-21) 320 3116

Figure Skating
International Skating Union (ISU)
Chemin de Primerose 2, 1007 Lausanne, Switzerland
Tel: (41-21) 612 6666 Fax: (41-21) 612 6677

Football (Soccer)
Fédération Internationale de Football Association (FIFA)
Hitzigweg 11, C.P. 85, 8030 Zürich, Switzerland
Tel: (41-1) 384 9595 Fax: (41-1) 384 9696

Gymnastics
Fédération Internationale de Gymnastique (FIG)
Rue des Oeuches 10, C.P. 359, 2740 Moutier 1, Switzerland
Tel: (41-32) 494 6410 Fax: (41-32) 494 6419

Handball
Fédération Internationale de Handball (IHF)
C.P. 312, 4020 Basle, Switzerland
Tel: (41-61) 272 1300 Fax: (41-61) 272 1344

Hockey
Fédération Internationale de Hockey (FIH)
Avenue des Arts 1, B.P. 5, 1210 Bruxelles, Belgium
Tel: (32-2) 219 4537 Fax: (32-2) 219 2761

Ice Hockey
International Ice Hockey Federation (IIHF)
Parkring 11, 8002 Zürich, Switzerland
Tel: (41-1) 289 8600 Fax: (41-1) 289 8629

Judo
International Judo Federation (IJF)
33rd Floor Doosan Tower, 18-12, Ulchi-ro, 6 ka,
Chung-Ku, Seoul, Korea
Tel: (82-2) 759 6936 Fax: (82-2) 754 1075

Lugeing
Fédération Internationale de Luge de Course (FIL)
Rathausplatz 9, 83471 Berchtesgaden, Germany
Tel: (49-8652) 669 60 Fax: (49-8652) 669 69

Modern
Pentathlon Union Internationale de Pentathlon
Moderne (UIPM)
Stade Louis II - Entrance E, 13 avenue des Castelans,
98000 Monaco
Tel: (377) 97-77 8555 Fax: (377) 97-77 8550

Rowing
Fédération Internationale des Sociétés d'Aviron
(FISA)
Avenue de Cour 135, C.P. 18, 1000 Lausanne 3,
Switzerland
Tel: (41-21) 617 8373 Fax: (41-21) 617 8375

Shooting
Fédération Internationale de Tir Sportif (ISSF)
Bavariaring 21, 80336 Münich, Germany
Tel: (49-89) 544 3550 Fax: (49-89) 544 35544

Skiing
Fédération Internationale de Ski (FIS)
Blochstrasse 2, 3653 Oberhofen/Thunersee,
Switzerland
Tel: (41-33) 244 6161 Fax: (41-33) 243 5353

Softball
International Softball Federation (ISF)
4141 NW Expressway, Suite 340, Oklahoma City, OK
73116-1675, USA
Tel: (405) 879 2004 Fax: (405) 879 9801

Swimming
Fédération Internationale de Natation Amateur
(FINA)
Avenue de Beaumont 9, Rez-de-Chaussée, 1012
Lausanne, Switzerland
Tel: (41-21) 312 6602 Fax: (41-21) 312 6610

Table Tennis
International Table Tennis Federation (ITTF)
53 London Road, St Leonards-on-Sea, East Sussex
TN37 6AY, United Kingdom
Tel: (44) (0)1424- 721414 Fax: (44) (0)1424 431871

Tae kwon do
World Tae kwon do Federation (WTF)
635 Yuksam-dong, Kangnam-ku, Seoul 135-080,
Korea
Tel: (82-2) 566 2505 Fax: (82-2) 553 4728

Tennis
International Tennis Federation (ITF)
Bank Lane, Roehampton, London SW15 5XZ, United
Kingdom
Tel: (44) (0)20878 6464 Fax: (44) (0)20878 7799

Triathlon
International Triathlon Union (ITU)
1154 West 24th Street, North Vancouver, BC V7P
2J2, Canada
Tel: (604) 926 7250 Fax: (604) 608 3195

Volleyball
Fédération Internationale de Volleyball (FIVB)
Avenue de la Gare 12, 1003 Lausanne, Switzerland
Tel: (41-21) 345 3535 Fax: (41-21) 345 3545

Weightlifting
International Weightlifting Federation (IWF)
Hold u. 1, 1054 Budapest, Hungary
Tel: (36-1) 331 8153 Fax: (36-1) 269 0208

Wrestling
Fédération Internationale de Luttes Associées (FILA)
Avenue Juste-Olivier 17, 1006 Lausanne, Switzerland
Tel: (41-21) 312 8426 Fax: (41-21) 323 6073

Yachting
International Sailing Federation (ISAF)
Ariadne House, Town Quay, Southampton,
Hampshire SO14 2AQ, United Kingdom
Tel: (44) 023-8063 5111 Fax: (44) 023-8063 5789

This index is an alphabetical name index comprising participants and key people involved with the Olympic Games. Names of, e.g., yachts and horses are also included. The index only refers to names which appear in the 'encyclopaedic' part of the book, namely pages 1–131. To locate individual events, sports, venues or medallists, please use the contents listing on pages v and vi and the medal tables by sport and year on pages 132–252. A listing of international sporting bodies can be found on pages 252–254.

Index

Date of birth/death given in brackets, where known.